한국문제 관련 유엔문서 자료집(下)

경희대학교 한국현대사연구원
현대사 자료총서 2-2

한국문제 관련 유엔문서 자료집(下)

유엔한국임시위원단 보고서(1948)

제3차 유엔총회 회의록(1948)

유엔한국위원단 보고서(1949)

경희대학교 한국현대사연구원

권재원 · 김재웅 · 안소영 · 유지아

경인문화사

제2부 유엔총회 회의록(1948)

제3부 유엔한국위원단 보고서(1949)

제2부 | 유엔총회 회의록(1948)

1. 본 자료집은 운석 장면기념사업회가 소장하고 있는 유엔 제3차 총회의 한국 관련 문서 중 총회 회의기록, 유엔사무총장보고서, 유엔한국임시위원단 보고서, 유엔한국위원단 보고서 등 총 22건, 929매에 이르는 문서 원문을 정리하고 이를 건별로 해제한 것이다. 이 가운데 유엔한국 임시위원단 및 위원단 보고서가 공간·번역된 바 있으나(국회도서관 입법조사국 편, 『1948年度 國際聯合 韓國臨時委員團 報告書(第1部 第1卷)』, 1965; 국회도서관 입법조사국 편, 『國際聯合 韓國委員團報告書, 1949~1950』, 1965), 이는 전체보고서의 일부에 해당하는 문서이다. 따라서 본 자료집은 이들 위원단의 일련의 보고서 전체와 위원단 활동에 관련된 유엔총회 및 '제1위원회' 회의기록 등을 망라하여, 제3차 및 제4차 유엔총회 시기의 한국문제에 관한 문서와 해제를 첨부해 수록하였다.

2. 편집은 각 문서별로 해제문을 앞에 배치하고 영인한 영문 원문을 그 뒤에 실었다. 지금까지 한국관련 유엔총회 및 산하위원회의 회의기록, 그리고 유엔한국 임시위원단 및 위원단 보고서가 문서별로 상세하게 해제·공간된 적은 없었다.

3. 편집 자료의 선정기준은 기존에 공간·번역되지 않은 문서를 중심으로 했다. 아울러 한국현대사 연구의 기초자료라 할 만한 문건과 정치학·법학·사회학 등 학제적 연구에 필요한 자료를 포함해서, 당시 유엔이 개입한 국제정치와 관련된 자료도 선정되었다. 또한 내용에 관한 이해를 돕기 위해 필요한 경우 각주를 첨부하였다.

4. 해제문은 가급적 원문의 형식을 따라 작성하고자 하였다. 회의록이나 보고서 등 원 사료의 형식은 물론, 내용구분 방식이나 기호를 원문대로 유지함으로써, 해제와 원문의 대조를 용이하게 하여 본 자료집을 활용할 연구자의 편의를 도모하고자 하였다.

5. 인명, 단체명, 직명 등의 용어는 관련 연구논저와 당시 신문, 국사편찬위원회가 발간한 문헌, 온라인 검색상의 용례(用例), 대한민국 외교부의 유엔문서 소개사이트 등을 참고하여 최대한 정확도를 높였고 표기는 가급적 원어 발음에 준하였다.

6. 특히 본 자료집의 중요 부분인 유엔한국위원단의 대표단 인명 및 사무국 직위는 동아일보(1948.1.8, "유엔朝鮮委員團 今夕入京豫定")와 경향신문(1948.1.7, "獨立朝鮮誕生의 前夜") 기사에 소개된 위원단 관련 정보에 근거하여 기재되었다. 현지채용 직원의 경우 영문 표기만 기록되어 있어 정확한 한글 이름을 확인하기 어렵지만 영문발음으로 추정한 한글인명과 원문에 나오는 이름을 병기하였다.

1. 제3차 유엔총회 소총회 문서

(1) 제3차 유엔총회 소총회 제6회 회의 요약

해제문서 6 : A/AC.18/SR.6 (Interim Committee of The General Aessmbly, Summary Record of The Sixth Meeting)

문서명	Interim Committee of the General Assembly, Summary Record of the Sixth Meeting		
	제3차 유엔총회 소총회 제6회 회의 요약 기록		
발신		생성일시	1948년 2월 24일 오전 11시
		발신일시	
수신		수신일시	
		문서번호	A/AC.18/SR.6
문서형태	회의록 (요약)	문서분량	14쪽
주제명	한국의 독립에 관한 문제: 1947년 11월 14일의 총회 결의안에 대한 협의 내용		
주요내용	한국독립 문제에 관해 1947년 11월 14일 총회 결의안을 적용한 유엔총회 소총회와 유엔한국임시위원단의 협의. 상세한 내용은 본문 참조.		
검색어	유엔한국임시위원단, 유엔총회 소총회, 제섭(Philip Jessup, 미국 대표), Matienzo(볼리비아 대표), 치앙(Tingfu. F. Tsiang, 중국 대표), 호메로 비테리 라프론테(Homero Viteri Lafronte, 에콰도르 대표)		

한국독립 문제에 관해 1947년 11월 14일 총회 결의안을 적용한 유엔총회 소총회(Interim Committee of the General Assembly)와 유엔한국임시위원단의 협의 내용임.

미국 대표는 1947년 11월 14일의 총회 결의안에서 유엔이 한국인의 자유와 독립을 되찾아 주기 위하여 온 힘을 다할 것을 명시했다고 말함. 그리고 미국 대표는 소련 역시 이와 비슷한 내용의 결의안을 제출했음에도 불구하고, 어째서 소련대표가 총회 결정을 반대하고 임시위원단 소련 점령지역 내에서 활동하는 것을 거부하는지 그 이유를 이해하지 못하겠다고 함. 또한 그는 미국이 임의로 지정한 38도선을 영속시킬 마음이 없으며 유엔총회에 대해 한국인의 직접 투표로 선출한 국회를 빨리 만들어야 한다고 촉구함. 다행히도 전체인구의 3분의 2가 살고 있는 미군점령지역에서는 투표가 가능하다는 사실을 알려줌. 그리고 한국 내에 자유로운 선거분위기를 조성하기 위해 미군이 전적인 도움을 주기로 약속했다고 전함. 3일 후 하지 중장은 표현, 언론, 집회 등의 기본자유를 보장하는 특히 선거 준비기간 동안을 염두에 둔 개별 명령을 발포했다고 전함. 이어서 점령지역으로부터 동시철수를 주장하는 소련의 제안을 거절하며 통일된 중앙정부가 수립되면 그 후에 철수하겠다고 주장함. 그 기간 동안 한국에 대한 미국의 정책 목표는 한국인들의 의지를 자유롭게 표출할 수 있는 자치정부를 수립하고 경제수준을 높이기 위해 원조하며 미래를 위한 적절한 교육 시스템을 만드는 것이라고 밝힘.

임시위원단과의 협의에 대해서는 지금 그들이 겪고 있는 내부적, 대외적 의견 충돌과 미군정 내의 활동의 어려움 등은 애초에 예상된 문제들이고 앞으로의 문제는 소련의 태도에 달려있다고 말하며, 소련이 한국의 진정한 독립에 장애가 될 것이라고 거듭 주장함. 이어 미국 정부는 한국민 스스로가 통일을 이루기를 바란다고 말하며 그것을 이루기 위해서는 유엔이 감찰하고 한국인의 3분의 2가 선출한 정부가 큰 도움이 될 것이라고 말함. 마지막으로 미국 대표는 미국의 유엔총회 결의안에 온전히 협조하겠다는 약속과 함께 발언을 마무리함.

중국 대표는 독립된 통일 한국의 건설이 매우 중요하다고 말함. 그리고 소련의 반대는 제3차 유엔총회 제1위원회와 총회에서도 있었던 일이고 예상된 일이므로 지금에 와서 소련의 주장이 총회 결의안의 실행에 영향을 주어서는 안 된다고 말함. 또한 그 어떤 것도 남북한의 분단을 조장해서는 안 된다고 말하고 위원단이 총회 결의안에 구상된 바의 선거를 투명하게 실시해야하며 선거 전후에 남북한 대표와 만나 충분한 토의를 나누어야 한다고 말함. 또 한국이 어떤 상황이든지 간에 결의안 2절에 명시된 프로그램을 시행하는 것이 임시위원단의 임무라고 주장함.

볼리비아 대표는 유엔과 관련된 문제는 특히 복합적으로 접근하고 보편적으로 해결해야 하므로 현재 한국 독립과 관련된 유엔 결의안의 문제에 대해 위원회는 유엔 헌장의 원칙에 따라 소련의 협조를 정식으로 요청해야한다고 주장함.

에콰도르 대표는 한반도 전역에 걸친 투표 가능성에 대해 설명하였으며 북한 지역의 점령당국, 인민정권, 그리고 인민들 이 세 가지 요소가 이를 방해할 것이라고 설명함. 한 지역에 국회가 선출되고 다른 지역에 이미 자유선거를 통해 수립된 정부가 존재한다면 그 의회를 중앙정부로 만들려는 시도는 한반도 분단에 영속성을 부여하는 일이 될 수도 있다고 하면서, 어떠한 정부가 수립되든 통일된 정부가 아니면 임시적인 형태여야 한다고 주장함. 위원회에 제시될 초기형태는 임시적인 것이어야 하며 궁극적 목표는 통일 독립된 한국의 모습이어야 한다고 주장함.

오후 1시 30분에 정회함.

United Nations

GENERAL ASSEMBLY

Nations Unies

ASSEMBLEE GENERALE

UNRESTRICTED

A/AC.18/SR.6
26 February 1948

ORIGINAL: ENGLISH

INTERIM COMMITTEE OF THE GENERAL ASSEMBLY

SUMMARY RECORD OF THE SIXTH MEETING

Lake Success, New York
Tuesday, 24 February 1948, at 11 a.m.

Chairman: Mr. L. PADILLA NERVO (Mexico)

OPENING OF THE MEETING

The CHAIRMAN recalled that, at its fourth meeting on 9 January 1948, the Interim Committee had adjourned until 24 February, on which date any proposals which had been submitted concerning the implementation of paragraph 2(c) of the General Assembly resolution of 13 November 1947 were to be considered. In the meantime, however, the Interim Committee had been convened on 19 February to consider the request made by the Temporary Commission on Korea for consultation in the light of developments, and had heard an exhaustive statement on the situation by Mr. K. P. S. Menon, Chairman of the Temporary Commission. This same item had been placed first on the agenda of the present meeting, and the Committee would proceed to its consideration.

PROBLEM OF THE INDEPENDENCE OF KOREA: CONSULTATION BY THE
UNITED NATIONS TEMPORARY COMMISSION ON KOREA WITH THE INTERIM
COMMITTEE ON THE APPLICATION OF THE GENERAL ASSEMBLY RESOLUTION
OF 13 NOVEMBER 1947 IN THE LIGHT OF DEVELOPMENTS

Mr. JESSUP (United States of America), after paying
tribute to the judicial spirit and fine impartiality of Mr. Menon's
address, drew attention to the specific questions before the
Committee, contained in document A/AC.18/27. The Interim
Committee was not asked to enter into a full debate on the
question of the independence of Korea, but to consider those
questions.

The General Assembly resolution of 14 November 1947 stated
clearly the objective of the United Nations with regard to Korea,
which was to restore to the Korean people their freedom and
independence. Since the Union of Soviet Socialist Republics had
declared that to be also the objective of its own resolution
presented to the General Assembly, and which had been accepted in
principle though not in the exact form in which it had been
presented, the United States delegation could not understand why
the USSR opposed the decision of the General Assembly and refused
to allow the Temporary Commission on Korea to exercise its
functions in that zone of Korea which was under USSR occupation.

The United States had no desire to perpetuate the arbitrary
division of Korea along the line of the 38th parallel, which was
a fortuitous division resulting from the war. It urged, as it
had urged in the General Assembly, that a National Assembly
representing all Korea should be elected by the people of Korea
on the basis of population. Fortunately that election could be
carried out in that part of the country occupied by the
United States forces, which contained two-thirds of the
population. As an indication of the readiness of the

/United States

United States authorities to cooperate in putting into effect the will of the United Nations, Mr. Jessup quoted a public statement made on 24 January 1948 by General Hodge, who commanded the United States occupation forces in Korea, to the effect that the United States fully supported the declaration of the Chairman of the Temporary Commission on Korea regarding the necessity of a free atmosphere for the election and that the United States Command in Korea would lend all possible assistance. Three days later, General Hodge had issued a special order to the Provincial Governors and the Mayor of Seoul reiterating the policy of the United States Government that the rights of freedom of speech, press and assembly, particularly during the period of preparation for the election be recognized, respected and safeguarded.

Continuing, Mr. Jessup outlined the series of events which had led to the adoption of the General Assembly resolution, from the Cairo Declaration of 1943, to which the USSR had agreed at Potsdam in 1945, to the request of the United States Government to have the problem of Korean independence placed upon the agenda of the General Assembly at its second session in 1948. It was only after that request had been made that the USSR delegation had proposed the simultaneous withdrawal of USSR and United States troops from Korea, to which the United States Government had replied that such a withdrawal should follow the establishment of a single independent Korean Government.

Throughout that whole period, the policy of the United States towards Korea had been based upon the objectives of establishing a self-governing, sovereign Korea, ensuring that the national government so established should be fully representative of the freely expressed will of the Korean people, and assisting the Koreans to establish a sound *economy*

/and an

and an adequate educational system as the basis of an independent, democratic State. The United States had never lost sight of the fact that Korea was a liberated and not a conquered country.

The Temporary Commission on Korea had asked for consultation with the Interim Committee; such a request was in accordance with the General Assembly resolution, which authorized the Commission to consult with the Interim Committee "in the light of developments". Was there, however, anything in those developments which could not have been foreseen? The Commission had duly gone to Korea, and although one member, namely, the member from the Ukrainian Soviet Socialist Republic, had declined to take his place on the Commission, that action was not unexpected in view of the attitude of the Ukrainian delegation at the second session of the Assembly. Secondly, the fact that consultations between the Commission and individual Korean leaders had revealed a certain lack of unanimity among the latter concerning the methods of establishing an independent government could not be considered unexpected; the operation of every democratic government revealed the same phenomenon. In the third place, the difficulties mentioned by the Chairman of the Commission as arising out of the occupation of South Korea by military forces of the United States did not constitute an unexpected development. The United States had never claimed perfection in the administration of its zone in Korea, as was borne out by the statement of Mr. Dulles in the First Committee of the General Assembly on 4 November 1947. A fourth development which could not have been unforeseen was the "negative attitude" of the USSR Government; that attitude had already been obvious at an early stage in the debates in the First Committee and the General Assembly.

The United States fully associated itself with the statement made by the Chairman of the Temporary Commission on Korea at a

/mass

mass meeting in Seoul, that without unity there could be no
independence. Indeed, it had diligently sought to secure such
unity by means of conversations with the USSR, but to no avail.
Difficulties had invariably arisen on the question of which
Korean organizations should participate in the consultations
concerning the political future of Korea, the United States
maintaining the view that a democratic government was one freely
elected by the people, while the USSR refused to allow joint
consultations with any political party which had at any time voiced
opposition to trusteeship for Korea. Nor did Four-Power consultation offer a solution, since such a method, suggested by the
United States, had met with USSR opposition. The United States
Government hoped that the efforts of the Korean people themselves
might help to achieve unity, but it felt that such efforts would
be more likely to succeed if backed by the authority of a
government elected under United Nations observation by two-thirds
of the people of Korea.

The statement of the Chairman of the Commission had implied
that some members of the Commission thought that resolutions I and
II were separable. Mr. Jessup wished to point out that the two
resolutions had been presented together and adopted by a single
vote, and that nothing in the legislative history of the
discussions in the General Assembly and its Committees supported
the theory that they were separable. They must be considered as
a single plan, envisaging one election. Indeed, resolution II
said that the Commission should "facilitate and expedite the
fulfilment of the foregoing programme", which obviously referred
to the complete programme contained in resolutions I and II.

In the opinion of the United States delegation, it was
incumbent on the Commission to proceed with the task allotted to
it. He would therefore suggest the following course of action.

/The

The Commission on Korea might decide, in consultation with the occupying authorities, upon an election law and procedures, designate the voting areas, and fix the date for the election. Since it was recognized that the Commission and its staff was not large enough to observe the elections in all areas simultaneously, it might announce that elections would be observed seriatim, perhaps starting in the South and working towards the North. The Commission might immediately announce that the purpose of the election was to choose representatives to constitute a National Assembly, with which the Commission might consult with regard to the prompt attainment of freedom and independence for the Korean people and which might establish a National Government of Korea.

The Commission might then proceed to observe the elections. It might be hoped that it would not be obstructed in its work when it reached the 38th parallel, but even if that should prove to be the case, two-thirds of the Korean people would have elected their proportional share of the National Assembly. One-third of the people would have been denied the opportunity of electing their own representatives to the Assembly, and the Korean people and the whole world would know who had denied them that opportunity. Nevertheless, a Korean National Assembly would exist, would be in a position to consult with the Commission on the establishment of a National Government of Korea, as envisaged in the General Assembly resolution, and might be able to negotiate with Koreans in the North regarding their participation in the National Government.

In conclusion, Mr. Jessup pledged the cooperation of the United States in the fulfilment of all parts of the General Assembly resolution. The views of the United States delegation,

/which

which were embodied in the draft resolution he was presenting
(document A/AC.18/31), were that the first question put to the
Interim Committee should be answered in the affirmative, thereby
leaving no need for an answer to the second question.

Mr. TSIANG (China), sketching briefly the past history
of Korea, stated that the Chinese Government regarded the
establishment of an independent and united Korea as a matter of
the greatest importance, which would serve the highest interests
of the whole world. Despite the many declarations and agreements
concerning Korea during and after World War II, the situation in
Korea had resulted in a deadlock, which had caused the United
States to place the question of Korean independence before the
General Assembly.

The Temporary Commission on Korea had given as its chief
reason for consulting the Interim Committee the "negative
attitude" of the USSR authorities with regard to the work of the
Commission. That, however, was no new development; such an
attitude had been made clear in both the First Committee and the
General Assembly. He could not, therefore, subscribe to the view
that the negative attitude of the USSR could be advanced as a
reason for changing the action contemplated in the General
Assembly resolution.

Mr. Tsiang paid tribute to the statement of the Chairman
of the Commission, which had shown a sympathetic understanding of
the legitimate aspirations and noble qualities of the Korean
people and had stressed their desire for unity. He shared the
feelings of the Commission that nothing should be done to
crystallize the division between North and South Korea, which
had not existed until the Powers had established the artificial
line of the 38th parallel. He saw no prospect, however, of that

/division

division disappearing of itself, and if, therefore, the Commission were to allow that division to prevent it from taking action, it would be tantamount to an acceptance and approval of the division of Korea into North and South. That would be to accept defeat, to sacrifice the deepest interests of the Korean people, and to perpetuate a great source of danger to peace.

In his opinion, the Commission should proceed with the elections envisaged in the General Assembly resolution, making it clear to the whole world that the participation of the people of Northern Korea was desired, and that if they were prevented from participating at the present time, they would be welcome at any later time. The Commission should encourage all possible consultations between leaders from North and South, both before and after the elections.

A government created through a free election would certainly be regarded by the people of Korea as their national government, and time would work in favour of such a government. Although it was hoped that Korea might, by one step, achieve freedom and unity, history had shown that it was often the fate of a nation to achieve unity through a succession of steps. Meanwhile, he wished to make it clear that the Chinese Government had no desire to see a national government of Korea adopt an anti-Soviet policy, but hoped rather that it would cultivate the most friendly relations with the USSR.

To sum up, the Chinese delegation felt that it was incumbent upon the Temporary Commission on Korea to implement the programme outlined in resolution II wherever the circumstances in Korea permitted.

Mr. MATIENZO (Bolivia) said that nations which aspired

/to see

to see the Organization acquiring political force and moral
ascendency on a legal basis should adjust their actions to
Article 2, paragraph 5, of the Charter. The members of the
Committee were in a privileged position which allowed them to
observe the fact that the machinery of international organization
did not function as it should. They should not pass by in
silence, but should express their principles and ideas.

No situation was more representative than that in Korea.
He paid a tribute to the Chairman of the Temporary Commission for
his admirable speech at the previous meeting. The general
impression given by the speech was one of perplexity that a
problem which was rather human than political should encounter
obstacles that were illogical and unjustified. The question
should be examined from the point of view of its general
implications for the United Nations. In the first phase, the
possibilities open to the Interim Committee were limited, since
it was empowered only to make recommendations to the General
Assembly.

One view was that the Temporary Commission had the power
to carry out the programme provided for in the second part of
the General Assembly resolution in that area of Korea occupied
by the United States, and that it should do so. He commended
the correctness of the procedure followed by the United States
authorities, which had of their own initiative indicated that
solution, accepting the ex officio mediation of the United
Nations in an attempt to achieve impartiality in guaranteeing
democratic processes in Korea. He could not avoid contrasting
the attitude of the USSR authorities, which had so far refused
to reply to a cordial and courteous message from the Chairman
of a Commission appointed by a majority of the Members of the

/United

제2부 유엔총회 회의록(1948)

United Nations.

Passing from the particular to the fundamental, he was not entirely satisfied that the holding of elections for constituting an Assembly would be in conformity with the resolution of 14 November, which expressed the desire to assist Korea to achieve independence, bearing in mind the unity and the political aspirations of the country. That initial step towards independence would be in accordance with democratic principles, inasmuch as South Korea was inhabited by two-thirds of the total population.

The Committee was in danger of finding itself in an impasse, and it would be neither wise nor correct to neglect the opinion of those best qualified to give advice. The Chairman of the Temporary Commission was in the best position to appreciate the aspirations of the Korean people.

From the general point of view of the interests of the United Nations, he would refer to one of the gravest and most persistent facts - the obstruction of Commissions appointed by the United Nations to deal with international problems in various parts of the world. The international situation was delicate, and even dangerous, and could not be allowed to remain as it was. It was quite contrary to international law and order that resolutions approved by three-fourths of the Members of the General Assembly should become a dead letter by the action of a minority claiming acquired rights.

No means were provided by which a majority could oblige Members to carry out resolutions of the United Nations. A more general and fundamental problem consequently arose: whether resolutions approved by a majority of the Members of the United Nations should be considered as having the same legality and

/Juridical

juridical force as resolutions approved unanimously. That in turn led to the problem of the veto and the unanimity rule.

Members of the United Nations should attempt to put into practice the idea that the Organization worked, not in the interests of one State or another, but in the interests of an international society and with no other view than the common good of all peoples. It was in that spirit that the United Nations had been established. The Organization was more than a club for economic and social cooperation; it must limit the individual action of States to ensure multi-lateral cooperation. Therefore recommendations should have binding force.

He would add his vote to a majority resolution on consultation with the Interim Committee, because that would be in accordance with the spirit of cooperation. He hoped it would be possible to smooth out the antagonisms prevailing in the world. The principles of international cooperation must unite all the nations of the world in the United Nations Assembly, in the hope that it would ensure peace.

Problems facing the United Nations must be approached in their complexity and solved on the basis of universality; and in the name of that universality he would advance a proposal to the effect that, whatever resolution was finally adopted by the General Assembly in connexion with the problem of Korea, the Interim Committee should make an appeal, based on the principles of the Charter, requesting the cooperation of the USSR in the matter. Ex officio mediation might perhaps be requested by a majority resolution which must be implemented if peace was to be assured in that part of the world. If the appeal met with a favourable response, the apprehensions of the peoples would be tranquillized and the United Nations would be strengthened.

/Mr. VITERI-LAFRONTE (Ecuador)

Mr. VITERI-LAFRONTE (Ecuador) did not consider that the Committee should open a general debate on the question of the independence of Korea. The matter had been decided upon in a series of agreements between the Powers from the time of the Cairo Conference. The Committee should limit itself to the recommendations of the General Assembly resolution, which were clear. It should reply to the request for a consultative opinion; to do more would be outside its competence. The difficulty which had caused the Commission to ask for an advisory opinion was simply the fact that a Member of the United Nations, which occupied part of Korea, did not recognize the existence of the Temporary Commission. It was regrettable that the matter should be discussed without the presence of a nation so important in international affairs.

This was not an isolated case; it was one more instance of failure to implement United Nations resolutions with the good will and the cooperative spirit which the world expected, since the United Nations was its only hope of avoiding future wars.

The most serious aspect of the matter was that various nations - not only one nation - had at one time or another objected to or criticized resolutions approved by the General Assembly or other organs of the United Nations. The matter was therefore fundamental and the reply to be given to the Temporary Commission should be carefully weighed, since it was a question of determining the validity and effectiveness of decisions reached by the majority of the United Nations.

The de facto situation was that in other cases, where the United Nations had been in favour of partition, there had been resistance; in the present instance, where the United Nations sought to achieve the unity and independence of Korea, there was

/resistance

resistance to unity and action in favour of partition.

The action of the Commission had been wise and consistent, but had been insufficient to achieve understanding with the authorities in Northern Korea. It was the definite opinion of the Commission that it was impossible in the present circumstances to proceed to the election of a national government and to hold elections in North and South Korea, in accordance with the decision of the General Assembly. The concrete question was whether it was possible to hold elections at all. There were three factors in Northern Korea: (1) the occupation forces; (2) the civil government; (3) the people. The Committee had no knowledge of the attitude and point of view of the occupation authorities or of the government that had been established, or of the general opinion of the Korean people concerning the situation.

With regard to Southern Korea, the Commission stated that there was a number of parties, that political questions were openly discussed and grievances expressed. It was materially impossible to carry out the General Assembly resolution in its entirety, but the possibility of holding an election in Southern Korea was provided for, the limit being the provisional military line, i.e. the 38th parallel. He hoped the Interim Committee would advise in the sense of holding elections in Southern Korea in the atmosphere of freedom referred to in the General Assembly.

The speaker raised the question whether the assembly could be considered a national assembly if constituted in part only of Korea. Territorially speaking the country was equally divided, but Southern Korea contained a population of nineteen million – two-thirds of the total population. In view of the fact that the elections would be held in only half the territory and among only a relative majority of the inhabitants, it would not be a national assembly; nevertheless the people should be allowed to

/take

take a step towards the establishment of democratic government
and the elections should be held. He emphasized that no individual
should be excluded from voting on the grounds of his allegiance
to any political party.

There was one further point. If an assembly were elected
in one part of the territory while another part claimed to have
already set up a government through free elections, any attempt
to represent that assembly as a national government might legalize
the division of Korea and even give it permanence. It should be
made clear that the government would be a provisional one. During
the course of the discussion, he would make concrete proposals
to the effect that the advice given to the Commission should
include a suggestion that the initial measures should be
characterized as provisional and that the final purpose was a
united and independent Korea.

The meeting rose at 1.30 p.m.

(2) 제3차 유엔총회 소총회 제7회 회의 요약

해제문서 7 : A/AC.18/SR.7 (Interim Committee of The General Aessmbly, Summary Record of The Seventh Meeting)

문서명	Interim Committee of the General Assembly, Summary Record of the Seventh Meeting		
	제3차 유엔총회 소총회 제7회 회의 요약 기록		
발신		생성일시	1948년 2월 24일 오후 3시 15분
		발신일시	
수신		수신일시	
		문서번호	A/AC.18/SR.7
문서형태	회의록(요약)	문서분량	5쪽
주제명	한국의 독립에 관한 문제: 1947년 11월 14일의 총회 결의안에 대한 협의 내용		
주요내용	한국독립에 관한 1947년 11월 14일의 총회 결의안을 적용한 유엔총회 소총회와 유엔한국임시위원단의 협의. 상세한 내용은 본문 참조.		
검색어	유엔한국임시위원단, 유엔총회 소총회, Muniz(브라질 대표), 피어슨(Lester P. Pearson, 캐나다 대표), Sarper(터키 대표), Arce(아르헨티나 대표), Aguilar(엘살바도르 대표)		

한국독립에 관한 1947년 11월 14일 유엔총회 결의안을 적용한 유엔총회 소총회와 유엔한국임시위원단의 협의 내용(Documents A/AC.18/27, A/AC.18/28, A/AC.18/28 Add.1 Corr.1).

브라질 대표는 위원단과 입장을 같이 한다고 말함. 또한 그는 1947년 11월 14일에 총회가 결의안을 통과시켰을 때 총회는 이미 소련의 반대 의견에 대해 알고 있었기 때문에 소련이 어떤 장애가 되더라도 단 한 국가가 유엔총회의 최종 결정에 영향을 미치게 해서는 안 된다고 말함. 또한 유엔한국임시위원단은 총회뿐만 아니라 한국국민들에게도 불가피한 책임감을 가지고 있다고 말하며 위원단이 한국 내에서의 임무를 지체 없이 최대한 수행해야 한다고 주장함. 그리고 그는 위원단의 활동이 현재 남한에 집중될 수밖에 없다는 것을 알지만 그래도 그 활동이 최대한 포괄적으로 진행되어야 한다고 지적함.

캐나다 대표는 이와 같은 사태에 대해 소총회가 할 수 있는 일은 유엔한국임시위원단 의장의 발언을 받아들여 이를 다음 총회에 보고하거나 총회에 특별 세션을 요청하는 것이라고 언급함.

호주 대표는 남한에 중앙정부를 세우는 일은 유엔총회가 원하는 형태의 결과를 가져오지 못할 것이며 오히려 북한에도 비슷한 결과를 만들어 남북한의 통일이 아닌 영구적인 분단을 초래할 수 있다는 것을 임시위원단의 위원들 대부분이 예상하고 있다고 말함. 이어 한반도 전체의 선거를 통한 중앙정부수립이 불가능해졌기 때문에 철수하게 된 임시위원단이 철수를 철회하고 한국에 남아서 진행 상황을 유엔 총회에 보고하고 조언하는 방식의 임무를 맡을 것을 제안함. 그런 연유로 해서 임시위원단에 대해 남한에서의 선거를 기획하고 자문기관으로서 그 선거가 완전한 자유 아래 실시되고 있는지를 감독하는 역할을 부여하도록 하자고 주장함. 또한 이 기관은 행정 업무를 맡되 중앙정부에 참여하지는 않고 이 기관을 통해 한국인들이 자신들의 대표로 하여금 자신들이 원하는 것을 점령당국과 유엔총회 소총회 모두 전달할 수 있도록 가교 역할을 하며, 남북한의 통합을 지원하고 두 열강의 협의 가능성을 창출하는 일을 하는 위원회로 만들자고 주장함.

　터키 대표는 불변의 평화의 원칙을 언급하면서 한국인들도 다른 모든 사람들처럼 독립과 통일의 권리를 갖고 있다고 말하고 유엔이 그 원칙을 지키기 위해 노력해야 한다고 주장함.

　아르헨티나 대표는 즉각적으로 선거가 실시되어야 하며 임시위원단은 한국에 남아서 유엔 총회에 도움이 되는 임무를 수행해야 한다고 주장함.

　엘살바도르 대표는 소련의 불참이 1947년 11월 14일의 총회 결의안을 실행하는데 큰 걸림돌이 될 것이라고 강조했지만, 이로 인해 한국의 중앙정부를 만드는 일을 늦춰서는 안 된다고 말함. 그리고 유엔이 세계대전 후 한국인에게 약속한 독립을 하루빨리 달성해야 한다고 주장하면서 최대한 빠른 시일 안에 선거를 실시해야 한다고 말함.

　오후 4시40분에 정회함.

United Nations

GENERAL ASSEMBLY

Nations Unies

ASSEMBLEE GENERALE

UNRESTRICTED
A/AC.18/SR.7
28 February 1948
ENGLISH
ORIGINAL: FRENCH

INTERIM COMMITTEE OF THE GENERAL ASSEMBLY

SUMMARY RECORD OF THE SEVENTH MEETING

Held at Lake Success
Tuesday, 24 February 1948 at 3.15 p.m.

Chairman: Mr. L. PADILLA NERVO (Mexico)

PROBLEM OF THE INDEPENDENCE OF KOREA: CONSULTATION BY THE UNITED NATIONS TEMPORARY COMMISSION ON KOREA WITH THE INTERIM COMMITTEE ON THE APPLICATION IN THE LIGHT OF DEVELOPMENTS OF THE GENERAL ASSEMBLY RESOLUTION OF 14 NOVEMBER 1947, (Documents A/AC.18/27, A/AC.18/28, A/AC.18/28 Add.1 Corr.1) (Continued)

Mr. MUNIZ (Brazil) said that it was not easy to reply to the questions raised by the Temporary Commission without taking into account the essential aspects of the problem, which showed that the difficulties were not solely of a legal nature.

It was important to note that the Commission had unanimously rejected a solution consisting in the admission that it was unable to fulfil its task. The members of the Interim Committee ought to keep constantly in mind this sentiment of the Commission's, which the delegation of Brazil, for its part, entirely shared.

There could be no doubt that, when it adopted the resolution of 14 November 1947, the General Assembly was perfectly aware of the obstacles in the way of their application, since it already knew the attitude of the Union of Soviet Socialist Republics.

The Assembly thereby declared its conviction that the unilateral action of some Powers could not and should not constitute an obstacle to the realization of its high aims. Whatever the obstacles raised by the Union of Soviet Socialist Republics, the United Nations could not permit that country to dictate the final decision. In accepting its task the Commission had assumed a responsibility not only towards the General Assembly but also towards the Korean people; and this responsibility it could not evade.

It was the duty of the United Nations Temporary Commission on Korea to fulfil its mission as far as possible, and it must be recognized that the

/action

action recommended in the General Assembly's resolutions could be achieved
to a large extent. If, therefore, the Commission was convinced of the
necessity of the task prescribed, it should proceed to carry it out
without delay.

Elections to establish a purely consultative body would be contrary
to the spirit and letter of the General Assembly resolutions, and Brazil
would oppose that interpretation.

The Interim Committee, for its part, must come to an agreement on
what action could be undertaken but it would necessarily be the Temporary
Commission's task to ascertain on the spot what measures could actually
be applied. It was clear that for the moment at least any action might
have to be limited to South Korea, but such action should be as comprehensive
as possible. The Brazilian delegation did not believe that the adoption
of such a plan would preclude the possibility of a subsequent agreement
with regard to North Korea; an agreement which might be achieved, as
suggested by Mr. Menon, by means of conferences with the political leaders
of the Northern zone, and which might subsequently lead to the unification
of the whole country.

Mr. PEARSON (Canada) considered, as regards the two questions on which
the Temporary Commission wished to consult with the Interim Committee of
the General Assembly, that the reply to the questions contained in
paragraph 1 and paragraph 2 (a) must be negative. The attitude of Canada,
which was represented in the Temporary Commission on Korea, would at
least have the advantage of proving the unwarranted nature of certain
allegations to the effect that the Temporary Commission was in the service
of United States of America.

From the legal standpoint the action of the Temporary Commission on
Korea was based on the two General Assembly resolutions of 14 November 1947.
Paragraph 4 of Resolution II made it clear that the Commission could not
confine its activities to Southern Korea. The Temporary Commission could
not violate its terms of reference, and the Interim Committee - which could
only "consider and report with its conclusions, to the General Assembly on
such matters as have been referred to it by the General Assembly" - was not
competent to change them. The Temporary Commission was entitled to consult
with the Interim Committee, but the latter had no authority to extend its
powers.

The Interim Committee had the choice between two methods: (1) to
consider the statement of the Chairman of the Temporary Commission on
Korea and report to the next General Assembly, with its conclusions; (2) to
recommend convening an extraordinary session of the General Assembly to

/consider

consider the possibility of amending the resolution of 14 November 1947 in the light of developments.

With regard to Resolution I of the General Assembly, he thought that that resolution had to be considered in conjunction with Resolution II, and that it did not empower the Temporary Commission to hold elections in Southern Korea only, even for purely consultative purposes. Resolution I provided for the election of representatives of the Korean people, who were to be invited to take part in the consideration of the Korean question. In the course of discussions in the First Committee of the General Assembly, the representative of China had stressed the need to obtain representation from the Korean people as a whole, and not from only one of the two zones. The Canadian representative in the First Committee shared that opinion and had voted for the resolutions because he believed that they expressed that point of view. The Canadian representative in the Temporary Commission on Korea had constantly upheld that interpretation of the resolutions of 14 November, and the consequent impossibility of confining the Commission's functions and powers to the Southern Zone.

If as some representatives declared, the discussion in the General Assembly had made it clear that the Commission would be prevented from exercising its powers in North Korea, it was unfortunate that these representatives, since they expected such opposition, did not attempt to have the resolutions amended to take that fact into account.

The Temporary Commission was not at present able to fulfil its task in Korea. The responsibility for that regrettable situation must be ascribed to the Union of Soviet Socialist Republics, which opposed the establishment of a free, united and democratic Korea, and whose obstructive policy was to be condemned.

He regretted that he was obliged to oppose the United States resolution, which called upon the Temporary Commission to take action it was not entitled to take under its terms of reference. The General Assembly resolutions of 14 November 1947 did not authorize the Commission to take action in Southern Korea only.

Mr. FORSYTH (Australia) said that owing to her geographical situation, Australia took a special interest in any country in the Pacific region. His Government considered that Korea's independence and unity were essential to the stability of that region.

The two General Assembly resolutions and the debate which had preceded their adoption ruled out any possibility of partial application. To arrange elections in Southern Korea, as the representative of the United States of America had proposed, would be contrary to the Assembly resolutions, since a Government thus elected could not, in the Australian delegation's view, have any pretensions to the status of a national Government. The

/Temporary

Temporary Commission was almost unanimous in thinking that such a Government would not have the character which the General Assembly had wished to give it. The establishment of a national Government in the South might give rise to similar action in the North, and he warned the Interim Committee against any solution which, instead of facilitating the unification of Korea, might perpetuate its division.

Considering the other solutions proposed, the Australian delegation did not think that the Temporary Commission should withdraw after finding that it was not possible to organize elections throughout Korea with a view to the formation of a national Government. He thought that to advise the Temporary Commission to remain in Korea to inform the General Assembly of the course of events, since it was unable to fulfil its task, was not going far enough, since it would not be making the best use of the Temporary Commission's presence on the spot. It was desirable for the Temporary Commission to remain in Korea in order to seize every opportunity of fulfilling its task.

The Interim Committee had no power either to alter resolutions adopted by the Assembly, or to modify the Temporary Commission's terms of reference, but it could give its views on the most appropriate method of enabling the Commission to fulfil its task. In this connection, it might suggest that elections be arranged in Southern Korea, making sure that they took place in absolute freedom, in order to set up an advisory body, also possessing administrative functions, which would, however, take care to make no claims to be a national Government. This body would nevertheless enable the Koreans to make their wishes known through their representatives, both to the occupying authorities and to the United Nations Temporary Commission. Its constitution would leave the door open for a fusion of the South and the North, and it was precisely in order to detect any favourable symptoms in this connection and to report to the General Assembly on the course of events in Korea that the Temporary Commission should remain there. In the meantime, the two Great Powers concerned might again consider the possibility of reaching agreement, either by direct negotiation or at the Conference of Pacific Powers.

Mr. SARPER (Turkey) stressed the principle of the **indivisibility of** peace, and stated that although his country was far distant from Korea, it was none the less concerned in an equitable solution of the problem.

The Korean people, like all the peoples of the world, had a right to independence and unity. That was a fundamental principle of the Charter, and no exception could be made to that principle on account of objections raised by a Member or by a minority. Such a proceeding would jeopardize the very existence of the United Nations. The latter must, on the contrary,

/take definite

take definite action to ensure the application of the principles for which it stood. Hence, the Turkish delegation would support the United States proposal, which it considered to be perfectly feasible.

Mr. ARCE (Argentina) pointed out that Korea was not an enemy country, and that elections should therefore have taken place immediately after the disarmament of the Japanese troops.

The Argentine delegation would vote for the adoption of the draft resolution submitted by the United States, in order that elections might take place in Korea in accordance with the General Assembly's wishes and that a national assembly guiding the destinies of the Korean people might be established there as soon as possible. The Temporary Commission should remain in Korea in order to report to the next General Assembly on the progress it had made in fulfilling its task.

Mr. AGUILAR (El Salvador) emphasized that the USSR refusal to co-operate in the task undertaken by the United Nations and the Temporary Commission on Korea represented the main obstacle to the application of the General Assembly's resolutions of 14 November 1947.

He thought, however, that this should not prevent the Temporary Commission from making an effort to facilitate the establishment of a national Government elected by two-thirds of the Korean people. The United States representative had given an assurance that the armed forces of his country would provide the Commission with every facility and guarantee for seeing that the elections took place in an atmosphere of freedom. The Commission had already undertaken a study of the electoral laws of Korea in considering the possibilities of modifying the existing administrative regime, and its presence during the elections should dispel the doubts which certain members of the Korean Commission seemed to feel with regard to the conditions in which these elections took place.

Since the end of the war, all efforts to enable the Korean people to regain the independence which had so long been promised them had failed. The United Nations should try to fulfil its obligations towards the Korean people.

In the interest, both of the Korean people and of the prestige of the United Nations, El Salvador hoped that the Interim Committee would send a reply to the Temporary Commission to the effect that national elections should be organized as soon as possible in all parts of Korea which the Commission could reach and in which it could supervise the elections, in accordance with Resolution II of the General Assembly of 14 November 1947.

The meeting rose at 4.40 p.m.

(3) 한국 독립 문제에 관한 제3차 유엔총회 소총회 회의록

해제문서 8 : A/AC.18/32 (Interim Committee of the General Assembly, Problem of the Independence of Korea)

문서명	Interim Committee of the General Assembly, Problem of the Independence of Korea		
	유엔총회 소총회: 한국 독립문제		
발신		생성일시	1948년 2월 25일
		발신일시	
수신		수신일시	
		문서번호	A/AC.18/32
문서형태	회의록(요약)	문서분량	2쪽
주제명	1. 유엔한국임시위원단의 권한문제 2. 한국의 국회의원 선거 및 그들의 한국수립 과정에서의 역할		
주요내용	1947년 11월 14일 유엔총회 결의안의 적용에 관한 유엔총회 소총회와 유엔한국임시위원단(UNTCOK)의 협의. 상세한 내용은 본문 참조.		
검색어	유엔한국임시위원단, 한국 국회, 유엔총회 소총회		

1947년 11월 14일 유엔총회 결의안의 적용에 관한 유엔총회 소총회와 유엔한국임시위원단(UNTCOK)의 협의.

미국은 1948년 2월 25일 제8차 회의에서 소총회에 제출한 제안에 관해 설명함(A/AC.18/31 문서로 제출된 결의안 초안이 소총회에서 채택된 것처럼 이 제안은 승인 가능한 형태로 초안되어 있음).

소총회는 유엔한국임시위원단이 제기한 첫 번째 질문에 대한 답변으로, 위원회의 견해를 표명한 결의안에 덧붙여 아래의 사항을 고려하였음.

1. 유엔한국임시위원단이 감독하는 한국에서의 선거는 표현의 자유, 집회의 자유, 언론의 자유 등 민주주의적 권리가 보장되는 분위기 하에서 실시되어야 하며 미국 대표가 미국 정부의 적극적인 지원을 받기로 약속했다는 내용.

2. 향후 선출될 국회의원들로 구성된 국회가 한국 정부 형성의 첫 번째 단계가 될 것이며, 그 형태는 그들 스스로가 정해야 할 것임. 그러기 위해서 국회를 구성하는 대표들은 유엔한국임시위원단과 자유롭게 의견을 조율할 것이고 그들이 원한다면 선거에 참가하지 않은 어떤 다른 단체와도 협상할 수 있으며, 거기에는 향후 설립될 정부의 형태와 이들 단체들의 참가 여부 등도 포함될 것임. 유엔총회 소총회는 한국의 통일을 달성하기 위해서 가능한 모든 범위의 설득과 모든 평화적 방법이 사용될 것이라고 확신함.

3. 유엔총회 소총회는 유엔한국임시위원단이 한반도의 전 지역에서 상황이 허락하는 한 자신의 임무를 수행할 권한(authority)과 결정권을 갖고 있다는 점을 승인함.

유엔총회 소총회에서 채택된 이 결의안과 다른 견해를 일부 대표자들이 표명함.

1. 소련 측은 유엔한국임시위원단이 유엔총회 결의안의 엄격한 법적 해석의 범위 내에서 남한만의 선거를 적절히 수행할 수 있을 것인가에 대한 의구심을

표명함. 이러한 관점에서 오직 자문적 목적의 선거만이 가능할 것이라는 의견들이 있었음.

2. 유엔총회 결의안의 해석과 관련해, 유엔총회 소총회 능력에 대한 회의적 견해가 제기됨.

3. 이러한 관점에서 모든 문제는 유엔총회 특별회기에서 다루어져야 한다는 제안이 제출됨.

United Nations **Nations Unies**

GENERAL ASSEMBLY **ASSEMBLEE GENERALE**

UNRESTRICTED
A/AC.18/32
25 February 1948
ORIGINAL: ENGLISH

INTERIM COMMITTEE OF THE GENERAL ASSEMBLY

PROBLEM OF THE INDEPENDENCE OF KOREA

CONSULTATION BY THE UNITED NATIONS TEMPORARY COMMISSION ON KOREA WITH THE INTERIM COMMITTEE ON THE APPLICATION OF THE GENERAL ASSEMBLY RESOLUTION OF 14 NOVEMBER 1947 IN THE LIGHT OF DEVELOPMENTS

UNITED STATES OF AMERICA: EXPLANATION OF THE SUGGESTIONS MADE TO THE INTERIM COMMITTEE DURING ITS EIGHTH MEETING ON 25 FEBRUARY 1948, PREPARED IN RESPONSE TO A REQUEST OF THE COMMITTEE

NOTE: This paper is drafted in a form in which it could be approved if the draft resolution submitted as document A/AC.18/31 is adopted by the Interim Committee.

The Interim Committee decided to answer in the affirmative the first question propounded to it by the United Nations Temporary Commission on Korea, having in mind the following considerations in addition to those stated in the resolution whereby it expressed its views:

1. The elections to be observed by the United Nations Temporary Commission on Korea should be held in a free atmosphere wherein the democratic rights of freedom of speech, press, and assembly would be recognized and respected. In this connection the Interim Committee took note of the assurance given by the representative of the United States that authorities of the United States in Korea would co-operate to the fullest extent to that end.

2. The National Assembly to which representatives are to be elected would be a stage in the formation of a Korean Government, the form of which is to be determined by the Korean people themselves. In reaching this conclusion, the Interim Committee noted that the representatives constituting the National Assembly would be entirely free to consult with the United Nations Temporary Commission on Korea and to carry on such negotiations as they wished with any other Korean groups which might not have participated in the elections, regarding the form of government to be established and the participation of those groups therein. The Interim Committee entertained the hope

/...

that in these consultations and negotiations, the Korean representatives
in the National Assembly would be able to secure through their efforts
the full co-operation in their government of all Koreans. The Interim
Committee was confident that all peaceful methods of persuasion
would thus be used to the greatest possible extent for the attainment
of Korean unity.

3.   The Interim Committee recognized that the United Nations
Temporary Commission on Korea itself has the authority and discretion
to discharge its duties in Korea wherever and to the extent that
circumstances permit.

Certain representatives expressed views which differed from those
embodied in the resolution adopted by the Committee. These views may be
summarized as follows:

1.   In the light of the "negative attitude" of the Soviet Union,
doubt was expressed as to whether the United Nations Temporary
Commission on Korea could properly hold elections in South Korea
alone within the strict legal interpretation of the General Assembly
resolution. A variation of this view was that elections for
consultative purposes only could be held.

2.   Doubt was further raised concerning the competence of the Interim
Committee to express a view which might be regarded as an interpretation
of the General Assembly resolution.

3.   It was also suggested in view of developments that the whole
matter should be referred to a special session of the General Assembly.

-----

2. 제3차 유엔총회 제1위원회 문서

(1) 제3차 유엔총회 제1위원회 제229차 회의 요약

해제문서 9 : A/C.1/SR 229 (Third Session, First Committee, Summary Record of the Two Hundred and Twenty Ninth Meeting)

문서명	Third Session, First Committee, Summary Record of the Two Hundred and Twenty Ninth Meeting		
	제3차 유엔총회 제1위원회 제229차 회의 요약 기록		
발신		생성일시	1948년 12월 6일 오전 10시 30분
		발신일시	
수신		수신일시	
		문서번호	A/C.1/SR 229
문서형태	회의록(요약)	문서분량	16쪽
주제명	1. 이탈리아의 구식민지 처리 문제 2. 조선민주주의인민공화국 대표의 유엔 회의 참석 여부		
주요내용	1948년 12월 6일 오전 10:30 프랑스 파리에서 개최된 제3차 유엔총회 제1위원회 제229차 회의록. 상세한 내용은 본문 참조.		
검색어	유엔한국임시위원단, 제1위원회, 휘슬러(James Abott Mcneil Whistler, 영국 대표), 덜레스(John Dulles, 미국 대표), Fernandez(칠레 대표), 말리크(Yakov Aleksandrovich Malik, 소련 대표), 치앙(Tingfu. F. Tsiang, 중국 대표), Medhen(이디오피아 대표), Arce(아르젠티나 대표), 매뉴일스키(Manuilsky, 우크라이나 대표), Houdek(체코슬로바키아 대표), Zebrowski(폴란드 대표), Kiselev(백러시아 대표), Franzer(뉴질랜드 대표), Fawzi(이집트 대표), Cicmil(유고슬라비아 대표)		

1948년 12월 6일 오전 10시 30분 프랑스 파리에서 개최된 제1위원회 제229차 회의록.

유엔한국임시위원단과 함께 유엔총회 소총회의 보고서(A/575 및 A583)와 그 주제의 항목별 논의 순서에 대한 제안들을 토론함.

영국 대표는 한국 독립문제와 이탈리아의 구식민지 문제를 동시에 다룰 것을 제안하였으나 미국 대표가 이에 동의하지 않음.

소련 대표는 이탈리아문제가 외상회의에서 충분히 논의된 바 있고 한국문제는 복잡하고 유엔한국임시위원단 보고서가 수 천 장에 달하는 분량인 만큼, 3주간에 걸쳐 논의된 팔레스타인 문제만큼의 시간이 필요하므로 이탈리아 식민지문제를 먼저 다루고, 한국문제는 회기 두 번째 기간에 논의하는 것이 바람직하며, 보고서 내용을 분석하기 위해 연설에 제한을 두지 말자고 제안함.

중국 대표는 영국과 소련의 제안을 모두 거부하고, 한국문제는 극동지역에 직접적으로 관련된 총회의 어젠다(의제)라고 규정함.

반대 32표, 찬성 8표, 기권 9표로 소련의 제안은 기각됨.

회의에서는 체코슬로바키아가 제안한 유엔의 한반도문제 회의에 북한 대표를 초청할지 여부에 관한 문제(A/C.1/367)를 논의함.

체코슬로바키아 대표는 북한 대표를 초청하는 것에 관한 안건을 제의함.

체코슬로바키아 대표의 발언에 이어, 중국 대표는 이미 제2차 총회 결의안에 따라 한국문제 관련 논의를 위해서는 선출된 한국국민의 대표가 참석해야 하며 합법적 절차에 따라 선출된 유엔대표 장면 박사가 남한 측 대표로 제3차 총회에 참석하고 있지만, 북한 측의 정부수립 과정에서는 체코슬로바키아만이 그 과정을 참관했을 뿐이므로 유엔이 그 정당성을 확인할 수 없고 따라서 절차상의 문제가 있기 때문에 북한 대표가 유엔총회에 참석하는 것은 온당하지 못하다는 의견을 제시함.

미국대표는 제2차 회의에서 체코슬로바키아가 제안한 북한 대표 초청 안이 부결되었음을 공표함.

폴란드 대표는 안건에 대한 표결을 주장하였으나 미국 대표가 북한 선거과정의 문제점을 제기하며 북한 대표의 대표성을 부인함. 이에 우크라이나, 백러시아 사회주의공화국 대표가 중국 발언에 반대의사를 표명함.

뉴질랜드 대표는 북한 선거에서 북한주민이 자유의사를 표명하였다는 증거를 제출하도록 요청함.

이집트는 북한 선거가 유엔 결의안을 준수했다는 전제하에 본 안건에 대한 지지 의사를 밝혔으며, 유고슬라비아 대표는 북한 선거의 정당성을 인정하며 본 안건을 지지함.

이어서 소련 대표는 북한 선거의 정당성을 입증하는 발언과 함께 본 안건 상정이 부당하다는 미국대표의 발언에 대해 반박함.

오후 1시 10분에 정회함.

United Nations　Nations Unies

**GENERAL
ASSEMBLY**

**ASSEMBLEE
GENERALE**

UNRESTRICTED

A/C.1/SR 229
7 December 1948

ORIGINAL: ENGLISH

<u>Dual distribution</u>

Third Session

FIRST COMMITTEE

SUMMARY RECORD OF THE TWO HUNDRED AND TWENTY NINTH MEETING

Held at the Palais de Chaillot, Paris,
on Monday, 6 December 1948, at 10.30 a.m.

CONTENTS:

Reports of the United Nations Temporary Commission on Korea
and of the Interim Committee of the General Assembly: (A/575
and A/583) (Discussion of porposals on the order of consideration
of the items on the agenda:

Dicaussion of the Czechoslovak proposal to invite the delegation
of the Korean People's Democratic Republic to participate in the
discussion A/C.1/367)

<u>Chairman:</u>	Mr. H. SPAAK	Belgium
<u>Rapporteur:</u>	Mr. S. SARPER	Turkey

Any corrections of this record should be submitted in writing, in
either of the working language (English or French), and within two
working days, to Mr. E. Delavenay, Director, Official Records Division,
Room 3015, Palais de Chaillot.　Corrections should be accompanied by or
incorporated in a letter, on headed notepaper, bearing the approprıate
symbol number and enclosed in an envelope marked "Urgent".. Corrections
can be dealt with more speedily by the services concerned if delegations
will be good enough also to incorporate them in a mimeographed copy of
the record.

REPORTS OF THE UNITED NATIONS TEMPORARY COMMISSION ON KOREA AND OF THE
INTERIM COMMITTEE OF THE GENERAL ASSEMBLY: (A/575 and A/583)

DISCUSSION OF PROPOSALS ON THE ORDER OF CONSIDERATION OF THE ITEMS ON
THE AGENDA:

Mr. McNEIL (United Kingdom) suggested that the Committee might
consider the problem of the independence of Korea and the question of the
disposal of the former Italian Colonies concurrently by discussing them
at alternate meetings. He said that he made the suggestion only in order
that the Committee could use the time which remained to the best advantage
and pointed out that if only one question were considered, the Committee
might be faced with the same situation which had occurred during the
discussion of the Palestinian question when it had wasted time because
there were no speakers. If the procedure he suggested were adopted, it
should be possible to complete a consideration of both Questions before
the adjournment of the General Assembly. He added, however, that he did
not wish to make his proposal formal, and would not press it if there
were any opposition to it.

Mr. DULLES (United States of America) expressed regret that his
delegation could not accept the suggestion of the United Kingdom representative. He thought that the Committee must assume that the General Assembly
would accept the recommendations of the General Committee to adjourn at
the end of the present week, in which case, an attempt to discuss both
these items would result in no action on either item. If, however, the
Committee concentrated on the question of Korea, it should be possible to
complete this item before the adjournment. The United States delegation
attached great importance to constructive action on this question. He
pointed out that the Committee had already dealt with two questions concerning the Mediterranean theatre and expressed the opinion that there
would be unfortunate repercussions in the Far East if the question of Korea
were not dealt with. He assured Mr. McNeil that if the Committtee temporarily
ran out of speakers on the Korean question, his delegation would ask that
the United Kingdom delegation be allowed to speak on the question of the
former Italian Colonies.

/The CHAIRMAN

The CHAIRMAN pointed out that the Committee might lose a further meeting if the question of the order of items were discussed at length. He suggested that it might be better to agree to limit speeches to one half-hour for a first statement or ten minutes for a rebuttal, but said he would withdraw this suggestion if there were any objections.

Mr. FERNANDEZ (Chile) regretted that he also must oppose the suggestion of the United Kingdom. He explained that the Government of Chile wished to help the Government of Italy in the question of the former Italian Colonies but would need time to discuss this question with other Foreign Offices. Therefore, he did not think the Assembly could take action on this question of the former Italian Colonies before adjournment.

Mr. MALIK (USSR) said that since the question of the former Italian Colonies had been fully discussed by the Council of Foreign Ministers and their Deputies, it should not require much discussion and the Assembly might therefore be able to complete consideration of this question before its adjournment. On the other hand, the Korean question was very complicated, and the Report of the Temporary Commission alone ran into thousands of pages. It would therefore require at least as much time for discussion as the Palestinian question which had been discussed for three weeks. He therefore suggested that the Committee begin consideration of the question of the former Italian Colonies and leave the Korean question until the second part of the session. He could not agree to the Chairman's suggestion for limiting speeches since it would be necessary to analyse the Korean situation at length, including the reports of the Temporary Commission and the Interim Committee.

Mr. TSIANG (China) said he could not accept the suggestion of either the United Kingdom delegation or the USSR delegation, and could see no need for changing the order of consideration of items. The Korean question was the only problem on the Assembly's agenda relating directly to the Far East and if its consideration was postponed, the Assembly could be accused of neglecting this area. Furthermore, if the Committee should try to consider both questions alternately, it would be able to finish neither of them.

Mr. MEDHEN (Ethiopia) supported the suggestion of the United Kingdom representative. He said that his delegation considered the question of the disposal of the former Italian Colonies would take a

/relatively

제2부 유엔총회 회의록(1948)

relatively short time since it had been thoroughly studied and discussed and was now merely a question of decision.

Mr. ARCE (Argentina) expressed himself in favour of maintaining the present order of consideration of items. He did not think that the question of the former Italian Colonies could be dealt with quickly although it had been thoroughly studied by the Foreign Ministers, since there were other Members of the United Nations interested in this question, who were not all thoroughly acquainted with its details. The views of the delegation of Ethiopia must be considered and consultation with the Trusteeship Council might be useful, all of which would take considerable time.

Mr. McNEIL (United Kingdom) said that since the Committee was clearly divided on his suggestion, he would withdraw it, but would take up the suggestion of the United States representative to speak on the question of the former Italian Colonies if there were a pause in the debate on the Korean question.

Mr. MANUILSKY (Ukrainian Soviet Socialist Republic) said that he saw a dangerous tendency in the statement of the United States representative to limit the discussion on the Korean question. The Temporary Commission on Korea had submitted voluminous material on which many delegations would have a number of comments. Furthermore, there had been a proposal by the Czechoslovak delegation some time ago to invite a representative of the Korean Peoples' Democratic Republic to participate in the discussion. Now there was also a proposal by the Chinese delegation to invite a Dr. Chang of the so-called Government of the Republic of Korea, to participate in the debate. In regard to the proposal of the Chinese delegation he could prove that there was no such thing as a Government of the Republic of Korea in southern Korea. He was opposed to any attempt to cut off discussion on the Korean question and, therefore, he objected to the proposals of the US delegation to proceed with the consideration of the Korean question without hearing the views of the true representatives of the Korean people, for it was obvious that they would require a certain time to be present. He quoted a statement by the Chairman of the Temporary Commission on Korea to the effect that no Government which would arise as a result of elections in Southern Korea alone could be called a National Government, either from a geographical or a political point of view. It was, in his opinion, essential that the true representatives of the Korean people be invited to participate in the discussion rather than a usurper. His delegation,

/therefore

therefore, insisted that the Committee deal first with the question of the former Italian Colonies and then take immediate steps to invite the representatives of the Korean people to participate in the discussion.

The CHAIRMAN then put to the vote the USSR proposal to take up immediately the question of the disposal of the former Italian Colonies.

A vote was taken by show of hands; the proposal was rejected by 32 votes to 8, with 9 abstentions.

DISCUSSION OF THE CZECHOSLOVAK PROPOSAL TO INVITE THE DELEGATION OF THE KOREAN PEOPLES' DEMOCRATIC REPUBLIC TO PARTICIPATE IN THE DISCUSSION: (A/C.1/367)

Mr. HOUDEK (Czechoslovakia) recalled that the Czechoslovakian delegation submitted for consideration of the Committee a draft resolution (A/C.1/367), calling for the invitation of representatives of the Government of the Korean Peoples' Republic to participate in a discussion on the Korean problem. He read excerpts from the cablegram dated 8 October from the Minister of Foreign Affairs of the Democratic Peoples' Republic of Korea, to the Secretary-General (A/C.1/366), requesting to be allowed to participate in the discussion of this question, on which the Czechoslovak proposal was based. He thought the Committee would agree on the necessity of considering all aspects of the problem, and since the representatives of southern Korea were already in Paris available for invitation by the Committee, he thought the same opportunity should be given to representatives from northern Korea.

Mr. TSIANG (China) read Resolution 112A adopted at the Assembly's second Session concerning the participation of elected representatives of the Korean people in the consideration of the Korean question, and noted that the proposal of the Chinese delegation (A/C.1/395) to invite the delegation of the Government of the Republic of Korea was based on the results of this Resolution. Dr. Chang was an elected representative of the Korean National Assembly and had been appointed as the Chairman of the delegation by the Government of the Republic of Korea, which had resulted from the election held pursuant to the Assembly's Resolution. On the other hand, only the Czechoslovakian delegation knew where and how the election of the representative of **northern** Korea took place and the United Nations Commission had not been able to observe that election. While he   that several delegations would like to give a hearing to

/both

both parties in accordance with the normal democratic procedure, he would
like to point out that such a procedure would not be in accord with the
previous Assembly Resolution and would not promote the cause of democracy.
In this situation, one region of Korea was co-operating with the United
Nations while the other had opposed the United Nations from the very
beginning and any recognition of the representative of northern Korea
might be misinterpreted in Korea with disastrous psychological reactions.

Mr. DULLES (United States) speaking on a point of order, read
from page 20 of the verbatim record of the 200th meeting of the Committee
which he thought showed that the Czechoslovak draft resolution had been
voted down and could not therefore be reconsidered unless the Committee so
decided by a two-thirds vote.

The CHAIRMAN replied that the excerpt from the verbatim record
quoted by Mr. Dulles did not accurately reflect what had happened for the
Committee had merely decided not to take up the Czechoslovak proposal at
that time and had not dealt with its substance. In this connection, he
quoted the official summary record which, in his opinion, made this clear.

Mr. ZEBROWSKI (Poland) expressed regret that the Czechoslovak
proposal had been given such summary treatment when it had been introduced
on 15 November for if it had been adopted at that time, the Committee
would have saved itself valuable time and would have made a substantial
contribution for the proper solution of the Korean problem. As background to the present situation he recalled that at the 89th and 90th
meetings of the First Committee during the second session, the USSR
delegation had submitted a proposal to invite elected representatives of
the Korean people to participate in the discussion. As the Polish
representative had stated at the time, it was obvious there was no party
more closely connected with the problem independence than the Korean
people themselves, but while many representatives paid tribute to the
principle, only a few representatives were not afraid to listen to the
views of the representatives of the Korean people. Other delegations
attempted to drown the principle in a flood of technicalities and the
United States delegation introduced a rider to the USSR proposal calling
for a Temporary Commission in Korea, thus preventing the admission of
representatives of Korea at the second session.

While he would reserve his right to deal with the results of this
Commission at a later stage he wished to meet the objection of the United

/States

States representative, made when the Czechoslovak proposal was introduced on 15 November, that the Peoples' Democratic Republic had adopted a hostile attitude towards the Commission. It should be added that all political parties and groups in the US Occupation Zone in Korea had also boycotted the Commission, with the exception of the most reactionary and subservient political organisations. Nothing else could have been expected for no nation could acquiesce to such an outside interference with its vital development, without at least having been previously consulted. Having prevented Korean representatives from attending the second session the US delegation could not therefore complain that the Peoples' Democratic Republic had not co-operated with the Commission.

If the Committee now really wished to aid Korean independence, the Polish delegation called upon it to show its respect for the principle of democratic equality by voting for the Czechoslovak proposal. It hardly seemed necessary to consider the many minor objections which were being raised. The decision must be based on a few simple facts. The Korean people had never co-operated with the enemies of the United Nations and had suffered much from their resistance to Japanese militarism. The Government of the Korean Peoples' Democratic Republic was the direct descendant of the most ardent fighters and the continuation of a spontaneous movement of the Korean people to form their own representative democratic institution, a movement which had unfortunately been suppressed in the United States Zone of occupation. It was an orderly Government elected not only by the people of northern Korea but also by the majority of people in southern Korea and even the Commission could not deny that it represented the true interests of the Korean people. For all these reasons the Polish delegation would vote for the czechoslovak proposal and he hoped that other delegations would not be sidetracked by irrelevant considerations.

Mr. DULLES (United States) read the operative part of the Assembly's Resolution 112A of the Second Session concerning the participation of Korean representatives in the Assembly's discussion, interpreting it to mean that the Assembly had decided on representation for the Korean people and sent a Credentials Committee to Korea to ensure that real representatives of the Korean people were chosen. The Temporary Commission on Korea had not been allowed to observe the election of representatives in northern Korea yet now, those nations which were largely responsible for having refused the Commission access were saying that the Committee should hear representatives from northern Korea without knowing whether they had been legally elected. He felt strongly that it would be beneath the Assembly's dignity to give such a privilege to those who had defied the Assembly's
/organ

제2부 유엔총회 회의록(1948)

organ in this matter. While he understood and subscribed to the strong
desire to have all sides fully heard, he thought there was no doubt that the
case of the regime in northern Korea would be fully presented by the
representatives of the occupying power there. Therefore, the Czechoslovak
proposal would not really enlighten the Committee and since it involved
condoning a defiance of the prior will of the Assembly, the United States
delegation would oppose it.

/ Mr. Manuilsky

Mr. MANUILSKY (Ukrainian SSR) urged the Committee to reject the Chinese draft resolution. He recalled how the Korean question had first come to the attention of the Assembly and how the USSR had submitted at that time a proposal for the withdrawal of all foreign troops from the country so that the Korean people could determine their own political future free from any possibility of foreign interference. At that time, the United States had not wished to see a resolution adopted calling for the withdrawal of Soviet and American troops occupying Korea, but it did not declare openly its unwillingness to debate the matter because it recognized that the proposal of the USSR was fully in accordance with the principles of the Charter. Hence, it had endeavoured to conceal its negative attitude to that proposal under the pretext that it was a procedural question. The United States had put forward the argument that it was necessary for representatives of the Korean people to be present and that, since there were no elected representatives in Southern Korea, it was essential to set up a Commission which would observe or supervise the election of the representatives, so that those elected could be invited to participate. It was with the same end in view that the United States was now pressing for the recognition of the representative of the Southern Korean Government as spokesman for the Korean people although the only body which was entitled to perform that role was the Government of the People's Democratic Republic.

Mr. Manuilsky said that there was ample evidence, including the testimony of unbiased eye-witnesses, which proved that the Government of Southern Korea had not been freely elected by the inhabitants of the United States Zone. For example, the Syrian representative on the Temporary Commission, who could not be described as a supporter of the USSR, had stated at the eighth meeting of the Commission that the situation in the Southern Zone, where people were being thrown into prison for long periods without a trial solely on the orders of the United States military government, and where the population was living in continuous fear, made it impossible to ensure free elections. That view had also been expressed by the Indian and Chinese representatives.

Faced, therefore, with the existence of terrorism and widespread arrests the Commission had decided that it was unable to hold elections. It had reversed that decision only on instruction of the Interim Committee. Mr. Manuilsky drew attention to the statements of the Commission's Chairman and the Canadian representative contained in the record of the twenty-second meeting held on 30 March. The Chairman had said that the Interim Committee's instruction came as a bombshell

/to the Commission

제2부 유엔총회 회의록(1948)

to the Commission and he doubted the wisdom of the Committee's action.
The Canadian representative had voted against obeying the order of the
Interim Committee and had stigmatized the Committee's decision as
"inappropriate and unconstitutional".

Mr. Manuilsky said that it was a scandal that the First Committee
should now, in effect, be asked to endorse the Interim Committee's
"unconstitutional" decision by admitting the representative of the
Southern Korean Government to speak on behalf of the Korean people.
He found the evidence proved without doubt that the Government whose
election the Temporary Commission had supervised was not a representative
one.   It was certain that world public opinion would consider the
elections in the Southern Zone to be a mockery just as were the
plebiscites which were held in Hitlerite Germany.

On the other hand there could be no doubt that the Government of
the People's Democratic Republic could truly claim to represent the
Korean people.   That was demonstrated by the fact that nearly 99%
of the population of Northern Korea had participated in the vote and
the USSR Government was already withdrawing its occupying forces from
the Northern Zone.   Mr. Manuilsky, therefore, appealed to the Committee
to reject the Chinese proposal in favour of the draft resolution
submitted by Czechoslovakia.

Mr. KISELEV (Byelorussian SSR) also opposed the Chinese draft
resolution because he considered that it was the People's Democratic
Republic which truly represented the Korean people.   He found it
difficult to understand how the Chinese representative could say that
he was not aware of any elections which had been held in Northern
Korea because they had been freely reported in the world press.
Mr. Kiselev assured the Chinese representative that the elections
which had been held in August 1948, unlike those which had led to the
establishment of the Southern Government, had been perfectly free and
unhampered.   The Government of the Democratic Republic, which had been
established by the National Assembly held in Pengyar, had received the
support of 85% of the Korean people not only in Northern Korea but also
in the Southern Zone.   Mr. Kiselev asked whether the Chinese
representative wished to deny those figures which were official and
had been published in the world's press.

The representative of the Byelorussian SSR thought that when the
United States representative had tried to show that the Czechoslovak
draft resolution had already been rejected, he had done so as a
manoeuvre designed to prevent its acceptance.   Now that the manoeuvre

/had failed

had failed because the Chairman had shown that the draft resolution had
not been rejected, Mr. Dulles was endeavouring to obtain the same
objective by casting doubts on the legitimacy of the Government of the
People's Democratic Republic.   He had based his argument on the fact
that the Temporary Commission had not been permitted to enter the USSR
occupation zone in order to observe the election there.   However, that
did not change the fact that the elections had been held under conditions
of complete freedom.   It had not been like the earlier election in the
Southern Zone which had taken place in an atmosphere of terror as could
be seen from the documents of the Commission itself.   The majority of
the democratic parties, including all shades of opinion, with the
exception of the extreme right wing led by Syghman Rhee, had protested
against holding a separate election in the United States Zone.   Their
protest was a demonstration of majority public opinion throughout the
land.   The Korean people did not want their land to be artificially
divided under two Governments.   What they wanted was a single election
throughout Korea and it was in order to obtain that end that the
democratic parties had united in appealing for the withdrawal of all
occupation troops.   It was therefore quite incorrect for Mr. Dulles
to say that the Southern Government had been established in accordance
with the desires of the Korean people.   The fact was that the
Government was being supported by the United States occupation forces.
Mr. Kiselev added that, for its part, the USSR was complying with
majority public opinion in Korea and was withdrawing its troops from
the Northern Zone.

      In view of all the preceding facts, Mr. Kiselev urged the Committee
to adopt the Czechoslovakian draft resolution and to admit the delegation
from Northern Korea to speak on behalf of the Korean people.

      Mr. FRAZER (New Zealand) regretted that the preceding speakers
who favoured the admission of the delegation of the People's Democratic
Republic had failed to adduce any concrete evidence to show that it
really represented the Korean people.   It was not enough to assert
that the Government of Southern Korea had been elected in an atmosphere
of terror.   Denunciations and diatribes could not take the place of
evidence.   What the New Zealand delegation desired was proof that the
Government of the People's Democratic Republic had been elected under
fair conditions and truly represented the people over whom it claimed
authority.   Mr. Frazer asked when the elections which had led to its
establishment had been held and who had supervised them in order to
ensure that no pressure was brought to bear on the electorate.

/Furthermore,

Furthermore, before the Committee could agree to recognize the
Government of the People's Democratic Republic it was essential that it
should formally state that it respected the authority of the United
Nations and the General Assembly.   The United Nations might just as
well abandon its attempts to promote peaceful co-operation if it was
prepared to recognize a Government which flouted its decisions.   If
satisfactory evidence was adduced to prove that the Government was
truly representative and if the latter formally accepted the authority
of the United Nations then the New Zealand delegation would not oppose
the participation of the Northern Korean representative in the Committee's
debate.   It was notable however that the supporters of the People's
Democratic Republic, far from denying that it had flouted the General
Assembly's decision, had endeavoured to justify that attitude.

Preceding speakers had also made allegations against the
Government of Southern Korea.   Here again, Mr. Frazer asked for
proof.   The USSR representative had stated that the United States
military authorities had arrested individuals for politcal reasons
but that was scarcely evidence of terrorism, for all military
governments of occupation maintained their authority by political
arrests.   Political arrests were a regrettable but inevitable
consequence of military occupation.   In the absence of any other
concrete evidence the Committee must be bound by the statements of
the Temporary Commission that the elections in the Southern Zone
were held under fair conditions.   Mr. Frazer thought that the
rhetorical nature of the preceding statements showed that there was
no evidence to the contrary and that diatribes were intended to
take the place of proof.   Mr. Frazer stated that his delegation
was quite convinced of the legitimacy of the Southern Government.
It was, however, waiting to be convinced that the same was true of
the People's Democratic Republic.

Mr. FAWZI (Egypt) said that his delegation would have been quite
prepared to support the Czechoslovakian draft resolution had the
elections in Northern Korea not been conducted in defiance of the
General Assembly's desire.   Nothing would have been more pleasing
to the Egyptian delegation than to have seen Korea united under a single
Government.   However, under existing conditions Egypt would vote against
the Czechoslovakian draft resolution.

/Mr. CICMIL

Mr. CICMIL (Yugoslavia) warmly supported the Czechoslovakian draft resolution because the Government of the People's Democratic Republic of Korea had been elected by 99 per cent of the population of the Northern zone and 72 per cent of the inhabitants of the Southern zone and was therefore fully representative of the Korean people.   He stated that the People's Democratic Republic had been recognized by Yugoslavia together with other Powers.

Mr. MALIK (USSR) said that he would do his best to satisfy the New Zealand representative's request for concrete evidence which would enable him to support the admission of the delegation of the Government of the People's Democratic Republic.

To begin with, however, it was necessary to comment on the attempt of the United States representative to show that the Czechoslovakian draft resolution had already been rejected and should not be discussed. The fact was that the previous decision of the Committee had related only to the question of whether or not the Czechoslovakian proposal should be considered before the Committee opened its debate on the substance of the Korean question.   The Committee had decided not to examine the proposal at that time.   It was true that the Journal of 16 November erroneously stated that the draft resolution had been rejected but there had been a corrigendum in the following issue. However, Mr. Dulles, dealing with the first report, did not refer to the corrigendum and asserted that the Czechoslovak proposal was rejected. Mr. Malik asked the Secretariat for an explanation of the original error.

Turning to the question of the elections in Southern Korea Mr. Malik said that perusal of the Temporary Commission's records, and especially of the records of Sub-Committee 2 which dealt with public opinion, showed that the overwhelming majority of all the political parties and social organizations in Southern Korea had been against a separate election in the Southern Zone.   It was also a fact that many rightist leaders had boycotted the Southern elections as an expression of their disapproval.   Two such leaders of right-wing parties, Kim Koo and Kim Kiusic, had submitted a plan to the Commission for the convocation of a conference of political parties which would pave the way for the establishment of a single Korean Government.   The plan had called for the withdrawal of foreign troops as a prerequisite for the Government's creation.   At first the Commission had been sympathetic towards the plan which had the support of all Korean public opinion. However the Commission had failed to implement it.

Subsequently an all-Korean Conference was held in the Northern
Zone in which 56 political parties and social organizations took part.
The only organizations which did not participate were two extreme rightist
reactionary groups, the so-called Hangkok party which was supported
by the United States administration and a certain militarist clique.
The Conference adopted three resolutions.   The first was a declaration
on behalf of the Korean people objecting to the carrying out of
separate elections in the two zones. The second was an appeal to the
USSR and the United States to withdraw their armies of occupation.
The third resolution dealt with the political situation in Korea.
It was as a consequence of the second resolution that the USSR
decided to withdraw its troops from Northern Korea by 1 January 1949.
Mr. Malik considered that the failure of the United States to do likewise
resulted from its desire to hold Southern Korea as a springboard for
possible military action in Asia and to permit its commerical monopolies
freedom to operate in the area.

Later, towards the end of April a further conference was held, this
time comprised of 33 political parties and social organizations.   It
was at that conference that the declaration of 30 April was drawn
up by Kim Koo and Kim Kiusic which provided for a political programme
as follows: first, all foreign troops were to be withdrawn from
Korea.   Then an all-Korean Congress was to be convoked to establish
a temporary Government and to institute elections for a Legislative
organ on the basis of direct universal franchise and a secret ballot.
The legislative organ thus elected was to have the task of drawing up
a constitution on the basis of which a permanent Government would be
established.

Despite the fact that the programme clearly expressed the will of
the whole Korean people the United States had insisted on the elections
being held in the Southern Zone as a result of which the Government of
the zone was entrusted to the Hangkok party. The Temporary Commission,
which had agreed to the all-Korean conference found itself subjected
to a three-fold pressure by those of its members which desired to please
the United States, by the Interim Committee, and by the United States
Military Government.   That pressure had induced the Commission to
ignore the desires of the Korean people as expressed by the conference
and to agree to observe the elections in the Southern Zone.   Mr. Malik
noted that the Indian representative on the Commission had stated that
he was voting in favour of holding the Southern elections, although he
was actually opposed to the measure, because of the instruction received
from the Interim Committee.   Mr. Malik considered that the decision to
hold elections, taken as it was by a simple majority, was a violation of

The USSR representative also cited the statement of the American Military Commander in Southern Korea that he considered it impossible to guarantee free elections in the Zone.   That statement of General Hodges was contained on page 34, volume III, Part I of the Commission's Report. Mr. Malik asked whether the New Zealand representative would describe the Temporary Commission's action in permitting elections to be carried on after, having heard such a statement, as calculated to maintain the prestige of the United Nations.   For his part, Mr. Malik believed that such an action was itself a violation of the General Assembly resolution on the Korean question and dealt a blow to the authority of the United Nations.

It was only to be expected that the political parties which took part in the two preceding all-Korean conferences should take appropriate measures to counter the United States action.   At a further all-Korean Congress they decided to hold a second election throughout both the Zones.   In Northern Korea that election took place unhampered while in Southern Korea the United States attempted to prevent them from being carried out.   However in spite of the efforts of the United States indirect elections were held in the Southern Zone and the Congress of Popular   Representatives which met in Chai Su in August truly represented the Korean people.   Of the delegates to that Congress 1002 came from Southern Korea, 48 were arrested by the United States authorities and others died on the way.   On 25 August the Congress elected 360 delegates from Southern Korea to the Supreme Popular Assembly.   On the same day direct elections were held in Northern Korea by secret ballot and on the basis of universal franchise.   Of all the electors in the Northern Zone 99.7 per cent took part in the vote while 77.52 per cent participated in the Southern Zone.   As a whole, 85.2 per cent of the Korean people took part in the elections.   Thus, the Korean people, freely and enthusiastically recorded their protest against the separate elections which had been held by the United States Administration.   The elections showed the indominitable will of the Korean people for a united and independent nation. The Supreme Assembly of all-Korea, which they elected, was the only genuine legislative organ for the whole country. As evidence of the democratic and representative composition of the Assembly Mr. Malik explained that of the 572 deputies, 120 were labourers, 194 peasants, 152 clerical workers, 33 intellectuals, and 22 trades people. Among the deputies, 69 of whom were women, 287 had participated in the resistance against Japanese agression.   The deputies came from all social classes and political parties throughout Korea.   Mr. Malik thought that

/the composition of

the composition of the Assembly should, in itself satisfy the New Zealand delegate's doubts as to its representative character.

The fact that the Temporary Commission did not observe the elections of the Government of the People's Democratic Republic could not conceivable be proof that they were not held under fair conditions. Similarly the existence of a Government in the Southern Zone only proved that the United States had been successful in inducing the Commission to accept its policy. The Commission had given way to United States pressure although many members had realized that the Southern election was illegal and violated the General Assembly's resolution.

Mr. PROTITCH (Secretariat) gave an explanation of the error in the Journal with regard to the Czechoslovak draft resolution. He said that the significance of the decision taken at the 200th meeting was ambiguous in both the French and English verbatim records. In fact, the verbatim records were not official and the Secretariat of the Committee was not responsible for them. The only official record of the meeting was the summary record (document A/C.1/SR 200) which stated perfectly clearly on page 6 that the "vote was taken on the proposal to consider the Czechoslovakian draft resolution at that time" and the proposal "was rejected by 38 votes to 6 with 6 abstentions". Mr. Protitch pointed out that the error in the Journal, which again was not an official record, had been corrected in the following issue of 17 November, as soon as the Secretariat had discovered the inaccuracy.

The meeting rose at 1.10 p.m.

(2) 제3차 유엔총회 제1위원회 제230차 회의 요약

해제문서 10 : A/C.1/SR 230 (Third Session, First Committee, Summary
Record of the Two Hundred and Thirtieth Meeting)

문서명	Third Session, First Committee, Summary Record of the Two Hundred and Thirtieth Meeting		
	제3차 유엔총회 제1위원회 제230차 회의 요약 기록		
발신		생성일시	1948년 12월 6일 오후 3시
		발신일시	
수신		수신일시	
		문서번호	A/C.1/SR 230
문서형태	회의록(요약)	문서분량	13쪽
주제명	조선민주주의인민공화국 대표의 유엔 회의 참석 여부		
주요내용	1948년 12월 6일 오후 3시 프랑스 파리에서 열린 제3차 유엔총회 제1위원회 제230차 회의 회의록. 상세한 내용은 본문 참조.		
검색어	조선민주주의인민공화국(the Democratic Peoples's Republic of Korea), 유엔한국임시위원단, 제1위원회, 말리크(Yakov Aleksandrovich Malik, 소련 대표), Castro(엘살바도르 대표), 피어슨(Lester P. Pearson, 캐나다 대표), Zebrowski(폴란드 대표), Lopez(필리핀 대표), Wold(노르웨이 대표), Manuilsky(우크라이나 대표), El Khouri(시리아 대표), Fraser(뉴질랜드 대표), 고든 워커 (Gordon Walker, 영국 대표), Ugon(우루과이 대표)		

1948년 12월 6일 오후 3시 프랑스 파리에서 열린 제3차 유엔총회 제1위원회 제230차 회의 회의록.

제229차 회의 안건으로, 체코슬로바키아가 제안한 북한 대표의 유엔 회의 참석 건에 대해 소련 대표는 조선민주주의인민공화국이 수립된 배경을 설명하면서 오전회의에 이어 북한대표의 유엔회의 참석 문제에 대해 지지 발언을 계속함. 그에 반해 남한 대표단이 유엔회의에 참석하기 위해 초청되어야 한다는 중국의 제안은 받아들일 수 없다고 하고 그 이유는 남한 정부의 설립은 자유선거의 결과에 의한 것이 아니기 때문이라고 주장함.

엘살바도르 대표는 중국대표가 발의한 남한 대표단이 제1위원회 회의에 투표권 없이 초청되어야 한다는 제안과 남한 정부가 유엔의 지도하에 수립되었다는 사실을 지적함으로써 남한정부의 합법성을 부인한 반면, 북한정부가 한국인 전체를 대표한다는 체코의 의견을 지지함. 그는 소련점령군이 유엔한국임시위원단이 북한지역에 접근하는 것을 거부했기 때문에 북한 선거에 관한 임시위원단의 보고는 신뢰하기 어렵다고 주장함.

캐나다는 조선민주주의인민공화국은 민주적인 절차에 의해 수립된 것이 아니라는 이유로 체코의 안건에 반대하였으며, 폴란드는 북한이 유엔에 참석하면 소련과 함께 점령군 철수를 지지할 것이라는 점을 우려해서 북한의 유엔 회의 참석을 반대하는 것은 옳지 않다고 하면서 북한 대표의 유엔회의 참석을 지지함.

필리핀 및 노르웨이는 북한이 자유로운 선거에 의해 선출된 합법적인 대표가 아니라는 이유로 반대하였고, 우크라이나는 지지를 표명하였으며, 시리아는 남한 대표를 점령군인 미국이 보증하여 참가할 수 있다면 북한은 점령군인 소련이 보증하기 때문에 참가할 수 있다는 것을 이유로 들어 북한의 유엔회의 참석을 지지함.

뉴질랜드는 증거를 더 제출해야한다고 말하면서 결론을 유보하였고, 영국은 모든 면에서 남한은 완벽하지만 북한은 무시무시하다는 이유로 반대함.

우루과이는 유엔회의는 그것이 결정되기 이전으로 돌아갈 수 없다는 이유로 체코슬로바키아의 제안 자체를 반대한다는 입장을 표명함.

마지막으로 소련 대표가 북한지역의 선거과정에 유엔감시단의 입국을 거부한 이유와 그 배경을 설명함.

안건에 대한 표결결과 찬성 6, 반대 34, 불참 8로 체코슬로바키아의 안건은 부결되었으며 북한 대표를 유엔총회에 초청하지 못하게 됨.

중국의 수정안에 대해서 찬성 39, 반대 6 불참 1로 가결함. 따라서 남한은 한반도의 유일한 합법 정부로 인정받고 유엔총회에 참석할 수 있게 됨.

오후 5시 55분에 정회함.

United Nations   Nations Unies   UNRESTRICTED

GENERAL   ASSEMBLEE   A/C.1/SR 230
ASSEMBLY   GENERALE   8 December 1948

ENGLISH
ORIGINAL: FRENCH

Dual distribution

Third Session

FIRST COMMITTEE

SUMMARY RECORD OF THE TWO HUNDRED AND THIRTIETH MEETING

Held at the Palais de Chaillot, Paris,
on Monday, 6 December 1948, at 3 p.m.

CONTENTS: The problem of the independence of Korea

Chairman:	Mr. P. H. SPAAK	Belgium
Rapporteur:	Mr. S. SARPER	Turkey

Any corrections of this record should be submitted in writing, in
either of the working languages (English or French), and within two working
days, to Mr. Delavenay, Director, Official Records Division, Room 3015,
Palais de Chaillot. Corrections should be accompanied by or incorporated
in a letter, on headed notepaper, bearing the appropriate symbol number
and enclosed in an envelope marked "Urgent". Corrections can be dealt
with more speedily by the services concerned if delegations will be good
enough also to incorporate them in a mimeographed copy of the record.

THE PROBLEM OF THE INDEPENDENCE OF KOREA

Mr. MALIK (Union of Soviet Socialist Republics) recalled that he had given figures at the previous meeting to illustrate the circumstances in which the Parliament of the People's Republic of Korea had been elected and a Government set up. He then read to the Committee an appeal from the Minister of Foreign Affairs of that Government, referring to the general elections of August 1948, which he had described as a free expression of the Korean people's desire to establish a unitary democratic State. An absolute majority of the population of the South and the North had taken part in the elections and the Government had drawn up a democratic programme. In addition, the Government of the People's Republic of Korea had requested the Union of Soviet Socialist Republics and the United States of America to withdraw their occupation forces from the entire Korean territory.

The USSR delegation, Mr. Malik continued, had stated in November 1947 that the problem of Korean independence was a matter for the Korean people themselves, and that it could not be solved without an expression of opinion by the representatives of that people. The view expressed by the USSR delegation had been reflected in the preamble of the resolution adopted by the Assembly on 14 November 1947. The delegation of the USSR was still of the same opinion and proposed that delegates of the People's Republic of Korea should be invited to take part in the discussion. The USSR delegation therefore supported the Czechoslovak proposal.

The Chinese proposal that representatives of South Korea should be invited to take part in the Committee's deliberations was not acceptable, since the establishment of the Government of South Korea was not the result of free elections. The Temporary Commission of the United Nations, in its decision regarding the elections in South Korea, had not paid sufficient attention to the facts, which were, however, sufficiently plain from the records of the Commission containing the evidence and statements of Korean politicians. The Supreme Judge of South Korea, Mr. Kim Koo, Mr. Kim Kiusic and other political figures had informed the Temporary Commission that the holding of free elections in South Korea was out of the question.

In fact, South Korea was a police State under the control of the United States of America. Fifty-three per cent of the police officers had collaborated with the Japanese occupying forces and had taken part in repressive measures against democratic organizations. The chief

/of police

dd

of police of South Korea, who was connected with the clique of Syngman
Rhee and with the allegedly democratic party of Hankook, had contributed
to the falsification of the elections of 10 May.   The other political
parties had incidentally boycotted those elections.   The representative
of Canada had observed that the Seoul Assembly, though including a
number of so-called independents, was solely represented by the parties
of Hankook and Syngman Rhee.   For his part, General Hodge had himself
stated that the conditions were not such as to allow the holding of
free elections.   Finally, in a memorandum of 2 July 1948, addressed to
the secretary of the United Nations Temporary Commission, the chief
of the United States police in South Korea had admitted that between
7 February and 14 May, 758 persons had been injured and 416 killed and
that, during the four days following the elections of 10 May, 137 persons
had been injured and 128 killed.   That was surely an admission that the
elections had not been free, but had taken place under a system of
police terrorism.

Mr. Malik referred to the claim made by the United Nations
Commission that the elections had been held in an atmosphere of freedom.
Four members of the Commission -- El Salvador, India, Canada and Australia --
had however declared before the elections that the creation of a Government tt
of South Korea would not be in conformity with the recommendation of the
General Assembly.   It was only by four votes, and one abstention, that
the Temporary Commission, which consisted of nine members, had decided
the fate of the elections and of South Korea, contrary to the recommendation
of the General Assembly.   The documents reproduced by the Commission
established the fact that the elections had not been held in a democratic
atmosphere, that the results had been falsified and, finally, that the
present Government of South Korea was not a legal Government.   For those
reasons, the delegation of the USSR was opposed to inviting representatives
of the Seoul Government to take part in the deliberations of the First
Committee, since, far from representing the people of Korea as a whole,
they did not even represent the people of South Korea.

Mr. CASTRO (El Salvador) pointed out that the Chinese proposal
was that a delegation from South Korea should be invited to take part in
the Committee's discussions without the right to vote, the Government of
South Korea having been set up under the auspices of the United Nations.
The Czechoslovak proposal, on the contrary denied the legality of that
Government and maintained that the Government of North Korea represented the
Korean nation as a whole.   It was not difficult to form an opinion on
those two proposals in view of the fact that the occupation forces of
the USSR had refused the Temporary Commission all access to the territory
dd
/of North Korea

of North Korea and that there was no trustworthy report on the situation there.

Mr. PEARSONS (Canada) considered that the Czechoslovak proposal was unacceptable. He informed Mr. Manuilsky that the Canadian delegation to the United Nations Temporary Commission on Korea had not always voted with the delegation of the United States. He added, however, that when the Canadian delegation had been in a minority, it had accepted the views of the majority after the vote. It was true that the Canadian delegation had opposed elections in South Korea for the reason that the USSR had prevented elections in Korea as a whole. In any event, after the elections had been held in South Korea, the Canadian delegation had noted that they had been carried through normally and had expressed the wishes of the population. It had therefore accepted the report of the Temporary Commission. On the contrary, the United Nations had been given no information on events in North Korea. How had the representatives of the People's Republic been selected? Whom did they represent? No verification of the answers given to those questions was possible. It was therefore natural to conclude that the elections in that part of Korea had not been held in a democratic manner. For that reason it was quite impossible to accord the representatives of North Korea the same status as the representatives of South Korea. The delegation of Canada would vote against the Czechoslovak proposal.

Mr. ZEBROWSKI (Poland) regretted that his speech at the previous meeting had roused such indignation in the representative of New Zealand. He thought, however, that such indignation would have been more appropriately directed against those who by-passed the opinion of the United Nations, overlooked the right of peoples to self-determination and misused the United Nations by creating organs which favoured the selfish interests of certain States. He pointed out that his speech had not been an appeal to anarchy but had merely stressed the tendency to domination shown by certain delegations. Why was it necessary to establish a United Nations commission to confirm the democratic nature of the regime in North Korea? Such a step was no more necessary in North Korea than in New Zealand, for example. The delegations of Poland and of the USSR had furnished evidence and data on the subject. The truth was that certain delegations feared the facts, and if representatives of Korea had been invited to take part in the Assembly in 1947, they would certainly have requested the withdrawal of the forces of occupation, as the delegation of the USSR had proposed.

dd

/Mr. LOPEZ

Mr. LOPEZ (Philippines) held that, if the Committee had adopted the proposal that the representatives of North Korea should be invited as representing the only legal Korean Government, it would be virtually granting recognition to that Government, which would be contrary to the will of the Assembly. It was to say the least surprising that representatives who had refused to appear before the Temporary Commission should now be willing to appear before the First Committee. If, however, their wish to be given a hearing was made in good faith, they should be heard in accordance with the normal procedure in such cases.

He was further surprised that only those delegations which had voted against the principle of the Temporary Commission and which had refused to take part in its work were giving their support to the representatives of North Korea. His delegation was unable to accept the Czechoslovak proposal.

Mr. WOLD (Norway) opposed the Czechoslovak proposal because there was no proof that the representatives of North Korea had been freely elected and had not simply been nominated by the military authorities. In fact, the United Nations Temporary Commission had not been authorized to find out whether those representatives had been freely elected. Moreover, to invite representatives of North Korea would be to confer on that State a status in contradiction with the Charter of the United Nations.

Mr. MANUILSKY (Ukrainian Soviet Socialist Republic) said that the representative of the USSR had submitted incontrovertible facts to prove that elections had taken place in North Korea and that sixty-six per cent of the population had taken part. No speaker had been able to deny those facts. It had, however, been asserted that representatives of Korea could not be heard since the United Nations Temporary Commission had not been granted access to the territory of North Korea. It was known that the Commission did not represent all the United Nations, but merely served as a starting-point from which the United States might impose its expansionist policy on the people of Korea. No article of the Charter provided that an organ established by a group of Members of the United Nations could be regarded as an organ of the United Nations. Furthermore, the first question with which the Committee had found itself faced was that of its own legality. On 4 February (Verbatim Summary Record of the 8th meeting of the Commission) the representative of the Philippines had stated that the General Assembly

dd

/had created

had created a legal fiction by its adoption of the resolution of
14 November: it had decided that elections should be held throughout
Korea, while well aware that elections could not be held in North Korea.
Was there in the circumstances any cause for surprise that the United
Nations Temporary Commission, a simple legal fiction, should not have
been admitted to North Korea?   Those who supported the contrary thesis
wished to create an atmosphere of confusion in order to prevent the
representatives of North Korea from obtaining a hearing.

The representative of the Ukraine also recalled Mr. Fraser's claim
that South Korea had a democratic regime.   In that connexion he quoted
the record of the Temporary Commission's examination of the chief of
police of Seoul (First Part of the Report of the United Nations Temporary
Commission on Korea, Volume III, Annexes IX to XII, page 116), from which
it appeared that the official in question had been appointed by the
American General Hodge and that he had then been responsible to
General Dean, Military Governor of South Korea, for exercising his
functions.   Dozens of similar examples could be given in proof of the
anti-democratic character of the regime in South Korea.

Mr. Manuilsky went on to emphasize the contempt for the Korean people
displayed in a statement made by General Hodge to the Temporary Commission.
General Hodge had declared that the people of Korea were a decadent
nation without the slightest concept of political life and without any
idea of the responsibilities inherent in the basic freedoms.   Was it to
be expected, under such circumstances, that the Korean people would
receive any guarantees?   The philosophy of racial superiority proclaimed
by General Hodge was reflected in the result of the falsified elections
held in South Korea.   There was thus ample proof that the Government of
South Korea did not represent the free will of the population.

It would be an insult to the Korean people if its voice was not
heard.   It was not possible to trifle with a people that was moving
forward.   The delegation of the Ukraine supported the Czechoslovak
proposal, which was both just and reasonable.

Mr. El KHOURI (Syria) observed that the Chinese and Czechoslovak
proposals were not necessarily contradictory.   The existence of a
National Assembly and of a regular Government in South Korea was proved
by the evidence of the American occupying authorities and by the report
of the United Nations Temporary Commission.   The existence of a National
Assembly and of a regular Government in North Korea was similarly
supported by proof submitted by the USSR, which had occupied it by its

military forces.   Such proofs could not be regarded as valueless
because the United States and the USSR had agreed to divide Korea and
to administer one part each.

If the General Assembly had not set up the United Nations Commission
in 1947, that evidence would have been sufficient, since the testimony
of the Government charged with the administration of a territory was
generally regarded as conclusive.   The Assembly had nevertheless set
up the Commission and all its members had made every effort to ensure
the full application of the Assembly's resolution, in conformity with
the desire of the population.   It was obvious that the Koreans did
not wish to be divided.   The partition had not been made in their
interest, but solely in the interest of other Powers.   There were at
present unfortunately two Governments in Korea, both of which claimed
authority over the whole country.   In fact, the two parts of the
country were not in disagreement, but were kept down by foreign
authorities which held them under their control.   To invite both
parties to take part in discussions on the question would not facilitate
any rapprochement.   The unification of Korea could only take place if
the occupying Powers withdrew their forces of occupation.   Those
Powers had committed an error in occupying the different parts of Korea.
It was another error to prevent the United Nations Temporary Commission
from entering the northern part of the country in order to ascertain
the situation there.   For that reason it was now difficult to intervene
in the question except in the case of South Korea, which the Commission
had been able to visit and on which it had submitted a report.

Mr. FRASER (New Zealand) said that one of the excerpts just
quoted by Mr. Manuilsky was likely to mislead the Committee.   That
quotation implied that the United States authorities still exercised
absolute military control in South Korea.   However, it was stated on
page 13 in Volume I of the Second Report that "the Government established
by the elected representatives has assumed the functions previously
operated by the Military Government of the United States and the armed
forces of Korea, and a progressive and orderly transition of these
functions is reaching its final stage."   Mr. Manuilsky would have been
wiser to refer to the report dated 15 October 1948 than to a text issued
several months earlier.

Was there any evidence to support the belief that the elections in
South Korea had not been held in accordance with democratic procedure?
Mr. Manuilsky had no doubt tried to prove that General Hodge had allowed

dd   /a state

a state of terrorism to prevail, but here again the meaning of a
quotation had been distorted, for, in view of outside influence,
General Hodge could obviously not guarantee in advance that the elections
would be held in an atmosphere of absolute freedom; nevertheless, he
had said neither that the elections would not take place, nor that they
would be held in an atmosphere of terror.   In fact, he had neglected
nothing to make an atmosphere of freedom prevail, and he had splendidly
accomplished his task.   On the other hand, that did not signify in any
way that holding new elections and strengthening the Government might
nor further improve the state of things.   It would, however, be
incorrect to assert that the authority of the Government of South Korea
extended to North Korea.   What was certain was that South Korea was run
by a democratically elected Government.   Could the same be said of
North Korea?   It was true that Mr. Malik had given some assurances to
that effect, but no one could be certain of what went on in North Korea
since its Government, as well as that of the Union of Soviet Socialist
Republics, had most reprehensibly refused access to an organ of the
United Nations.

Thus, in spite of the assurances given by Mr. Malik that the
elections were held by secret ballot and on the basis of universal
suffrage, there were doubts concerning the situation in North Korea.
Moreover, Mr. Malik had not gone so far as to assert that the population
of South Korea, which had allegedly participated in the elections in
the North, had done so individually and by secret ballot; on the
contrary, Mr. Malik had stated that the people of South Korea had
participated through the intermediary of representatives who had, it
seemed, assisted on its behalf at a Conference.   But by whom had those
representatives of South Korea been elected?   Did they represent the
whole of the population of South Korea?   Regardless of the confidence
one might have in Mr. Malik, that was not the correct way to proceed in
electing the representatives of a whole people.   Instead of claiming
that certain organizations in North Korea were equally representative
of the South, it would be better to confine oneself to giving valid
proof at least as regards the North.   It would be better also if the
authorities of North Korea gave assurances concerning the respect that
was due the United Nations and its organs.

Concerning, further, Mr. Malik's quotation of a statement of
Mr. Kim Koo (page 66 of the First Part of the Report, Volume III), if
his intention had been to prove that a democratic Government existed in
North Korea, he had fallen far short of the mark.   Mr. Kim Koo had

dd

/stated that,

stated that, in his opinion, the elections held in North Korea had not been free, because they had been held under Soviet pressure and because the voters had had no possibility of choosing from among several parties.

In South Korea, on the contrary, the Commission had been able to note that the procedure followed had been fair and that the elected authorities were gradually assuming various administrative functions, including that of the police.

In conclusion, the New Zealand delegation was ready to vote either way, according to the evidence which would be furnished; but what it did not wish, was to see the authority of the United States flouted.

Mr. WALKER (United Kingdom) said that his delegation would vote against the draft resolution submitted by Czechoslovakia, but not because it believed that everything in South Korea was perfect and everything in North Korea monstrous. As the representative of Syria had pointed out, one could feel nothing but sympathy for the people of North Korea.

The essential difference, however, was that, thanks to the United Nations Temporary Commission, one at least knew the position in South Korea; the representative of New Zealand was justified in asking for evidence concerning North Korea. Undoubtedly, evidence in such matters was difficult to come by, but that merely confirmed the wisdom of the decision relating to the appointment of a Commission which was originally supposed to ensure the fairness of the elections in the whole of the country. The speech of the USSR representative about the elections, the all-Korean Parliament and the Conference of the organizations representing North Korea, inevitably made one think of the methods of the Communist Party in the United Kingdom, where the Labour Party had succeeded in reducing the Communists to complete insignificance. For in England, as in North Korea, the Communists assigned great importance to delegations which supposedly represented all but one or two parties of the country, parties which were scornfully qualified as reactionary and which in reality were backed by all the democratic forces of the country.

The only way the United Nations could have found out the true situation in North Korea was by sending a Commission there; it had been denied that possibility by the Soviet Union. And now the Czechoslovak and the USSR draft resolutions offered the members of the First Committee the alternatives of either standing by the United Nations Commission, or ignoring its conclusions. The United Kingdom delegation would

dd

/consequently

consequently vote against the Czechoslovak proposal.

Mr. UGON (Uruguay) stated that his delegation would vote against the Czechoslovak draft resolution to invite a would-be Government of the Korean People's Republic.

There must, of course, be valid reasons for making an exception to the principle that interested parties should be heard.   That was precisely the case here, however, since one of the parties had flouted the authority of the United Nations.   That had also occurred in the question of Greece as well as in that of Korea.

The Charter itself stipulated that a non-Member State which asked to be heard must undertake to comply with its principles.   One could therefore conclude that whoever did not recognize the authority of the United Nations could not claim the right to be heard.   Would it not be absurd to place on an equal footing those who had recognized the authority of the United Nations and those who had repudiated it?

There were other reasons why the Czechoslovak proposal should be rejected: to accept it would be to go against a decision taken by a two-thirds majority in the General Assembly.

In accordance with the resolution of 14 November 1947, a United Nations Commission had gone to Korea.   What happened then?   While the authorities in one of the zones had prevented the entry of the United Nations Commission, which consequently could not carry out its instructions, elections had taken place in the other zone where the people, that is t o-thirds of the Korean population, had freely expressed their will.   Consequently if the United Nations wished to be consistent, it could only invite the representatives of that part of Korea where free elections had been held.   On the other hand, the principle according to which matters of concern to a nation should be discussed in the presence of its representatives could not hold in the case of the would-be representatives of the Korean People's Democratic Republic.   For since the elections in North Korea had been held without any supervision, there was no way of knowing what those persons really represented.   As a matter of fact, that was the very difficulty which the appointment of a United Nations Commission was to have obviated.

In conclusion, the delegation of Uruguay considered that the General Assembly could not go back on its decision of the previous year, nor could it give an advantage to those who had scorned its authority over those who had respected it.

dd   /Mr. MALIK

Mr. MALIK (Union of Soviet Socialist Republics), referring
to the recent speech of the Philippines representative, quoted a
statement made by the Chairman of the Temporary Commission on Korea
upon his return from the bargain, in which he had expressed doubts
concerning the possibility of holding free elections in South Korea.
How then could Mr. Luna have spoken of civil liberty in South Korea
when Mr. Kim Koo and Mr. Kim Kiusic, to cite specific instances, had not
participated in the elections?

As regards the fact that the authorities in North Korea had denied
the United Nations Commission access to their territory, certain points
should be noted. Fifty-six political and social organizations of
North and South Korea had called a conference with the authorization of
the United Nations Commission. At the end of the conference it was
announced that agreement had been reached on various matters: (a) The
immediate and simultaneous withdrawal of the American and Soviet forces
was the only possible solution, and an appeal to that effect would be
addressed to the United States and the Soviet Union. (b) Once the
foreign forces had withdrawn, the Korean people would not allow a
fratricidal war to break out. (c) The different parties and organizations would set up a democratic Government representing all Korean
organizations, with the primary task of organizing free and direct
elections on the basis of universal suffrage and a secret ballot, in
order to draft a Constitution and essential legislation.

Two Korean political leaders, Mr. Kim Koo and Mr. Kim Sung Soo,
representing the North and the South respectively, and consequently the
spokesmen of the general opinion of the Korean people, had expressed
their opposition to the setting up of separate Governments. The United
Nations Temporary Commission had, however, ignored their declarations
and had proceeded to arrange separate elections in South Korea, an
action which was likely to injure the prestige of the United Nations.
Thus there had been no single election for the whole of Korea.

Those were the reasons why the authorities in North Korea had
refused to let the Commission enter that part of the country. In doing
that, the authorities of North Korea had been working for the liberation
of the Korean people.

As regards the situation in South Korea which, according to the
United Kingdom representative, was excellent, he would merely point out
that a person belonging to the Right like Mr. Kim Koo had declared to
the press his return from North Korea that the latter was progressing
and that the same could not be said of the South. Since Mr. Kim Koo

could not be suspected of Communist leanings, his statement needed no comment.

Furthermore, the representative of New Zealand, in speaking of the two zones in Korea, had seemed to forget what his Government had said on that subject the previous year.

Those were the facts which must be taken into account if there was a desire to see the Korean people really represented in the First Committee, and compared with those facts the procedural quibbles of the representative of Uruguay had very little weight. Fifty-six political parties, representing ten million members, had stated their wishes. How then could anyone refuse to listen? The basic principle of the United Nations was the liberty and independence of peoples who must be given the opportunity to take their affairs into their own hands. If his conscience allowed him, the representative of Uruguay was free to refuse to hear the representatives of the Korean People's Democratic Republic, but the delegation of the Soviet Union would not, by its vote, deny a hearing to those representatives.

The CHAIRMAN put to the vote the draft resolution submitted by Czechoslovakia (A/C.1/367).

Upon the request of the representative of Czechoslovakia, <u>a vote by roll-call was taken as follows</u>:

<u>Saudi Arabia</u>, having been drawn by lot by the Chairman, was called upon to vote first.

> <u>In favour</u>: Byelorussian Soviet Socialist Republic, Czechoslovakia, Poland, Ukrainian Soviet Socialist Republic, Union of Soviet Socialist Republics, Yugoslavia.
>
> <u>Against</u>: Australia, Belgium, Brazil, Canada, Chile, China, Colombia, Costa Rica, Cuba, Denmark, Dominican Republic, Egypt, El Salvador, Ethiopia, France, Greece, Haiti, Honduras, India, Liberia, Luxembourg, Netherlands, New Zealand, Norway, Pakistan, Paraguay, Peru, Philippines, Siam, Turkey, Union of South Africa, United Kingdom, United States of America, Uruguay.
>
> <u>Abstaining</u>: Afghanistan, Burma, Iran, Iraq, Sweden, Syria, Venezuela, Yemen.

<u>The Czechoslovak proposal was rejected by 34 votes to 6, with 8 abstentions.</u>

dd

/The CHAIRMAN

The CHAIRMAN put to the vote the Chinese draft resolution (A/C.1/395).

Mr. PLIMSOLL (Australia) said that his delegation would suggest that the following words should be added after the word "delegation" in the second paragraph of the Chinese draft resolution: "of the Government of the Republic of Korea".

Mr. TSIANG (China) on behalf of his delegation, accepted the amendment.

The CHAIRMAN put to the vote the Chinese draft resolution as amended by the Australian delegation.

A vote was taken by show of hands. The proposal was adopted by 39 votes to 6, with 1 abstention.

The CHAIRMAN recalled that Mr. Spaak had said at the morning meeting that the Committee would have to consider whether to ask the Rapporteur of the United Nations Temporary Commission on Korea himself to submit his report.

It was so decided.

The meeting rose at 5.55 p.m.

(3) 제3차 유엔총회 제1위원회 제231차 회의 요약

해제문서 11 : A/C.1/SR 231 (Third Session, First Committee, Summary
Record of the Two Hundred and Thirty First Meeting)

문서명	Third Session, First Committee, Summary Record of the Two Hundred and Thirty First Meeting		
	제3차 유엔총회 제1위원회 제231차 회의 요약 기록		
발신		생성일시	1948년 12월 7일 오전 11시
		발신일시	
수신		수신일시	
		문서번호	A/C.1/SR 232
문서형태	회의록(요약)	문서분량	10쪽
주제명	1. 유엔한국임시위원단의 한반도 내 선거 관련 활동 결과에 관한 보고와 그에 대한 논의 2. 한반도 통일 문제		
주요내용	1948년 12월 6일부터 7일 오전 11시까지 프랑스 파리에서 개최된 제3차 유엔총회 제1위원회 제231차 회의록. 상세한 내용은 본문 참조.		
검색어	유엔한국임시위원단, 한국 국회, 제1위원회, 리우 위안(Liu Yu-Wan, 유엔한국임시위원단 조사위원), 카를로스 로물로(Carlos Romulo, 필리핀 대표), 플림솔(J. Plimsoll, 호주 대표), 덜레스(John Dulles, 미국 대표), 카를로스 뮤니츠(J. Carlos Muniz, 브라질 대표)		

1948년 12월 6일부터 7일 오전 11시까지 프랑스 파리에서 개최된 제3차 유엔총회 제1위원회 제231차 회의록.

의장은 한국 문제에 관해 향후 6차례의 회의만이 가능하다는 점을 밝혔으며 유엔한국임시위원단의 리우 위안 보고관은 위원단의 보고서가 1948년 1월 12일부터 5월 24일까지의 첫 번째 기간을 다룬 부분과 1948년 5월 25일부터 10월14일까지를 다룬 두 번째 부분으로 구성되어 있다고 설명함.

리우 위안 보고관은 발표에서 유엔한국임시위원단은 1947년 11월 14일의 유엔 결의안 112호에 따른 총선거 감시, 한국 정부에 대한 자문의 실시, 유엔총회에 보고서를 제출하는 것의 세 가지 임무를 띠고 있었으며, 결의안의 목적은 유엔과 한국 국민의 공동의 노력으로 한국의 독립을 보장하는 것이라고 말함. 그러한 목적에 따라 위원단은 총선거가 정상적으로 실시되었으며, 한국 대표는 한국국민들의 자유로운 선거에 의해 선출되었고 군정에 의해 임명된 것이 아니라는 사실을 확인함. 위원단은 선출된 한국 국회의원들과 연락망을 구축하였으며, 한국 정부가 원하는 바의 자문을 제공하도록 하였다고 말함. 그리고 1948년 1월 12일 서울에서 열린 제1차 회의 이래로 위원단은 북한 당국과의 협력을 시도하였으나 2월 26일 북한 당국이 협조를 거부하였다는 점을 고려하여, 위원단은 1948년 11월 12일의 유엔총회 결정이 한반도 내의 접근 가능한 지역에 한해 적용될 것으로 결정하였다고 말함.

리우 보고관은 유엔한국임시위원단이 남한에서 실시된 총선거 과정을 감시하였으며 전체 한국인 중 3분의 2에 해당하는 남한 주민의 자유의사가 합법적으로 표명되었다는 결론에 도달하였고 또한 총선 이후 한국에서의 사태 진전을 주시하면서, 수립된 한국 정부에 자문을 제공하고 유엔총회에 보고서를 제출하였다고 말함. 하지만 북한은 위원단의 방문을 거부했기 때문에 1948년 11월 12일의 유엔총회의 결의에 따를 수밖에 없었다고 함. 위원단은 한국인들을 위해 한반도가 통일되어야 한다는 의견을 밝히는 한편, 유엔한국임시위원단은 남한 정부가 한반도를 대표하는 정부임을 승인하였으나 이 문제에 대해서는 총회에서 추가로 논의할 필요가 있다고 말함.

필리핀 대표는 총회 이전에 진정한 문제는 한국의 통일문제라는 점을 지적함. 한국의 분단이 부자연스럽고 현재의 한반도의 분단 상황이 미국과 소련 양국 간의 정치적인 문제로 인해 발생된 부당한 상황임을 강조함. 또한 유엔한국임시위원단이 유엔 임시총회의 승인 하에 남한 내 총선을 실시하고 이를 감시하여 자유롭고 합법적인 선거가 진행되었다는 사실을 인정하기 때문에, 남한 정부를 한반도내 유일한 합법적인 정부로서 한반도를 대표하는 정부로 지지한다는 취지의 발언을 함.

호주 대표는 유엔한국임시위원단의 보고서 내용을 지지하며 소련대표의 반대 발언이 잘못되었음을 지적함.

미국대표는 유엔한국임시위원단의 정당성을 주장하며 북한 내 소련의 행위를 비난하는 발언을 하였고 또한 유엔은 한반도의 독립과 통일을 위한 임무를 완수해야한다고 주장함.

마지막으로 브라질 대표가 한반도의 통일을 지지하는 발언을 함.

오후 1시 5분에 정회함.

Third Session
FIRST COMMITTEE

SUMMARY RECORD OF THE TWO HUNDRED AND THIRTY-FIRST MEETING
Held at the Palais de Chaillot, Paris,
on Tuesday, 7 December 1948, at 11 a.m.

CONTENTS:

Question of the independence of Korea (continuation)

Chairman: Mr. SPAAK   Belgium

Rapporteur: Mr. SARPER   Turkey

The CHAIRMAN announced that the Committee could devote only six more meetings to discussion of the Korean problem. He therefore asked the speakers to be brief.

Mr. LIU, Rapporteur of the United Nations Temporary Commission on Korea, said that the Commission's report consisted of two parts: one covering the period 12 January 1948 - 24 May 1948; the other the period 25 May 1948 - 14 October 1948.

According to its terms of reference as defined by resolution 112 of 14 November 1947, the Temporary Commission had three main tasks: to observe events; to consult with the Korean authorities; and to submit a report to the General Assembly. The purpose of the resolution of 14 November 1947 was to secure the independence of Korea by the concerted efforts of the United Nations and the Korean people. To that end, the Commission was to ensure that the elections proceeded normally, and that the Korean representatives were chosen freely by the people themselves, and not appointed by the military authorities. The Commission was further to establish contact with the elected representatives of Korea, and place its services at the disposal of the Korean government in a consultative capacity. Ever since the first meeting, held at Seoul on 12 January 1948, the Commission had sought to co-operate with the authorities of Northern Korea. On 26 February, however, the Commission decided, in view of the refusal of the Northern Korean authorities to co-operate, to apply the decision taken by the General Assembly on 14 November to those parts of Korea to which it had access.

The Rapporteur stated that the Temporary Commission had observed the progress of the elections which were held in Southern Korea on 10 May 1948, and had reached the conclusion that those elections represented a valid expression of the free will of the people of Southern Korea, who formed two-thirds of the population of the whole of Korea. The Commission had also observed the development of the situation in Korea since the elections, and had had advisory consultations with the Government which had been set up. Finally, the Commission had submitted its report to the General Assembly, as instructed.

Mr. Liu said that, in a general way, the Temporary Commission had studied the situation of the whole of Korea. The Commission regretted that it had been refused access to Northern Korea, and considered that, for the good of the Korean people, the whole of Korea should be unified. On the other hand, it must be pointed out that two-thirds of the population of Korea had elected their representatives under the control

dd   /of the

of the Temporary Commission and had formed a National Assembly and a
Government, to which the United States forces of occupation had progressively
transferred governmental and administrative functions.   It was the
opinion of the Temporary Commission that, when the transfer of authority
was completed, and a Korean security force had been formed, the support
of the Korean people for that government would be such as to allow it
to fulfil its mission.   A representative government had in fact been
established in Korea.   The Commission had taken note of that fact in
its report, and had discussed all the factors in support of the claim
of the government to represent the whole of Korea.   That was however a
question for the First Committee to discuss and solve.   Finally, the
Temporary Commission regretted to have to state that it had not been
able to complete all the tasks conferred on it by the General Assembly
resolution of 14 November 1947.   The First Committee would have to decide
whether the programme laid down by the General Assembly in the preceding
year should be completed, and if so, by what body.   The Temporary
Commission had decided not to make any recommendation which might
prejudice the position of the General Assembly.   The Commission was
of course at the disposal of the Assembly and was ready to help that
body to find a solution for outstanding questions.

Mr. ROMULO (Philippines) stated that the real problem before
the Assembly was that of the unification of Korea.   The partition of
Korea, which was unnatural and which, moreover, was contrary to the
declarations made by the Great Powers in Cairo and in Moscow, arose
from factors which were preventing Korea from being free and independent.
The continued occupation of a country which should be free was unjustified,
especially as Korea had become the scene of conflict between the policies
of the two occupying Powers.   The United States, having failed to reach
an agreement with the USSR to give the Korean people liberty and
independence, had appealed to the United Nations to solve the problem.
It would be remembered that after the adoption of the General Assembly
resolution of 14 November 1947, the USSR had refused to co-operate with
the Temporary Commission; the Ukrainian SSR which was elected a member
of the Commission, had refused to send a representative; and the USSR
occupation forces had refused to allow the Commission to enter the
territory of Northern Korea.   As a result, the Commission, convinced
that it would never be able to carry out its mandate in full, had asked
the Interim Committee of the General Assembly whether the terms of
reference which it had received under the General Assembly resolution
dd
/allowed

allowed no grace time to carry out its task in accordance to the
decision. If the reply to the first question was negative, the Temporary
Commission should nevertheless follow the elections of Korean representatives and observe whether they were held in an atmosphere of ... The Secretary-General of the General Assembly had instructed the Temporary Commission to fulfill its mandate in those parts of Korea which it could accede and to follow the elections taking place there. In acting thus, the Interim Committee of the General Assembly had merely applied the direct view of the resolution of 14 November 1947, the purpose of which was to find a way out of the impasse into which the negative attitude assumed by the USSR had brought the problem of the independence of Korea.

Mr. Romulo pointed out that the conclusions of the Temporary Commission showed clearly that the elections of 10 May had been held in conditions which, in the circumstances, must be regarded as satisfactory; 75 per cent of the electorate went to the polls in an atmosphere of enthusiasm, despite isolated cases of threats and coercion. On the basis of its observations, the Temporary Commission had concluded that in Southern Korea, both before and during the elections, there had been a fair degree of freedom of speech, press and assembly, and that the results of the elections were the expression of the free will of the electorate of Southern Korea, which represented about two-thirds of the total electorate of all Korea. In the second part of its report, the Temporary Commission maintained, in reply to complaints which had been submitted, that the elections had taken place in normal conditions. The Temporary Commission while recognizing the right of the elected representatives of Southern Korea to form a National Assembly had however not expressed any opinion as to whether the Seoul Government could be regarded as the Government of Korea, as contemplated by resolution 112 of the General Assembly, for the Commission felt that it was for the General Assembly to take a decision on that point. It was not certain whether the Assembly elected in Southern Korea could be regarded as a national assembly, as neither the inhabitants of Northern Korea nor the members of certain political parties in Southern Korea had taken part in the elections. At the same time, the Government had been established on the basis of the majority rule. In short, it was for the present General Assembly to decide whether the Korean Government set up on 5 August 1948 could be considered as the government of the whole of Korea. That was the political side of the question of the unification of Korea.

dd

/The view

In view of the fact that the National Assembly had been elected
under the supervision of the Temporary Commission of the United Nations,
and that the occupying Power -- the United States of America -- had
handed over the administrative functions to the Korean Government, the
President of the Philippines had on 19 August 1948, virtually accorded
de jure recognition to the government of Korea. Four days later,
the Ministry of Foreign Affairs of the Philippines had made a public
statement to the effect that in its view the Government of the Korean
Republic should be recognized as the Government of Korea in accordance
with the terms of the General Assembly resolution of 14 November 1947.

The problem now was therefore no longer that of the independence of
Korea, but of the unification of Korea. Southern and Northern Korea
formed a single economic unit. A political division of the country
would create an untenable economic situation. The Korean leaders had
made supreme efforts to avoid accentuating the division of the country,
by inviting Northern Korea also to hold free elections and to send her
freely elected representatives to occupy the seats reserved for them in
the Korean National Assembly.

In the meantime, progress had been made in connexion with the
formation of local security forces and the transfer of the government
functions from the occupation authorities to the Korean Government.
There was however still much to be done in order to bring about the
unification of Korea.

The Philippines delegation supported the draft resolution submitted
by Australia, China and the United States (A/C.1/426).

The Philippines delegation had taken part in the work of the Temporary
Commission because it wished to help the Korean people to realize their
national aspirations. The Philippines delegation appealed to the United
Nations to give the Korean people the possibility of establishing a regime
of freedom and justice.

dd   /Mr. PLIMSOLL

Mr. PLIMSOLL (Australia) pointed out that the Korean question was
primarily of concern to the countries of the Far East.   It was in that part
of the world that the most important political and social changes were
taking place.   It was essential that those changes should be made
peacefully and should lead to the advancement of personal freedom and the
principles of democracy.   From the Potsdam and Moscow Declarations, it had
been possible to contemplate the establishment of an independent Korean State.
The fact that the question of the unification of Korea had arisen later was
due to the artificial and temporary partition of the country between the
United States and the Union of Soviet Socialist Republics.   Such a division
defied geography, economic laws, and the ethnical requirements of Korea.

The United Nations Temporary Commission appointed by the General Assembly
in 194 had been able to observe the situation in Southern Korea and to
co-operate with the United States which exercised authority there.   But it
had not been able to verify what was happening in Northern Korea;   it had no
information, although certain delegations were now alleging, without however,
offering any proof, that the government of that part of Korea represented
the entire Korean people.   Those same delegations had used the Temporary
Commission's report to claim that the regime in Southern Korea was not
democratic.   That only proved that the Commission had been objective and
gave so much more weight to its conclusions, which had been adopted
unanimously.

The Australian representative went on to point out that the statement
of the USSR representative to the effect that the Southern Korean elections
had not been free was based on remarks made by certain members of the
Temporary Commission during the first few weeks of its existence.   That
fact alone showed that the members of the Temporary Commission had not been
the instrument of any power, that they had had no preconceived ideas and that
they had begun their work with an open mind.   Furthermore, the Committee
should keep in mind that the Commission had decided unanimously that the
elections had been free, that there had been no interference on the part of
the military authorities of the occupying Power and that the elected
government represented the freely-expressed will of the Korean people.   In
addition, the Temporary Commission had made every effort to see that a
greater degree of liberty prevailed before the elections and to quicken
the democratization process in Southern Korea.   The second part of the
report of the Commission showed that the measures taken in Southern Korea
had improved the situation and had removed the causes for criticism.

dd   /It was

It was true the General Assembly resolution of 14 November had now resulted in the unification of Korea. But information had been collected and a democratic Government had been formed in Southern Korea. The Australian delegation wished to pay a tribute to the officials of the Korean Government who, in spite of forty years of Japanese dictatorship, had been able to bring about the independence of their country in a remarkable manner.

According to the Australian, Chinese and United States draft resolution, the Government of Southern Korea should be considered as the only free Government and the Government of Northern Korea could in no way be considered to have jurisdiction over Southern Korea. Furthermore, a United Nations Commission should continue the work begun by the Temporary Commission in Southern Korea. The resolution of the three Powers left the way open for the unification of Korea by providing for a withdrawal of the armies of occupation. In short, that resolution would promote the establishment of the independence of a democratic and unified Korea.

Mr. DULLES (United States of America) reminded the Committee that five years ago the victorious Powers had promised the independence to the thirty million inhabitants of Korea. As they had not been able to keep their promise, the United Nations had been forced to deal with the question. In 1947, the Assembly had decided by 43 votes to none, with 6 abstentions, to set up the Temporary Commission to consult with the elected representatives of the Korean people, to verify that those representatives were really elected by the people and not just nominated by the military authorities. The Commission was also to verify whether the regularly elected National Assembly was going to set up a national Government. The Government, in turn, was to organize forces to maintain national security, dissolve other military or semi-military groups, progressively take over the functions of government and make arrangements with the occupying Powers for the withdrawal of their armed forces.

It was regrettable that the Commission had not been able to visit Northern Korea which was occupied by the USSR. That had meant that the United Nations had not been able to make sure that the elections which had been held in that part of Korea had been free and that the people had participated in the formation of a national Government. It seemed, on the contrary, that Northern Korea was dominated by a communist regime which has pretentions to govern the whole of Korea and threatened to back its pretentions by force. That regime had already perpetrated acts of terrorism. It had, however, already been recognized by the USSR, Czechoslovakia and Poland and was assured, it would seem, of the moral and

dd

/material support

material support of the forces of the USSR in Northern Korea.   It was
regrettable that the Korean people, after forty years of Japanese oppression
should again be threatened by acts of terrorism from the North.   It was also
a serious matter for the United Nations that one of the General Assembly
recommendations, adopted by 43 votes to none, should be nullified by certain
of its Members.

The United States representative pointed out, however, that in
Southern Korea the Commission had had all the necessary facilities to carry
out its mission.   The elections which had been held under the supervision
of the Commission were striking proof of the ability of the Korean people
to create a representative and responsible Government.   Almost 80 per cent
of the electorate had registered and 95 per cent of the registered voters
had voted.   The result of the elections was a balanced assembly which
reflected the will of the people.   The Government appointed by that
Assembly was now in authority and was maintaining law and order in spite of
the efforts of certain subversive elements.   In short, a legal Government
controlled the most populous part of Korea.   Based on elections considered
as a valid expression of the free will of the voting populace, it was the
only such government in Korea.

Mr. Dulles predicted that, as happened last year, **glowing statements**
would be made about the wonders of Northern Korea.   But the Committee could
not take any account of such statements, because the Temporary Commission
had been refused access to the territory of Northern Korea.

The representative of the United States found, moreover, that the
United Nations should complete its attempt to assure independence and unity
for Korea.   The Government of the Republic of Korea should be recognized so
that, stamped with the seal of legitimacy, it could maintain its prestige and
authority in Korea and throughout the rest of the world.   Furthermore, the
United Nations should send a Commission to Korea to assist the new Government
to end the war-time military occupation.   The forces of occupation should be
withdrawn as soon as possible and that withdrawal should be of such a nature
that the Korean people would really be masters in their own house and would
not be terrorized by elements receiving their orders from a foreign country.
Finally, the United Nations Commission should help the Korean people to
reunite and to rid themselves of economic barriers and fears of civil war
of which they were the victims.   Just as in Greece, the communists were
trying to impose their will by force with the support of neighbouring
communist elements.   The presence of a United Nations Commission in Korea
would make it possible to ensure that the people of Northern and Southern
Korea practiced tolerance and lived in peace with their neighbours.   By its
good offices, the Commission could break down the barrier which was

jd   /obstructing

obstructing friendly relations between Northern and Southern Korea.

The resolution proposed by Australia, China and the United States would allow the United Nations to achieve its avowed objectives. That resolution should be adopted by an overwhelming majority because the principle behind it was of concern not only to Korea but also to all non-communist States threatened by violence, terrorism and internal division. Against that danger there was one elemental defence and that was to show, through the United Nations, that other States offered moral support to those who, in violation of the United Nations Charter, were the object of such measures of violence.

The communist States were not hated because they were communist but because they used methods of coercion, of terrorism and of violence and because members of the Party were taught to use such methods. The greatest service which the United Nations could render in that respect was to demonstrate that whenever these methods were used on an international plane, the rest of the States of the world would close their ranks and prevent such methods from succeeding by using all the pacific means put at their disposal by the Charter. In that way it would perhaps finally be realized that the use of violence or terrorism to achieve certain international objectives provoked such consequences that it was preferable to abandon all such methods.

In conclusion, Mr. Dulles said that in the interest of the Korean people, and in the interest of each of the Members of the United Nations desirous of defending its independence, it was important to give some token of solidarity to the Government of the Republic of Korea, which, although newly formed was already being threatened.

Mr. MUNIZ (Brazil) stated that, although his Government had no direct interest in Korea, it considered it unfortunate and very disquieting that the recommendations of the United Nations had not been observed by Members of the United Nations. The United Nations now had only moral authority. If decisions taken by the majority were scorned by the minority, the very existence of the Organization would be threatened.

In the case of Korea, the action of the United Nations was perfectly justified; the Temporary Commission had carried out its task to ensure respect for the decisions of the Assembly. Consequently the First Committee had no choice; it should apply the conclusions of the Temporary Commission, and put an end to the division of Korea which had become the battlefield for two ideologies.

The representative of Brazil added that the assertions made on the subject of conditions in Northern Korea were not admissible because they

had not been proved, especially insofar as concerned the very high
percentage of the population which according to the representative of the
USSR had participated in the elections.   Such assertions would have been
more convincing if the Temporary Commission had been able to take note of
the facts on the spot.   The Brazilian delegation considered that, in such
circumstances, it was strange that Northern Korea had been recognized by
certain members of the United Nations.

The proposal made by Australia, China and the United States was
reasonable.   The Brazilian delegation supported that resolution and hoped
that the new commission would receive the support of all the Members of
the United Nations in an effort to bring the problem of the unification of
Korea to a successful conclusion.

The meeting rose at 1.05 p.m.

(4) 제3차 유엔총회 제1위원회 제232차 회의 요약

해제문서 12 : A/C.1/SR 232 (Third Session, First Committee, Summary Record of the Two Hundred and Thirty Second Meeting)

문서명	Third Session, First Committee, Summary Record of the Two Hundred and Thirty Second Meeting		
	제3차 유엔총회 제1위원회 제232차 회의 요약 기록		
발신		생성일시	1948년 12월 7일 오후 3시
		발신일시	
수신		수신일시	
		문서번호	A/C.1/SR 232
문서형태	회의록(요약)	문서분량	17쪽
주제명	1. 유엔한국대표 장면 박사의 연설 2. 한국의 독립문제		
주요내용	1948년 12월 7일 오후 3시 프랑스 파리에서 개최된 제3차 유엔총회 제1위원회 제232차 회의록. 상세한 내용은 본문 참조.		
검색어	유엔한국임시위원단, 한국 국회, 제1위원회, 장면(John M. Chang, 한국 대표), 무기르(Mughir, 시리아 대표), 치앙(Tingfu. F. Tsiang, 중국 대표), Setalavad(인도 대표), 토넬리(De La Tournelle, 프랑스 대표), Sandler(스웨덴 대표), U Pe Kin(버마 대표), Snouck Hurgronje(네덜란드 대표), Balaguer(도미니크 공화국)		

1948년 12월 7일 오후 3시 프랑스 파리에서 개최된 제3차 유엔총회 제1위원회 제232차 회의록.

한국독립문제에 관한 유엔한국임시위원단과 유엔총회 소총회의 보고 (A/575 및 A/583)가 속개된 것임.

제3차 유엔총회에 참석한 한국대표단의 장면 대표는 식민지 시기 이전부터 한국은 독립국이었으며 일본 식민지 치하에서도 한국인들은 독립의지를 굳건히 견지해 왔음을 밝힘.

또한 일본으로부터 독립한 후 3년이 지난 시점에도 여전히 한국은 완전한 독립국가를 이루지 못하고 있다는 사실, 미소 양국에 의해 북위 38도에 설정된 분단선의 부당함 등을 강조하며 분단선을 철폐하고자하는 미국의 의지에 반대하는 소련의 행동을 비난함.

이어서 남한에서의 총선거 과정의 합법성과 정당성을 강조하고 북한 정부가 불법적으로 구성된 경위를 설명하여, 대한민국 정부가 한반도 내의 유일한 합법적 정부임을 주장함. 따라서 대한민국정부가 한반도를 대표하여 외교권을 행사하는 것뿐만 아니라 한국 정부를 유엔대표로 인정해 줄 것을 요청함.

북한지역에서 3년 넘게 실시되어 온 소련군에 의한 군사 지원 및 훈련에 대해 언급하고 이로 인한 남북한 군사력의 비대칭성이 존재함을 주장하며 이를 해소하기 위해 미군이 남한에 주둔하여 한국의 군사력을 육성해 줄 것을 요청함.

호주, 중국, 미국이 제안한 결의안에 대해 언급하고 결의안 3항에 대한 수정안을 제시함. 유엔이 대한민국정부(the Republic of Korea)를 인정하는 것이 한반도의 독립에 크게 도움이 될 것이라고 주장함. 이를 반대하는 소련과 비합법적인 북한정권을 비판하는 한편, 대한민국 정부는 유엔 결의안을 준수하며 한국의 독립과 대한민국의 주권을 수호하겠다는 의지를 밝히며 연설을 마무리함.

각국 대표가 한국 독립문제에 대한 의견을 밝힘.

시리아 대표는 유엔총회에 참석한 각국 대표의 의견을 요약하며 남한정부의 합법성과 대표성을 인정하지 않는 국가들의 견해는 위험한 것이라며 남한정부의 합법성을 주장하였고, 남한정부가 유일하게 한반도를 대표하는 정부임을 강조함. 또한 한반도의 분단 상황은 종결되어야 한다고 주장함.

이어 중국 대표와 인도 대표는 한국임시위원단의 보고서 내용을 지지하며 대한민국정부의 대표성을 인정한다는 견해를 밝힘.

프랑스 대표는 한국인이 처한 상황을 고려하여 한국의 독립과 통일을 지지하고 수정결의안에 찬성의사를 밝힘.

스웨덴 대표는 현재의 안건은 평화협정과 연계되어 있다며 기권의사를 밝혔고 버마 대표도 기권의사를 밝힘.

네덜란드 대표는 수정결의안에 의해 구성될 한국위원단의 규모를 확대할 것을 건의함.

도미니크 공화국 대표는 한반도에 한국인이 자유롭게 의사결정을 할 수 있는 환경이 조성되어야 한다는 취지의 발언을 함.

오후 5시 45분에 정회함.

United Nations   Nations Unies   UNRESTRICTED

GENERAL ASSEMBLY

ASSEMBLEE GENERALE

A/C.1/SR 232
7 December 1948

ORIGINAL: ENGLISH

Dual distribution

Third Session

FIRST COMMITTEE

SUMMARY RECORD OF THE TWO HUNDRED AND THIRTY-SECOND MEETING

Held at the Palais de Chaillot, Paris,
on Tuesday, 7 December 1948, at 3 p.m.

CONTENTS:

The problem of the independence of Korea: Reports of the United
Nations Temporary Commission on Korea and of the Interim Committee
of the General Assembly; (A/575 and A/583)
Continuation of the Discussion

Chairman:	Mr. H. SPAAK	Belgium
Rapporteur:	Mr. S. SARPER	Turkey

THE PROBLEM OF THE INDEPENDENCE OF KOREA: REPORTS OF THE UNITED NATIONS
TEMPORARY COMMISSION ON KOREA AND OF THE INTERIM COMMITTEE OF THE GENERAL
ASSEMBLY: (A/575 AND A/583)
(CONTINUATION OF THE GENERAL DISCUSSION)

Dr. John M. CHANG (Korea) said that he was honoured to speak
before the United Nations on behalf of justice and liberty for the
Korean people, who regarded the United Nations as their greatest hope.
Throughout unbearable years of bondage the Korean people had kept alive
their deep longing for the restoration of their sovereign independence,
but although the Japanese enemy had been defeated more than three years
ago, the freedom of Korea remained incomplete. Korea had an ancient
civilization, an ancient history of sovereignty and independence, a common
language, complete racial homogeneity, and clearly recognized frontiers,
and its people were devoted to the cause of their national independence.
While, like many other free nations, Korea had its fifth columnists,
they were few in number and exercised their power through the military
assistance of a foreign government against the will of the overwhelming
mass of the Korean people. During the forty years of Japanese domination, which had begun for Korea long before the Nazi and Japanese
blitzkriegs had erupted over Europe and Asia, an active movement for
independence had been maintained at home and abroad.

The present circumstances of the Republic of Korea were far from
perfect, but surely the Assembly would not fail to approve the Republic,
which had been established in conformity with the Assembly's will,
because one power had defied the Assembly's clear mandate. The international pledges for Korean independence and sovereignty, such as those
at Cairo in 1943 and at Potsdam in July 1945, were so numerous that no-
one contested Korea's abstract rights. When the war with Japan had
ended, the Korean people welcomed the Americans and the Russians as
liberators, but few then thought that they would stay on indefinitely.
However, a military dividing line was arbitrarily established at the
38th parallel, a line without political, topographical or economic
meaning which swiftly froze into a barrier to the flow of commerce, of
persons, of railway and highway traffic of every kind. The Korean
people had had no part in this monstrous division of their country and
still suffered from its many evils. It was only fair to say that once
having become a party to this division, the United States Government had
done everything within its power to lift the barrier, both by direct
appeals from their Commanding General in Korea and in several conferences.
The Russians, on the other hand, refused to consider any political

id
/unification

unification which would not in effect, establish the Communist party
in control and failing a political agreement, would not even discuss
relaxation of the economic barricade.

The obvious injustices done to the Korean people caused the General
Assembly to adopt its two resolutions concerning Korea of 14 November 1947.
However, the Soviet Government boycotted the Temporary Commission
established by one of these resolutions and refused either to permit any
member of the Commission to enter North Korea and to receive its
communications, but with the permission of the Interim Committee, the
Temporary Commission proceeded with its work and reported that the
result of the election of 10 May 1948 was a valid expression of the free
will of the electorate in those parts of Korea which were accessible to
the Commission.   Should the Government established by more than two-
thirds of the Korean people go unrecognized because a foreign power had
arbitrarily refused to permit the other third to join in the elections?
Although the Korean people had never before participated in popular
elections approximately 80 per cent of the potential electorate registered
and over 95 per cent of the registered electorate cast their ballots in
complete freedom and absolute secrecy, despite every foul means attempted
by the Communists to disrupt the elections.   The elected representatives,
among which he himself and his alternate representative, were included,
assembled on 31 May 1948 at the Korean National Assembly and adopted the
constitution of the Republic of Korea.   Under this constitution a
President, and a Vice-President were elected, and a Government formed and
inaugurate⁷ on 15 August 1948 to which governmental powers had been
conferred by United States military authorities.   It was the aim of this
Government to secure a similar transference of powers from the occupation
authorities north of the 38th parallel.   The Korean people well knew
that mere residence north of an artificial line had not made aliens and
Communists of the patriotic Korean people and were holding vacant
approximately one-third of the seats in the National Assembly until
such time as elections could be held in the north.   This urgent desire
of the Assembly for national unity was clearly expressed in a resolution
of 12 June 1948 which had been widely publicised.

Mr. Chang traced the establishment of what he called a Communist
dictatorship under Soviet sponsorship based on the northern city of
Pyong Yang, and supported by Russian trained military forces.   He said
that a small group of Korean Communists had organized an administrative
committee, re-named the Communist party, and created numerous other
organizations under Communist control.   They had then conducted a so-
called election by placing their own names on a ballot and requiring all

/citizens

citizens to indicate their favour or disapproval of this single list
by placing it either in a white or a black box.   Fear of reprisals
was such that few persons dared to drop the list in the black box, yet
this procedure had been referred to by some representatives to the
General Assembly as the holding of democratic elections.   Last July
the self-appointed Communist leaders had declared in force a Soviet
type constitution and had designated 25 August as the date for further
elections.   It was now claimed that these elections were also held
in South Korea and that the new Communist Government was inclusive of
North and South Korea but such statements were extraordinary departures
from truth.   The Temporary Commission, the Consular officials of the
United Kingdom, China, France and the United States, the civilian and
military officials of the United States occupation force and he himself
were all in Korea in August 1948 and saw no elections.   Despite this
independent testimony, it was claimed that 77.52% of the people living
south of the 38th parallel, that is, over 6 million people, went to
the polls to vote, secretly and unseen by anyone.

The essential facts of the present situation were that the
Government of the Republic of Korea had been established as a result
of the election of 10 May 1948, was based on constitutional safeguards of
civil liberty and public participation in government had the essential
bases for economic stability and maintenance of public peace, and had
already received the provisional recognition of the United States, China
and the Philippine Republic.   Following its approval by the General
Assembly this Government looked forward to the establishment of normal
diplomatic relations with most of the nations of the world and to formal
membership in the United Nations.

Because of the conduct of the Soviet military forces and of
Korean Communists acting under their directions, several millions of
Korean citizens from every strata of society had been displaced from
their homes and forced to take refuge south of the 38th parallel.   The
Korean people sympathised deeply with these refugees and some of them
were participating in the Government, but they created a serious
economic dislocation.

Some time must pass for the Republic of Korea to train properly
and equip an adequate military force for its defence.   The United States
Army in Korea had begun the organization of a small constabulary which
was now being expanded and trained as a regular military body, but was
still in the early stages of training.   On the other hand, very large
military forces had been trained and equipped by the Soviet army for
over three years in the northern part of Korea.   Military weakness in

/the Republic

the Republic would be an invitation to the northern leaders to use
their well-trained forces as they had threatened.   It seemed
reasonable, therefore, that the Assembly should give friendly
consideration to the Republic's desire to have adequate time to train
its security forces.   The National Assembly and the Government of the
Republic had requested the United States to retain a small tactical
force in Korea to serve as a school force and to give the necessary
moral backing to Korean troops during their training period.   While
this question primarily concerned the Government of the Republic and of
the United States, they would not wish to act in this manner without the
moral support of the free nations, and he therefore urged the continued
interest of the General Assembly in this problem.

Mr. Chang said that his delegation considered the joint resolution
submitted by the delegations of Australia, China and United States
(A/C.1/426) as a possible measure for the solution of Korean problems,
but wished to make several specific comments.   Referring to paragraph 2,
he expressed the desire that suitable changes be made to confirm the
claims of the Republic of Korea that it was the Government envisaged
in the Assembly's Resolution of 14 November 1947, that it was only
prevented from exercising its jurisdiction over all Korea by force
measure and that the whole sovereignty of the Korean nation resided in
it.   He asked that paragraph 3 should be amended by the addition of the
words, "bearing in mind the completion of the training and equipment of
an adequate security force for the Government of the Republic of Korea".

He said that his delegation understood paragraph 4 (c) to apply to
the people north of the 38th parallel, but that in the meantime, the
Korean people had a representative Government in the Government of the
Republic of Korea, based upon the freely expressed will of the people
and with a democratic constitution, as testified by the Temporary
Commission in their reports.   He said that his delegation understood
paragraph 8 to mean that Member States should refrain from any acts
derogatory to the results achieved by the United Nations in assisting
in the creation of the Republic of Korea, and from any further results
which the Commission might achieve in bringing independence to the
people in northern Korea, so that they might unite with southern Korea
in one nation.

He expressed regret that paragraph 9 did not use more precise
language in calling for recognition of the Government of the Republic
of Korea by Member States, but interpreted this to be the meaning of
the paragraph.

Mr. Chang thought that the greatest aid to unification of Korea

/would be

would be the approval by the General Assembly of the Government of the
Republic of Korea and its subsequent general recognition, for such
recognition would attract the loyal adherence of millions of men and women
in the north.   In the meantime, it would be unfair to hold against the
Korean people a geographical division imposed upon by them without their
prior consent, and even more unfair to withhold the diplomatic intercourse
simply because one Member of the United Nations had defied the rest.   For
the General Assembly to fail to approve of the Government of the Republic
of Korea as that contemplated in its Resolution of 14 November 1947
because the Soviet Government had boycotted the Commission and because of
the establishment of the self-appointed northern regime, would be to
reward the guilty and punish the innocent and would be an admission that
the defiant political group at Pyong Yang had the Assembly's support.
The Korean people had complied with the Assembly's mandates and would
maintain their independence and sovereignty against any challenge.

        Mr. MUGHIZ (Syria) recalled briefly the periods of Japanese
domination and of liberation by the United States and USSR forces in order
to point out that Korea in 1948 was no better off than it was before the
Japanese surrendered and in fact, now faced the new difficulty of division
at the 38th parallel.   In the face of this difficulty the urge of unity
had been so compelling that when it became clear to the United Nations
Temporary Commission that its work was necessarily confined to one part
of Korea, several members expressed reluctance to proceed with the
implementation of the Assembly's Resolution of 14 November 1947.   In
support of this he cited a statement of the Chairman of the Commission to
the Interim Committee that a separate government in South Korea could
not be a national government as defined in the Assembly's Resolution,
the objections of the Canadian representative on the Interim Committee to
any election confined to one part of Korea, and the criticism by the
Australian representative on the Commission of the Interim Committee's
resolution.   He also quoted the explanation of the Syrian representative
on the Commission of his abstention from voting on the Interim Committee's
Resolution of 26 February 1948, pointing out the dangers involved in any
scheme of partition of Korea, and his statement at a later meeting that
opposition to any work of the Commission would mean that the present
situation would remain as it was.   He added that the Syrian Government
had had bitter experience with partition in Palestine and did not wish the
same fate to overtake Korea.

        The consequences of the division economically could not be over
                                                        /emphasized

emphasized, for the agricultural south and the industrial north were
inter-dependent.   Thus neither could enjoy economic stability and
independence without substantial foreign aid, and politically and
socially the division had been most disrupting.   These considerations
had induced the Syrian delegation to the Korean Commission to advocate
a cautious course of action and the linking of the question of
independence with that of unity.   The division was the result of
power politics, self-interest and foreign intervention and in this
connection he quoted the statement of a well-known Korean personality
before Sub-Committee 2 of the Commission, to the effect that the Korean
problem was a reflection of the natural antagonism between Soviet Russia
and America.   The negative attitude of the USSR to the Assembly's
Resolution of November 1947 had therefore put the Commission in a very
precarious situation and in the circumstances, the Syrian delegation
chose to co-operate with the Commission to the fullest extent possible
but only on the explicit condition that a free atmosphere for elections
should be assured before any observation of elections took place.

The need for this free atmosphere was acknowledged by the Commission
in its Resolution of 12 March in which it decided to accept the advice
of the Interim Committee to hold elections in South Korea only.   It
calculated that a free election in the south might induce the people in
the north to adhere to the programme of the United Nations and reconsider
the possibility of joining the South Korean government.   The United States
military authorities did their best to correct existing conditions in
the south and to secure free and unfettered elections.   Undoubtedly,
the election had not been perfect, taking into account that this was the
first election in Korea and that a perfect election was practically
unthinkable even in the most democratic societies.   The Syrian Government
subscribed to the conclusion reached by the Commission that "there existed
a reasonable degree of free atmosphere wherein the democratic rights of
freedom of speech, right and assembly were respected".

Out of this election a Korean Government was established and the
legal grounds for its claims to be the Government for the whole of Korea
had been pointed out.   The advice of the Interim Committee, the findings
of the Commission on the results of the elections, and its readiness
to enter into consultation with the Korean National Assembly were grounds
for the claim that the Government in South Korea had been legally
established for the whole of Korea.   Since this Government had been
established in accordance with the Assembly's Resolution of 14 November 1947,
it deserved the support and the assistance of the Assembly, although it
was not yet an effective Government for the whole of Korea.   It would

dd   /serve

serve as the basis for further efforts towards the unification of Korea
and the Syrian Government now advocated extending help and recognition to
this Government for practical and moral considerations as well as for legal
reasons.   This Government had acquired all the prerequisites of an
accepted and accredited Government and its constitution stressed the
paramount importance of the consolidation of national unity "by justice,
humanity, brotherly love and the elimination of all kinds of social evils".

The Syrian delegation did not wish to question the legality of the
Government which had reportedly been established in Northern Korea and
to which some Governments had already given full de jure recognition,
nor to raise doubts as to the way in which the elections for this
Government had been held.   But it could not help asking why the leaders
in the north, if they were certain that they commanded the majority of
the Korean people had opposed any compromise with the southern leaders
under the auspices of the United Nations Commission.   Furthermore,
why did certain members of the United Nations not only boycott the
Commission but deny it access to territories under their occupation
when they had been so enthusiastic in the defence of another Assembly
resolution adopted hastily by a weak and artificial majority?   Whatever
the considerations, the Government of the Republic of Korea was the
one authority which constituted a basis for the unification of Korea
and for the formation of a Government as envisaged in the Assembly's
resolution of 14 November 1947, but recognition of this Government
should be conditional upon its efforts for unification of the country
by peaceful means.   The United Nations should remain seized of the
problem, but in the final analysis, however, its solution was possible
only by agreement between the United States and the USSR.   Dr. Kim Kiusic,
a well-known leader of moderate leanings, had suggested at a Sub-Committee
of the Korean Commission that the United Nations should request either
the USSR or the United States and the USSR together to solve the problem
which they had created and the Syrian delegation endorsed this request.

Mr. TSIANG (China) said that the two fundamental elements
in the Korean question were the universal recognition that Korea should
be united and independent and the insistence of the Korean people that
this should come about as soon as possible.   The 38th parallel, which
had become an iron curtain between northern and southern Korea and was
the symbol of the differences between the United States and the Soviet
Union, had become a bar to Korean unity and independence.   In the
circumstances the United States had properly brought the question to
the General Assembly, recognizing it as the final court of appeal in the

dd

/next van

post-war world.   By its resolution of 14 November 1947 the Assembly
had decided on the only possible course, that the Korean people themselves
should decide their own fate by holding elections; by the same resolution
it had sent a Temporary Commission to Korea with the duty of observing
these elections.

The Report of the Temporary Commission stated that 75 per cent of
the potential electorate in South Korea took part in the elections and
that the population in this area represented approximately two-thirds
of the population of Korea.   The Commission unanimously recorded its
judgment that the elections were a valid expression of the free will
of the electorate in this area.   The Report demonstrated beyond any
doubt that the members of the Commission were devoted to democratic aims
and procedures and spared no effort in seeing that they were scrupulously
observed.   The Commission rightly assumed that the election laws and
regulations were of basic importance and in Volume II, Annex 4 of the
First Part of the Report there were 36 recommendations, many of which
were further sub-divided, calling for amendments to the draft electoral
law.   To show the spirit and method of work of the Commission, Mr. Tsiang
called attention to a number of recommendations of the Commission which he
had singled out at random.

The Temporary Commission had been well aware that a good electoral law was not itself a sufficient guarantee of a free election and it had devoted much of its efforts to ensuring what it called a "free atmosphere". One of its main concerns in that respect had been to ensure against any possible interference by the police. To achieve that end the Commission had provided that the police should not be permitted inside the polling offices except when expressly called upon by the Chairman of the Election Committee to maintain order. The Commission had also forbidden the police to make any arrests under the election law without a court writ except in cases of emergency.

The Commission had moreover been worried by the Korean people's lack of experience in the matter of general elections in view of the fact that this was the first one to be held in the country. In particular, it had been worried lest the traditional respect for age in Korea should permit the heads of families and village elders to exercise an undue influence on those under their authority. The Commission had realized that the solution lay partly in legal and administrative measures and partly in an educational programme. In connexion with the latter, the United States occupation authorities had done valuable work. Mr. Tsiang quoted from the record of the meeting of Committee I on 1 February 1948 at which the representative of General Hodge had informed the Committee that the United States authorities had already prepared a comprehensive programme to familiarize the population with the purposes and procedures of the election, utilizing for this purpose the press, radio talks and leaflets to be dropped by aeroplanes. The Commission had been told that the United States authorities had supervised the preparation, by Koreans, of a film which would be shown in every town and village before the election. The United States military spokesman had invited the Commission to examine the film and to suggest any changes which it deemed desirable. Commenting on the spokesman's statement, the Chairman of the Commission had said that he was very encouraged by the United States attitude of co-operation. Mr. Tsiang added that General Hodge himself declared before the Commission that he was particularly interested in ensuring that the election should be held under conditions of complete freedom. To achieve that end the United States authorities had carefully studied the experience gained during the Nicaraguan plebiscite in 1930 and the Saar plebiscite of 1935. After reading the Commission's report Mr. Tsiang was convinced that the United States authorities had co-operated to the greatest possible extent.

The report of the Temporary Commission showed that the Commission had based its conclusions that the election results fully expressed the free-will of the Korean population on the most carefully observations. The Commission

/had divided

divided itself into small groups to observe first the registration of voters, then the registration of candidates and finally the plebiscite which was held on 10 May. The Commission certified that the National Assembly, which resulted from the election was not dominated by any part or combination of parties. In fact, the majority of the Assembly's members were either independents or representatives of minor political groups. The Hankook Democratic Party which had nominated 100 candidates had succeeded in having only 28 elected. The National Association for the Rapid Realization of Korean Independence, led by Syghman Rhee, the President of the Government, out of a total of 247 candidates had only 55 members in the Assembly.

In conclusion, Mr. Tsiang said that the Government of Southern Korea was a representative and democratic Government, as was also the National Assembly. He thought that the United Nations could be proud of its part in the establishment of that Government and that the Temporary Commission deserved the thanks of the General Assembly. The work, however, was not yet complete and Mr. Tsiang hoped that the Committee would approve the joint draft resolution by a large majority.

Mr. SETALAVAD (India) said that his delegation was interested in the Korean question not only because India had been a member of the Temporary Commission but also because it felt a deep concern for the fate of an Asiatic country which possessed an ancient and rich civilization.

In explaining his delegation's attitude towards the Korean problem, Mr. Setalavad reviewed the events which had followed the Assembly's resolution of 14 November 1947. The Temporary Commission's mandate had been to supervise elections throughout the whole of Korea. However, soon after its arrival in Seoul, the Commission had realized that it could not carry out its task in respect of the northern zone and, through the intermediary of the Chairman, who, at that time, was the Indian representative, had placed the whole issue before the Interim Committee with a request for instructions on its future course of action. The Chairman had explained to the Interim Committee that the Commission, while unanimous in thinking that no real national Government, as envisaged in the Assembly's resolution, could possibly be created on the basis of an election in the southern zone alone, nevertheless believed that it should continue its efforts so long as there was any hope that a national Government could eventually be established as a result of conciliation. In reply, the Interim Committee had instructed the Commission to carry on its task in those areas in which it was able to gain admission in the hope that the representatives elected to the National Assembly from the **southern zone** would be **able to establish** contact with the political parties of the northern zone and induce them to co-operate in forming an all-Korean Government. In other words, the Interim Committee had been anxious to ensure that all possible means of persuasion should be employed to bring about Korean unity.

Mr. Setalavad explained that the Indian delegation had supported the Interim Committee's decision, which was transmitted in a letter to the Chairman of the Commission for reasons similar to those outlined above. While it did not believe that any Government created as a result of the elections held in the southern zone could possibly be regarded as a national Government of all Korea, it hoped that the authority which would be elected would be able to enter into relations with the regime in the northern zone so that the two might finally be merged to form the real national Government. The Indian representative on the Commission had stated the belief that the Commission was perfectly free to call a halt in its work whenever it found that it could go no further in implementing the 14 November resolution. Mr. Setalavad regretted that the objective of the Indian delegation had not been reached. Between the election of the National Assembly on 31 May and the formation in the southern zone of the Government which claimed to represent the whole of Korea, no real effort appeared to have been made to bring into the Government any of the major parties in the south which had refused to participate in the election. Moreover, except for a general radio appeal to the people of northern Korea, no attempts had been made to bring about a rapprochment or reconciliation with the northern regime.

That was the background against which the Temporary Commission had had to consider the southern Government's request that the Commission recognize it as the national Government of Korea and authorize it to take over the functions of administration as envisaged in paragraph 4 of the 14 November resolution. The Indian representative on the Commission had voted against such action and had urged the Commission to abandon any further implementation of the General Assembly's resolution because it had believed that the recognition of the new regime as the national Government was too grave a step for the Commission to take without first giving the Assembly an opportunity to reconsider the whole Korean question. Mr. Setalavad explained that the attitude taken by his delegation was not due to any doubt as to the democratic character of the southern Government or the efficiency with which the Commission had done its work. The Indian delegation had voted to suspend the work because the Commission had from the first been placed under a serious handicap by reason of its inability to visit northern Korea and to undertake direct conciliation between the political parties in the two zones and because the establishment of two regimes had confronted it with a _fait accompli_.

/The problem

The problem had therefore been thrown back into the lap of the General Assembly and the latter had to decide what future action it should take. In reaching its decision the Assembly should be guided by three considerations: first, the independence of the whole of Korea must be achieved with the least possible delay; second, independence must be granted to Korea as an integral unit, and the Assembly should not approve any arrangement which might weaken the prospects of realizing that aim   third, the Assembly should lend the fullest support to ensure that every effort was made at conciliation between the peoples of the two zones. In the light of the preceding considerations the Indian delegation believed that the Assembly should determine its action with the greatest possible care. It was necessary that nothing should be done, either directly or indirectly, which might strengthen the unnatural gulf between the two zones.

In that connection, Mr. Setalavad observed that the Commission had emphasized the urgency for instituting peaceful negotiations before the forces of occupation were evacuated from Korea. If negotiations were not instigated before the evacuation, Korea might become a centre of internecine strife between rival political regimes.

In conclusion Mr. Setalavad said that the independence of Korea was long overdue and the Government of India, which feared lest the artificial division of Korea might jeopardize stability in the Far East, was prepared to support any proposal which would bring peace to Korea on the basis of national unity. It was for that reason that India supported the substance of the joint draft resolution. It had, however, some reservations in respect of paragraph 2 because it felt that the paragraph might be interpreted to imply recognition of the southern Government envisaged in the 14 November resolution.

Mr DE LA TOURNELLE (France) expressed the French delegation's deep regret that it had not been possible for representatives of the people of northern Korea to participate in the Committee's debates. However, their absence was not the fault of the Committee or of the Temporary Commission. Mr. de la Tournelle considered that the elections which had taken place in northern Korea constituted a challenge to the authority of the United Nations. The assertion that 99.7% of the voters had participated in the election could scarcely serve to re-assure the peoples of democratic states. The result might have been more acceptable if only 80% or 90% had taken part. Mr. de la Tournelle said that the world had already seen elections in

/Berlin

Berlin where the local authority, which was supported unanimously at one meeting, was next day rejected by the freely expressed will of the Berlin people. It had been asserted that the election in northern Korea took place under free conditions but the fact remained that it had been held under a pall of secrecy and the Commission had been carefully prevented from observing it.

The French representative rejected the accusations which had been made against the Temporary Commission. Previous speakers had based their criticism of it on the testimony of those members of the Commission who had disagreed with their colleagues on certain points. But the very fact that members of the Commission had been free to express their own opinions and to criticize the work which was being done was excellent proof of the Commission's democratic nature. Mr. de la Tournelle considered that the Commission should be congratulated upon the work which it had done.

It was true that the French delegation considered that the Commission had failed insofar as it had been unable to carry out the task of creating a unified independent Korea as the Assembly had intended. But that was not the Commission's fault for no Assembly resolution had any value unless it was accepted by the parties concerned, no matter how large a majority voted in its favour. The refusal of the USSR to co-operate with the Commission was nothing less than a projection into the Assembly of the "veto" which had so greatly impaired the effectiveness of the Security Council. If the Assembly admitted the right of any Member to "veto" its recommendations that would constitute a violation of the Charter.

The consequences of the refusal to accept the Assembly's decision had been tragic for the people of Korea as the representative of southern Korea had so eloquently shewn. It was sad that the Korean people, who had endured the Japanese yoke, should find that their will to national unity was not respected by the liberators.

Mr. de la Tournelle said that his delegation would support the joint draft resolution because it was compatible not only with the Charter and the 14 November resolution, but also with the recommendations of the Temporary Commission. However, if the new Commission which it was prepared to create was faced with the same lack of co-operation as the previous body, then the French delegation feared that it would not be successful. Mr. de la Tournelle hoped that his fears would prove groundless and that if there were a minority which opposed the resolution, the latter would respect the will of the majority in accordance with the Charter.

/Mr. SANDLER

Mr. SANDLER (Sweden) said that, in line with the course of
action which it had taken in earlier debates on the Korean question,
the Swedish delegation would abstain from voting on the joint draft
resolution because the subject with which it dealt was closely linked
with the peace settlements.   In doing so, however, the Swedish delegation reserved its right to take a positive stand on any future
problems of a similar character if it deemed it necessary to intervene.
Mr. Sandler added that his delegation's abstention in the forthcoming
vote should not be taken to mean that it did not hold any views on
the Korean question.   He thought it was deplorable that the
authorities in northern Korea had refused to co operate with the
Tempoary Commission.   The Swedish delegation could not approve such
treatment of a United Nations organ.

Mr. U PE KIN (Burma) expressed his nation's sympathy with the
Korean people who were suffering as a result of a situation which was
not of their own making.   While he did not wish to recapitulate the
series of events which had followed the 14 November resolution and
which had already been adequately described by the representative of
the Philippines, he felt bound to state that his delegation considered
that it was extremely unfortunate that the authorities in the northern
zone of Korea had refused to co-operate with the Temporary Commission,
thus preventing a satisfactory solution.

Mr. U Pe Kin said that his delegation was extremely perturbed at
the tendency among certain Powers to take the easiest course in solving
a difficult situation like that in Korea, by proposing the partition
of a country into separate zones.   The Burmese delegation had noticed
with anxiety the enthusiasm with which some delegations had favoured
partitioning Palestine and he hoped that that decision would not be
taken as a precedent in the case of Korea, especially since the
Committee had just heard the representative of the southern Government
deploring the artificial division of his country.   Mr U Pe Kin
wondered whether the omission of any reference in paragraph 2 of the joint
draft resolution to the northern zone of Korea was not a sign that the
division might become permanent.   It was because the Burmese
delegation opposed any measure which might increase the division
between northern and southern Korea that it had abstained from
voting on the Czechoslovakian proposal for the admission of the
northern representative.   The Burmese delegation had not been
convinced by the arguments adduced by either of the two sides in the

/Committee.

Committee. It did not agree with the argument that the Assembly could
not admit those representatives of a regime which had flouted the
authority of the United Nations and refused to co operate with the
Commission, for had not the Assembly done precisely that when it admitted the representatives of Bulgaria and Albania in the Greek case
and the Jews and the Arabs in connection with Palestine? Nobody
would deny that they had all flouted the authority of the United
Nations at one time or another. The Burmese delegation had also
abstained because the refusal to admit the Temporary Commission to
northern Korea made it impossible to obtain sufficient data to form
a satisfactory opinion on the prevailing conditions in that area.

Mr. U Pe Kin desired nothing more than to see Korea united.
But he believed that the only solution which could being about such
unity was the withdrawal of all the forces of occupation. He
fervently hoped that the two great powers concerned would make an effort
to compose their differences at the earliest possible date so that
their troops might be withdrawn, leaving the Korean people free to
determine their own destiny.

The Burmese representative approved of the substance of the
joint draft resolution, in particular the proposal for a new body
to carry on the work of the Temporary Commission. However, he
reserved his right to speak again on paragraph 2 and he stated that
the Burmese delegation would abstain from voting on that paragraph
if the Committee decided to vote each paragraph separately.

Mr. SNOUCK HURGRONJE (Netherlands) said that the Temporary
Commission's report gave a very clear picture of what had happened
since the adoption of the 14 November resolution. He deeply regretted
that it had not been possible to realize the aim of unifying the
two zones owing to the absence of co-operation by the authorities
of northern Korea. He considered that the measures taken by the
Commission to observe the elections in the southern zone were
completely satisfactory because they were free and democratic.

The Netherlands delegation would support the joint draft
resolution and in particular, the terms of reference of the proposed
Commission which were contained in paragraph 4. However, Mr. Snouck
Hurgronje had some doubt as to whether it was right to refer to the
southern Government as "the Government of the Korean Republic". He
hoped that after the occupying armies had been withdrawn, the people
of northern Korea would be able to express their wishes freely in
elections supervised by the Commission so that unification of Korea
could be achieved

/Mr. Snouck Hurgronje

Mr. Snouck Hurgronje also said that his delegation would prefer a larger Commission than that proposed in the draft resolution. He suggested that 9 or 11 members would be appropriate.

Mr. BALAGUER (Dominican Republic) contrasted the situation in Korea with that in Greece. Here for the first time was a recommendation for troop withdrawal which neither of the States concerned could reject on the grounds that the other's troops would be allowed to remain. It was a test of the sincerity of the USSR's appeal for the withdrawal of all national armed forces. Acceptance would mean that the inhabitants of both zones of Korea would be left free to determine their own political future. Mr. Balaguer earnestly hoped that this would be achieved for the Korean people deserved their freedom after having so long endured the Japanese yoke. He hoped also that the regime which had been set up in North Korea would not endeavour to impose its own political system on the country against the will of the majority of Koreans.

After a discussion on procedure, the meeting rose at 5:45 p.m.

(5) 제3차 유엔총회 제1위원회 제233차 회의 요약

해제문서 13 : A/C.1/SR 233 (Third Session, First Committee, Summary Record of the Two Hundred and Thirty Third Meeting)

문서명	Third Session, First Committee, Summary Record of the Two Hundred and Thirty Third Meeting		
	제3차 유엔총회 제1위원회 제233차 회의 요약 기록		
발신		생성일시	1948년 12월 7일 오후 8시 30분
		발신일시	
수신		수신일시	
		문서번호	A/C.1/SR 233
문서형태	회의록(요약)	문서분량	16쪽
주제명	한국문제 관련 미국의 태도에 대한 비판적 의견 및 토론 내용 1. 한국 독립 문제에 관한 미국 및 유엔의 절차상 문제 2. 남한 현 정부의 합법성 문제		
주요내용	1948년 12월 7일 오후 8시 30분에 프랑스 파리에서 개최된 제3차 유엔총회 제1위원회 제233차 회의 회의록. 상세한 내용은 본문 참조.		
검색어	유엔한국임시위원단, 제1위원회, Kovalenko(우크라이나 대표), Zebrowski (폴란드 대표), 고든 워커(Gordon Walker, 영국 대표)		

1948년 12월 7일 오후 8시 30분에 프랑스 파리에서 개최된 제3차 유엔총회 제1위원회 제233차 회의 회의록으로, 제232차 회의에 이어서 한국 독립문제 안건에 대해 우크라이나 대표의 발언을 시작으로 진행됨.

장시간에 걸쳐 발언을 이어간 우크라이나 대표는 한반도 문제 해결과정에서 미국이 보여준 태도를 비난하고 유엔한국임시위원단의 임무수행과정과 북한의 입국거부로 인해 남한 단독정부 구성을 승인한 유엔총회 의결과정의 문제점을 지적함. 그리고 미국을 지지하는 다수의 국가대표들이 소련의 제안을 거부하고 군대철수를 무기한으로 연기하고 총칼 아래에서 치러진 선거에 의해 꼭두각시 같은 한국 정부를 수립할 수 있는 미국의 제안을 받아들였다고 비난함. 또한 미국의 정책은 오로지 한국이 미국의 이익을 위해 희생하면서 소련에 동조하는 것을 막는 것이라고 주장함.

우크라이나의 의견에 동조하는 대표들은 1948년 5월 9일[1] 선거가 경찰과 미군에 의해서 강압적으로 이루어진 부정선거였다고 주장하면서, 민주적이지 못한 선거에 의해 성립된 정부는 남한을 대표한다고 할 수 없다고 말함.

이어진 폴란드 대표의 발언은 우크라이나 대표가 발언한 내용과 유사한 것으로, 미국이 한반도를 점령할 당시 한반도에는 이미 국민 정부가 활동하고 있었으나, 하지 장군은 정무총감을 포함한 일본인의 지위를 유지하도록 선언했으며 미국은 유엔 제2차 총회에서 미군정 연장을 위한 안건을 제출한 사실을 지적함. 폴란드 대표는 이러한 제안이 한 민족의 운명을 그들의 대표들에게 물어보지 않고서는 결정할 수 없다는 유엔헌장의 조항에 위반되는 것이며, 유엔한국임시위원단의 구성이 유엔헌장뿐만이 아니라 포츠담회담과 모스크바삼상협정의 위반이며, 유엔이 아닌 외상 위원회와 같은 조직이 전후 처리를 담당해야 한다고 주장함. 그리고 폴란드 대표는 유엔한국임시위원단의 한국 시찰·조사과정에서 한국이 군사독재 치하에 있음을 확인하였고, 유엔한국임시위원단이 서울에 도착했을 때 개인의 자유나 표현의 자유가 없었으며, 남한(South

---

1 A/AC.19/W.55.Add.1.

Korea)의 상황은 경찰국가·군사독재와 다름없었다고 주장함. 남한의 정부수립 과정에서 유엔과 유엔한국임시위원단에 대한 미국의 영향력과 대한민국 정부수립 과정의 불법성을 주장하며 이에 대한 모든 책임은 미국에 있으며 한반도에서 유일한 합법적인 정부는 북한 정부임을 주장하고 남한 정부의 합법성을 부정함.

영국대표는 호주, 중국, 미국 대표가 제출한 결의안이 제2차 유엔총회가 채택한 정책에 따라 구성된 것이라고 주장함. 통일된 한국을 위한 결정을 지지하지만 분단은 현실이며 남한에서 현 정권이 자유선거에 기초한 유일한 정부임이 확실하다고 말함. 소련 대표 및 소련의 우방인 우크라이나와 폴란드의 발언 내용은 근거가 부족하므로 수용할 수 없고 유엔한국임시위원단의 보고 내용을 지지하며 호주, 중국, 미국이 제안한 수정결의안에 찬성한다는 의사를 밝힘.

오후 10시 57분에 정회함.

United Nations　　　Nations Unies　UNRESTRICTED

GENERAL　　　ASSEMBLEE　A/C.1/SR 233
　　　　　　　　　　　　　　　　　12 December 1948
ASSEMBLY　　　GENERALE　ENGLISH
　　　　　　　　　　　　　　　　　ORIGINAL: FRENCH

Dual_distribution

Third Session

FIRST COMMITTEE

SUMMARY RECORD OF THE TWO HUNDRED AND THIRTY-THIRD MEETING

Held at the Palais de Chaillot, Paris,
on Tuesday, 7 December 1948, at 8.30 p.m.

CONTENTS:

The Problem of the Independence of Korea (continued)

Chairman:　　　　　　Mr. SPAAK　　　　　　Belgium

Rapporteur:　　　　　Mr. SARPER　　　　　Turkey

Mr. KOVALENKO (Ukrainian Soviet Socialist Republic) stated that, at the second regular session of the General Assembly, the United Kingdom and the United States had brought pressure to bear on the United Nations to induce it, by a further violation of the Charter, to examine the question of Korea.

Apart from the fact that the attention of the United Nations was in that way diverted from more important problems, the examination by the United Nations of a question outside its competence was bound to cause discord.

The United States, having succeeded in getting the question put on the agenda, had tried to prevent it from being dealt with adequately. Taking advantage of their mechanical majority, they had hastened to obtain a decision of substance in the guise of a procedural decision, and the rights of the Korean people had been outrageously disregarded.

The mechanical majority, faithful to the United States, had also, during the same session, rejected the USSR proposal and had adopted an American proposal to enable the United States, by organizing elections at the point of the bayonet, to set up a puppet Korean Government and postpone indefinitely the withdrawal of their troops, which had been provided for by the USSR proposal.

United States policy was aimed solely at abrogating the Moscow agreement on Korea, which was thus sacrificed to American strategic interests. As that policy of disregard for the Korean people had, however, to be camouflaged, a United Nations Temporary Commission had been created as a result of Anglo-American pressure. On 2 November 1947, even a right wing Korean paper had published a declaration by the Korean Centre Labour party to the effect that the submission of the Korean question to the United Nations had been designed merely to postpone the establishment of Korean independence. As regards the dispatch of a Commission to Korea, the Centre Labour Party could only regret that that method had been adopted, instead of representatives of the country participating directly in the solution of the Korean problem. The Labour party had added that, though the United Nations, with United States and USSR co-operation, was doubtless capable of settling the Korean question, it would be preferable for it to be solved by a truly national authority.

Unfortunately the General Assembly, at its second session, had decided not to hear the representatives of the Korean people, but had set up a Temporary Commission to assume full responsibility for the policy of the American military authorities in South Korea, which consisted in the organization of the elections, the designation of a Government of hirelings and the indefinite extension of the American occupation.

/On that

On that account the Ukrainian Soviet Socialist Republic had refused to participate in the work of the Temporary Commission. The Ukrainian Soviet Socialist Republic had not wished its name to be used to cover and camouflage the United States colonial policy in South Korea. Moreover, the Temporary Commission had itself, on arrival in Seoul, expressed serious doubts regarding its right to implement the General Assembly decision in South Korea alone, and regarding the possibility, in view of existing conditions, of holding free elections in South Korea. The Indian representative in particular had declared that a Government established on the basis of elections held in South Korea could not be described as a national Government in the sense of the General Assembly resolution, and he had recalled the statement by Dr. Syngman Rhee before the Temporary Commission that, if a Government were set up in South Korea, it would always need the support of American troops. A Government thus proposed up by the bayonets of the United States, or perhaps of the United Nations, could be nothing else than a Government in tutelage.

Similar views were expressed by the representatives of Australia, Syria Canada and El Salvador, and the last-named proposed that the work of the Commission should be suspended.

Similarly, the representatives of India, Syria and China had declared that it had been impossible to create an atmosphere of freedom in which to hold the elections.

The Interim Committee, on being consulted by the Temporary Commission, had taken a decision, without hearing the representatives of the Korean people or even the members of the Temporary Commission, which was equivalent to a veritable abrogation of the General Assembly's decisions, since it had requested the Temporary Commission to implement in South Korea a decision which had been meant to apply to the whole of Korea. It was again United States pressure that was responsible for this new legal fiction.

It should be noted that the decisions of the Temporary Commission with respect to consulting the Interim Committee and implementing the latter's decision had only been taken by an affirmative vote of four out of nine members, owing to the fact that the members of the Temporary Commission had felt that they did not have the right to implement the resolution of the General Assembly in respect of South Korea alone, and that they had seriously doubted the possibility of holding free elections. Thus the representatives of Canada and Australia in particular had stated that the decision of the Interim Committee was irregular and illegal.

/What had

제2부 유엔총회 회의록(1948)

What had happened? What had caused the Commission to change its views? It had had three sources of information: Korean organizations and private persons; its own observations; and, lastly, the American authorities. The answer was to be found in the documents of the Temporary Commission.

From the very first day of occupation, the American authorities had launched an anti-democratic campaign. They had refused to recognize the Government of the People's Republic elected on 6 September 1945 by an assembly of delegates of national committees of democratic parties and of social organizations. More than that, the Americans had suppressed the democratic popular movement which had arisen as a result of the defeat of Japan and had supported pro-Japanese elements. They had set up an advisory council headed by Kim Suk Soo, former Secretary of the League of National Mobilization, a reactionary pro-Japanese party which had incited Korean youth to murder American and British nationals. Moreover, the statistics of December 1947 showed that the Americans were maintaining the Japanese administrative machinery: twenty per cent of those holding high posts in the Korean administration had occupied the same posts under the Japanese regime; eighty-three per cent of the members of the Temporary Legislative Assembly, fifty-three per cent of the police officials, and seventy-nine per cent of the magistrates were former collaborators. The situation as regards the police force was especially significant, since the matter was an independent body responsible solely to the American military command. Its chief, Chough Pyung Oh, had held a high post in one of the principal pro-Japanese organizations. It was quite natural, therefore, that he should have asked the United Nations Commission to re-establish in North Korea the situation which had prevailed prior to the liberation -- which meant that in South Korea that state of affairs had been faithfully preserved.

Besides the all-powerful police, consisting of traitors, the American authorities had protected terrorist organizations headed by Syngman Rhee and others. It was true that they called themselves youth or athletic organizations. In point of fact, however, they engaged in murdering true Korean patriots. Yet the deputy United States Commander had said in 1947 that those very youth organizations constituted an official branch of the activity of the United States and were designed to prepare young people between 18 and 35 for participation in the administration and the democratic government of their country. The youth organization, which had its own training school, had 300,000 members, while the police and the constabulary numbered 30,000 and 23,000 respectively; the Americans resorted to the same police and administrative machinery as their Japanese predecessors and used the same mercenaries.

/Furthermore,

. Furthermore, economic exploitation took the same forms as under the Japanese: thus the former Company for the Development of the Far East had merely changed its name and the New Korean Company controlled 70 per cent of the mines, 70 per cent of the industry and more than one-eighth of the arable land, including one-sixth of the rice fields. Finally, in South Korea the great land owners held 63 per cent of the land, while 83 per cent of the farmers were in reality share-croppers or even day labourers.

Again, the Americans were perpetuating the miserable status of office employees. The Americans considered Korea merely as a market: trade had revived to the extent of only 27 per cent, and only 5 per cent of the enterprises operating in 1937 were still in existence. The workers were in miserable circumstances and inflation was constantly increasing.

From the cultural point of view, the region had reverted to the dark ages; the so-called National University was attended only by those who were prepared to support the American military authorities.

As regards the political situation, democratic parties and organizations which had had six million members had been driven underground. Among them were the Workers' Party, the Confederation of Labour and the Peasants' Union. The Korean National Union of Youth, which had comprised 800,000 members, had been dissolved by the police. The leaders of those democratic organizations had been arrested or exiled. The press had been subjected to persecution and such democratic newspapers as the "Toiling Masses", the "Cultural News" and the "International News" had been suppressed.

At the moment, according to certain newspapers, there were 30,000 political prisoners in South Korea, including the heads of the Labour Party, the Popular Republican Party and the Democratic Peasants Union. Generally speaking, the people of South Korea were being subjected to arrest, torture and murder. Terrorists were wrecking the headquarters of democratic organizations; terror, instigated by Syngman Rhee and his henchmen. reigned in South Korea, as could be gathered from the documents of the Temporary Commission itself, and in particular from the figures supplied by the Democratic Popular Front.

In order to cover up that situation, the United States of America had submitted the Korean question to the United Nations. Thirteen Korean parties of the Right and the Centre had, on 17 November 1947, violently criticized the decision taken by the General Assembly without the participation of the people of Korea. They had stated they would not take part in elections controlled by foreign authorities. In conclusion,

/the thirteen

the thirteen Korean parties had declared that the interference of the
Temporary Commission diminished the chances of agreement between the
Great Powers and could not but aggravate the division between the north
and the south. That was precisely the aim pursued by the United States
of America, as was evident from the fact that, ever since the time of
the joint USSR-United States Commission, the United States Military
High Command had been preparing the establishment of a separate
Government in South Korea.

The United States Military Authorities had, since 1946, encouraged
the Korean reactionaries and had, in 1947, set up a central committee
to control the elections. The latter had, however, been delayed until
the decision of the General Assembly had resulted in placing the sham
plebiscite under the auspices of the United Nations.

Neither the opinions of political parties, nor the complaints which
had been made, were taken into consideration by the Temporary Commission
or the occupying authorities, as the report on Korean public opinion,
contained in a document of the Commission itself (A/575/Add.1), had shown.
That document had indicated that, of ten parties and organizations
extending from the right to the left, only two parties of the extreme
right had been in favour of separate elections in South Korea and had
stated that free elections were possible. The Commission had not taken
that verdict into account; he wondered whether its own observations
had enabled it to state that the views of those two parties of the
extreme right were justified. The documents of the Commission and
the reports of the observation groups did, however, show that police
and terrorist organizations had not hesitated to exert pressure on
the electors from the moment electoral registration had started. Thus
observation group No. 3 had reported the complaints of the inhabitants
of Seoul who were being forced to vote or have their ration cards
confiscated. That was only one of many examples. Moreover, terrorist
organizations were taking the people of Korea to the polling booths by
force.

The whole electoral campaign had been carried out in an atmosphere
of terror; Kim Kiuskik had told the Commission that the election had
been faked beforehand by the manner in which the campaign had been
conducted and by the fact that the police had chosen beforehand the
candidates to be elected. The electors had, therefore, only to
support mechanically the choice made by the police.

/The Commission

The Commission had been content to transmit those complaints to the United States Command which, in its turn, had declared that it had not sufficient personnel to carry out the necessary enquiries; that those complaints were in most cases imaginary or had been made by Communists, and that in those last cases it had not been necessary to undertake any enquiries. The whole affair had therefore been in the hands of the pro-Japanese element.

As the date of the elections drew near, in 1948, the situation had become more serious. On 9 May, according to a Reuter telegram, a police force of 60,000 men had invaded towns and villages to supervise the elections and some hundreds of thousands of volunteers had helped the police to carry out mass arrests. A few risings had been quickly suppressed. The electors themselves had stated that there had been no real secret ballot. Thus in a great many cases the voting papers had been numbered so as to permit of the voters being identified. Moreover, it was the case that the United States forces, police agents and youth organizations had dragged electors by force to the polling booths and had closely watched their movements. Finally, electoral corruption had taken place on a large scale.

It was not surprising then that a Chinese newspaper had said the elections in South Korea were undemocratic, since only one-third of a population of 21,000,000 had been given the right to vote. Moreover, the elections had taken place under the watchful eye of police forces numbering 60,000 and of a million volunteers. Kim Koo and Kim Kiusik had been opposed to the elections, in which only two groups of any importance had taken part, including that of Syngham Rhee. In those circumstances, even if South Korea had been able to hold free elections, it would only have been able to choose between the Syngham Rhee group and the pro-Japanese Kim Sung Soo group.

The particulars he had given were taken from the Commission's documents or were facts known to the Commission. The elections in South Korea had been manipulated and had taken place in an atmosphere of terror. The Government established as a result of those elections could not therefore be considered as representing South Korea, and still less the people of Korea as a whole.

Nevertheless, the Temporary Commission had not hesitated, in defiance of common sense and of the facts before it, suddenly to turn right-about face. It was not the freedom of the Korean people that had benefited by its activities, but the United States.

Those were the views of the Ukrainian SSR regarding the elections in South Korea and the activities of the Temporary Commission on Korea.

The Ukrainian SSR reserved the right to speak later on the various proposals submitted to the First Committee.   /Mr. ZEBROWSKI

Mr. ZEBROWSKI (Poland) recalled that at the second ordinary session he had raised the question whether the United States, in bringing the question of Korea before the United Nations, had really had in view the interests of the Korean people; shortly before the beginning of the second session, the representative of the United States had in fact declared at a press conference that the people of Korea had not been previously consulted. It was known to all that, until the end of the Second World War, very few Americans had taken any interest in Korea. The United States had "discovered" Korea when their troops had entered that country on 7 and 8 September 1945, well after the surrender of the Japanese forces.

What had been the situation in Korea at that date? A national administration and a national Government were already at work. The Koreans undoubtedly hailed the United States troops as friends, but the Americans had believed that they were being greeted as conquerors. It was true that the Japanese and the collaborators had hoped for something quite definite from the Americans: that they should save them from just punishment.

When the Americans arrived, people's committees had been set up in 145,000 villages, and on 6 September 600 delegates had taken part in a National Assembly at Seoul for the purpose of forming a central authority. General Hodge had announced from the start that independence could not be granted to Korea, and that in order to avoid what he called chaos he would temporarily retain in office the Japanese, including the Governor General. Collaborators and Japanese officials had been immediately reinstated, and power had been restored to the Japanese police. Thus, when the Koreans had acclaimed the United States troops when they landed, the Japanese police had opened fire on the crowd.

Moreover, the local government organizations set up after the surrender of the Japanese had been dissolved, freedom of party politics had been restricted, and the trade unions themselves no longer had the right to organize freely. All power was centralized around the American Military Command which ruled the Korean people through the Japanese.

In order to maintain that regime, the United States made its proposal at the second session of the General Assembly.

At that time, the Polish delegation had advocated the withdrawal of all foreign troops, and it had stressed the fact that it was in contradiction with the terms of the Charter to decide the fate of a people without consulting its representatives. The constitution of a Temporary Commission was a violation of the Potsdam and Moscow agreements, as well as of the Charter, according to which an organ other than the United Nations, namely the Council of Foreign Ministers, had to deal with and liquidate the consequences of the war.

/In reality,

In reality, in Korea as in Greece, American imperialism on the look-
out for new bases situated for preference near to the territories of the
USSR, had used an organ of the United Nations as a screen. In both those
countries, as in Germany, the idea was to build up a vast American empire
and to call to order those who were not attracted by the American way of
life.

Events had confirmed the Polish predictions regarding the fate of
the Koreans, the establishment of American rule and the role of the Temporary Commission.

Firstly, the Temporary Commission, upon arrival at Seoul, had found
that neither individual freedom nor freedom of expression had been in the
slightest degree guaranteed.   South Korea was nothing but a police State,
a military dictatorship.   Moreover, all parties, both of the Right and
of the Left, with the exception of two Right-wing parties, had been opposed
to separate elections being held in South Korea.   Consequently, on
19 February 1948, the Chairman of the Temporary Commission, Mr. Menon,
had stated in the Interim Committee that the formation of a separate
Government in South Korea would be contrary to the objectives of paragraph 5 of the General Assembly resolution; that was, contrary to the
national independence of Korea and to the withdrawal of the occupation
troops.   Mr. Menon had added that a mass of evidence had been produced
regarding restrictions on civil liberties, which General Hodge had attributed to the threat of a communist conspiracy, and that the Chief Justice
had had to admit the non-existence of habeas corpus in South Korea and had
even recognized that every Korean was at the mercy of the police.
Mr. Menon had for his part concluded that it might be detrimental to the
interest of Korea and inconsistent with the terms of the General Assembly
resolution to carry out in South Korea alone the programme outlined in
the resolution of November 1947 relating to Korea.

That point of view had also been shared by the representatives of
Canada, Australia, Egypt and Brazil, while Bolivia had made reservations
on the subject.   In any case, led by the United States delegation and
against the opinion of the Temporary Commission itself, the Interim Committee,
with eleven abstentions, had decided that the Temporary Commission should
hold elections in South Korea.   Moreover, that had been a decision taken
by an illegal body in response to doubts expressed by another illegal body
in violation of a decision of the General Assembly, which had not provided
that elections should take place in one part of Korea only.

That decision had opened a new chapter in American activities in
South Korea.   Although on 26 April 1948, at a meeting of political leaders
of the whole of Korea, agreement had been reached with a view to achieving

/the unity

제2부 유엔총회 회의록(1948)

the unity of the country, General Hodge had fixed the date of 9 May for separate elections in South Korea, in order to perpetuate the division of the Korean people. The Commission, which had at first been displeased, had finally been obliged to give way.

In general, if the task of the Commission had been to supply the United Nations with the basic information for the solution of the Korean question, it must be recognized that, despite the tributes paid to the members of the Commission and to the elaborate machinery they had set in motion, the Commission had failed miserably. That fact could not surprise those who, like the Polish representative, had long had doubts upon the subject and who had realized that the true task of the Temporary Commission had been to serve as a screen for the imperialistic activities of the Americans.

The members of the Commission had been better diplomats and officials than investigators. They had paid too much attention to what had been told them by the American Military Government, the Korean authorities and members of the privileged classes of Korean society. They had not understood that all constitutional and electoral rules were powerless when thwarted by petty politicians, vested interests, a ruthless police force and organized thugs. Moreover, the Temporary Commission had not gone far enough in its enquiries for its findings to serve as a basis upon which to pass judgment on the true freedom of the elections in South Korea.

Fortunately there was other evidence about South Korea besides the report of the Temporary Commission. Certain American correspondents had managed to overcome the obstacles placed in their way by the American Military Intelligence and from their evidence the conclusion could be drawn that in spite of the Cairo and Potsdam agreements, the American authorities in South Korea had never considered the Korean people as a friendly nation. The "conquerors" had been afraid of the people, and for that reason they had dissolved the People's Committees and had maintained the brutal Japanese-trained police force which had been guilty of treachery to the nation. The Americans had depended on reactionary forces and on those who had been tools of the Japanese, and they had opposed such measures as the abolition of child labour and agrarian reform. Yet there were vast estates of several thousand acres in South Korea, and an owner of five acres sometimes had five or six share-croppers who paid him, by way of rent, half the proceeds of their labour.

In general, the Koreans had been considered as contemptible creatures by the Americans, their new masters. Moreover, the mismanagement of the Americans, the lack of food and the wretched conditions had resulted in a revolt shortly before the opening of the second session. Workers, share-croppers and intellectuals had been imprisoned by the thousand and

/subjected to

subjected to the brutalities of the police in conditions similar to those
of the German concentration camps. Sentences of years of imprisonment
had been meted out by the American Military Courts on the slightest pretext, while Mr. Rhee's henchmen had organized units of vigilantes under
the benevolent eye of the officers of the American military administration.
A "political machine" had been formed by reactionary politicians and
bands of vigilantes: such had been the prelude to the "free" elections
in South Korea which had taken place some months later.

It was then that the United Nations Commission had arrived. It had
made enquiries of those who were responsible for the conditions, and needless to say, it had discovered that things were not going so badly. The
American Military Government had then proclaimed a certain number of
"freedoms", which were quite inoperative in that their implementation
had been placed in the hands of those who had been violating them for
so long on the slightest pretext. Moreover, even if the decrees of the
American Military Government had been prompted by the best intentions in
the world, it was too late to change the political atmosphere a few weeks
before the elctions. Beaten, tortured and terrorized, the Koreans had
finally "confessed" on the day of the elections, in the same way as they
had been forced to do by the tortures of the Japanese. Mr. Rhee and
other reactionaries had been elected. But had the Commission thought
fit to visit the places where the worst atrocities had been committed,
after the revolt had been put down? Furthermore, how had the Commission
understood its work in the case of the youth organization mentioned on
pages 13 and 42 of the first volume of the Report? While the Report merely
mentioned the fact that an organization known as "The National Youth Organization" was under the patronage of the American military authorities,
Mr. Mark Gayn, correspondent of the "Chicago Sun" and of "Newsweek", had
related that General Lee Bum Suk had told him that in Korea, as in Germany
in 1919, there were conflicting ideologies, national discord and an economic crisis, and that only the National Youth Organization was able to
remedy those evils. According to General Lee Bum Suk, therefore, the
United Youth school for leaders should be given full confidence. The
chief thing the students learned in that school, which was under the supervision of an American officer, Colonel Voss, was how to combat strikes;
they were also taught the history of the Hitler Youth. The Military
Governor had given $333,000 to General Suk's movement in six months.
It would be interesting, therefore, for the Rapporteur of the Commission
to know some of the specific details concerning the introduction of Hitler's
methods into Korea, under the auspices of the United States Government.

/With regard

With regard to the elections themselves, a reign of terror had been
prevailing at the very time the Temporary Commission had been carrying
out its investigations.   Koreans who had not registered for voting had
been openly threatened, and their ration cards for rice had been confiscated.
Those who had been interrogated by the Temporary Commission had been arrested
and mishandled.   On the election day, some 150 persons had been killed by
the police.

I cument A/AC.19/SC 414 of 23 April 1948 contained a letter from the
Chairman of the Korean Public Opinion Association to the Temporary Commission concerning threats which had been uttered against that association
as a result of an investigation it had made with regard to registration on
the electoral lists in certain areas on 12 April 1948.   On 16 April 1948
the Department of Public Information had, however, stated that the results
of the investigation were contrary to public order.   According to an
investigation made on 15 April 1948 by the same Korean Public Opinion Association, on the basis of a questionnaire submitted to 1,262 persons, it
appeared that 91 per cent of the registrations had been made by force,
while 26 per cent of the persons interrogated had not registered at all.
It would seem, therefore, that if the Temporary Commission considered that
the elections had been "reasonably" free and had taken place in "general"
conformity with the electoral laws and regulations, the words "reasonable"
and "general" did not have the same meaning for the Temporary Commission
as for most people.

The Polish delegation considered that the elections in South Korea
had been a political fraud, as a result of which Mr. Singman Rhee, a
puppet of Washington, had become the "President" of South Korea.   It was
true that in October 1945 General Hodge had introduced Mr. Rhee as a great
man;   but in November 1947 Mark Gayn had pointed out in the American paper,
"P.M.", that Rhee had introduced his henchmen into the Korean police force
and, thanks to his organization of police and Military Government officials,
had won forty seats in elections which were a travesty of democratic methods.
Gayn had added that noted collaborators had been elected and that Rhee had
expressed his gratitude by stating his hope that the American Army would
remain in Korea for strategic purposes.

/According to

125

According to the "New York Times of 1 June 1948, Mr. Rhee had
expressed the hope that the American forces would remain until the Korean
Government had organized its own forces. It was a fact that the Greek
Government also wanted the American army to remain in Greece. It was
always the same procedure and the same objectives. Had not Mr. Rhee's
Minister of Home Affairs, Yeon Tchi Yang, stated, according to the "Korean
Independence" of 8 September 1948, that the Americans should remain in
Korea in order to train and arm a force which would be capable of occupying
the whole of North Korea in two weeks? On 18 February 1948, the "American
Journal" had stated that a Rightist Government in Korea would grant military
and naval bases to the United States; and finally, Mr. R.T. Oliver had said
in the paper "Plain Talk" of 19 May 1947 that if the United States possessed
permanent bases in Korea, the latter would be a loaded pistol pointed at
Russia's doorway to the Pacific, and that, apart from its military
significance, Korea was a rich economic prize.

In Greece as in China, the imperialists were always acquiring new
territories and subjecting more Governments to their will, under the pretext
of "containing" Communism. That was the method Hitler had used, and the
language employed was no different. The Chairman of the Temporary Commission
had told the Interim Committee that a high American authority had described
the Korean people as a "decadent nation" which had not the slightest
conception of political life. It was not surprising, therefore, that the
United Nations had hastened to dissolve the first body elected by the Korean
people and to form a reactionary control directed by the police and the so-
called legislative assembly. It was sufficient to refer to the first volume
of part I of the report of the Temporary Commission, where pages 9 and 10
in particular showed that the United States had recognized that Mr. Rhee,
who was of the extreme Right, had not been able to provide the basis for a
stable and representative political coalition. That had been written, it
was true, before General Hodge had changed his mind and had chosen Mr. Rhee,
who had been nominated President.

The Charter could not allow a nation that had been liberated from
Japanese occupation to achieve nothing but a change of masters. There
were still foreign troops in Korea, and the 38th parallel divided into
two a country which, both ethnically and economically, constituted an
indivisible whole.

From the day of liberation the Korean people had been working for the
establishment of an independent democratic State. Elections had been held
in North and South Korea in August 1945, which had been an expression of
the free will of the electors and of the desire of the whole Korean nation
for liberty and independence. It was to be noted that in South Korea the

elections had had to be held in secret because of the attitude of the
American occupation authorities. The result had been the election of a
national assembly that was the truly representative and supreme legislative
body in all Korea. The Korean Government had recently been recognized by
Poland, with which it maintained diplomatic relations; on 10 September
1948, that Government, together with the Grand National Assembly, had
appealed to the Governments of the United States and the Union of Soviet
Socialist Republics for foreign troops to be withdrawn and for the people
of Korea to be allowed to lead a free and independent existence. The Soviet
Union was actually withdrawing its troops from North Korea at the present
time.

The Polish delegation felt bound to stress the following facts:
(1) By rejecting the USSR proposal for the simultaneous withdrawal of USSR
and American troops from Korea, the General Assembly had delayed the
achievement of Korean independence. (2) The Temporary Commission had
ultimately become the tool of American politics against the freedom and
independence of the Korean people, as also against the USSR, China and
other Far Eastern countries. (3) In pursuing that policy, the Temporary
Commission had disregarded its terms of reference in order to achieve the
results sought by the State Department. (4) The elections in South Korea
had been held under a reign of terror and virtual martial law; they had
been boycotted by all but extreme and unrepresentative Right-wing parties.
(5) The Government of South Korea was not only reactionary; it had no
support from the people, and it was only maintained in office by the
American army. The leading posts were held by one-time collaborators,
and the answer of Rhee's regime to the discontent of the Korean people
had been to institute a reign of terror. The newspaper "Le Monde" of that
very day stated that vast police operations had taken place in South Korea
and that hundreds of suspects had been arrested in Seoul. (6) The full and
entire responsibility for that situation rested with the Military Government
of the United States in Seoul. The American authorities had declared that
until the withdrawal of the American army the Seoul police and constabulary
would be responsible to the American Military Government. (7) The report
of the Temporary Commission, which revealed, especially in its first part,
the anti-democratic and oppressive character of the American-sponsored
regime in Seoul, was in striking contradiction with the activities of the
Commission, as well as with its conclusions. (8) The only Korean authority
that had been elected and supported by the overwhelming majority of the
nation was the Government of the Korean People's Democratic Republic, which
should be recognized by all Members of the United Nations. (9) The true
reason for the American occupation of South Korea was the desire of the

/United States

United States to secure strategic and economic positions in that country.
The question of Korea had been brought before the United Nations the previous
year because the United States had been unwilling to withdraw its forces
from Korea; at the present day, the only solution still was to leave Korea
to the Koreans and to accept the USSR proposal and the appeal of the
Grand National Assembly of Korea to withdraw all foreign troops from that
country immediately.

The only desire of the Korean people was to live in independence and
peace. That country had, however, been the victim of the United States
power politics. The First Committee and the United Nations should therefore
help the Koreans to gain that independence that had been denied them
successively by the Japanese and the Americans.

Mr. WALKER (United Kingdom) said that the resolution submitted
by the delegations of Australia, China and the United States of America
implied the continuation of the policy adopted by the General Assembly at
its second ordinary session. Although he would have preferred to support
a resolution in favour of a united Korea, the following facts had to be
faced: (1) Regrettable as it might be, Korea was actually divided. (2) The
present regime in South Korea was beyond all doubt the only one based on
free elections. That was the real basis of the joint draft resolution, as
the preamble indicated and as the whole of the resolution implied.

The USSR representative and his two partners had above all tried to
deny the fact that the regime in South Korea was the only one which had
emerged from free and democratic elections. The USSR and the Ukrainian SSR
representatives had claimed that the elections in South Korea had been held
under the protection of American bayonets, but the Temporary Commission,
whose evidence was first-hand, had from its observations formed a different
opinion. How then could the many allegations made by the last two speakers,
which were based on second-hand evidence, be accepted? On the other hand,
those speakers had referred to elections which had been held secretly in
South Korea. Those two assertions were contradictory. If there was a police
regime in South Korea how could anyone believe that secret elections could
be held, in which 70 per cent of the population had taken part, without the
police having noticed anything? The USSR representative would have to choose
between those two assertions. Moreover, those alleged secret elections in
South Korea were a fraud. The United Kingdom delegation possessed alleged
ballot papers from Communist partisans in South Korea which had been sent to
North Korea to be counted. Among those ballot papers there were a number of
palpable and impudent forgeries. There were in fact a whole series of names

/of alleged

of alleged electors all in the same handwriting and with finger prints
which it was absolutely impossible to identity. In addition, the names
of prominent anti-Communists were included, and in particular that of the
present Prime Minister of the Republic of Korea. One of the names was that
of a historical novel. Others were the names of months, of deceased people,
and of one of the members of the Korean deputation to the First Committee.
It would be wiser therefore if the USSR delegation did not dwell on the
subject of the alleged "election".

The United Kingdom delegation would support the joint draft resolution
submitted by the delegations of Australia, China and the United States of
America because, as the Philippines representative had stated, it considered
that the Korean question could only be settled in one way -- by the
unification of the country. Anything designed to achieve that objective
would therefore receive the approval of the United Kingdom delegation,
which considered that the proposals contained in the joint draft resolution
were a necessary first step.

The United Kingdom Government felt that there were three aspects of
the Korean problem: (1) The local problem. The sympathies of the United
Kingdom were with the population of Korea which was an indivisible whole
and whose interests were covered by the joint draft resolution. (2) Far
Eastern affairs, in which the United Kingdom took the greatest interest
and on which the solution of the Korean question must necessarily, for
geographical reasons, have important repercussions. (3) The United Nations.
The Commission, if set up, would have to lend its good offices to bring
about the unification of Korea. The new commission would be authorized to
travel throughout Korea and paragraph 7, which was very important, invited
interested States Members to lend all help and aid to the new commission.

It was possible to speak, as the representative of the Ukrainian Soviet
Socialist Republic had done, of obedient majorities and mechanical voting,
but the fact was that if a majority of the General Assembly adopted the
resolution it would represent the views of the United Nations. Accordingly,
any country which decided to defy the clearly expressed will of the United
Nations would assume a grave responsibility. The USSR representative should
bear in mind the closing words of the Polish representative, who had asked
all members of the First Committee to disregard any ideas of bases and
strategic positions. The United Kingdom delegation expressed the hope
that the Union of Soviet Socialist Republics would hesitate before it
put imperialist and expansionist interests against the clear views of
the United Nations.

The meeting rose at 10.57 p.m.

(6) 제3차 유엔총회 제1위원회 제234차 회의 요약

해제문서 14 : A/C.1/SR 234 (Third Session, First Committee, Summary Record of the Two Hundred and Thirty Fourth Meeting)

문서명	Third Session, First Committee, Summary Record of the Two Hundred and Thirty Fourth Meeting		
	제3차 유엔총회 제1위원회 제234차 회의 요약 기록		
발신		생성일시	1948년 12월 8일 오전 10시 30분
		발신일시	
수신		수신일시	
		문서번호	A/C.1/SR 234
문서형태	회의록(요약)	문서분량	14쪽
주제명	한국문제 관련 소련 대표의 의견 제시 및 단독 결의안(A/C.1/427) 발의 1. 한국 독립문제 관련 소련 대표의 의견 2. 유엔한국임시위원단에 관한 결의안		
주요내용	1948년 12월 8일 오전 10시 30분에 프랑스 파리에서 개최된 제3차 유엔총회 제1위원회 제234차 회의록. 상세한 내용은 본문 참조.		
검색어	유엔한국임시위원단, 제1위원회, 말리크(Yakov Aleksandrovich Malik, 소련 대표)		

1948년 12월 8일 오전 10시 30분 프랑스 파리에서 개최된 제3차 유엔총회 제1위원회 제234차 회의록으로 소련대표가 단독으로 발언한 내용임.

소련대표는 앞서 제233차 회의에서 우크라이나 대표와 폴란드 대표가 발언한 내용과 유사한 주장을 펼쳤으며, 앞선 회의에서 발언한 각국 대표의 발언내용에 대해 조목조목 반론을 제기함. 특히 한국대표의 유엔총회 발언내용을 언급하는 가운데 한국대표의 발언이 한국 국민의 의사를 대표하는 것이라고 볼 수 없으며 미국의 견해를 대변한 것에 불과하다고 폄하함.

소련 대표는 호주, 미국, 중국이 공동으로 발의한 수정결의안에 대한 대안으로 단독 결의안(A/C.1/427)을 발의하였으며, 그 가운데서 유엔한국임시위원단은 남한에서 실시된 총선거가 공권력의 강제에 의해 실시되는 것을 묵인함으로써 반동적인 정권이 수립되도록 하였기 때문에 유엔한국임시위원단을 해산해야 한다고 주장함.

그리고 남한의 선거운동 기간 동안 수천 명의 정치범이 투옥되고 고문이나 죽임을 당한 사실을 지적하면서 남한에는 자유나 민주주의가 존재하지 않는다고 주장함. 또한 남한 정부의 특징인 테러리즘이나 억압적 통치의 일익을 담당하고 있는, 과거 일본에 의해 훈련된 경찰을 유엔은 인정할 수 없다고 주장하며, 위원단이 남한 정부를 인정한다면 이는 곧 테러리즘에 합법성을 부여하는 것이라고 말함.

소련대표는 단독결의안이 남한정부뿐만 아니라 미국에 의해 점령된 지역을 유지하기 위해서도 위원단의 승인을 얻고자 한다고 하면서, 미국은 남한 점령을 연장하는 것이 분명한 목표이기 때문에 말로는 되도록 빨리 남한에서 군대를 철수하자고 하면서도 한국의 상황을 복잡하게 만들어 남한을 반식민지화하려는 것이라고 주장함.

또한 미국은 한국에서 임무를 수행할 새 위원회를 설립하는 제안을 지지할 것이 분명하다고 말하고 그 이유는 이들이 한국에서 미국의 정책을 지지하기 위해 마련되고 선출된 멤버라고 생각하고 있기 때문이라고 함. 제안된 위원회는 미국의 비민주적인 행동을 은폐하는 수단이 될 것이며, 미군정 권력의 비호를 받는 반동적인 꼭두각시 정부에 대해 도덕적 지지를 제공하게 될 것이라고 주장함. 미국은 이러한 연막을 필요로 하며 그 이유는 20세기에 민족자결(self determination)의 권리는 국제적으로 승인된 원칙이며, 이 점이 한국에서의 식민정책을 정당화하기 어렵게 만들기 때문이라고 함. 이것이 바로 그리스, 인도네시아, 일본, 독일에 적용한 방법이라고 주장함.

오후 1시에 정회함.

United Nations   Nations Unies   UNRESTRICTED

GENERAL   ASSEMBLEE   A/C.1/SR 234
ASSEMBLY   GENERALE   9 December 1948

                                              ORIGINAL: ENGLISH

Dual distribution

Third Session

FIRST COMMITTEE

SUMMARY RECORD OF THE TWO HUNDRED AND THIRTY-FOURTH MEETING

Held at the Palais de Chaillot, Paris,
on Wednesday, 8 December 1948, at 10.30 a.m.

CONTENTS:

The problem of the independence of Korea: Reports of the
United Nations Temporary Commission on Korea and of the
Interim Committee of the General Assembly (A/575 and A/583)
Continuation of the Discussion.

Chairman: Mr. H. PAAK   Belgium
Rapporteur: Mr. S. SARPER   Turkey

Mr. MALIK (USSR) said that his delegation had to draw attention to the blatant injustice done by the First Committee in refusing to admit representatives of the Democratic Peoples Republic of Korea whose Government had been elected by the people in Southern as well as Northern Korea. This refusal had been made under the pressure of the United States which seemed to fear that the true voice of the people might be heard telling the truth about the military administration in Southern Korea. However, the truth would be discovered by public opinion.

The Korean Question had been on the United Nations agenda, for over a year, having originally been brought up by the United States. While the question now appeared in the form of reports from the Temporary Commission on Korea and from the Interim Committee, it continued to be a fact that the question came before the Assembly illegally. However, experience had shown that it was the policy of the United States to place items on their agenda illegally and in defiance of wartime agreements. Other examples of this policy were United States action in connextion with Greece and Berlin. The United States was making use of the United Nations to oppress the people of Korea and counted upon the support of the majority to screen its expansionist policy in Southern Korea. Rather than make an immediate withdrawal from the South as the Soviet Union was in the process of doing from the North, the United States brought the question before the United Nations in order to postpone a solution and delay the unification of Korea. The United States had not only promoted the formation of the Temporary Commission which was established in violation of international agreements and lacked any legal or constitutional basis. The United States also managed to get the question before the Interim Committee. These manoeuvres were made to conceal the regime of police terror which had been inaugurated by the United States. In these circumstances, the main function of the Temporary Commission was to camouflage the activities of the American military command. Falsified elections were held and a Government of puppets and former collaborationists was established in Southern Korea with the connivance of the Commission.

At the previous Assembly and again at the present session, the USSR delegation had maintained in the debate upon the agenda that the question ought not to be discussed in the Assembly since it was a part of the post-war settlement and should be dealt with by the responsible Allied Governments. Mr. Malik wished to repeat to the First Committee this view that the question was outside the competence of the United Nations. However, as the majority had forced the question into the Assembly, the USSR delegation would present their views and intended to submit concrete proposals.

An examination of the documents of the Temporary Commission revealed that it had discovered and reported upon the fact that the United States military authorities had converted Southern Korea into a police State. Despite their attempt to ornament the truth, the Commission had been unable to conceal the facts in its records which showed that Southern Korea was a police preserve where the forces of reaction used Fascist Japanese methods for the suppression of democratic movements and did so with the connivance of the military authorities. Thus the Commission confirmed the piecemeal reports in the press which showed that when the United States Army arrived in August, 1945, their Commander established an occupation regime although Southern Korea was territory liberated from enemy occupation. After their deliverance from colonial slavery, the Koreans set up their own democratic organs but these were destroyed by the United States who reimposed the Japanese kind of military Government and put quislings and collaborationists in power.

In order to justify their policy, circulation was given to the thesis that the Koreans were unable to govern themselves and were not ready for a democratic system. The representative of the Ukraine had already dealt with the insulting remarks of General Hodge. The Koreans had struggled for democracy for almost a half century under the Japanese and then "friends", such as this General with his racial theories, tried to keep them enslaved. This anti-democratic theory was accepted by the Temporary Commission as could be seen in Chapter VI of Volume I of the First Part of their Report. This was an attempt to justify the United States regime. However, the slanderous character of the theory was evidenced by the development of democracy in northern Korea where there were no impediments presented.

From the very beginning, the USSR military command had assisted in the liquidation of the colonial type of administration and in preparations for self-government. Important progressive legislation such as that concerning the equality of women had been achieved with the aid of the USSR authorities. The composition of all organs from purely local ones up to the National Committee were constituted democratically. By an agrarian reform, thousands of families had received land from the great estates. Labour had been given the eight hour day. By means of educational reforms, illiteracy was being stamped out. In these circumstances, leaders had come forward capable of running the administration and promoting far-reaching endeavours of a social and cultural nature.

These events served to refute the Hodge theory and showed that the Korean people were capable of the political organization required for self-government.   Experience in Northern Korea showed that there was no problem surrounding the broad participation of various parties in the Government.   This, too, could have been achieved in Southern Korea. The system being followed in the North could have been the basis for a unified and independent Korea.   The United States objected to this however for its military and capitalistic imperialistic circles choose to ignore the will of the Korean people.   The United States was trying to make a colony and strategic base out of Southern Korea.

The main tool of the United States policy was their police machine which was an enlargement of the old Japanese machine.   The Report of the Temporary Commission showed that the police forces had been quadrupled and that over half of the responsible posts were held by former collaborationists.   The full details could be found in the record of the 14th meeting of Sub-committee 2 at which evidence was given by the Director of the National Police.   This could be found in Annex 10 in Volume III of the First Part of the Report.   At that same meeting, it was observed by the Australian representative that in Southern Korea, the police were still using Japanese methods and possessed unlimited power.   There was no necessity to have warrants for arrest and the idea of introducing habeas corpus had been rejected by the United States authorities.   The Director of Police had testified that there was nothing to prevent arrest without a warrant and this was confirmed by the Chief Justice of the Supreme Court.   The orders issued in March 1948 by the United States military command, did not appreciably modify the police system because of the many reservations and qualifications contained in the orders.

The first part of the Commission's Report referred to the huge terroristic organization of reactionary Fascist youth although it tried to camouflage its nature.   Nevertheless the Report in paragraph 25 of Chapter VI of Volume I of the First Part shows the connexion of this organization with political parties and its intolerance towards political opponents.   The organization which was the off-shoot of Japanese reaction terrorized popular democratic elements and developed the practice of beating up its opponents as was clear from the seventh meeting of Sub-committee 2, the record of which could be found in Volme III of the First Part of the Report.   The Director of the Police had admitted that this Organization was financed by the United States military authorities.   Its quasi-governmental nature made it a source of anxiety to the people of Southern Korea.

This was indicative of the dark forces which were being used by
the United States.   In the record of this same meeting of Sub-committee
2 it could be seen how people with known democratic views were detained
or limited as to their freedom.   It was shown by the Commission in
the records of interviews with Koreans how democratic movements had been
suppressed.   Some men were arrested when entering the Commission's
building and others, because of fear for their lives, did not wish
their names or the organizations they represented to be published
in the records.   The South Korean jails were full and the records
showed that some 30,000 democratic leaders had been incarcerated.
It could be read in the Report that political leaders who had been
imprisoned by the Japanese because of their struggle for freedom had
never been released by the United States authorities because the
collaborationists did not wish to let them out.   According to the
data presented by the Commission, thousand had been arrested in
connexion with strikes.   Only during August 1948 11,139 were arrested,
453 were subjected to terroristic methods while others were fired from
their jobs.   In February 1948, over 8,000 were thrown into prison for
this reason and the bashful attempt of the Commission to secure action
for their release by the United States authorities had had scandalous
results.   The military commanders had undertaken to grant certain
amnesties by the 1st of April.   What happened on that date was that,
among the 3,000 odd who were released, there were included 1,253 political
prisoners who had served their sentences.   The details could be read
in Chapter V of Volume I of the First Part of the Report.   It was a
barefaced falsification to include these numbers in what was termed
an amnesty.   The fact was that the amnesty failed to release true
political prisoners but the Commission took no notice of this move to
enlarge the figure of the numbers pardoned.   The Commission did recognize
the fact that the reactionary Hankook Party and the National Association for
the Rapid Realization of Korean Independence were in control in Southern
Korea.   It could be noted that the Hankook Party was very small but at the
same time powerful because many wealthy landowners and merchants were
members.   This Party and the United States administration gave each
other mutual support.   The Head of the Party was a well-known
collaborationist and the honorary President was a former Japanese
puppet.   The fact that the Director of Police had connexions with these
two parties went a long way towards explaining the strangle hold which
they have upon Southern Korea.   The United States Administration was
based upon the support of organizations of this type and any attempts
to reform the political or governmental machinery was opposed by the
military commander

In November 1946 a puppet Interim Legislative Assembly was set up
in conditions of oppression as was noted in the Commission's documents.
Even that Assembly attempted to pass legislation with regard to
collaborationists but the military administration refused to confirm such
acts.   The military administration also refused to withhold the
franchise from the collaborationists despite the views of the Commission.
Thus the country was being controlled and democratic forces suppressed
through the medium of collaborationists as was being done by the
United States in Greece, Germany, and Japan.

The entire record was one of horror.   The facts given in the
Commissions documents could be used as a basis for judging conditions.
Nevertheless the Commission found it possible to give the approval of
the United Nations to the conditions established for election.   Such
conduct could only undermine the prestige of the United Nations.   The
approval of the United Nations was given by a vote which found only four
out of the nine members of the Commission favouring the decision but
this minority became a majority because of abstentions.   With regard
to the actual conditions, the representative of Australia had observed
in Sub-Committee 2 that the elections would be under the control of a
single party, that the opposition would have no chance, and that the
party concerned was full of collaborationist reactionaries.   It was
noted that the pursuit of the United States policy would lead to the
establishment of an extreme rightist administration.   This explained why
the United States had wrecked the work of the USSR-United States Joint
Commission which was to have aided the establishment of a unified and
democratic government.   It also showed why the United States was insisting
upon placing the question before the United Nations.   The Temporary
Commission was needed to camouflage the reactionary policies of the
United States Administration and to conduct "free and impartial" elections
which would establish a reactionary Government.   At a congress of
democratic parties held in April 1948, all party leaders indicated that
they were opposed to separate elections in Southern Korea.   The
Temporary Commission recognized, as was shown in Appendix I to Annex VI
in Volume III of the First Part of the Report, that all except the
Rightist Parties were opposed to holding elections in the circumstances
having regard to the restriction on civil liberties which indicated that
free elections could not be insured and that the results would not be
representative.   Even leaders well to right of center agreed that only
the extreme Right could profit from such elections.   The Commission had
been informed of the unfortunate consequences which would follow the
elections.   Indeed, the representatives for certain consitituencies
had already been assigned and the Youth Organizations had prepared for

terroristic activity.   There was general protest throughout South Korea
on the question of elections.

Faced with this situation, the Temporary Commission turned to
the Interim Committee for advice.   The reply, given under United States
pressure, was that elections should be observed in Southern Korea only.
The Interim Committee thus arrogated to itself the right to decide
a question which was not within the competence of the Assembly.   Thus,
the Interim Committee and the Temporary Commission promoted elections
in conditions of police terrorism.   This would only undermine the
authority of the United Nations and show that it was becoming the tool
of the expansionist aims of one Great Power.

It was clear that the Interim Committee had no right to give advice
in this sense quite apart from the illegality of its own constitution.
The representative of Canada on the Commission had been of the opinion
that the recommendation was neither proper nor constitutional.   The
representative of Australia had foreseen that the elections would be
boycotted by all but the extreme Right and this in fact had occurred.
The Temporary Commission decided to observe the elections by a vote of
four in favour, two against, two abstaining, and one not participating
out of a total of nine members.   Three of those favouring the procedure
were dependents of the United States.   The fourth was the representative
of India, who at the same time stated that one could hardly fail to share
the doubts of the representative of Canada as to the legal propriety of
the action of the Interim Committee.   He had also observed that when
the question had been laid before the Interim Committee, a negative reply
had been expected.   He further had expressed doubts that the move could
lead to the unification or independence of Korea or that free elections
could be insured.   This statement was made in March 1948 on the eve of
the election.

The action of the Commission in holding elections in the existing
conditions could not be justified.   The United States recognized the
fact that protests on the part of the people could lead to the failure of
the elections and accordingly took measures to ensure the participation of
voters.   General Hodge issued an appropriate order which could be
found in paragraph 79 of Chapter III of Volume 1 of the First Part of
the Report.   This stated "Anyone abstaining from voting forfeits his
right to complain of actions or policies of a Government resulting from
an election in which he did not participate".   In the last few days before
the election, thousands were arrested and many more injured and killed for
their opposition.   Although the United States representative in the

/Interim

Interim Committee had said that freedom of the election would be ensured,
the measures to this end turned out to be mass arrests and terrorism.
Quite apart from the pressure exerted by the police, and the youth
organizations, there was throughout the election period the menace of
United States Army, Navy, and Air Forces.   Indeed, the elections in
Southern Korea were reminiscent of the Italian elections with their
intimidating demonstrations of military might.   Korean newspapers
reported incidents of threats of death against those who would not vote.

The Commission recognized that electoral laws and its own
recommendations had been violated.   There was pressure from the youth
organizations at the polling places and balloting was not always secret.
Observation by the Commission was restricted by the American Commander.
The Commission was able to visit only 2% of the precincts.   It therefore
could not be said that the elections really had been observed.   On the
Election Board were sitting Japanese collaborators who had been
nominated by the United States Administration but there were no
democratic representatives.   The forces of reaction were in control of
the elections, even in the local and provincial boards.

James Rowe, the United Press correspondent, had written reports
upon the intimidation caused by the armed constabulary and display of
military force.   On a visit to one precinct, the Principal Secretary
of the Commission had seen one voter being beaten.   In another dispatch,
James Rowe had dealt in detail with the circumstances in Seoul, recounting
how the streets had been barricaded and hooligans with blackjacks
were at the polls.   The police had been armed by the United States
Administration.   On the polling day, an atmosphere of oppression
prevailed.   It should be added that Rowe was by no means inclined to
the left politically.

/There was

There was ample evidence to support the assertion of the all-Korean Congress of Political and Social Organizations that the election in the southern zone had been conducted under conditions of police terror, and that the statistics had been falsified. As proof of the latter, Mr. Malik recalled that the Central Board of Electors on 11 May declared that 72 per cent of the registered voters took part in the election of the preceding day and that in the island of Kyosai To, off Korea, 70 per cent of the voters took part. However, it became clear subsequently that there had been no vote at all in two of three precincts into which the island was divided and the United States authorities had been obliged to make fresh arrangements for a new election in June. This fact cast some light upon all the figures supplied. The percentage given for all Korea had been falsified. Nevertheless, the Commission took these figures for whole cloth and included them blithely in its Report. In order to ensure the election of their principal puppets the United States authorities decided that if only one candidate were running in a certain precinct he would be elected without a ballot, since there was no opposing candidate. All the preceding facts showed that the elections in southern Korea had been conducted in defiance of the will of the Korean people and under conditions of police terror and repression.

Mr. Malik said that there was no lack of testimony by impartial observers to prove that the election had not been free. He cited the statement of Roger Baldwin, the leader of the American Civil Liberties Union, who was reported by the United Press on 28 June as saying that the military occupation authorities had set up a police State, led by a clique of ex-Japanese collaborators who was suppressing all progressive movements in Southern Korea.

Even the majority of the members of the Temporary Commission had been forced to realize that their work served only to place new obstacles in the way of Korean independence. Looking back on what had been done, it was clear that the Commission had helped the United States Government to achieve its aim of obtaining control of southern Korean. so that it could become a springboard for military aggression in Asia and a field for exploitation by American monopolies. But the conscience of the General Assembly could not permit an organ of the United Nations to serve the imperialist interests of a great Power in such a way and, therefore, it must refuse to recognize the validity of the election in the southern zone. The Commission had been guilty of a series of unconstitutional acts, not least of which was its decision to permit the election, which should not have been taken on the basis of a simple

/majority vote

majority vote in which only 4 out of the 9 members of the Commission
supported the proposal. In sanctioning the election the Commission
had contravened the Charter and had violated the Assembly's resolution
which provided for a free election covering the whole of Korea. The
Commission had been used as a smokescreen to conceal the illegal action
of the military authorities in establishing an anti-democratic regime,
in violation of the rights of the Korean people and in contradiction
with one of the basic principles of the Charter.

Mr. Malik submitted a draft resolution (A/C.1/427) to the effect
that that the Assembly recognized that the Temporary Commission had
permitted an election to be held under conditions of police terror and
oppression which had resulted in the establishment of a reactionary
regime and therefore decided that the Temporary Commission should be
dissolved.

Many of the preceding speakers had made grandiloquent statements
of their desire to establish freedom and democracy in Korea but it was
apparent that none of them had taken the trouble to examine the documents
of the Temporary Commission. Had they done so they would have realized
that there was no freedom or democracy in southern Korea, that the will
of the people was being suppressed, that ex-Japanese collaborators were
still in power and that supporters of democracy were being presented and
driven underground or were imprisoned. The failure of the preceding
speakers to take account of these facts could only be interpreted as a
conspiracy of silence aimed at concealing the facts from world opinion.
Who, after studying the documents of the Temporary Commission, could
believe the United States representative's assertion that his Government
"hated terror and oppression"? One had only to look at the statistics
which showed that scores of thousands of political prisoners were
incarcerated in the gaols of southern Korea. Many had been arrested
and even tortured and killed during the electoral campaign. Mr. Malik
drew attention to document A/AC.19/W.22/ADD.5 in which it was reported
that the head of the Farmers' Union had been tortured and had almost
died during an interrogation.

The United States representative had spoken with approval of the
police of southern Korea. But it was that very Japanese trained police
force which was responsible for the terrorism and oppression which
characterized the southern regime, and made it so unacceptable to the
United Nations. If the Committee were to recognize the southern Government
it would be putting the stamp of legality on that terrorism. It could
not take such a step, for the southern regime was guilty of all the
oppression which Mr. Dulles had so wrongly ascribed to the Communist States.

/Mr. Malik

Mr. Malik said that the stories of Communist persecution, which were repeated in the Press of the United States and other countries were fairy tales designed to camouflage and justify United States imperialism in Korea, Greece and elsewhere.

The USSR representative considered that the joint draft resolution was designed to obtain the Committee's sanction not only for the regime in southern Korea but also for a continued occupation of the zone by the United States. The aim of the latter was perfectly clear. Its sole purpose was to prolong the occupation. That could be seen from the vagueness of the references to troop withdrawal both in the original resolution of 14 November and in the present joint draft resolution. The latter said that troops should be withdrawn at the earliest practicable date. The United States was endeavouring to confuse the situation in Korea and had used the Temporary Commission to conceal the fact that southern Korea was being made into a quasi-colony. Only recently a financial agreement had been entered into with the southern Government, the terms of which had been so outrageous that they had even roused the indignation of some of the representatives in the puppet National Assembly who had pointed out that it placed the southern Koreans in the position of tenants of the United States. The agreement had been accepted only after the President, Mr. Sygman Rhee had gone to the rostrum in person to point out that its ratification was essential if southern Korea was to obtain United States support at the third session of the General Assembly. The agreement was therefore nothing less than a cynical bargain. The United States was to support the reactionary government in return for being given control over southern Korea for an unlimited time. In fact, the agreement was confirmed by a minority vote of only 78 out of the 198 members of the National Assembly. Now, after having concluded a slave agreement with the Koreans, the United States was making hypocritical statements about respect for the principles of the Charter and was asking the General Assembly to place the stamp of legality on its actions.

It was obvious that the United States was supporting the proposal to establish a new Commission to carry on the work in Korea because it felt sure that the members who would be elected would be quite prepared to support United States policy in Korea. The proposed Commission would be a tool of the United States to cover up its anti-democratic activites in southern Korea and to give the moral support of world public opinion to the reactionary puppet government whose authority, so far, rested solely on the support of United States military occupation forces. The United States

/found it

found it necessary to provide itself with such a smoke screen, because
in the 20th century the right of peoples to self-determination had
become a universally accepted principle, and it was increasingly
difficult to justify a colonial policy in Korea. That was precisely
the method which had been adopted in the cases of Greece, Indonesia,
Japan and Germany.

The Philippine representative on the Commission had said that the
election in the southern zone was conducted in conformity with the
standards generally accepted throughout the world. But if that was so,
then the delegation of the USSR could not accept such standards. The
Philippine representative had also said that the Commission had taken
notice of the complaints of the Korean population. It was true that
the Commission had received such complaint but could anyone say that
it had acted democratically in transmitting them to the United States
military authorities who were the very people complained against?
There could be no doubt that hundreds and thousands of the people who
had submitted complaint were now incarcerated in gaols and concentration
camps because of their action.

A number of assertions had been made to the effect that southern
Korea contained two-thirds of the population of the entire country and
an effort had been made to prove on the basis of that assertion that
the southern Government was representative of the majority of the
Korean people. In fact, the assertion was incorrect for it had been
recognized at the joint meeting of the United States and Union of Soviet
Socialist Republics occupation authorities in 1946 that the population
of the southern zone amounted to only three-fifths of the total.

Mr. Malik turned to the statement of the representative of the
southern Korean Government. The latter had claimed to speak on behalf
of the people of Korea but any unbiassed person would have realized
that he was really speaking on behalf of the United States. However,
on one point in his statement he had been correct, namely, the
assertion that there were few Koreans who placed the interests of a
foreign country above their own. It was true that patriotism was a
characteristic of the overwhelming majority of Korean people, as it was
of every other people. That was why the United States had felt
obliged to seek the General Assembly's endorsement of its continued
occupation of southern Korea and of the puppet government which it had
established there. That was also why the southern Government was so
anxious to assure itself of continued foreign support. It feared
the withdrawal of United States occupation forces which were the basis
of its authority.

/The real

The real voice of the Korean people had been heard in the declaration of the all-Korean conference when representatives of 56 political parties had adopted the proclamation calling for the immediate withdrawal of foreign troops. The USSR Government had complied with that request and by 1 January 194, all USSR troops would have left Korean soil. The United States on the other hand, was asking the General Assembly to endorse the continuation of its occupation. That, Mr. Malik believed, was the sole object of the present debate. He considered that the United States delegation had been very clever in bringing Korean representatives to support its request. However, the Korean spokesman had exceeded all normal bounds, in asking the General Assembly to recognise his regime as the legal Government of all Korea. The people of Korea would never accept the southern Government for they had already elected their own representatives in the Government of the Peoples' Democratic Republic.

The Chinese representative had gone to great lengths in an attempt to prove that the results of the election carried out by the United States authorities truly represented the desires of the Korean people. He had shown how the Temporary Commission had obtained the extension of the franchise to deaf and dumb persons, while, at the same time, recommending the exclusion of ex-Japanese collaborators. However, he had not mentioned that the United States authorities had refused to deprive Japanese collaborators of the franchise on the excuse that it was impossible to ascertain who was a collaborator and who was not. That, of course, was not the real reason for the refusal. The United States had been unwilling to withdraw the franchise from the collaborationists because they constituted the principle support of the military Government and the puppet regime.

The Chinese representative had also adduced as evidence of the United States co-operation the fact that the military Government had carefully studied the experience of the Saar Plebiscite before drawing up the election plans. Mr. Malik wondered what the French delegation thought of that fact, for the French people would scarcely regard the Saar Plebiscite as a good model for a democratic election. The Saar plebiscite was an outstanding instance of the use of terrorism, coercion, and propoganda. The people of the Saar had voted for their incorporation in Germany because of the pressure exerted by the Nazis who had employed as propogandists French traitors such as Laval and the Comte de Polignac. The League of Nations had been induced to approve the results of the plebiscite through political pressure. The experience of the Saar had therefore proved a good model for the election in southern Korea. But the USSR delegation could not be a party to the attempt which was now being made to induce the United Nations to follow the example of the League by approving the Korean elections.

The Chinese representative had also said that the representative character of the southern National Assembly could be seen from the fact that the majority of its members were independent of representatives of minor political parties. But anyone who read paragraph 23, Volume I, Part II of the Temporary Commission's Report would see that the independent candidates who had been successful in the election were closely linked with the Hankook Party and the National Association for the Rapid Realisation of Korean Independence. It was well known that these last were parties of the extreme right wing and that many of their members had obtained election by passing themselves off in the guise of independents. In fact, the majority of the representatives were not independents at all.

Mr. Malik refuted the United Kingdom representative's attempt to cast doubt on the validity of the election in northern Korea. Mr. Walker had spoken of false ballots. But his evidence was no more to be accepted than the notorious "Protocol M". He had also said that there could not have been any election for the Democratic Assembly in South Korea because had there been, the police would have known of it and would have taken counter measures. Mr. Malik drew the United Kingdom representative's attention to the Seoul Times of 25 August which reported that thousands of people had been arrested by the police for participating in the election. The fact was that the Japanese trained police had been unable to prevent the people of south Korea from participating in the election and demonstrating their desire for an independent and democratic Government of the whole of Korea.

There followed a lengthy discussion on procedure during which it was proposed that, in view of the short time available to the Committee in which to complete its work, members should agree to limit their statements to thirty minutes. After taking the sense of the Committee, the CHAIRMAN decided not to put the suggestion to a vote.

The meeting rose at 1.0 p.m.

(7) 제3차 유엔총회 제1위원회 제235차 회의 요약

해제문서 15 : A/C.1/SR 235 (Third Session, First Committee, Summary Record of the Two Hundred and Thirty Fifth Meeting)

문서명	Third Session, First Committee, Summary Record of the Two Hundred and Thirty Fifth Meeting		
	제3차 유엔총회 제1위원회의 제235차 회의 요약 기록		
발신		생성일시	1948년 12월 8일 오후 3시
		발신일시	
수신		수신일시	
		문서번호	A/C.1/SR 235
문서형태	회의록(요약)	문서분량	19쪽
주제명	유엔한국임시위원단의 한반도 내의 선거관련 활동 결과보고 및 한반도 통일 문제		
주요내용	1948년 12월 8일 오후 3시 프랑스 파리에서 개최된 제3차 유엔총회 제1위원회 제235차 회의 회의록. 상세한 내용은 본문 참조.		
검색어	유엔한국임시위원단, 제1위원회, Houdek(체코슬로바키아 대표), Cic Mil(유고슬라비아 대표), Kisselev(백러시아 사회주의공화국 대표), Fraser(뉴질랜드 대표), Castro(엘살바도르 대표), 피어슨(Lester P. Pearson, 캐나다 대표)		

1948년 12월 8일 오후 3시 프랑스 파리에서 개최된 제3차 유엔총회 제1위원회 제235차 회의에 관한 요약.

체코슬로바키아 대표의 발언으로 회의가 속개됨. 체코슬로바키아 대표는 유엔한국임시위원단이 한반도 문제를 확대하여 문제 해결을 지연시키고 있으므로 이에 반대하며, 한반도 문제는 유엔 영역 밖의 일이므로 미·소 양국의 협의 하에 해결해야 한다고 주장하고 한국 해방 이후 미·소 양국의 한반도 문제 해결 과정을 소개함.

유고슬라비아 대표 역시 유엔한국임시위원단에 대해 반대 의사를 표하며 미군이 한반도에 진주하기 전에 이미 한국은 인민공화국을 선포한 상태였으나 미군정이 이를 제압하고 반동분자들을 동원해 현재의 정부를 구성하였으며 미군이 체포한 정치범이 28,000명에 이르고 대한민국 정부는 미국의 조종을 받고 있다고 주장함. 또한 남한의 총선거 과정에서의 외압과 부당한 점을 지적하고 대한민국 정부는 합법성을 결여하고 있으므로 합법적인 정부로 인정할 수 없다고 주장하였으며, 미·소 양국 점령군의 철수를 주장한 소련군은 이미 철수를 시작하였다는 사실을 강조하고 소련의 수정결의안을 지지함.

백러시아 사회주의공화국 대표는 유엔한국임시위원단의 보고 내용을 면밀하게 검토해 봐야 한다고 말하고 남한 단독의 총선거를 결정하기 위하여 유엔총회에서 각국 대표단이 발언한 내용을 소개함. 그리고 유엔한국임시위원단은 유엔총회임시위원회에 대해 남한의 총선거에 관한 자문을 구했으며, 미국 대표는 이 위원회에서 남한에서의 총선거는 국회의 설립이라는 관점에서 진행되어야 하고 유엔총회가 부여하는 한반도 전체에 대한 통치권(mandate)을 유엔한국임시위원단에 위임하는 결의안을 제출하였다고 말함. 이 미국 대표의 결의안에 대해 캐나다 대표가 남한 인민 다수가 미국의 계획을 지지하는지 확신할 수 없다고 선언한 사실을 환기함.

노르웨이 대표도 미국 안을 채택하는 것은 유엔총회임시위원회의 권한을 넘어서는 일이라고 하고 스칸디나비아 대표도 소련의 불참 하에 한국문제를 결정할 수 없다는 사실을 고려해야 한다고 하면서, 유엔한국임시위원단 의장도 남한 국회 구성의 유일한 지지자들은 대지주 및 자본가 대표인 이승만, 김성수[2]이고 좌우의 보통 사람들은 한국 분단을 가속화시키게 될 선거에 반대하고 있다는 점, 위원단이 한민당과 협력하는 것에 대해 불만이 있다고 듣고 있다는 사실 등을 지적하고[3] 이승만, 김성수 등과 같은 지주계급이나 기업가의 견해가 한국인 전체의 의견이 될 수는 없을 것이라고 강조함. 또한 총선거 실시 전야의 남한사회의 혼란을 예로 들어 선거가 공정하게 추진되지 못했다고 주장함. 이승만을 친미, 극우, 기회주의자, 지주계급이라고 비판하고 김규식, 김구 등이 총선을 반대한 것과 같이 남한사회에서 총선에 반대한 움직임에 대해 상세하게 설명함.

백러시아 사회주의공화국 대표는 호주, 미국, 중국 공동 수정 결의안을 조목조목 반박하며 반대의사를 표명한 후 소련의 결의안을 지지함.

뉴질랜드 대표는 소련이 제2차 세계대전 종전 직전에 태평양 전쟁에 참여한 국가로서 그 이전에 많은 희생을 감수하며 태평양전쟁을 수행한 미국을 비난할 자격이 없으며 소련은 한반도에 대한 지배권을 주장할 권리도 없다고 주장함. 또한 소련을 추종하는 국가들은 모두 동일한 내용의 근거 없는 주장을 되풀이하고 있다고 비난함. 유엔이 확보한 증거에 의하면 한반도 내의 유일한 테러세력은 총선을 거부한 세력이므로 남한 정부의 합법성과 정당성을 인정하고 남한정부체제로 유엔감시하의 남북한 총선을 실시하자고 주장함.

엘살바도르 대표는 소련의 유엔 내에서의 방해 활동을 비난하며 소련의 협조를 촉구함.

캐나다 대표는 소련을 추종하는 국가들의 발언을 제한하고 정회를 제청하였으며 소련과 폴란드 대표가 이의를 제기하였으나 의장은 정회를 표결에 부칠

---

2 원문에는 Kim Sing Koo로 표기되어 있으나, 당시 남한총선거를 지지한 세력이 이승만 및 한민당 계열이었음을 고려할 때 김성수를 지칭하는 것으로 보인다.
3 원문에는 Hankuk party로 표기되어 있으나 한민당의 오기로 추정된다.

것을 선언하여 표결 결과, 찬성 35, 반대 6, 불참 7로 가결됨.

오후 6시15분에 정회함.

United Nations

GENERAL
ASSEMBLY

Nations Unies

ASSEMBLEE
GENERALE

UNRESTRICTED

A/C.1/SR.235
14 December 1948.

ENGLISH
ORIGINAL: FRENCH

Dual distribution

Third Session

FIRST COMMITTEE

SUMMARY RECORD OF THE TWO HUNDRED AND THIRTY FIFTH MEETING

Held at the Palais de Chaillot, Paris,
on Wednesday, 8 December 1948, at 3 p.m.

CONTENTS:

Question of the independence of Korea (discussion continued)

Chairman: Mr. P.H. SPAAK   Belgium
Rapporteur: Mr. S. SARPER   Turkey

Any corrections of this record should be submitted in writing, in
either of the working languages (English or French), and within two
working days, to Mr. E. Delavenay, Director, Official Records Division,
Room 3015, Palais de Chaillot. Corrections should be accompanied by
or incorporated in a letter, on headed notepaper, bearing the appropriate
symbol number and enclosed in an envelope marked "Urgent". Corrections
can be dealt with more speedily by the services concerned if delegations
will be good enough also to incorporate them in a mimeographed copy
of the record.

Mr. HOUDEK (Czechoslovakia) recalled that in 1947 his delegation had maintained that the problem of Korean independence did not fall within the competence of the United Nations, but should be decided by the United States and the Union of Soviet Socialist Republics on the basis of the agreements between them. The Czechoslovak delegation had opposed the establishment of the Temporary Commission, which could only aggravate the problem and delay a final solution. The report of that Commission had served to confirm the doubts and misgivings of the Czechoslovak delegation.

Mr. Houdek went on to make a brief historical survey of the question. It had been decided in Moscow, in December 1945, to set up a United States-Soviet Joint Commission entrusted with the task of co-operation with the democratic parties in Korea for the purpose of establishing Korean independence and of laying the foundations for a provisional Korean democratic government. That Commission met between 20 March and 8 May 1946 and adjourned sine die following differences of opinion between the two States on the question of the Korean organizations to be consulted. While the USSR wanted to establish relations with the democratic and social organizations, the United States proposed consultations with isolated groups and refused to consult with democratic and social groups such as the Korean Trade Union Federation and the All-Korean Peasant Union. In November 1946, the USSR put forward concrete proposals which might have provided a basis for a resumption of work by the Joint Commission, namely that the latter should consult only with those organizations and parties, which were not opposed to the Moscow decisions and which were willing to pledge themselves not to oppose them in future, nor to incite others to do so. The United States accepted that view on the 24 December, 1946, but no meeting of the Joint Commission took place. On the contrary, on 28 August, 1947, the United States proposed that separate elections should be held in the two zones. The USSR replied on 4 September, 1947 that such a proposal could only emphasize the division of Korea at a time when it was vital that it should remain united. Despite the tendency shown by the United States to follow an independent and selfish policy in Korea, the USSR consented to form a Joint Commission together with the United States on condition that the Commission should assist in the formation of an all-Korean government and that United States and Soviet troops should be withdrawn from Korean territory. Once formed, however, the Commission disregarded the proposals of the USSR and suggested that a United Nations Commission should be set up. The Czechoslovak delegation

/opposed the

opposed the formation of a Temporary Commission, which had not justified itself from the very start, and, as subsequent events served to prove, held out no hope of a solution of the problem. For that reason, the Czechoslovak delegation supported the USSR proposal to abolish the Temporary Commission for Korea.

As an example of the atmosphere prevalent in South Korea at the time of the elections, Mr. Houdek quoted a declaration by Mr. Min Won Sik, chairman of the Korean journal "The Seoul Times", which was reproduced on page 156 of Volume III of the Report of the Temporary Commission. It appeared from that declaration that all Koreans with progressive ideas or opposed to the right-wing parties were taxed as Communists and had been forced to take to the hills. There could be no liberty in South Korea, since the United States Army was in control and its inhabitants were without legal protection. The Czechoslovak delegation considered that such a declaration was sufficient evidence of the atmosphere in which the elections took place in South Korea.

Mr. Houdek said that, both in 1947 and 1948, his delegation had asked that representatives of the Korean people should take part in the discussions. It was not surprising that the representatives of South Korea should have been able to attack the regime of North Korea, since no representative of North Korea had been present at the discussions. What was, however, surprising, was the fact that it was precisely the self-styled champions of freedom of speech, who opposed the participation of North Korea in the present discussions.

There was another and no less significant fact. In 1947, the USSR proposal that all occupying forces should be withdrawn from Korea simultaneously, had been rejected. In the present year the situation was simpler, since the USSR, in response to a request made on 10 September, 1948 by the Supreme National Assembly of Korea had decided on 20 September, 1948 to evacuate Soviet troops from North Korea as from the 1 January, 1949. While the USSR had been able to secure the necessary conditions for the withdrawal of its troops and had thus made it possible for the people of North Korea to decide the form of their future government without the slightest trace of foreign interference, the Temporary Commission had been unable to ensure similar conditions in South Korea, since it considered that the occupying forces should not be withdrawn until circumstances permitted.

He was of the opinion that if the representatives of North Korea had not been given a hearing, it was because most of the States who formed part of the majority had been afraid of the consequences.

/Mr. CIC MIL

Mr. CIC MTL (Yugoslavia) recalled the statement made by the
Yugoslav delegation in 1947 that the decision to set up a Temporary
Commission was directed against the interests of Korea and against
the maintenance of peace in that part of the world.   Facts had
confirmed the view of the Yugoslav delegation.

The representative of the Ukraine had been justified in the statement
he made in 1947 that the Commission would have one purpose only: that
of advancing the interests of the United States in Korea.   To understand the problem, it must be remembered that the United States forces
entered Korea in 8 November 1945 without striking a single blow, since
the Japanese forces had already been defeated by the Korean people.
Until September of that year, the people had proclaimed in Seoul a
People's Republic of Korea, which had immediately restored peace and
internal order.   The United States forces of occupation suppressed the
People's Committees. which exercised power in Korea, took power into
their own hands and entrusted the execution of their orders to the
former Japanese administration.   On 4 September, 1945, popular
demonstrations took place in Seoul, but the demands put forward went
unheeded.   The United States military authorities then had recourse
to the appointment of a body of Korean Councillors, eleven reactionary
collaborators headed by the notorious Kim Song Soo.   That Council
made every effort to turn Southern Korea into a "place d'armes" and
colony of the Americans.   The United States did not abolish the
Japanese colonial regime. but merely transformed it to suit themselves.
All property confiscated by the Japanese in Korea, a large part of
the land, and commercial and industrial undertakings were regarded as
war booty by the United States and were subsequently distributed to
Korean capitalist concerns.   Thus the commercial company "New Asia"
which was created, was indistinguishable from the previous Japanese
commercial companies.

In both the political and economic spheres the United States
exercised similar pressure.   To strengthen the position of the Korean
reactionaries, a parody of an election was held in 1946.   Out of
ninety deputies, forty-five were appointed by the United States while
forty five others were elected by indirect voting.   It was to be
noted that 70 per cent of the electors abstained from voting and of
the ninety deputies, twenty-seven were former collaborators, seventeen
prominent industrialists and twenty-eight big landowners.   It was
therefore, obvious that the Korean people had not taken part in the
election.   Only fifty-seven deputies took part in the work of that
Assembly and, when the Temporary Commission arrived, a certain number

/left the

left the Assembly as a sign of protest. What was more, the remnants of that parliament had little or no power. The Temporary Commission was of the opinion that the presence of United States officials in the central administration would reduce even more the authority of the Government of South Korea. Thus, the legislative and executive power was in fact in the hands of the United States.

In March, 1947, a large number of democratic leaders had been arrested by the United States authorities. In August of the same year, when the Koreans learned that the United States had decided to abandon the Moscow Declaration as a basis for the solution of the Korean question, fresh reprisals had taken place against the progressive and democratic parties. In October 1947 there were in South Korea twenty-eight thousand persons in prison for political reasons, more than at any time during the Japanese occupation. A delegation from the World Federation of Trade Unions was unable to fulfil its task when visiting Korea in 1947 on account of persecution by the United States authorities. When the delegation returned to Europe, Mr. Saillant, Secretary-General of the Federation, stated that the regime in South Korea was an arbitrary and harsh regime under the control of the United States, that prisons were full to overflowing, that thirty-three thousand policemen and twenty-three thousand gendarmes were required to maintain order, that democratic organizations had been disbanded and that youth terrorist organizations were actively occupied. There had been many demonstrations and protests against the division of Korea and the transformation of South Korea into a colony of the United States. Clashes between the people and the police were a daily occurrence. More than two hundred and forty persons had been killed and five hundred and fifty injured between 9 February and 9 May, 1948. The elections which, according to the decision of the General Assembly, should have been held on 31 March, 1948, were postponed until 10 May.

/neither the

Neither the Korean people nor the representatives of the Temporary Commission had any illusions as to the methods employed in preparing for those elections, the results of which had been nullified by the decision of the Interim Committee of the General Assembly. In deciding that elections could be held in South Korea, the Interim Committee had in fact usurped the functions of the General Assembly.

The Interim Committee, whose very constitution was illegal, altered the meaning of the General Assembly's resolution of 14 November by its resolution of 26 February. By virtue of the latter resolution, the Temporary Commission assumed the right to control the elections in South Korea, but was unable to obtain the United States' consent to the deletion of collaborators and traitors from the electoral lists since the United States military authorities alleged it was impossible to verify the antecedents of electors.

Reviewing the conditions under which the elections took place, the Yugoslav representative pointed out that the democratic leaders had either been arrested or were in flight, that the moderate parties had refused to vote in order to avoid accentuating the division between the north and south of the country, and that only the parties of the extreme right had taken part in the elections, as, for example, the party of Hankuk, the best organized right-wing party, which (according to the report of the Temporary Commission) had the support of the big landowners and the police. Moreover, the United States authorities had feared that a large number of Koreans would boycott the elections, and General Hodge had accordingly announced in a declaration of 3 March, 1948 that all who failed to vote would be outlawed. The elections had been supervised by 60,000 armed police and by a million volunteers, who had been the moving force behind many disturbances.

Despite terrorism and pressure, 20 per cent of the population had not registered for inclusion on electoral lists, while 5 per cent of those registered had failed to vote and 9 per cent of those who had actually voted had cast blank voting papers. The Temporary Commission nevertheless concluded that the preparations for the elections in South Korea took place in an atmosphere of reasonable liberty. That may have been the opinion of the United States and the police, but it was certainly not that of the Korean people. The National Assembly was not representative of the people as a whole, but was the docile instrument of United States policy. When the Government of South Korea was set up, 92 deputies failed to appear and of the 78 deputies present, 28 left the assembly hall. The Government of South Korea therefore represented no one but the United States, which was striving to give the impression that the government reflected the

/freely-

freely-expressed will of the Korean people.

Mr. Houdek attempted to show the economic plight of South Korea.   No
effective reforms, whether political, social or economic, had been
carried out.   The peasants were over-burdened with taxes.,   Between
December 1945 and January 1948 prices had multiplied 21 times, and
salaries only 7 times.   There were 2 million unemployed in South Korea
and industrial production was 20 per cent below the pre-war level.   As
long as Korea was divided, its economy would remain chaotic.   Such was
the situation created in Korea by the United States of America as revealed
by the report of the Temporary Commission, although that report attempted
to give the opposite impression.   There was only one solution to the
problem -- the United States must withdraw its troops from South Korea
just as the USSR had withdrawn its troops from the North.

The people of both zones of Korea had made their desire for unity plain
at the time of the elections to the Constituent Assembly on August 12, 1948.
77.5 per cent of the electors of South Korea and 99 per cent of the
electors of North Korea had taken part in the elections which had culminated
in the formation of a Constituent Assembly.   That Assembly had adopted
a constitution and appointed a popular government.   The Korean people
had established their own State in moral and political unity.   On
10 September, the National Assembly had requested the United States and the
USSR to withdraw their forces of occupation.   The USSR had given a
favourable reply, whereas the United States still maintained its forces in
South Korea.   The people of Korea had proved that they were capable of
governing their country.   An agrarian reform act had transferred ownership
of the land to those who cultivated it.   A national economy plan had been
put into effect;   laws on social insurance had been enacted and educational
reforms had completed the task of national regeneration.   The USSR
had begun the withdrawal of its troops on 15 October to ensure its
completion by 1 January 1949.   The United States, on the other hand,
had stated on the 20 September that the withdrawal of troops was only
one aspect of the solution of the problem of Korea.   The United States
was thus anxious to profit by its majority in the General Assembly of the
United Nations in order to perpetuate the present situation into Korea.
As in Greece, the United States had created an impotent government which was
entirely dependent upon it and which was thus obliged in order to remain in
power to request the United States to maintain its forces in Korea.

The representative of Yugoslavia thought the sole question at issue in
Korea was that of the withdrawal of troops.   As long as South Korea
remained under occupation, there was no possibility, as Mr. Marshall had
stated in the General Assembly, of creating an independent and united Korea
with a constitutional government elected by the Koreans themselves after
/genuinely

2. 제3차 유엔총회 제1위원회 및 문서

157

genuinely free elections. The withdrawal of Soviet troops from North
Korea showed the course which should be followed to enable Korea to
acquire national sovereignty. Yugoslavia could accept no solution
which did not correspond to the interests of the Korean people, namely,
the withdrawal of the forces of occupation to enable the Korean people
to organize itself and to administer its country as an independent
and sovereign State, which might become a member of the United Nations.

The Yugoslav delegation therefore supported the resolution of the USSR,
which alone would enable a solution to be found of the question of the
independence and unity of Korea.

Mr. KISSELEV (Byelorussian Soviet Socialist Republic) noted that
the United Nations Temporary Commission on Korea aimed to prove that the
elections of 10 May 1948 had taken place in normal conditions, and were
the legal expression of the will of the electors. The report even
claimed that the democratic rights of freedom of speech of the press and
of assembly had been guaranteed. In order to check whether the Temporary
Commission's conclusions were accurate, however, its record must be
examined. That Commission, realizing that both the political parties
and the Korean people as a whole were opposed to elections for the
establishment of a South Korean government, had consulted the Interim
Committee of the General Assembly. The United States representative
on that Committee had expressed the wish that elections should be held
in South Korea with a view to the establishment of a National Assembly,
and had proposed a resolution giving the Temporary Commission power to
implement in South Korea the mandate conferred on it by the General
Assembly for the whole of Korea. That resolution had been adopted by
31 votes to 2, with 11 abstentions. The Canadian representative on the
Interim Committee had declared that he was not convinced that the majority
of the people in South Korea supported the United States plan. The
Norwegian representative had been of the opinion that, in adopting the
United States plan, the Interim Committee would be exceeding the powers
vested in it by the General Assembly. The representatives of the
Scandinavian countries had thought that the Korean problem could not be
solved in the absence of the USSR. Mr. Melon, Chairman of the Temporary
Commission, had stated before the Interim Committee that the sole
advocates of the establishment of a National Assembly in Southern Korea
were Syngman Rhee and Kim Sing Koo, both representatives of the big
landowners and Korean businessmen. He had stressed that many moderate
men of both left and right were opposed to elections which could only
result in accentuating the division of Korea. The Chairman of the
Temporary Commission had added that the Commission had received complaints

/about

about its co-operation with the Hankuk party, and complaints to the
effect that the inhabitants of South Korea did not consider that the
elections would be free, because the country was occupied by United
States troops.

Mr. Kisselev pointed out, further, that, on the eve of the elections,
the United States, in co-operation with Korean reactionaries, had
resorted to political pressure of all kinds. Patriots had been
imprisoned, 500 men had been killed, 60,000 police and countless so-
called volunteers of the extreme right wing had been mobilized. In
Seoul, martial law had been proclaimed.

On 10 May 1948, the day of the elections, the police had forced the
people to go to the polling-booths, subjected them to systematic search,
and instructed them how to vote. On this subject, the United Press
correspondent had written that the violation of electoral rights was so
blatant that even the Principal Secretary of the Temporary Commission had
been constrained to declare that the elections could not be regarded as
free if the electors were searched; and the Chairman of the Commission
had stated that certain reservations must be made about the way in which
the elections had been held. There had been patrols, American military
police, Korean police and "volunteers" everywhere. The American troops
had been placed on a war footing, and even the members of the United Nations
Commission had been "protected". On 10 May, the correspondent of "France
Presse" had reported on the activities of the Youth Organization, members
of which had searched the electors and arrested suspects. Reuter's
correspondent had reported that, on 10 May, fifteen persons had been
killed in a single district.

Directly the polling booths were closed, all the ballot boxes had had
to be taken to the central offices, and the results had not been announced
until 12 May. The whole of the Korean press had agreed that the
separate elections held in South Korea had taken place in an atmosphere
of terror. Police detachments and "volunteers" of extreme rightist
convictions had forced the electors to vote. In the towns, the elections
had been directly controlled by American troops.

The Seoul correspondent of the "New York Times" had reported the presence
in Korean waters of an American light cruiser and two destroyers.
Popular opposition had, however, been very strong, so that the American
High Command had been forced to admit that the situation was more
critical than at any time since the beginning of the occupation.

Such was the atmosphere in which the elections of 10 May 1948 had in
fact taken place. In addition all the parties and organizations in

/South

South Korea, including rightists like Kim Koo and Kim Kiusik had
boycotted the elections, asserting that the true purpose was to dismember
Korea.   The only exceptions were Syngman Rhee, a devoted partisan of
the United States, and the pro-Japanese group of Kim Sung Koo.   Syngman
Rhee, for his part had said to a representative of the United Press
that he had represented Korea, and that he had against him only
the Communists and unimportant members of the left and centre: when
the Korean Government was reconstituted, it would ask the USSR to
evacuate Korea and the United States to remain.

Who was Syngman Rhee?   On 23 June 1948, in "Far Eastern Survey"
the journalist Benjamin Weems had recalled that Rhee had returned to
Korea in 1945 after an absence of thirty-five years.   Rhee regarded
himself as the representative of the provisional Korean Government in
Washington, and had become, on his return to Korea, the leader of a
party formed of the enemies of Communism, landowners opportunists and
pro-Japanese elements.   At the beginning of 1947, a campaign had been
started for holding separate elections in South Korea.

Benjamin Weems added that the elections which were held while the Commission
was in Korea had resulted in a large majority of extreme rightists being
returned;   the leftists, including Kim Kiusik and Kim Koo, had boycotted
the elections.   Kim Kiusik and Kim Koo had regarded the elections as an
obstacle to the unification and independence of Korea.

Such was the report given by Benjamin Weems, a man who had lived in
Korea for twenty years.   The Buddhist Society of Korea had likewise
declared that the elections had taken place under the threat of armed force.

The South Korean police force had on its strength 6,000 men who had
served under the Japanese. Democratic organizations were persecuted and
there was a ban on the democratic press.   Thousands of patriots were
being imprisoned and tortured;   others were fleeing to the forests and
mountains or taking refuge in North Korea.

No less a person than the Chief Justice of South Korea had told the Commission that if they wanted to hold free elections, the system in force would have to be reformed; in particular, the police would have to be prevented from interfering with the political parties and imprisoning people for months on all kinds of pretexts.

The United Nations Commission must be aware of the fact that, during two and a half years of American domination, no democratic measures had been taken and the land was still in the hands of the big landowners, to whom the peasants had to pay exorbitant rents.

It was not only the peasants who were suffering: workmen and employees were in a similar position, as inflation and unemployment were rife. It was true that there were in South Korea six metalurgical factories which, at the time the Japanese left, had had enough raw material for six years' work. But the Americans had shipped those raw materials to Japan.

There was in South Korea no security and no social insurance; and speculators were growing rich at the expense of their fellow countrymen.

On 28 April 1948, Kim Kiusik, chief of the League of National Independence, which comprised a whole group of centre and rightist parties, had declared that the decision of the Interim Committee regarding separate elections had been illegal. Kim Kiusik had supported the Soviet proposal for the simultaneous withdrawal of troops which, he had said, would make possible the unification of Korea. Finally, he had stressed the contrast between the progress made in North Korea and the deplorable conditions in South Korea, where every person lived in fear of terrorist attacks. Yet no one could claim that Kim Kiusik had any particular sympathy for North Korea.

Though the Commission had been aware of the Korean people's opposition to separate elections, it had obeyed the orders of the United States. On page 29 of its report (Russian text) the Commission had noted accusations to the effect that it had helped the reactionaries, the police, and the American authorities to bully the leftist parties and to create conditions such that free democratic electi.. were out of the question. Those criticisms had been all too well founded.

It was true that the Commission's report contained recommendations about freedom of speech, of the press and of assembly, all of which were essential for the holding of free elections, but the Commission had done nothing to ensure those freedoms, so that the elections had been held in an atmosphere of unprecedented terrorism. Thus even the Commission itself had not been free to make contacts as desired. On 6 March 1948, a Sub-Committee had investigated two cases of the arrest of Koreans trying to make contact with the Commission. At the request of the latter, the Chairman had written to the American Commander stating that Koreans should be entirely free to make contact with the Commission. How could there be any talk of free elections when even the Commission itself had to apply to the Americans?

A sub-committee of the Temporary Commission, having decided to issue invitations to a number of representatives of leftist-organizations who had been either under arrest or under police or military supervision had applied to the American authorities to obtain certain assurances for them. The guarantees given were, however, not sufficient to satisfy the Korean representatives, all of whom had refused the Commission's invitation thinking that acceptance might cost them their lives.

As regards supervision of the elections themselves, the nine groups of the Commission, which had included incidentally, American officials, had inspected only 277 polling centres out of a total of 13,272, i.e. 2%.

The Temporary Commission would go down in Korean history as having helped the United States to violate elementary rights.

The representative of the Seoul Government on the First Committee had no doubt ventured to slander the Soviet Union; but he had not breathed a word about the responsibilities of the United States. Yet the latter had one aim only: to maintain their troops in Korea in violation of the Moscow agreement, and to submit the Korean question, illegally, to the United Nations. The United Nations had also acted illegally in setting up a Temporary Commission. The United States had then submitted to the Interim Committee a resolution regarding' separate elections in South Korea, the only desire of Wall Street being to substitute American domination for that of the Germans or the Japanese. It was not an accident that the United States had proposed a ten-year trusteeship and wanted to appoint a High Commissioner in Korea. The United States had not evacuated their troops, and all their statements about the independence of Korea were merely a cloak for their real intention -- to turn Korea into an American colony. Thanks to manipulated elections, the preliminary economic conditions had been created and the country split into two parts. But the whole Korean people demanded the withdrawal of the American troops: genuine elections would then be held, and a legislative assembly would set up a national Government for the whole of Korea.

Whereas the USSR was striving to remove the effects of Japanese domination, the United States Government was striving to stifle Korean democracy. But the Korean people now knew the true position: the colonial aims of the United States were based on strategic and economic factors.

/The United Kingdom

제2부 유엔총회 회의록(1948)

The United Kingdom representative had denied that the elections in South Korea had been held under the threat of armed force, and had asserted that the statements made by the Soviet representatives could not compel belief because those representatives had not been on the spot. But if the United Kingdom representative had been present at the elections, why had he not described the terror which had reigned in South Korea? The British correspondents after all knew about it.

As for the documents mentioned by the United Kingdom representative, they were doubtless products of the British Intelligence Service, made famous by the case of protocol M.

As regards the text of the joint draft resolution submitted by Australia, China and the United States, the first operative paragraph expressed approval of the conclusions contained in the reports of the Temporary Commission. But, as already pointed out by the representatives of the Union of Soviet Socialist Republics, the Ukrainian Soviet Socialist Republic, Poland, Czechoslovakia and Yugoslavia, those conclusions were entirely unfounded. What newspapers or other publications could assert that the democratic freedoms had been guaranteed on the day of the elections in South Korea? The democratic newspapers had in fact been banned.

The second operative paragraph referred to the "free will of the electorate". But the majority of the parties and democratic organizations had refused to take part in those "free" elections. The fact was that there had been the most atrocious terrorism, under the aegis of the American occupation troops instead of any "free will of the electorate".

The third operative paragraph contained a recommendation to the occupying Powers to withdraw their troops as soon as possible. As stated in the press, the USSR was about to complete the withdrawal of its troops, but the Koreans and the world in general wished very much to know when the withdrawal of the United States troops would be completed. Instead of using a vague term like "as soon as possible", it would be better to specify a date such as 1 February 1949.

In that connexion, the information service of the Staff Headquarters of the 21st Corps of the United States Army, in a press survey dated 14 October 1948, had mentioned that the newspaper "Cha Yu Chin Min" had given a summary of a meeting held by the National Assembly on 13 October, in the course of which forty members had submitted a resolution calling for the immediate withdrawal of foreign troops. The resolution also mentioned the creation of a Republic of Korea, in accordance with the General Assembly Resolution; a protest was made against the

occupation, which was considered as a step towards the establishment of a
trusteeship system, and the hope was expressed that the United States and
the USSR should carry out the provisions of the Resolution of
14 November 1947, dealing with the withdrawal of foreign troops.

According to the newspaper "Cha Yu Chin Min", the discussion
of that resolution at the "National" Assembly of Seoul degenerated
into a free fight and the consideration of the question was postponed.

Thus, even within the "National" Assembly of Seoul, the idea
of the withdrawal of the United States troops was sufficient to cause
a free fight.

The fourth operative paragraph of the joint draft resolution
dealt with the establishment of a new commission for Korea and
defined the functions of that new body. The delegation of the
Byelorussian SSR categorically opposed the establishment of a new
commission, as the Koreans should be free to decide their future
for themselves, without the presence of United States troops, and
to create a fully independent and unified democratic State. They
had deserved this, after four decades of heroic struggle against
the yoke of Japanese colonialism.

The Byelorussian SSR delegation formally objected to the whole
of the draft resolution submitted by the delegations of Australia,
China and the United States. The adoption of that resolution would
be an insult to the people of Korea. His delegation gave its full
support to the USSR resolution.

Mr. FRASER (New Zealand) said that the speech made by
the representative of the Byelorussian SSR was simply a mass of
purely verbal accusations without a shred of evidence to support
them.

In particular, the First Committee had been asked to accept a
completely unreal picture of the United States. However, at a time
when it could have kept out of the Second World War, as the USSR
was doing, the United States had acted in a way which was quite
without precedent for a non-belligerent country, by helping the
United Kingdom in its struggle for mankind. In spite of the small
groups of isolationists, President Roosevelt had given encouragement
and material aid to the British Commonwealth.

Moreover, when the war had broken out in the Pacific, the United States had borne the brunt of the struggle against Japanese tyranny and terrorism.

The exploits of the Red Army and the Russian people would certainly not be forgotten by posterity, but the USSR had only come into the war in the Pacific two days before the atomic bomb brought about the cessation of hostilities. New Zealand could not, therefore, tolerate any insults against the United States, whose sons had fought shoulder to shoulder with the Australians and the New Zealanders right up to the time when peace was imposed upon Japan.

As for the claim made by the USSR that it had forced the Japanese out of Korea, or even that it had defeated the Japanese, the Soviet group itself knew quite well that the USSR had no military grounds for making claims in Korea. It was true that the United Kingdom and the United States made no claim on the basis of military achievement either.

What could not be permitted was that the policy of a country that had given its wealth and its men, both in the Pacific and in Europe, should be misrepresented, a country which was still helping Western Europe to help itself. New Zealand for its part owed a debt of gratitude to the United States.

The Soviet group -- for in reality each delegation simply repeated what the others had already said -- had also spoken of terrorism in South Korea. But what was happening in North Korea? That Republic might be truly representative of the people, but the United Nations had no means of knowing whether it was or not.

Furthermore, those who considered that every type of revolutionary violence was justified in order to overthrow a government they considered to be tyrannical were hardly fitted to plead in favour of legality. For the Soviet group there was only one criterion of legality and that was their own convenience.

Certain parties in Europe were being dangerously obdurate: was it to be permitted that similar conditions should be imposed upon Korea? The United States hoped for a settlement in Korea and no evidence to the contrary had been produced, whereas the USSR, or its military leaders, had been obdurate. What then could the United States do? Wait until a certain Government changed its attitude. The United States had turned to the rest of the world, that is to say the United Nations, which was superior to the Soviet group. The United Nations was in fact paramount, and it was the authority of the United Nations which was at present at stake as well as the fate of the people of Korea.

/Where was

Where was the proof for the accusations made against the United States?
The United Nations had received no evidence of ulterior motives on the
part of the United States nor of the alleged reign of terror in South Korea.
Neither had it any evidence that there was no reign of terror in North
Korea, where it had not had access.

It had of course been said that the Temporary Commission had been
refused access to North Korea because its establishment had been illegal.
But what right had any group of countries to take upon itself to decide
what was legal and what was not?

In reality, the only acts of terrorism that had been proved in South
Korea had been provoked by those who had abstained from voting in the election.
That was clear from the evidence submitted by the United Nations Commission,
evidence which, though sparse on certain points, was all that the United
Nations had to go upon.   It was, moreover, impossible to imagine that
a Commission set up by the General Assembly would deliberately distort the
facts or would come to conclusions without sufficient evidence.   If the
Temporary Commission were considered in that light, suspicion would be
introduced into international relationships.   The Assembly should therefore
accept the conclusions reached by the Temporary Commission, according to
which there had only been one type of terrorism in South Korea, namely that
brought about by the groups opposed to the holding of the elections.   As
for the police, it had not interfered unjustifiably and it had proved
impartial, as was shown by the evidence of the Temporary Commission itself.

The New Zealand delegation did not consider that the authority of the
Government of the South extended over North Korea.   It was self-evident
that it did not, and the resolution implied nothing of the kind.   Thus the
resolution recognized the Republican Government of the South, in the regions
over which it had control, in the hope that its authority would be extended
and that an agreement would be reached between the North and the South.
For that it was not essential that the present Government of South Korea
should extend its authority over the North.   If the USSR would ask the
United Nations to send a commission to North Korea to find out who did
really represent the people in that area, the two Governments could be
merged and elections could be held under the new authority which would be
set up.

It was most important that the election should be carried out fairly, as
had been done in South Korea, according to the evidence before the United
Nations.

/If the

If the members of the Soviet group were to produce more facts and fewer unfounded assertions, their cause would be better served, at least as far as the continuation of investigation in Korea was concerned. But the fact that they were unable to prove the truth of their accusations justified the adoption of the joint draft resolution submitted by the delegations of Australia, China and the United States and the rejection of the USSR draft resolution.

Mr. CASTRO (El Salvador) said that the question of Korea, whose territorial integrity and unity were in danger, was the most difficult problem that had ever come before the United Nations, that almost universal Organization.

North Korea, which was the industrial area, was cut off from the rest of the world. The north was closely related to the south, which was an agricultural region, and only if they were united could the political and economic stability of Korea be ensured.

What was worse, there existed a blatant antagonism, which would eventually turn the population of the north into a satellite of the USSR, while the south would develop on its own.

That situation had arisen because of one of those unhappy compromises made between certain of the Great Powers at the end of the World War. Although the USSR had not really contributed to the victory of the United Nations in Asia, it had not wished to be absent at the time of the final settlement. One of the consequences of that last-minute intervention had been the partition of Korea.

Why did the USSR persist in isolating all the territories under its military control from the rest of the world? Why too did that Power, which had contributed most decisively to the success of the Allies in Europe, persist in refusing to co-operate in the work for peace, whose programme had been drawn up at San Francisco?

The Soviet Union had opposed the most constructive resolutions of the Assembly and, in the Security Council, it had used its right of veto to excess. In the course of the Third Regular Session the USSR had voted against the most important resolutions of the First Committee, such as the resolutions concerning Greece, atomic energy and disarmament.

Palestine had been the only question on which the USSR had voted in the same way as the other members of the Security Council. In general, as long as the conflict continued between the USSR and the nations associated with it on the one hand, and the other Members of the United Nations on the other, the success of the United Nations would be very problematical.

/However, it

However, it was certain that the people of the USSR earnestly desired an atmosphere of international peace and security, so that they could devote themselves to economic reconstruction and enjoy all their rights.

When the USSR had completed its work of reconstruction, an era of prosperity and happiness would open up before it, as long as it gave up its aims of expansion. That was indeed an essential prerequisite for the success of the United Nations and the solution of all international problems. In Korea, in particular, national unity would eventually have to be restored and preliminary and provisional steps should already be taken to that end.

The delegation of El Salvador would favour the report of the Temporary Commission and would support the operative part of the joint draft resolution submitted by the delegations of Australia, China and the United States, which provided that a new Commission for Korea should carry on the work of the Temporary Commission.

With regard to the withdrawal of troops, the delegation of El Salvador considered that the troops should not be withdrawn from South Korea until stability and security had been re-established. It was well known that, for more than a year, there had been a well-organized army numbering at least 170,000 in North Korea. Consequently, as long as South Korea did not possess a similar army capable of maintaining security, the troops which were there should not be withdrawn. His delegation further considered that the drafting of paragraph 3 was not explicit enough and should be altered.

Mr. PEARSON (Canada) pointed out that the Committee had only a few hours before it in which to complete its work. In order to help to bring about unification and understanding in Korea, his delegation would therefore be prepared to refrain from speaking at present, if that gesture would result in the closure of the general debate.

The CHAIRMAN said that the representative of the Ukrainian SSR and the USSR had placed their names on the list of speakers.

Mr. PEARSON (Canada) re-emphasized the fact that the Committee had very little time left. The two representatives mentioned had already spoken at length that day and he proposed the closure of the debate in accordance with rule 106 of the rules of procedure.

/Mr. RADIONOV

Mr. RADIONOV (Union of Soviet Socialist Republics) said that his delegation was opposed to the closure of the debate. He proposed that the list of speakers should be closed.

Mr. ZEBROWSKY(Poland) was opposed to the motion for closure submitted by the representative of Canada. While several speakers had spoken against the Temporary Commission's report today, nearly all the speakers had spoken in favour of that report on the previous day, but that had been no reason for closing the debate.

The Polish delegation considered that the representatives who were opposed to the report should be given the opportunity to reply to the criticisms that had been made against them. Perhaps it would be sufficient if the list of speakers were closed.

The CHAIRMAN put the motion for closure to the vote.

A vote was taken by show of hands.

The motion was adopted by 35 votes to 6, with 7 abstentions.

The meeting rose at 6.15 p.m.

(8) 제3차 유엔총회 제1위원회 제236차 회의 요약

해제문서 16 : A/C.1/SR 236 (Third Session, First Committee, Summary Record of the Two Hundred and Thirty Sixth Meeting)

문서명	Third Session, First Committee, Summary Record of the Two Hundred and Thirty Sixth Meeting		
	제3차 유엔총회 제1위원회 제236차 회의 요약 기록		
발신		생성일시	1948년 12월 8일 오후 8시 30분
		발신일시	
수신		수신일시	
		문서번호	A/C.1/SR 236
문서형태	회의록(요약)	문서분량	13쪽
주제명	한국의 독립문제		
주요내용	1948년 12월 8일 오후 8시 30분 프랑스 파리에서 개최된 제3차 유엔총회 제1위원회 제236차 회의 회의록. 상세한 내용은 본문 참조.		
검색어	유엔한국임시위원단, 제1위원회, Radionov(소련 대표), Khalidy(이라크 대표), Wilson(뉴질랜드 대표), Manuilsky(우크라이나 대표), Castro(엘살바도르 대표), Mughiz(시리아 대표), 덜레스(John Dulles, 미국 대표), Kisselev(백러시아 대표), Zebrowski(폴란드 대표), 피어슨(Lester P. Pearson, 캐나다 대표), 토넬리(De La Tournelle, 프랑스 대표), 고든 워커(Gordon Walker, 영국 대표)		

1948년 12월 8일 오후 8시 30분 프랑스 파리에서 개최된 제3차 유엔총회 제1위원회 제236차 회의 회의록.

소련 대표의 발언으로 회의가 속개됨.

소련 대표는 제235차 회의에서 뉴질랜드 대표가 발언한 내용에 반론을 제기하였고 이에 이라크 대표가 회의 안건에 대해 토론할 것을 요청함.

소련 대표는 이어서 호주, 중국, 미국 공동결의안이 유엔총회 결의안에 위배된다고 주장함.

엘살바도르 대표, 시리아 대표는 공동결의안을 지지하였으나 우크라이나 대표는 공동결의안을 면밀히 검토할 것을 제안하고 남한의 총선거 과정에 위법행위가 있었다고 주장함.

미국 대표는 공동결의안 각 조항은 확인된 사실에 근거해서 작성되었음을 강조함.

백러시아 사회주의공화국 대표와 폴란드 대표는 결의안 일부 조항의 문제점을 지적하며 결의안에 대한 반대 의사를 표명하고 소련이 제안한 결의안을 지지함.

소련 대표는 공동결의안 표결 시에 기권 의사를 밝혔으며 폴란드 대표도 소련 결의안에 대한 지지의사를 밝힘.

미국의 제안에 대해 위원회 멤버들의 거수로 투표가 진행됨.

호주, 중국, 미국이 제출한 공동결의안(A/C.1/426)에 대한 표결 결과 찬성 41, 반대 6, 불참 2로 공동결의안이 가결됨.

미국 대표는 유엔한국임시위원단 위원국 구성 선정 문제에 관해 가결된 공동결의안에 "유엔한국임시위원단 위원국과 동일한 국가로 위원회를 구성한다"는 문구를 삽입할 것을 제의하였고 이를 표결에 부친 결과 찬성 41, 반대 0, 불참 1로 가결됨.

소련이 제의한 결의안(A/C.1/427/Corr.1)은 표결 결과 반대 42, 찬성 6, 불참 3으로 부결됨.

이에 의장은 제3차 유엔총회 제1위원회의 종료를 선언함.

22시 48분에 정회함.

United Nations　　　　Nations Unies

UNRESTRICTED

GENERAL
ASSEMBLY

ASSEMBLEE
GENERALE

A/C.1/SR 236
9 December 1948
ORIGINAL: ENGLISH

Dual distribution

Third Session

FIRST COMMITTEE

SUMMARY RECORD OF THE TWO HUNDRED AND THIRTY-SIXTH MEETING

Held at the Palais de Chaillot, Paris,
on Wednesday, 8 December 1948, at 8.30 p.m.

CONTENTS:

· The problem of the independence of Korea.

Chairman:	Mr. P.H. SPAAK	Belgium
Rapporteur:	Mr. S. SARPER	Turkey

Mr. RADIONOV (Union of Soviet Socialist Republics) said
that the statement made by the representative of New Zealand called
for comment as it had distorted the truth in an attempt to deny the
contribution of the USSR to the collapse of Japan. The representative
of New Zealand had said that the USSR had fought only for two days.
The facts were well known and Mr. Radionov would refer only to three
specific points. Firstly, the USSR had entered the war on 8 August
and the Japanese surrender was not until 3 September. Moreover,
after that date the Red Army had to continue fighting against the
Kwantung Army. However, the date were not as important as the results.
During four years of the war with Germany, the finest Japanese Army
stayed on the borders of the USSR. In accordance with its obligations,
the USSR built up the strength of its Eastern Armies and thus served to
pin down an important part of the Japanese forces which as a result
could not be used against the forces of the United States, New Zealand
and Australia. There could be little doubt that this diversion of
the Kwantung Army had saved New Zealand from invasion. Secondly,
the official figures showed that between 9 August and 9 September,
the attack by the Red Army upon the Kwantung Army resulted in over
six hundred and seventy-four thousand Japanese casualties while the
USSR casualties were over thirty thousand. Thirdly, the representative
of New Zealand had claimed that the atomic bomb forced the surrender
of Japan. The facts were that the Japanese General Staff had
prepared plans to continue the war on the mainland even if the Islands
had to be evacuated. Only the intervention of the USSR prevented
this plan being carried out.

Mr. KHALIDY (Iraq) observed that the representatives of over
fifty States had come to the meeting of the First Committee and they
should keep to the matter on the agenda. The representative of
New Zealand had brought up unnecessary points and praised one of the
belligerents in the recent war. The other representatives were not
interested in this sort of statement which did not refer to the agenda.
Mr. Khalidy was of the opinion that such remarks were out of order.

Mr. WILSON (New Zealand) said he reserved the right of
Mr. Frazer to make a reply since reference had been made to his
statement.

Mr. MANUILSKY (Ukrainian Soviet Socialist Republic) said that
he would confine his remarks to discussion of the draft resolution
presented by Australia, China, and the United States (document A/C.1/426).

This draft resolution overturned logic, facts, the meaning of the Charter and the decisions of the General Assembly. The essential question which should have been dealt with in the resolution was the withdrawal of foreign troops from Korea. It was well known that during 1947 the Government of the USSR had met with opposition from the United States in its attempts to settle the Korean problem and establish a democratic government in accordance with the obligations of the Moscow Conference of 1945. When the United States proceeded to transfer the question to the General Assembly, the Government of the USSR proposed on 26 September 1947 the simultaneous withdrawal of the occupation forces of the two Powers. The USSR also proposed that the Korean people should be allowed to decide their future political structure on the basis of self-determination. It was answered that the USSR was not ready to withdraw and was only executing a manoeuvre to put the United States in an awkward position. However, during the year of the Temporary Commission's activity, it was the USSR which took the important decision to withdraw its forces. There could be no doubt that a majority of the world public would endorse this USSR decision. There could be no doubt after reading the documents of the Temporary Commission that a majority of the Korean people of all political parties wished to see the United States troops leave. The most equitable solution of the Korean Question and the most acceptable to a majority of the delegations present would be the withdrawal of foreign troops.

It had been claimed that those who were opposed to the draft resolution and did not support the conclusions of the Temporary Commission were undermining the work of the General Assembly and of the Temporary Commission. The representative of El Salvador had spoken along these lines. The Ukrainian delegation looked with respect upon any statement or criticism from any representative, since they based their position upon principle. However, there was special status reserved for the representative of El Salvador who continually was hurling abuse at the USSR. Moreover when attempts were being made to achieve a peace settlement and to liquidate fascism, the representative of El Salvador, during the discussion of the Spanish Question, had defended the Franco Regime. The words of this representative therefore could not hope for a respectful hearing from the Ukrainian SSR delegation.

An examination of the Temporary Commission's documents would show who was doing the undermining. The Chairman of the Commission had observed that it was the opinion of the Commission that the creation

/of a separate

of a separate government in Southern Korea would not further the aims
of the Assembly's Resolution of 14 November 1947, namely, independence
and the withdrawal of troops.   The Chairman had further said that
he had informed the Interim Committee that such a government would not
be the national government contemplated in the Assembly's Resolution.
Nevertheless, some delegations were now calling for support for a
draft resolution which said that the Government of Southern Korea
was representative of the Korean people.

Mr. Manuilsky wished to draw attention to another statement
concerning a violation of the Assembly Resolution of 14 November 1947.
In a meeting of the Temporary Commission on 20 August 1948, it was
made clear that negotiations which had been conducted with the
United States military authorities had not been directed towards the
withdrawal of troops.   There had been statements made against the
Assembly decision that troops should be withdrawn within ninety days
of the establishment of a government for Korea.   It was claimed
that a government had been established and then an attempt was made
to violate the Assembly decision that troops should be withdrawn
within ninety days.   The puppet Government of Southern Korea, which
was reminiscent of the Government of Manchuko, was induced to request
the United States troops to remain.   The procedure had been a farce
for only eighty-eight out of two hundred representatives in the
Interim Legislative Assembly had voted in favour and the others had
left the Assembly Chamber.   Furthermore, sixteen representatives of
the Korean Assembly had published a statement on 21 September concerning
occupying forces.   They had said that the decision of the Assembly
to ask the United States forces to remain was against the interests
of Korea and pointed out that never before in history had occupying
powers been asked to stay.

Despite the clear facts that the Assembly decision had been
violated, that the rights of the Korean people had been trampled upon,
and that even the Legislative Assembly had been unable to accept the
retention of occupying troops, the draft resolution stated that a
lawful government had been established in Southern Korea and controlled
that part in which the Commission had been able to observe.   It was
evident that this question and indeed, the entire resolution, was
connected with the unification of Northern and Southern Korea.   This
was one point upon which all political parties were in agreement,
for those of the Right and Centre as well as those of the Left stood
for unification.   The draft resolution suggested, however, that

The documents of the Temporary Commission recording the interview with Korean political leaders showed a unanimous request for self-determination.   The representative of Canada in the course of the interviews had asked the leader of a moderate party what would be the effect of separate elections upon the unification of the country. The answer had been given that the results would be most unfortunate and would lead to a division of Korea into two separate nations. The Chairman had then inquired what could improve the situation and the answer had been that if the Korean people were left alone, they could settle the matter but that it was hard to do so while intervention continued.   Clearly, the wish of the Korean people was to be left alone.   The resolution did not have this as its object.   Rather it would keep the United States forces there and send out a new Commission.

It had frequently been pointed out that the Temporary Commission had been unable to visit Northern Korea.   There was, however, the view that the Commission was a legal fiction.   Any government would wish to protect itself from the interference of a juridically baseless body which wanted to enter the country and carry out fictitious elections.

The new Commission which was proposed would serve to impede the unification of Korea and hinder the self-determination of the people. The functions of the new Commission were unclear.   It was said that it could supervise elections although it had been claimed that these had taken place.   Again it might exercise functions in Korea, as suggested by the Chairman of the Temporary Commission, which would be similar to those exercised under the Trusteeship System.   However, there was no decision to transform Korea into a non-self-governing territory.

The Ukrainian delegation had arrived at four principal conclusions. Firstly, the Temporary Commission had not really been an organ of the United Nations but only a tool of United States policy for the transformation of Korea into a colony of monopolistic capitalistic interests. Secondly, there had been no free elections held in Southern Korea. Thirdly, the so-called Government of Southern Korea comprised only puppets and their voices should not be heeded by the Assembly. Fourthly, the objects of the Commission which was now being proposed would be to maintain the existing division in Korea, to prevent the unification of the country, and preclude the principle of self-determination.   The Ukrainian delegation could not vote for the three-Power draft resolution as it was contrary to the Charter and ran counter

The CHAIRMAN said that they should settle the question of
their procedure.   Either they should discuss the resolution as a whole
or deal with each article individually but they should not conduct
both sorts of discussions.   If they were to discuss the resolution as
a whole, they would not be prevented from voting paragraph by paragraph
if this were desired.   As no amendment had been offered, there seemed
to be no need to proceed paragraph by paragraph.   The Chairman
therefore proposed that they discuss the resolution as a whole.   He
would call speakers to order if they diverged too much from the question
before them.

Mr. CASTRO (El Salvador) said his delegation supported the
three-Power draft resolution.   They hoped, however, that the
third paragraph which dealt with the withdrawal of troops would be
modified since the withdrawal ought not to take place until the Government
of Southern Korea had established its own armed forces.   There was an
army of about one hundred and seventy thousand in Northern Korea and
if the United States forces withdrew prematurely, it was clear that
this army would come down from the North and the tragedy of other
countries would be repeated.

The delegation of El Salvador had always been opposed to interference
in the internal affairs of states.   Accordingly, they had opposed the
imposition upon Spain of any decision concerning its own Government.
The USSR had intervened in Spain previously and the present regime
there had defeated the interests of the USSR.   The USSR was now trying
to regain its influence and the delegation of El Salvador would resist
any attempt at intervention.

The representative of the Ukraine had claimed that world public
opinion would support his views.   Mr. Castro believed however that
a majority in the First Committee were more representative of world
opinion that were any six countries.   The resolution which was adopted
by the Committee would show who was right.   El Salvador supported the
three-Power draft resolution and opposed that of the USSR.

Mr. MUGHIZ (Syria) said that the views of his delegation had
already been presented.   They believed that the United Nations should
continue to keep the Korean problem before them.   The three-Power
draft gave expression to the concern and the wishes of the majority.
It set forth the essential objective which was the unification of Korea.
The Syrian delegation therefore would support this resolution and would
oppose the USSR draft, firstly, because it criticized the Temporary

/Commission and

제2부 유엔총회 회의록(1948)

Commission and minimized its achievements and second, becuase it
failed to present any positive plan and only recommended the abolition
of the Temporary Commission.

Mr. MANUILSKY (Ukrainian Soviet Socialist Republic)said
he had hoped that the resolution would be considered point by point
but in view of the Chairman's ruling, he would now give his further
observations.   First of all, he would like to remark that the
representative of Syria was inconsistent in his opinions.   While in
Korea, he had not considered the elections which had been held to have
been valid.   Then in the First Committee, he had said that he
recognized the validity of these elections.   The theory seemed to
be that because the elections had in fact been held, they became lawful.
It was not clear however how elections which had not been legal acquired
legitimacy ex post facto.

It was also claimed that the Government in Southern Korea was
the Government of the whole and was representative of the Korean people.
The Ukrainian delegation held a different view.   They believed that
the Government which was based upon elections throughout the country
and in which 99 per cent of the people had participated was the real
Government.   The representative of the USSR had pointed out that
these elections had taken place not only in Northern Korea but also
clandestinely in Southern Korea.   The representative of the United
Kingdom had objected to this claim on the grounds that the representative
of the USSR was inconsistent when he said both that there had been
widespread terror and a universal secret election in Southern Korea.
Mr. Manuilsky pointed out that, despite the German terrorism during
the occupation of France and Belgium, the Resistance Movements had
found support and aid from all the people.   It could be assumed
that if the United Kingdom also had unfortunately been occupied by
the Nazis, the inhabitants would have resisted despite the terror
and carried on democratic activities and discovered the will of the
people through a plebiscite.

The representative of the United Kingdom had displayed photographs
purporting to show that the names of candidates were not always on
the ballots and that sometimes the names of members of the Temporary
Commission were on the ballots.   Mr. Manuilsky recalled that the
photograph of a famous protocol had proved to be a forgery and he
said that the photographs produced by the representative of the
United Kingdom were also forgeries.   The elections in Korea had been
held before the arrival of the Temporary Commission which showed

how clumsy had been the agents who prepared the photographs.   The
elections in Northern Korea had been conducted under conditions of
full freedom and secrecy.   On the other hand, the elections in
Southern Korea had been carried out under the terror regime, where
76 per cent of the population was excluded.   A government elected
in this manner could not be accepted even for Southern Korea.

MrMr. DULLES (United States of America) pointed out that
paragraph 2 of the joint draft resolution (A/C.1/426) had been carefully
worded to state only what was indisputably true and did not assert that
the present Government was in fact the Government of all Korea nor deny
that another regime existed in certain parts of Korea.   It was a
carefully drawn statement which had been considered very thoroughly
by the sponsors of the resolution and he thought it was responsive to
the thought expressed by the representative of New Zealand.

Referring to paragraph 3 and paragraph 4 (d), Mr. Dulles expressed
his belief that if the USSR would co-operate with these provisions for
an observed withdrawal of occupying forces, as he was prepared to pledge
that the United States would co-operate, one of the problems concerned
would be resolved and it would be practical to leave the situation in
the hands of the Government of the Republic of Korea.

Referring to paragraphs 4 (a) and (b), he stated the opinion that
the existence of a United Nations Commission in Korea, exercising the
function of good offices, would be able to supplement the efforts of the
Government of Korea and bring about the unification of Korea.

To fill in the blank left in paragraph 4 of the resolution, Mr. Dulles
suggested that the Commission should consist of the same Member States
as composed the present United Nations Temporary Commission on Korea.

Mr. KISSELEV (Byelorussian Soviet Socialist Republic) referring
to paragraph 3 of the joint draft resolution, asked Mr. Dulles to state
exactly when the armed forces of the United States would withdraw from
Southern Korea as desired by the Korean people and expressed the opinion
that this paragraph actually said nothing at all on this point.   It was
well-known that the withdrawal of USSR forces would be completed by
1 January 1949 and that no concealing manoeuvres were possible in this
connection.   The joint resolution stated that one of the tasks of the
Commission was to observe the actual withdrawal of the occupying forces
but no mention was made of when United States forces would be withdrawn
from Southern Korea.

Referring to paragraph 4, Mr. Kisselev asked what the functions of
the new Commission would be.   The Commission would be empowered to make
observations throughout Korea but the present Commission had not even
been able to make a serious report to the Political Committee; its
Rapporteur was forced to cover up the events which took place in Korea
during the elections by remaining silent in the face of the various
questions which had been directed at him.   The Temporary Commission had
only approved and supported the terroristic regime which prevailed in

/Southern Korea

Southern Korea during the elections, the facts of which could be seen
from the reports of the various press agencies which had representatives
there at the time. Such a policy did harm to the cause of Korean
independence. If the Commission had been politically responsible, it
would have reported that the elections in Southern Korea were far from
free. Free elections had already been held in Northern Korea and he
thus could not understand the functions of the new Commission.

He therefore thought that a new Commission would be completely useless
and that it would have no chance of solving the most important political
problem of Korea, which fell within the purview of the United States,
the United Kingdom, the USSR and China. For these reasons the Byelorussian
delegation would vote against the joint draft resolution.

Mr. ZEBROWSKI (Poland) thought that the joint resolution was
the direct consequence of the action taken by the Assembly at its
Second Session, which his delegation had considered was in violation of
the Charter and of international agreements concerning Korea. Being
mindful of its obligations under Article 2, Paragraph 5 of the Charter,
the Polish Government had as excellent a record as any Government for
implementing the decisions and recommendations of the United Nations and
had refrained from any action that was contrary to the spirit of the
Charter or to international agreements. Its objected to the Assembly's
resolution of 14 November 1947 because it was in violation of Article 107
of the Charter since the fate of Korea had been decided in the Potsdam
and Moscow Agreements.

In reply to the request of the Chairman at this point not to re-open
the general debate, Mr. Zebrowski pointed out that the new draft
resolution was based on the Assembly's resolution of 14 November 1947 and
that he must therefore deal with the latter. In his opinion the previous
Assembly resolution was contrary to the principles of the Charter,
particularly to the principle of self-determination mentioned in Article 2,
paragraph 2.

Referring to paragraph 1 of the joint resolution, he noted that he
had been the only member of the Committee who had even quoted
the report of the Temporary Commission and therefore he did not think it
was right for the Committee to approve automatically the conclusions of
the reports without any proper consideration.

He expressed the opinion that paragraph 3 of the joint resolution was
merely a smoke-screen to hide the fact that the occupation forces of the
USSR would be withdrawn by the end of 1948 while the Government of the
United States had evaded the request that its forces be withdrawn
dd
/simultaneously.

simultaneously. The wording "as early as practicable" was evasive
and meant that United States forces would remain in Korea as long as it
was suitable for the reactionary Government there, while the majority of
the people wished both occupying Powers to withdraw their forces.
Furthermore, the organization of armed forces by the United States in
Southern Korea, mentioned by the representative of El Salvador, would
perpetuate the division of Korea and was drawing the United Nations into
a new civil war. He warned the United Nations against aiding the United
States' attempts to interfere with the people of Asia.

Mr. RADIONOV (Union of Soviet Socialist Republic) said that
he saw no reason to dwell on the slanderous statement of the representative
of El Salvador since the policy of the USSR was well-known and the representative of the Ukrainian Soviet Socialist Republic had already replied.
In regard to the joint resolution, the USSR delegation considered that the
recommendations contained therein could not be reconciled with the
principles of the United Nations and had already expressed its view that
the Commission on Korea had been and would be used to conceal the
activities of the reactionary Government in Southern Korea and to split
Korea. In conclusion, Mr. Radionov stated that the USSR delegation
would not take part in any vote on the separate paragraphs of the joint
draft resolution and would vote against it as a whole.

Mr. MANUILSKY (Ukrainian Soviet Socialist Republic) declared
that his delegation would also refrain from taking part in a vote on the
joint resolution by paragraphs and would vote against the resolution
as a whole. Furthermore, his Government stood by its refusal to
participate in the activities of the Temporary Commission and would not
take part in any new Commission which might be set up.

Mr. ZEBROWSKI (Poland) stated that his delegation would join
in the procedure of voting announced by the USSR delegate.

A vote was taken by show of hands on the joint draft resolution submitted
by the delegations of Australia, China, and the United States of America
(A/C.1/426). The resolution was adopted by 41 votes to 6 with 2 abstentions.

Mr. DULLES (United States of America) asked whether the vote
which had just been taken included his suggestion for the membership of
the Commission and when the Chairman gave his opinion that a separate
vote was necessary, Mr. Dulles moved the addition of the following words
to fill the blank in paragraph 4 of the resolution: "consisting of the same
member States which composed the United Nations Temporary Commission on Korea.

Mr. PEARSON (Canada) said that he did not wish to oppose this motion but would like to reserve the right of his delegation to move an amendment on this matter when it was considered at a plenary meeting of the Assembly. His delegation had some doubts as to the practicability of a Commission consisting of 8 members, in effect, although there were 9 in theory.

Mr. DE LA TOURNELLE (France) thought it might be more desirable to leave the text as it had been adopted and allow the General Assembly to take a decision on the membership of the Commission at a plenary meeting. However, at the request of the representative of the United States, Mr. de la Tournelle agreed to accept the United States proposal on membership with the understanding that amendments could be proposed at the plenary meeting.

A vote was taken by show of hands on the United States proposal for the membership of the Commission, set out above. The proposal was adopted by 41 votes to none with 1 abstention.

The CHAIRMAN noted statements by the representatives of the Union of Soviet Socialist Republics, Ukrainian Soviet Socialist Republic, Poland, Byelorussian Soviet Socialist Republic, Czechoslovakia and Yugoslavia that they did not take part in the vote.

A vote was taken by show of hands on the draft resolution submitted by the USSR delegation (A/C.1/427/Corr.1). It was rejected by 42 votes to 6 with 3 abstentions.

The CHAIRMAN noted that the work of the First Committee for the Third Session of the General Assembly had been completed. He expressed his thanks to Mr. Costa du Rels, the Vice-Chairman, who had aided the work of the Committee so much during the Chairman's absence. On behalf of the Committee, he sincerely thanked the Secretary of the Committee, who had given the Chair very valuable support and aid during the many long meetings, and he also added his thanks to the members of the Secretariat of the Committee and to all the members of the staff who had helped in the Committee's work.

Mr. GORDON WALKER (United Kingdom) pointed out that the First Committee still had the question of disposal of the former Italian Colonies on its agenda and had not therefore completed its business. When the Chairman replied that the question of the former Italian colonies was not on the agenda for the present meeting and that there were no further meetings of the First Committee scheduled for the present session,

/Mr. Tomlinson

Mr. Tomlinson said he would like to reserve any rights which his delegation might have in this matter. He did not think that the mere fact that further meetings were not fixed was necessarily decisive.

Mr. DULLES (United States of America) wished to express the appreciation of the Committee for the work of the officers of the Committee as well as the members of the staff. He thought the Committee had done a task which had thrown a very heavy burden on all those who served it.

Mr. MEDHEN (Ethiopia) reserved the position of his delegation on the question of consideration of the item on the former Italian colonies.

Mr. STEPHEN (Haiti) recalled that the General Assembly had rejected the recommendation of the General Committee to refer the question of the former Italian colonies to the <u>Ad Hoc</u> Committee and had resolved that this question should be deferred until the second part of the Third Session. He therefore, did not think the Committee should return to this question. He also wished to associate himself with the tributes paid to the work of the officers of the Committee and to the Secretariat.

<u>The meeting rose at 22.48 hours.</u>

(9) 제3차 유엔총회 제1위원회 : 한국 독립문제에 관한 유엔총회 소총회에 제출된 유엔한국임시위원단 보고서

해제문서 17 : A/C.1/366 (Third Session, First Committee, The Problem of The Independence of Korea: Reports of The United Nations Temporary Commission on Korea and of The Interim Committee of The General Assembly)[4]

문서명	Third Session, First Committee, The Problem of the Independence of Korea: Reports of the United Nations Temporary Commission on Korea and of the Interim Committee of the General Assembly		
	제3차 유엔총회 제1위원회 : 한국 독립문제에 대한 유엔한국임시위원단과 유엔총회 소총회 회의 보고		
발신		생성일시	1948년 11월 4일
		발신일시	
수신		수신일시	
		문서번호	A/C.1/366
문서형태	보고서	문서분량	2쪽
주제명	북한의 한국 문제 관련 유엔총회 참석 문제		
주요내용	1948년 10월 8일자로 조선민주주의인민공화국(the Democratic Peoples's Republic of Korea) 외무상(Minister of Foreign Affairs)이 유엔사무총장에게 보낸 전보. 상세한 내용은 본문 참조.		
검색어	조선민주주의인민공화국(the Democratic Peoples's Republic of Korea), 외무상(Minister of Foreign Affairs), 박헌영		

4　이하의 문서는 박헌영이 10월 7일자로 유엔 사무총장에게, 10월 9일자로 유엔총회 제3차 회의 의장에게 보낸 동일한 전문의 내용이다. 유엔 사무총장이 제3차 유엔총회 제1위원회 에서 한국문제를 다룰 때 이를 회람할 것을 약속했고, 아래 문서는 그 회람 회의에 관한 회 의록이다. 이정박헌영전집편집위원회, 『박헌영전집』 9권, 역사비평사, 412~413쪽.

1948년 10월 8일자로 조선민주주의인민공화국(the Democratic Peoples's Republic of Korea) 외무상(Minister of Foreign Affairs)이 유엔사무총장에게 보낸 전보.

1948년 10월 7일 평양

조선민주주의인민공화국 내각 외무상으로서 각하에게 질의함. 조선(Korea)이 연합국 군대에 의해서 해방된 후 많은 역사적 변화를 겪었으며, 이러한 변화는 주권 국가를 급속히 세워서 경제, 문화적 재건과 국가의 주권을 회복하고자 한 조선인민들의 투쟁의 결과임.

우리는 남북한을 아울러 1948년 8월에 선거를 치렀으며 남북한 선거인의 85.2%가 참가하였음. 이 선거는 자유롭고 합법적인 인민 의지의 표현이며, 통일 투쟁을 위한 인민의 힘과 결단력을 세계에 보여준 것임.

최고인민회의와 내각 등 최고 입법 기구와 최고 집행기구가 이 선거에 기초해 세워졌으며, 여기에는 모든 주요 정당들과 사회단체들, 전 사회계층이 망라되어 있음. 내각의 위임을 받아 조선민주주의인민공화국 대표가 한국문제에 대한 유엔 총회 회의에 참가할 수 있도록 조정해줄 것을 요청함.

각 국가의 문제는 해당 국가의 합법적 대표들의 참가 하에 논의되고 조정되어야만 한다는 원칙을 거부할 수는 없을 것이라고 믿고 있음.

박헌영(PAK NUN YUNG)[5], 조선민주주의인민공화국 외무상

---

5   원문에는 PAK NUN YUNG으로 표기되어 있으나, 이는 박헌영의 전문(電文)상의 오기인 것으로 보인다. 조선민주주의인민공화국의 제1대 외무상 (1948년 9월 2일~1953년 8월)이 박헌영이고 내각을 대표하여 유엔사무총장에게 공식 요청 전문을 보낼 수 있는 위치에 있던 인물은 1948년 당시 부수상 겸 외무상을 지낸 박헌영이라는 점에서 합리적 추정으로 판단되기 때문이다.

Dual_Distribution

Third session

First Committee

THE PROBLEM OF THE INDEPENDENCE OF KOREA: REPORTS OF THE UNITED NATIONS
TEMPORARY COMMISSION ON KOREA AND OF THE INTERIM COMMITTEE OF THE
GENERAL ASSEMBLY

Cable dated 8 October 1948 from the Minister of Foreign Affairs of
the Democratic People's Republic of Korea to the Secretary-General

PYENGYANG, 7 OCTOBER 1948

ON BEHALF OF MY GOVERNMENT I, MINISTER OF FOREIGN AFFAIRS OF THE
DEMOCRATIC PEOPLE'S REPUBLIC OF KOREA, HAVE THE HONOUR OF ASKING YOUR
EXCELLENCY AS FOLLOWS:

SINCE KOREA'S LIBERATION FROM THE YOKE OF LONG COLONIAL OPPRESSION OF
JAPANESE IMPERIALISM BY THE ARMS OF THE ALLIES, CHANGES OF GREAT HISTORIC
SIGNIFICANCE HAVE TAKEN PLACE IN OUR COUNTRY. THESE CHANGES ARE THE RESULT
OF THE KOREAN PEOPLE'S STRUGGLE FOR THE RESTORATION OF ECONOMY, CULTURE,
AND SOVEREIGNTY OF THEIR NATION IN ORDER TO RAPIDLY ESTABLISH KVA* SOVEREIGN
STATE WHICH HAD BEEN THE TARGET OF OUR SANGUINARY STRUGGLES AGAINST THE
JAPANESE INVADERS FOR AS LONG AS FORTY YEARS. WE CARRIED OUT IN AUGUST 1948
GENERAL ELECTIONS THROUGHOUT NORTH AND SOUTH KOREA IN WHICH 85.2 PER CENT
OF THE ENTIRE ELECTORATES OF NORTH AND SOUTH KOREA TOOK PART. THESE
ELECTIONS WERE THE FREE AND LAWFUL EXPRESSION OF THE WILL OF OUR PEOPLE.
AT THE SAME TIME THE ELECTIONS HAVE SHOWN TO THE WHOLE WORLD THE STRENGTH AND
DETERMINATION OF OUR PEOPLE IN OUR STRUGGLE FOR THE UNITY OF THE COUNTRY.
ON THE BASIS OF THESE ELECTIONS THE HIGHEST LEGISLATIVE ORGAN AND THE HIGHEST
EXECUTIVE ORGAN, i.e. THE SUPREME PEOPLE'S ASSEMBLY AND THE UNITED GOVERNMENT
OF THE DEMOCRATIC PEOPLE'S REPUBLIC OF KOREA, WHICH HAD BEEN A LONG
CHERISHED DESIRE OF OUR PEOPLE HAVE BEEN ESTABLISHED. THEY CONSIST OF THE
REPRESENTATIVES OF ALL THE MAIN POLITICAL PARTIES AND SOCIAL ORGANIZATIONS AS
WELL AS OF ALL THE STRATA OF THE PEOPLE WITH VARIOUS POLITICAL VIEWS IN NORTH
AND SOUTH KOREA.

/IN VIEW OF

———————
* Subject to correction

IN VIEW OF THESE FACTS AS MENTIONED ABOVE, GOVERNMENT OF THE
DEMOCRATIC PEOPLE'S REPUBLIC OF KOREA ENTRUSTED ME WITH THE MATTER OF ASKING
YOUR EXCELLENCY SECRETARY-GENERAL TO ARRANGE FOR THE REPRESENTATIVES OF THE
GOVERNMENT OF THE DEMOCRATIC PEOPLE'S REPUBLIC OF KOREA THE POSSIBILITY
OF PARTICIPATING IN THE DISCUSSION OF KOREA PROBLEM AT THE SESSION OF THE
UN GENERAL ASSEMBLY.   WE FIRMLY BELIEVE THAT THERE WILL BE NOBODY WHO CAN
REJECT THE PRINCIPLE THAT PROBLEMS OF EACH NATION MUST BE CONSIDERED AND
SETTLED WITH THE PARTICIPATION OF LAWFUL REPRESENTATIVES OF THE SAME NATION.
I HOPE THAT YOUR EXCELLENCY SECRETARY-GENERAL WILL NOT REFUSE THE ABOVE-
MENTIONED REQUEST OF THE GOVERNMENT OF THE DEMOCRATIC PEOPLE'S REPUBLIC OF
KOREA AND WILL LET ME KNOW OF YOUR DECISION.

SINCERELY YOURS

PAK NUN YUNG
MINISTER OF FOREIGN AFFAIRS OF
THE DEMOCRATIC PEOPLE'S
REPUBLIC OF KOREA
PYENGYANG KOREA

- - - - -

3. 유엔 사무총장 보고서

유엔 사무총장의 연례활동 보고서(1947.7.1~1948.6.30)

해제문서 18 : A/565 (Annual Report of The Secretary-General on The Work of The Organization 1 July 1947-30 June 1948)

문서명	Annual Report of the Secretary-General on the Work of the Organization 1 July 1947-30 June 1948		
	유엔 사무총장의 연례 활동보고서 (1947.7.1~1948.6.30)		
발신	유엔 사무총장	생성일시	1948
		발신일시	1948
수신		수신일시	
		문서번호	Official Records: Third Session Supplement No.1 (A/565)
문서형태	보고서	문서분량	153쪽
주제명	한국의 독립문제		
주요내용	1948년 뉴욕 레이크 석세스(Lake Success)에서 발간된 보고서로, 1947년 7월 1일부터 1948년 6월 30일까지 1년간의 유엔 활동에 대해 주제 별로 요약한 내용이 기술되어 있음. 한국 독립문제는 "Ⅰ.정치안보문제" 가운데 J항(The problem of the independence of Korea)으로 정리되어 있음. 상세한 내용은 본문 참조.		
검색어	유엔한국임시위원단, 미소공동위원회, 모스크바 3상회의, 남한정부, 유엔총회 소총회 , 분과위원회, 주한미군사령관, 총선거		

<h1 align="center">〈구성 및 개요〉</h1>

Ⅰ. 정치안보문제

파키스탄, 그리스, 이집트, 인도네시아의 정치안보문제와 관련된 유엔의 활동 및 토의 등이 주요 내용임. 여기에 특히 한국 독립문제에 관한 내용이 언급되어 있으며, 독립 직후 유엔한국임시위원단의 설치로부터 이 위원단이 시도한 소련, 우크라이나, 북한 정권과의 협상 노력을 설명하고 위원단이 남한에서 대통령 선거를 성공적으로 이끌어냈다고 서술함. 또한 이 선거의 영향력이 현재 소련 점령군의 존재로 인해 북한까지는 미치지 못했다는 것, 이는 강대국 간의 영향력 경쟁에서 비롯된 것이라고 말함.

Ⅱ. 경제사회문제

당시 세계 경제의 동향과 지역 경제에 대한 내용, 국제 무역이나 개발도상국의 경제발전 등 세계 경제의 전반적인 내용들을 다루고 있으며 인권이나 복지, 마약 유통 및 인구 변화와 같은 사회문제도 전 세계적인 관점에서 다룸.

Ⅲ. 신탁통치 및 비(非) 자치지역 문제

유엔의 신탁통치제도에 관한 문제와 관련된 논의를 비롯하여 신탁통치제도의 확대 및 운용에 관한 내용, 비 자치지역에 관한 전반적인 정보와 그 지역 내에서 실시되고 있는 제반 개발 문제에 관한 내용이 기술되어 있음.

Ⅳ. 법률문제

국제사법재판소의 설립과 그 역할, 국제법의 개발 및 체계화에 관한 논의가 주된 내용임.

Ⅴ. 유엔에 대한 대중의 이해

유엔에 대한 대중의 이해에 관한 전반적인 의견 교환과 대중의 이해를 제고하기 위한 방법 등에 관한 논의.

Ⅵ. 유엔 조직, 행정 및 재정

유엔 사무국의 조직과 구조, 사무국 운영, 뉴욕 유엔본부 건설, 그리고 유엔의 재정 등 유엔 내부의 행정문제에 관한 내용.

I. 정치안보문제

(중략)

J. 한국 독립문제
(The problem of the independence of Korea)

〈목차〉

(a) 제2차 본회의에서 논의된 총회의 검토사항

(b) 유엔한국임시위원단의 조직

(c) 소련, 우크라이나, 북한정권과의 접촉

(d) 유엔총회 소총회와의 협의

(e) 소총회의 건의에 대한 임시위원단의 결정

(f) 분과위원회의 임무(자유로운 선거분위기, 선거법, 구술 청취)

(g) 선거 감시

(h) 총회 제출을 위한 임시위원단의 보고서 작성

(a) 제2차 본회의에서 논의된 총회의 검토사항

1947년 8월에 열린 미소공동위원회에서 소련과의 협의가 결렬 된 후 미국은 1947년 9월 17일 한국 독립에 관한 문제를 유엔총회 제2차 본회의 의제로 상정하자는 의견을 제시함.

같은 해 9월 23일 총회는 이 문제를 본회의 의제로 채택하기로 하고 제1위원회(First Committee)에 이 문제에 대한 조사와 보고를 맡기기로 결정함. 제1위원회는 1947년 10월 28일부터 11월 1일까지 회의를 속개하고 한국의 독립문제에 관해 논의함.

10월 17일 미국 대표는 점령당사국은 자국 관리하의 지역에서 유엔 감시하에 늦어도 1948년 3월 31일까지 선거를 실시해야 한다는 내용의 제안과 대강의 결의안 초안을 제출함. 또한 이 결의안 초안은 한국 군대의 자립과 점령당국과의 협상에 의해 한국 내 미군과 소련군의 완전한 철수를 실시할 수 있는 '한국 정부'의 수립이 필요하다고 제안함.

한국 문제를 처리할 유엔한국임시위원단이 조직됨. 이 위원단은 첫째 한반도 전체를 감독하고 이동할 권한을 보유하고 선거기간 동안 각자 맡은 지역에 상주해야 하며, 둘째 선거와 관련된 협의, 국회 구성에 관한 협의, 중앙정부 조직에 관한 협의, 점령국 군대의 철수에 관한 협의 과정에 참여할 수 있어야 한다고 함.

1947년 10월 28일에 열린 제1위원회 회의에서 두 가지 문제가 제기되었으며, 첫째는 선거에 의해 선출된 한국 대표들의 총회 참석에 관한 것이고, 둘째는 한반도에 주둔한 소련군과 미군의 철수에 관한 문제임. 소련 및 소련을 지지하는 국가 대표들은 한국 문제는 유엔 관할권 밖의 문제이며 미국이 모스크바 3상회의 결정을 위반했음에도 불구하고 협상 결렬에 대한 책임을 전부 소련에게 전가하고 있다고 말함. 또 오히려 미국이 한반도에서 진정한 민주주의 국가의 탄생을 가로막고 있다고 비난하고 한국 문제를 해결할 수 있는 다른 결의안을 제출할 것이라고 함. 선거실시에 앞서 먼저 점령군의 철수가 이루어져야 한다고 주장하는 한편, 한국정부의 수립은 전적으로 한국 국민 자신의 손에 의해 이루어져야 한다는 견해를 밝힘. 그러나 점령군의 철수가 선거 실시 후에 이루어져야한다는 본래의 견해는 제1위원회의 대다수 구성원에 의해서 고수됨.

한국 대표의 유엔총회 참석 문제에 대해 백러시아 사회주의공화국은 한국 대표가 제1위원회 회의 및 유엔 총회에도 참석해야 한다는 내용의 개정안을 제출했으나, 1947년 10월 30일 제1위원회는 한국 대표와의 협의는 한국 내에서 유엔한국임시위원단과 이루어져야 한다는 결정을 내림. 이러한 결정으로 인해 소련과 다른 5개국 대표들은 미국 제안에 대한 표결에서 기권을 표명함. 소련은 한국 대표를 유엔총회에 참석시키자는 자신들의 제안이 받아들여지지 않았다는 이유로 유엔한국임시위원단의 활동에 일체 참여하지 않겠다고 말함. 제92차 회의에서 미국 대표는 개정된 결의안 초안을 제출했고 11월 5일에 찬성 46표, 반대 0, 기권 4표로 통과됨. 그 후 우크라이나 대표는 한국 대표의 참석이 거부되었다는 이유로 유엔한국임시위원단 활동에 참여하지 않겠다는 의사를 표명함.

유엔 총회는 제1위원회의 보고를 토대로 1947년 11월 13일, 14일에 한국의 독립문제에 관해 토의함. 제1위원회에 상정된 결의안은 개정 없이 찬성 43표, 기권 6표(백러시아, 체코, 폴란드, 우크라이나, 소련, 유고슬라비아)로 1947년 11월 14일에 통과됨. 결의안의 주요 내용은 첫째, 유엔한국임시위원단은 호주, 캐나다, 중국, 엘살바도르, 프랑스, 인도, 필리핀, 시리아, 그리고 우크라이나 대표로 구성되며 둘째, 위원단은 한국의 독립과 자유에 대하여 논의할 수 있으며 중앙정부를 수립할 수 있는 대표를 뽑는 선거는 늦어도 1948년 3월 31일 이전에 실시되어야 하며 셋째, 선거 후 최대한 빠른 시일 내에 국회를 소집하고 중앙정부를 설립한 후 임시위원단에 통보하고 넷째, 중앙정부 수립 과정에서 국방의 자립을 도모하고 남북한에 있는 기존 정부는 권력을 이양하고, 그리고 점령당국의 군대 철수문제를 임시위원단과 협의하며 다섯째, 임시위원단은 이 결의안에 대해 유엔총회 소총회(interim committee)와 협의할 수 있으며, 마지막으로 회원국들은 임시위원단이 자신의 목표를 모두 달성할 수 있도록 지원해야 한다는 내용임.

제1위원회 결의안이 통과된 후 총회에서는 1948년 초에 소련, 미국 양국 군대가 한국으로부터 동시에 철수하자는 내용의 소련 측 결의안 초안을 표결에 회부했으며 반대 33표, 찬성 7표, 기권 16표로 기각됨.

(b) 유엔한국임시위원단의 조직

유엔한국임시위원단의 첫 번째 회의가 1948년 1월 12일에 개최됨. 인도 대표가 첫 임시 대표로 선출되었고, 2월 4일에 정식대표로 추대됨. 인도 대표가 서울을 떠난 후 위원단 의장을 15일마다 한 사람씩 돌아가며 맡는 방식으로 변경됨. 위원단은 분과위원회와 기타 부속기구를 설치함.

(c) 소련, 우크라이나, 북한군정과의 접촉

1948년 1월 13일 임시위원단은 위원단 활동이 남한뿐만 아니라 한반도 전역에 걸쳐 이루어져야 한다는 호주 대표의 제안을 명시하는 결의안 초안을 채택하였으며, 1월 16일에는 미국과 소련 양국의 점령군 사령관에게 임시위원단 대표의 방문 의사를 밝히는 서한을 보내기로 함. 1월 19일 남한의 미군정사령관은 이에 대한 답장을 보냈으며 다음날 위원단 대표가 사령관을 예방함. 북한의 소련군 사령관에게서는 회신이 오지 않음.

임시위원단은 유엔 사무총장에게 남북한 사령관 간의 대화를 촉구하는 내용의 의사를 소련대표에게 전달해달라고 요청했으나 1948년 1월 22일 소련대표는 임시위원단 조직 당시의 경위를 들어 부정적 태도를 나타냄. 같은 날 위원단은 소련대표에게 '회원국들은 임시위원단이 자신들의 목표를 달성할 수 있도록 지원해야 한다'고 하는 제2결의안 6조의 내용을 상기시켜 줄 것을 사무총장에게 요청함.

우크라이나의 불참에 대해 유감을 표하고 우크라이나의 임시위원단 참여의 중요성을 강조한 시리아 측 결의안이 통과되었으나 1948년 1월 25일 우크라이나 정부는 제2차 총회에서와 마찬가지로 불참의사를 밝힘.

북한지역 출입 승인을 포함한 유엔한국임시위원단 문서가 평양에 도착했으나, 소련 당국이 이를 거절했다는 사무국의 보고에 대해 임시위원단은 1948년 2월 6일 북한 군정당국의 비협조적 태도에 대한 유감성명을 발표함.

(d) 유엔총회 소총회(Interim Committee of the General Assembly)와의 협의

1947년 11월 14일 총회에서 채택된 결의안을 이행하기 위해 파견된 위원단이 북한지역에 출입하지 못하는 문제에 대해 1948년 2월 6일 유엔총회 소총회와 상세한 토론을 거친 후 위원단은 다음과 같은 결의안을 통과시킴. 첫째 1947년 11월 14일에 총회에서 채택된 결의안은 소련의 비협조적인 태도로 인하여 소련군이 점령하고 있는 지역에서는 이행할 수가 없음. 둘째 위원단은 발전적 견지에서 유엔총회 소총회와 협의할 것이며 소총회가 이 문제의 해결책을 강구하는 동안 의장이 위원단을 대표하기로 함.

2월 11일 위원단은 첫째 이 결의안의 이행이 미군 점령지역에서는 가능한가, 또 이는 위원단의 의무인지 만약 아니라면 위원단은 자유로운 선거 분위기 속에서 선거가 이루어질 수 있는지를 감독해야 하는 것인가, 또 위원단이 목적을 이루기 위해 다른 방안을 이용해도 되는가라는 문제에 대해 소총회와 협의하겠다고 함.

소총회는 이러한 문제에 대한 답을 찾기 위해 여섯 번의 회합을 가졌으며 자신들에게 주어진 권한이 부족하므로 한국 독립에 관한 문제로 들어가기 전에 이 질문에만 답하기로 함.

1948년 2월 19일 임시위원단 대표는 한국의 정치상황과 위원들의 의견에 대해 자세히 발표하고 임시위원단은 다음 조치들 중 한 가지를 채택할 필요가 있다고 말함. 1) 오직 남한 지역에서의 선거와 중앙정부 수립만을 감찰 2) 한국 대표들과 협의된 제한된 목적을 달성하기 위한 선거 감시 3) 임무가 실행될 수 없음을 밝히고 총회에 권한을 반납. 그러나 소총회는 이러한 해결책이 위원단 내부에서 이미 만장일치로 거부되었음을 밝히고 소총회는 오직 총회에 대해서만 제안을 할 수 있기 때문에 다음과 같이 제안함. 1) 위원단 대표의 제안에 대해 고민해 보고 다음 정기회의 때까지 결론을 내릴 것 2) 중앙정부 형태가 아닌, 행정적인 업무나 자신들의 입장을 점령국과 유엔에 전달하는 정부를 수립하기 위한 남한 지역만의 선거를 하자는 제안 3) 원래의 결의안을 개정하여 두 강대국 대표들의 참여를 확실히 보장할 수 있는 특별회의 소집을 제안함.

그러나 현재의 상황은 남북한 공동선거에 의한 정부 수립이 불가능하며, 남한에서의 선거는 가능하지만 이 또한 유엔 총회 결의안의 취지에 반(反)하는 내용이라는 사실에 대부분의 소총회 위원들도 동의하고 있음.

1948년 2월 26일 소총회는 위원단의 질의에 찬성 33표, 반대 2표, 기권 11표로 '유엔한국임시위원단은 1947년 11월 14일 유엔총회에서 채택된 결의안에 따라 위원단이 출입할 수 있는 지역에 한해서 결의안 II에 명시된 프로그램을 실행할 의무를 지닌다'는 것을 확인함.

1948년 3월에 소총회 대표는 유엔한국임시위원단 대표에게 위원단의 질문에 대한 답변과 위원단 결의안에 대해 다음과 같은 견해의 서한을 보냄.

1. 소총회가 확인한 결과 남한의 미군정은 결의안에 명시된 한국에서의 선거가 집회, 언론, 출판의 자유가 허용되는 자유로운 분위기에서 이루어지고 있는지를 감찰하는 임시위원단의 활동에 무한한 협조를 할 것이라고 함.

2. 한국의 국회 대표들과 유엔한국임시위원단의 협의가 자유롭게 이루어져야 하며, 이를 통해 한국 국회의원들은 모든 한국인들의 국정 참여를 이끌어내고 한반도의 통일을 위한 최대한의 평화적 노력과 설득을 시도할 것이라고 말함.

3. 소총회는 유엔한국임시위원단은 자신들이 원하고 상황이 허락할 때 언제든 자신들의 의무를 이행할 권리를 갖고 있다고 말함.

(e) 소총회의 결의에 대한 유엔한국임시위원단의 결정

2월 26일의 소총회의 결의안 채택에 따라, 위원단 의장 및 캐나다 대표의 부재 가운데 현재 서울에 있는 임시위원단 대표들은 비공식 회의를 갖고 유엔한국임시위원단은 위원단이 접근 가능한 한반도의 지역에 한정하여, 늦어도 1948년 5월 10일까지는 선거가 실시되는 것을 감독하겠다는 성명을 발표함. 심도 있는 토론을 거친 후 1948년 3월 12일, 마침내 임시위원단은 주한미군 총사령관이 발표한 1948년 5월 9일에 열릴 선거가 집회, 언론, 출판의 자유가 허용되는 자유로운 환경에서 이루어지는지를 감독하겠다는 내용의 결의안을 발표함.

(f) 분과위원회의 임무(자유로운 선거분위기, 선거법, 구술 청취)

유엔임시위원단은 선거 준비를 위해 일해 왔으며 그 중 많은 부분이 다음과 같이 3개 분과위원회와 여타의 산하 조직들을 통해 처리됨.

첫째 제1분과위원회는 주로 자유로운 선거분위기 조성을 위한 임무를 담당했으며 이와 같은 분위기 조성에 필요한 기본 조건으로 '언론의 자유, 출판 및 정보의 자유, 집회결사의 자유, 이전의 자유, 임의적인 체포와 구금으로부터의 보호, 폭력 및 폭력에 대한 위협으로부터의 보호' 등을 규정함. 이 위원회는 이와 같이 임시위원단이 정한 자유로운 선거의 전제조건에 관한 기준을 주한미군 총사령관에게 제시했고 그 결과 1948년 4월 8일 총사령관은 '한국 국민의 권리에 관한 선언문' 사본을 위원단에 전달함. 4월 5일에 공표된 이 선언에는 일반적인 민주주의 국가에 널리 확산되어 있는 헌법상의 권리와 자유가 포함되어 있음. 제1분과위원회는 또한 정치범 사면에 대한 위원단의 권고를 주한미군 총사령관에게 전달했고, 3월 31일 군정장관이 3,140명을 사면함으로써 이들은 시민권과 투표권을 완전히 회복하였으며 본인이 원할 경우 후보자 등록도

가능하도록 함.

둘째 제2분과위원회는 다양한 경로로 유입된 문서들을 검토하고 한국의 요인들의 성명을 수집하여 위원단이 임무를 수행하는 데에 유용하게 쓰일 정보를 정리하는 임무를 담당함. 이렇게 수집된 정보는 임시위원단 대표에게 전달되었으며 유엔총회 소총회와의 협의 과정에서 유용하게 사용됨.

셋째 제3분과위원회는 남북한 선거법 및 규정을 검토하고 한국과 소련 및 미국인 관료들과 전문가들의 견해를 파악하는 임무를 담당함. 이 위원회는 북한이나 소련 전문가들과는 협의할 수도, 정보를 얻을 수도 없었지만 북한의 라디오 방송을 통해 남한 선거법에 대한 북한 고위층의 비판을 들을 수 있었음. 또한 제3분과위원회는 자신들의 권고의 목적은 성인 투표권, 무기명 투표의 비밀유지, 한국 내 각 선거구의 대표권, 인구비례에 따른 선거원칙, 그리고 민의의 표현을 최대한으로 발현시키는 총회 결의안에 더욱 충실한 임시위원단의 선거 준비 감독을 위한 것이라고 설명함.

(g) 선거 감시

3월 30일 선거관리위원회는 선거 날짜를 5월 9일에서 5월24일로 연기하고 싶다고 요청했으나 임시위원단은 심사숙고 끝에 자신들은 선거일을 5월 9일로 유지하고자 한다는 의사를 사령관에게 전달함. 4월 2일 사령관은 서신을 보내, 선거는 5월 9일에 그대로 진행될 것이라고 말함. 그러나 위원단은 사령관의 요청을 받아들여 선거날짜를 하루 연기한 1948년 5월 10일에 실시하기로 결정함. 1948년 4월 29일 위원단은 중국 대표가 발표한 '남한에는 집회, 언론, 출판의 자유가 허용되는 자유로운 환경이 조성되어 있다'는 결의안의 내용을 채택하였으며 위원단은 사령관이 발표한 1948년 5월 10일 선거에 대한 감독을 실시할 것이라고 발표함.

1948년 3월 20일, 위원단은 현재의 각 분과위원회 임무를 그대로 유지한 채, 하나로 통합하여 중앙위원회를 만들고 이들에게 서울의 중앙 선거관리위원회와 지속적으로 연락을 취하면서 불평불만을 접수하여 이를 검토하며 선거 실시와 관련된 각종 정보를 교환하고 자유로운 선거를 위한 분위기를 파악하고 검토하는 임무를 맡게 함.

또한 선거감찰을 세 단계로 나누어 실시할 것이라고 하여 이를 선거(유권자)등록 기간, 후보자 등록 기간, 선거당일 및 전후의 세 단계로 구분함.

첫째, 선거등록 기간인 4월 5일부터 10일까지의 첫 번째 단계에서는 세 그룹의 선거감시단을 9개의 도(道)와 서울로 각각 파견하여 그들로 하여금 선거등록 현황을 파악하고 선거등록 장소를 방문해서 등록 진행 상황을 직접 확인하게 함. 아울러 선거를 위한 자유로운 분위기가 존재하는지에 대한 심도 있는 조사활동도 빠뜨리지 않음.

둘째, 4월 19일부터 24일에 걸친 두 번째 단계는 후보자 등록이 끝난 3일 뒤에 시작됨. 임시위원단과 사무국은 네 개의 그룹으로 나뉘어 서울을 포함한 모든 지방을 돌아다니며 등록에 대한 상세하고 최종적인 정보를 수집했으며 대체로 90%이상 어떤 곳은 100% 목표달성을 한 곳도 있음을 확인함.

셋째, 선거 당일에 집중된 세 번째 기간의 감찰은 5월 7일부터 5월 11일에 걸쳐 진행됨. 임시위원단과 사무국은 9개의 선거감시단으로 나뉘어 서울을 포함한 남한의 각 도(道)를 돌아다녔으며 세 부문에 걸친 감찰을 실시함. 첫 번째는 투표소 설치를 참관하고 선거 방해 움직임이 있는지를 조사함. 두 번째는 5월 10일 선거 당일, 수백 곳의 투표소를 돌아다니며 실제로 진행되고 있는 투표상황을 참관함. 마지막으로 투표 당일 밤과 이튿날, 각지에서 투표함 개봉과 개표 현황을 지켜봄.

(h) 유엔총회에 제출하기 위한 임시위원단의 보고서 작성

1948년 5월 1일 임시위원단은 다음과 같은 시리아 대표의 결의안을 수리함.

1. 현 상황에서는 예비 결론을 내리는 것이 바람직하고 선거를 포함한 지금 까지의 상황을 담은 총회 제출용 보고서의 첫 부분을 준비해야 한다.

2. 이 작업에 집중하기 위해 서울이 아닌 다른 곳으로 가는 것이 바람직하다.

3. 5월 15일 동경으로 이동하여 지금까지의 활동을 기록한 보고서를 작성한다.

4. 6월 첫째 주에 서울로 돌아온다.

1948년 5월 12일, 위원단은 동경으로 이동하자는 결정을 재고하여 5월 18일 전에 상하이로 떠나 6월 첫째 주에 돌아오는 내용의 결의안을 통과시킴. 상하이에 체류한 5월 18일부터 6월 7일 사이에 위원단은 총회에 제출할 처음 다섯개의 장(chapter)으로 구성된 보고서를 첨부문서 목록과 함께 작성함.

6월 7일 위원단은 서울로 돌아왔고 6월 10일에는 1947년 11월 14일 유엔 총회에서 채택된 결의안에 명기된 바의 협의가 이제 가능하다는 내용을 당선된 대표에게 전달함. 6월 25일 위원단은 1948년 5월 10일에 실시된 무기명 투표는 위원단의 출입이 가능하고 한반도 전체 인구의 3분의 2가 살고 있는 지역 유권자들의 자유로운 의사의 표현이라는 견해를 기록하기로 결의함.

UNITED NATIONS

ANNUAL REPORT OF THE SECRETARY-GENERAL ON THE WORK OF THE ORGANIZATION

1 JULY 1947-30 JUNE 1948

GENERAL ASSEMBLY

OFFICIAL RECORDS : THIRD SESSION

SUPPLEMENT No. 1 (A/565)

LAKE SUCCESS, NEW YORK, 1948

(152 p.)

UNITED NATIONS

ANNUAL REPORT OF
THE SECRETARY-GENERAL
ON THE
WORK OF THE ORGANIZATION
1 JULY 1947-30 JUNE 1948

GENERAL ASSEMBLY

OFFICIAL RECORDS : THIRD SESSION

SUPPLEMENT No. 1 (A/565)

LAKE SUCCESS, NEW YORK, 1948

Contents

Introduction

This is my third report as Secretary-General of the United Nations.

That historic day, 26 June 1945, when representatives of fifty nations signed the Charter at San Francisco, came not a moment too soon.

The wartime alliance from which the United Nations was born started to pull apart all too quickly and, had the establishment of the United Nations been delayed even a few months, the Organization might never have been created. But today, the peoples of the world possess a world law—the Charter, machinery for constructive co-operation—the Organization, and a flag—the United Nations flag—under which they have a good chance to maintain a lasting peace and build a world that is fit for all men to live in.

UNITED NATIONS CHIEF FORCE HOLDING WORLD TOGETHER

A great deal has been said to the effect that the United Nations was based on the assumption of agreement among the great Powers, that it was not created to make peace but to keep it after it was made, and that in general the Organization has been submitted to strains it was not equipped to bear.

However true this may be, I believe it is time to think of the United Nations in other terms than of an infant which must be protected from the harsh realities of world politics. It is time to stop justifying the setbacks experienced in the work of the United Nations. I believe that we should start by recognizing that the United Nations has become the chief force that holds the world together against all the conflicting strains and stresses that are pulling it apart. The United Nations has interposed law and human decency and the processes of conciliation and co-operation between the world's peoples and the naked, lawless use of power. The United Nations has continued to stand for brotherhood in the midst of all the voices that talk of national policy in terms of military strategy and tactics—as if the building of peace were a matter of offensives and counter-offensives, of break-throughs and infiltrations, of blockades and ideological Maginot Lines.

Indeed, the organs of the United Nations are now virtually the only places where regular contact and discussion have been maintained on a continuous basis between the Western Powers and the Union of Soviet Socialist Republics. The Council of Foreign Ministers has not met since December 1947 and negotiations for a peace treaty with Germany have been in a state of suspense since then. The conflict between East and West has been the cause, direct or indirect, of many setbacks and disappointments in the work of the United Nations during the past year; yet it is equally true, though far less often admitted, that the United Nations in its turn has acted as a restraining and conciliating influence upon the parties to this conflict. Before the General Assembly and the Councils of the United Nations every nation must justify its policies in the light of the Charter and for the judgment of world opinion. Around the tables of council chamber and committee room the pressure is always in the direction of agreement and the peaceful processes of settlement, even when agreement is not reached. The United Nations does not provide a favourable atmosphere for ultimatums or conspiracy. Its growing influence is unceasingly in the direction of peace and away from war.

WORLD IN MIDST OF PROFOUND SOCIAL AND POLITICAL CHANGE

Many things have happened both inside and outside the United Nations during the past year that should remind us not to over-simplify the world picture. The present tension between the two mightiest nations—the United States of America and the Union of Soviet Socialist Republics—is not the only factor likely to have a powerful influence on history.

The position of the other three permanent members of the Security Council, which, under the Charter, are on a basis of equality with the two already mentioned, symbolizes some of the other forces at work. Of these three Powers, the United Kingdom and France represent Europe, which was the main battlefield of the last war. Europe was deeply shaken politically and spiritually and its peoples suffered immense material losses. In the struggle for economic recovery and political stability a new European pattern is emerging. Its outlines are not yet clearly and definitely fixed, but it is already evident that the new forces at work among the four hundred million people in Europe give promise of restoring their political and economic influence.

The remaining permanent member is China, the largest country in Asia. The war began earlier in Asia than in Europe and ended later. It brought about severe disturbances in Asia's basic food production and this had catastrophic results for the peoples, from which recovery has not yet been made. Politically, the war left many parts of Asia in turmoil and ferment, but it has greatly hastened the process of emancipation of the Asiatic peoples from positions of dependence and inferior status. Their position as equal partners in world affairs is now being recognized as a matter of principle and, step by step, is being put into practice.

When the United Nations Charter was signed, China was the only fully independent nation of Eastern Asia among the signatories. Within three years Burma, India, Pakistan and the Philippines have become fully independent and all are now Members of the United Nations, India and the Philippines being original Members. Siam has also been admitted and Ceylon has applied for admission to the United Nations. The emerging United States of Indonesia is a potential applicant for membership. Further north in Asia, the Mongolian People's Republic has sent in its application. In the United Nations Economic Commission for Asia and the Far East representatives of Cambodia, Ceylon, Hong Kong, Laos and the group of territories comprising the Malayan Union, Singapore, North Borneo, Brunei and Sarawak sit as associate members. Of the countries of Western Asia, Afghanistan and Yemen are already Members of the United Nations, and Transjordan has applied for membership.

Thus, in three years some twelve or more of the rising nations in Asia, which altogether has a population greater than that of Europe and the Western Hemisphere combined, have in varying degree begun to make their influence felt in the work of the United Nations.

The American continents, with their rich resources, and, in their northern part, highly developed economy, have proved to be in peace as well as in war a vast reservoir of material assistance for less fortunate lands. Nevertheless, the wealth of the Americas is very unevenly distributed among their countries, and economic development which will raise the standard of living is a necessity for most of the American republics if their peoples are to gain equal opportunities for social and economic advancement. Politically, the inter-American system of consultation and pacific settlement of disputes has been further developed during the past year as a result of the conferences of Rio de Janeiro and Bogota.

Regional arrangements can never be a substitute for world organization, but if they are kept carefully within the framework of the United Nations, and subordinate to it, as the Charter provides, they can play a most important role in the gradual strengthening of the structure of peace.

The peoples of Africa are but sparsely represented in the United Nations and many of them have a long road to travel in the development of the great natural resources of their continent and toward political and economic independence. In these regions, the provisions of the Charter relating to Non-Self-Governing Peoples and to the trusteeship system have potentially their greatest significance. Through this machinery the people of Africa can bring their case to the attention of the world with better hopes of help and justice and genuine respect for their equal rights as human beings than ever before. During the past year, for example, the Trusteeship Council has heard the petition of representatives of the Ewe people of West Africa for the unification of their land, now divided among the British Gold Coast Colony and the British and French Trust Territories of Togoland. The Council is also sending this summer its first regular visiting mission to East Africa, where it will inspect conditions in Tanganyika under British administration and Ruanda-Urundi under Belgian administration.

It would be a grave mistake to believe that most of the world has any intention of accepting any single economic system, whether based on the communist doctrine of the classless society or the most extreme American capitalist version of a free enterprise system. In a world where so many forces are at work and so many different civilizations and cultural traditions are stirring and intermingling, domination by any single ideology, whether it be religious, or political, or economic, is unthinkable and impossible. It is equally unthinkable that any one nation or group of nations could establish and maintain in such a world a new empire resting on either economic power or military might.

UNITED NATIONS ADAPTED TO CHANGING WORLD

It is for this new world that is gradually rising from the ruins and bitter memories of the war that the United Nations was conceived. The United Nations has been constructed to embrace the whole world, because anything less would destroy the hope of preventing war by dividing the world into rival military alliances. Because the United Nations must embrace the whole world—a world of nations differing profoundly in culture and interests, each sensitive of its sovereignty—its possibilities of action have been subjected to important limitations, such as the unanimity rule for the permanent members of the Security Council and the fact that decisions of the General Assembly are in the form of recommendations only. The world has been made physically one by modern technology, but its peoples must be given time and freedom to search out the common ground afforded to them by the loosely-knit United Nations of today in order to develop the stronger unity that the United Nations of tomorrow can achieve.

Finally, the United Nations has been designed above all for a changing world. It has been so framed and so constructed that change can be brought about peacefully instead of by force of arms. It has been so built that the old nationalisms of the western world and the rising new nationalisms of Asia and the Far East can adjust themselves peacefully to each other. It has been built to contain within peaceful bounds any kind of ideological competition, among capitalists, communist socialists, social democrats, or adherents to any other economic or political faith, provided that one group does not attempt to impose its will upon the others by the threat or use of force.

I can understand that the procedures required of Member States in the United Nations may sometimes seem irksome and limiting compared with the greater freedom of traditional methods of diplomacy. But this discipline, which the Member States have imposed upon themselves by their adherence to the Charter, and this submission to the processes of open debate and public criticism and the vote, even by the greatest and most powerful of nations, constitute the essential minimum if change is to be kept within peaceful channels and if all manner of men and nations are to learn to live together without destroying each other. Constant use of the machinery of the United Nations by the Member States, and a growing tradition among them of respect for and observance of its decisions and recommendations, is the way to strengthen the Organization and to develop its powers.

I submit that all that has happened during the past year has shown more conclusively than ever that the road laid out by the United Nations Charter is not only the right road, but the only road now available to a permanently peaceful world.

The record of the United Nations, generally speaking, has been more encouraging than might have been expected in a year of adverse political circumstances.

Let us look for a moment at that record.

Palestine

This was a problem that had defied all efforts to solve it extending over the past thirty years. It was brought to the United Nations for settlement by the Mandatory Power, the United Kingdom, which announced its intention of giving up the Mandate. Last November the General Assembly, at its second regular session, adopted, by the necessary two-thirds majority, a recommendation for the partition of Palestine between Arab and Jewish States, with an economic union, and for the internationalization of the City of Jerusalem under the United Nations. A Commission was established by the Assembly to supervise the implementation of the plan. The Arab States refused to accept the recommendation and declared that they would oppose by force any attempt to impose its terms. The United Kingdom would accept no responsibility for the implementation of the recommendation against the will of either party. Finally, the United States of America, which had supported the partition plan, opposed the use of force to carry it out and asked for the appointment of a Truce Commission and for a special session of the General Assembly to consider the question of establishing instead a temporary trusteeship, without prejudice to the ultimate solution.

The special session met from 16 April to 14 May 1948. The trusteeship proposal was dropped, but the Assembly decided that a Mediator for Palestine should be appointed. Count Folke Bernadotte of Sweden was subsequently chosen to act in that capacity. Meanwhile, the Mandate came to an end on 15 May in accordance with the decision of the Mandatory Power. The Jews, at that moment, proclaimed the State of Israel within the limits of the boundaries recommended by the General Assembly. Armed forces of the Arab League States then moved across the borders of Palestine. There was widespread fighting between Arab and Israeli forces, particularly in Jerusalem. Two truce appeals by the Security Council failed and only five votes were cast in favour of action under Chapter VII of the Charter, which would have had the force of a command but might have required the sending of armed forces which the Security Council did not possess. Finally, both sides agreed to a four-weeks truce under terms worked out by the Mediator in accordance with a third Security Council resolution.

The members of the Security Council's Truce Commission—Belgium, France and the United States of America—supplied ninety-three military observers and military and naval equipment and personnel for use in the supervision of the truce. A unit of fifty men, members of the

United Nations Security Guard, reinforced by other Secretariat members, volunteered for service in Palestine. Forty other members of the Secretariat were despatched to assist the Mediator in various capacities and at key points. Meanwhile the Mediator started negotiations for an extension of the truce and for a lasting settlement of the problem.

At the time of writing, the final outcome cannot be foreseen, but these facts stand out. The General Assembly recommended the creation of a Jewish State in Palestine, as well as of an Arab State. The Jewish State, Israel, has been proclaimed. The carrying out of the Assembly recommendation was resisted by force by some Member States. Some other Member States, when faced with force, sought to change the recommendation rather than use force themselves to implement it.

Indonesia and Kashmir

The Security Council has not yet been able to act as an agency for the enforcement of peace, but it is achieving increasing success as a mediator and conciliator. The two outstanding cases of this kind, apart from Palestine, have been those of Indonesia and Kashmir.

In Indonesia the Committee of Good Offices established by the Security Council, after five months of persistent efforts to secure full observance of a "cease-fire", brought about a truce last January which, since then, has prevented the renewal of a major civil war between forces of the Netherlands and of the Republic of Indonesia that threatened to involve seventy million people. It secured agreement at the same time on political principles as the basis for a final settlement. These principles provided, among other things, for the establishment of a sovereign federal United States of Indonesia linked with other parts of the Kingdom of the Netherlands. Negotiations for a final settlement on the basis of these principles have continued unremittingly since January through the Committee of Good Offices. Many difficulties remain to be overcome, but the work of conciliation goes on while men and women work at the tasks of peaceful reconstruction instead of killing and being killed.

In the case of Kashmir, a dispute that might otherwise have plunged the sub-continent of India, with its four hundred million people, into all the horrors of communal warfare has been, up to now, successfully diverted to the peaceful channels of Security Council debate. A Commission has now been despatched by the Council in the hope that it may be able to promote a final settlement of the disputes between India and Pakistan by negotiation and mediation on the spot.

Greece and Korea

The cases of Greece and Korea are in a somewhat different, but related, category. Here the United Nations, partly by the mere fact of its watchful presence on the spot, is a constant influence on the side of peace. For the second year a United Nations group is watching the borders between Greece and her three northern neighbours. Last year the Security Council sent a commission, whose recommendations were not accepted by the Security Council due to the adverse vote of the Soviet Union. The case was then passed to the General Assembly which in its turn appointed, at its second regular session, a Special Committee on the Balkans. This Committee is now in Greece, watching for border violations and at the same time seeking to improve relations between Greece on the one hand, and on the other, Bulgaria, Yugoslavia and Albania, all of which have been accused of aiding the guerrilla forces which are engaged against the Greek Government.

In Korea, the United Nations Temporary Commission established by the Assembly has successfully supervised an election in the southern occupation zone, although it has not been granted permission by the occupying authority to enter the northern zone.

Both these cases, like that of Palestine, have involved a refusal or failure to accept or carry out a recommendation of the Assembly. In both cases the refusal by certain Member States has taken the form of a boycott or non-co-operation. Both cases involve areas where the immediate interests and mutual fears of the two greatest Powers have reacted sharply upon each other.

Interim Committee

The Interim Committee of the General Assembly (in which the Byelorussian Soviet Socialist Republic, Czechoslovakia, Poland, Ukrainian Soviet Socialist Republic, Union of Soviet Socialist Republics and Yugoslavia have not participated on the ground that the Committee was, in effect, an illegal rival of the Security Council) has concentrated its attention on problems of voting in the Security Council and on proposals for new machinery for mediation and conciliation of disputes. It has adopted recommendations aimed at restricting the application of the veto in the field of pacific settlement of disputes, this restriction to be achieved by agreement among the great Powers on procedures and not by amendment of the Charter. Other recommendations on this matter have emphasized the importance of advance consultations among the great Powers before votes are taken in the Security Council, in order to avoid, wherever possible, the use of the veto.

Atomic energy and regulation of armaments

One of the most discouraging aspects of United Nations work during the year under review has been the failure of the Atomic Energy Commission, the Commission for Conventional Armaments and the Military Staff Committee to make any real progress.

The Atomic Energy Commission reported to the Security Council in May last that it was useless to continue its work until a political accord had been reached between the Western Powers and the Union of Soviet Socialist Republics. The Commission, therefore, proposed to suspend its sessions. This resolution was opposed and vetoed by the Soviet Union in the Security Council, but the whole matter was then referred without objection to the coming session of the General Assembly, which will have an opportunity of reviewing the lack of progress in dealing with this urgent problem.

The Commission for Conventional Armaments has not yet formally suspended its work, but it has held few meetings and has never got beyond discussion of a few general principles and the definition of weapons of mass destruction, which are the responsibility of the Atomic Energy Commission. In the meantime, the armaments race among the great Powers continues and the United Nations has taken no practical step to halt it.

The prolonged debate on the control of atomic energy and the demonstrations of the tremendously destructive power of atomic weapons that the United States has given to the world have distracted attention from developments in the field of bacteriological and lethal-chemical weapons. Whatever the situation regarding atomic weapons may have been or still may be, there has never been any effective monopoly of bacteriological and chemical weapons. Some of these weapons are probably potentially as destructive of human life as atomic weapons but not a single proposal has been made by any of the Member nations for any system of preventing or controlling their manufacture, nor has there been any discussion or study of the problem in the United Nations. Meanwhile, it is not too much to assume that, as in the case of atomic bombs, stocks of these weapons are piling up and that new discoveries are constantly being made that render them more deadly.

Nevertheless, all Members of the United Nations, including the great Powers, remain bound by their solemn pledge, made at the first session of the General Assembly almost two years ago, to eliminate all weapons of mass destruction and to reduce and regulate other armaments and, as an essential step to this end, to establish effective systems of international control, which will provide practical and effective safeguards, by way of inspection and other means, against the hazards of violations and evasions.

International Court of Justice

It is encouraging for the development of world law that the International Court of Justice now has its first case and has also rendered its first advisory opinion.

The case is that of the Corfu Channel, first brought against Albania by the United Kingdom in the Security Council last year. The Security Council recommended that the parties refer the case to the Court. Albania objected to the admission by the Court of the United Kingdom's application, but the Court ruled against this objection, on the ground that its jurisdiction had been accepted by Albania when replying to the application. The Court's judgment was rendered with the unanimous agreement of all fifteen of its regular judges. Albania and the United Kingdom concluded a special agreement which now forms the basis of further proceedings before the Court. The case will be argued this autumn on its merits.

The first advisory opinion of the Court, requested by the General Assembly, concerned the question of membership in the United Nations. By nine votes to six the Court declared its opinion that a Member of the United Nations is not juridically entitled to make its consent to the admission of a State dependent on conditions not expressly provided for in Article 4 of the Charter, which states that "Membership in the United Nations is open to all other peace-loving States which accept the obligations contained in the present Charter, and, in the judgment of the Organization, are able and willing to carry out these obligations", and that, in particular, no Member State can, while it recognizes the conditions set forth in Article 4 as fulfilled, subject its affirmative vote to the additional condition that another State be admitted.

In addition to the General Assembly and the Security Council, which are authorized by the Charter to ask the Court for advisory opinions, the Economic and Social Council, the Trusteeship Council and certain specialized agencies have now also been authorized by the General Assembly to ask the Court for advisory opinions. I therefore hope that increasing use may be made of the principal judicial organ of the United Nations.

In the course of last year, six States (Brazil, Honduras, Mexico, Pakistan, Philippines and Belgium) accepted the compulsory jurisdiction of the Court, bringing the total number of States accepting the compulsory jurisdiction of the

제2부 우엔총회 회의록(1948)

Court, either by declaration made since the establishment of the International Court of Justice or by application of paragraph 5 of Article 36 of the Statute of the International Court to thirty-two, namely, Australia, Belgium, Brazil, Canada, China, Colombia, Denmark, Dominican Republic, El Salvador, France, Guatemala, Haiti, Honduras, India, Iran, Luxembourg, Mexico, Netherlands, New Zealand, Nicaragua, Norway, Pakistan, Panama, Paraguay, Philippines, Siam, Sweden, Turkey, Union of South Africa, United Kingdom, United States of America and Uruguay. Many other Member States have not yet taken action in the matter. This is another example of the slow but steady pace of progress in developing the authority of the United Nations and of the need both for patience and for persistent and repeated effort in this direction.

General Convention on the privileges and immunities of the United Nations

The accession to the Convention on the Privileges and Immunities of the United Nations by the Governments of the United Kingdom, the Dominican Republic, Liberia, Iran and Panama, reported previously to the General Assembly, has been followed by the accessions of Honduras, El Salvador, Guatemala, Ethiopia, Haiti, France, Norway, Sweden, Afghanistan, Philippines, Nicaragua, New Zealand, Greece, Poland, Canada, Iceland, Netherlands, India and Denmark. It is hoped that the instruments of accession of the other Members of the Organization will be deposited at as early a date as possible. However, only by the accession of the United States of America will the arrangements relating to the status of the Organization at its headquarters produce their full effects. The General Assembly itself has repeatedly stressed the importance, for the effective functioning of the Organization, of the acceptance of the Convention, which was unanimously adopted by the General Assembly and by the host State, as well as by all the other Members of the United Nations.

International law

The General Assembly will, at its third session, elect the fifteen members of the International Law Commission which was created at its last regular session. It is important that this Commission should begin its work on the development and codification of international law. To this end, preliminary studies have been prepared by the Secretariat on the draft declaration on the rights and duties of States, and on the formulation of the principles of the Charter of the Nürnberg Tribunal. A draft convention on genocide has also been completed by an *ad hoc* committee of the Economic and Social Council.

The object in view is to make international law apply to individuals as well as to States.

In the meantime the fact that multilateral conventions are among the most effective means for extending the scope of international law should not be overlooked. Outstanding examples of such conventions concluded during the past year are given later.

Non-Self-Governing Peoples

This year the new machinery, established by the second session of the General Assembly for the implementation of Chapter XI of the Charter, is being brought into operation. A standard form for the preparation of information on conditions in all Non-Self-Governing Territories outside the trusteeship system has been established. The Secretary-General will summarize and analyse for the General Assembly the information received from Member Governments. In addition, a Special Committee of the General Assembly will meet before the third session to examine this information. The Special Committee is authorized to make procedural recommendations and also substantive recommendations to the General Assembly relating to functional fields generally, but not to individual Territories.

The decision of the Soviet Union to take its seat in the Trusteeship Council has been an encouraging development and will strengthen the Council, since all five of the permanent members are now, for the first time, actively participating in its work, as the Charter intended them to do.

I have already referred to the oral petition of the Ewe peoples and to the first regular visiting mission which the Trusteeship Council is sending out this summer to Tanganyika and Ruanda-Urundi. Last summer the Council sent a special mission to Western Samoa whose people had petitioned for a greater measure of self-government. As a result of that mission, and with the full sympathetic co-operation of New Zealand, the Administering Authority, reforms are being made which will result in more rapid progress in the development of institutions of self-government for the people of Western Samoa.

The Administering Authorities responsible for the administration of the Trust Territories of New Guinea, Western Samoa, Ruanda-Urundi, Tanganyika, Cameroons under British administration and Togoland under British administration, have submitted annual reports on the administration of those Territories. The Trusteeship Council has examined the reports on New Guinea and Western Samoa, and, at the present time, is examining the reports on Ruanda-Urundi and Tanganyika.

The economic recovery of the world from the great devastation and dislocations of the war has been slow and painful. Yet, some remarkable results have been achieved by courageous national effort and by international co-operation (through UNRRA, through bilateral loans and trade agreements, etc.). Since the abandonment of the internationally administered relief and rehabilitation programme carried on by UNRRA, no comparable world-wide effort for recovery has been made. However, this year, the European Recovery Programme, under which sixteen nations of Western Europe have joined hands in a common programme financed by the United States of America, has been set up.

This programme holds great promise for the restoration of Western Europe to economic and political stability, but it can have lasting results only if present political divisions are not permitted to block co-ordinated action within Europe as a whole and an increase of trade between Eastern and Western Europe.

World-wide and regional economic co-operation

A very useful contribution to the economic reconstruction and rehabilitation of Europe as a whole is made by the Economic Commission for Europe, the first of the regional commissions to be set up. Within its framework, all European States—whether participants or not in the European Recovery Programme—work jointly and in a practical way towards the solution of the numerous economic problems with which the continent is beset.

The Commission has made good progress during the past year. It is helping to break such bottle-necks in production as the coal, steel and transport shortages and is facilitating, through its research work, a continental attack upon the problems of inflation and balance of payments.

The Economic Commission for Asia and the Far East was established last year and is now passing from the planning stage to the stage of positive programmes.

The Economic Commission for Latin America, established this year, will be concerned mainly with raising the level of economic activity within that region. A recommendation for the establishment of a similar economic commission for the Middle East will be before the Economic and Social Council at its seventh session to be held in Geneva in July.

These regional bodies, as well as the other economic Commissions of the Council, have encountered vast gaps in the knowledge of economic conditions in many parts of the world. Without reliable data, reliable planning is, of course, impossible, whether it be national, regional or world planning.

The Secretariat has played an important part in the resumption of world statistical services after an interruption of nearly ten years. Its efforts toward the development of common statistical standards are providing a basis for notable advances in the near future. One project which should greatly contribute to all economic work depending upon a sound knowledge of facts, consists in the censuses of population and agriculture which are to be made throughout the whole world, if possible, in or about 1950. The Secretariat, the interested specialized agencies and other inter-governmental organizations are collaborating to encourage and assist this important undertaking.

Another outstanding achievement of the Secretariat has been the publication of a series of studies on economic conditions that have already proved to be extremely useful. These studies include: *Economic Report—Salient Features of the World Economic Situation 1945-1947*, a best-seller, *Survey of Current Inflationary and Deflationary Tendencies, Economic Development in Selected Countries* and *Survey of the Economic Situation and Prospects of Europe*, as well as others.

The Havana Charter on Trade and Employment, completed under the auspices of the United Nations after more than two years of work, constitutes an important landmark in the long struggle towards promoting international trade and has opened the way for the establishment of an international trade organization. Meanwhile, under the General Agreement on Tariffs and Trade, extensive tariff concessions have been made among countries having more than two-thirds of the world's trade.

Similarly, a conference called by the United Nations has adopted a convention for the establishment of an Inter-Governmental Maritime Consultative Organization which will concern itself with the technical aspects of maritime navigation and with the removal of discriminatory action and unnecessary restrictions affecting shipping engaged in international trade.

The Economic and Employment Commission has recommended the organization of international teams of experts drawn from the United Nations and the specialized agencies who would be made available to the less-developed countries for technical assistance in developing their production and resources; action is being undertaken to implement this recommendation.

It is by unspectacular means such as these that the United Nations, its commissions and the specialized agencies are doing some of their most constructive long-range work, the object of which is to remove the underlying causes of war and to improve the living conditions of the vast masses of the human race. Many new tools of international co-operation are slowly being fashioned and these are adding greatly to the ability of mankind to improve the lot of all its members.

Human rights

After two years of labour, the Commission on Human Rights has completed a draft declaration on human rights for submission to the Economic and Social Council and later to the General Assembly. This declaration, the first attempt in history to write a "Bill of Rights" for the whole world, is an important first step in the direction of implementing the general pledges of the Charter concerning human rights.

A covenant on human rights, which would be in the form of a multilateral treaty, is also in the drafting stage. Finally, active study continues on the question of establishing international machinery for the implementation and supervision of provisions on human rights.

In the field of freedom of information—a specific aspect of the human rights programme—definite progress has been made. The Conference on Freedom of Information, held in Geneva this spring, in addition to framing some forty resolutions, adopted three draft conventions for submission to the Economic and Social Council and to the Members of the United Nations—one on the gathering and international transmission of news, one establishing an international right of correction of false news and a third affirming fundamental principles and rights in the field of freedom of information.

Full and free discussion among the Member States at this Conference has by no means produced a synthesis but will in the long run, I believe, serve to promote greater mutual understanding of different concepts and customs.

Improving social conditions

The United Nations, with certain of the specialized agencies, has assumed leadership in many phases of the world movement towards better social conditions. The matters with which the United Nations itself is primarily concerned relate to social welfare (including child and family welfare), emergency child relief, social defence (including prevention of crime and treatment of offenders, and the suppression of traffic in women and children), the international control of narcotics, the securing of equal rights for women, standards of living and housing, migration and population problems. In each of

these fields, useful and encouraging results have been recorded in the past year and in certain fields in which international control machinery already operates, as in the case of narcotics, steps have been taken to strengthen it and widen its scope.

Special mention should be made of the operational programmes, which comprise the International Children's Emergency Fund, the United Nations Appeal for Children and the provision of social welfare advisory services to Governments.

The International Children's Emergency Fund, which is very largely financed by government contributions, was designed to continue a minimum of help to those who were most affected by the cessation of UNRRA aid, namely, the needy children in war-devastated countries. Contributions so far received, or promised, from twenty-one Governments are enabling the Fund to provide, in addition to certain other supplies, a daily supplementary meal of protective foods for more than four million children in Europe and the Far East, while in Europe alone some fifteen million children exposed to tuberculosis infection are being immunized by BCG serum.

Under the United Nations Appeal for Children—the world-wide appeal for contributions from private individuals in favour of the International Children's Emergency Fund and other important child relief efforts—national campaigns have been launched in no less than forty-five countries, together with a number of colonial territories. This in itself is a remarkable achievement; its effect on the general understanding of United Nations work throughout the world and on the general awareness of the problems of child welfare should not be underestimated.

Under the programme of social welfare advisory services, thirty-two countries asked for and received assistance during 1947; in the current year this number has already been exceeded and is likely to reach forty-nine. These services include the provision of expert consultants in various fields of social welfare, arrangements for fellowships for field observations abroad, the loan of demonstration equipment for physically handicapped persons and the organization of regional seminars for key social welfare personnel.

While the primary responsibility in regard to refugees and displaced persons lies with the Preparatory Commission for the International Refugee Organization, the General Assembly entrusted to me, in collaboration with the Executive Secretary of that Commission, a special task in this field, namely, to submit a report on the progress and prospects of repatriation, resettlement and immigration of the refugees and displaced persons. As the report which I am submitting to the seventh session of the Economic and Social Council makes clear, unless Governments do far more than they have so far done in opening their doors to displaced persons and refugees, the existence of the International Refugee Organization will not prevent the perpetuation of a very serious problem.

Specialized agencies and the question of co-ordination

The specialized agencies, membership in which is not compulsory and varies from one agency to another, carry on a very important part of the work of the United Nations in the economic and social fields.

Thirteen organizations already exist in either a preparatory or final form and most of them have been established since the San Francisco Conference.

They are as follows:

International Labour Organisation (ILO)
Food and Agriculture Organization (FAO)
United Nations Educational, Scientific and Cultural Organization (UNESCO)
International Civil Aviation Organization (ICAO)
International Bank for Reconstruction and Development
International Monetary Fund
World Health Organization (WHO)
Universal Postal Union (UPU)
International Telecommunications Union (ITU)
International Refugee Organization (IRO)
International Trade Organization (ITO)
Inter-Governmental Maritime Consultative Organization
World Meteorological Organization.

The existence of so many agencies covering such varied fields inevitably calls for effective co-ordination of their work with that of the organs of the United Nations itself. The Co-ordination Committee, which was set up under direction of the Economic and Social Council and which is composed of myself and the chief administrative officers of each of the agencies, has been meeting regularly. It has made considerable progress not only in administrative co-ordination but also in assisting the Economic and Social Council in carrying out the responsibilities for co-ordination entrusted to it under the Charter. It has not only contributed—through its meetings and through those of its several technical subsidiary bodies—to the prevention of unnecessary duplication of work, but

also to a spirit of mutual assistance among the various organizations within the United Nations family. Such efforts are helping to promote the best and most efficient use of the resources of the United Nations and the specialized agencies.

PROPOSALS FOR FURTHER STRENGTHENING OF THE UNITED NATIONS

In the face of the continuing political tension between the East and West, the first concern of all the Member States at this time should be to find ways and means by which the United Nations can continue to gather strength during the coming months and be able to exert that strength with greater authority on the side of peace.

First of all, if there is the slightest prospect that progress can be made I would urge a resumption of negotiations between the United States of America, the United Kingdom, the Union of Soviet Socialist Republics and France on the future of Germany. Nothing would contribute more to the effectiveness of the United Nations than a settlement of this problem. It is difficult for me to judge whether any of the machinery for mediation and conciliation possessed by the Security Council and the General Assembly would be helpful or not in the settlement of these differences. If consideration is given to bringing the whole problem of Germany before the United Nations, I can only urge in the strongest terms that it be done only in the spirit of a genuine attempt to reach a settlement.

I would also urge upon the Members fuller use of the existing powers of the Security Council for the settlement of international disputes and for the preservation of peace. Much has been said about the alleged helplessness of the United Nations, and particularly of the Security Council. I respectfully submit, however, that the powers contained in the Charter would have been more than sufficient to deal with every situation which has come before the Security Council to date, had they been invoked.

One act which would strengthen the authority of the Security Council would be the provision of the armed forces called for by Article 43 of the Charter. I hope that the great Powers will make renewed efforts to break the deadlocks which have blocked all progress in the Military Staff Committee during the past year, although I realize that the political differences between the Powers are the real cause of the delay.

I have under study proposals for the creation of a small United Nations Guard Force which could be recruited by the Secretary-General and placed at the disposal of the Security Council and the General Assembly. Such a force would not be used as a substitute for the forces contemplated in Articles 42 and 43. It would not be a striking force, but purely a guard force. It could be used for guard duty with United Nations missions, in the conduct of plebiscites under the supervision of the United Nations and in the administration of truce terms. It could be used as a constabulary under the Security Council or the Trusteeship Council in cities like Jerusalem and Trieste during the establishment of international regimes. It might also be called upon by the Security Council under Article 40 of the Charter, which provides for provisional measures to prevent the aggravation of a situation threatening the peace.

There are many uses for such a force. If it had existed during the past year it would, I believe, have greatly increased the effectiveness of the work of the Security Council, and have saved many lives, particularly in Indonesia and Palestine. It should not be a large force—from one thousand to five thousand men would be sufficient—because it would have behind it all the authority of the United Nations.

The General Assembly will have before it reports of lack of progress toward the control of atomic energy and the control of conventional armaments. In considering these reports, I believe that the Assembly should give special attention to the problem of the control of other weapons of mass destruction. As I have pointed out, nothing whatever has even been proposed regarding those other weapons. Pending a break in the present deadlock between the majority and the minority over methods of control of atomic energy, it might be fruitful to begin a study of some of the problems involved in the control of bacteriological and lethal-chemical weapons.

I believe that the United Nations should continue to move as rapidly as possible toward universality of membership. Eight States have been admitted since the San Francisco Conference, but there are now eleven States whose applications for admission have not been the subject of any recommendation by the Security Council. These eleven are: Albania, Austria, Bulgaria, Finland, Hungary, Ireland, Italy, Mongolian People's Republic, Portugal, Roumania and Transjordan. As will be seen, nine of these are European States whose absence leaves that continent under-represented. I hope that the permanent members on the Council will be able to come to an agreement so that all applicants can be admitted at the coming session of the General Assembly.

Finally, I would urge once again upon Member Governments the importance to the future of the United Nations and to the more rapid development of world law, and respect for law, of giving all possible weight and support to the decisions of the General Assembly and of the Councils, even though they be in the form of recommendations to the Member States.

The growth in effectiveness of the Organization will be measured by the extent to which it draws upon and adapts to new uses the rich reservoir of historical experience in parliamentary institutions and the other institutions of democratic government. It is necessary that the practice of observing the will of the General Assembly should be extended and more firmly established year by year. Only in this way can we advance toward that world rule of law, which is the ultimate objective of us all.

Trygve LIE
Secretary-General

5 July 1948

Chapter I

POLITICAL AND SECURITY QUESTIONS

This chapter gives an account of the work of the Organization on political and security matters between 1 July 1947 and 30 June 1948. It includes action taken by the General Assembly at its second regular session and its second special session, by the Security Council, the Military Staff Committee, the Atomic Energy Commission, the Commission for Conventional Armaments and by the Interim Committee of the General Assembly.

With respect to membership of the Security Council, it is recalled that, at its 92nd plenary meeting on 30 September 1947, the Assembly elected Argentina and Canada, and at its 109th plenary meeting on 13 November 1947 the Ukrainian Soviet Socialist Republic, for a term of two years to replace Australia, Brazil and Poland as from 1 January 1948.

A. The question of Palestine

(a) UNITED NATIONS SPECIAL COMMITTEE ON PALESTINE

The United Nations Special Committee on Palestine, constituted by the first special session of the General Assembly and composed of representatives of Australia, Canada, Czechoslovakia, Guatemala, India, Iran, Netherlands, Peru, Sweden, Uruguay and Yugoslavia met from 27 May to 3 September 1947, at Lake Success, Jerusalem, Beirut, and Geneva. A ten-member Sub-Committee spent one week investigating the problem of the Jewish displaced persons and refugees in Austria and Germany.

The Special Committee submitted a report to the Assembly containing twelve general recommendations unanimously agreed to for a solution of the question of Palestine. The main recommendations were that the Mandate for Palestine should be terminated and that independence should be granted to Palestine at the earliest practicable date. During the transitional period ending on 1 September 1949, the administrative authority in Palestine should be responsible to the United Nations.

Seven members of the Special Committee (Canada, Czechoslovakia, Guatemala, Netherlands, Peru, Sweden and Uruguay) recommended a plan for the partition of Palestine into an Arab State and a Jewish State bound together by an economic union. The City of Jerusalem, including Bethlehem, was to be placed under international trusteeship, with the United Nations as the Administering Authority. During the transitional period, Palestine would be administered by the present Mandatory Power under the auspices of the United Nations, either alone or assisted by one or more Members of the United Nations. During that period, 150,000 Jewish immigrants would be admitted.

Three members of the Committee (India, Iran and Yugoslavia) recommended a plan for the establishment, within three years, of an independent, federal State comprising an Arab State and a Jewish State, under a federal government.

One member of the Committee (Australia) did not express its support of either plan.

(b) SECOND REGULAR SESSION OF THE GENERAL ASSEMBLY: *ad hoc* COMMITTEE ON THE PALESTINIAN QUESTION

The General Assembly, on 23 September 1947, established an *ad hoc* Committee on the Palestinian Question on which all Members of the Assembly were entitled to representation. This Committee dealt with all items on the agenda of the Assembly related to the question: (1) question of Palestine proposed by the United Kingdom (document A/286); (2) report of the Special Committee on Palestine (document A/364); (3) termination of the Mandate over and the recognition of its independence as one State, as proposed by Saudi Arabia and Iraq (documents A/317 and

A/328). Following an invitation from the *ad hoc* Committee, representatives of the Jewish Agency for Palestine and the Arab Higher Committee attended its meetings and participated in its work.

At the second meeting, the representative of the United Kingdom declared that his Government would not oppose any decision the Assembly might take with regard to the future of Palestine, but that it was not prepared to impose by force a settlement which was not acceptable to both Arabs and Jews of Palestine and that, in the absence of an agreed settlement, it must plan for an early withdrawal of British forces and British administration from Palestine.

During the general discussion, the *ad hoc* Committee heard statements from the representative of the Arab Higher Committee, who rejected the recommendations of the Special Committee on Palestine and advocated the establishment, in the whole of Palestine, of an Arab State "which would protect the legitimate rights and interests of all minorities". The representative of the Jewish Agency stated that the Agency was ready to accept, with some modifications, the majority plan of the Special Committee.

Seventeen draft resolutions were submitted during the general debate. At its nineteenth meeting, the *ad hoc* Committee established:

(*a*) A Conciliation Group entrusted with the task of bringing together the parties;

(*b*) Sub-Committee 1 to draw up a detailed plan based on the majority proposal of the Special Committee;

(*c*) Sub-Committee 2 to draw up a detailed plan for the recognition of Palestine as an independent unitary State.

The reports of Sub-Committees 1 and 2 were submitted to the *ad hoc* Committee on 19 November 1947. The Chairman of the *ad hoc* Committee, who was also the Chairman of the Conciliation Group composed of himself, the Vice-Chairman and the Rapporteur, informed the Committee that the efforts of the Conciliation Group had not been fruitful.

The report of Sub-Committee 1 recommended the adoption of a draft resolution embodying a plan of partition with economic union. The plan followed, in its general lines, the proposal of the majority of the Special Committee on Palestine. In view of the statements of policy made by the representative of the Mandatory Power, a new solution was proposed for the problem of implementation. A Commission of five members to be appointed by the General Assembly would be sent to Palestine and would perform, under the guidance of the Security Council, the functions assigned to it by the General Assembly.

The report of Sub-Committee 2 recommended the adoption of three draft resolutions:

(*a*) That before the General Assembly recommended a solution of the Palestine question, it should request the International Court of Justice to give an advisory opinion on certain legal questions connected with or arising from the problem, including questions concerning the competence of the United Nations to recommend or enforce any solution contrary to the wishes of the majority of the people of Palestine.

(*b*) That a settlement of the problem of Jewish refugees and displaced persons on an international basis should be recommended.

(*c*) That a provisional government, representative of the people of Palestine, should be created, to which the authority of the Mandatory Power would be transferred preparatory to the setting up of an elected constituent assembly.

During the discussion of the two reports in the *ad hoc* Committee, a number of amendments were introduced to the draft resolution proposed by Sub-Committee 1. In particular, changes were made revising the boundaries of the two proposed States. The Jewish Agency agreed to a transfer to the Arab State of a part of the Beersheba area and a portion of the Negeb area along the Egyptian frontier, in order to satisfy certain delegations which were in favour of partition but had suggested an extension of the territory of the Arab State in the south of Palestine.

The proposals of Sub-Committee 2 were not accepted by the *ad hoc* Committee.

The draft resolution proposed by Sub-Committee 1, embodying the Plan of Partition with Economic Union, to which various amendments had been introduced, was adopted by twenty-five votes in favour to thirteen against, with seventeen abstentions, and was included in the report of the *ad hoc* Committee to the General Assembly.

(*c*) GENERAL ASSEMBLY RESOLUTION 181(II) OF 29 NOVEMBER 1947

At the 128th plenary meeting of the General Assembly on 29 November 1947, the General Assembly considered the report of the *ad hoc* Committee and adopted the resolution on the future government of Palestine by thirty-three votes in favour, thirteen against, with ten abstentions, as follows:

In favour: Australia, Belgium, Bolivia, Brazil, Byelorussian Soviet Socialist Republic, Canada, Costa Rica, Czechoslovakia, Denmark, Dominican Republic, Ecuador, France, Guatemala, Haiti, Iceland, Liberia, Luxembourg, Netherlands, New Zealand, Nicaragua, Norway, Panama, Paraguay, Peru, Philippines, Poland, Sweden, Ukrainian Soviet Socialist Republic, Union of South Africa, Union of Soviet Socialist Republics, United States of America, Uruguay, Venezuela.

Against: Afghanistan, Cuba, Egypt, Greece, India, Iran, Iraq, Lebanon, Pakistan, Saudi Arabia, Syria, Turkey, Yemen.

Abstained: Argentina, Chile, China, Colombia, El Salvador, Ethiopia, Honduras, Mexico, United Kingdom, Yugoslavia.

At the same meeting the General Assembly elected Bolivia, Czechoslovakia, Denmark, Panama and the Philippines as members of the United Nations Palestine Commission charged with implementing the resolution. It also authorized the Secretary-General to draw from the Working Capital Fund a sum not to exceed $2,000,000 for the purposes set forth in the last paragraph of the resolution on the future government of Palestine.

(d) United Nations Palestine Commission

The United Nations Palestine Commission was charged with direct responsibility for implementing the measures recommended by the General Assembly. On 29 January 1948, the Commission submitted to the Security Council its first monthly progress report (as provided for in part I, section B, paragraph 14 of the Assembly resolution).

On 16 February 1948, the Palestine Commission presented to the Security Council a special report on the problem of security in Palestine, with particular reference to the maintenance of law and order and to the implementation of the resolution of the General Assembly on the future government of Palestine. In this report, the Commission called upon the Security Council for assistance in the discharge of its duties, having stated that "the Commission now finds itself confronted with an attempt to defy its purposes, and to nullify the resolution of the General Assembly". It referred to the Security Council the "problem of providing that armed assistance which alone would enable the Commission to discharge its responsibilities on the termination of the Mandate", and emphasized the need for prompt action in order to avert bloodshed and to assist in the implementation of the resolution. Finding that it would be unable to establish security and maintain law and order unless military forces in adequate strength were made available to it, the Commiss. . stated also that "powerful Arab interests, both inside and outside Palestine, are defying the resolution of the General Assembly and are engaged in a deliberate effort to alter by force the settlement envisaged therein".

On 15 March 1948, the Palestine Commission submitted its second monthly progress report to the Security Council in which it concluded that, in view of the policy of the Mandatory Power not to co-operate in the implementation of the plan adopted by the General Assembly, a satisfactory co-ordination of the plans of the Commission with those of the Mandatory Power in many vital respects was precluded. It stated also that, in accordance with the information which it had received from the advance party of the Secretariat in Jerusalem, the conclusions of the Commission outlined in the special report mentioned above had been reaffirmed and that, unless security was restored in Palestine, implementation of the resolution would not be possible.

The Mandatory Power had informed the Palestine Commission that it would not regard favourably a decision of the Commission to go to Palestine earlier than two weeks before the date of termination of the Mandate, but had agreed that the Commission might send a few members of its staff "for the purpose of finding accommodations and making arrangements for necessary facilities" with the Palestine Government. The Commission accordingly sent an advance party to Palestine composed of six members of the Secretariat for the purpose of observation and exploratory discussions, but made it clear to the Mandatory Power that the presence of this advance party should not be interpreted as an acceptable alternative to the presence in Palestine of the Commission itself, even for the preparatory work.

The advance party of the Secretariat arrived in Jerusalem on 3 March 1948. It conducted a number of conversations with the Government of Palestine relating to matters which would arise on the assumption by the Palestine Commission of the responsibilities assigned to it by the General Assembly resolution. Fulfilling also the task of observation, the group kept the Palestine Commission informed of the general situation in Palestine, particularly with regard to matters of order and security. In order to have first-hand information, the Palestine Commission recalled two members of the advance party to Lake Success to be available during the consideration of the Palestine question by the second special session[1] of the Assembly. The remaining four continued to fulfil their functions in Palestine.

On 2 April 1948, the Commission took note of the resolution of the Security Council of 1 April calling for a truce in Palestine and requesting the Secretary-General to convoke a special session of the General Assembly to consider further the question of the future government of Palestine. The Commission resolved to continue its

[1] See page 6.

work on the understanding that all its decisions would be subject to final action by the forthcoming special session of the General Assembly. Pursuant to the same resolution, the Commission prepared a report to the General Assembly which was circulated to Members on 10 April 1948.

In its report, the Commission gave an account of its work and of the major difficulties which had prevented the implementation of the resolution of 29 November 1947. In its conclusions, the Commission presented a review of the problems which required an urgent solution, irrespective of the ultimate decision of the General Assembly on the future government of Palestine. These problems fell into three groups: security, administrative, and economic and financial. In particular, the Commission drew the attention of the Assembly to the critical food situation in Palestine upon the termination of the Mandate, and to the question of the security of the City of Jerusalem.

On 14 April 1948, the Palestine Commission submitted to the Security Council a second special report which related to the food situation in Palestine. In that report, the Commission once more stressed that a serious food situation existed in Palestine, and that the steps which should have been taken to place orders for essential foods, and to make arrangements for their shipment, had not been taken. On 5 May 1948, the Commission informed the Security Council that it had been successful in making arrangements for the importation into Palestine of such essential foods as would meet the pressing needs of the country until about the middle of July.

The Chairman of the Commission participated, during the second special session of the General Assembly, in the deliberations of the First Committee and of its Sub-Committee 9. In adopting the resolution by which it appointed a United Nations Mediator in Palestine, the General Assembly decided, at its 135th plenary meeting on 14 May 1948, to relieve the Palestine Commission from the further exercise of responsibilities under resolution 181(II), and expressed its full appreciation for the work performed by the Palestine Commission in pursuance of its mandate from the General Assembly.

(e) TRUSTEESHIP COUNCIL

Under the terms of part III of the Plan of Partition with Economic Union annexed to its resolution of 29 November 1947 on the future government of Palestine, the General Assembly decided that the municipal area of Jerusalem together with certain adjacent towns and villages should be established as a *corpus separatum* under a special international regime and should be administered by the United Nations.

It was provided that the Trusteeship Council should first elaborate and approve a detailed Statute for the City and should subsequently, on or shortly before 1 October 1948, assume the functions of Administering Authority in the name of the United Nations. The Plan indicated certain provisions to be included in the Statute. The most important provisions were for the appointment of a Governor with wide executive and certain legislative powers, for a Legislative Council elected by proportional representation, for safeguards for human rights and fundamental freedoms, and for the protection of Holy Places, religious buildings and sites.

The Trusteeship Council, during its second session, considered the question of drafting a Statute for the City, and for that purpose set up a Working Committee on Jerusalem. During January 1948, this Committee examined a preliminary draft Statute prepared by groups of experts, and with certain amendments approved it for submission to the Trusteeship Council.

The Working Committee heard the views of representatives of the Jewish Agency, of Agudath Israel World Organization and of the Patriarch of Jerusalem (Greek Orthodox Church). The Arab Higher Committee was also given an opportunity to state its views, but did not avail itself of the opportunity.

The Trusteeship Council examined the draft in detail at the second part of its second session (18 February to 10 March 1948), and with some modifications accepted it as being in satisfactory form. However, the Council decided that the question of the formal approval of the Statute should be taken up shortly before 29 April 1948, by which date the Council was required to take such action under the terms of the Plan. When the Council reconvened on 20 April 1948, the General Assembly was already undertaking, at its second special session, a further consideration of the question of the future government of Palestine. In view of this fact, the Council decided to refer the question of the Statute to the General Assembly for such further instructions as it might see fit to give. The General Assembly did not consider this matter at its second special session, and in the absence of instructions the Trusteeship Council has taken no further action on the Statute.

At the first meeting of the third session of the Trusteeship Council held on 16 June 1948, the representative of the Union of Soviet Socialist Republics proposed that the question of the implementation of part III of the General Assembly's resolution of 29 November 1947, pertaining to the Statute for Jerusalem, should be included in the agenda as an additional item, and considered by the Council. He added that the Council should deal with this question during the present session and report to the next regular session of the General Assembly. After a discussion, during which opposing views were expressed by a number of delegations, a French amendment was adopted which provided that item 9(a) of the agenda of the third session of the Trusteeship Council would read, "Present state of the question of the Statute for Jerusalem". The Council has not yet considered this question.

(f) ECONOMIC AND SOCIAL COUNCIL

Part I, section D, paragraph 3 of the Plan of Partition provided for the establishment of a Joint Economic Board, consisting of "three representatives of each of the two States and three foreign members appointed by the Economic and Social Council of the United Nations". The foreign members were to be appointed, in the first instance, for a term of three years; they were to serve as individuals and not as representatives of States.

On 11 March 1948, the Economic and Social Council adopted a resolution requesting the Member States to submit names of candidates to the Secretary-General before 15 June 1948. It requested the Secretary-General to consult with the Palestine Commission on the terms and conditions of service, and to submit a list of nominees to the seventh session of the Economic and Social Council. In view of subsequent developments, no further action on this matter is contemplated.

(g) SECURITY COUNCIL

On 2 December 1947, the Secretary-General addressed a letter to the President of the Security Council transmitting the General Assembly resolution concerning the future government of Palestine. At its meeting on 9 December 1947, the Security Council took note of the Assembly resolution and, from that date, was seized of the Palestine question.

On 24 February 1948, the Security Council began the consideration of the General Assembly resolution, together with the first monthly report and the special report on the problem of security in Palestine which had been submitted to it by the Palestine Commission. The Council invited the Chairman of the Palestine Commission, the representatives of Egypt and Lebanon, and of the Jewish Agency for Palestine and the Arab Higher Committee to participate in its deliberations. The Arab Higher Committee, however, did not avail itself of this opportunity until 1 April 1948, when the Security Council requested the presence of a representative in connexion with intended arrangements for a truce.

On 5 March 1948, the Council adopted a resolution calling upon the permanent members to consult and inform the Council regarding the situation with respect to Palestine, and to make recommendations to it regarding the guidance and instructions which the Council might usefully give to the Palestine Commission with a view to implementing the resolution of the General Assembly. The Council also appealed to all Governments and peoples to take all possible action to prevent or reduce disorders occurring in Palestine.

On 19 March 1948, those permanent members of the Council which participated in the consultations (the United States of America, China, France and the Union of Soviet Socialist Republics) reported to the Council. (The representative of the United States reported also on behalf of the representatives of China and France.) The report was limited in the main to the first part of the Security Council's resolution of 5 March 1948, and gave information in regard to the situation in Palestine. In that part of the report which was unanimously agreed to, the permanent members recommended that the Security Council should make it clear to the parties and to the Governments concerned that the Council was determined not to permit the existence in Palestine of any threats to the peace, and that it would take further action by all means available to it to bring about the immediate cessation of violence and the restoration of peace in Palestine. Brief consultations in respect of the remaining part of the Council resolution also took place.

On 19 March 1948, at the 271st meeting of the Council, the United States delegation stated that, since it had become clear that the Assembly resolution could not be implemented by peaceful means and that the Security Council would not be prepared to implement it, the Council should recommend a temporary trusteeship for Palestine under the Trusteeship Council; further, the Council should request the convocation of a special session of the General Assembly and, pending the meeting of the special session, should instruct the Palestine Commission to suspend its efforts to implement the Partition Plan.

At its meeting on 24 March 1948, the representative of the Jewish Agency for Palestine informed the Council of a statement, adopted on 23 March by the Jewish Agency for Palestine and the National Council of Jews (Vaad Leumi). This declaration stated, among other things, that the Jewish people would oppose any proposal designed to prevent or postpone the establishment of the Jewish State; that they rejected a trusteeship regime for Palestine; that the Provisional Council of Government of the

Jewish State should be recognized by the Palestine Commission without delay; and that upon the termination of the Mandatory Administration, and not later than 16 May 1948, a Provisional Jewish Government would commence to function in co-operation with the representatives of the United Nations then in Palestine.

On 1 April 1948, the United States delegation introduced two resolutions. The first, calling for a truce in Palestine, was adopted unanimously by the Council. The second, adopted by nine votes in favour, with two abstentions (Ukrainian SSR and the Soviet Union), requested the Secretary-General to convoke a special session of the General Assembly to consider further the question of the future government of Palestine.

In accordance with the terms of the first resolution adopted by the Security Council on 1 April 1948, the Arab Higher Committee and the Jewish Agency for Palestine appointed representatives who met with the President of the Security Council to discuss arrangements for a truce in Palestine. After the first meeting, during which the representatives of the Jewish Agency and the Arab Higher Committee agreed on the procedure for negotiating, the President held two conversations with each representative separately. These conversations did not lead to any agreement between the parties, and no basis for the truce could be worked out.

During informal conversations held among the members of the Security Council after the President had reported upon the results of his conversations with the parties, a number of delegations made suggestions for a basis of a truce and for the machinery to be employed in the arrangement thereof.

At the 282nd meeting of the Council, the President reported upon the result of these conversations. He also submitted, on behalf of the Colombian delegation, a draft resolution outlining the principles and machinery for a truce in Palestine.

At its next meeting held on 17 April 1948, the Council adopted by nine votes in favour with two abstentions (Ukrainian SSR and the Soviet Union) an amended version of the Colombian draft resolution. It called upon all persons and organizations in Palestine, especially the Arab Higher Committee and the Jewish Agency for Palestine, to cease all activities of a military or para-military nature, as well as acts of violence, terrorism and sabotage, and also requested the United Kingdom Government, as long as it remained the Mandatory Power, to use its best efforts to bring all those concerned in Palestine to accept these measures. All Governments, and particularly those of the countries neighbouring upon Palestine, were asked to assist in the implementation of this resolution.

On 23 April 1948, on the basis of a resolution introduced by the United States of America, the Council established a Truce Commission for Palestine composed of representatives of those members of the Security Council which had career consular officers in Jerusalem, namely Belgium, France and the United States of America (Syria having indicated that it was not prepared to serve on the Commission), to assist the Security Council in supervising the implementation by the parties of the Council's resolution of 17 April 1948. This resolution was adopted by nine votes in favour with two abstentions (Ukrainian SSR and the Soviet Union).

On 1 May, the Jewish Agency addressed a telegram to the President of the Security Council drawing the Council's attention to reports of the invasion of Palestine by the regular forces of Syria and Lebanon across the northern border, and by Egyptian forces across the southern border.

In response to an inquiry sent by the President of the Council to the Mandatory Power and to the Truce Commission, the Council was informed that there was no confirmation of the alleged invasion of Palestine by the armed forces of the above-mentioned countries. The Council took note of all these communications, and requested the President to ask the Truce Commission to keep it constantly and currently informed of the situation in Palestine.

On 12 May 1948, the Council took note of two telegrams received from the Truce Commission concerning its negotiations for a truce for the City of Jerusalem. The Council discussed various points raised in those communications, in particular the suggestion of associating the International Red Cross with the machinery to be employed for a truce in the City. The Council authorized the President to advise the Truce Commission that it should explore and adopt such means of assistance as it might require in the performance of its functions.

(*h*) Second special session of the General Assembly

In accordance with the decision of the Security Council at its meeting on 1 April 1948[1] the Secretary-General, acting under the provisions of rules 7 and 9 of the rules of procedure of the General Assembly, convoked the second special session of the General Assembly to meet on 16 April 1948 "to consider further the question of the future government of Palestine".

---

[1] See column 1, this page.

On 19 April 1948, the General Assembly referred this item to the First Committee for consideration and report.

The representative of the United States of America, who had submitted in the Security Council the initial draft resolution suggesting a special session of the General Assembly, invited the members of the Security Council to discuss informally, prior to the convocation of the General Assembly, a proposal to be submitted to the special session on the subject of trusteeship. The representative of the Soviet Union did not participate in these informal conversations.

The General Assembly had before it a report by the United Nations Palestine Commission giving an account of its activities up to 10 April 1948.[1]

The First Committee, at its first meeting, invited the Chairman of the United Nations Palestine Commission and the representatives of the Arab Higher Committee and of the Jewish Agency for Palestine to participate in its discussions and to render such assistance as the Committee might require.

At the opening of the general debate in the Committee, the representative of the United States of America introduced a draft Trusteeship Agreement for Palestine in the form of a working paper. At the end of the general debate on the working paper, the Committee decided to discuss in detail the draft Trusteeship Agreement. During that discussion, which concentrated upon a list of selected topics prepared by the Chairman of the Committee, various delegations sought clarification of crucial aspects of the agreement, particularly of the type of Administering Authority, the duration of the Trusteeship, the selection of the countries to become signatory to the Agreement, and means of implementation. The representatives of the Arab Higher Committee and of the Arab States were prepared to discuss in detail the draft Trusteeship Agreement, upon clarification of the essential points and upon receipt of an assurance that the resolution of the General Assembly of 29 November 1947 would not be implemented. The representative of the Jewish Agency rejected the draft Trusteeship Agreement as contrary to that resolution and as ignoring the legitimate rights and aspirations of the Jewish people in Palestine for independence.

A draft resolution submitted by the delegation of Guatemala proposed the appointment of a sub-committee which, after hearing the United Nations Palestine Commission, the Mandatory Power, the Arab Higher Committee, the Jewish Agency for Palestine and various experts, would report to the First Committee its findings with respect to the question whether trusteeship was desired and would be acceptable to the population of Palestine, and whether it was possible to implement trusteeship and make it workable. The Guatemalan resolution was adopted in an amended form, and Sub-Committee 9 was established on 4 May. It was composed of the officers of the First Committee and of the representatives of Argentina, Belgium, Canada, Cuba, Guatemala, France, India, Soviet Union and the United States of America. The Sub-Committee was instructed to study the situation in Palestine in the light of the existing circumstances, and to formulate a proposal for a provisional regime in Palestine.

Sub-Committee 9 reported back to the First Committee on 13 May. The resolution contained in its report, as amended by Greece and France, was adopted by the First Committee and transmitted to the General Assembly for approval.

In the course of the general debate in the First Committee, the representative of France submitted, on 22 April 1948, a draft resolution stating that the maintenance of order and security in Jerusalem was an urgent question requiring immediate attention, and that the Trusteeship Council should be asked to study and, in consultation with the Mandatory Power and the interested parties, take suitable measures for the protection of the City of Jerusalem and its inhabitants. The French resolution, as amended by the delegation of Sweden, was adopted; the General Assembly referred it to the Trusteeship Council on 26 April 1948.

The Trusteeship Council considered various proposals, such as that submitted by France for dispatching to Jerusalem a United Nations official with powers to recruit, organize and maintain an international police force of 1,000 men. The Council also considered a United States proposal to place Jerusalem under temporary trusteeship, with provisions for the maintenance of law and order, and an Australian proposal for the adoption of the draft Statute for Jerusalem as prepared previously by the Trusteeship Council.[1] On 5 May 1948, the Trusteeship Council informed the General Assembly that the Arab Higher Committee and the Jewish Agency for Palestine, on 2 May 1948, had ordered a cease-fire within the Walled City of Jerusalem, that the specific terms of a truce would be elaborated in Jerusalem in consultation with the High Commissioner for Palestine, and that the Council had been informed that the Mandatory Power was willing to appoint under Palestine legislation, before 15 May 1948, a neutral acceptable to both Arabs and Jews, as Special Municipal Commissioner. This Com-

[1] See page 4.

[1] See page 8.

missioner was to carry out, with the co-operation of the community committees already existing in Jerusalem, the functions hitherto performed by the Municipal Commission. The Trusteeship Council, while recognizing that the measure did not provide adequately for the protection of the City and its inhabitants, recommended the approval of this suggestion by the General Assembly.

On 6 May 1948, the General Assembly approved the conclusions and the recommendations of the Trusteeship Council, and recommended that the Mandatory Power appoint a Municipal Commissioner in accordance with the conditions proposed by the Trusteeship Council. Subsequently, Mr. Harold Evans was appointed on 13 May 1948 as the Municipal Commissioner of Jerusalem. He left New York on 22 May on his way to Jerusalem, where, in his absence, Mr. P. Azcarate (Secretariat) was acting, upon appointment by the High Commissioner of Palestine, as Deputy Municipal Commissioner.

The Municipal Commissioner did not proceed to Jerusalem but remained in Cairo, since he considered it inadvisable to take up his duties in Jerusalem as long as no truce was established. According to information available to the Municipal Commissioner on 9 June 1948 (the date of the acceptance by all parties of the Security Council's truce resolution), the Arab authorities were unwilling to co-operate, under existing conditions, with any Jerusalem Commissioner appointed by the United Nations, while the Jewish authorities had declared their readiness to co-operate with him. In these circumstances, and considering that full co-operation by both sides was essential, the Municipal Commissioner decided to postpone his departure for Jerusalem and was, in the meantime, assisting the Mediator. He nevertheless informed all the authorities concerned that he was prepared to proceed to Jerusalem as soon as possible, and asked them to advise him how soon he could be of assistance to them. On 21 June 1948, he returned to the United Nations headquarters for consultation.

The General Assembly, on 6 May, also requested the First Committee or its subsidiary bodies to give continued urgent attention to the question of further measures for the protection of Jerusalem and its inhabitants. On 11 May 1948, the First Committee adopted a draft resolution proposed by the United States, as subsequently amended by France and Guatemala, for the establishment of Sub-Committee 10, which was instructed to report to the Committee appropriate recommendations for the protection of the City of Jerusalem and its inhabitants. The Sub-Committee was composed of representatives of the States members of the Trusteeship Council

and of representatives of Brazil, Iran and Sweden. Sub-Committee 10 recommended to the First Committee the adoption of a joint United States and French proposal, as amended by other delegations, for a temporary international regime for Jerusalem, based on Chapter XII of the Charter. According to this proposal, the protection of Jerusalem and its inhabitants was to be entrusted temporarily to the responsibility of a United Nations Commissioner nominated by the United Nations and placed under the supreme authority of the Trusteeship Council. On 14 May 1948, this proposal was considered in the General Assembly without any recommendations for its adoption from the First Committee and, having failed to receive the necessary two-thirds majority, was not adopted.

On 14 May 1948, the General Assembly adopted, by thirty-one votes in favour to seven against, with sixteen abstentions, the following resolution:

"*The General Assembly,*

"*Taking account* of the present situation in regard to Palestine,

I

"*Strongly affirms* its support of the efforts of the Security Council to secure a truce in Palestine and calls upon all Governments, organizations and persons to co-operate in making effective such a truce;

II

"1. *Empowers* a United Nations Mediator in Palestine, to be chosen by a committee of the General Assembly composed of representatives of China, France, the Union of Soviet Socialist Republics, the United Kingdom and the United States of America, to exercise the following functions:

"(*a*) To use his good offices with the local and community authorities in Palestine to:

"(*i*) Arrange for the operation of common services necessary to the safety and well-being of the population of Palestine;

"(*ii*) Assure the protection of the Holy Places, religious buildings and sites in Palestine;

"(*iii*) Promote a peaceful adjustment of the future situation of Palestine;

"(*b*) To co-operate with the Truce Commission for Palestine appointed by the Security Council in its resolution of 23 April 1948;

"(*c*) To invite, as seems to him advisable, with a view to the promotion of the welfare of the inhabitants of Palestine, the assistance and co-operation of appropriate specialized agencies of the United Nations, such as the World Health Organization, of the International Red Cross, and of other governmental or non-governmental organizations of a humanitarian and non-political character;

"2. *Instructs* the United Nations Mediator to render progress reports monthly, or more frequently as he deems necessary, to the Security Council and to the Secretary-General for transmission to the Members of the United Nations;

"3. *Directs* the United Nations Mediator to conform in his activities with the provisions of this resolution, and with such instructions as the General Assembly or the Security Council may issue;

"4. *Authorizes* the Secretary-General to pay the United Nations Mediator an emolument equal to that paid to the President of the International Court of Justice, and to provide the Mediator with the necessary staff to assist in carrying out the functions assigned to the Mediator by the General Assembly;

III

"*Relieves* the Palestine Commission from the further exercise of responsibilities under resolution 181 (II) of 29 November 1947."

At the same time the General Assembly adopted unanimously the following resolution concerning the United Nations Palestine Commission:

"*The General Assembly,*

"*Having adopted* a resolution providing for the appointment of a United Nations Mediator in Palestine, which relieves the United Nations Palestine Commission from further exercise of its responsibilities,

"*Resolves* to express its full appreciation for the work performed by the Palestine Commission in pursuance of its mandate from the General Assembly."

On 20 May 1948, the Committee of the General Assembly composed of the representatives of China, France, the Union of Soviet Socialist Republics, the United Kingdom and the United States of America, in accordance with part II of the General Assembly resolution, chose Count Folke Bernadotte, Vice-President of the International Red Cross, as the United Nations Mediator in Palestine. On 25 May he arrived in Paris, where he was joined by the Secretariat assigned to him by the Secretary-General; on 27 May, arrived in Cairo, where he opened consultations with the representatives of the Egyptian Government and other representatives of the Arab States on the basis of the Assembly resolution. Subsequently, he established contact with the representatives of the Provisional Government of Israel in Tel Aviv.

(*i*) ACTION BY THE SECURITY COUNCIL SUBSEQUENT TO THE SECOND SPECIAL SESSION OF THE GENERAL ASSEMBLY

On 15 May 1948, the Council received a telegram from the Minister of Foreign Affairs of Egypt declaring that Egyptian armed forces had crossed the border of Palestine for the purpose of establishing security and order. The same day the Secretary-General of the Arab League informed the Council that the Arab States members of the League, recognizing that the independence and sovereignty of Palestine became a fact upon the termination of the Mandate, were compelled to intervene in Palestine because the disturbances there constituted a serious and direct threat to peace and security within the territories of the Arab States, and in order to restore peace and establish law in Palestine. The Jewish Agency for Palestine brought to the attention of the Council two telegrams from the Foreign Secretary of the State of Israel in which he requested urgent action by the Security Council, as a result of the invasion of Palestine and armed attack upon the territory of Israel, including air bombardment of Tel Aviv by the Egyptian forces. The Council was also informed, by King Abdullah of Transjordan, of the intervention of Transjordan armed forces in Palestine, and by the Jewish Provisional Government, of the intervention of armed forces of Lebanon and Iraq.

In the course of the discussion, the United States delegation introduced a draft resolution asking the Security Council to determine that the situation in Palestine constituted a threat to the peace and a breach of the peace within the meaning of Article 39 of the Charter, and ordering all Governments and authorities to cease any hostile military action and to issue a cease-fire order, to become effective within thirty-six hours after the adoption of the resolution. The delegation of the United Kingdom submitted a series of amendments to the draft resolution. The main points of these amendments were the omission of any determination by the Council that the situation in Palestine constituted a threat to the peace or breach of the peace and the substitution for the cease-fire order of a call upon the parties to the same effect.

At the suggestion of the United States delegation, the Council on 18 May 1948 addressed a number of questions to the Governments of Egypt, Iraq, Lebanon, Saudi Arabia, Syria, Transjordan and Yemen, also to the Arab Higher Committee and the Jewish authorities in Palestine, for the purpose of clarifying the situation subsequent to the armed intervention of the Arab States in Palestine. The Council requested replies to these questions within forty-eight hours as from noon, 19 May 1948, New York Standard Time. The replies were delivered to the Council either orally in the course of the meeting of the Council held on 22 May, or by cable. The Government of Transjordan advised the Council of its refusal to answer the questions addressed to it.

The proposal of the United States calling upon the Council to determine the existence of a threat to the peace and a breach of the peace in Palestine, failed to receive the required number of votes; five members (Colombia, France, Ukrainian SSR, Soviet Union and the United States of America) voted in favour and the remaining six abstained. The United States resolution, as amended by the United Kingdom and other members of the Council, was adopted on 22 May by eight votes in favour with three abstentions (Syria, Ukrainian SSR and the Soviet Union). The Council called upon all Governments and authorities to abstain from any hostile military action in Palestine and to issue a cease-fire order to their military and para-military forces to become effective thirty-six hours after midnight, 22 May, New York Standard Time. At the request of the Arab States, the Council at its meeting on 24 May 1948 granted an extension of forty-eight hours ending 26 May 1948, noon, New York Standard Time.

The Truce Commission, in face of the increasing violence and rapidly deteriorating situation, continued its efforts for the establishment of a truce for the City of Jerusalem. The Commission felt that the only effective measure which could bring about an immediate cessation of hostilities in the Holy City was the employment of a neutral force strong enough to compel the parties to refrain from fighting, and that, in view of the extreme gravity of the situation, the Council should explore all remedies provided for in Articles 41 and 42 of the Charter which could be immediately and effectively applied. Members of the Truce Commission, in an effort to bring about a truce, were crossing the battle lines at great personal risk; during the performance of his duties, the Chairman of the Truce Commission, Mr. Thomas Wasson, lost his life.

The Provisional Government of Israel, on 24 May 1948, communicated its acceptance of the resolution of 22 May, and informed the Council that it had decided to issue a cease-fire order on all fronts operative from noon 24 May, New York Standard Time, provided the other party acted likewise. On 26 May, the Provisional Government communicated its decision to re-issue that order operative from noon, 26 May 1948.

On 26 May, the representative of Iraq submitted, on behalf of the Arab States, a reply to the Council resolution of 22 May. He stated that the Arab States were anxious to restore peace in Palestine and willing to co-operate with the Council to that end. They considered, how-

ever, that the 17 April resolution of the Council should be observed so that the cease-fire might lead to a just and lasting solution. They also considered that the terms of the Council's resolution of 22 May did not guarantee safety for Palestine or for neighbouring Arab States.

On 27 May 1948, the Soviet delegation submitted a draft proposal (revised on 29 May) stating that the resolution of the Security Council of 22 May had not been carried out in view of the refusal of the Arab States to comply with it, and considering that, as a result of increased fighting in Palestine, the situation constituted a threat to peace and security within the meaning of Article 39, called on the Security Council to order the parties concerned to secure the cessation of military operations within thirty-six hours after the adoption of the resolution. The resoluiton received five votes in favour (Colombia, France, Ukrainian SSR, Soviet Union and the United States of America) except for the sentence ascribing the failure of the earlier resolution to the refusal of the Arab States to comply with it. That sentence was supported by two votes (Ukrainian SSR and the Soviet Union) and was not adopted.

On 27 May, the representative of the United Kingdom submitted a draft resolution which provided, among other things, for the cessation of hostilities in Palestine for a period of four weeks, and instructed the United Nations Mediator for Palestine, appointed in virtue of the General Assembly resolution of 14 May,[1] to make contact with both parties, as soon as the cease-fire was in force, with a view to making recommendations to the Security Council about an eventual settlement for Palestine. The draft resolution also provided that, should the resolution be rejected, repudiated or violated by either party or both, the situation in Palestine would be reconsidered with a view to action under Chapter VII of the Charter. That resolution, as amended by the United States of America, France and Canada, was adopted on 29 May 1948. Pursuant to its provisions, the Arab States and the Jewish and Arab authorities in Palestine communicated their acceptance of this resolution to the Security Council by 6 p.m., New York Standard Time, on 1 June 1948.

On 2 June 1948, the Security Council acknowledged the acceptance by the parties concerned of its resolution of 29 May 1948, the President making a statement to the effect that it was the Council's understanding that the terms of the resolution had been accepted unconditionally by all parties. In accordance with the suggestion made on 2 June by the United Nations Mediator in Palestine, the Council in-

[1] See page 8.

structed him to arrange, in consultation with the two parties and the Truce Commission, for the effective date of the cease-fire. The Council added that the cease-fire should be arranged as quickly as possible, taking into account the considerations attendant upon the problem of control. All parties concerned and the Truce Commission have been informed of this decision of the Security Council.

On 3 June 1948, the Council agreed that the Mediator should be authorized to interpret the text of the resolution as he deemed correct. Should his interpretation be challenged, the Council would then give further consideration to the point on which there were conflicting views. The Council also felt that no specific instructions should be given to the Mediator, and that he should have full authority to act within the framework of the resolutions of the General Assembly and the Security Council.

On 4 June 1948, the United Nations Mediator informed the Council that, in the negotiations for a truce, a difficulty had arisen with regard to the interpretation of the phrases, used in paragraphs 3 and 4 of the resolution of the Council of 29 May, referring to "fighting personnel" and "men of military age". His inquiry sought to establish whether the resolution permitted Jewish immigration of men of military age during the truce, provided that they were not mobilized or submitted to military training, or whether its purpose was to exclude, during this period, all men of military age. In reply, the President of the Council informed the Mediator of the previous decision of the Council giving him full authority to interpret the resolution as he deemed appropriate.

After further negotiations with the interested parties, the Mediator on 7 June, sent a note to the Arab States and to the Provisional Government of Israel requesting them to notify him by noon on 9 June 1948 of their acceptance or rejection of the truce proposals contained in the note. The effective date and hour of the cease-fire and truce, including the application of supervision envisaged in the resolution of 29 May 1948, was set for 11 June at 6 a.m. Greenwich Mean Time. By 9 June the Mediator had received the unconditional acceptance of his proposals by all interested parties and consequently the cease-fire and the truce were ordered for 11 June 1948 at 6 a.m. G.M.T.

In accordance with the suggestion of the Mediator, the Council approved the procedure for the handling of all communications from interested parties concerning the execution of the truce agreement. It was agreed that all such communications would be submitted to the Mediator, and that he would exercise his discre-

tion in reporting to the Council all information with respect to enforcement. In approving the procedure, the Council understood that it would not preclude the parties from addressing any communications directly to the Council should they feel it necessary.

A number of reports on incidents which occurred during the first few days of the truce were brought to the attention of the Mediator and were investigated by military observers.

On 17 June, the Mediator requested the Secretary-General to supply him with further personnel required for the supervision of the truce in general, and of the supply route between Tel Aviv and Jerusalem in particular. Accordingly, the Secretary-General put at his disposal fifty uniformed United Nations guards. They were dispatched to Palestine on 19 June 1948.

In the second week of the existence of the truce, no significant violations or incidents took place. The machinery for the supervision and control of the truce was perfected and organized on a much larger scale.

On 22 June, the headquarters for supervision of the truce were established at Haifa, which was centrally located and afforded a good access to several fronts. Colonel Thord Bonde (Sweden), acting as the Mediator's personal deputy in charge of these activities, was assisted by the military observers supplied by Belgium, France and the United States of America, and by the staff from the United Nations Secretariat furnished by the Secretary-General.

On 25 June 1948, the Mediator reported to the Council a serious incident at Negba (Negeb) in which the Egyptian armed forces were involved and during which the United Nations observer's plane was fired upon. The Mediator requested explanations from the Egyptian Government. After having received them, he expressed the hope that further incidents of this nature would be avoided, and that difficulties over interpretation of the truce agreement might be amicably settled.

On 15 June the Mediator requested the Council to ask the Member States to report on the steps they had taken for the implementation of the Council resolution of 29 May, to draw their attention, as well as that of non-member States from which substantial immigration to Palestine or to the Arab States might emanate, to paragraph 6 of the truce proposals, and to request them to extend co-operation and assistance to him in the implementation of the provisions of those proposals. The Council approved that request on the same day, and the Secretary-General accordingly notified the States in question.

In its resolution of 29 May, the Council instructed the Mediator, in concert with the Truce Commission, to supervise the observance of the truce. It decided also that they should be provided with a sufficient number of military observers. The Mediator approached the Governments of Belgium, France and the United States of America, members of the Truce Commission, requesting that he be supplied with a number of military observers and with other means necessary for the supervision of the cease-fire and the truce. In response to this request, these Governments put at his disposal a number of military observers and a few patrol vessels and planes.

The representative of the Soviet Union considered that membership in the Truce Commission had nothing to do with the selection of the States which were to furnish military observers to the Mediator, and that the Council was obliged to take a specific decision in accordance with the resolution of 29 May. He stated also that the Soviet Government was prepared to participate, together with other Governments, in supplying the Mediator with the necessary number of military observers. On 15 June, he submitted a draft resolution to the effect that the Mediator should be provided with military observers in accordance with the Council's resolution of 29 May, and that they should be appointed by States members of the Security Council who wished to participate in the designation of such observers, excluding Syria. This resolution received two votes in favour (Ukrainian SSR and Soviet Union) with nine abstentions, and was not adopted.

As soon as the truce had been established, the United Nations Mediator turned his attention to the broader aspects of his task under the resolution of the General Assembly of 14 May, namely, the promotion of a peaceful adjustment of the future situation of Palestine. He established special headquarters for mediation on the island of Rhodes.

On 15 and 16 June, he met in Cairo the Political Committee of the Arab League for exploratory conversations, during which he exchanged views with representatives of the Arab States, but offered no proposals. During that meeting it was arranged that the Political Committee should designate four Arab experts on the working level to be available to the Mediator at Rhodes for non-political consultation and for supplying information when initial suggestions and proposals were to be worked out by him. On 17 June, he met the Prime Minister and Foreign Minister of the Provisional Government of Israel in Tel Aviv and held conversations of the same nature with them. As a result

three Jewish experts of the same status as the Arabs were sent to the Mediator's headquarters at Rhodes.

On 28 June, the Mediator, through his representatives, submitted to all parties concerned, in Cairo and Tel Aviv, suggestions for a peaceful settlement of the dispute. While submitting these suggestions, the Mediator stressed that both parties would be free to make any comments or counter-suggestions. The Mediator decided not to release the details of his suggestions until he had received the comments and reactions of the parties thereon, and had had an opportunity of discussing with the parties the advisability of so releasing them.

B. The Greek question

(a) CONSIDERATION OF THE REPORT OF THE COMMISSION OF INVESTIGATION CONCERNING GREEK FRONTIER INCIDENTS

On 27 June 1947, the Rapporteur of the Commission of Investigation concerning Greek Frontier Incidents presented the Commission's report to the Security Council at its 147th meeting.

A number of resolutions were introduced during the debate, none of which, however, was adopted by the Council. The representative of the United States of America, who opened the general discussion, introduced a draft resolution, based on the conclusions and recommendations submitted to the Council by the majority of the members of the Commission. Several amendments submitted by the representatives of France and the United Kingdom were incorporated in this draft resolution. The representatives of Colombia, Australia and Syria also made some suggestions which were included, in part, in the proposal. The revised draft resolution received nine votes in favour and two against (Poland and the Soviet Union). Inasmuch as one of the negative votes was cast by a permanent member, the draft resolution was not adopted.

The representative of the Union of Soviet Socialist Republics, who disagreed with the conclusions and recommendations of the majority of the Commission, submitted a proposal based on different considerations, which was rejected by the Council by two votes in favour (Poland and the Soviet Union) and nine votes against.

After the two above-mentioned proposals were rejected, the representative of Poland submitted another, limited only to the recommendations which had received general approval, such as the conclusion of new and the renewal of old frontier conventions, and the establishment of normal diplomatic relations among the countries concerned. This proposal was rejected by the Council by two votes in favour and nine against.

On 31 July 1947, the representative of Greece submitted to the Council a letter from the Foreign Minister of Greece, requesting the Council to treat the Greek question as a threat to the peace, within the meaning of Chapter VII of the Charter. He made an explanatory statement at the meeting of the Council held on 6 August 1947.

At the same meeting, the representative of Australia submitted a proposal requesting the Council to determine that a threat to the peace existed within the meaning of Article 39, and to adopt measures leading to the removal of this threat. This proposal received nine votes in favour and two against (Poland and the Soviet Union). Since one of the negative votes was cast by a permanent member, the proposal was not adopted.

On the suggestion of the representative of Colombia, the Council, on 6 August 1947, appointed a Sub-Committee, composed of the representatives of Australia, Colombia, France, Poland, the United Kingdom, the Union of Soviet Socialist Republics and the United States of America. The Sub-Committee was requested to ascertain the possibility of formulating a new draft resolution which it could recommend for the approval of the Council. The Sub-Committee, having met twice, reported to the Council that it was unable to make any proposal.

On 12 August 1947, the United States delegation submitted a new draft resolution charging that Albania, Bulgaria and Yugoslavia had given assistance and support to the guerrillas fighting against the Greek Government, and requesting a decision by the Council that this assistance constituted a threat to the peace within the meaning of Chapter VII of the Charter. This draft resolution, which suggested a number of measures to be taken for the removal of this threat to the peace, received nine votes in favour and two against (Poland and the Soviet Union). Inasmuch as one of the permanent members cast a negative vote, the draft resolution was not adopted.

At this stage, the President of the Council declared that, since the Council was unable to adopt any proposal, the consideration of the question was concluded. The matter would, however, remain on the agenda of the Council, and could be taken up again at any time at the request of any member.

(b) REMOVAL OF THE GREEK QUESTION FROM THE AGENDA OF THE SECURITY COUNCIL

On 15 September 1947, the representative of the United States of America submitted to the Security Council a draft resolution requesting the General Assembly to consider the dispute between Greece on the one hand, and Albania, Yugoslavia and Bulgaria on the other, and to make any appropriate recommendations. This draft resolution received nine votes in favour and two against (Poland and the Soviet Union). Since one permanent member opposed the resolution, it was not adopted.

Finally, the Council decided at the same meeting, by nine votes in favour and two against (Poland and the Soviet Union), that the dispute should be taken off the list of matters of which the Council was seized, and requested the Secretary-General to place all relev records and documents at the disposal of t eneral Assembly.

(c) GENERAL ASSEMBLY RESOLUTION 109(II) OF 21 OCTOBER 1947

At the request of the delegation of the United States of America, the question "Threats to the political independence and territorial integrity of Greece" was placed on the agenda of the second regular session of the General Assembly. The matter was discussed by the First Committee and by the General Assembly in plenary meeting.

The discussion in the First Committee began on 25 September 1947. Draft resolutions were introduced by the representatives of the Soviet Union and of the United States of America. The United States draft resolutions, as amended by the representatives of Canada, France and the United Kingdom, was adopted by the First Committee by thirty-six votes in favour to six against, with ten abstentions.

The report of the First Committee was discussed by the General Assembly at great length, and was finally adopted by the Assembly on 21 October 1947 by forty votes in favour to six against, with eleven abstentions. The Assembly called upon Albania, Bulgaria and Yugoslavia to do nothing which would furnish aid and assistance to the guerrillas fighting against the Greek Government. It also called upon Albania, Bulgaria and Yugoslavia, on the one hand, and Greece, on the other hand, to co-operate in the settlement of their disputes by peaceful means. The Assembly made recommendations with a view to the establishment of normal diplomatic and good neighbourly relations, on frontier conventions, voluntary repatriation of refugees, voluntary transfer of minorities, and on preventing refugees from participating in political and military activities. It established a Special Committee to observe the compliance, by the four Governments concerned, with its recommendations and to be available to assist them in the implementation of the recommendations. The General Assembly also decided that the Special Committee should consist of the representatives of Australia, Brazil, China, France, Mexico, the Netherlands, Pakistan, the United Kingdom and the United States of America; seats were held open for Poland and the Union of Soviet Socialist Republics.

The representatives of the Byelorussian Soviet Socialist Republic, Czechoslovakia, the Ukrainian Soviet Socialist Republic, Poland, the Union of Soviet Socialist Republics and Yugoslavia declared that the Special Committee constituted by this resolution had been given functions and terms of reference which were incompatible with the sovereignty of States as set forth by the Charter, and that it contradicted the principles which were the basis of the United Nations Organization. Because of the above considerations, the representatives of Poland and the Soviet Union declared that they would not participate in the work of the Special Committee.

A resolution, submitted by the delegation of Poland during the ninety-seventh meeting of the General Assembly on 20 October 1947, and recommending a withdrawal from Greece of all foreign troops, military missions, instructors and other military experts, was rejected, on 21 October 1947, by seven votes in favour to thirty-four against, with sixteen abstentions. A Soviet proposal, recommending, among other things, the establishment of a special commission to guarantee by supervision that foreign economic aid was used solely in the interests of the Greek people, was rejected at the same meeting by six votes in favour to forty-one against, with ten abstentions.

(d) United Nations Special Committee on the Balkans

The United Nations Special Committee on the Balkans, constituted by the resolution of the General Assembly, held its first meeting in Paris on 21 November 1947 and has met continuously since 1 December 1947 at Salonika, its principal headquarters.

In accordance with their declarations made during the second regular session of the General Assembly, Poland and the Soviet Union did not participate in the work of the Committee; Albania, Bulgaria and Yugoslavia informed the Secretary-General that they would not co-operate with or extend any facilities to it. The Government of Bulgaria, however, in one instance pertaining to the Evros River frontier incident, permitted investigation on its territory.

(i) *Question of the resumption of diplomatic relations of Bulgaria and Albania with Greece*

By letters dated 20 April and 2 May 1948, respectively, the Governments of Bulgaria and Albania informed the Secretary-General, who transmitted their declarations to the Special Committee, that they were prepared to re-establish diplomatic relations with Greece. The Special Committee, pursuant to these declarations, on 22 May informed the Government of Bulgaria that it was willing to offer its good offices to facilitate negotiations between Bulgaria and Greece leading to the re-establishment of diplomatic relations. The Special Committee suggested a general discussion of this subject between its representatives and those of the Bulgarian Government, at a time and place the latter might indicate. On 8 June 1948, the Bulgarian Government informed the Secretary-General that, in order to facilitate negotiations for the re-establishment of diplomatic relations between Bulgaria and Greece, it proposed that the Greek and Bulgarian diplomatic representatives in Washington, D. C., should start conversations on the conditions under which the objective could be attained. In conformity with the request of the Bulgarian Government, the Secretary-General transmitted this proposal to the Greek Government, which notified him on 12 June of its acceptance thereof and that it had instructed the Greek Ambassador in Washington accordingly.

On 25 June 1948, the Bulgarian Minister to the United States informed the Secretary-General that the negotiations with the Greek Ambassador to the United States regarding the resumption of diplomatic relations between Bulgaria and Greece had reached a deadlock at the first meeting. He attributed the suspension of the negotiations to the refusal of the Greek Ambassador to discuss anything else but the technical aspects of the resumption of diplomatic relations, to the exclusion of all substantive questions pertaining to the relations between the two countries.

On 29 June, the permanent representative of Greece to the United Nations communicated to the Secretary-General a statement issued by the Greek Ministry of Foreign Affairs expressing the attitude of the Greek Government on the subject of the negotiations for the resumption of diplomatic relations between Greece and Bulgaria. In this statement, the Greek Government declared that it was prepared to resume immediately diplomatic relations with Bulgaria without putting forward any terms or conditions whatever, but that it was not prepared to accept any terms or conditions.

The Secretary-General transmitted these two communications to the respective Governments, and to the United Nations Special Committee on the Balkans for its information.

On 28 May 1948, the Special Committee discussed the Albanian communication and decided to consider it further in the light of information supplied by the Greek delegation. An *ad hoc* committee, comꞁ ꞁed of the representatives of China, Pakistan and the United States of America, was constituted to study these communications and submit recommendations to the Special Committee. No final action has yet been taken by the Special Committee on this matter.

(ii) *Work of the Special Committee*

The Special Committee set up three standing Sub-Committees, later merged into two, which, under the guidance of and subject to final decisions by the Special Committee, dealt with different aspects of the Committee's work. The Committee also organized a number of observation groups. The actual number in the field varied from time to time; the highest number simultaneously in the field was five. These groups were assigned zones of responsibility and posted along the northern frontier of Greece; they were instructed to observe the compliance by the four countries concerned with the General Assembly resolution, and to report continuously to the Special Committee on the extent to which good neighbourly relations existed on the frontiers between Greece and its northern neighbours.

The Special Committee endeavoured to advance the solution of the problem of frontier conventions between Greece and its northern neighbours. The inability of the Special Committee, however, to approach and establish contact with Albania, Bulgaria and Yugoslavia made any real progress in this field impossible.

The Special Committee was also handicapped in working out a solution for the problem of refugees. Although the international refugee problem could not be settled by the Special Committee within its terms of reference, attempts have been made to settle the problem of international refugees in Greece. Having made a thorough study of this problem, the Special Committee approached the Preparatory Commission for the International Refugee Organization and some Governments, either directly or through the Secretary-General, with a view to enabling these refugees to emigrate from Greece. The Special Committee likewise found itself unable to make a proper examination of the question of minorities or a study of the practicability of concluding agreements for their voluntary transfer.

In accordance with paragraph 9 (3) of the General Assembly resolution, the Special Committee has thus far prepared two interim reports, transmitted to all Members of the United Nations, and will submit a report to the next regular session of the General Assembly containing a detailed account of its activities. This report is now being prepared in Geneva by a Drafting Committee, which on 10 June 1948 was joined by the whole Committee, the latter having decided to move temporarily to Geneva in order to expedite the preparation and adoption of the report. During its absence, a special *ad hoc* Committee was constituted to continue the functions of the Special Committee in Salonika and to advise and instruct the observation groups which continued to operate in the field. On 14 June, the Special Committee decided that, while maintaining its principal headquarters in Salonika where it will assemble from time to time, it will hold its meetings in Athens, commencing in July 1948, until otherwise decided.

C. The question of the appointment of a Governor of the Free Territory of Trieste

As indicated in the previous report, the Security Council, on 10 January 1947, approved the Instrument for the Provisional Regime of the Free Territory of Trieste, the Permanent Statute and the Instrument for the Free Port and "accepted the responsibilities devolving upon it under the same".

The representative of the United Kingdom, in a letter dated 13 June 1947, requested the Security Council to consider the question of the appointment of a Governor of the Free Territory of Trieste, in accordance with article 11, paragraph 1 of the Permanent Statute. The Security Council first discussed the matter on 20 June 1947. It decided, on 10 July 1947, to establish a Sub-Committee composed of the representatives of Australia, Colombia and Poland to collect additional information about the candidates already suggested, as well as other possible candidates, and to report to the Security Council.

The Sub-Committee submitted to the Security Council on 10 September a report containing information on the candidates who had been proposed up to that date, and recommended certain names for the consideration of the Council. An additional candidate was later proposed by the representative of China.

On 24 September 1947, the Security Council considered the report of the Sub-Committee, following a request by the representative of Australia that the Council should fulfil its responsibility to appoint a Governor to assume office in the Free Territory at the earliest possible moment after the coming into force of the Peace Treaty with Italy. After some discussion, the Council decided to ask the permanent members to hold an informal consultation on the subject.

On 18 December 1947, the Security Council heard a report on the results of the informal consultation among the permanent members and resumed its consideration of the matter. It decided to request the Governments of Yugoslavia and Italy to consult with each other, in an effort to agree on a candidate for Governor of the Free Territory of Trieste, and to report to the Council not later than 5 January 1948.

The Italian observer to the United Nations, in letters dated 12 and 15 January 1948, informed the Secretary-General that the direct conversations between the two Governments had not reached any practical results.

The permanent representative of Yugoslavia, in a letter dated 15 January 1948 to the Secretary-General, transmitted a reply from the Government of Yugoslavia which stated that its efforts to achieve agreement with the Government of Italy on the person for Governor of the Free Territory of Trieste had met with no success.

The Security Council, on 23 January 1948, resumed its discussion of the question of the appointment of a Governor of the Free Territory. The replies from the Governments of Italy and Yugoslavia to the Security Council's request of 18 December 1947 were discussed. The Council decided to ask the permanent members to hold further consultations on the matter, and decided also to discuss it again as soon as possible.

On 9 March 1948, the Security Council resumed its consideration of the question, but after some discussion agreed to postpone the matter and to take it up again at the request of any member of the Council.

D. The Egyptian question

(a) DISCUSSION OF THE EGYPTIAN APPLICATION

In a letter dated 8 July 1947 to the Secretary-General, the Prime Minister and Foreign Minister of Egypt stated that British troops were maintained in Egypt against the will of the people, contrary to the Charter and to the General Assembly's resolution of 14 December 1946. He also complained of British policy in relation to the Sudan. A dispute between Egypt and the United Kingdom had resulted, the continuance of which was likely to endanger the maintenance of international peace and security. Negotiations

had been attempted pursuant to Article 33 of the Charter, but had failed. Consequently, Egypt was bringing its dispute with the United Kingdom to the Security Council under Articles 35 and 37, and requested the Security Council to direct: (1) the total and immediate evacuation of British troops from Egypt, including the Sudan; (2) the termination of the present administrative regime in the Sudan.

The Egyptian application was included in the Security Council's agenda on 17 July 1947, but consideration was postponed until 5 August 1947. The representative of Egypt was invited to the Council table, and amplified the statements made in the Egyptian Prime Minister's letter of 8 July. He maintained that the Anglo-Egyptian Treaty of 1936 had been negotiated under pressure, that it was in contradiction to the Charter, and that it had outlived its purpose. He held that the valley of the Nile formed a physical, economic and racial entity. The British had no legal or political claims with respect to the Sudan.

At the next meeting, held on the same date, the representative of the United Kingdom contended that there was no proof of a threat to the peace, and that, consequently, Articles 35 and 37 were not applicable. Negotiations for a new treaty in 1946 had broken down over a provision in the British draft of the Protocol relating to the Sudan, which proposed recognition of the right of the Sudanese themselves to choose the future status of their country. The Egyptian Government had ignored the British offer to negotiate separately the questions of the evacuation of British troops and of the Sudan. Hence, the Treaty of 1936, which had been freely adopted by the Egyptian Parliament, remained in effect.

The representative of the United Kingdom submitted that the Security Council, in view of its duty to settle disputes in accordance with international law, should find that the Egyptian Government had failed to make its case. The only issue before the Security Council was the legal question of the validity of the 1936 Treaty.

The representative of Egypt, on 11 August, refuted the United Kingdom representative's statements, and contended that it was the duty of the Security Council to deal with the situation brought before it. The Council could not evade its responsibility for the maintenance of peace and security on the grounds of legal arguments. A threat to the peace was involved, as British interference in Egypt created a situation which could not be tolerated any longer.

The representative of the United Kingdom agreed that the primary duty of the Security Council was to maintain international peace and security, but cautioned against the dangers involved in the Council not considering itself bound by international law. All outstanding questions between Egypt and the United Kingdom had been settled by the negotiations in 1946, except the matter of the future status of the Sudan.

The representative of Egypt refuted the British contentions, and urged the Council to carry out the requests made in the original letter from the Egyptian Prime Minister.

(b) Consideration of draft resolutions

During the general discussion several draft resolutions were presented.

(i) *Draft resolution submitted by the representative of Brazil*

The representative of Brazil submitted a draft resolution and accepted amendments proposed by the representative of China. The draft resolution, as amended, took note of the partial withdrawal of British troops from Egypt and of the willingness of the United Kingdom Government to negotiate on the completion of evacuation.

It recommended, in broad terms,

(1) The resumption of direct negotiations between Egypt and the United Kingdom; .

(2) Keeping the Security Council informed of such negotiations, and reporting on them not later than 1 January 1948.

The representative of Belgium submitted an amendment advising consultation with the International Court of Justice, in the case of another breakdown in negotiations, as to the validity of the 1936 Treaty.

The representative of Australia submitted three amendments to the draft resolution, two involving changes in wording, and the third providing for consultation with the Sudanese in so far as the future of the Sudan might be affected by the Anglo-Egyptian negotiations.

The Brazilian draft resolution as amended by China, together with Australian and Belgian amendments, was put to a vote on 28 August but did not receive enough affirmative votes to be accepted.

(ii) *Draft resolution submitted by the representative of Colombia*

The representative of Colombia, on 28 August, submitted a draft resolution which called on the United Kingdom and Egypt to resume direct negotiations with a view to

(1) Completing the evacuation of all British forces from Egypt at the earliest possible date, mutual assistance being provided to safeguard the liberty and security of navigation of the Suez Canal in time of war or imminent threat of war;

(2) Termination of the joint administration of the Sudan, due regard being given to the rights of the Sudanese.

In addition, the Security Council was to be kept informed of negotiations.

The Colombian draft resolution was voted on paragraph by paragraph on 29 August. All paragraphs failed to obtain the required number of affirmative votes, and the resolution was not adopted.

(iii) *Draft resolution submitted by the representative of China*

On 10 September, the representative of China introduced a draft resolution which, while recognizing the natural and reasonable desire of the Egyptian Government for the early and complete evacuation of British troops from Egypt, did not go into the question of how the outstanding issue should be solved, beyond recommending the resumption of direct negotiations.

The representative of Australia submitted an amendment to the Chinese draft expressing confidence in the solution of all issues in dispute

Neither the Australian amendment nor the Chinese draft resolution obtained enough votes to be accepted.

The Security Council remains seized of the question.

E. The Indonesian question

(a) Applications of Australia and India of 30 July 1947

By a letter dated 30 July 1947, addressed to the Secretary-General, the acting representative of Australia stated that his Government considered that the hostilities in progress in Java and Sumatra constituted a breach of the peace under Article 39 of the Charter, and urged the Council to take immediate action to restore international peace and security. As a provisional measure, the Australian Government proposed that the Council should call upon the Governments of the Netherlands and of the Republic of Indonesia to cease hostilities forthwith and to commence arbitration in accordance with article 17 of the Linggadjati agreement.

By a letter dated 30 July 1947 to the Secretary-General, the permanent liaison officer of the Government of India with the United Nations drew the attention of the Council, under Article 35, paragraph 1, of the Charter, to the situation in Indonesia and requested the Security Council to take the necessary measures provided by the Charter to put an end to the situation.

(*b*) Security Council resolution of 1 August 1947 calling for a cessation of hostilities

The two above-mentioned applications were included in the Council's agenda on 31 July 1947, the President having ruled that this action would not prejudice the Council's competence or the merits of the case. The representative of Australia submitted a draft resolution according to which the Council determined that the hostilities constituted a breach of the peace, under Article 39 of the Charter, and called upon the Governments of the Netherlands and the Republic of Indonesia, under Article 40 of the Charter, to cease hostilities forthwith and to settle their disputes by arbitration in accordance with article 17 of the Linggadjati agreement. The representative of India supported the Australian position and suggested, in addition, that the Council ask the parties to revert to the positions they had occupied when hostilities broke out, to avoid undue advantage to the Dutch in negotiations. The representative of the Netherlands replied on the facts, arguing that the Netherlands was sovereign in the region concerned and that the matter was solely within the domestic jurisdiction of the Netherlands. However, his Government was prepared to invite a number of other Governments to send representatives to the Republic, East Indonesia and Borneo, to report on the situation. The representative of the United States of America said that his Government had tendered its good offices in the matter.

At two meetings held on 1 August 1947, discussion was continued on the question of jurisdiction, and various amendments were submitted to the Australian proposal. The representative of the Netherlands said that his Government accepted the United States offer of good offices.

The Council rejected a Soviet amendment stating that the Council considered it necessary that the troops of both sides be withdrawn immediately to the positions they had occupied before the beginning of military operations. This amendment received two votes in favour (Poland and the Soviet Union) with nine abstentions.

After voting upon it paragraph by paragraph, the Council adopted a resolution which was based upon United States amendments to the original Australian draft resolution and deleted the references to Articles 39 and 40 of the Charter. The resolution called upon the parties to cease hostilities forthwith, to settle their disputes by arbitration or by other peaceful means and to keep the Council informed of the progress of the settlement. The President immediately forwarded this resolution to the parties.

On 4 August 1947, the Council discussed questions arising from difficulties in transmission of the above resolution to the parties, and methods by which the Council could be kept informed of developments in Indonesia.

(*c*) Participation of non-members in the Security Council discussions

At its first meeting at which the Indonesian question was discussed, on 31 July 1947, the Council invited the representatives of the Netherlands and India to participate in its discussions.

On 7 August 1947, the Council rejected the request of the Philippines to participate, there being six votes in favour, with five abstentions (Belgium, France, Poland, United Kingdom and the Soviet Union). On 14 August, by nine votes in favour with two abstentions (Poland and the Soviet Union), the Council invited the representative of the Philippines to participate in the discussion, following upon a further application of the Philippines and the new reasons advanced therein.

By a letter dated 12 August 1947 to the President of the Council, the representative of the Republic of Indonesia submitted his Government's request to participate in the Council's discussions without vote. The letter stated that, for the purposes of this dispute, the Republic accepted in advance the obligations of a Member of the United Nations. The legal basis for the Republic's participation was discussed on 31 July and 12 August, and it was agreed, by eight votes in favour to three against (Belgium, France and the United Kingdom) to send an invitation to the Republic of Indonesia.

After discussion on 12 and 14 August 1947, the Council rejected, by four votes in favour (Belgium, France, United Kingdom and United States of America) with seven abstentions, a proposal to invite the representatives of East Indonesia and Borneo to participate in its work. After further discussion on 22 August, the Council rejected by the same number of votes a proposal to invite representatives of East Indonesia and Borneo to participate in its work on the same basis as the representative of the Republic of Indonesia.

(*d*) Establishment of a Consular Commission and of a Committee of Good Offices: resolutions of 25 and 26 August and 3 October 1947

By a letter dated 3 August 1947, the representative of the Netherlands stated that his Government, although persisting in its denial of the Council's jurisdiction in this matter, fully understood its desire to see the use of arms come to an end, and had instructed the Lieutenant

Governor-General of the Netherlands Indies to enter into contact with the authorities of the Republic with a view to the cessation of hostilities in Indonesia.

By a cable dated 5 August, the Prime Minister of the Republic of Indonesia informed the Security Council that, pursuant to the Council's decision of 1 August 1947, the Government of Indonesia had decided to order all Republican armed forces to cease hostilities on 4 August.

By a cable dated 6 August, the Vice-Premier of the Republic of Indonesia communicated details of continued Netherlands military operations.

At the Council's meeting on 7 August, several representatives pointed out that each party claimed that the other had continued hostilities after the cease-fire order was supposed to have become effective. On 12, 14, 15 and 19 August, there was general discussion of the question of the Council's jurisdiction; of the short-term measures to be taken to implement the cease-fire order of 1 August; and of the long-term problems of arbitration and mediation.

The representative of Australia submitted a proposal for the establishment of a Commission, consisting of the representatives of countries to be determined by the Council, which would report directly to the Council on the situation in the Republic of Indonesia following upon the resolution of 1 August. As to the long-term problem, his Government wished the negotiations to start as soon as possible, and would be prepared to act jointly with the United States Government as mediator and arbitrator.

The representative of the Republic of Indonesia urged withdrawal of Netherlands troops to the positions allocated by the Truce Agreement of October 1946; he asked the Council to appoint a commission to proceed immediately to Indonesia to supervise the implementation of the resolution of 1 August. He suggested that the Council should appoint a commission to arbitrate on all points of dispute between the parties, and announced that his Government accepted the offers of United States good offices and of Australia's mediation or arbitration as constructive steps toward the setting up of such a commission.

The representative of the Netherlands maintained his objections to the Council's jurisdiction. He said, however, that his Government was prepared to propose to the Republic that each should designate one State, and that the two States so designated should appoint a third impartial State, which would send a commission of its nationals to inquire into the situation and supervise the cessation of hostilities. The Netherlands Government further proposed that the

career consuls in Batavia should immediately draw up a report on the situation in Java, Sumatra and Madura.

The representative of Poland submitted amendments to the Australian draft resolution providing that the proposed body should be a commission of the Security Council, and adding a provision establishing a second commission of the Council to act on its behalf as mediator and arbitrator.

The representative of China submitted an amendment to the Australian proposal deleting the provision for the appointment of a commission and providing that the Netherlands proposals for consular report and impartial inquiry and supervision be accepted by the Council as steps in the right direction; the amendment also provided that the consular body and the impartial State be requested to forward copies of their reports to the Council, which would consider the matter further if the situation required. This amendment was intended to avoid the delays which would result from further legal controversy and possible reference to the International Court of Justice.

The representative of the Republic of Indonesia said that the Netherlands military action aimed at the destruction of the Republic, which must base its hopes on action by the Council and not on direct negotiations with the Netherlands. He rejected the Netherlands suggestions and said that the United States and Australian offers would contribute to a stable solution only if they formed a continuing part of the action already taken by the Council.

The representative of the Netherlands outlined the unfortunate consequences of the cease-fire order, and said that the Republic had interpreted Netherlands compliance as an admission of defeat.

On the short-term problem, the representative of Australia, jointly with the representative of China, submitted a proposal for a report by the career consuls in Batavia. As to the long-term problem, the representative of Australia submitted a further draft resolution, requesting the parties to submit all matters in dispute to arbitration by a commission on which each party would select one arbitrator and the Security Council a third.

On the long-term problem, considering the doubts which had been expressed concerning the Council's jurisdiction and the undesirability of imposing a particular method of peaceful settlement upon the parties, the representative of the United States submitted a draft resolution according to which the Council tendered its good offices to the parties.

On 25 and 26 August 1947, the Council took its decisions on the above issues debated between 7 and 22 August. Since one of the permanent members voted in the negative, the Council did not adopt a Soviet amendment to the joint Australian-Chinese draft resolution. The amendment proposed the omission of certain sections of the joint proposal, called for the establishment of a commission composed of the States Members of the Council to supervise fulfilment of the decision of 1 August and for a decision to keep the Indonesian question on the Council's agenda. There were seven votes in favour, two against (France and Belgium) and two abstentions (China and United Kingdom).

The Australian proposal requesting the parties to submit all matters in dispute to an arbitration commission was rejected, there being three votes in favour (Australia, Colombia and Syria), and eight abstentions.

By a vote of three in favour (Poland, Syria and the Soviet Union) to four against (Belgium, France, United Kingdom and the United States of America) with four abstentions, the Council rejected a Polish amendment to the rejected Australian resolution providing for the establishment of a Security Council commission, consisting of its eleven members, to act on its behalf as mediator and arbitrator between the Governments of the Netherlands and the Republic of Indonesia.

By a vote of four in favour (Belgium, France, United Kingdom and the United States of America) and one against (Poland), with six abstentions, the Council rejected a Belgian proposal requesting the International Court of Justice, under Article 96 of the Charter, to give an advisory opinion as to whether the Council was competent to deal with the question.

The joint Australian-Chinese draft resolution was adopted by seven votes in favour with four abstentions (Colombia, Poland, United Kingdom and the Soviet Union). By this resolution the Council noted with satisfaction the steps taken by the parties to comply with the resolution of 1 August 1947 and the statement issued on 11 August by the Netherlands Government affirming its intention to organize a sovereign, democratic United States of Indonesia in accordance with the purposes of the Linggadjati agreement. The resolution requested the members of the Council having career consuls in Batavia to instruct them to prepare jointly, for the Council's information and guidance, reports on the situation in the Republic following the resolution of 1 August, such reports to cover the observance of the cease-fire order and the conditions prevailing in areas under military occupation or from which armed forces then in occupation might be withdrawn by agreement between the

parties. Finally, the resolution provided that the Council should consider the matter further should the situation so require.

By eight votes in favour with three abstentions (Poland, Syria and the Soviet Union), the Council adopted the United States draft resolution tendering the Council's good offices to the parties in order to assist in the pacific settlement of their dispute in accordance with the resolution of 1 August. The Council expressed its readiness, if the parties so requested, to assist in the settlement through a committee of the Council consisting of three of its members, each party selecting one and the third to be designated by the two so selected.

A Polish resolution was adopted by ten votes in favour with one abstention (United Kingdom). In this resolution the Council took into consideration the continuation of military operations in the territory of the Indonesian Republic, reminded the parties of the resolution of 1 August for the cessation of hostilities and a peaceful settlement of the dispute, and called upon them to adhere strictly to the recommendations of 1 August.

The representative of the Republic of Indonesia announced his delegation's acceptance of the Council's offer of good offices.

By a letter of 3 September 1947 to the Secretary-General, the representative of the Netherlands stated that his Government maintained its position as to the Council's jurisdiction, but believed that the tendency of the resolutions of 25 and 26 August was acceptable.

Pursuant to the resolution by which the Council had tendered its good offices, the Republic of Indonesia selected Australia as a member of the Committee; the Netherlands selected Belgium; and Australia and Belgium selected the United States of America as the third member.

On 24 September 1947, the Council received an interim report from the Consular Commission. This report noted that advances by Netherlands troops between 20 July and 4 August were in the nature of spearheads behind which considerable numbers of Republican troops had remained. On 29 August, the Netherlands Indies Government had declared its intention of completing the restoration of law and order within a demarcation line covering advanced Dutch positions. The Republic of Indonesia did not accept this demarcation line. The Commission found that the cease-fire order was not fully effective and that casualties and damage continued.

On 3 October 1947, after discussing this interim report, the Council adopted, by nine votes in favour with two abstentions (Poland and the Soviet Union) an Australian draft resolution requesting the Secretary-General to convene the Committee of Good Offices and to arrange for the organization of its work; and requesting the Committee to proceed to exercise its functions with the utmost dispatch.

The Committee of Good Offices assembled in Sydney, Australia, on 19 October. After holding organizational meetings, it commenced its work in Batavia on 27 October 1947.

(e) Question of the Withdrawal of Troops: Resolution of 1 November 1947

At various meetings in October 1947, the Security Council discussed proposals for the withdrawal of armed forces, to assist in arranging the cessation of hostilities and the commencement of just political negotiations. Discussion centred on the practicability of such withdrawals, the ability of the Republican authorities to maintain law and order in evacuated areas, the application of Article 40 of the Charter to the withdrawal of troops, the reports of the Consular Commission, the interpretation of the Council's cease-fire order, and the advisability of directing the parties to desist from inflammatory propaganda, provocation and retaliation, to release hostages and in other ways promote an atmosphere favourable to conciliation.

On 3 October, the representative of the Soviet Union submitted a draft resolution stating that the Council considered it necessary that the troops of both sides be immediately withdrawn to the positions they had occupied before the beginning of military operations.

On 11 October, the representative of Australia submitted a draft resolution calling upon the parties to withdraw their forces at least five kilometres behind the positions held at the time of the cease-fire order of 1 August.

On the same date, the representative of the United Kingdom submitted a draft resolution stating that, to ensure observance of the cease-fire order, the first step would be the establishment of a provisional demarcation line; and requesting the Committee of Good Offices to make this its first objective and to instruct the Consular Commission to make early proposals to that end.

By a letter dated 15 October 1947, the Government of the Republic of Indonesia urged the Security Council to direct the withdrawal of Dutch troops in Republican territory to their *ante bellum* positions. The Republican Government guaranteed safety, peace and order in all areas evacuated by Dutch troops, and accepted supervision as well as co-operation from the Council or any other international body set up for that purpose.

On 13 October 1947, the Council received a summary of the main points of the report by the Consular Commission on the observance of the cease-fire order in Java and Sumatra and on conditions prevailing in areas under military occupation or from which armed forces then in occupation might be withdrawn.

The full report, received on 21 October, stated that cease-fire orders had been issued but that there was no confidence by either party that the other would carry them out, and no attempts had been made to come to an agreement about means to give effect to the order. The Republican Government had ordered its troops to remain in their positions and cease hostilities; the Netherlands Indies Government had proceeded with the restoration of law and order within the limits of the lines laid down by it. The Dutch advance had by-passed considerable Republican forces, which were subject to mopping-up operations in accordance with the Dutch interpretation of the order. The Republican Government had directed its forces to defend themselves and to oppose movements within Dutch-held territory. The different interpretations of the cease-fire order thus made it impossible for the order to be observed.

On 27 October, the representative of the United States of America submitted a draft resolution replacing an earlier text. This draft resolution called upon the parties forthwith to consult with each other about the means to be employed to give effect to the cease-fire resolution and, pending agreement, to cease any activities contravening that resolution; requested the Committee of Good Offices to assist the parties in reaching agreement on an arrangement to ensure the observance of the cease-fire resolution; requested the Consular Commission to make its services available to the Committee; and stated that the resolution of 1 August should be interpreted as not permitting the use of the armed forces of either party to alter substantially by military action the territory under its control on 4 August 1947. The representative of the United Kingdom withdrew his draft resolution, since it was covered by the wider United States text.

On 29 October, the representative of Poland submitted a draft resolution finding that Netherlands forces had failed to comply with the resolutions of 1 and 26 August; calling upon the Government of the Netherlands to withdraw all armed forces and civil administration from the territory of the Republic; instructing the Consular Commission to supervise compliance by the parties with the Council's resolutions and to report to the Council; requesting the Committee of Good Offices to take into consideration, under

Article 40 of the Charter, the fact that the Netherlands Government had not complied with the resolutions of 1 and 26 August. The Polish draft resolution also called the attention of the Netherlands Government to the fact that failure to comply with the provisional measures should be taken into account by the Council under Article 40 of the Charter and that it created a situation which, under the Charter, might lead to the necessity of applying enforcement measures.

By a letter dated 28 October 1947, the Government of the Republic of Indonesia urged withdrawal of Dutch forces from Republican territory occupied after 21 July, and called upon the Council to appoint an international commission composed of representatives of the Council to observe conditions in and to supervise territories handed back to Republican control after the withdrawal of Dutch forces.

On 31 October, the representative of China submitted amendments to the United States draft resolution, providing *inter alia* that consultations should be either direct or through the Committee of Good Offices, and calling upon the parties to cease incitement to activities contravening the cease-fire resolution and to take appropriate measures for safeguarding life and property. On the same date, the representative of Belgium submitted an amendment to the same resolution providing that the cease-fire resolution should be interpreted as meaning that any substantial alteration of the territory occupied by the parties on 4 August would be inconsistent with the cease-fire resolution.

On 31 October, the Soviet draft resolution for withdrawal of troops was rejected, there being four votes in favour (Australia, Colombia, Poland and the Soviet Union), four votes against (Belgium, France, United Kingdom and the United States of America) with three abstentions.

The representative of Australia accepted a Soviet amendment to his draft resolution. The amendment substituted the distance of twenty-five kilometres for the original distance of five kilometres.

The above Australian draft resolution for withdrawal of troops, as amended, was rejected, there being five votes in favour (Australia, Colombia, Poland, Syria and the Soviet Union), one against (Belgium) with five abstentions.

The representative of Australia submitted an amendment to the United States draft resolution stating that any consolidation, control or acquisition of territory not occupied on 4 August 1947 would not be in conformity with the resolution of 1 August.

On 31 October, the Council adopted a United States proposal that a sub-committee be set up to consider the United States resolution and amendments thereto, with a view to reconciling the different texts. The representatives of Australia, Belgium, China and the United States were appointed to serve on this Sub-Committee.

On 1 November, the Sub-Committee presented an agreed text to the Council, and its members withdrew their previous proposal.

After further debate on the proposals before the Council, the representative of Colombia submitted an amendment to the revised United States text, deleting references to the failure of the parties to implement the resolution of 1 August, and adding a provision that the Council expected the two Governments to comply with that resolution fully and faithfully.

The Colombian amendment was rejected, there being five votes in favour (Australia, Brazil, China, Colombia and Syria) with six abstentions.

By seven votes in favour to one against (Poland) with three abstentions (Colombia, Syria and the Soviet Union), the Council adopted the draft resolution submitted by the Sub-Committee. This resolution called upon the parties forthwith to consult with each other, either directly or through the Committee of Good Offices, on the means to give effect to the cease-fire resolution and, pending agreement, to cease any activities or incitement to activities contravening that resolution and to take appropriate measures to safeguard life and property. The resolution also requested the Committee of Good Offices to assist the parties in reaching agreement on an arrangement to ensure observance of the cease-fire resolution; requested the Consular Commission to make its services available to the Committee; advised that the resolution of 1 August should be interpreted as meaning that the use of armed forces of either party to extend by hostile action its control over territory not occupied by it on 4 August 1947 was inconsistent with the resolution of 1 August and, should it appear that some withdrawals of armed forces were necessary, invited the parties to conclude as soon as possible the agreements referred to in the resolution of 25 August 1947.

The Polish draft resolution for the withdrawal of Netherlands armed forces and administration was rejected, there being two votes in favour (Poland and the Soviet Union), four votes against (Belgium, France, United Kingdom and the United States of America), and five abstentions.

After discussion on 9 and 19 December 1947, the President stated, as the Council's understanding, that the membership of the Committee of Good Offices should continue unchanged, notwithstanding the expiration of Australia's term of office on the Security Council.

(f) THE RENVILLE SETTLEMENT OF 17 AND 19 JANUARY 1948 AND SUBSEQUENT DEVELOPMENTS: RESOLUTIONS OF 28 FEBRUARY 1948

On 17 January 1948, the Committee of Good Offices informed the Security Council that the parties would on that day sign a truce agreement and an agreement on political principles as a basis of discussion for the settlement of the dispute.

On 10 February, the Committee of Good Offices submitted an interim report on its work; on the proceedings of the Special Committees established to implement the resolution of 1 November 1947; and on the negotiations leading up to the Truce Agreement of 17 January 1948 and the acceptance of the political principles of 17 and 19 January 1948. The Truce Agreement provided *inter alia*: that a stand-fast and cease-fire order should be issued by both parties; that demilitarized zones should be established in general conformity with the boundary lines of the areas described in the proclamation of the Netherlands Indies Government of 29 August; for the withdrawal of Republican military forces continuing to offer resistance behind forward Netherlands positions; for the maintenance of law and order; and that trade and intercourse between all areas should be permitted as far as possible. The political principles provided that the Republic of Indonesia should be a State within a sovereign, federal United States of Indonesia; and for a Union of the United States of Indonesia and other parts of the Kingdom of the Netherlands under the King of the Netherlands. The principles also dealt with many specific questions such as conditions of plebiscites, democratic guarantees, resumption of trade, transport and communications, etc.

On 17 February 1948, the Council approved a request by the representative of Australia that his country be invited to participate in the Council's discussion.

During various meetings in February, the Council discussed the interim report; the terms of the agreements; the possibility of giving the Committee of Good Offices the power to arbitrate, interpret the agreements and make and publish suggestions to the parties on its own initiative; the maintenance of democratic liberties and promotion of conditions for an equitable settlement; movements for the creation of new States in Dutch-controlled territory, more particularly in West Java, Madura and East Sumatra, and the extent to which these movements were spontaneous or Netherlands-inspired or con-

trolled; and the extent to which the Renville political principles were being observed.

On 28 February, by seven votes in favour to none against, with four abstentions (Colombia, Syria, Ukrainian SSR and the Soviet Union), the Council adopted a Canadian draft resolution noting with satisfaction the signing of the Truce Agreement and the agreement on political principles, maintaining the Council's offer of good offices in its resolution of 25 August and, to that end, requesting both parties and the Committee of Good Offices to keep it directly informed about the progress of the political settlement in Indonesia.

The Council rejected Colombian amendments to the Canadian draft resolution adding an invitation to the parties to direct their efforts to the early and full implementation of the agreed bases for a political settlement and to avail themselves of the Committee's services in connexion with differences in interpreting and applying these principles; and requesting the Committee to continue, by the means it considered appropriate, to assist the parties to attain the above ends.

The representative of Australia submitted an amendment to the Canadian draft resolution adding a provision that the Council considered that it was for the Committee itself to determine whether it should make and, at its discretion, publish suggestions to the parties to help them in reaching a political settlement, without necessarily waiting for the parties to request it to do so. The representative of Australia later stated that, in view of the statements made by members of the Council and by the Chairman of the Committee, he did not feel it necessary to urge adoption of this amendment.

By eight votes in favour with three abstentions (Argentina, Ukrainian SSR and the Soviet Union), the Council adopted a Chinese draft resolution requesting the Committee of Good Offices to pay particular attention to the political developments in West Java and Madura and to report to the Council thereon at frequent intervals.

On 16 March 1948, the Committee of Good Offices reported to the Council on the programme of points for discussion submitted by the parties. On 23 April, the Committee forwarded its report on political developments in West Java and, on 18 May, its report on political developments in Madura. On 19 May, the Committee forwarded its second interim report which described the organization of its work, the activities of its Political, Economic and Financial, Social and Administrative, and Security Committees, and its consideration of letters from the Republican delegation concerning the formation of a provisional federal government for

Indonesia and the formation of an East Sumatra State. On 4 June, the Committee forwarded its report on the Federal Conference which opened at Bandoeng on 27 May 1948.

On 10, 17 and 23 June, the Council continued its discussion, with particular reference to political developments in Java, Madura and East Sumatra; to a projected amendment to the Netherlands Constitution in relation to the Netherlands-Indonesian Union; to the allegation that the Bandoeng Conference was a Netherlands-inspired constitutional convention; to the setting up of an interim federal government; and the Netherlands air and naval blockade. The Council discussed the serious difficulties which had arisen in the negotiations, which were attributed by the Republican representative to Netherlands attempts to eliminate the Republic by circumvention of the actual negotiations. These difficulties were attributed by the Netherlands representative to the Republic's negative attitude to previous agreements for a federal Indonesian State and for a Union of the Netherlands and the United States of Indonesia. On 17 June 1948, the Council discussed reports that negotiations had been suspended, and the President inquired of the Committee of Good Offices concerning the cause, justification and duration of this suspension.

On 22, 23 and 29 June, the Committee submitted reports on the circumstances of the suspension, the resumption of discussions and the continuing difficulties in determining the basis for further negotiations. After discussion on 23 June 1948, the President requested the Committee of Good Offices to continue its efforts to attain a peaceful adjustment between the parties, and to keep the Council informed.

On 21 June 1948, the Council received the first chapter of the Committee's third interim report. This chapter gave a general estimate of the situation and described the serious problems remaining unsolved. The Committee expressed the hope that the parties would be able to re-examine their positions and, with the Committee's assistance, find a formula for harmonizing them. The Committee stated that, in conformity with its mission of good offices, and guided by the Renville principles, it was considering further ways and means of assisting the parties to this end.

F. The India-Pakistan question

(a) APPLICATION OF INDIA AND REPLY OF PAKISTAN

In a letter dated 1 January 1948 to the President of the Security Council, the representative of India to the United Nations stated that a situation the continuation of which was likely to endanger international peace and security existed between India and Pakistan resulting from the aid that invaders, comprising Pakistan nationals and tribesmen from areas adjacent to Pakistan, were drawing from Pakistan for operations against the State of Jammu and Kashmir. He requested the Security Council to call on Pakistan immediately to stop giving such assistance, as it was an act of aggression against India. If Pakistan did not desist from such action, the Government of India might be compelled in self-defence to enter Pakistan territory to take military action against the invaders. The matter therefore was of extreme urgency, and called for immediate action by the Security Council to avoid a breach of international peace.

On 6 January 1948, the Council decided to place this question on its agenda, and invited the representatives of India and Pakistan to participate in the discussion.

At the request of the representative of Pakistan, the Security Council decided to postpone its consideration of the matter until a date not later than 15 January.

Under cover of a letter addressed to the Secretary-General, the Foreign Minister of Pakistan submitted documents giving Pakistan's reply to India's charges and making counter-charges. He called on the Council to take action on the latter. The main points of the counter-charges concerned the Indian Government's action in Kashmir and Jammu, the unlawful occupation of the State of Junagadh and other States by Indian forces, mass destruction of Muslims in a pre-arranged programme of genocide, and failure to implement agreements between the two countries.

(b) SECURITY COUNCIL RESOLUTION OF 17 JANUARY 1948

After hearing representatives of the two parties at meetings held on 15, 16 and 17 January 1948, the Council, on 17 January, adopted by nine votes in favour to none against, with two abstentions, a resolution recognizing the urgency of the situation and calling upon the Governments of India and Pakistan to take all measures to improve the situation and to refrain from making statements or allowing acts which might aggravate it.

The resolution also requested the two Governments to inform the Council immediately of material changes in the situation, actual or anticipated, and to consult with the Council on such changes while the matter was under its consideration.

(c) SECURITY COUNCIL RESOLUTION OF 20 JANUARY 1948

Following discussions between the President of the Security Council and representatives of both parties, the Security Council on 20 January 1948, adopted, by nine votes in favour to none against, with two abstentions, a resolution submitted by the President of the Council.

This resolution established a Commission to be composed of representatives of three Members of the United Nations, one to be selected by India, one to be selected by Pakistan, and the third to be designated by the two so selected. The Commission was to proceed to the spot as quickly as possible. It was to act under the authority of the Security Council and in accordance with the directions it might receive from it. It was to keep the Security Council currently informed of its activities and of the development of the situation. It was to report to the Security Council regularly, submitting its conclusions and proposals.

The Commission was invested with a dual function: (1) to investigate the facts pursuant to Article 34 of the Charter; (2) to exercise, without interrupting the work of the Security Council, any mediatory influence likely to smooth away difficulties, and to report how far the advice and direction, if any, of the Security Council had been carried out. These functions were to be performed in regard to the situation in Jammu and Kashmir State, and in regard to other situations in the India-Pakistan question when the Security Council so directed.

(d) CONTINUATION OF THE DISCUSSIONS

Discussion of the Jammu-Kashmir question was continued in the Security Council at various meetings held between 20 January and 12 February 1948.

During this period, several draft resolutions came before the Council, but failed to prove acceptable to both the parties concerned. The main issues on which differences remained were:

(1) The disposition of the Dominion of India troops then in Kashmir; and

(2) The question of the administrative regime in Kashmir in the period preceding the plebiscite.

The delegation of India took the position that the disposition of the Dominion of India troops was an internal matter for the Dominion of India and the State of Jammu and Kashmir, since this State had become part of the Dominion with its accession thereto, and would so remain until that accession might be reversed by plebiscite. Dominion of India troops were required in Kashmir to maintain law and order. With re-

gard to the setting up of an impartial administration, the delegation of India took the position that the Security Council had not the right to make recommendations that would infringe upon the sovereignty of the State of Jammu and Kashmir. These matters should be left to the good faith of the Government of India and the State Government.

The delegation of Pakistan contended that the presence of Dominion of India troops in Kashmir would react against a free plebiscite, and held that their presence there would be unnecessary when Pakistan took the action it would be called upon to take. The Government of India was said to have pledged withdrawal of these troops before the plebiscite. An impartial administration was also vital to the freedom of the plebiscite, it was held, and the Pakistan delegation brought forward evidence to show the partisan character of the existing administration. The question of constitutionality gave rise to no difficulties, as the external sovereignty only of the State was involved.

On 12 February, the Security Council adjourned consideration of the Kashmir issue to enable the representative of India to report to and consult his Government. It turned its attention to issues other than that of Kashmir and Jammu and, at meetings held on 18 and 26 February and 8 March, took up the question of Junagadh.

On 10 March 1948, after the return of the representative of India, the Security Council resumed its consideration of the Kashmir and Jammu question. Discussions between the President of the Security Council and the parties concerned were continued. A further draft resolution resulted from these conversations but, like the previous proposals brought before the Council, it failed to prove satisfactory to both parties concerned.

(e) SECURITY COUNCIL RESOLUTION OF 21 APRIL 1948

On 21 April, despite the opposition of the representatives of both India and Pakistan, the Security Council adopted a joint resolution, sponsored by six of its members—Belgium, Canada, China, Colombia, United Kingdom and the United States of America.

Under the terms of this resolution, the membership of the Commission established by the Council's resolution of 20 January 1948 was increased to five, one member to be selected by India, one by Pakistan, and three by the Security Council. The Commission was instructed to proceed at once to the sub-continent of India to place its good offices at the disposal of the two Governments in order to fulfil the Council's recommendations for a peaceful settlement. These recommendations concerned (1) the restoration of peace and order, and (2) the plebiscite to decide the issue of the accession of the State of Jammu and Kashmir.

Under (1) above, the Government of Pakistan was to endeavour to secure withdrawal from Jammu and Kashmir of tribesmen and Pakistan nationals not normally resident therein, to prevent any intrusion into the State of such elements and any furnishing of material aid to those fighting in the State. When it was established to the satisfaction of the Commission that withdrawal was taking place and that arrangements for the cessation of the fighting had become effective, the Government of India was to put into operation, in consultation with the Commission, a plan for withdrawing its own forces from Jammu and Kashmir, and reducing them progressively to the minimum strength required for the support of the civil power in the maintenance of law and order. When this had been accomplished, the Government of India was to arrange, in consultation with the Commission, to station its remaining forces in accordance with the principles that the presence of troops should not afford any intimidation or appearance of intimidation to the inhabitants of the State, that as small a number as possible should be retained in forward areas, and that any reserve included in the total strength should be located in their present base area. Personnel recruited locally in each district were to be utilized as far as possible for the re-establishment and maintenance of law, but if these local forces were found to be inadequate, the Commission, subject to the agreement of the Governments of both India and Pakistan, was to arrange for the use of such forces of either Dominion as it deemed effective for the purpose of pacification.

Under (2) above, the Government of India was to ensure that the Government of the State included, in the administration, responsible representatives of the major political groups and was to undertake that such powers as the Plebiscite Administration considered necessary for holding a fair plebiscite would be delegated to it by the State, including, for that purpose only, the direction and supervision of the State forces and police. The Government of India was to make available at the request of the Plebiscite Administration such assistance as the latter might require for the performance of its functions.

A plebiscite administrator was to be nominated by the Secretary-General of the United Nations. He would act as an officer of the State of Jammu and Kashmir, and his nominees and draft regulations would be formally appointed and promulgated by the State of Jammu and Kashmir.

The administrator was to have the right to communicate direct with the Government of the State and with the Commission of the Security Council and, through the Commission, with the Governments of India and Pakistan. Other provisions of the resolution provided against coercion, intimidation, and bribery of voters, and for full freedom of expression, Press, speech, assembly and travel. Withdrawal of Indian nationals not normally resident in Kashmir, release of political prisoners, freedom for citizens of the State to return to their homes, absence of victimization and protection of minorities were also to be ensured.

The Governments of India and Pakistan were each to be invited to nominate a representative to be attached to the Commission for such assistance as it might require in the performance of its task.

This resolution was a result of the conversations held with the two parties by four successive Presidents of the Council (the representatives of Belgium, Canada, China and Colombia), and of the consultations of the Presidents with the representatives of the United Kingdom and the United States of America.

The countries represented on this Commission are: Czechoslovakia (selected by India); Argentina (selected by Pakistan); Belgium, Colombia and the United States of America (selected by the Security Council).

The other charges involved in the Pakistan complaint, namely those of genocide and of non-implementation of agreements, were considered by the Security Council on 7 May 1948, when the two parties presented their cases.

(f) SECURITY COUNCIL RESOLUTION OF 3 JUNE 1948

On 3 June 1948, the Council adopted, by eight votes in favour to none against, with three abstentions, a resolution submitted by the President, which reaffirmed its resolutions of 17 and 20 January and 21 April 1948, directed the Commission to proceed without delay to the areas of dispute with a view to accomplishing in priority the duties assigned to it, and directed the Commission further to study and report to the Security Council, when it considered it appropriate, on the matters in the India-Pakistan question other than the question of Kashmir.

The Council remains seized of the India-Pakistan question.

G. The Czechoslovakian situation

By a letter dated 12 March 1948, the representative of Chile informed the Secretary-General that his Government had "noted that on

10 March 1948, Mr. Jan Papanek, permanent representative of Czechoslovakia accredited to the United Nations, had sent a communication to the Secretary-General", alleging that the political independence of Czechoslovakia had been violated by the threat of the use of force by the Union of Soviet Socialist Republics; and that this situation endangered the maintenance of international peace and security and should be brought to the attention of the Security Council. In accordance with Article 35, paragraph 1, of the Charter, the representative of Chile requested the Secretary-General to refer to the Security Council the question raised in Mr. Papanek's letter. In the name of his Government, he requested that the Council should investigate the situation in accordance with Article 34.

By a letter dated 15 March 1948, the representative of Chile communicated to the Secretary-General Mr. Papanek's letter of 10 March, since he considered it a complementary part of his first letter.

On 17 March, the Security Council decided, by nine votes in favour to two against, to include in its agenda the Chilean communication of 12 March 1948.

It was further decided, by nine votes in favour to two against, to invite the representative of Chile to participate in the Council's discussions on this matter.

On 22 March, the Council decided, by nine votes in favour to two against, to invite Mr. Papanek to take part in the discussion, which was continued on 23 and 31 March.

On 6 April, the Security Council decided to send an official invitation to the Government of Czechoslovakia to send a representative to take part in its proceedings. To that end, the Council adopted, by nine votes in favour to two against, an amended form of a draft resolution proposed by the representative of the United States of America, as follows:

"The Government of Czechoslovakia is invited to participate without vote in the discussion of the Czechoslovak question now under consideration by the Security Council, and the Secretary-General is instructed to notify the Czechoslovak representative to the United Nations accordingly."

In reply to this invitation the representative of Czechoslovakia appointed to replace Mr. Papanek stated that his Government did not find it possible in any way to take part in the discussion. The matters involved were exclusively within the domestic jurisdiction of Czechoslovakia, which rejected with indignation the unfounded complaint which had been put before the Council. Discussion of these internal questions, he added, was contrary to the Charter.

At the meeting of the Council on 6 April, the representative of Chile submitted a draft resolution proposing the appointment of a sub-committee, with a membership to be determined by the Council, to receive and hear evidence, statements and testimonies and to report to the Council at the earliest possible time. This action was to be without prejudice to any decisions which might be taken in accordance with Article 34.

The discussion was continued at meetings held on 12 and 29 April. The representative of Argentina asked that the Chilean proposal be put to the vote under rule 38 of the Council's rules of procedure, and suggested that the sub-committee should be composed of three members of the Council.

After further discussion on 21 and 24 May, the preliminary question was raised as to whether the vote to be taken on the Chilean draft resolution should be considered as a matter of procedure. Eight votes were cast in favour, two against (Ukrainian SSR and the Soviet Union), and there was one abstention (France).

The President interpreted this vote as a decision to regard the draft resolution as a matter of substance, since a permanent member had voted negatively on the preliminary question.

Several representatives opposed this ruling, and the President submitted it to a vote. Six votes were cast to annul the ruling, two votes were cast against its annulment (Ukrainian SSR and the Soviet Union) and there were three abstentions (France, United Kingdom and the United States of America). The President announced that his ruling stood.

The Chilean draft resolution, as completed by the representative of Argentina, read as follows:

"*Whereas* the attention of the Security Council has been drawn by a Member of the United Nations, in accordance with Articles 34 and 35 of the Charter, to the situation in Czechoslovakia which may endanger international peace and security; and the Security Council has been asked to investigate this situation; and

"*Whereas* during the debate which took place in the Council the existence of further testimonial and documentary evidence with regard to this situation has been announced;

"*Whereas* the Security Council considers it advisable that such further testimonial and documentary evidence should be heard;

"*Therefore to this end,* and without prejudice of any decisions which may be taken in accordance with Article 34 of the Charter,

"The Security Council

"Resolves to appoint a sub-committee of three members and instruct this sub-committee to receive or to hear such evidence, statements and testimonies and to report to the Security Council at the earliest possible time."

When put to the vote on 24 May, the draft resolution received nine votes in favour and two against (Ukrainian SSR and the Soviet Union). Since a permanent member had voted against the draft, it was rejected.

The discussion was continued on 26 May, when the representative of Argentina submitted the following resolution:

"The Security Council,

"Whereas it has given consideration to the matter brought to its attention by the representative of Chile regarding recent changes in the Government of Czechoslovakia;

(1) *Considers* it advisable to obtain further testimonial evidence, both oral and written, regarding that situation;

"(2) *Entrusts* its Committee of Experts with the task of obtaining such testimonial evidence and to report back to the Security Council at the earliest opportunity."

H. Relations of Members of the United Nations with Spain

On 23 September 1947, the General Assembly decided to refer to its First Committee, for consideration and report, the question of "Relations of Members of the United Nations with Spain". During the debate in the First Committee on the question, a number of draft resolutions and amendments were introduced, and a Sub-Committee was set up to prepare a joint resolution. On 12 November, the First Committee, after voting upon the draft joint resolution paragraph by paragraph, approved its report to the General Assembly.

After having eliminated the second paragraph of the draft resolution proposed by the First Committee, the Assembly, on 17 November 1947, adopted resolution 114(II). This resolution noted the information given by the Secretary-General in his annual report on the steps taken by Members in pursuance of the Assembly's recommendations of 12 December 1946, and expressed its confidence that the Security Council would exercise its responsibilities under the Charter as soon as it considered the situation in regard to Spain so required.

By a letter of 13 December 1947, the Secretary-General transmitted the Assembly resolution to the President of the Security Council.

On 25 June 1948, the Secretary-General's letter was placed on the provisional agenda of the Security Council. After a brief discussion, the Council decided not to include this question in its agenda.

I. Measures to be taken against propaganda and the inciters of a new war

The question of "Measures to be taken against propaganda and the inciters of a new war" was first submitted to the General Assembly in the form of a draft resolution by the delegation of the Union of Soviet Socialist Republics. The Assembly, having decided to place this question on its agenda, referred it to the First Committee for consideration and report.

The First Committee first discussed this question on 22 October 1947. A general discussion ensued in which more than thirty countries participated. Amendments and draft resolutions were introduced by the representatives of Australia, Canada, France, Venezuela and Poland. After the rejection of the original draft resolution proposed by the Soviet Union, the Committee voted upon a draft joint resolution submitted by the representatives of Australia, Canada and France. This draft joint resolution, amended by the representative of the United States of America, was unanimously adopted by the Committee.

On 3 November 1947, the Assembly adopted unanimously the draft resolution submitted by the First Committee. This resolution condemned all forms of propaganda, wherever conducted, which was either designed or likely to provoke or encourage any threat to the peace, breach of the peace or act of aggression. The resolution requested the Government of each Member to take appropriate steps within its constitutional limits to promote friendly relations among nations, based on the purposes and principles of the Charter, by all available means of publicity and propaganda. Further, the Governments were requested to encourage the dissemination of all information designed to give expression to the undoubted desire of all peoples for peace.

Lastly, the Assembly directed that this resolution should be communicated to the Conference on Freedom of Information.

The Secretary-General, on 13 November 1947, circulated the text of the resolution to Member Governments of the United Nations.

In accordance with paragraph 3, the resolution was also transmitted to the Conference on Freedom of Information, which met in Geneva from 23 March to 21 April 1948.

The Conference unanimously adopted a resolution endorsing the resolution of the General

Assembly. It declared that all war propaganda and reports were contrary to the purposes of the United Nations as defined in the Charter and constituted a problem calling for urgent corrective action. The resolution appealed to all information personnel to serve the aims of friendship, understanding and peace; expressed the conviction that only organs of information which are 'free to seek and to disseminate the truth can greatly contribute to the counteracting of nazi, fascist or any other propaganda of aggression; and finally recommended that all countries take within their respective territories the measures which they might consider necessary to give effect to the resolution.

In another resolution, the Conference took further note of the significance of its resolution mentioned above and emphasized that all appropriate steps should be taken to implement it. Accordingly, the Conference decided:

(*a*) To transmit the said resolution to the Economic and Social Council;

(*b*) To recommend that all countries should promptly inform the Secretary-General of the United Nations of any measures taken by them to give effect to the resolution;

(*c*) To recommend that appropriate national bodies should supplement the work of information agencies and associations of journalists and of others engaged in the collection, publication and dissemination of news, in ensuring the impartial presentation of news and opinion;

(*d*) To recommend that the Members of the United Nations should give consideration to means by which they may be able to assist in implementing the resolution; and further

(*e*) To recommend that the Sub-Commission on Freedom of Information and of the Press, in carrying out the functions which may be assigned to it in accordance with the recommendations of the Conference, should consider appropriate means by which measures taken to give effect to the resolution may be co-ordinated.

J. The problem of the independence of Korea

(*a*) CONSIDERATION BY THE GENERAL ASSEMBLY AT ITS SECOND REGULAR SESSION

After the breakdown of negotiations in the American-Soviet Joint Commission on Korea in August 1947 the Government of the United States of America, on 17 September 1947, submitted the problem of the independence of Korea to the Secretary-General for inclusion in the agenda of the second regular session of the General Assembly.

On 23 September, the General Assembly, on the recommendation of the General Committee, decided to place this item on its agenda and referred it to the First Committee for consideration and report. The First Committee discussed the question of Korea at meetings held between 28 October and 5 November 1947.

Meanwhile, on 17 October, the United States representative had submitted an outline of suggestions and a draft resolution recommending that the occupying Powers should hold elections in their respective zones not later than 31 March 1948 under the observation of the United Nations, "as the initial step leading to the creation of a National Assembly and the establishment of a National Government of Korea" in conformity with a procedure set out in an annex to that resolution.

The draft resolution further recommended the establishment of "the National Government of Korea", which would constitute its own national security forces and would arrange with the occupying Powers for the early and complete withdrawal from Korea of the armed forces of the Union of Soviet Socialist Republics and the United States of America.

In addition, a United Nations Temporary Commission on Korea would be established which would, *inter alia:*

"1. Be present in Korea during the elections in each zone with the right of freedom of travel and observation throughout all Korea;

"2. Be available for such consultations as might be appropriate in connexion with the elections, organization of the National Assembly, the formation of the National Government and the conclusion of agreements for the withdrawal of occupying forces."

During the general discussion in the First Committee on 28 October 1947, two main problems emerged: (*a*) the participation of elected representatives of the Korean people in the discussion, and (*b*) the withdrawal of United States and Soviet troops from Korea.

During the above-mentioned discussions, the Soviet representative and other representatives supporting him maintained that the problem of Korea, like other questions connected with the conclusion of the peace treaties, did not fall within the jurisdiction of the United Nations. He also stated that the United States was not abiding by the Moscow Agreement and was trying to put the blame for the breakdown of negotiations on the Soviet Union, while, in his opinion, the creation of a really democratic Korean Government had been prevented by United States action. The Soviet representative went on to say that now that the proposal had been put on the agenda he would submit his own proposals for the resolution of the Korean problem. In his opinion, and in that of the representatives supporting him, it was essential that the occupying Powers should withdraw and that thereafter it should be left to the Korean people themselves to establish a National Government of Korea. However, the United States representative maintained that the elections should be held first and that, after successful completion of these elections, discussions should be initiated, under the auspices of the United Nations Commission, for the withdrawal of troops. The latter point of view was upheld by the majority of the First Committee.

On the question of the participation of elected representatives of the Korean people in the discussions of the First Committee, the representative of the Byelorussian Soviet Socialist Republic submitted a proposal in the form of an amendment to the United States draft resolution, to the effect that these representatives of the Korean people be invited to take part in the consideration of the question both in the First Committee and at the plenary meetings of the General Assembly. However, the First Committee, on 30 October 1947, decided that consultation with representatives of the Korean people should take place in Korea itself and notably by the United Nations Korean Commission. This decision of the First Committee caused the representatives of the Soviet Union and five other States to abstain from voting on the United States proposal. When the Committee rejected a Soviet Union proposal which would have invited representatives of the Korean people to Lake Success, the representative of the Union of Soviet Socialist Republics stated that, if a United Nations Temporary Commission on Korea were to be set up after the General Assembly had considered the question without the participation in the latter's discussion of representatives of the Korean people, the Soviet Union would not be able to take part in the work of the Commission.

In the meantime, at the ninety-second meeting, the representative of the United States of America presented a revised draft resolution, which incorporated, *inter alia,* parts of the resolution which the First Committee had adopted at its ninetieth meeting on 30 October and suggestions made by several delegations during the previous debate. This text, divided into two resolutions, and further amended by Chinese, French, Philippine and Indian amendments, was adopted on 5 November by forty-six votes in favour to none against, with four abstentions; the Soviet Union, the Byelorussian Soviet Socialist Republic, Czechoslovakia, Poland, the Ukrainian Soviet Socialist Republic and Yugoslavia did not vote because, in their opinion, the

Korean question could not be discussed without the participation of Korean representatives.

Before the close of the debate, the representative of the Ukrainian Soviet Socialist Republic had declared that his country could not take part in the United Nations Temporary Commission on Korea, as proposed in the United States resolution, because no representatives of Korea had been invited to attend the debate.

The General Assembly, on 13 and 14 November 1947, discussed the problem of the independence of Korea on the basis of the report received from the First Committee. The resolutions recommended by the First Committee were adopted on 14 November 1947, without amendment, by forty-three votes in favour to none against, with six abstentions. The following countries did not vote: Byelorussian Soviet Socialist Republic, Czechoslovakia, Poland, Ukrainian Soviet Socialist Republic, Union of Soviet Socialist Republics and Yugoslavia.

The main provisions of these resolutions were as follows:

1. The United Nations Temporary Commission on Korea should consist of representatives of Australia, Canada, China, El Salvador, France, India, Philippines, Syria, and Ukrainian Soviet Socialist Republic;

2. Elections should be held not later than 31 March 1948 "to choose representatives with whom the Commission may consult regarding the prompt attainment of the freedom and independence of the Korean people and which representatives, constituting a National Assembly, may establish a National Government of Korea";

3. As soon as possible after the elections, the National Assembly should convene and form a National Government and notify the Commission of its formation;

4. Upon the establishment of a National Government, that Government should, in consultation with the Commission: (*a*) constitute its own national security forces and dissolve all military or semi-military formations not included therein; (*b*) take over the functions of government from the military commands and civilian authorities of North and South Korea; and (*c*) arrange with the occupying Powers for the complete withdrawal from Korea of their armed forces as early as practicable, and if possible, within ninety days.

5. The Commission might consult with the Interim Committee with respect to the application of the resolution in the light of developments.

6. The Member States concerned should afford every assistance and facility to the Commission in the fulfilment of its responsibilities.

After adopting the resolution proposed by the First Committee, the General Assembly took a vote on a Soviet draft resolution concerning the simultaneous evacuation of the United States and Soviet troops from Korea at the beginning of 1948. The draft resolution was rejected by thirty-four votes in favour to seven against, with sixteen abstentions.

(b) ORGANIZATION OF THE UNITED NATIONS TEMPORARY COMMISSION ON KOREA

The first meeting of the Commission was held in Seoul, Korea, on 12 January 1948. The representative of India was first elected temporary Chairman and, on 4 February 1948, permanent Chairman. On his departure from Seoul, the Commission decided to have a rotating chairmanship for periods of fifteen days. The representative of China was elected Rapporteur.

The Commission established sub-committees and other subsidiary bodies. The work of these organs is summarized below, under (f) "Work of the Sub-Committees", and (g) "Observation of the elections"

(c) APPROACHES TO THE UNION OF SOVIET SOCIALIST REPUBLICS, THE UKRAINIAN SOVIET SOCIALIST REPUBLIC, AND THE MILITARY AUTHORITIES IN NORTH KOREA

On 13 January 1948, the Commission adopted an Australian draft resolution recommending that steps be taken to guard against any misconstruction which might be placed upon the initial presence of the Commission in South Korea, and that "every opportunity be taken to make it clear that the sphere of this Commission is the whole of Korea and not merely a section of Korea".

On 16 January 1948, the Commission decided to address a letter to the military commanders of the armed forces in North and South Korea, stating that the Chairman, accompanied by one member of the Secretariat of the Commission, wished to pay immediate courtesy calls upon the commanders. The Commanding General in South Korea replied to this communication on 19 January and a courtesy call was made on the following day. No reply was received from the Commanding General in North Korea.

At the same time, the Commission cabled the Secretary-General of the United Nations, asking him to request the permanent representative of the Union of Soviet Socialist Republics to the United Nations to transmit to Moscow the communication of the Commission concerning the exchange of courtesies with the General Officers commanding the forces in North and South Korea. In his reply to the Secretary-General on 22 January 1948, the permanent representative of the Union of Soviet Socialist Republics referred to the "negative attitude" taken by the Soviet Government during the second session of the General Assembly towards the establishment of the United Nations Temporary Commission on Korea.

At the same meeting, it was also decided to send a cable to the Secretary-General, asking him to remind the Government of the Soviet Union of the letter of the Secretary-General dated 24 November 1947, drawing attention to paragraph 6 of resolution II of the General Assembly, calling on all Member States concerned to afford every assistance and facility to the Commission in the fulfilment of its responsibilities. No reply was received from the Soviet Government.

A Syrian resolution was also adopted recording the Commission's regret at the absence of the representative of the Ukrainian Soviet Socialist Republic, and stressing the importance of the participation of the Ukrainian SSR in the work of the Commission. On 25 January 1948, a reply was received stating that the attitude of the Government of the Ukrainian Soviet Socialist Republic remained the same as that presented by the Ukrainian delegation at the second session of the General Assembly.

The Secretariat of the Commission subsequently reported that the letter addressed to the Commanding General of the Soviet Forces in North Korea, requesting an exchange of courtesies, together with other United Nations Commission documents, had arrived at Pyongyang, North Korea, but had not been accepted by the Soviet authorities. As a consequence of the negative results of the above approaches, the Commission, on 6 February 1948, adopted a statement concerning the non-co-operation of the military authorities in North Korea.

(d) CONSULTATION WITH THE INTERIM COMMITTEE OF THE GENERAL ASSEMBLY

The question of consultation with the Interim Committee, as provided in resolution 112 (II), arose out of the inability of the Commission to enter North Korea for the purpose of implementing the terms of reference of the resolutions adopted by the General Assembly on 14 November 1947. After a detailed discussion, the Commission adopted, on 6 February 1948, a resolution stating:

"(a) That the negative attitude of the Soviet authorities with regard to the work of the Commission has made it clear that it will not be possible for the Commission to exercise, for the time being, the functions conferred upon it by the General Assembly under the resolutions of 14 November 1947 in the part of Korea occupied by the armed forces of the Union of Soviet Socialist Republics;

"(*b*) That the Commission shall consult with the Interim Committee of the General Assembly in the light of developments, and the Chairman, accompanied by the Assistant Secretary-General, shall represent the Commission during the consideration of this question by the Interim Committee."

The Commission decided, on 11 February, that this consultation should take place on the following questions:

"1. Is it open to or incumbent upon the Commission, under the terms of the General Assembly resolutions of 14 November 1947, and in the light of developments in the situation with respect to Korea since that date, to implement the programme as outlined in resolution II in that part of Korea which is occupied by the armed forces of the United States of America?

"2. If not,

"(*a*) Should the Commission observe the election of Korean representatives to take part in the consideration of the Korean question, as outlined in resolution I of 14 November 1947, provided that it has determined that elections can be held in a free atmosphere? and

"(*b*) Should the Commission consider such other measures as may be possible and advisable with a view to the attainment of its objectives?"

The Interim Committee devoted six meetings to consideration of the questions referred to it by the Temporary Commission. It was agreed at the outset that possibilities open to the Interim Committee were limited, and that it would attempt only to reply to the request for consultation without going into the problem of the independence of Korea.

On 19 February 1948, the Chairman of the Temporary Commission gave a detailed survey of the political situation in Korea and of the views of the various representatives on the Commission. He explained in particular that the Commission had been faced with the necessity to decide between the following possible actions:

(1) To observe elections and facilitate the establishment of a National Government in South Korea only;

(2) To observe elections for the limited purpose of consultation with the elected representatives of the Korean people;

(3) To express its inability to carry out its mission and to return its mandate to the General Assembly.

The Interim Committee took note of the fact that the Temporary Commission itself had unanimously rejected the last of these three possible solutions.

In view of the fact that the Interim Committee should only make recommendations to the Assembly itself, it was suggested during the consideration of the matter that the Interim Committee should limit its action to the following alternatives:

(1) To consider the statement of the Chairman of the Temporary Commission on Korea and to report to the next regular session of the General Assembly with its conclusions;

(2) To suggest that elections be organized in South Korea in order to set up an advisory body with administrative functions, making it clear that this body did not constitute a National Government, but would be established only for consultative purposes to enable the Koreans to make their wishes known through their representatives, both to the occupying authorities and to the United Nations Commission;

(3) To recommend the summoning of a special session of the General Assembly to consider the possibility of amending the resolution of 14 November 1947 in the light of developments, which would offer the possibility of ensuring participation of representatives of the two great Powers concerned and of qualified representatives of Korea.

However, the majority of the Interim Committee agreed that the recommendations of the General Assembly were quite clear and that, if it were, in the present circumstances, impossible to proceed to the election of a National Government and to hold elections in both North and South Korea, it would be possible nevertheless to hold such elections in South Korea, whereas elections to establish a purely consultative body would be contrary to the spirit and letter of the General Assembly resolution.

After a thorough consideration of the views expressed, the Interim Committee on 26 February 1948 decided, by a vote of thirty-one in favour to two against, with eleven abstentions, to answer the questions brought before it as follows:

"That in its view, it is incumbent upon the United Nations Temporary Commission on Korea, under the terms of the General Assembly resolution of 14 November 1947, and in the light of developments in the situation with respect to Korea since that date, to implement the programme as outlined in resolution II in such parts of Korea as are accessible to the Commission."

In a letter dated 1 March 1948 to the Chairman of the Temporary Commission, the Chairman of the Interim Committee stated that, in deciding to answer in the affirmative the first question asked by the Commission, the Interim

Committee had in mind the following principal considerations, in addition to those stated in the resolution:

"1. The elections to be observed by the United Nations Temporary Commission on Korea should be held in a free atmosphere wherein the democratic rights of freedom of speech, Press and assembly would be recognized and respected. In this connexion, the Interim Committee took note of the assurance given by the representative of the United States that authorities of the United States in Korea would co-operate to the fullest extent to that end.

"2. The National Assembly to which representatives are to be elected would be a stage in the formation of a Korean Government, the form of which is to be determined by the Korean people themselves. In reaching this conclusion, the Interim Committee noted that the representatives constituting the National Assembly would be entirely free to consult with the United Nations Temporary Commission on Korea and to carry on such negotiations as they wished with any other Korean groups which might not have participated in the elections, regarding the form of government to be established and the participation of those groups therein. The Interim Committee entertained the hope that, in these consultations and negotiations, the Korean representatives in the National Assembly would be able to secure through their efforts the full co-operation in the government of all Koreans. The Interim Committee was confident that all peaceful methods of persuasion would thus be used to the greatest possible extent for the attainment of Korean unity.

"3. The Interim Committee recognized that the United Nations Temporary Commission on Korea itself has the authority and discretion to discharge its duties in Korea wherever and to the extent that circumstances permit."

(*e*) DECISIONS OF THE TEMPORARY COMMISSION CONCERNING IMPLEMENTATION OF THE INTERIM COMMITTEE RESOLUTION

Following the adoption of the Interim Committee's resolution of 26 February, and in the absence of the Chairman of the Commission and the representative of Canada, the representatives on the Commission present in Seoul unanimously decided, at an informal meeting, to issue a public statement to the effect that the United Nations Temporary Commission on Korea would observe elections in such parts of Korea as were accessible to the Commission, not later than 10 May 1948, according to the terms of reference of the resolutions of the General Assembly, and taking into account the recommendations made by the Interim Committee as

to the conditions to be fulfilled for such elections.

After a detailed discussion, the Commission finally adopted, on 12 March 1948, a resolution stating that the Commission would observe elections announced by the Commanding General of the United States Army Forces in Korea, to be held on 9 May 1948, provided the Commission had ascertained that the elections would be held in a free atmosphere wherein the democratic rights of freedom of speech, Press and assembly would be recognized and respected.

(*f*) WORK OF THE SUB-COMMITTEES (FREE ATMOSPHERE FOR ELECTIONS; HEARINGS; ELECTION LAWS)

In the meantime, the Commission considered all the necessary preparatory work connected with the elections. A large part of this work was done by three sub-committees and other subsidiary bodies created by the Commission.

Sub-Committee 1 was mainly concerned with the consideration of a free atmosphere for elections, the minimum requirements for which it defined as follows:

"Freedom of expression, freedom of the Press and information, freedom of assembly and association, freedom of movement, protection against arbitrary arrest and detention, and protection against violence or threats of violence."

The Sub-Committee drafted recommendations concerning the requirements for a free atmosphere which were adopted by the Commission and transmitted to the Commanding General, United States Army Forces in Korea. As a result of these discussions and recommendations, the Commanding General transmitted to the Commission, on 8 April 1948, a copy of a "Proclamation of the Rights of the Korean People". Issued on 5 April, it contained the ordinary constitutional rights and freedoms such as generally prevail in democratic countries.

Sub-Committee 1 was also concerned with the question of political prisoners. As a result of the recommendations made by the Commission for pardoning of political prisoners, a letter from the Commanding General, United States Army Forces in Korea, was received on 8 April informing the Commission that on 31 March 1948 the Military Governor had issued 3,140 pardons. The pardons restored full civil rights to those released and allowed them to register as voters and to stand as candidates if they so desired.

Sub-Committee 2 was charged with examining documents already received or which might be received from Korean sources by the Secretariat, and with securing statements from Korean personalities whose views might be helpful to the Commission in the discharge of its duties.

A survey was made of the information thus collected, and was handed to the Chairman of the Commission for his guidance during the discussions with the Interim Committee of the General Assembly.

Sub-Committee 3 was established for the purpose of examining the electoral laws and regulations of North and South Korea, and of acquainting itself with the views of Korean, Soviet and United States officials and experts.

This Sub-Committee was unable to consult with North Korean or Soviet experts, or to receive information regarding the application of the electoral regulations in force in North Korea. Its members, however, had cognizance of the transcripts of broadcasts from the North Korean radio, which were circulated by the Secretariat, including the main points of criticism made by North Korean authorities of the election law in force in South Korea.

In its report to the Commission, Sub-Committee 3 stated that the purpose of its recommendations was to bring the electoral provisions which would govern the elections to be held under the observation of the Commission into greater conformity with the General Assembly's resolution concerning adult suffrage, secrecy of the ballot, representation of the Korean people from each voting area or zone proportionate with the population and, in general, to promote as complete and as free an expression of popular will as possible.

(g) Observance of the elections

A request from the National Election Committee for the postponement of the election date from 9 May to 24 May 1948 was considered by the Commission on 30 March; it was decided to inform the Commanding General that it was still the wish of the Commission that the elections should be held on 9 May. On 2 April 1948, the Commanding General stated by letter that he had noted the wish of the Commission that the elections be held on 9 May 1948. However, the Commission later decided to concur in a request of the Commanding General for a one-day postponement of the elections, that is, from 9 to 10 May 1948.

After discussing the question whether there were sufficient grounds to state that a free atmosphere for elections existed in South Korea, the Commission, on 29 April 1948, adopted a resolution proposed by the representative of China which stated that the Commission had satisfied itself, as a result of its extensive field observations in the various key districts in South Korea, "that there exists in South Korea a reasonable degree of free atmosphere wherein the democratic rights of freedom of speech, Press

and assembly are recognized and respected". The Commission resolved "to confirm that it will observe the elections announced by the Commanding General of the United States Army Forces in Korea to be held on 10 May 1948".

As a result of the report of an *ad hoc* Sub-Committee, which considered the methods of observation during the election period, the Commission decided, on 20 March 1948, to establish a Main Committee, into which the existing Sub-Committees were merged and whose activities were to include, among others, the maintenance of permanent liaison with the National Election Committee in Seoul, the receiving and examining of complaints and general information concerning the conduct of the elections, and the examining of and reporting to the Commission on conditions relating to a free atmosphere for the holding of elections. It was further agreed that there should be three periods of observation: (a) the registration period; (b) the period following the registration of candidates; and (c) the election day and the days immediately preceding and following that day.

During the first period, 5 to 10 April inclusive, three field observation groups were sent out covering all nine provinces and the city of Seoul. These groups checked the progress of the registration at that stage and visited a number of registration places to observe the procedure at first hand. They also made detailed inquiries into the existence of a free atmosphere for the elections.

The second period of observation, which took place from 19 to 24 April 1948, began three days after the registration of candidates had closed. The Commission and the Secretariat were in this period divided into four groups, and all provinces and the city of Seoul were visited. The groups received detailed and final information about the results of the registration, which normally ran over 90 per cent, and in some cases close to 100 per cent.

The third period of observation, devoted exclusively to the elections, took place in the period from 7 to 11 May 1948. The Commission and the Secretariat were divided into nine observation groups, which visited all provinces and the city of Seoul. The observations of these nine groups can be divided into three phases, namely: (a) the pre-election days, when most groups witnessed the erecting of polling places and were able to observe the extent to which attempts had been made to sabotage the elections; (b) election day itself, Monday 10 May, when several hundreds of polling places were visited and the actual voting was observed; and finally, (*c*) that same night and the following day, when, at a number of places, the opening of the poll boxes and the counting of ι .'ots were witnessed.

(*h*) PREPARATION OF THE REPORT OF THE TEMPORARY COMMISSION TO THE GENERAL ASSEMBLY

On 1 May 1948, the Commission adopted a Syrian resolution stating: (*a*) that it would be advisable at this time to reach certain preliminary conclusions, and to prepare the first part of its report to the General Assembly to cover the period up to and including the elections; (*b*) that advantages would be gained through concentration on this phase of its task in some centre removed from Seoul; (*c*) that it proceed from Seoul to Tokyo on 15 May 1948 for the purpose of preparing its report on the work covered so far; and (*d*) that it return to Seoul during the first week of June.

On 12 May 1948, the Commission reconsidered its decision to proceed to Tokyo. It adopted a resolution whereby it decided to leave for Shanghai not later than 18 May 1948, and to return to Seoul during the first week of June.

During its stay in Shanghai from 18 May to 7 June, the Commission adopted, in final reading, the first five chapters of the report to the General Assembly, together with a list of annexes.

On 7 June the Commission returned to Seoul. On 10 June it decided that notice should be sent to the elected representatives, stating that the Commission was now ready for such consultation as they might request concerning the further implementation of the Commission's terms of reference, as defined in the resolution adopted, on 14 November 1947, by the General Assembly.

On 25 June 1948, the Commission resolved to record as its opinion that the results of the ballot of 10 May 1948 were a valid expression of the free will of the electorate in those parts of Korea accessible to the Commission, parts in which the inhabitants constituted approximately two-thirds of the population of all Korea.

K. The problem of voting in the Security Council

(*a*) CONSIDERATION BY THE GENERAL ASSEMBLY AND BY THE SECURITY COUNCIL

By a letter dated 3 January 1947, the Secretary-General transmitted to the Security Council resolution 40 (I) adopted by the General Assembly on 13 December 1946. This resolution recommended to the Security Council "the early adoption of practices and procedures, consistent with the Charter, to assist in reducing the difficulties in the application of Article 27 and to ensure the prompt and effective exercise by the Security Council of its functions".

The Security Council discussed the matter on 27 August 1947, and decided to refer it to its Committee of Experts. The Committee was instructed to submit to the Council its recommendations on the measures which the latter should adopt in view of the Assembly's recommendation.

The representative of the United States of America on the Committee of Experts on 2 September 1947, submitted draft rules of procedure for the Security Council relating to voting. The Committee of Experts, however, has not yet begun examination of this question.

Two items relating to the problem of voting in the Security Council were placed on the agenda of the second regular session of the General Assembly. The first, requested by Argentina, proposed the convocation of a General Conference of Members to amend the privilege of the veto. The second, requested by Australia, concerned the extent to which the recommendations contained in resolution 40 (I) in relation to the exercise of the veto had been carried out.

In the course of discussion in the First Committee, the representative of the United States of America submitted a draft resolution providing, in the first place, that the question of voting procedure in the Security Council should be referred to the Interim Committee for its consideration and report and requesting it to consult with any committee which the Council might designate to co-operate with it in the study of the problem. Secondly, the draft resolution invited the permanent members of the Security Council to consult with one another in order to secure agreement on measures to ensure the prompt and effective functioning of the Council. The draft resolution was adopted by the First Committee, and was subsequently adopted by the General Assembly on 21 November 1947 (resolution 117 (II)).

The Secretary-General transmitted the resolution adopted by the General Assembly to the Security Council on 21 November 1947, and, on 10 December 1947, to the permanent members of the Council, pursuant to the last paragraph of the resolution.

On 19 December 1947, the Security Council decided that "the letter from the Secretary-General conveying the resolution be received by the Security Council".

(*b*) CONSIDERATION BY THE INTERIM COMMITTEE

To give effect to the provisions of the General Assembly resolution of 21 November 1947, which requested the Interim Committee to "consider the problem of voting in the Security Council", the Committee, following a general discussion at its twelfth meeting on 15 March 1948, appointed a Sub-Committee to examine and analyse all proposals submitted during the second regular session of the General Assembly, or which might be submitted to the Interim Committee or to the Sub-Committee, and to make a preliminary report thereon.

The Sub-Committee held seven meetings during which proposals submitted by Argentina, China, the United Kingdom, New Zealand, the United States of America, Canada, Belgium and Turkey were considered. These proposals may be classified under five general headings:

(i) Liberalization of the voting procedure in the Security Council by means of interpretation of the Charter;

(ii) Improvement of the functioning of the Security Council on the basis of agreement among the permanent members of the Council;

(iii) Amendment to Article 27 of the Charter with a view to eliminating or modifying the provision requiring the unanimity of the permanent members of the Security Council;

(iv) Convocation of a General Conference to consider whether the proper time had arrived for reviewing the Charter;

(v) Recourse to an advisory opinion of the International Court of Justice, by a procedural vote of the Security Council, whenever a permanent member invokes its "veto" privilege, in an attempt to prevent a request for such an opinion.

Before considering in detail these various proposals, and in particular, the list of Security Council decisions which the United States proposal recommended should be taken by any seven members of the Council, the Sub-Committee examined a list of ninety-eight possible decisions which were "adopted or might be adopted by the Security Council in application of the Charter or the Statute of the International Court of Justice". In studying this list, the Sub-Committee first sought to determine which decisions were procedural within the meaning of Article 27, paragraph 2, of the Charter. The conclusions reached by the Sub-Committee on this subject were based on the following criteria:

(i) All decisions of the Security Council adopted in application of provisions which appear in the Charter under the sub-heading "Procedure", and all decisions which relate to the internal functioning of the Security Council and the conduct of its business are procedural and, as such, are governed by a procedural vote.

(ii) All decisions which concern the relationship between the Security Council and other organs of the United Nations, and those bearing a close analogy to them relate to the internal procedure of the United Nations, and, consequently, are subject to a procedural vote.

(iii) Certain decisions which are instrumental in arriving at or in following up a procedural decision are procedural.

The Sub-Committee then sought to determine which decisions, whether considered procedural or non-procedural, should in its opinion be decided by the vote of any seven members of the Security Council. The conclusions reached by the Sub-Committee on this subject were based on the consideration whether these decisions, if taken by a vote of any seven members, would improve the functioning of the Council and permit it, promptly and effectively, to fulfil its responsibilities under the Charter.

In its report to the Interim Committee, the Sub-Committee recommended:

(1) That, in the list of ninety-eight possible decisions of the Security Council, thirty-six should be regarded as procedural; and

(2) That twenty-one possible decisions relating to the various Chapters of the Charter, including Chapter VI on pacific settlement of disputes, should be taken by a vote of any seven members of the Council.

No recommendation was made on the other possible decisions and, in particular, on those concerning the application of Chapter VII of the Charter.

As to the implementation of its conclusions, the Sub-Committee proposed to the Interim Committee that the General Assembly should recommend to the members of the Security Council that the thirty-six possible Council decisions mentioned in (1) above are procedural, and that the permanent members and other members of the Security Council should agree to steps being taken between them to make this agreement effective and conduct their business accordingly.

The Sub-Committee also proposed that the General Assembly should recommend to the permanent members of the Security Council that they agree that the possible decisions of the Security Council mentioned in (2) above should be adopted by the vote of any seven members, whether these decisions are considered as procedural or non-procedural, and that steps should be taken to make this agreement effective.

In addition, the Sub-Committee proposed that the General Assembly should recommend to the permanent members of the Security Council that:

(i) Whenever possible, consultations should take place among them concerning important decisions to be taken by the Security Council;

(ii) They should agree among themselves to consult with one another where possible, before a vote is taken, if their unanimity is required to enable the Council to function effectively;

(iii) If there is not unanimity, it should be agreed that the minority of the permanent members, mindful of the fact that they are acting on behalf of all the United Nations, would exercise the "veto" only when they consider the question of vital importance to the United Nations as a whole, and that they would explain on what grounds they consider this condition to be present;

(iv) They should agree that they will not exercise their "veto" against a proposal simply because it does not go far enough to satisfy them;

(v) They should agree on the definition of a "dispute" for the purpose of Article 27, paragraph 3 of the Charter.

Finally, the Sub-Committee proposed that the General Assembly should "recommend to the Members of the United Nations that, in agreements conferring functions on the Security Council, such conditions of voting within this body be provided as would exclude the application of the existing rule of unanimity".

The report of the Sub-Committee is at present under consideration by the Interim Committee and will, in accordance with the General Assembly resolution, be "transmitted to the Secretary-General not later than 15 July 1948, and by the Secretary-General to the Member States and to the General Assembly".

L. The Interim Committee of the General Assembly

(a) PROPOSAL FOR THE ESTABLISHMENT OF AN INTERIM COMMITTEE OF THE GENERAL ASSEMBLY ON PEACE AND SECURITY

At its second regular session, the General Assembly included in its agenda a proposal submitted by the United States of America for the creation of a subsidiary organ of the General Assembly which would function between sessions in order to assist the Assembly in the discharge of the responsibilities conferred upon it by the Charter in the field of peace and security. The proposed body was intended to assist the Assembly by considering and making recommendations to it on questions arising within the purview of Article 14 or on such questions as might be brought before the General Assembly by the Security Council pursuant to Article 11, paragraph 2, and by making recommendations thereon to the Assembly. The proposed body was also to consider the general principles of co-operation in the maintenance of international peace and

security under Article 11, paragraph 1, and to initiate studies and make recommendations for the promotion of international co-operation in the political field under Article 13, paragraph 1a.

This proposal gave rise to extensive debates in the First Committee and in the Sub-Committee which was set up to study the various proposals submitted on the subject, as well as in the Assembly itself. The proposal was opposed on the ground that to confer such powers upon a committee of the Assembly was contrary to the Charter. This opposition led the representatives of the Byelorussian Soviet Socialist Republic, Czechoslovakia, Poland, the Ukrainian Soviet Socialist Republic, the Union of Soviet Socialist Republics and Yugoslavia to declare that it would not be possible for their delegations to participate in the work of any such body if it were established. In accordance with this statement, the representatives of the Soviet Union and Czechoslovakia, who were appointed to serve on the Sub-Committee of the First Committee, did not attend its meetings; their seats remained vacant throughout the work of the Sub-Committee.

During the debates in the Sub-Committee, the necessity was emphasized of ensuring that the mandate of the proposed body should in no way encroach upon that of any other organ of the United Nations. Great care was taken in drafting its terms of reference to ensure that no such encroachment would occur. Thus, very significant limitations were incorporated in the draft resolution elaborated by the Sub-Committee and later approved by the First Committee.

(b) ESTABLISHMENT OF THE INTERIM COMMITTEE

On 13 November 1947, the General Assembly, by forty-one votes in favour to six against, with six abstentions, decided as follows (resolution 111 (II)):

"1. There shall be established, for the period between the closing of the present session and the opening of the next regular session of the General Assembly, an Interim Committee on which each Member of the General Assembly shall have the right to appoint one representative;

"2. The Interim Committee, as a subsidiary organ of the General Assembly established in accordance with Article 22 of the Charter, shall assist the General Assembly in the performance of its functions by discharging the following duties;

"(a) To consider and report, with its conclusions, to the General Assembly on such matters as have been referred to it by the General Assembly;

"(*b*) To consider and report with its conclusions to the General Assembly on any dispute or any situation which, in virtue of Articles 11 (paragraph 2), 14 or 35 of the Charter, has been proposed for inclusion in the agenda of the General Assembly by any Member of the United Nations or brought before the General Assembly by the Security Council, provided the Committee previously determines the matter to be both important and requiring preliminary study. Such determination shall be made by a majority of two-thirds of the members present and voting, unless the matter is one referred by the Security Council under Article 11 (paragraph 2), in which case a simple majority will suffice;

"(*c*) To consider, as it deems useful and advisable, and report with its conclusions to the General Assembly on methods to be adopted to give effect to that part of Article 11 (paragraph 1) which deals with the general principles of co-operation in the maintenance of international peace and security, and to that part of Article 13 (paragraph 1a) which deals with the promotion of international co-operation in the political field.

"(*d*) To consider, in connexion with any matter under discussion by the Interim Committee, whether occasion may require the summoning of a special session of the General Assembly and, if it deems that such session is required, so to advise the Secretary-General in order that he may obtain the views of the Members of the United Nations thereon;

"(*e*) To conduct investigations and appoint commissions of inquiry within the scope of its duties, as it may deem useful and necessary, provided that decisions to conduct such investigations or inquiries shall be made by a two-thirds majority of the members present and voting. An investigation or inquiry elsewhere than at the headquarters of the United Nations shall not be conducted without the consent of the State or States in whose territory it is to take place;

"(*f*) To report to the next regular session of the General Assembly on the advisability of establishing a permanent committee of the General Assembly to perform the duties of the Interim Committee as stated above, with any changes considered desirable in the light of experience."

The Assembly explicitly stipulated in the same resolution that the Interim Committee should, at all times, take into account the responsibilities of the Security Council for the maintenance of international peace and security, as well as the duties assigned by the Charter, by the General Assembly or by the Security Council to other Councils, or to any committee or commission.

(*c*) CONVENING OF THE INTERIM COMMITTEE

The first meeting of the Interim Committee was convened on 5 January 1948 at Lake Success, in accordance with the terms of the Assembly resolution, which required that the Committee should meet not later than six weeks after the close of the second regular session of the Assembly.

The six Members of the General Assembly which, during the second regular session, did not participate in the elaboration of terms of reference for the Interim Committee, decided to maintain their previous attitude, and have not taken part in the work of the Committee.

(*d*) SPECIFIC MATTERS REFERRED TO THE INTERIM COMMITTEE BY THE GENERAL ASSEMBLY

(i) *Consultation by the United Nations Temporary Commission on Korea*

Within a few weeks after it had been convened for the first time, the Interim Committee devoted six meetings to a thorough consideration of the application—in the light of developments—of General Assembly resolution 112 (II) establishing the United Nations Temporary Commission on Korea, in order to supply the advice and guidance sought by that Commission, which had called for consultation with the Interim Committee in conformity with the resolution. An account of this consultation is included in this chapter in section J, "The Problem of the Independence of Korea".[1]

(ii) *The Problem of Voting in the Security Council*

The problem of voting in the Security Council was referred to the Interim Committee by the General Assembly in its resolution 117 (II) of 21 November 1947. A sub-committee (Sub-Committee 3) was established by the Interim Committee to study this question. An account of its work is included in this chapter in section K, "The Problem of Voting in the Security Council".[2]

(*e*) MATTERS SUBMITTED FOR THE AGENDA OF THE GENERAL ASSEMBLY UNDER ARTICLES 11, 14 OR 35 OF THE CHARTER

The Interim Committee, in the second field of activity conferred upon it, has not so far made use of its power to undertake the preparatory consideration of important disputes and situations submitted for inclusion in the agenda of the Assembly under Articles 11 (paragraph 2), 14 or 35 of the Charter.

---

[1] See page 29.
[2] See page 35.

(f) PROMOTION OF INTERNATIONAL CO-OPERATION IN THE POLITICAL FIELD

The third task conferred upon the Interim Committee is related to the responsibilities placed upon the General Assembly by Articles 11 (paragraph 2) and 13 (paragraph 1a) of the Charter, under which the Assembly may consider the general principles of co-operation in the maintenance of peace and security and initiate studies for the purpose of promoting international co-operation in the political field.

The work already accomplished by Sub-Committee 2, which was established to prepare these subjects for consideration by the Interim Committee, has laid a foundation for further study. Such study would presumably lead to the adoption of methods whereby the General Assembly would be better enabled to carry out its functions in these fields. The Sub-Committee has made a general recommendation to the effect that the studies already initiated, in particular in respect to pacific settlement of disputes, should be continued by some organ like the Interim Committee on which all Members of the United Nations would be entitled to representation.

(g) ADVISABILITY OF ESTABLISHING A PERMANENT COMMITTEE OF THE GENERAL ASSEMBLY

A special Sub-Committee (Sub-Committee 4) was established to study the overall operation of the Interim Committee, to elaborate the functions that might usefully be performed by a standing committee of the Assembly and to determine the field of activity in which these functions should be exercised. Two working groups were set up by the Sub-Committee to study the functions of preparation and implementation that might be undertaken by such an organ. In addition to powers substantially the same as those of the Interim Committee, the reports of the working groups contained suggestions that the powers of such a subsidiary organ should be extended to cover items submitted for inclusion in the agenda of the General Assembly in certain fields other than the political field. The Sub-Committee has further suggested that the proposed committee should be empowered to undertake functions of implementation of Assembly resolutions. It was agreed, however, that the committee would exercise these functions only with regard to those resolutions in which specific provision to that effect had been included by the Assembly.

While agreement has not yet been reached on the fields of activity in which a new interim committee should be empowered to function, Sub-Committee 4 has already decided to propose in its report that an interim committee, on which all Members would be entitled to be represented, should be established during the third regular session for another experimental year.

M. Military Staff Committee

It is recalled that the Military Staff Committee, in a letter of 30 April 1947 to the Secretary-General, forwarded to the Council its report on "General Principles governing the organization of the Armed Forces made available to the Security Council by Member nations of the United Nations".

The Security Council began its consideration of the report on 4 June 1947. In the course of the debate, various questions raised in the discussion were referred to the Military Staff Committee.

As the result of a request from the Security Council on 26 June 1947, the Military Staff Committee submitted to the Council an estimate of the overall strength of the armed forces to be made available to the Security Council including the strength and composition of the separate components and the proportions that should be provided by the five permanent members.

The report and estimate of the Military Staff Committee are still under consideration by the Security Council.

Pending the completion of the examination by the Security Council of the report and estimate, the Military Staff Committee has undertaken a provisional consideration of the "overall strength and composition" of these forces, as outlined in a programme of work adopted by the Military Staff Committee on 16 May 1947.

The question of the overall strength and composition of the armed forces to be made available to the Security Council was the subject of informal discussions by a Sub-Committee from May to December 1947, with a view to reconciling the provisional estimates submitted by the various delegations. On 23 December 1947, the Sub-Committee submitted the results of its deliberations to the Military Staff Committee. Since that date, the Military Staff Committee has had the report under consideration; but, owing to the thorough examination and extensive discussion which it necessitates, the work has not yet been completed.

N. Commission for Conventional Armaments

The Commission for Conventional Armaments, set up by the Council in pursuance of resolution 41 (I) adopted by the General Assembly on 14 December 1946, submitted to the Security Council, on 25 June 1947, a plan for the organization of its work. The Council having approved the plan on 8 July 1947, the Commission, at its tenth meeting held on 16 July 1947, adopted unanimously the following resolution establishing the Working Committee of the Whole provided for in its original plan of 25 June:

"The Commission for Conventional Armaments resolves:

"To establish the Working Committee of the Whole provided by the resolution of 25 June 1947. The Committee shall have as its terms of reference the plan of work approved by the Security Council at its 152nd meeting. The Working Committee will be authorized to establish such sub-committees from time to time as it may deem necessary and to define their terms of reference. The Chairman of the Commission for Conventional Armaments shall act as Chairman of the Working Committee."

The Working Committee met in closed session on 20 August 1947. Between that time and 30 June 1948, it was found possible to hold only sixteen meetings, owing to the requirements of the General Assembly and the heavy commitments of the Security Council and Atomic Energy Commission.

At its fourth meeting, on 9 September 1947, the Committee completed consideration of item 1 of the plan of work and adopted the following resolution defining the jurisdiction of the Commission:

"The Working Committee resolves to advise the Security Council:

"(1) That it considers that all armaments and armed forces, except atomic weapons and weapons of mass destruction, fall within its jurisdiction and that weapons of mass destruction should be defined to include atomic explosive weapons, radio-active material weapons, lethal chemical and biological weapons, and any weapons developed in the future which have characteristics comparable in destructive effect to those of the atomic bomb or other weapons mentioned above.

"(2) That it proposes to proceed with its work on the basis of the above definition."

The following meetings were devoted to a detailed discussion of proposals submitted by each delegation relating to items 2 and 3 of the plan of work. Draft resolutions were submitted by France and Syria, Australia, and the United Kingdom aiming at the crystallization of points on which there had been majority agreement. These texts were later withdrawn in favour of a revised United Kingdom draft resolution. Amendments have been submitted to this draft

resolution by the United States of America, Canada and Colombia. The amendments of the first two delegations have been accepted by the United Kingdom.

O. Atomic Energy Commission

The Secretary-General's report of last year indicated the nature and direction of the programme of the Atomic Energy Commission during the summer of 1947. Two committees were pursuing concurrent discussions: The Working Committee (Committee 1) was considering amendments and additions to the first report proposed on 18 February 1947 by the representative of the Union of Soviet Socialist Republics; and Committee 2 was formulating specific proposals for the international control of atomic energy following the "list of principal subjects" which had been adopted in April 1947 as a guide to discussion. In addition, the Committee had before it the Soviet proposals of 11 June 1947 as a further matter for consideration.

The Working Committee completed its examination of the Soviet amendments and additions on 23 July 1947, and instructed the Secretariat to draw up an account of the discussions. The Committee then turned its attention to the preparation of a second report, in accordance with the request made by the Security Council in its resolution of 10 March 1947. On 4 August 1947, the procedures to be followed were agreed upon and a drafting sub-committee was established.

During July, Committee 2 continued, through its working groups and by means of informal conversations, with the formulation of specific proposals regarding control. By 31 July 1947, a series of six documents had been presented to Committee 2 under the following titles:

(1) Functions of the international agency in relation to research and development activities;

(2) Functions of the international agency in relation to location and mining of ores;

(3) Functions of the international agency in relation to processing and purification of source material;

(4) Functions of the international agency in relation to stockpiling, production and distribution of nuclear fuels and the design, construction and operation of isotope separation plants and of nuclear reactors;

(5) Operational and developmental functions of the international agency and its relation to planning, co-ordination and direction of atomic activities;

(6) Rights of and limitations on the international agency in relation to inspections, surveys and explorations.

Formal consideration of these documents was postponed until the end of August, in order that the representatives might consult their Governments and give expression to official views.

In the meantime, Committee 2 embarked upon a preliminary debate on the Soviet proposals of 11 June 1947, in the course of which each delegation made a general statement. On 15 August, the Committee adopted a resolution to the effect that these proposals, as then constituted, did not provide an adequate basis for the development of specific proposals for an effective system of international control. Several delegations expressed a desire to have various points clarified, however, and it was understood that debate upon the proposals should not be considered terminated. In particular, on 11 August 1947, the representative of the United Kingdom addressed to the representative of the Soviet Union a letter containing eleven questions. These were answered by the representative of the Soviet Union in a reply dated 5 September 1947; however, in view of the intention to produce the second report before the General Assembly convened, discussion of the questions and answers was postponed.

In the latter part of August and early September, the Commission proceeded with the compilation of its second report. The six documents prepared by Committee 2 were the subject of formal debate and amendment, after which they were assembled under the title "Operational and developmental functions of the international control agency" and submitted as part II of the report. This part, together with part I (proceedings), part III ("Report on the deliberations of the Working Committee concerning the amendments and additions to the first report submitted by the representative of the Union of Soviet Socialist Republics at the hundred and eighth meeting of the Security Council"), part IV ("Report on the consideration of the proposals of the Union of Soviet Socialist Republics of 11 June 1947"), and an introduction, were reviewed in the Working Committee and forwarded to the Commission as the draft second report.

The Commission considered the draft report on 10 and 11 September 1947. At the conclusion of the debate, the report was adopted by ten affirmative votes, the representative of the Soviet Union voting in the negative, and the representative of Poland abstaining. The report was then forwarded to the Security Council by the Chairman.

After the second regular session of the General Assembly, during which no meetings were held, the Working Committee met on 18 December 1947 to consider its future method of work as well as that of Committee 2. A two-fold programme was again decided upon: the Working

Committee would discuss the Soviet proposals of 11 June 1947 in the light of the questions submitted by the representative of the United Kingdom and the replies thereto by the representative of the Soviet Union; Committee 2 would continue the examination of items on its "list of principal subjects", beginning with a study of the organizational structure of the control organ.

On 1 January 1948, in accordance with the changes in membership of the Security Council, the representatives of Australia, Brazil and Poland retired from the Commission and the representatives of Argentina and the Ukrainian Soviet Socialist Republic were added. The third new non-permanent member appointed to the Council was Canada, already a member of the Commission.

On 16 January 1948, the Working Committee resumed its study of the Soviet proposals of 11 June 1947 and devoted seven meetings to their examination. At the conclusion of the detailed discussion, the Committee proceeded to review the proposals as a whole, devoting three additional meetings to this task. During the general discussion, on 29 March 1948, the representative of the United Kingdom presented, on behalf of his own delegation and those of Canada, China and France, a joint statement analysing the proposals and submitting a resolution concerning them. This statement and the resolution were adopted by the Committee on 5 April, by nine votes in favour to two against (Ukrainian SSR and the Soviet Union).

In resuming its work on 19 January 1948, Committee 2 agreed that, for the time being, it should confine its activity to sub-heading "(a) Organizational structure" and invite appropriate experts on staffing and organization to give evidence. The next two meetings were devoted to examining experts and an informal conversation also was held, as well as a number of private and unofficial gatherings of the delegations. At the Committee's meeting on 30 March 1948, it appeared to the majority of the members that the question of organization could not be clearly defined unless there was prior agreement upon the functions and powers of the international control agency. No formal decision was taken, but Committee 2 on that date adjourned *sine die*.

On 7 May 1948, the Commission met to receive and discuss a statement presented by the representative of France on behalf of his own delegation and those of the United Kingdom and the United States of America. This statement outlined the reasons why the Commission's work had been interrupted and the conditions which would be necessary in order to resume consideration of its task, and summarized the work which had been accomplished. At the same time, the representative of France circulated "A summary of the majority plan of control". The statement and the recommendations contained therein were considered further by the Commission on 17 May, and were adopted by nine votes in favour to two against (Ukrainian SSR and the Soviet Union).

At the same meeting, the Commission discussed the compilation of its third report. Members agreed upon a table of contents which included the three-nation statement, "Report and recommendations of the Atomic Energy Commission" (part I), proceedings (part II), and the annexes.

Part I of the third report concludes with the following recommendation:

"*The Atomic Energy Commission,* therefore

"*Recommends* that, until such time as the General Assembly finds that this situation no longer exists, or until such time as the sponsors of the General Assembly resolution of 24 January 1946, who are the permanent members of the Atomic Energy Commission, find, through prior consultation, that there exists a basis for agreement on the international control of atomic energy, negotiations in the Atomic Energy Commission be suspended.

"In accordance with its terms of reference, the Atomic Energy Commission submits this report and recommendation to the Security Council for consideration, and

"*Recommends* that they be transmitted, along with the two previous reports of the Commission, to the next regular session of the General Assembly as a matter of special concern."

The Security Council began consideration of the third report of the Atomic Energy Commission on 11 June 1948. At that meeting, the representative of the United States submitted a draft resolution which would have indicated that the Security Council had received, examined, accepted, approved certain sections of, and directed the Secretary-General to transmit, the Atomic Energy Commission's three reports to the General Assembly, together with the record of the Security Council's approval thereof. The debate in the Security Council occupied two more meetings. During these meetings, the representatives of the United Kingdom, Canada, France, China, Belgium and Colombia stated that they were in general agreement with the substance of the third report, while the representatives of the Union of Soviet Socialist Republics and the Ukrainian Soviet Socialist Republic expressed their disagreement with it. At the second meeting, on 22 June, the Security Council voted on the draft resolution submitted by the representative of the United States, which received nine votes in favour and two against (Ukrainian SSR and the Soviet Union) and was not adopted.

After the United States draft resolution had been defeated, the representative of Canada submitted a draft resolution which was adopted by nine votes in favour with two abstentions (Ukrainian SSR and the Soviet Union) reading as follows:

"*The Security Council,*

"Having received and examined the first, second and third reports of the United Nations Atomic Energy Commission,

"*Directs* the Secretary-General to transmit to the General Assembly and to the Member nations of the United Nations, the first, second and third reports of the Atomic Energy Commission, together with the record of the deliberations of the Security Council on this subject, as a matter of special concern."

In addition to serving the Atomic Energy Commission and its Committees, the Atomic Energy Commission Group has undertaken certain research projects in connexion with the drafting of its three reports. It is now engaged in compiling two bibliographies on atomic energy —one on its political, economic and social aspects, and the other on its scientific aspects.

P. Admission of new Members

(a) APPLICATIONS FOR ADMISSION

At the time of the preparation of the last report on the work of the Organization, the following countries had applied for admission to the United Nations:

	Date of application
The People's Republic of Albania	25 January 1946
Mongolian People's Republic	24 June 1946
Afghanistan	2 July 1946
Ireland	2 July 1946
The Hashemite Kingdom of Transjordan	8 July 1946
Portugal	2 August 1946
The Republic of Iceland	2 August 1946
Siam	5 August 1946
Sweden	9 August 1946

At the second part of the first session, the General Assembly, on the recommendation of the Security Council, decided to admit as Members of the United Nations the following countries:

Afghanistan, the Republic of Iceland, Siam and Sweden.

Between the close of the second part of the first session of the Assembly and the date of preparation of the present report, applications were received from the following countries:

	Date of application
Hungary	22 April 1947
Italy	7 May 1947
Austria	2 July 1947
Roumania	10 July 1947
Yemen	21 July 1947
Bulgaria	26 July 1947
Pakistan	15 August 1947
Finland	19 September 1947
Burma	27 February 1948
Ceylon	25 May 1948

(b) CONSIDERATION OF APPLICATIONS BY THE SECURITY COUNCIL

The General Assembly, at the second part of its first session, recommended (resolution 35 (I) of 19 November 1946) that the Security Council re-examine the applications for membership in the United Nations of the People's Republic of Albania, the Mongolian People's Republic, the Hashemite Kingdom of Transjordan, Ireland and Portugal on their respective merits as measured by the yardstick of the Charter, in accordance with Article 4. The Security Council accepted the recommendation of the Assembly and instructed its Committee on the Admission of New Members to re-examine the applications of the above-mentioned States.

The Security Council also resolved to refer to the same Committee for study and report, the applications of Hungary, Italy, Austria, Roumania, Yemen and Bulgaria.

The Committee duly considered the applications enumerated above, and submitted its report to the Security Council on 18 August 1947.

During that meeting, the President informed the Council that an application for membership had been received from Pakistan. The Council agreed that this application should be considered without being referred to the Committee on the Admission of New Members.

On 21 August 1947, the Security Council resolved to recommend to the General Assembly the admission of Yemen and Pakistan to membership in the United Nations. No recommendation was made by the Security Council in respect of the other applications.

The decision of the Council was communicated to the Secretary-General in a letter dated 21 August 1947, which was duly transmitted to the Members of the Assembly.

After its decision had been transmitted to the Assembly, the Security Council received three more communications: (1) a cablegram dated 19 September 1947 from the Minister of Foreign Affairs of Finland requesting that Finland be admitted to membership in the United Nations; (2) a letter dated 20 September 1947 from the deputy representative of the United States requesting that the application of Italy be reconsidered; (3) a letter dated 22 September 1947 from the Minister of Foreign Affairs of Poland requesting that the applications of Hungary, Italy, Roumania and Bulgaria be reconsidered and that Finland be admitted to membership in the United Nations.

These communications were discussed by the Security Council on 25 and 29 September and 1 October 1947. After a discussion of the applications of Hungary, Italy, Roumania, Bulgaria and Finland, the Council proceeded to vote on them individually. None of the applications obtained the necessary majority to enable the Council to make a recommendation.

An account of the relevant proceedings of the Security Council was transmitted to the General Assembly in a special report.

(c) CONSIDERATION OF APPLICATIONS BY THE GENERAL ASSEMBLY

The General Assembly, on 23 September 1947, decided to refer to the First Committee the report of the Security Council on the admission of new Members.

The First Committee, on 24 September 1947, considered that part of the Security Council's report which recommended the admission of Yemen and Pakistan, and decided to recommend to the General Assembly that these countries should be admitted to membership. This recommendation was adopted by the Assembly on 30 September 1947, on which date Yemen and Pakistan became Members of the United Nations.

During the debate in the First Committee, which extended over six meetings, a number of proposals, draft resolutions and amendments were submitted. On 10 November, the First Committee adopted a series of eight resolutions for submission to the Assembly. The Assembly, on 17 November 1947, adopted the resolutions proposed by the First Committee.

As regards resolution B, requesting the International Court of Justice to give an advisory opinion, an account of the action taken by the Court is given in Chapter IV of this report.

In the resolutions dealing with the applications of Transjordan and Italy, the Security Council was requested to reconsider the applications of these two countries before the end of the second regular session of the Assembly.

(d) RECONSIDERATION OF THE APPLICATIONS OF TRANSJORDAN AND ITALY BY THE SECURITY COUNCIL

As requested by the General Assembly, the Security Council, on 22 November 1947, reconsidered the applications of Transjordan and

Italy. It decided to report to the General Assembly that the reconsideration of these applications by the Security Council had indicated that none of the members had changed its position and that this recommendation of the General Assembly had therefore not produced any result. The Security Council decided to postpone further consideration of these two applications to allow consultation among the permanent members.

This decision of the Security Council was reported to the President of the General Assembly in a letter dated 22 November 1947 from the President of the Security Council, and was duly transmitted to the Members of the Assembly.

(e) REQUESTS FOR THE RECONSIDERATION OF APPLICATIONS

By letters dated 3 and 7 April 1948 respectively, addressed to the President of the Security Council, the representatives of France, the United Kingdom and the United States of America requested the reconsideration of the applications of Austria, Ireland, Italy, Portugal and Transjordan. By a letter dated 5 April 1948 to the Secretary-General, the representative of the Ukrainian Soviet Socialist Republic requested the reconsideration of the applications of the People's Republic of Albania, Bulgaria, Finland, Hungary, Italy, the Mongolian People's Republic and Roumania.

On 10 April 1948, the Security Council reconsidered the applications of these States. After a discussion, the Council voted on the proposal to recommend the admission of Italy to the United Nations. The result of the vote was nine in favour and two against (Ukrainian SSR and the Soviet Union). As one of the permanent members voted against the proposal, it was not adopted.

At its next meeting held on the same date, the Security Council reconsidered the other ten applications. Since none of the members had changed its position with regard to these applications, the Security Council decided so to report to the General Assembly and adjourned its discussion on the matter indefinitely.

(f) APPLICATION OF THE UNION OF BURMA

By a letter dated 27 February 1948 to the Secretary-General, the Ambassador of the Union of Burma to the United States of America applied, on behalf of his Government, for the admission of Burma to membership in the United Nations. On 17 March 1948 a declaration of acceptance of the obligations contained in the Charter of the United Nations was also submitted. The application, together with the declaration, was transmitted to the Members of the United Nations by the Secretary-General in a letter dated 22 March 1948.

The Security Council, on 3 April 1948, referred the application of the Union of Burma to its Committee on the Admission of New Members for examination and report.

On 10 April 1948, the Security Council considered the report of the Committee and adopted, by ten votes in favour to none against, with one abstention (Argentina), a resolution recommending to the General Assembly that the Union of Burma should be admitted to membership.

Following requests made by the representatives of China and India, the General Assembly decided to include this item on the agenda of the second special session, which had been convened to give further consideration to the question of the future government of Palestine.

The recommendation of the Security Council was accepted by the Assembly on 19 April 1948; on that date, the Union of Burma became a Member of the United Nations.

(g) APPLICATION OF CEYLON

By a letter dated 25 May 1948 and addressed to the Secretary-General, the Prime Minister and Minister of External Affairs of Ceylon applied on behalf of his Government for the admission of Ceylon to membership in the United Nations. On 16 June, a declaration of acceptance of the obligations contained in the Charter of the United Nations was also submitted

The application, together with the declaration, was transmitted to the Members of the United Nations by the Secretary-General in a note dated 28 June 1948.

The Security Council, on 11 June 1948, referred the application of Ceylon to its Committee on the Admission of new Members for examination and report.

The Committee met on 29 June to examine the application and, in accordance with its request, its Chairman will report thereon to the Security Council.

Q. Rules governing the admission of new Members

Under the terms of resolution 36 (I) of 19 November 1946, the General Assembly and the Security Council each appointed a committee jointly to confer with a view to the preparation of rules governing the admission of new Members which would be acceptable both to the Assembly and to the Council.

On 29 November 1946, the Security Council instructed its Committee of Experts to appoint a sub-committee from their number to meet with the committee appointed by the Assembly and to report back any proposals to the Council for instructions.

The Committee of Experts submitted its report to the Security Council on 25 August 1947.

On 27 August 1947, the Security Council adopted the report of the Committee of Experts and also a resolution which summed up its essential points, and instructed the sub-committee of the Committee of Experts to negotiate with the General Assembly's committee for its acceptance of changes made by the Security Council.

All these changes were incorporated in a report of the Assembly's committee, which was considered by the Assembly on 21 November 1947. The Assembly, at that meeting, thereupon adopted new rules on the admission of new Members, which have since been included in its revised rules of procedure.

For its part, the Security Council approved amended new rules to be inserted in its own rules of procedure.

Chapter II

ECONOMIC AND
SOCIAL QUESTIONS

In the last annual report on the work of the Organization, it was possible to state that "with the co-operation of Member Governments, the United Nations is ready to undertake responsibility for the handling of problems in the economic and social fields". Since then, further progress has been made in setting up a comprehensive international machinery for this purpose and in approaching the fundamental economic and social tasks set out broadly in the Charter.

In the economic field, it has become apparent that an essential prerequisite for action was the definition of problems, and the study and analysis of the salient economic factors underlying those problems. To this end, and in response to requests made by the competent economic organs of the United Nations, the Secretariat embarked on the publication of a series of economic surveys and analyses. On the one hand, the first issue of a comprehensive world economic report was prepared and published in close collaboration with the specialized agencies. This report was followed by regional economic surveys of Europe, and of Asia and the Far East, in the "war-devastated areas" for which regional economic commissions had already been established. On the other hand, a number of special technical publications on specific problems were produced, including a survey of current inflationary and deflationary tendencies, a study of the plans and programmes for economic development in certain selected countries, an international standard industrial classification, and so forth. These studies will be continued and extended, and will constitute basic documentation for the economic work of the Economic and Social Council and its various subsidiary functional and regional economic commissions.

The problems of the areas devastated by the war continue to occupy a place in the forefront of the world economic situation. The United Nations has contributed to the solution of these problems through the regional machinery of the Economic Commissions for Europe, and for Asia and the Far East. Both these Commissions, in widely differing circumstances, have achieved considerable success.

In view of the growing interest in the regional approach to economic problems, further steps have been taken by the Council. At its sixth session, it created an Economic Commission for Latin America and, in response to a resolution of the General Assembly, charged an *ad hoc* committee with the study of factors bearing upon the establishment of an economic commission for the Middle East. This committee has reported favourably.

Together with the economic organs at headquarters these regional commissions are served by a single economic secretariat. The staffs of the regions are made directly responsible to headquarters, and in this way unified policy and control are achieved. Not later than 1951, the Economic and Social Council is to make a special review of the work of the regional economic commissions in order to determine whether they should be terminated or continued. Meanwhile much thought has been given to the matter of their relationship to the functional commissions, and here there is clearly a problem which will have to be solved in the light of further experience.

In the social field, encouraging results have been achieved within the past year. As regards the broad range of problems covered by the Social Commission and the corresponding division of the Secretariat, the programme of work itself, and the manner in which the Organization can most effectively assist Governments in regard to each item of that programme, have become more clearly defined. Among the features of the year's work, the following deserve particular attention: the successful development of three important operational programmes—the International Children's Emergency Fund, the United Nations Appeal for Children, and the provision to Governments of advisory social welfare services; advances in the human rights programmes, including the adoption by the competent commission of a draft Declaration on Human Rights and the adoption by the International Conference on Freedom of Information of three draft conventions and a number of significant resolutions; progress made towards an extension of the scope of the international control of narcotics and the assistance given to a Member State in re-organizing its narcotics administration; the report, submitted to the Economic and Social Council, on the progress and prospect of repatriation, resettlement and immigration of refugees and displaced persons; and closer co-ordination within the United Nations Organization itself and between the United Nations and the specialized agencies, in respect of work on a number of social problems.

Five agreements with specialized agencies were approved by the General Assembly at the second regular session, thus bringing to nine the number of specialized agencies now within the United Nations family. Negotiations are under way with four other organizations.

Not only has the number of specialized agencies been augmented; co-operative relationships among themselves and between them and the United Nations are being multiplied and improved, and the mechanism and procedures for bringing about more effective co-ordination of their work are being steadily developed. The Coordination Committee, under the chairmanship of the Secretary-General, has given attention throughout the year to co-ordination not only in the administrative sense, but also in terms of activities and work programmes. Consultative committees and working groups have been created to promote co-ordination of the work of the various bodies in fields such as statistics, migration, housing and town and country planning.

Definite progress has been made through these mechanisms and the broader task of the Economic and Social Council thereby facilitated. At its sixth session, the Council paid close attention to the question of co-ordination, and more particularly the co-ordination of programmes. At its seventh session, it is to give further detailed consideration to the whole matter.

1. ECONOMIC QUESTIONS

A. Surveys of world economic conditions and trends

During the past year, the Secretariat began its general task of preparing reports on world economic conditions and trends. The Economic and Employment Commission, the Economic and Social Council and the General Assembly all recognized the need for an appraisal of world economic conditions and trends as a prerequisite for recommendations as to concerted national and international action in the economic field. At its second session the General Assembly, on 31 October 1947, adopted a resolution to this effect (118 (II)), and at the same time requested the Secretary-General to assist the Council and its subsidiary organs "by providing factual surveys and analyses". The first issue of a world economic survey was released in January 1948 under the title *Economic Report—Salient Features of the World Economic Situation, 1945-47*. The report was the result of the effective co-ordination existing between the staffs of the United Nations and the specialized agencies, co-ordination which enabled the Secretariat to issue this report in a period of only a few months.

In this initial issue of the *Economic Report,* an attempt has been made to describe economic conditions in most parts of the world and to bring forward those economic problems which require urgent national and international attention. It was found and recorded in the report that the first twelve to eighteen months after the end of the Second World War were months of rapid economic reconstruction and recovery. Nevertheless, the world's production of key industrial commodities in 1947 was still below the pre-war level, and the world food situation was as critical as at any time since the end of hostilities. The report also dealt with major obstacles to the expansion of world production and the inflationary pressures generally prevailing.

The report pointed out the need for co-ordinated national and international action which would result in increased production of food and fuel. It stressed particularly the need for action involving the production and distribution of food. Calling attention to the fact that a shortage of food in the world is likely to continue and thus would constitute a serious obstacle to economic recovery, it asked for action "which will facilitate increased production of food as quickly as possible and will ensure a better distribution of the food available now, both within and among all countries".

The *Economic Report* received world-wide attention and numerous comments from Member Governments and the public.

During the sixth session of the Economic and Social Council, the *Economic Report* served as a basis of extended discussion of world economic conditions, and this discussion was subsequently published as a supplement to the report. Several Commissions and Sub-Commissions of the Council also had the report before them during their deliberations, and the factual data and analyses contained in it guided them in their conclusions and recommendations to the Council.

Concerning the continuing world food crisis, the Council, at its sixth session, taking note of memoranda submitted by the Food and Agriculture Organization, called upon Member States to "give serious consideration to the continuing world food shortage and take measures individually and in co-operation with the FAO, and, where appropriate, with other international agencies and organizations of which they are members, to contribute to the solution of this problem".

The Council also invited the specialized agencies concerned and the regional economic commissions, in consultation with the FAO, to study suitable measures to bring about an increase in food production by the elimination of supply shortages such as those of oil, coal, steel, electricity, chemicals, which directly or indirectly affect the production of fertilizers, agricultural machinery and the availability of transport. The Food and Agriculture Organization was requested to report to the seventh session of the Council on progress achieved in the co-ordination of these studies, and to present a report to the first session of the Council following the 1948 annual conference of the FAO on measures taken by Member States, regional commissions and specialized agencies to alleviate the world food crisis.

The Economic Commission for Europe, at its third session, acted on this question by establishing an *ad hoc* committee on agricultural problems of common concern to the Commission and the FAO to recommend the best means of securing the necessary co-operation in this field. This matter also came before the third session of the Economic Commission for Asia and the Far East, which established a joint working party of ECAFE and FAO to consider problems relating to agricultural requisites, and the reduction of prices of essential commodities.[1]

B. Inflation

The *Economic Report* also dealt, at some length, with the manner in which the scarcities of goods and inflationary situations in many countries had inter-acted upon one another and had thus tended to spread the inflationary pressures around the globe. The Secretariat has considered current inflationary phenomena as one of the most important current world economic problems. In that connexion, it has prepared a

[1] See page 53.

special *Survey of Current Inflationary and Deflationary Tendencies*. This survey analysed for selected countries the problems of deficiency or excess in effective demand, leading to unemployment or inflation respectively. Another survey is now in preparation.

The problem of inflation and anti-inflationary remedies was also the main subject of the first and second sessions of the Sub-Commission on Employment and Economic Stability, which met in November 1947 and March 1948. The report of that Sub-Commission was considered by the Economic and Employment Commission at its third session in April 1948, and the Commission presented its views to the seventh session of the Economic and Social Council.

The Commission drew attention to differences in the patterns of inflation and relative rates of economic growth in various countries, and to such important factors contributing toward inflation as excessive military expenditure and the activities of speculators. The Commission stressed particularly the need for a positive approach toward fighting inflation through emphasis on economic action designed to increase the production of essential goods, especially as international efforts could be more easily applied in that direction than in the direction of reducing demand. As regards national action in the latter respect, the Commission suggested that the countries concerned should undertake effective measures to halt domestic inflationary processes, for example, by the rationing of essential goods, coupled with price control, and by progressive income taxation. It was considered that such measures should be applied in such a way as not to cause unemployment.

Recognizing the urgent nature of the problem of food and coal shortages, the Secretariat, in addition to the analyses of this problem in its *Economic Report*, undertook a special study which has now been completed and is ready for publication.

C. Regional economic surveys

Surveys of economic conditions and trends have also been produced during 1948 by the staffs of the Economic Commissions for Europe, and for Asia and the Far East, to provide background material for the deliberations of these Commissions at their third sessions. These surveys deal in detail with the specific impact on Europe, and on Asia and the Far East respectively, of the world-wide problems analysed in general in the *Economic Report* to which reference has already been made. (See also the following section on regional commissions.)

D. Reconstruction and the regional economic commissions

The reconstruction of the war-devastated areas continues to be one of the world's most important current economic problems. The *Economic Report* pointed out, with respect to Europe, that it had become apparent by the end of 1947 that "post-war economic reconstruction would require a longer period of time and be more difficult to achieve than the early progress of European recovery had led many to expect". Of Asia and the Far East, the report stated: "In this region, which at the time it was drawn into the Second World War had not yet as a whole achieved any high degree of economic advancement—the vast majority of its predominantly agricultural population still living on a bare subsistence level—the various countries are struggling arduously with the difficulties of rehabilitating their war-shattered economies."

During the past year, national Governments have been taking action, individually and collectively, to solve these continuing problems of reconstruction which affect all countries of the world directly or indirectly. The United Nations is assisting in the solution of these problems through the machinery created by the Economic and Social Council for this specific purpose— namely, the Economic Commissions for Europe, and for Asia and the Far East.

(a) ECONOMIC COMMISSION FOR EUROPE

The Economic Commission for Europe, established by a resolution adopted on 28 March 1947 at the fourth session of the Economic and Social Council, has held three sessions, all at Geneva. The first session took place from 2 to 14 May 1947, the second from 5 to 16 July 1947 and the third from 26 April to 8 May 1948.

The members of the Commission are the European Members of the United Nations and the United States of America. The Executive Secretary of the Commission has exercised his discretion under the Commission's terms of reference to invite European non-members of the United Nations to participate in the work of the Commission and of its subsidiary organs in a consultative capacity. In addition, certain non-European Members of the United Nations have participated in the work of those technical committees of the Commission in which they have a special interest.

At its first and second sessions, the Commission made the organizational arrangements necessary to implement its terms of reference as laid down by the Council. In particular, the Commission took over most of the activities and all the essential work of the Emergency Economic Committee for Europe (EECE), the European Coal Organization (ECO) and the European Central Inland Transport Organization (ECITO).

The Commission had been instructed by the Council to give prior consideration during its initial stages to measures to facilitate the economic reconstruction of devastated countries of Europe which are Members of the United Nations. To this end, the Commission, at its second session, established a number of committees and sub-committees to consider the technical problems involved in European reconstruction. These committees began their practical work during September 1947. The committees in some cases found it necessary to set up certain subsidiary bodies of experts to discuss and report on a number of restricted technical questions. The reports of the activities of the committees and their subsidiary bodies were reviewed by the Commission at its third session. At the end of that session of the Commission, there existed the following main committees: Coal, Inland Transport, Industry and Materials, Electric Power, Timber, Steel, and Man-power.

During the third session, the Commission decided to extend its activities into two other fields. It instructed an *ad hoc* committee to examine the functions which the Commission might appropriately undertake in order to promote the industrial reconstruction and development of war-devastated and under-developed countries and expand international trade between the countries of Europe and also between European countries and countries outside Europe. Furthermore, an *ad hoc* committee was established to consider agricultural problems of common concern to the Commission and the Food and Agriculture Organization. This committee is called upon to determine those problems militating against the development and rehabilitation of European agriculture, the solution of which will be facilitated by co-operative measures on the part of FAO and ECE, and to make recommendations in this field.

In its annual report to the seventh session of the Economic and Social Council, the Commission has placed on record its substantial achievements to date in facilitating the reconstruction of Europe.

(i) *General*

In the first two years after the war, the pace of European recovery was set by the available supplies of food, fuel and power, and materials, and by the limits imposed by transport conditions. The main difficulties occurred during this period in the early stages of the production process, and the industries producing finished goods were revived at a greater speed than the basic industries providing them with materials. Thus the engineering industries reached a higher level of production than the iron and steel industry, while the iron and steel industry itself recovered faster than the coal industry.

The committee structure of the Economic Commission for Europe, to which reference has already been made, has reflected this fundamental situation in European production. The committees and their subsidiary bodies, the work of which is briefly described below, have had before them as their main task the promotion of concerted action to increase the production of commodities in short supply.

Some success has already been achieved in this task, as a result of both national and international action. At the beginning of 1948, considerable changes were beginning to appear. The coal shortage, for example, has been largely overcome. As the problems of basic industrial production are progressively solved, the bottlenecks are appearing more and more in the later production stages, such as the engineering industries. In addition, there are a number of serious problems connected with trade and currency difficulties. Recent additions to and changes in the committee structure of the Economic Commission for Europe, such as the setting up of an *ad hoc* Committee on Trade and Development, and the recent transforming of the Sub-Committee on Steel into a full committee, are designed to take account of these developments in the European economic situation.

An account will now be given of the broad progress in the work of the Economic Commission for Europe during the past year.

(ii) *Problems of coal*

With the aid of an allocations sub-committee, the Coal Committee has carried out its important function of recommending allocations of available solid fuels to European importing countries. The allocations for the second quarter of 1948 were notable in that they took into account a significant agreement reached in respect of the allocation of metallurgical fuels in such a way as to make possible an increase in European steel production. Agreements were also reached on the allocation of domestic fuels to timber-producing countries to encourage the export of the maximum quantities of timber, including pitwood.

In considering allocations for the third quarter of 1948, the allocations sub-committee was confronted by a situation in which shortages of particular qualities of fuels were becoming more significant than the overall supply position. As a result, the sub-committee took the first steps

towards a method of allocating by qualities; and substantial progress has already been made towards evolving an acceptable allocations procedure on this basis.

The Coal Committee has also dealt, through subsidiary bodies, with questions concerning mining equipment, pitwood and statistical information.

(iii) *Problems of inland transport*

A large number of measures have been undertaken by the Inland Transport Committee directed toward the speediest possible restoration of European inland transport facilities, and their most effective use. Considerable progress has been made in re-establishing the "Regulations on the Reciprocal Use of Wagons in International Traffic" (RIV), and a large number of European countries are applying these regulations in a manner consistent with the recommendations of the Inland Transport Committee. This should make it possible for the exchange of railway wagons in international traffic to be undertaken in an orderly manner over the greater part of Europe, thus allowing the more efficient use of rolling stock available. Moreover, the situation regarding the substantial wagon debts owed by certain countries to the Wagon Exchange Commission in Paris had now been substantially improved.

In the field of road transport, the most substantial achievement has been the lifting of restrictions on freedom of the road, to which a large number of European Governments have agreed.

Periodic BIDAC[1] meetings, within the framework of the Inland Transport Committee, have taken responsibility for allocating available transport facilities within the occupation zones of Germany and Austria to the various countries requesting freight shipments into or across these zones.

Amongst other questions discussed by the Inland Transport Committee have been the taking of a census of floating equipment on the waterways of Europe, and the overcoming of difficulties due to key shortages in the repair, maintenance and renewal of European transport equipment.

(iv) *Problems of industry and materials*

The Industry and Materials Committee is concerned with a number of key shortages in European production. For example, the main factors limiting the production of fertilizers in Europe have been examined, and recommendations have been made with the aim of increasing the pro-

---

[1] Conferences where programmes and the routing of transit traffic through occupation zones of Germany and Austria are considered.

duction of nitrogen. Agreement has been reached on special coal allocations for this purpose. The Committee also established working parties to review the situation in respect of the supply of certain engineering products.

At future meetings, the Committee will deal with problems of specific equipment shortages referred to it by other technical committees, together with questions involved in European housing requirements.

(v) *Problems of electric power*

The Electric Power Committee has directed its efforts in part toward the study of the best means of effecting the co-ordinated development of European electric power resources. Problems of the supply of important items of power equipment were brought to the attention of the Sub-Committee on Steel. The Electric Power Committee has also helped to facilitate the negotiation of international agreements for the supply and exchange of electrical energy. Finally, preliminary steps have been taken in surveying requirements of electrical energy; and regional studies have been made in the Rhineland, Silesian, Alpine and Danubian areas of the possibilities of power development.

(vi) *Problems of timber*

At the third session of the Commission, the sub-committee on timber was transformed into a full committee without any change in its terms of reference. This body, dealing with matters of common concern to FAO and ECE, is serviced by a joint secretariat of the two bodies.

A survey was made of the supplies of and requirements for timber in Europe. Informal agreement was reached by importing countries not to exceed specific purchasing ceilings for the period up to 1 July 1948, when the situation would be again reviewed. Exporting countries were requested to continue their efforts to produce more timber for export. It was noted that certain of the major difficulties involved in the European timber situation were a result of currency problems and, in particular, of certain shortages of equipment. The Executive Secretary was requested to bring these difficulties to the attention of the International Bank for Reconstruction and Development, the International Monetary Fund, and any other interested international agencies. Discussions are at present in progress regarding methods whereby these difficulties may be eased and the European timber deficit thereby reduced.

In addition, the coal allocation sub-committee recommended the allocation of extra domestic coke to Sweden in exchange for a commitment to increase the export of pitprops.

(vii) *Problems of steel*

At the third session of the Commission, the Sub-Committee on Steel was transformed into a full committee without any change in its terms of reference.

Data have been assembled on requirements for coke, consequent upon the urgent need to increase the European production of steel for reconstruction. Acting on the basis of principles laid down by the steel sub-committee, the coal allocation sub-committee recommended, for the second quarter of 1948, allocations of coal designed to permit an increase of about 400,000 tons in steel production in that quarter.

At its May session, the Steel Committee planned for a further increase of some 500,000 tons in the rate of European steel production in the third quarter, over and above that of the second quarter. This was achieved by means of an agreement to divert more domestic coke to metallurgical uses.

A survey was made of the difficulties encountered by certain countries in obtaining the necessary equipment for their steel industries; and Governments were urged to make the utmost effort to expedite deliveries of equipment and to suggest any measure which could be taken to ease financing of equipment purchases.

(viii) *Problems of man-power*

At the third session of the Commission, the sub-committee on man-power was given the status of a full committee without any change in its terms of reference.

The International Labour Office was requested to develop quarterly statistics setting out the surpluses of man-power available for emigration against deficits to be covered by immigration, and to take certain steps towards improvement of existing manpower statistics. The sub-committee on man-power also recommended that arrangements be made by the International Labour Office for the exchange of information and experience on all questions related to training and re-training. In addition, the attention of the International Labour Office was drawn to the need for minimum standards for migration in Europe and for the acceleration of migration between European countries.

These recommendations were accepted by the Governing Body of the International Labour Organisation in March 1948, and steps have been taken to put the necessary work in hand.

(ix) *Survey of the economic situation and prospects of Europe*

In addition to the considerable volume of studies produced by the Secretariat for the work of the Committees, sub-committees and working parties of the Commission, a *Survey of the Economic Situation and Prospects of Europe* was published in April 1948 at Geneva. The *Survey* contains a comprehensive analysis of Europe's most pressing economic problems, and is designed to provide essential basic information for the work of the Commission and its subsidiary bodies.

The four main sections of the *Survey* deal with the recovery of production, the recovery of trade, the balance of payments and problems of European reconstruction. It was found that, although there had been a remarkable industrial recovery in Europe during the eighteen months following the cessation of hostilities, the following nine months had revealed little further progress over a large part of Europe. Similarly, after a fairly rapid recovery in 1946, the foreign trade of many European countries had shown only moderate progress in 1947. The solution of the crucial problems resulting from the huge deficit in the European overseas balance of payments was shown to require an expansion not only of production, but of intra-European trade.

(x) *Collection of data*

The requirements for economic and statistical data for the technical committees of the Economic Commission for Europe have naturally been considerable. As in the case of the Economic Commission for Asia and the Far East, the Commission's staff has confined itself to the assembling of data necessary for special studies, leaving the continuous collection of basic series to the Statistical Office at headquarters.

At its third session, the Statistical Commission had under consideration the availability of compararable statistics in connexion with the activities of the Economic Commission for Europe. The Statistical Commission recommended to the Economic and Social Council that it request the Secretary-General to encourage and facilitate consultation upon statistical questions among representatives of the statistical agencies of European Governments. The Statistical Commission considered that reports of such consultations, together with any proposed actions affecting the responsibilities of the Statistical Commission, should be referred to that Commission in order to secure the necessary co-ordination and international comparability.

(*b*) Economic Commission for Asia and the Far East

The Economic Commission for Asia and the Far East, established by a resolution adopted at the fourth session of the Economic and Social Council on 28 March 1947, has held three sessions. The first session met in Shanghai, China, on 16 June 1947; the second session met in Baguio, Philippines, on 24 November 1947, and the third session at Ootacamund, India, on 1 June 1948.

The Commission was originally composed of representatives of the following countries: Australia, China, France, India, Netherlands, Philippines, Siam, Union of Soviet Socialist Republics, United Kingdom and the United States of America.

As a result of its entry into membership in the United Nations, Pakistan became a member of the Commission and was represented at its second session. Similarly, the Union of Burma, having been represented as an associate member at the second session, was represented as a full member at the third session, following upon the Union's admission to membership in the United Nations. New Zealand has also been admitted to membership of the Commission and was represented at its third session.

At its fifth session, the Economic and Social Council amended the terms of reference of the Commission to provide for the inclusion, as associate members, of representatives of any of the following territories, or part or group of such territories, namely, North Borneo, Brunei and Sarawak, Burma, Ceylon, the Indochinese Federation, Hong Kong, the Malayan Union and Singapore, and the Netherlands Indies. Such associate members enjoy the right to participate fully in the work of the Commission, excepting only that they are not entitled to vote in plenary meetings. The present associate members are Cambodia, Ceylon, Hong Kong, Laos and the group of territories comprising the Malayan Union, Singapore, North Borneo, Brunei and Sarawak. The question of the way in which the Indonesian Republic should be represented was discussed at the second and third sessions, and has been deferred for further consideration at the fourth session of the Commission.

The Economic Commission for Asia and the Far East operates in an environment in which distances in the region with which it is concerned are great, the transport conditions difficult, and data on economic matters very scarce. Moreover, there were not at the time of the creation of the Commisssion any pre-existent international bodies, the functions of which could have been taken over by it, as was the case with the Economic Commission for Europe.

(i) *General*

The most urgent task of the Commission, at the time of its creation, was to provide itself and the countries for which it was to work with the essential prerequisites for co-ordinated action in the economic field, that is to say with the information on the situation prevailing at the present time, which would allow for a diagnosis of this situation and for the determination of the measures necessary to remedy it. Accordingly, the Secretariat undertook, in conformity with the decisions taken by the Commission at its first session in June 1947, a series of studies, both at headquarters and in the field, in order to procure this information.

At its second session, in November 1947, the Commission had before it a survey of reconstruction problems and needs which had been prepared by the Secretariat on the basis of the above studies. This survey brought out the basic requirements of the region in food, transport facilities, manufactured goods, coal and power, foreign exchange, etc., and proposed a series of measures to be taken by the Commission, either alone or in conjunction with specialized agencies (and more particularly with the FAO) for the purpose of determining the possibility of satisfying these requirements. Moreover, a special report was made to the Commission on the very important problems of the training in the economic field of administrative and technical personnel of the countries concerned, and of the securing of technical assistance from outside the region. On the basis of these studies, the Commission, at its second session, adopted a series of resolutions. Some account will now be given of the action taken as a result of these resolutions.

(ii) *Problems of food*

In the all-important realm of food problems, the necessity for close co-ordination between the activities of the Commission and those of the FAO is apparent. The responsibility for the promotion of agricultural production must rest primarily with the FAO, but the Commission can contribute to the improvement of the present very unsatisfactory situation by working towards increasing the availability of industrial supplies affecting food production (agricultural machinery, fertilizers, insecticides, etc.).

The Food and Agriculture Organization has been called upon by the Commission to initiate a series of activities in the field of food and agriculture in the Far East. Acting on the basis of experience acquired in a series of food conferences held in 1947 and at the beginning of 1948, the FAO prepared a statement for the third session of the Commission which indicated principles for the formulation of food production campaigns, outlined the action to be undertaken by the FAO on a series of problems, and warmly welcomed the co-operation of the Commission. In connexion with the question of agricultural requisites, the establishment of a joint FAO and ECAFE working party was proposed, to study the production and distribution of these requisites and promote concerted action for increasing supplies. At its third session, the Economic Commission for Asia and the Far East called for continued co-operation between the Commission and the FAO, and established a joint working party of these bodies to discuss problems relating to agricultural requisites and the reduction of prices of essential commodities.

Co-operation is also envisaged between the Food and Agriculture Organization and the Commission for the creation of a regional fisheries' council and for the calling of a technical conference on timber which is to take place in 1949.

(iii) *Problems of industrial development*

As far as industrial development is concerned, a working party of experts nominated by Governments was established at the second session of the Commission. It met in March 1948 and proceeded, on the basis of official and unofficial documentation supplied to it, to analyse the industrial development plans existing in each country of the area, to examine the basic factors involved and the effect of development on the social and economic structure of the countries concerned.

The report of the working party was submitted to the Commission at its third session. It stressed the need for co-ordinated action and embodied a series of general recommendations on the pattern of future work for the study and promotion of industrial development in the region, and on the measures to be taken in connexion with a series of important factors such as material requirements, technical personnel, finance, utilization of Japanese capacity and availability of incentive to enterprise.

At its third session, the Commission appealed to the advanced industrial countries to supply capital goods and other basic requirements to countries in the region of Asia and the Far East, in order to assist them in their industrial rehabilitation. The Commission requested the countries in the area to specify the nature of their short-term requirements, and their long-term plans for development. The industrial working party was empowered to study the financial requirements of the region; and a clear statement was sought from the Governments concerned as to their financial, fiscal and industrial policies in relation to foreign investment.

(iv) *Problems of trade*

A very important measure for raising the level of economic activity of the area served by the Commission is the promotion of trade within the region. Accordingly, a specialized section has been created within the Secretariat to consider ways and means for the early augmentation of trade between countries of Asia and the Far East, and between them and other parts of the world. The Commission intends, eventually in consultation with the International Trade Organization, to make recommendations to the Member Governments on the organization of national trade promotion agencies which could collaborate with the Economic Commission for Asia and the Far East.

A report on the situation and prospects of trade and on the trade promotion machinery existing in the countries of the region was drafted on the basis of information received by the Secretariat from the Member Governments, and was submitted to the Commission at its third session. It indicated the possibility of a strong development of intra-regional trade, especially on the assumption of the realization of the various development programmes which are being drawn up and implemented at the present time. The report also stressed the urgency of the solution of a series of financial and transport problems, and suggested certain specific measures such as the creation of a permanent Trade Promotion Bureau. The Commission, at its third session, called for further study of these matters, and suggested various measures designed to promote intra-regional trade.

(v) *Problems of transport*

The lack of transport facilities in Asia and the Far East handicaps industrial development, food distribution and trade. The convening of a group of experts to study the problems of the rehabilitation and co-ordinated development of transport in Asia and the Far East and the means best suited to promote the solution of these problems, was recommended by the Transport and Communications Commission at its second session. This proposal received the approval of the Economic Commission for Asia and the Far East at its third session.

(vi) *Problems of flood control*

The problem of the control of floods is particularly important in the area under review, and conditions both the physical security of the population and the production of food. The Economic and Social Council, acting on the basis of a recommendation made by the Commission at its second session, resolved that the question of the creation of a bureau of flood control should be studied and proposals made to the Council at its seventh session. A draft note prepared for the third session of the Commission outlined the main functions of the proposed bureau, including *inter alia* research, field investigation, advice to Governments, technical assistance, training and dissemination of information. The Commission decided at its third session to establish this bureau.

(vii) *Problems of technical training and expert assistance*

The setting up, in co-operation with the specialized agencies concerned and particularly with the International Labour Organisation, of an appropriate machinery to deal with questions of technical training and expert assistance was advocated at the second session of the Commission. Thus, the necessary information as to the existing facilities will be furnished to Member Governments and measures taken which will contribute towards increasing these facilities. An interim report was prepared by the Secretariat and was considered at the third session of the Commission.

(viii) *The problem of Japan*

At its third session, the Commission called upon member Governments to give immediate consideration to the possibility of exchanging with Japan raw materials against capital goods. The principle was adopted that plans for Japanese trade and industry should be adjusted to the needs of the countries of Asia and the Far East, within the limits allowed by the Far Eastern Commission and any peace treaty which might be concluded with Japan.

(ix) *Problems of economic and statistical documentation*

In order to facilitate the accomplishment of the various tasks of the Commission, the Secretariat has proceeded with the collection and dissemination of economic and statistical documentation. The Secretariat has been specifically instructed to publish a comprehensive annual survey on economic conditions and problems of the countries within the scope of the Economic Commission for Asia and the Far East, and to assemble and make available to Members documentation and reports on economic questions. The first edition of the survey will appear shortly; a preliminary issue was circulated at the third session of the Commission.

As far as statistics are concerned, great care has been taken to ensure the utmost co-operation with the Statistical Office at Lake Success and, through that Office, with the specialized agencies. The Economic Commission for Asia and the Far East has confined itself mainly to the collection of data which are necessary for special studies, leaving the continuous collection of basic series to the Statistical Office at headquarters.

E. Relief needs after the termination of UNRRA

In the last annual report to the General Assembly, it was stated that, pursuant to resolution 48 (I) on relief needs after the termination of UNRRA (United Nations Relief and Rehabilitation Administration), adopted by the General Assembly on 11 December 1946, plans designed to meet somewhat over one-half of the total financial assistance estimated by the Special Technical Committee to be required for 1947 were receiving the consideration of Member Governments. On the basis of information subsequently received, a report was made to the fifth session of the Economic and Social Council indicating that the assistance planned ranged from about sixty to seventy per cent of the total estimated requirements of $583,000,000 (U. S.) (not including China).

Information which has since become available as to the magnitude, character and distribution of the relief assistance actually provided does not appear to call for any change in the observations previously made on the plans announced in response to the estimated requirements established by the Technical Committee.

Since the above report was noted by the Economic and Social Council and referred to the attention of the General Assembly at its second regular session, the following additional information has become available:

(i). *United States of America.* As of 31 December 1947, the sum of nearly 304 million dollars was earmarked for post-UNRRA relief of which 280.3 million had been programmed for procurement and 229.5 million actually shipped. The amounts programmed by country were as follows (in thousands of U. S. dollars): Austria, $87,113; China, $27,49? (exclusive of 18 million dollars specifically appropriated for China but unprogrammed); Greece, $37,887; Italy, $118,696; Trieste, $9,071.

(ii) *Australia.* On 19 March 1948, the Government of Australia advised that it was offering raw wool to the value of 1.1 million Australian pounds to the six European countries designated by the Special Technical Committee as requiring relief assistance. This amount was to be allocated as follows: £A.150,000 each to

Austria, Greece, Hungary and Yugoslavia, and £A.250,000 each to Italy and Poland.

Such further information on this subject as Governments provide pursuant to resolution 119 (II), adopted by the General Assembly on 31 October 1947, will be submitted to the Economic and Social Council.

F. New regional economic commissions

During the past year, the original conception of regional economic commissions as organs designed primarily to facilitate the reconstruction of war-devastated areas has become modified and extended. It has been recognized by the Economic and Social Council that certain areas of the world, though not the victims of physical devastation during the war, did suffer substantial economic losses as a direct result of the war. The Council has consequently had under consideration the establishment of regional economic commissions to deal with the economic problems of such areas.

At the fifth session of the Council, an *ad hoc* Committee was set up "to consider the factors bearing upon the establishment of an Economic Commission for Latin America within the framework of the United Nations and . . . present to the Council a report with recommendations concerning the creation of such a Commission"

The Secretariat prepared studies dealing with the economic situation in Latin America to assist the Committee in its consideration of the urgent economic problems bearing upon the creation of an Economic Commission for Latin America. At its sixth session, the Economic and Social Council, acting on the unanimous recommendation of the *ad hoc* Committee, created an Economic Commission for Latin America with terms of reference largely based on those of the regional commissions already in existence.

The first session of the Commission began on 7 June 1948 at Santiago, Chile. Arrangements were made by the Secretariat with a number of specialized agencies so that information concerning their current activities in Latin America in so far as they related to the Commission's terms of reference could be available to the Commission.

The major business before the Commission at its first session was the consideration of the plan of work to be undertaken in implementation of its terms of reference, whereby the Commission was to "initiate and participate in measures for facilitating concerted action for dealing with urgent economic problems arising out of the

---

[1] Data available from the second report to Congress on the United States foreign relief programme, U. S. Department of State, April 1948.

The remainder of the appropriation of 350 million dollars was programmed as follows:

(a) International Children's Emergency Fund, $40 million (maximum);

(b) Voluntary Relief Agency Transportation Fund, $35 million; and

(c) Administrative Expenses (State Dept.) and Citizens' Food Committee, $1.1 million.

war and for raising the level of economic activity in Latin America and for maintaining and strengthening the economic relations of the Latin American countries both among themselves and with other countries of the world". The Commission had before it several papers prepared by the Secretariat on the scope and functions of the Commission, on proposals for an economic report on Latin America, and on the provision of expert assistance and technical training as a function of the Commission. In formulating its programme of work, the Commission had clearly before it the need for the fullest co-ordination of its activities with the Inter-American System in order to avoid wasteful duplication of effort. This was not only required by its terms of reference but had also been the subject of discussion at the Ninth International Conference of American States at Bogota in 1948.

At the time when it established the Economic Commission for Latin America, the Economic and Social Council decided to consider the question of creating an Economic Commission for the Middle East. It was guided by resolution 120 (II) of the General Assembly in which the Assembly invited the Council "to study the factors bearing upon the establishment of an Economic Commission for the Middle East".

The Council followed the pattern it had established in its consideration of the need for an Economic Commission for Latin America. At its sixth session, it created an *ad hoc* Committee with terms of reference closely resembling those of the *ad hoc* Committee for Latin America. To facilitate the work of this *ad hoc* Committee, the Secretariat prepared several studies on the situation in the Middle East. These enabled the Committee to examine the economic problems facing the Middle East to-day, arising from the impact of the war and from the lack of sufficient economic development of the countries in that area. The *ad hoc* Committee has decided to recommend to the Economic and Social Council that it establish an Economic Commission for the Middle East.

G. Maintenance of full employment

In spite of the fact that most of the countries of the world have suffered, to a greater or lesser degree, from the effects of inflation during the post-war period, the United Nations has not lost sight of the possibility of a fall in effective demand in some countries in the near future which would lead to unemployment. The *Survey of Current Inflationary and Deflationary Tendencies* and the *Economic Report*[1] both referred to

this problem and to conditions under which the problems of a deficiency in effective demand and of unemployment might arise. This matter was also raised by the United Nations Conference on Trade and Employment, and was referred by the Conference to the Economic and Social Council. The Council, at its sixth session, discussed the question and considered that attention should be given now to methods of ensuring that high levels of employment and economic activity will be maintained even when special factors of temporary duration now prevailing in many countries have ceased to operate.

The Secretariat is, at the Council's request, undertaking an inquiry into the problems involved in preventing a decline in effective demand and an increase in unemployment in the near future. A questionnaire soliciting information concerning national plans in this field is being circulated to Member nations. Concurrently, an inquiry is being conducted to ascertain the extent to which international action by the specialized agencies would contribute towards maintaining full employment and effective demand. The analyses of the results of these inquiries will be published in due course. The Sub-Commission on Employment and Economic Stability has also decided to devote its third session, to be held in 1949, to the study of the long-term problems of the maintenance of full employment and has arranged for the preparation of various studies by its members. The Economic and Employment Commission has fully endorsed this work programme of the Sub-Commission.

H. Economic development of under-developed areas

The promotion of the economic development of hitherto under-developed countries and regions has continued to engage the attention of the United Nations.

The Sub-Commission on Economic Development devoted its first session, in November 1947, to a clarification of the general principles which should govern the economic development of under-developed countries and of the character of international action in this field. The Sub-Commission also gave attention to some of the immediately urgent problems confronting the under-developed countries of the world. On both these subjects, a report was made to the Economic and Employment Commission. On the immediate problems, three recommendations were made for the consideration of the parent body. These dealt respectively with assistance to under-developed countries by way of finance, food and equipment, with the ascertainment of

[1] See pages 47 and 48.

the immediate requirements of the various countries by the United Nations regional economic commissions (present and future), and with the importance of mutual consultation and agreements among the various under-developed countries themselves.

The Economic and Employment Commission, with the report of the Sub-Commission before it, discussed development problems extensively during its third session. The Commission expressed a broad measure of agreement with the general principles enunciated by its Sub-Commission and presented several recommendations and draft resolutions to the seventh session of the Economic and Social Council. The Commission also suggested that the Sub-Commission, at its second session in June 1948, should consider problems of international assistance in the mobilization of the national resources of under-developed countries for their economic development.

Now that the general principles have been clarified and a wide measure of agreement reached, the main problem which is coming to the forefront in the work of the Organization is that of technical assistance to be rendered to under-developed countries under international auspices. Carrying further the action previously taken by the General Assembly at its first session and by the Economic and Social Council at its fourth and fifth sessions, the Economic and Employment Commission has recommended that the Economic and Social Council should inform those countries which require expert assistance for economic development that the Secretary-General may, upon request, organize international teams composed of experts furnished by or through the United Nations and the specialized agencies "for the purpose of advising them in connexion with their economic development". The organization of such teams would, of course, not preclude direct invitation of experts from specialized agencies in connexion with problems in the fields of those specialized agencies. The Secretary-General is asked in this recommendation to publicize among Member Governments knowledge of the kind of expert assistance available to them and the terms under which it can be made available. This question of technical assistance and its proper organization was one of the chief subjects for discussion at the second session of the Sub-Commission on Economic Development in June 1948. The Secretariat has undertaken the required studies to enable the Sub-Commission to arrive at concrete suggestions on this matter.

The problem of economic development came up for extended consideration at the United

Nations Conference on Trade and Employment.[1] The draft charter placed before that Conference contained important provisions on this subject; and it was recognized by the Conference that no long-term plans for the expansion of international trade could be made without taking parallel account of the needs of the economically less developed areas of the world. The Interim Commission established by the Conference was directed to examine, among other things, "the powers, responsibilities and activities, in the field of industrial and general economic development and reconstruction, of the United Nations, of the specialized agencies and of other inter-governmental organizations, including regional organizations", and in the light of this examination to report upon "the working relations with the United Nations, the specialized agencies, and other inter-governmental organizations, including regional organizations, which will enable the International Trade Organization most effectively to carry out its positive functions for the promotion of the economic development and reconstruction of Members".

Many of the specialized agencies also have important functions to perform, under their basic instruments, in respect of economic development. Moreover, the regional economic commissions of the Economic and Social Council are beginning to consider the particular developmental problems of their areas.

It will be necessary to ensure the closest possible co-ordination of all these activities in the sphere of economic development in general, and of technical assistance to under-developed countries in particular. It is only by actual experience that the international organizations can demonstrate their worth in this field, and establish a routine for dealing with requests from Governments in a satisfactory way. The United Nations is, however, now ready, in co-operation with the specialized agencies, to place its services at the disposal of Members wishing to explore the possibilities in this field.

The Secretariat study entitled *Economic Development in Selected Countries,* published last year, has had a wide circulation. A second volume dealing with the plans and programmes of a number of other under-developed countries not included in the first volume will be published this year. A number of other studies on problems related to economic development are also in course of preparation both at headquarters and by the staffs of the regional economic commissions.

[1] See page 59.

I. United Nations Scientific Conference on the Conservation and Utilization of Resources

Another way in which the United Nations is helping to promote economic development is by the preparation of the United Nations Scientific Conference on the Conservation and Utilization of Resources. At its fourth session, the Economic and Social Council adopted a resolution to call such a conference, and the Secretary-General was requested to undertake the necessary preparatory work and was authorized to establish a committee of experts to advise and assist him in this task. Accordingly, an advisory committee, consisting of representatives of the specialized agencies concerned and of individual experts, met five times from September 1947 to February 1948 to consider the conference programme. With the advice and assistance of this committee, the Secretariat prepared a provisional programme which has been sent to Member Governments for their comments and suggestions.

At its sixth session, the Economic and Social Council considered a progress report from the Secretary-General concerning the preparations for the Conference, and requested him "to proceed with plans for the Conference, keeping in mind that the task of the Conference is to be limited to an exchange of experience in the techniques of the conservation and utilization of resources".

The Secretary-General, with the advice and assistance of a preparatory committee, is now engaged in the revision of the provisional programme in the light of the comments and suggestions of Member Governments. This Committee is also selecting authors to be invited to contribute papers to the Conference.

The Conference is tentatively scheduled to convene in June 1949.

The mobilization of knowledge concerning the most recent advances in the techniques of resource conservation and utilization and an evaluation of their economic effectiveness are tasks for which the Conference will assemble the world's leading authorities. Since such a mobilization is fundamental for economic development, it is expected that the Conference and the records of its proceedings will constitute a major contribution by the United Nations to the progress of economic development in all countries, particularly in the less developed countries.

J. International financial and commercial relations

In addition to the several studies described above relating the problems either of economic stability and full employment or of economic development, the Secretariat has also been engaged on some major investigations which are expected to contribute to the activities of the United Nations in both these fields.

In relation to the general conditions for international economic equilibrium, the Secretariat, after consultation with the International Monetary Fund, has begun research into the system of multilateral settlement of accounts. This work involves the examination of the historical development and subsequent decline of this system in the past, and of current or planned changes in economic activities related to multilateral settlement. It is expected that the study will also contribute to the Secretariat's work in the field of factual surveys and analyses of world economic conditions and trends.

A second subject of international concern is the movement of capital between countries. Not only are capital movements an element in the settlement of international accounts, but new foreign investments in under-developed or devastated countries have a function to fulfil in the return to international equilibrium and the promotion of sound economic growth. In this connexion, mention should be made of the request of the Economic and Social Council and the Economic and Employment Commission concerning the need for an international code relating to foreign investments in a number of countries, taking into account the points of view of both borrowing and lending countries. The study made in response to this request will also give consideration to the international movements of capital during the inter-war period and the experience gained by the debtor and creditor countries during this period.

These studies are being carried out in consultation with the International Bank for Reconstruction and Development, which is also concerned with these questions. The International Trade Organization, when established, will also, under the terms of its charter, have a direct interest in problems connected with foreign investments. Activities in this field are thus likely to depend on the joint efforts of the Economic and Social Council and the two specialized agencies to which reference has just been made.

The Secretariat has also been collaborating actively with the International Monetary Fund on current work on balance of payments questions. At its fourth session, the Economic and Social Council requested the Secretary-General "to make the necessary arrangements for full and regular reports on analyses of balances of payments", in order to assist the Economic and Employment Commission and its Sub-Commissions in considering economic problems related to or arising out of balances of payments. During the past year, the Secretariat contributed to the elaboration of a manual on *Balance of Payments,* the preparation of which was undertaken by the staff of the International Monetary Fund. The manual has been distributed to Governments, and the Fund is planning to issue at regular intervals a publication presenting balance of payments statements. It should be noted that one of the agreed purposes of the International Monetary Fund is "to shorten the duration and lessen the degree of dis-equilibrium in the international balance of payments" of its members.

K. International trade conferences

The work of bringing into being an International Trade Organization, which was initiated on 18 February 1946 by a resolution of the Economic and Social Council, has made substantial progress and there only remains the ratification by the required number of nations of the charter drawn up at the Havana Conference.

At the time when the annual report of the Secretary-General was issued last year, the Preparatory Committee for the United Nations Conference on Trade and Employment was still holding its second session at Geneva. That session ended successfully on 30 October 1947.

During its second session, the Preparatory Committee submitted to the fifth session of the Economic and Social Council an interim report which indicated the proposed outline of the annotated draft agenda and convention then being prepared for the full Conference. The interim report also contained recommendations as to the date and place of the Conference, and as to which non-members of the United Nations might be invited to attend. In the light of this report, the Economic and Social Council resolved, on 28 July 1947, that the United Nations Conference on Trade and Employment should be convened on 21 November 1947 in Havana, Cuba, and also approved the agenda of the Conference as presented by the Preparatory Committee. Further, on 1 August 1947, the Economic and Social Council adopted a resolution concerning voting rights at the Conference and invitations to it.

At its second session, the Preparatory Committee reached a large measure of agreement on the text of the draft charter to be recommended to the full Conference, although the text approved was accompanied by a number of notes showing the reservations which had been made and the interpretations of the text which were thought necessary in order to make the exact intention clear.

At its first session, the Preparatory Committee, considering that the task of the proposed Conference would be facilitated if concrete action were taken by the principal trading nations to enter into negotiations directed to the substantial reduction of tariffs and the elimination of preferences on a mutually advantageous basis, recommended that such negotiations should be carried out between the members of the Preparatory Committee as part of the work of the second session. In accordance with this recommendation, a General Agreement on Tariffs and Trade was negotiated during the second session.

In addition to the members of the Preparatory Committee represented at Geneva, Pakistan, Syria, Burma, Ceylon and Southern Rhodesia took part in the tariff negotiations, owing to their close economic connexion with certain members of the Preparatory Committee.

These negotiations, the complexity and magnitude of which have no precedent, were, successfully concluded; and a Final Act relating to the General Agreement on Tariffs and Trade, incorporating a number of important general provisions in the field of trade together with lengthy schedules of tariff reductions, was signed at Geneva on 30 October 1947. A total of one-hundred and twenty-three agreements were negotiated and completed amongst the participants. This is an achievement without parallel in the history of tariff negotiations. Taken as a whole, about two-thirds of the import trade of the countries concerned was covered by tariff reductions or by the binding of tariff rates. Over forty-five thousand items were included in the schedules which formed part of the General Agreement. The completed negotiations had special significance, for they demonstrated the desire of Governments representing a major share of the world's trade to negotiate with each other for the substantial reduction of tariffs and elimination of preferences, in accordance with one of the most important articles incorporated in the charter of the Havana Conference.

The General Agreement on Tariffs and Trade, which is already being applied by most of the signatories to the Final Act, is an important and concrete factor in the reduction of trade barriers and will contribute to expanding trade among nations.

The United Nations Conference on Trade and Employment opened in Havana on 21 November 1947, and ended on 24 March 1948 with the completion of the charter for an International Trade Organization. Fifty-seven nations, including ten non-members of the United Nations, took part in the work of the Conference, and fifty-three nations signed the Final Act.

The charter groups its hundred and six articles into nine chapters, dealing with: Purposes and objectives; Employment and economic activity; Economic development and reconstruction; Commercial policy; Restrictive business practices; Inter-governmental commodity agreements; The International Trade Organization; Settlement of differences; General provisions.

As well as completing the text of the charter, the Conference adopted a resolution establishing an Interim Commission for the International Trade Organization. Fifty-two delegations approved this resolution, by which the Commission is charged with preparing the ground for the International Trade Organization.

Resolutions were also adopted regarding the relations of the International Trade Organization and the International Court of Justice, regarding the Interim Co-ordinating Committee for international commodity arrangements, and regarding employment, economic development and reconstruction.

During the Havana Conference, the first session of the contracting parties of the General Agreement on Tariffs and Trade was held from 28 February to 24 March 1948. As a result of this meeting, four protocols and one declaration were signed in respect of the General Agreement on Tariffs and Trade.

It remains for the necessary instruments of acceptance of the charter to be deposited for the International Trade Organization to come into being and to fulfil the functions and responsibilities laid upon it by the charter.

L. Fiscal problems

During the past year, fiscal problems have continued to be of great concern in the efforts of Governments to balance their national economies and to promote industrial development and foreign trade. In most if not all countries, a need was felt to bring about greater equilibrium in the national budget, to combat inflation through fiscal means and, at the same time, to create the fiscal conditions necessary to economic progress. In addition, many economically less-advanced countries have found that one of the factors hampering their economic development is connected with shortcomings in their fiscal systems and administration.

At recent international conferences, such as the United Nations Conference on Trade and Employment and the Conference of American States at Bogota, emphasis was placed on the importance of removing, by international agreements, certain tax obstacles to international trade, foreign investment and economic develop-ment. At the Havana Conference, particular reference was made to the desirability of pursuing the programme of work of the Fiscal Commission in the field of international fiscal problems.

The work of the Secretariat on fiscal problems has followed the lines laid down by the recommendations contained in the report of the Fiscal Commission on the work of its first session, and by resolution 67 (V) of the Economic and Social Council of 24 July 1947.

As a basis for its work, the Secretariat has undertaken to establish an international fiscal information centre to assemble from all over the world documentary material on all problems within its jurisdiction. In this endeavour the Secretariat has enlisted, in accordance with a suggestion of the Fiscal Commission, the help of liaison officers designated by Member Governments. It is the double purpose of this centre to assemble the material needed in the current research of the Secretariat, and to equip itself to give advice and information on fiscal problems to international agencies or Member Governments which may request it.

In the field of public finance in general, the Secretariat has undertaken to prepare a series of reports under the heading *Public Finance Survey* which is ultimately to cover some sixty countries. This survey will review for each country the development of government expenditure, revenue and borrowing and summarize fiscal legislation and policy, with particular reference to war finance.

As a further reference work on public finance, the volume *Public Debt 1914-1947* will be available in the near future. It will contain tables giving comprehensive information on the public debt—long-term and short-term, domestic and foreign—of some sixty countries during the last thirty-year period.

In the field of international tax relations, the Secretariat has undertaken to collect from all Member Governments complete information on the tax treatment accorded, in each country, to foreign nationals, foreign assets and international transactions. This information is being collected by means of circular letters, questionnaires and missions. Numerous partial answers have already been received from Member Governments, and are now being completed and analysed before submission to the Fiscal Commission.

Comments have been received from Member Governments on the London and Mexico Model Tax Conventions prepared by the League of Nations in 1943 and 1946. The comparative analysis of these comments should serve as a useful aid in the negotiation of further tax agreements among Member Governments.

A *Collection of International Tax Agreements* is now in the process of being printed. This collection of almost one hundred new tax agreements concluded during the last twelve to fifteen years will bring up to date the collection previously started by the League of Nations.

In accordance with the emphasis placed by the General Assembly and the Economic and Social Council on the granting of technical assistance to Member Governments, the Secretariat has been active in giving such assistance to the Government of Venezuela, at its request, in a fundamental reform of its fiscal system and administration. In this connexion, the Secretariat has sent missions to Venezuela and has also assisted that Government in selecting foreign experts for long-term assignments.

M. Transport and communications

(*a*) DEVELOPMENTS IN RESPECT OF INTERNATIONAL ORGANIZED COLLABORATION IN THE FIELD OF TRANSPORT AND COMMUNICATIONS

During the past year, considerable progress has been made in giving a more definite shape to international organization in the field of transport and communications, on lines laid down in the United Nations Charter.

Two further inter-governmental organizations with world-wide responsibilities were brought into relationship with the United Nations, as specialized agencies, under Article 57 of the Charter. An agreement was negotiated with the Universal Postal Union during the Twelfth Universal Postal Congress, held in Paris in the spring and summer of 1947. This agreement was subsequently approved both by the Universal Postal Congress and by the United Nations General Assembly at its second session. Thus, one of the oldest international agencies was brought into the United Nations family. Similarly, negotiations conducted with the International Telecommunications Union at its Conference held at Atlantic City in the summer of 1947 resulted in an agreement subsequently approved by the Conference and by the United Nations General Assembly at its second session.

In another sphere of transport—that of maritime navigation—provision was made for the creation of a new world-wide inter-governmental agency at the United Nations Maritime Conference convened at Geneva in February 1948, as a result of a decision of the Economic and Social Council. This is the only transport field in which no inter-governmental organization existed, though the need for it was apparent. As a result of the Conference, a Convention was concluded for the establishment of the Inter-Governmental Maritime Consultative Organization. The constitution of the new agency provides for an Assembly, in which all the Governments members of the organization will be represented, and a Council of sixteen member nations, eight of which will represent the most important providers of international shipping, and the other eight the most important consumers of international shipping facilities.

The main purposes of the new organization, the character of which is consultative and advisory, are, according to the Convention, to deal with the technical aspects of maritime navigation and safety, to encourage the removal of discriminatory action and unnecessary restrictions by Governments affecting shipping engaged in international trade, and to provide for the consideration by the organization of matters concerning unfair restrictive practices by shipping concerns. The Convention will enter into force and the Inter-Governmental Maritime Consultative Organization will formally be established when twenty-one States, of which seven shall each have a total tonnage of not less than one million gross tons of shipping, have become parties to the Convention. The Conference established a Preparatory Committee of the new organization to operate during the interim period. This Committee, which is for the time being serviced by the Division of Transport and Communications of the United Nations Secretariat, will prepare for the first Assembly of the Inter-Governmental Maritime Consultative Organization, to be convened after the entry into force of the Convention.

The Conference also adopted the text of a draft agreement to be concluded in order to bring the new organization into relationship with the United Nations as a specialized agency. The Preparatory Committee was empowered to enter into negotiations with the United Nations, using as a basis the draft agreement approved by the Conference.

In the sphere of meteorology a new inter-governmental agency, the World Meteorological Organization, was established by a convention concluded in Washington in September 1947, thus superseding the International Meteorological Organization. The text of a draft agreement with the United Nations was also adopted. Thus, a new specialized agency covering this important field closely related to transport and communications may soon be added to the other world-wide agencies within the United Nations framework.

The Economic and Social Council has taken the view that problems of inland transport should be considered, in the first instance, on a regional basis. Progress achieved during the past year was especially significant in Europe, where the activities of the competent organs of the Economic Commission for Europe in the inland transport field were very numerous and permitted a solution of many important practical issues[1].

The examination of problems of regional concern in the inland transport field is also one of the responsibilities of the Economic Commission for Asia and the Far East. In addition, these problems will no doubt come before the newly established Economic Commission for Latin America and any other regional economic commission that may be created. A preliminary study of the inland transport problems of the African continent is now in preparation by the Secretariat.

Acting on the view that those problems in the inland transport field which have a world-wide character should be discussed on a universal basis, the Transport and Communications Commission has recommended to the Economic and Social Council the convening of a conference of Governments with the purpose of concluding a new world-wide convention on road and motor transport.

(b) Resumption of facilities in international travel

As a result of the recommendation adopted by the meeting of governmental experts on passport and frontier formalities, convened in Geneva in the spring of 1947, the Economic and Social Council requested the Secretary-General to make a comparative analysis of the relation between the practices of Member Governments and the recommendation of the Geneva meeting of experts and of the extent to which Members have indicated willingness to change their present practices to conform with the recommendations of the experts. The Transport and Communications Commission, after having considered at its second session the study presented by the Secretariat on this subject, stated in its recommendation to the Council that neither a world conference nor another meeting of experts is required in the immediate future, but that all Member Governments should be encouraged to reduce, simplify and unify passport and frontier formalities to the extent consistent with national security. The Commission also requested the Council to instruct the Secretary-General to report to the next meeting of the Commission as to the progress made by Member Governments in the above respect. This recommendation of the Commission will be considered by the Economic and Social Council at its seventh session.

[1] See page 50.

N. Statistical services of the United Nations

The activities of the statistical services of the United Nations during the past year have included three closely related aspects of the work of an international centre responsible for the development of statistics comparable for international purposes. The first involves planning and research toward the development of international standards of definitions and practices and of uniform systems of statistical classification. The second relates to the collection, compilation and publication of available statistics necessary to the programmes of the United Nations and the specialized agencies. The third is the arrangement among the United Nations and the specialized agencies of programmes for the collection and publication of statistics and research on their development which will promote an integrated system of statistical data, a maximum utilization of the available resources and a minimum burden on Governments supplying statistics to international organizations. The responsibility for these activities is shared by the Statistical Commission, the Sub-Commission on Statistical Sampling and the Statistical Office of the United Nations.

(a) International statistical standards

At its second (August-September 1947) and third (April-May 1948) sessions, the Statistical Commission studied the work of previous international organizations dealing with statistics, and recommended to the Economic and Social Council a series of steps in a programme of statistical activities designed to achieve much-needed levels of international comparability and standards.

As a first step, it was recommended that the United Nations should assume the responsibilities for research and administration previously vested in the League of Nations by the International Convention relating to Economic Statistics (1928). A World Statistical Congress was convened in September 1947 to acquaint leading statisticians and responsible officials in national statistical services with the statistical work and requirements of the United Nations and the specialized agencies, as well as to promote the exchange of professional and technical experience on statistical methods and problems which had been in suspense for nearly ten years.

On the recommendation of the Commission, a draft international standard classification of types of economic activities was circulated to all Governments for their comments. This classification proposed a system whereby the statistics of all branches of economic activity of a nation could be classified so as to achieve international comparability of such data when national statistics were compiled for international purposes. The comments received from the Governments were reviewed by a group of experts and a revised *International Standard Industrial Classification of all Economic Activities* was adopted by the Statistical Commission. Similar studies on basic statistical classification relating to international trade statistics and to commodity statistics are being undertaken by the Statistical Office. A proposed classification of occupational status is being prepared by the International Labour Organisation, and will be considered by the Statistical Commission at its fourth session.

In view of the plans on the part of many Governments to conduct national censuses of population in or about 1950, the Statistical Commission has recommended that all countries taking censuses should try to provide comparable data on a number of basic items. As part of the endeavour to develop comparable census data for all countries, the Statistical Office and the Population Division of the Secretariat, in collaboration with some of the specialized agencies, are issuing a series of *Studies of Census Methods*. Five studies have been published and others are in preparation.

The Sub-Commission on Statistical Sampling has suggested the possibility of using sampling methods in population censuses as well as in many other fields of inquiry. As a preliminary guide in the development of sample surveys, the Sub-Commission approved the publication of a *Brief Statement on the Uses of Sampling in Censuses of Population, Agriculture, Public Health and Commerce*. A special manual dealing with agricultural sample surveys is now in preparation. A study is being undertaken by the Statistical Office on the types and methods of current sampling projects in different countries and in different subject fields, with the purpose of disseminating among all interested countries information on the practical aspects of sampling technique.

An analytical study of the concepts of national income, including a compilation of the available statistics of national income for different countries, has been undertaken by the Statistical Office. The results of this study are to be published in a volume entitled *National Income Statistics of Various Countries, 1938-1947*. This is a first step in the process of formulating and recommending standard definitions of statistics in this field.

The Statistical Commission has also recommended a review of the problems in two of the basic fields of economic statistics, that of prices and price index numbers and that of indices of industrial production. Studies are in progress on the extent and availability of price statistics, and the scope and content of price index numbers, especially those relating to imports and exports. A similar review is being undertaken of the use and composition of indices of industrial production. These studies are being made with a view to formulating recommendations to Governments regarding these basic statistical tools of economic analysis.

(*b*) Collection and publication of statistics

In the collection and publication of available important current statistics, the Statistical Office has been able to develop and publish approximately eighteen hundred statistical series covering more than seventy countries in the *Monthly Bulletin of Statistics*. This programme has involved the co-operative effort of a number of the specialized agencies, notably the International Labour Organisation, the Food and Agriculture Organization, the International Civil Aviation Organization and the International Monetary Fund. The contents of the *Monthly Bulletin* have been continuously expanded during the past year, and adapted more and more to the needs for comparable statistics for general economic analysis. A large number of changes have been made in order to present comparable statistical series for different countries. A supplement to the *Monthly Bulletin* has been issued giving descriptive analyses of the structure, scope and limitations of each of the national series published in the bulletin.

One result of the work connected with the collection of this large volume of statistical data from many countries is the greatly improved facilities for the preparation of special *ad hoc* studies for various purposes. Not only the various organs and departments of the United Nations, but also other international organizations, national Governments, and non-governmental organizations have at various times called upon the Statistical Office for information available in its files. The development and recognition of the central statistical functions of the Statistical Office fulfil in large measure the original conception of the Economic and Social Council in establishing the Office.

A special project is now in progress to compile, on a current basis, statistics relating to external trade in important commodities, with a view to resuming the special trade publications of the League of Nations. Statistics will soon be available for the principal commodities in international trade relating to a large number of countries, as well as for the commodities entering into the external trade of the principal countries.

A *Statistical Yearbook* is also in preparation, covering a wider range of subjects than the statistical yearbooks formerly published by the League of Nations. The Statistical Office, in co-operation with the Population Division and with some of the specialized agencies, is also preparing for publication a *Demographic Yearbook* containing the latest available information on population and vital statistics for all countries. These yearbooks, in conjunction with other specialized yearbooks now in print or to be issued by various specialized agencies, will provide, for the first time in many years, important reference volumes containing the basic statistical data for the analysis of social and economic problems.

(c) An integrated statistical programme

Co-operative planning of the statistical activities of the United Nations and the specialized agencies has been achieved in several phases of the collection, publication and research programmes of these international agencies. Periodic meetings of the Consultative Committee on Statistical Matters, as well as *ad hoc* meetings on special problems, have enabled the various agencies to co-ordinate their statistical activities, to agree upon common practices in collecting and publishing statistics, and to develop a co-operative programme of research in fields of mutual interest.

The establishment, during the past year, of the regional economic commissions with statistical responsibilities created the need to relate statistical work at headquarters with that being undertaken in the offices of the regional commissions. Suitable arrangements for co-ordination and for the allocation of responsibilities are rapidly being made. These arrangements assure the necessary degree of centralized responsibility without preventing the regional offices from conducting the statistical work necessary for their purposes.

Through agreement among the specialized agencies, a procedure has been established whereby the Statistical Office serves as a clearing house for the circulation of statistical questionnaires among all agencies prior to their issuance to national Governments. This practice has resulted not only in improvements in the questionnaires themselves but also in a satisfactory co-ordination of agency requests for statistics and a lessening of this burden on Governments.

The collection of statistical information by Governments for domestic and international use is a highly technical function requiring the services of experts in various administrative and technically specialized positions. When there is a shortage of such trained and experienced personnel in any country, the United Nations and other inter-governmental organizations are seriously handicapped in receiving needed information. For this reason, the Statistical Office of the United Nations hopes to have adequate resources by means of which the Organization can respond promptly to reque of Member Governments for expert assistance in statistical matters.

In conducting the work directed towards an integrated statistical programme, with improved comparability and availability of statistics for international use, the United Nations has made solid technical progress. Communications have been established with most countries where the national statistical services have been restored after the war years or established for the first time. With continued efforts and the co-operation of Member Governments as well as other international agencies, it will be possible to assemble a sufficient wealth of timely, reliable and internationally comparable statistics for the use of all national and international organizations.

2. SOCIAL QUESTIONS

A. Operational programme

(a) International Children's Emergency Fund

The International Children's Emergency Fund, set up by the General Assembly in December 1946, received its first governmental contribution, an initial grant of $15,000,000 from the United States of America, in July 1947. With this support and other that was promised, the Fund was able to begin its major work of procurement and allocation of supplies for a feeding programme which, within less than six months, was reaching children in twelve European countries. By June 1948, this programme was in full operation for more than 4,000,000 children and pregnant and nursing women; in addition, food supplies were on their way to China for an initial programme there. Many other child health and child welfare projects were either being launched or planned, including a mass anti-tuberculosis vaccination project.

This far-reaching programme of child-aid is carried out under the direction of an Executive Board composed of representatives of twenty-six countries. At its meeting in June 1947, the Board established policies and principles to be followed in allocating the Fund's resources, and otherwise prepared the way for actual operations. In August 1947, the Programme Committee met in Paris and considered plans of operations for the European countries as well as reports on a number of countries requesting aid.

The Committee also had before it a special report of July 1947 on nutrition and feeding, made at the Fund's request by a Committee of the Food and Agriculture Organization and the Interim Commission of the World Health Organization. During five sessions subsequently held by the Executive Board, the programme of the Children's Fund has been expanded in line with the Fund's increased resources and the numerous demands made upon it for child-aid projects of many kinds.

Missions composed of international personnel are working in the twelve European countries in which the Fund is operating, and in China, while there are representatives of the Fund in Australia and Latin America. In the spring of 1948, special missions were sent to the Far East, and into the American, British and French occupation zones of Germany, to report to the Board on a possible extension of the Fund's programme to those areas.

A sub-committee of the Programme Committee has medical projects under consideration, and a group of technical experts from a number of countries and from the Food and Agriculture Organization has been in consultation with Fund officials, to consider what might be done to increase local supplies of milk for the children in recipient countries.

Reports from all these groups and missions are being presented to the Programme Committee which is meeting in Paris on 3 July, and recommendations are being made for action by the Executive Board at its next session in Geneva on 16 July.

The primary operation of the Fund is the feeding of children, which was the greatest need disclosed in a survey made by the Fund prior to the setting up of its programmes. One meal per day is provided, consisting of from 400 to 600 calories, of which the Fund supplies the protective foods—milk, meat, fish, fats and fish-liver oils. The Fund's contribution is matched by contributions of indigenous foods from the Governments of the assisted countries and from voluntary agencies of those countries. The children are fed at schools, day nurseries, children's institutions, mothers' clinics, etc. This supplementary meal is provided through approximately 30,000 feeding centres in Europe.

More than 40,000 tons of supplies from ten countries had been shipped by the Fund up to June 1948. Of this amount, 65 per cent, or over 26,000 tons, consisted of powdered milk; 15 per cent, or slightly less than 6,000 tons, of fats; 18 per cent, or over 7,000 tons, of meats and fish; and 2 per cent, or 700 tons, of fish-liver oil. None of the receiving countries has an adequate indigenous source of supply for these special

protective foods that make up the greater part of these shipments, nor are they able to import such foods in sufficient quantities, because of high costs and lack of foreign exchange.

The Fund is also attempting to meet the great need for children's clothing. For this purpose, the sum of $3,400,000 has been allocated to purchase cotton, wool and leather for processing by the receiving countries into children's diapers, clothing and shoes. A considerable part of the cotton and wool will be made into sheets and blankets for children's institutions.

The medical programmes in which the Fund is participating are principally of the type in which help is given to Governments in developing projects of both immediate importance and lasting value in rehabilitation and disease prevention. The principal activity of the Fund in this field is the mass vaccination project previously mentioned, which calls for the testing of 50,000,000 children in Europe alone, and the inoculation of all those found free of infection, and therefore "vaccinateable". The objective is to prevent tuberculosis in children through vaccination with BCG (Bacillus-Calmette-Guerin) serum. Four million dollars have been allocated for the undertaking, $2,000,000 for Europe and $2,000,000 for countries outside Europe. In countries where a mass vaccination campaign is not immediately practicable, equipment, technical services and facilities for training will be provided.

This vaccination project is a joint enterprise carried on with the Danish Red Cross and its Scandinavian associates and the World Health Organization. The Danish Red Cross began the work soon after the close of the war. The World Health Organization, through its Interim Commission, has been associated with the Children's Fund in working out plans for taking over and expanding the undertaking. The medical officer directing the BCG programme is, at the same time, the chairman of the World Health Organization's committee of experts on tuberculosis.

The Executive Board, besides offering its help in the prevention of tuberculosis, will consider projects for helping Governments to eradicate syphilis among children and expectant mothers.

In setting up and operating these various child-aid projects, one other great need common to all the assisted countries has been brought to the foreground. Shortages in trained personnel are making it difficult to develop adequate programmes of child health and child welfare. France and Switzerland, as a contribution to the Fund, offered their help in providing training facilities, including short courses and observation tours, for pediatricians, pediatric nurses, social workers, architects of children's institutions and educators. During the spring and summer of 1948, some 150 persons received such training.

In addition to its programmes in Europe and China, the Executive Board of the Fund has set aside $3,000,000 for programmes to be developed in countries of the Far East other than China. The Fund is also consulting with appropriate international organizations in the Americas concerning needs of children in the Western Hemisphere, and on possibilities of furthering their health and welfare through co-operation with such organizations.

As of 15 June 1948, contributions and pledges to the Fund amounted to approximately $70,000,000. Of. this amount, $51,000,000 or 73 per cent, came from Governments; $17,900,000 or 26 per cent, from UNRRA residual assets; and $713,000, or 1 per cent, from voluntary private contributions. The figure for private contributions does not include the Fund's share of the current national campaigns of the United Nations Appeal for Children.

Contributions and pledges to the Fund have been received from twenty-one Governments: Australia, Austria, Canada, Czechoslovakia, Denmark, Dominican Republic, France, Hungary, Iceland, Italy, Luxembourg, Newfoundland, New Zealand, Norway, Poland, Switzerland, Union of South Africa, United Kingdom, United States of America, Uruguay, and Yugoslavia. Each sum of $100 contributed by other Governments is matched by a sum of $257 from the United States Government, up to $75,000,000, under the formula established by the United States Congress, to be operative through 30 June 1949.

Under the terms of Assembly resolution 57 (I) of 11 December 1946, the Children's Fund is administered in accordance with principles laid down by the Economic and Social Council and the Social Commission. The latter, in reviewing the work of the Fund in April 1948, recommended that "the Fund's programmes of BCG vaccination, control of syphilis, and fellowships for the training of medical and auxiliary personnel be considered by the first World Health Assembly with a view to determining the ability of the World Health Organization to administer programmes in these fields". The Social Commission, while emphasizing the value of the Fund's achievements, also recommended that the Fund's special projects in the welfare field should be planned and administered in co-operation with permanent organizations in order that such projects might be absorbed and become part of long-range programmes at the earliest possible date.

The Fund has made important strides toward attaining the objectives set before it by the General Assembly, but it has been able to reach only a fraction of the children in need. With its present resources, even its current programmes can be carried through for only a limited period. The Economic and Social Council, at its sixth session, in commending the Fund for its concrete accomplishments on behalf of children, once again invited all Governments to contribute to the Fund in the near future.

(b) United Nations Appeal for Children

The Economic and Social Council, at its fifth session, adopted a resolution approving the programme for the United Nations Appeal for Children contained in a report by the Secretary-General as modified by a report of the Committee of the Council.

The principal directives thus laid down by the Council were that the actual fund-raising should be left to the national committees; that countries whose own needs were exceptionally urgent could, to the extent agreed upon with the Secretary-General, use funds raised under the Appeal for the relief of their own children; that the Appeal was to be essentially non-governmental but that Governments would be expected to facilitate the implementation of the Appeal; that any appeals with which the United Nations Appeal for Children might be linked in any country should be consistent with the purposes and objectives of the Appeal; that, in principle, the major part of the amounts raised by national committees should go to the International Children's Emergency Fund or be distributed only in agreement with the Fund.

At the same session, the Council agreed that a representative group of distinguished sponsors should be invited to lend inspiration and support to the Appeal. Furthermore, the Council set up an International Advisory Committee and a Special Committee of the Council to give direct assistance to the Secretary-General.

The International Advisory Committee was chiefly composed of representatives of the non-governmental organizations in category A and the chairmen of national committees. The Committee's task was to "assist the Secretary-General in co-ordinating the national appeals and in his relations with the international organizations sponsoring the Appeal" and also "to advise him, at his request, on matters falling within his responsibility under the Council's resolutions".

The Special Committee, composed of seven of the Council's members, was entrusted with the task of assisting the Secretary-General between sessions of the Council in the practical application of the policies relating to the Appeal as set forth in the Council's resolutions.

The work of stimulating and co-ordinating the

Appeal throughout the world has been carried out by the Secretariat at headquarters and through the regional offices set up in London, Prague and Shanghai. In addition, special representatives of the Appeal have travelled throughout the various continents.

In negotiating agreements on the conditions governing the conduct of national campaigns, the Secretary-General has consistently emphasized the principle of non-discrimination and endeavoured to ensure that the major part of the proceeds should be allocated to the International Children's Emergency Fund or distributed in agreement with it. In view of the diverse needs of various countries, a considerable latitude had to be allowed when the allocation of the proceeds was negotiated. In most cases, however, it was possible to agree upon the allocation of a percentage of the proceeds to the Children's Fund and the balance to appropriate agencies engaged in child welfare work. All countries have accepted the clauses relating to the non-discriminatory character of the Appeal.

In all participating countries, valuable assistance was afforded by the Governments and, in most of them, many national branches of the principal international non-governmental organizations and other voluntary agencies actively supported the campaign. In a few countries, committees were set up under the leadership of government officials but, in the main, private individuals and organizations took the matter entirely into their hands after the first initiative by the Government. To date, national committees have been formed in the following countries:

Afghanistan, Australia, Austria, Belgium, Bolivia, Bulgaria, Canada, Chile, China, Cuba, Czechoslovakia, Denmark, Dominican Republic, Ecuador, Ethiopia, Finland, France, Great Britain, Greece, Guatemala, Honduras, Hungary, Iceland, India, Iran, Italy, Liechtenstein, Luxembourg, Mexico, Netherlands, New Zealand, Nicaragua, Norway, Pakistan, Panama, Peru, Philippines, San Marino, Siam, Sweden, Switzerland, Turkey, Union of South Africa, United States of America and Venezuela.

It had been decided by the Economic and Social Council that a special day for the observance of the Appeal should be fixed by the Secretary-General, and that people should be asked to sacrifice the income of that day to the cause of the needy children of the world. The date of 29 February 1948 was chosen. Because of the organizational difficulties encountered by many countries owing to the short time available, it did not prove feasible to organize a concentrated campaign period around this date in all participating countries. However, United Nations Appeal for Children Day was effectively observed by many countries as well as at Lake Success. In Finland, Luxembourg, Norway and Hungary, churches marked the day with special sermons and collections. In some countries the day marked the opening of the national campaign; in others, it was chosen as the climactic day of collection. There were children's parades in the Philippines, benefit sports events in Nicaragua, charity fetes in Panama, special radio programmes in Colombia, China and the United States of America. Thus, on this day the attention of the world was focussed upon the needs of children. At Lake Success, children of twenty-six nations successfully conducted a meeting on the purposes of the Appeal and clearly demonstrated their comprehension of the urgency of the problem.

At the time of writing, many campaigns are still under way and some countries have not yet begun operations. It may be stated, however, that provisional results reported so far from fifteen of the forty-five participating countries amount to the equivalent of approximately fifteen million dollars, computing the various national currencies at the official rate, and with many of the campaigns still continuing. Nearly all of the larger nations which have agreed to join the Appeal have so far not announced any definite or interim results.

In addition to supplementing the resources of the Children's Fund and other agencies engaged in child relief, the Appeal has been productive of other valuable results. There is no doubt that, through the Appeal, the plight of millions of children and the urgent obligation to remedy the situation have been brought to the attention of vast sections of the world's population. The conviction has also been strengthened that, where relief is required, the generosity of peoples is not confined within national boundaries. Furthermore, great numbers of people have learned through the Appeal to appreciate the purposes and objectives of the United Nations and the value of an organization which is working for the benefit of mankind through the concerted action of the majority of nations.

(c) ADVISORY SOCIAL WELFARE SERVICES PROGRAMME

The advisory social welfare services authorized by General Assembly resolution 58 (I) of 14 December 1946, and provided to Governments during 1947, included the following categories:

(i) Provision of social welfare experts;

(ii) Granting of fellowships to an appropriate number of suitably qualified social welfare officials to observe the experience of other countries in the field of technical social welfare;

(iii) Provision of advice and demonstrations in connexion with the manufacture of prosthetic appliances, and instruction in the vocational training of physically handicapped persons;

(iv) Furnishing of technical publications helpful in the training of social workers;

(v) Participation in two regional social welfare seminars held in Latin America (for social welfare officials from Latin American countries only);

(vi) Production of the film *First Steps* in the Chinese, Czech, English, French, Greek, Polish, Serbo-Croatian and Spanish languages, for workers concerned with the training of physically handicapped children, and of three films on child welfare prepared in India at the Indian Government's request and available for distribution to other countries.

Services under the above headings were provided to the following countries at their request:

Category (i)

Albania, Austria, China, Czechoslovakia, Greece, Hungary, Italy, Philippines, Poland;

Category (ii)

Albania, Austria, China, Czechoslovakia, Finland, Greece, Hungary, India, Italy, Philippines, Poland, Yugoslavia;

Category (iii)

Austria, China, Czechoslovakia, Finland, Hungary, Philippines, Poland, Yugoslavia;

Category (iv)

China, Czechoslovakia, Greece, Philippines, Poland, Yugoslavia;

Category (v)

Argentina, Bolivia, Brazil, Chile, Colombia, Costa Rica, Cuba, Dominican Republic, Ecuador, El Salvador, Guatemala, Haiti, Honduras, Mexico, Nicaragua, Panama, Paraguay, Peru, Uruguay, Venezuela;

Category (vi)

Albania, Austria, China, Czechoslovakia, Finland, Greece, Hungary, India, Italy, Philippines, Poland, Yugoslavia.

Expenditures in 1947 were approximately 45 per cent for fellowships, 31.6 per cent for consultants' services, 9 per cent for films, 7.5 per cent for seminars, 6.5 per cent for demonstration equipment for the handicapped, and 0.4 per cent for social welfare literature.

The General Assembly, at its second regular session, approved the continuance of the advisory social welfare services during 1948, and allocated for this purpose funds equivalent to those appropriated for the 1947 programme.

The Secretary-General reviewed the policies and procedures which had been followed in the implementation of the 1947 programme, and made appropriate revisions and changes based on the experience gained during the year's operations. The text of the revised policies and procedures was communicated to all Member Governments and to the five non-member Governments which had participated in the programme.

Immediate steps were taken to establish co-ordination of the fellowship programme; and an inter-departmental committee was set up to correlate activities between the various units of the United Nations and specialized agencies at the Secretariat level. A meeting, attended by representatives of the International Labour Office, the United Nations Educational, Scientific and Cultural Organization, the Food and Agriculture Organization, the World Health Organization and also of the International Children's Emergency Fund, was held at Lake Success in March 1948. The committee reported to the Social Commission and to the Co-ordination Committee. The co-operation of host countries receiving recipients of fellowships for observation purposes was also enlisted by means of a meeting held in Geneva and attended by representatives of such countries and of the Secretariat.

Requests for services in 1948 have been received from forty-nine countries as compared with thirty-two countries in 1947. The Secretariat is taking appropriate measures to comply with requests for services in the categories mentioned above which have been requested by the following countries:

Category (i)

Austria, Bolivia, China, Czechoslovakia, Ecuador, Greece, Guatemala, Haiti, Hungary, Italy, Philippines, Poland, United Kingdom;

Category (ii)

Austria, Bolivia, Chile, China, Czechoslovakia, Ecuador, Finland, Greece, Haiti, Hungary, India, Italy, Lebanon, Netherlands, Norway, Philippines, Poland, Turkey, Yugoslavia;

Category (iii)

China, Czechoslovakia, Philippines, Poland, Yugoslavia;

Category (iv)

Chile, China, Egypt, Greece, Pakistan, Philippines, Poland;

Category (v)

Four Social Welfare seminars are being planned:

Two in Latin America for twenty Latin American countries;

One in the Near East for the seven Arab League countries;

One in the Far East for eight countries;
(An additional seminar for countries in Eastern Europe is under consideration);

Category (vi)

Egypt, Greece, Pakistan, United States of America.

The Dominican Republic, Ethiopia and Honduras have requested services but have not determined the exact type desired. The Secretariat is, however, in consultation with these Governments with a view to meeting their wishes. The United States of America has asked for documents, bibliographies of technical social welfare publications, films and film catalogues, and has expressed its willingness to pay for such services.

Recipient countries have, at the request of the Secretary-General, substantially increased their financial participation which, in respect of experts, is an amount equal to that spent by the United Nations, and for fellowships ranges from 30 per cent to 50 per cent of the costs.

The increased number of requests for services, not only from Governments which participated in the programme during 1947 but also from other Governments, has demonstrated the usefulness of this programme. There remain, however, many difficulties for the United Nations and for the recipient and assisting countries, in planning and carrying out a programme which is authorized for only one year at a time on a fiscal year basis.

The Economic and Social Council, at its sixth session in March 1948, requested the Social Commission to submit to the Council at its seventh session a recommendation as to whether the advisory social welfare services should be continued in 1949 and, in the event of the recommendation being confirmed, to submit further proposals regarding the extent, administration and methods of financing these services, together with supporting facts. The Social Commission at its third session (April 1948) considered the pertinent facts and recommended that these services should be continued in 1949, that the programme should include the same basic services as those of 1948, and that the funds to be provided in 1949 should be at least equal to those appropriated in 1948. The Commission has also recommended that the programme should be administered in accordance with the policies and procedures in force in 1948, and that the Secretary-General should continue his efforts to bring about increased financial participation on the part of recipient Governments. The Social Commission further expressed the belief that this programme was one of the most effective and useful in the field of social activities undertaken by the United Nations.

(*d*) REFUGEES AND DISPLACED PERSONS

The period covered by the present report (1 July 1947 to 30 June 1948) coincides with the first year of operations of the Preparatory Commission for the International Refugee Organization.

Up to 15 June 1948, there were twenty-two signatures to the Constitution, of which thirteen, representing 72.64 per cent of the operational budget, were either made without reservation as to ratification or have since been ratified, and eight, representing 2.29 per cent, were conditional on ratification. In addition, the ratification of the French Government (whose contribution to the operational budget is 4.10 per cent), with a reservation as to the term of payment, has been received. For the into force of the Constitution, fifteen full signatures representing 75 per cent of the operational budget are required.

When the Preparatory Commission began its work on 1 July 1947, it was estimated that some 704,000 persons were receiving care and maintenance from the United Nations Relief and Rehabilitation Administration, the Inter-Governmental Committee on Refugees and other bodies whose responsibilities were taken over by the Preparatory Commission. Several hundred thousand more persons were, it was estimated, eligible for care and maintenance, and an even larger number were potentially eligible for some other form of aid.

During the first nine months of operations (1 July 1947 to 31 March 1948), approximately 217,000 refugees and displaced persons were assisted by all agencies to return to their homes or to be resettled. Of this total 72,000 were repatriated, 42,000 of whom had been receiving PCIRO care and maintenance or had been under its auspices, and 145,000 left for their places of resettlement, 98,000 of these with PCIRO participation. On 31 March 1948, there remained 625,200 refugees and displaced persons receiving PCIRO care and maintenance in Europe, the Middle East and the Far East.

The General Assembly on 17 November 1947, by resolution 136 (II), recommended Member nations to adopt urgent measures for the repatriation of the repatriable refugees and displaced persons and for settling a fair share of the non-repatriables in their respective countries, and to report to the Secretary-General. The latter drew the attention of all Members to the above resolution by a *note verbale* of 15 December 1947. Of the replies received, three give positive statements of the numbers of refugees and displaced persons received into the respective countries, one draws attention to the active participation of the country concerned in the work of the refugee organization, six countries express regret that they cannot receive immigrant refugees (although one of them is prepared to receive a limited number of industrial and social experts), two countries give details of what they have done in the way of repatriation, and one is interested in repatriating non-assimilable immigrant refugees and displaced persons.

The same resolution also requested the Secretary-General to submit to the Economic and Social Council, at its seventh session, in collaboration with the Executive Secretary of the Preparatory Commission of the IRO, a report on the progress and prospects of repatriation, resettlement and immigration of refugees and displaced persons. A report prepared by Mr. Carl Hambro and Mr. Pierce Williams has since been submitted. In addition to an analysis of the situation and prospects of the work of the Preparatory Commission, the report contains a number of recommendations: first, States should accept refugees without discrimination as to their usefulness; secondly, a strong appeal should be made to the States Members of the United Nations to join the International Refugee Organization and translate their declarations of support into action; thirdly, the Refugee Organization should take the initiative in planning for the liquidation of the refugee problem and not leave it to the haphazard and unconnected efforts of certain Governments; fourthly, a decision of principle should be taken concerning the fate of the children of foreign nationalities brought into Germany; and, fifthly, the international status of refugees should be considered and action taken to bring it up to date. Minor recommendations are also included in the report with a view to removing obstacles in connexion, for example, with the granting of visa facilities, with inadequate transport and emigration facilities, and with the processing of refugees and displaced persons.

With regard to prospects of further repatriation and resettlement, the report states that the Preparatory Commission considers it improbable that more than 45,000 persons will ask to be repatriated during the second year of operations, and estimates that 180,000 can be resettled overseas and an indefinite number in Western European countries. It is feared that the number in PCIRO assembly centres on 1 July 1949 is likely to be higher than previously estimated; the majority of these persons will consist of non-repatriables and, unless Governments change their present selection policy, the old, the disabled and the sick. The comparatively small change in the numbers receiving care and maintenance during the first nine months of operations in spite of the numbers repatriated and

resettled, and in the estimated numbers for the coming year, is due to a number of causes. The two most important are (*a*) the excess of births over deaths, and (*b*) the admission of a large number of hardship cases to care and maintenance. Under existing agreements originally negotiated between UNRRA and the military authorities, there were time-limits of 1 July 1946 in the British zone of Germany and of 21 April 1947 in the United States zone after which dates only cases which would otherwise suffer undue hardship would be admitted to care and maintenance.

Although a deadline has not yet been established by the Preparatory Commission, the latter has decided to recommend to the General Council of the International Refugee Organization, when it is finally constituted, the desirability of restricting the benefits of the organization, other than legal protection, to persons who had left their countries prior to 1 February 1948, except for "hardship" cases.

The situation of unaccompanied children in Germany as a result of the war is the subject of one chapter of the report mentioned above. This is in accordance with the request made by the Economic and Social Council on 1 March 1948 for a specific account and recommendations as to the most effective methods to be employed for expediting a final solution of this problem.

B. Human rights

Since the close of the second session of the General Assembly, the United Nations has made notable progress toward the goal, set by the Charter, of achieving international co-operation in promoting and encouraging respect for human rights and for fundamental freedoms for all without distinction as to race, sex, language or religion. The Commission on Human Rights has drawn up a draft Declaration and a draft Covenant on Human Rights, and has suggested the means whereby the terms of the Covenant might be implemented or enforced. An *ad hoc* committee of the Economic and Social Council has prepared a draft Convention on Genocide. The United Nations Conference on Freedom of Information not only made great progress in defining and clarifying the concept of the fundamental freedom of information, but proposed three draft conventions and adopted forty-three resolutions designed to make this concept a reality.

Further, voluminous documentation concerning human rights and fundamental freedoms has been collected and published, thousands of communications relating to these subjects have been analysed, studies in the field have been initiated, and a start has been made in examining the question of the prevention of discrimination and the protection of minorities.

In short, several of the most difficult preliminary steps toward a realization of the aims of the Charter with respect to human rights and fundamental freedoms have already been taken. Acceptance by Governments of the principles that have been so carefully formulated, and of the measures of implementation that have been proposed, may, by establishing international machinery for the protection of the rights and freedoms of individuals, remove one of the principal causes of war.

(a) INTERNATIONAL BILL OF HUMAN RIGHTS

At its fourth session, the Economic and Social Council established a procedure and a time-table for the formulation of an International Bill of Human Rights. This important work has progressed according to schedule, and it is expected that the Council will recommend such a Bill to the third session of the General Assembly.

At the request of the Council, the Secretariat supplied the documentation on the basis of which a Drafting Committee, composed of the representatives of eight States, prepared a preliminary draft of this Bill. The preliminary draft was considered by the Commission on Human Rights at its second session held at Geneva in December 1947.

The Commission decided to prepare as component parts of the Bill, a draft Declaration on Human Rights and a draft Covenant on Human Rights. The former was to take the form of a resolution of the General Assembly; the latter was to take the form of a convention or treaty to which States would accede.

The Commission also suggested certain measures for implementation as a third part of the International Bill of Human Rights. It indicated that such measures might eventually form part of the Covenant.

The draft Declaration prepared by the Commission is a simple statement defining "human rights and fundamental freedoms". Its force, upon adoption by the General Assembly, would be of a moral rather than a legal nature; the Declaration would establish standards and indicate goals rather than impose precise obligations upon States.

The draft Covenant, on the other hand, was visualized as an instrument which would legally bind the States acceding to it. Such States would undertake to make their national laws conform to its standards, and would agree to the imposition of sanctions in the case of violation of the rights enumerated therein. For this reason, the draft Covenant was prepared in more precise language than the draft Declaration, and its enumeration of the rights to be protected is not so far-reaching. It was anticipated, however, that in time this first convention would be followed by others giving legal effect to other rights enumerated in the Declaration, including those of an economic or social nature.

The measures of implementation put forward by the Commission relate only to the proposed Covenant, since the Declaration is not envisaged as establishing legally enforceable obligations. The Drafting Committee, considering this question at its first session, agreed that the international community must in some way ensure the observance of the rights to be included in an International Bill of Human Rights, but did not attempt to suggest the precise manner in which this objective might be attained. The Drafting Committee, however, expressed the opinion that in addition to enforcement measures the United Nations should promote through education the widest possible respect for human rights, and recognized that observance of human rights could not be completely assured unless conditions of social progress and better standards of life were established in larger freedom.

The Commission on Human Rights set up a working group to consider the question of implementation. Among the ideas put forward by the group were the following: (i) that each State should incorporate into its own national law the principles of the Covenant on Human Rights; (ii) that a standing committee should be appointed by the Economic and Social Council to mediate, conciliate and, if possible, rectify alleged violations of human rights; (iii) that disputes not settled by this means should be forwarded to the Commission on Human Rights, which would decide whether the case should be sent to an international tribunal; (iv) that an international tribunal should be empowered to give binding decisions on cases thus brought before it, establishing a body of law which would settle hundreds of similar cases; and (v) that the General Assembly, because of the powers conferred on it by the Charter with regard to questions of economic and social co-operation, should implement the decisions of the international tribunal in this field should the necessity arise.

At its sixth session, the Council directed the Commission on Human Rights, through its Drafting Committee and at its third session, to give particular attention to the implementation of the Bill of Human Rights, and to ensure that draft articles on implementation were submitted to Member Governments at the earliest possible date.

(b) Freedom of information

At the second part of its first session, the General Assembly instructed the Economic and Social Council to convoke a conference of all Members of the United Nations on freedom of information (resolution 59 (I)). At its second regular session, the General Assembly adopted two resolutions relating to freedom of information, one on "Measures to be taken against propaganda and the inciters of a new war" (resolution 110 (II)), and the second on "False or distorted reports" (resolution 127 (II)).

The Sub-Commission on Freedom of Information and of the Press formulated preliminary suggestions for the organization of the United Nations Conference on Freedom of Information, began the examination of the rights, obligations and practices which should be included in the concept of freedom of information, and prepared, with the help of the Secretariat, documentation on this question which later served as a basis for discussion in the Conference.

The Economic and Social Council at its fifth session prepared a final plan for the Conference, including a detailed agenda. It invited all States Members of the United Nations, thirteen non-member States, the specialized agencies, and a number of non-governmental organizations, to attend. At the request of the Council, the Secretary-General prepared the necessary detailed documentation on items of the proposed agenda, consisting largely of a compilation of existing practices and problems of the Governments with respect to freedom of information.

The United Nations Conference on Freedom of Information was held at the European headquarters of the United Nations, Geneva, from 23 March to 21 April 1948. Fifty-four countries, including nine non-member States, sent representatives, while three additional countries sent observers. A majority of the delegations included experts in press, radio, motion pictures and other media for the dissemination of information.

In accordance with the guiding principles laid down by the General Assembly, the Conference had as its basic purpose the formulation of views concerning the rights, obligations and practices which should be included in the concept of the freedom of information. The Conference, in addition to considering these general principles, took into account the last two Assembly resolutions mentioned above, and dealt with such technical phases of the subject of freedom of information as (i) measures to facilitate the gathering of information; (ii) measures to facilitate the international transmission of information; and (iii) measures concerning the free publication and reception of information. It proposed possible continuing machinery to promote the free flow of true information, and suggested the means of action by which its recommendations might best be put into effect.

The Conference prepared, at the request of the Economic and Social Council, draft articles on freedom of information for the draft Declaration and the draft Covenant on Human Rights. It adopted forty-three resolutions, largely designed to improve the facilities available to the various information media in performing their basic functions of gathering, transmitting and disseminating news and information without fetters. It transmitted to the Economic and Social Council, for examination at its seventh session in the light of the comments forwarded by Governments, three draft conventions covering various aspects of freedom of information. The Council was requested to submit to the General Assembly draft conventions on freedom of information which might be opened for signature or accession by those States entitled or willing to become parties thereto, and remain open subsequently for additional accessions.

(c) Prevention of discrimination and protection of minorities

At the second part of its first session, the General Assembly declared (resolution 103 (I)) that "it is in the higher interests of humanity to put an immediate end to religious and so-called racial persecution and discrimination". Steps toward this objective have been taken by the Economic and Social Council on the advice and recommendation of the Commission on Human Rights and the Sub-Commission on the Prevention of Discrimination and the Protection of Minorities.

The Sub-Commission, which held its first session at the European headquarters of the United Nations, Geneva, from 22 November to 6 December 1947, discussed the general principles to be applied in these fields and made suggestions as to the action which might be taken to give effect to such principles.

Following consideration of these recommendations by the Commission on Human Rights and by the Economic and Social Council at its sixth session, the Secretary-General has begun: (i) to organize studies and prepare analyses designed to assist the Sub-Commission in determining the main types of discrimination which impede the equal enjoyment by all of human rights and fundamental freedoms, and the causes of such discrimination; and (ii) to study the question of the extent to which the so-called "minorities treaties" should be regarded as still being in force. The Secretary-General will consider the desirability of formulating effective educational programmes in these fields, and will ask the

United Nations Educational, Scientific and Cultural Organization to collaborate in planning and initiating such programmes.

(d) THE CRIME OF GENOCIDE

At its second regular session, the General Assembly reaffirmed (resolution 180 (II)) its earlier resolution 96 (I) on the crime of genocide, which it had defined as a denial of the right of existence of entire human groups. It declared that genocide was an international crime entailing national and international responsibility on the part of individuals and States, and requested the Economic and Social Council to continue the work it had begun concerning the suppression of this crime, to proceed with the completion of a draft convention on this subject, and to submit the results of its work to the third session of the General Assembly.

Accordingly, the Council at its sixth session established an *ad hoc* committee, composed of the representatives of seven countries, to prepare the draft convention for consideration at the next session of the Council. The *ad hoc* committee met at the headquarters of the United Nations during the period from 5 April to 10 May 1948, and on the basis of a first draft suggested by the Secretariat, prepared a draft convention together with a report indicating the views of the members on articles which were not unanimously adopted. This draft convention will be forwarded to the General Assembly after consideration by the Economic and Social Council at its seventh session.

(e) COMMUNICATIONS CONCERNING HUMAN RIGHTS

As might be expected, the widespread public interest in the subject of human rights and fundamental freedoms has resulted in a large influx of communications from individuals and organizations all over the world, many petitioning for enforcement of particular rights or freedoms in specific areas. Having confirmed the opinion of the Commission on Human Rights "that it has no power to take any action in regard to any complaints concerning human rights", the Economic and Social Council advised the Secretary-General how to deal with communications.

The Secretary-General, in accordance with the suggested procedure, has compiled a confidential list of communications received, together with a short summary of the substance of each, and has furnished this list to the Commission on Human Rights in private meeting, so that the members of the Commission might on request consult the originals of the communications dealing with the principles involved in the promotion of universal respect for and observance of human rights. The Secretary-General has, moreover, acknowledged the receipt of the communications, and has furnished each Member State not represented on the Commission with a brief indication of the substance of any such communication which refers explicitly to that State or to territories under its jurisdiction. The names of the authors of such communications are not divulged, except in cases where the authors state that they have already divulged their names or that they have no objection to this being done.

A similar procedure has been followed by the Secretary-General regarding communications relating to the status of women, and to the prevention of discrimination and the protection of minorities.

(f) STATELESS PERSONS

As a result of its consideration of the draft Covenant on Human Rights, the Commission on Human Rights expressed the wish that the United Nations give early consideration to the legal status of persons who do not enjoy the protection of any Government, in particular pending the acquisition of nationality, as regards their legal and social protection and their documents, and make recommendations to Member States with a view to concluding conventions on nationality.

Recognizing that this problem demanded the adoption of interim measures to afford protection to stateless persons while further steps were being worked out to ensure that everyone should have an effective right to a nationality, the Secretary-General, in consultation with interested commissions and specialized agencies, has begun: (i) a study of the existing situation with regard to the protection of stateless persons by the issuance of necessary documents or by other measures, and to make recommendations to an early session of the Council on the interim measures which might be taken by the United Nations to further this object; and (ii) a study of national legislation and international agreements and conventions relevant to statelessness, and to submit recommendations to the Council as to the desirability of concluding a further convention on the subject.

C. Status of women

At its second session, held at the headquarters of the United Nations in January 1948, the Commission on the Status of Women was principally concerned with measures which might be taken to advance the political rights of women, to improve their educational opportunities, to raise the economic rights accorded them to a parity with those accorded to men, and to secure for them full equality in civil rights.

(a) POLITICAL RIGHTS OF WOMEN

Continuing its efforts to give effect to resolution 56 (I), adopted by the General Assembly on 11 December 1946, the Commission considered information on the political rights of women which had been compiled by the Secretary-General on the basis of replies to part I of the questionnaire on the legal status and treatment of women. The Commission noted with satisfaction that, since its first session, Argentina and Venezuela had granted women full political rights, and it expressed the hope that plans for similar action by Costa Rica, Colombia, Peru and Chile might be completed as soon as possible.

The Secretary-General, pursuant to a resolution adopted by the Economic and Social Council at its sixth session, will bring up to date a memorandum supplementing his preliminary report to the Commission on the political rights of women and their eligibility for public office, making reference to the action taken by Governments since the signing of the Charter, and will transmit this memorandum to the members of the General Assembly.

Similar material will be circulated annually to Members of the United Nations until such time as all women throughout the world have the same political rights as men.

The Commission also considered various problems relating to conflicts of laws in the fields of nationality, domicile, marriage and divorce. It pointed out the need for a thorough study of these problems, which might perhaps lead to the formulation of a convention on nationality. It also expressed the opinion that women should participate under conditions of equality in the international activities of Governments and particularly in the Secretariat of the United Nations. Women should have full and equal opportunities in the civil service, in all professions, in all diplomatic, consular and judicial spheres, and at all levels of governmental activity.

(b) EDUCATIONAL OPPORTUNITIES FOR WOMEN

The Commission discussed information gathered by the Secretary-General relating to educational opportunities for women, and considered a number of recommendations designed to improve these opportunities. As a result of its suggestions, the Economic and Social Council, at its sixth session, requested the Secretary-General to continue his compilation of such information and to circulate, for consideration at the third session of the Commission, a detailed comparative report showing the existing educational dis-

abilities of women. The Secretariat asked the Member States to submit this information before 1 June 1948.

The Secretary-General was also requested to make the replies of Governments on this subject available to the United Nations Educational, Scientific and Cultural Organization, with the consent of the Governments concerned, in order to facilitate that agency's work in areas where women and girls suffer disabilities in the field of education.

(c) QUESTIONNAIRE

The Secretary-General, in conformity with the desire expressed by the Commission for a greater amount of background data upon which to base its work, has invited Member Governments which have not yet done so to complete their replies to the questionnaire on the political rights of women by 1 December 1948.

(d) EQUAL PAY FOR EQUAL WORK

As a result of its examination of the economic rights of women, which was conducted in consultation with a representative of the International Labour Organisation, the Commission recommended that the Economic and Social Council call upon Governments to encourage by all possible means the establishment of the principle of equal pay for equal work for men and women workers. At its sixth session, the Council, having considered this recommendation in connexion with its examination of a similar item placed on its agenda at the request of the World Federation of Trade Unions, reaffirmed the principle of equal rights for men and women as laid down in the preamble to the United Nations Charter, approved the principle of equal remuneration for work of equal value for men and women workers, and called upon the States Members of the United Nations to implement the latter principle in every way, irrespective of nationality, race, language and religion. A memorandum on the subject submitted to the Council by the World Federation of Trade Unions was transmitted by the Secretariat to the Commission on the Status of Women for its consideration and for any suggestions which it might wish to make to the Council. Special attention will be given to this subject at the third session of the Commission.

(e) RESEARCH PROGRAMME

In accordance with the resolutions of the Economic and Social Council and the recommendations of the Commission on the Status of Women, the Secretariat has begun research to determine the position of women all over the world. To the material already received or which is already available to the Secretariat, it is hoped eventually to add the data to be collected in other countries.

In order to influence public opinion towards improving the condition of women, the Secretariat is preparing a pamphlet dealing with the work of the Commission. A publication on political rights accorded or denied women will be issued as soon as the research in this field is finished.

A series of lectures and round-table discussions on topics relating to the advancement of women is also being developed.

(f) PLANS FOR THE THIRD SESSION OF THE COMMISSION

The Commission received an invitation from the Government of Lebanon to hold its third session in that country. The Economic and Social Council approved the acceptance of this invitation at its sixth session, and requested the Secretary-General to make the necessary arrangements. It also noted with satisfaction the Commission's suggestion that official agencies, non-governmental organizations and others in the region convene a conference on the status of women, to be held at the same time.

D. Social welfare

(a) PROTECTION OF THE FAMILY, CHILDREN AND ADOLESCENTS

The Economic and Social Council, at its sixth session, adopted, on 1 March 1948, a resolution requesting the Social Commission to give priority to questions of child welfare. By the same resolution, the Economic and Social Council approved the child welfare programme contained in the report on the work of the second session (September 1947) of the Social Commission.

The work of the Social Commission and of the Secretariat has therefore been regulated since then by this principle of priority, and has to be considered as part of a long-term programme, the general lines of which were laid down by the Commission at its second session, while the various priorities for its execution in 1948-1949 were decided at its third session (April 1948).

The Social Commission's discussions of the programme showed that, on the one hand, the three terms, *family, children* and *adolescents,* formed an inseparable whole and that, on the other hand, there was a close connexion between child welfare and social welfare services in general.

Several questions on this programme have already been dealt with during 1947-1948;

others will be more particularly part of the work to be done in 1948-1949.

The Secretariat has thus continued to give effect to the resolution adopted by the Council on 29 March 1947 regarding the transfer of the functions of the League of Nations. By 1 May 1948, reports had been received from thirty Governments and the information contained therein was analysed with a view to the publication by the Secretariat of an annual report on the welfare of children and adolescents in various countries. This publication will be combined with a summary of the legislative series regarding the same questions, while the legislative series itself will be widened to cover social welfare as a whole.

Being desirous of having its basic information compiled as uniformly and systematically as possible, the Secretariat has sent to Governments a detailed model form for annual reports and a questionnaire on the organization and administration of child welfare. A study of the replies to these documents will enable the Secretariat to determine not only the situation and specific needs of countries, but also the best practical methods for dealing with them, and will thus enable the various countries to benefit by collective experience.

Furthermore, the Social Commission having repeatedly advocated close co-operation with the non-governmental organizations concerned with child welfare, the Secretariat has sent these organizations a detailed questionnaire on their activities. It has requested them to indicate, with a view to co-operating with the United Nations, those questions which would best lend themselves to international action and which merit prior attention.

Whilst laying down a solid foundation for its sources of information, the Social Commission was anxious to define the rights of the child in a charter which would be based on the declaration of the rights of the child, known as the Declaration of Geneva, worked out in 1923 by the International Save the Children Union and adopted by the League of Nations in 1924 and 1934. The Social Commission recommended the Secretariat to study this question, giving full weight both to the principles of the Declaration of Geneva and to the development of a newer concept of child welfare, so as to transform the Declaration of Geneva into a United Nations charter to be submitted to the Social Commission at its fourth session.

As regards studies and investigations, the Commission also considered that one of the most urgent was the study of the welfare of children who were victims of the war.

A still more general study, since it concerns

all countries, will deal with the welfare of homeless children in their country of origin and the most effective forms and methods of relief given in such cases. The work now being done by emergency relief organizations, such as the International Children's Emergency Fund, should, it is felt, be continued and consolidated in a permanent organization working on a long-term basis.

The Commission, noting the development of various forms of family assistance in several countries, requested the Secretary-General to study the measures of financial assistance (other than family allowances) and the various arrangements in force in different countries for improving family conditions, such as tax exemptions or reductions, housing facilities, issues of food and clothing, transport facilities, educational priorities and facilities for family leisure.

The Secretariat has begun the collection of information on family assistance programmes designed to increase the real earnings and to improve the living conditions of the family as compared with the earnings and living conditions of unmarried persons. The Secretariat proposes to submit the results of this inquiry to the Social Commission at its fourth session.

A special survey will be devoted to the best methods of providing assistance and social services to needy families.

In addition to this programme of financial and economic assistance, the Secretariat was instructed to study family social services as a whole as well as special social services for children and for handicapped groups.

The Secretariat, having collected preliminary information on the subject of adolescence, has been asked by the Commission to prepare a report on questions of particular importance to young persons. The Secretariat has, at the request of the Commission, approached youth organizations with a view to collecting information on their activities. A report will be prepared later on the basis of the information thus obtained.

(b) Social administration

The Economic and Social Council, on 29 March 1947, requested the Secretary-General, in co-operation with the specialized agencies concerned, to arrange for a study of:

(i) Methods of social welfare administration at present in use in different countries:

(ii) Methods of furnishing advice and information and providing experts for countries which request such assistance, with a view to helping them to organize the administration of their social services, including the training of social workers.

In connexion with (i) above, an annotated questionnaire was drawn up in consultation with members of the Social Commission and the specialized agencies, and was transmitted to the former requesting them to state the experience gained in their respective countries in this field. Replies already received from China, Czechoslovakia, Denmark, Greece, Netherlands, the Union of South Africa, the United Kingdom, the United States of America and Yugoslavia have encouraged the Secretary-General to extend the inquiry to all Member nations; a first reply to this second inquiry has been received from the Philippines. A report on the different methods used in various important aspects of social welfare administration is being prepared for consideration by the Social Commission at its fourth session, in 1949.

To assist in deciding policy covering social welfare advisory services (see (ii) above), essential questions have been listed, the experience gained by the United Nations has been analysed and the experience of Member Governments, specialized agencies and the International Children's Emergency Fund has been sought. On the basis of this factual material, a report on the organization of international social service advice and information is being prepared for consideration by the Social Commission at its fourth session.

(c) Training of social workers

In accordance with paragraph (c) of the resolution adopted on 29 March 1947, in which the Economic and Social Council requested that a study be made as to how a long-term welfare training programme of assistance to Governments may be developed and how international training fellowships may be established, a plan of study and questionnaires were prepared in the summer and autumn of 1947 in consultation with members of the Social Commission.

This plan, together with an explanation of the procedure to be followed, was then transmitted to Member Governments, while the relevant questionnaires were sent direct to social welfare advisers of the United Nations, professional associations of social workers and/or individual experts (including members of the Social Commission) in the various countries, and to more than two hundred schools of social work. Working groups, for the most part representative of all the social services, were organized in many countries to co-operate in the collection and utilization of the required information.

Twenty-eight countries have already submitted information regarding their present resources for the training and exchange of social welfare personnel and their views on international action in initiating or developing training and exchange facilities. Detailed data in regard to training already available in educational institutions for the preparation of social welfare personnel have been submitted by a hundred and fifteen schools of social work. The replies received indicate that the study has aroused keen interest in the possibility of constructive international action being initiated in regard to the training and exchange of social welfare personnel. A final report will be submitted to the Social Commission at its fourth session.

(d) INFORMATION AND TECHNICAL REFERENCE CENTRE

One of the many non-political functions of the League of Nations which the Secretary-General was authorized to assume and continue, under General Assembly resolution 51 (I) of 14 December 1946, was the League of Nations Child Welfare Information Centre. The desire of Governments to have advice and information on social services has been stressed on various occasions in resolutions of the Social Commission and the Economic and Social Council. Accordingly, an Information and Technical Reference Centre, covering a considerably wider field than the League institution, was set up and approved by the Social Commission at its third session, in April 1948. The Centre collects material for the various publications of legislative texts dealing with child welfare (proposed by the Social Commission), housing, social services and the prevention of crime. Much of the information so collected is disseminated by means of a quarterly bulletin.

E. Rise in standards of living

(a) STANDARDS OF LIVING

During its second session held in September 1947, the Social Commission suggested that, in centralizing documentary material and information relating to standards of living, particularly in under-developed countries and areas, the Secretary-General should pay special attention to studies carried out by the method of field survey. Effect has been given to this suggestion by the collection and analysis of information on the organization, methodology, scope and content of the relatively small number of intensive field inquiries into the living conditions of selected social groups which have been undertaken in the course of the past two decades in various under-developed areas. The results of these analyses will be made available to the Social Commission.

The Economic and Social Council, by a resolution of 1 March 1948, requested the Secretary-General to initiate immediate studies and to collect and disseminate information and reports with respect to social welfare administration, social services in relation to rural welfare, training of social welfare personnel and child welfare, including the prevention and treatment of juvenile delinquency, in under-developed areas and territories. The Council also requested the Social Commission "to advise the Secretary-General as to any other social problems which warrant special study and attention".

All the subjects specified in the above-mentioned resolution except the question of social services in relation to rural welfare were already being studied by the Secretariat on a world-wide basis, in virtue of earlier decisions taken by the General Assembly, by the Economic and Social Council and by the Social Commission.

The material thus assembled will form the basis for the further report requested by the Social Commission at its third session held in April 1948 "on a comprehensive programme in respect of equitable standards of living generally, but particularly in under-developed areas and territories regardless of their political status and where a low standard of living prevails so as to determine the causes thereof and the means of raising their standards of living". This report is to be prepared in conjunction with the specialized agencies so that it may contain joint recommendations as to the scope, methods and objectives envisaged for a practical programme in this field.

Recognizing that the promotion of improved standards of living is closely linked with economic planning to increase production, the Social Commission requested the Secretary-General also to report on methods of co-ordination in respect of work in this field. Steps are accordingly being taken to bring about a co-ordinated approach by organs of the United Nations as well as by the specialized agencies.

(b) HOUSING AND TOWN AND COUNTRY PLANNING

The Economic and Social Council, at its fourth session, in March 1947, instructed the Social Commission, in collaboration with the Economic and Employment Commission, to continue its study of housing problems in close co-operation with the specialized agencies and inter-governmental organizations concerned. The above-mentioned Commissions were also instructed to consider the desirability of holding an international conference of experts on housing.

The preliminary findings of the Social Commission, based on documentation prepared by the Secretariat, were embodied in certain principles set forth in a resolution on town and country planning contained in the report on the work of the second session of the Commission.

The Economic and Social Council, at its sixth session, approved these principles. It requested the Secretary-General, in the light of the widespread interest and activity in housing and town and country planning, to submit a report to its next session outlining in some detail the several activities of the specialized agencies, intergovernmental and non-governmental organizations and subsidiary organs of the Council in this field and the measures taken thus far toward their co-ordination.

Considerable progress has been made in co-ordination at the technical level. An inter-departmental committee on housing and town planning was set up by the Secretariat to correlate activities between the various units and specialized agencies at the working level. This Committee reports to the Co-ordination Committee. It proposes in the future to invite the participation of representatives of inter-governmental and non-governmental organizations.

The Social Commission, at its third session, accepted the view that, while the subject is urgent, it is one which is so complex that its solution must be mainly domestic. The most effective service the Secretariat could render would therefore be to collect and disseminate to Member Governments expert information for such application in their own countries as they may find appropriate and desirable.

As a means of supplying this information, the Secretariat will issue this year the first number of an international review on housing and town and country planning, the publication of which was recommended by the Social Commission at its second and third sessions.

Furthermore, arrangements are being made to publish during 1949 information dealing with the structure, aims and activities of international, national and regional housing and town planning institutions and agencies, and summaries of legislation relating to housing and town and country planning.

With regard to the proposed international conference of housing experts, a careful study of the various problems involved showed that the convening of such a conference at this juncture would be premature. The Social Commission, however, at its second session, recommended that small meetings of experts on specific problems and on problems arising in particular areas should be arranged. It considered that the question of housing standards came within its special field of interest, and referred specifically to tropical areas, war-devastated areas, economically under-developed areas and rural areas.

Accordingly, in December 1947, a meeting of experts on housing and town and country planning in tropical areas was convened by the Sec-retary-General in conjunction with the Government of Venezuela. At this meeting, in addition to formulating a more general programme to be followed at future meetings of experts, a wide range of topics calling for further study was also suggested.

The Economic and Social Council, at its sixth session, held in February-March 1948, further proposed that the Secretary-General should include in his budgetary estimates for 1949 provision for not more than two small meetings of experts on particular technical matters in the housing field. As such matters require careful long-range planning, the Secretariat, pending a decision by the General Assembly, has commenced preparatory arrangements for two meetings of experts on housing in humid tropical areas.

F. Cultural questions

One of the results of the present development of world society and increased knowledge of natural phenomena and technical means is that all fields of human activities involve cultural problems in a broad sense. Cultural factors must be considered whenever a solution of human problems of a long-range character is looked for. Cultural problems therefore arise in connexion with many of the activities of the United Nations and the specialized agencies, especially the United Nations Educational, Scientific and Cultural Organization.

The co-operation between the United Nations and these agencies is becoming closer and more effective. As a result of resolutions or recommendations passed by the General Assembly, the Economic and Social Council and its commissions, and various specialized agencies, co-ordinated activities are being pursued in many cultural, scientific and educational fields. These activities concern fellowships and advisory missions; personnel training and education and technical training; housing and town and country planning; application of technology and research; conservation and utilization of natural resources; removal of barriers impeding the interchange of persons and the free flow of cultural material; the philosophical principles of human rights; educational opportunities for women; expert advice and technical assistance.

(*a*) Scientific activities

(i) *United Nations research laboratories*

The Secretary-General has submitted a report to the Economic and Social Council regarding the problem of establishing United Nations research laboratories. The report contains extensive studies, comments and suggestions by the specialized agencies interested, by numerous international and national scientific organizations, and by many outstanding scientists and administrators of scientific research.

(ii) *Co-ordination of cartographic services and promotion of cartographic sciences*

The Economic and Social Council requested the Secretary-General to take action with a view to co-ordinating plans and programmes of the United Nations and specialized agencies in the field of cartography and recommending that Member Governments stimulate and encourage accurate cartographic services. The Secretary-General has invited Member Governments, specialized agencies and international organizations to inform him of the measures which have been taken to implement this resolution, and information is being received.

The Secretariat is making plans to consult, in the early part of 1949, experts in the cartographic field and representatives of specialized agencies and interested international organizations.

(*b*) EDUCATIONAL ACTIVITIES

The General Assembly at its second regular session adopted a resolution recommending that all Member Governments should encourage the teaching of the United Nations Charter, and of the purposes, principles and activities of the United Nations, in their schools and colleges, particularly in elementary and secondary schools. The United Nations Educational, Scientific and Cultural Organization was invited to help Member States, at their request, to carry out this programme and to report to the Economic and Social Council. The Secretary-General, on 19 December 1947, sent a communication to Member Governments asking them to report on the measures they were taking to encourage teaching on the subject of the activities of the United Nations. A letter was also sent, on 16 April, to Governments of Members which are not members of UNESCO, drawing their attention to the resolution adopted by the General Conference of UNESCO, which welcomed the resolution of the General Assembly and offered assistance in its implementation.

The United Nations, in consultation with UNESCO, has provided facilities for and co-operated with educational agencies in, among other things, establishing information centres for schools, preparing materials in a form suitable for schools and meeting requests from teachers and pupils. In the adult education field the United Nations has worked with non-governmental organizations.[1] The United Nations has

---

[1] See also page 119.

also participated in the organization of an international seminar, sponsored by UNESCO, which is to be held in Garden City, New York, in July and August 1948, on the subjects, "Teaching about the United Nations and its specialized agencies" and "Education for world society".

The Secretary-General has prepared a report for the seventh session of the Economic and Social Council which contains an account of activities carried out by Member Governments, in co-operation with the secretariats of the United Nations and of UNESCO. The report also contains a review of the experience of the League of Nations in regard to the dissemination of information about international co-operation, and of the recent programmes and activities of non-governmental organizations in this field.

G. Population trends

During the year under review, substantial progress has been made in assembling a staff of demographic experts, and in carrying out the programme of work that was initiated by the Population Commission at its first session in February 1947 and further developed during the second and third sessions in August 1947 and April 1948.

(*a*) DATA ON POPULATION GROWTH AND CHARACTERISTICS

The work of compiling and promoting the development of adequate, internationally comparable statistics on population has been done in close collaboration with the Statistical Office. This will result in the publication of the United Nations *Demographic Yearbook*—the first issue of which it is hoped will be ready in the latter part of 1948—and a file of data for the use of the various organs of the United Nations. In addition to assembling statistics from the official reports of the various Governments, the Secretariat has prepared preliminary estimates and forecasts where they were needed to fill important gaps in the available statistics, and has encouraged Governments to develop more adequate official data at such points.

A special aspect of the work on sources of data, which has formed a large part of the programme during the year under review, is the establishment of standards for censuses of population which will be taken in many countries in or around 1950. For this purpose, a series of technical reports on various aspects of census methodology has been prepared and distributed to Member Governments and to other interested authorities. On the basis of these studies, the Population Commission, at its third session, drew up a general set of recommendations regarding subjects to be covered by 1950 censuses and types of data to be obtained on each subject. The work of the Secretariat in this field will be developed during the coming year.

(b) RELATION OF POPULATION TRENDS TO ECONOMIC AND SOCIAL DEVELOPMENT

During the year, the Secretariat has published population studies for two Trust Territories: Western Samoa and Tanganyika. These studies are intended to assist the Economic and Social Council and the Trusteeship Council in promoting the social, economic and political advancement of the Trust Territories. They provide summaries of the basic facts of population characteristics and population dynamics in each Territory, and an interpretation of these facts with reference to outstanding social and economic problems.

The Population Commission recommended that studies should be made of the manner in which the interplay between demographic and economic and social factors in various types of situations could be analysed. The object of such analyses is to encourage Governments and research institutions to undertake studies in these fields, and thus to provide a scientific foundation for economic and social policies in matters which are significantly related to population changes. Substantial progress has been made in methods of identification of the principal types of demographic, economic and social situations which are found in different parts of the world, so that appropriate methods may be chosen for analysing the problems.

(c) MIGRATION

International migration is of world-wide concern in connexion with population problems (intensified by war casualties in many countries) and with problems of reconstruction, full employment and improvement of standards of living, and thus obviously raises many problems falling within the responsibilities of international organizations. At its fourth session, the Economic and Social Council, recognizing this fact, instructed the Population Commission and the Social Commission to report on a practical plan for the allocation of functions, without duplication of work, among the various organs concerned in the field of migration; and the Council requested the Secretary-General to make studies to facilitate the work of the Commission. A report was drafted in consultation with, and with the co-operation of, the interested specialized agencies. A working arrangement was concluded between the International Labour Office and the Secretariat of the United Nations regarding the allocation of responsibilities and the co-ordination of activities in the field of migration.

This was communicated to other interested specialized agencies, all of which agreed to the principles of the arrangement relating to coordination. Within the Secretariat, co-ordination is assured through an interdepartmental *ad hoc* technical committee on migration.

Studies of migration, as an aspect of population movements, have been made for the *Demographic Yearbook* now in preparation. Following the recommendations of the Population Commission at its second and third sessions, analytical work on selected aspects of migration is being undertaken. The analyses are designed to help the understanding of the conditions and implications of international migration in the present-day world.

The social aspects of migration were considered by the Social Commission at its third session, particularly with a view to ensuring migrants social and economic rights equal to those of the local populations. The Secretariat is expediting, in co-operation with specialized agencies, the development of a concrete programme in the field of migration in accordance with the decisions of the Economic and Social Council.

(d) ASSISTANCE TO INDIGENT FOREIGNERS

In pursuance of a resolution adopted by the Economic and Social Council on 29 March 1947, the Secretary-General transmitted to Member Governments in October 1947 a questionnaire on administrative practices with respect to assistance to indigent foreigners, in order to ascertain to what extent the Model Convention on Assistance to Indigent Foreigners (May 1938) corresponds to the exigencies of the present situation and what changes, if any, should be made in the Convention. As replies to the questionnaire are received, they are analysed for use in the preparation of a report to be submitted to the Social Commission and to the Economic and Social Council.

If the content of the replies justifies such action, a new text of an international convention on the subject will be prepared and submitted for consideration by the appropriate bodies.

(e) EXECUTION OF MAINTENANCE OBLIGATIONS ABROAD

The question of the execution of maintenance obligations abroad is one of the League of Nations activities which has been transferred to the United Nations. The Secretariat has taken up the study of the problem, which was begun as early as 1929 by the International Institute for the Unification of Private Law in Rome. Further developments depend on reaching a satisfactory arrangement for collaboration with the Institute in order that the text of an international convention may be worked out.

H. Social defence

(a) PREVENTION OF CRIME AND TREATMENT OF OFFENDERS

The Economic and Social Council, by a resolution of 29 March 1947, requested the Secretary-General to submit, at a future session of the Social Commission, a report on the prevention of crime and the treatment of offenders indicating which proposals would be suitable for international action and how they could effectively be carried out.

A number of steps have been taken to give effect to this resolution. A questionnaire on the state of crime and the treatment of offenders during the last ten years was drawn up and distributed to all Member States in May 1947. A preliminary report, prepared on the basis of the replies received, was approved in principle by the Social Commission at its second session; and the Secretary-General was requested to collaborate closely with the specialized agencies, with inter-governmental and non-governmental organizations working in the field of crime, and to seek the assistance of experts in regard to specific aspects of the problem.

The plan outlined by the Secretariat was subsequently submitted for comment to the leading organizations working in this field, to criminological institutes and to individual experts, with a view to enlisting their co-operation in carrying out the proposed plan. Collaboration has also been established with the interested specialized agencies. The World Health Organization, for instance, has appointed an expert to prepare a report on the medical and psychiatric aspects of crime and the treatment of offenders. Five international organizations actively concerned with the prevention of crime and the treatment of offenders have been granted consultative status by the Economic and Social Council, and a number of valuable reports have already been received from these organizations. Requests for information and advice have been addressed to experts in thirty-seven countries, and a large number of replies have been received. Working parties formed in several countries have submitted reports on certain questions of paramount importance, such as juvenile delinquency, treatment of the adolescent and adult offender, probation, etc.

On the basis of the material thus collected, the Secretariat has drawn up a list of topics which it considered particularly suitable for international inquiry. The revised plan of study

was reviewed and adopted with certain modifications by the Social Commission during its third session, in April 1948. The programme includes subjects of great practical value, on which the standards of penal administration largely depend, including the prevention and treatment of juvenile delinquency, the probation system in relation to short-term imprisonment and open penal institutions.

While fruitful co-operation has been initiated with certain of the inter-governmental organizations concerned, relationship with the International Penal and Penitentiary Commission has still to be established. The Social Commission was requested by the Economic and Social Council, in a resolution of 10 March 1948, to enter into consultation with the International Penal and Penitentiary Commission provided and as long as the Government of Franco Spain was not readmitted to membership in that Commission. The Secretary-General therefore communicated with the Commission and drew attention to the desirability, from the point of view of the United Nations, of its so amending its Constitution, at the earliest possible moment, as to control its membership. The Secretariat is now preparing a report for the next session of the Economic and Social Council concerning the result of these consultations and the most effective methods to be employed in the carrying out of international activities in the field of the prevention of crime and treatment of offenders.

(b) INTERNATIONAL CONVENTIONS ON TRAFFIC IN WOMEN AND CHILDREN AND ON OBSCENE PUBLICATIONS

In a resolution of 29 March 1947, the Economic and Social Council requested the Secretary-General to take the necessary steps to transfer, to the United Nations, the functions formerly exercised by the League of Nations under the Conventions of 30 September 1921 and 11 October 1933 relating to the suppression of the traffic in women and children, and the Convention of 12 September 1923 concerning the suppression of the circulation of and traffic in obscene publications. The transfer has now been completed. The necessary protocols relating thereto were approved by the General Assembly on 20 October 1947 (resolution 126 (II)) and were signed at Lake Success on 12 November 1947.

With regard to the transfer to the United Nations of the functions exercised by the French Government under the Agreement of 18 May 1904 and the Convention of 4 May 1910 for the suppression of the white slave traffic, and the Agreement of 4 May 1910 for the suppression of obscene publications, the Secretary-

General, in accordance with the terms of the resolution adopted by the Economic and Social Council on 14 August 1947, submitted a report to the third session of the Social Commission, in April 1948. The Commission has advised the Economic and Social Council to recommend the General Assembly to approve this transfer.

The resolution of the Council referred to at the beginning of this section instructed the Secretary-General to resume the study of the 1937 draft convention regarding the exploitation of the prostitution of others, to make any necessary amendments in order to bring it up to date and to take account of changes in the general situation. The modifications proposed by the Secretariat have been communicated to Member States and to certain international organizations for their observations. The Secretariat subsequently submitted a report to the third session of the Social Commission, which recommended that the study of the draft convention should be continued in conjunction with the study of the proposed consolidation of all existing instruments relating to the suppression of the traffic in women and children. A report on the latter subject arising out of a resolution adopted by the Economic and Social Council on 14 August 1947 is now being prepared for consideration by the Social Commission at its fourth session.

Annual reports from Governments on traffic in women and children and on obscene publications.

On the basis of replies received from Governments to a questionnaire circulated by the Secretariat, the first summaries of annual reports to be issued by the United Nations on traffic in women and children and on obscene publications are now being published. These reports refer to the year 1946-1947; subsequent reports are also being prepared covering the period 1947-1948.

(*c*) PREVENTION OF PROSTITUTION AND SUPPRESSION OF THE TRAFFIC IN WOMEN AND CHILDREN

A resolution adopted by the Economic and Social Council on 29 March 1947 requested the Secretary-General, *inter alia,* to consider:

(i) The possibility of implementing the proposal of the League of Nations to establish a bureau in the Far East for suppression of the traffic in women and children;

(ii) Suitable measures for an effective campaign against the traffic in women and children; and

(iii) Provisions to be contemplated for the prevention and suppression of prostitution.

The following preliminary steps have been taken to give effect to these recommendations:

(i) A report has been prepared by the Secretariat giving a brief survey of the main developments relating to this question. Before, however, making specific recommendations concerning the establishment of a bureau in the Far East, the views of the interested Governments and organizations are being sought in order that a plan may be outlined for consideration by the Social Commission at its fourth session.

(ii) A revision of the League of Nations questionnaire on traffic in women and children, which forms the basis of the annual reports from Governments on the traffic, has been undertaken in the light of post-war developments. Certain interested specialized agencies and national and international organizations have been invited to co-operate in this work.

(iii) A comprehensive study, undertaken by the League of Nations, on the prevention of prostitution was completed in 1939 but, owing to the course of events, was not published until 1943. Although the trend of prostitution has undergone certain changes since that date, the recommendations embodied in the report are of great value at the present time. As a preliminary step towards the implementation of the above-mentioned resolution on this question, an extract has been made of the report's main recommendations relating to the more direct measures of prevention of prostitution. Member States are to be requested to submit their observations as to the extent to which these recommendations are in operation in their countries. The views thus expressed will be submitted to the Social Commission for consideration at its fourth session.

I. Narcotic drugs and their international regime

The Commission on Narcotic Drugs of the Economic and Social Council held its second session from 24 July to 8 August 1947, and its third session from 3 to 22 May 1948.

On each of these occasions, it examined the whole field of the problems relating to the control of the international trade in narcotic drugs and took decisions governing the Secretariat's work for the period preceding the next session.

The primary task of the Commission is to examine the documents which Governments are required, under the terms of international conventions, to transmit regularly to the Secretary-General, namely, the annual reports, legislative texts and report on seizures. These documents are submitted to the Commission by the Secretariat both in their original form and in analytical summaries.

The Commission then studies the replies of Governments to special questionnaires, such as the questionnaire on the limitation of raw materials and that on drug addiction. To facilitate this task, the Secretariat provides it with analyses of the replies received.

Finally, the Commission recommends measures to strengthen the control system, such as the new protocol on synthetic drugs, and draws up a programme of future work. In 1948, for example, it is providing for a study of the codification of international instruments on narcotic drugs and of the simplification of international control.

The Secretariat is required to supply the Commission with any available materials which may facilitate its consideration of each question.

A summary outline of the main questions dealt with by the Commission at its second and third sessions follows.

(a) INTERNATIONAL INSTRUMENTS RELATING TO NARCOTIC DRUGS

On 9 September 1947, the Secretariat registered the accession of Ethiopia to the Conventions of 19 February 1925 and 26 June 1936. On the same date, the Ethiopian Government ratified the Convention of 13 July 1931.

All the amendments introduced by the Protocol of 11 December 1946 into the international agreements, conventions and protocols relating to narcotic drugs entered into force at the end of 1947 and the beginning of 1948. On 1 June 1948, forty-two countries were parties to the above-mentioned Protocol.

(b) RE-ESTABLISHMENT AND IMPROVEMENT OF THE INTERNATIONAL CONTROL OF NARCOTIC DRUGS

(i) *Annual reports*

The Secretary-General took the step of submitting to the Commission, at its second session, a detailed summary showing the countries and territories which had submitted their annual reports and those which had not as yet done so.

During the same session, the Commission noted with regret that, in spite of a telegraphic reminder and a *note verbale* addressed by the Secretary-General to all Governments, some countries had omitted—in some cases owing to conditions caused by the war—to comply with the obligation of communicating to him their annual reports. For the year 1945 the Commission had received only twenty-eight reports from sovereign countries and thirty from territories, that is, from just over a third of the total

of a hundred and eighty countries and territories.

On the Commission's recommendation, the Economic and Social Council adopted, on 2 March 1948, a resolution recognizing the importance, for the international control of narcotic drugs, of the regular dispatch of these reports by Governments.

The Council's resolution was circulated to Governments by the Secretary-General on 26 March 1948. The communication was preceded by a *note verbale*, with which was enclosed the form of annual reports prepared by the Secretariat and revised by the Commission.

At its third session, the Commission noted that ninety-four annual reports had been received for 1946, forty from sovereign countries and fifty-four from territories. This represents an improvement upon the figure for 1945 but is not yet considered entirely satisfactory. The Commission therefore asked the Secretary-General to remind Governments which had neglected to submit their reports of their treaty obligation.

The Commission was particularly concerned with the question of re-establishing the control system in the occupied territories. In pursuance of instructions given by the Commission at its first session, the Secretary-General in 1947 had asked the Chairman of the Allied Control Council in Germany and the Supreme Commander of the Allied Forces in Japan to submit annual reports and reports of seizures for the territories under their control. Annual reports for Japan for 1945 and 1946, and a report on the British zone in Germany for 1945 and 1946 and for the four zones for 1946 were received and examined by the Commission. Although some progress had been noted in the organization of the control of narcotics in Germany, the Commission considered that the system, particularly with regard to the illicit traffic, needed to be strengthened.

The Italian Government having adhered, on 28 March 1948, to the Protocol of 11 December 1946, the Secretary-General sent a note to the Italian Minister of Foreign Affairs on 12 April 19 drawing his attention to the obligations with regard to the maintenance of control which are incumbent on parties to international conventions on narcotic drugs.

(ii) *Illicit traffic*

The Commission gave special attention to illicit traffic. Noting that this traffic was on the increase and was beginning to develop along the lines typical of the period before the Second World War, the Secretariat had submitted, to the Commission, quarterly summaries of the reports of seizures, giving the total quantities of drugs seized, as notified by Governments, and memoranda on trends in the illicit traffic which emerged from the information available.

Between the Commission's second and third sessions, 216 reports of seizures were transmitted to the Secretary-General by twelve sovereign States and three territories. Of the 986 cases of illicit traffic reported, all except a dozen were notified by nine countries—Australia, Canada, China, Egypt, India, Italy, Palestine, United Kingdom and the United States of America.

As the existence of illicit traffic in other parts of the world is an incontrovertible fact, confirmed in the annual reports of various Governments, the Commission recommended that the Economic and Social Council should appeal to all Governments to fulfil their obligations under Article 23 of the 1931 Convention and to submit reports on illicit traffic to the Secretary-General.

The Commission then turned its attention to the sources of drugs seized in the illicit traffic and noted with regret that, in their reports, most Governments did not clearly indicate the origin of the drugs seized. It was therefore anxious that Governments should be informed of the essential points which should be included in the information given in reports of seizures, and proposed to the Economic and Social Council that it should adopt a resolution to this end.

The Secretary-General has been asked to communicate to all parties to the Conventions the chapter of the Commission's report on the work of its third session which deals with this question.

(iii) *Summary of laws and regulations*

During its third session, the Commission examined the first annual summary of the national laws and regulations on narcotic drugs prepared by the Secretariat. In pursuance of instructions given by the Commission at its first session, the Secretariat has also undertaken the preparation of a digest of national legislation on narcotic drugs, the Commission having expressed the view that a summary of this kind would prove invaluable to national administrations.

(iv) *Technical assistance furnished to the Government of Peru with a view to the reorganization of the control of narcotic drugs in Peruvian territory*

At the request of the Government of Peru, the Secretary-General sent to that country a mission consisting of three members of the Secretariat to study the system of narcotics control with a view to its reorganization. The mission went to Peru on 18 March 1948 and completed its work on 23 April; its report was submitted to the Secretary-General, who transmitted it to the Government of Peru.

(v) *Methods of determining the origin of seized opium by chemical and physical means*

A statement submitted by the United States representative, regarding new methods which make it possible to determine by physical and chemical means the origin of opium discovered in the illicit traffic, was received with the greatest interest. The Commission recommended that there should be an exchange of documentation and information on this subject between the Secretary-General and Governments; the latter —more particularly those with the necessary experts and laboratory facilities—should be invited to state whether they are prepared to take part in a joint research programme. For this purpose, Governments would be invited to furnish samples of the opium produced in their respective countries, subject to the provisions of chapter V of the 1925 Convention.

(vi) *Continuation of studies on Indian hemp*

The Commission requested the Secretariat to continue the studies on Indian hemp initiated by the League of Nations Advisory Committee on Opium, enlisting the services of an expert for this purpose if necessary.

(vii) *Questions relating to narcotic drugs included in the provisional questionnaire of the Trusteeship Council*

The Commission recommended that the Economic and Social Council should make certain alterations in the questions on narcotics included in the provisional questionnaire, as adopted by the Trusteeship Council and communicated to the Economic and Social Council for its advice.

(viii) *Protocol to bring under international control certain drugs outside the scope of the 1931 Convention*

In accordance with the Commission's recommendation, approved by the Council at its fifth session, the Secretary-General prepared and communicated to Governments, for their observations, a draft protocol to bring under international control drugs not covered by the 1931 Convention, in particular, synthetic drugs.

During its third session, the Commission examined the Secretary-General's draft, and drew up a text which took into account the observations received from Governments.

In accordance with the instructions of the Commission, the Secretary-General communicated the text in question to Governments on 9 June 1948, and requested them to submit to him any observations they wished to make before the seventh session of the Council.

(ix) *Codification of conventions, agreements and protocols on narcotics and simplification of the machinery of international control*

There are at present six international instruments governing the control of narcotics throughout the world. The protocol on synthetic narcotics will be the seventh, while a convention on the limitation of the production of raw materials would be the eighth.

It has been apparent for some time that there is a need to reduce the extreme complexity of the provisions of the existing conventions, agreements and protocols, which are the result of the evolution over the last thirty-five years of international legislation respecting narcotic drugs.

The hope was expressed by the Fifth Committee, during the second regular session of the General Assembly, that the Economic and Social Council would study the measures necessary to unify and simplify the control machinery.

During its third session, the Commission on Narcotic Drugs adopted a resolution requesting the Council to invite the Secretary-General to prepare a single draft convention providing for a single body to perform all control functions other than those which are now or may in the future be entrusted to the Commission on Narcotic Drugs.

This convention would replace the existing instruments and also include provisions for the limitation of the production of raw materials used in the manufacture of narcotics.

The Economic and Social Council will be invited to take a decision on this proposal during its seventh session.

The Secretariat has submitted various preliminary studies on these matters to the Commission, which has been able to realize the complexity of the task contemplated.

(c) LIMITATION OF THE PRODUCTION OF RAW MATERIALS

The limitation of the production of raw materials is still one of the major concerns of the Commission on Narcotic Drugs. It has taken into consideration the extensive information prepared by the Secretariat, and has discussed the problem at length.

As already stated, the Commission has recommended that the Secretary-General should prepare, for insertion in the future general convention, the text provisions relating to the limitation of the production of raw materials. To this end, the Secretary-General has been authorized to revise the draft convention drawn up in 1939 by the League of Nations Advisory Committee.

The Commission has requested the Secretariat to prepare estimates of world requirements of raw opium for medical use. It has also recommended that the Secretariat should undertake studies and investigations regarding the advisability of convening a conference of the countries producing opium and the countries using opium in the manufacture of drugs for medical or scientific purposes, with a view to concluding a provisional agreement limiting the production and export of opium to such needs, pending the adoption of a general convention.

The Commission has requested that the results of these studies and investigations be submitted to it at its next session.

The problem of the limitation of raw materials is not, however, confined to raw opium and poppy straw. It also includes the production and use of Indian hemp and coca leaf.

(d) COMMISSION OF INQUIRY ON THE EFFECTS OF COCA-LEAF CHEWING

During its second regular session, the General Assembly had drawn the attention of the Economic and Social Council to the request of the Government of Peru for the setting up of a committee or a group of experts to study the effects of coca-leaf chewing in certain regions in the Andes.

During its sixth session, the Council approved in principle the sending of such a commission to these areas. In accordance with the Council's request, the Secretary-General will submit to its seventh session a detailed plan, taking into account any requests which may be received from other countries interested in the matter.

This Commission would also study the possibility of limiting the production of coca leaf to medical and scientific needs.

(e) DRUG ADDICTION

During its third session, the Commission examined the replies of Governments to the "Special questionnaire regarding the legal and practical standpoint taken up regarding drug addiction and drug addicts". This questionnaire had been sent to them by the Secretary-General on 23 April 1947.

It was proposed that the Secretariat should analyse and classify the replies according to the various subjects dealt with in the questionnaire, and should submit the results of this study to the Commission at its next session.

(f) ABOLITION OF THE LEGAL USE OF SMOKING OPIUM IN THE FAR EAST

After studying a series of reports on this problem, the Commission found that, although a number of countries had declared their intention of abolishing the monopolies in opium for smoking in the Far East, the situation in certain of these territories had hardly improved at all. The Commission therefore recommended the Economic and Social Council to invite all countries in which the custom of opium smoking exists to take the necessary steps to suppress it; to request Governments which had announced their intention of suppressing it to submit to the Secretary-General, by 31 March of each year at the latest, a special annual report on the results obtained in this respect; and lastly, to request these Governments immediately to prohibit the importation of raw opium into their territories, except for medical and scientific purposes.

(g) Narcotic drugs and genocide

During its third session, the Commission examined a document submitted by the Government of the United States of America giving photographs and a detailed description of the factory constructed at Mukden by the Japanese authorities for the manufacture of narcotic drugs, which they had intended to distribute to the inhabitants of Manchuria.

The Commission was of the opinion that special provision should be made against crimes of this nature in the Convention on genocide, and that the Economic and Social Council should so act that the use of narcotic drugs as a means of endangering the physical and moral health of whole population groups would be covered by the Convention on the prevention and punishment of genocide.

(h) Permanent Central Opium Board and Supervisory Body

The Secretary-General was represented at the two sessions of the Permanent Central Opium Board which took place at Geneva from 14 to 19 April 1947, and from 13 to 20 October 1947, respectively.

The amendments made to the Geneva Convention of 1925 by the Protocol of 11 December 1946 having come into force on 3 March 1948, the Secretary-General submitted to the Economic and Social Council the information required with a view to reconstituting the Permanent Central Opium Board.

On the basis of this information, the Council appointed the following persons as members of the Board:

Professor Hans Fischer, *Switzerland;* Sir Harry Greenfield, *United Kingdom;* Mr. Herbert L. May, *United States of America;* Dr. Pedro Pernambuco Filho, *Brazil;* Mr. Paul Reuter, *France;* Mr. Milan Ristic, *Yugoslavia;* Professor Sedat Tavat, *Turkey;* Dr. Y. N. Yang, *China.*

The Supervisory Body held its twenty-eighth session at Geneva in October 1947 and its twenty-ninth in London in November 1947, and drew up a statement of estimated world requirements of narcotic drugs for 1948.

In accordance with the provisions of the Geneva Convention of 1925, amended by the Protocol of 11 December 1946, the World Health Organization elected Professor Hans Fischer (Switzerland) a member of the Supervisory Body and will later nominate a second member.

The Commission on Narcotic Drugs has appointed Colonel C. H. L. Sharman a member of the Supervisory Body. The Permanent Central Opium Board will appoint a fourth member to complete the membership of the reconstituted Supervisory Body.

(i) Reconstitution of the Commission on Narcotic Drugs

During its third session, the Commission considered that it was important to avoid any interval between the expiry of the term of office of the retiring members and the beginning of the term of the newly appointed members. It also recognized the importance, generally speaking, of ensuring the continuity of the Commission through its members, as far as was possible. Consequently, after studying the document prepared on this subject by the Secretariat, the Commission recommended that the Economic and Social Council fix the term of membership of its members at three years. The appointment of these members would be made by the Council every three years at its first session in the year; this procedure would come into force at the beginning of 1949. On the other hand, the mandate of the retiring members of the Commission would expire only on the eve of the first meeting of the Commission, following election of the new members.

The Commission further recommended the Council to draw the attention of Governments which are members of the Commission on Narcotic Drugs to the fact that, when appointing their representatives, they should give particular consideration to the fundamental problems of the international control of narcotic drugs, problems which can only be solved over a period of several years.

(j) Publication by the United Nations of a periodical on narcotic drugs

The Commission recognized the importance of the publication, by the United Nations Secretariat, of a periodical dealing with problems connected with narcotic drugs. It therefore recommended the Economic and Social Council to approve the publication of such a periodical and invite the Secretary-General to take the necessary steps to this effect.

3. CO-ORDINATION AND RELATIONS WITH SPECIALIZED AGENCIES

During the past year, additional specialized agencies have entered into agreements with the United Nations, and the machinery for co-operation between the United Nations and the agencies has been strengthened and improved. Within the framework of general policies laid down by the General Assembly, at its second regular session, and by the Economic and Social Council, at its sixth session, the Secretary-General and the chief administrative officers of the agencies have undertaken to deal with numerous issues of common concern through the Co-ordination Committee.

The desirability of consulting in advance on key policy matters, and of proceeding by accord on joint problems has been recognized by all organizations comprising the United Nations system. Arrangements for co-operative action on broad policy matters as well as on day-to-day technical matters are now considered adequate.

The concern of the Economic and Social Council to avoid overlapping of activities as the programmes of the several international organizations develop is shared by the Secretary-General and the Directors-General of the agencies. At the present stage of development, there would seem to be no significant duplication of work in the United Nations and the specialized agencies.

The most valuable type of co-ordination is, of course, that involved in settling day-to-day technical problems as they arise. The extent of such technical collaboration, as well as the more formal provisions for joint action with respect to particular economic and social problems, are dealt with in other sections of this report.

(a) STATUS OF AGREEMENTS

Five more agreements between the United Nations and specialized agencies were approved by the General Assembly at its second regular session, and action was taken by the Economic and Social Council to initiate negotiations for agreements with four other agencies, making a total of thirteen agencies with which the United Nations has negotiated or is negotiating agreements. The status of the agreements is as follows:

(i) Agreements are in force with the International Labour Organisation, the Food and Agriculture Organization, the United Nations Educational, Scientific and Cultural Organization, the International Civil Aviation Organization, the International Bank for Reconstruction and Development, and the International Monetary Fund;

(ii) Agreements with the International Telecommunications Union, the Universal Postal Union and the World Health Organization have been approved by the General Assembly, and are awaiting entry into force under the respective constitutional processes of each agency;

(iii) Negotiations are being initiated for agreements with the Inter-Governmental Maritime Consultative Organization, the International Refugee Organization, the International Trade Organization and the World Meteorological Organization.

(b) MACHINERY FOR CO-ORDINATION

Within the framework of the Co-ordination Committee set up by the Secretary-General in accordance with the request of the Economic and Social Council, further progress has been made in consolidating the machinery for co-ordination between the United Nations and the specialized agencies. A Preparatory Committee, composed of representatives of the chief administrative officers of the agencies, was established in February 1948 for the purpose of relieving the chief administrative officers of lesser matters of co-ordination, so that the latter can devote more attention to questions of higher policy. Subsidiary bodies now include three consultative committees (on administrative questions, statistical matters and public information), the United Nations Film Board, the Inter-Library Committee, two technical working groups (fellowships and housing), and one regional consultative committee (at Geneva). Each of these subsidiary bodies, composed of the respective technical officers of the various agencies, reports on the progress of its work to the Co-ordination Committee.

In addition to the framework of the Committee, other important liaison arrangements have been made under the agreements between the United Nations and the agencies, and between agency and agency, particularly with respect to the articles providing for exchange of information and documents and reciprocal representation at meetings. There has at the same time been steady progress as regards day-to-day contact at all Secretariat levels which is the indispensable basis of effective co-ordination.

(*c*) Administrative and programme co-ordination

Through the machinery of the Co-ordination Committee and its subsidiary bodies, inter-agency study has been given to the problems involved in such questions as a calendar of conferences, a co-ordinated policy for the sale and distribution of documents, issuance of non-statistical questionnaires, statistical programmes, public information and film production, as well as to the co-ordination of regional activities. Besides budgetary matters (which are dealt with in more detail below under D.), the Consultative Committee on Administrative Questions has undertaken inter-agency studies on the financing of common services, on salary scales and allowances, on a programme for the proposed International Civil Service Advisory Board, and on comparisons of administrative and financial systems.

In programme co-ordination, considerable impetus was given by the Economic and Social Council, in March 1948, to the efforts previously initiated by the Co-ordination Committee and by the General Assembly in its resolution 125 (II) of 20 November 1947, when it undertook a careful study of the problems of co-ordination between the United Nations and the agencies, with special reference to the transmittal, by agencies, of reports on their activities and work programmes. The resolution adopted by the Council on 10 March 1948 represents the cornerstone on which its efforts in co-ordination are being built, with the general purpose of indicating gaps and overlapping in the activities of the agencies and emphasizing objectives and priorities in their programmes.

At the suggestion of the Co-ordination Committee, the Secretary-General has arranged for a comparative review of the reports submitted by agencies to the Council which would take into account also the activities and programmes of the United Nations. The comparative review is to be considered by the Committee prior to submission to the seventh session of the Council. It is expected that, as the process of preparing the comparative review is developed and improved, it will provide a useful basis for determining gaps or overlapping in programmes.

(*d*) Budgetary and financial relations with the specialized agencies

(i) *Bases for budgetary relations of the United Nations and the specialized agencies*

The continuing interest of Member States in the question of budgetary co-ordination of the United Nations and the agencies was reflected in resolutions 125 (II) and 165 (II), adopted by the General Assembly on 20 November 1947.

These resolutions, based upon the responsibility of the General Assembly under Article 17, paragraph 3, of the Charter to examine the administrative budgets of the specialized agencies with a view to making recommendations to the agencies concerned, emphasized methods for improving the system of budgetary co-ordination. The resolutions also made certain specific recommendations to agencies whose 1948 estimates were examined at the second regular session.

Specialized agencies were requested to transmit their budgets or budgetary estimates for 1949 to the Secretary-General not later than 1 July 1948. They were also asked to provide for active consultation between their secretariats and the Secretariat of the United Nations during the period of preparation of their budgets. The importance of adequate budget justifications was also stressed. It was pointed out that estimates could not be appraised properly unless a statement of work to be done in the financial year under consideration was provided for each section or division of the budget. The relation of such a presentation of work projects to the co-ordination of work programmes by the Economic and Social Council was noted.

The Secretary-General was requested to report to the third regular session of the General Assembly on:

(*a*) Measures for achieving greater uniformity in presentation of the budgets of the United Nations and of the specialized agencies, with a view to providing a basis for comparison of the several budgets;

(*b*) The fiscal year and schedule of meetings of the specialized agencies in relation to the procedures of the Economic and Social Council and the General Assembly with respect to the specialized agencies;

(*c*) The feasibility of improved budgetary co-ordination between the United Nations and the specialized agencies; and

(*d*) Promotion of the development of similar budgetary, administrative and financial practices in the United Nations and the specialized agencies.

(ii) *Implementation of the General Assembly resolutions*

A detailed report on progress in implementing the General Assembly resolutions is being presented to the seventh session of the Economic and Social Council and will be transmitted to the General Assembly. It may be noted here that significant progress has been made in achieving a more uniform budget pattern, which is to be used in presenting an annex to the United Nations budget estimates for 1949, summarizing United Nations and specialized agency budgets according to a standard pattern of budget headings and objects of expenditures. Comparability in the form of the estimates, as all Members have recognized, is the prerequisite for budgetary co-ordination.

With the adoption by the second Assembly of the International Civil Aviation Organization of a fiscal year from 1 January to 31 December of each year, the United Nations and all specialized agencies financed through annual contributions by their members have achieved uniformity in the use of the calendar year as the fiscal period. This action, together with the co-ordination of the calendar of annual conferences, will remove most of the mechanical obstacles to improved budgetary co-ordination.

The question of an integrated or consolidated budget for the United Nations and the specialized agencies, to be approved by the General Assembly, was debated at considerable length at the latter's second regular session. A majority of Members favoured further study of the whole problem of the feasibility of improved budgetary co-ordination, including all reasonable alternatives to consolidation. The Secretary-General has explored the whole problem with the administrative heads of the specialized agencies and has concluded that, apart from any question of desirability, the constitutional and political prerequisites for a consolidated budget are not capable of immediate fulfilment. The Secretary-General and the heads of the specialized agencies concerned have agreed, in lieu of such integration, to ensure by all means within their power that available resources are wisely and prudently expended, with proper regard not only to the particular interests of one agency but equally to the wider interests of the United Nations as a whole. The Secretary-General, together with the Co-ordination Committee, therefore believes that, in the field of budgetary co-ordination, the United Nations and the specialized agencies should strive to give full effect to the recommendations and suggestions of the General Assembly, the Economic and Social Council and the Advisory Committee on Administrative and Budgetary Questions as well as to the policies and procedures agreed upon in the Co-ordination Committee and its subsidiary bodies, with special reference to:

(*a*) Implementation of recommendations which the General Assembly may make;

(*b*) Active consultation between the United Nations and the specialized agencies in the preparation (at all stages) of their budgets;

(*c*) The role which the Economic and Social Council should play in the development of an overall work programme, and the importance in relation thereto of adequate reports on activities and future programmes; and

(*d*) The desirability of achieving a greater measure of uniformity of administrative and financial practices and procedures, particularly with respect to internal financial controls and external audit arrangements.

(iii) *Other financial relations*

Loans to specialized agencies. Under the authority of General Assembly resolution 166 (II) of 20 November 1947 relating to the Budget and the Working Capital Fund, the Secretary-General has made available in 1948, with the concurrence of the Advisory Committee on Administrative and Budgetary Questions, loans from the Working Capital Fund to finance the initial operations of the Interim Commission of the World Health Organization, the International Conference on Trade and Employment and the Interim Commission of the International Trade Organization. The amount of these loans outstanding at 31 May 1948 was $2,950,137. Under the terms of the General Assembly resolution, these loans are repayable within two years.

Officials of the Interim Commission of the World Health Organization have requested consideration by the Secretary-General and the Advisory Committee of further loans to the Interim Commission and to the organization itself, which is expected to be formally established by 1 September 1948, to finance world health work, pending receipt of sufficient contributions under its first budget. The Secretary-General has recommended favourable action on such a loan.

Reimbursement for joint costs. The development of common administrative and fiscal services has been facilitated during the past year by agreement between the United Nations and the specialized agencies on the principles, methods and rates for sharing the costs of such services.

It is estimated that from 30 to 40 per cent of all conference activity at the Geneva Office of the United Nations is serviced on behalf of the specialized agencies. Their use of the interpreters, translation and documentary services, and fiscal services available at Lake Success has grown significantly over the past year. ·

Chapter III

QUESTIONS CONCERNING TRUSTEESHIP AND NON-SELF-GOVERNING TERRITORIES

A. Organization of the trusteeship system

The organization of the international trusteeship system has been laid down in the past year and the Trusteeship Council has, in the discharge of its responsibilities, assured itself of the co-operation of the Economic and Social Council and its Commissions and of the specialized agencies in particular fields. The sole remaining problem of importance is the application of the basic objectives of the international trusteeship system to strategic areas under Trusteeship. It is hoped that this problem may soon be solved.

(a) INCREASE IN THE MEMBERSHIP OF THE TRUSTEESHIP COUNCIL

The Trusteeship Agreement for the Trust Territory of the Pacific Islands entered into force on 18 July 1947, the date on which it was signed by the President of the United States of America. Under the terms of the agreement, the United States was designated as the Administering Authority. As the United States was already a member of the Trusteeship Council, by virtue of being mentioned by name in Article 23 of the Charter, for it to become a member administering a Trust Territory necessitated the election by the General Assembly of two members to the Trusteeship Council, in order to maintain the balance provided for in Article 86 of the Charter between those members which administer Trust Territories and those which do not. During its second regular session, the General Assembly elected Costa Rica and the Philippines. Thus the membership of the Council was increased to twelve. The newly-appointed members took their seats on the Council at its second session in November 1947; their appointments will expire on 31 December 1950.

(b) RELATIONS BETWEEN THE SECURITY COUNCIL AND THE TRUSTEESHIP COUNCIL

The question of the relations between the Security Council and the Trusteeship Council with regard to the trusteeship system as applied to strategic areas arose as a result of the entry into force of the Trusteeship Agreement for the Pacific Islands, and was brought to the attention of the Security Council by the Secretary-General in a letter dated 7 November 1947. In this letter, the Secretary-General pointed out the necessity for formulating procedures to govern the detailed application of Articles 87 and 88 of the Charter to the strategic areas.

On 15 November 1947, the Security Council decided to refer the whole question to its Committee of Experts.

The Committee of Experts devoted seven meetings to the consideration of the matter referred to it by the Security Council, and found it necessary to consider whether its terms of reference required it to make recommendations to the Security Council only in relation to the specific question of the Pacific Islands formerly under Japanese mandate, or whether it was entitled to recommend procedures applicable to strategic areas generally.

The Committee eventually decided to recommend to the Security Council the adoption of a resolution generally applicable to strategic areas under trusteeship.

The Committee of Experts also discussed whether it should recommend to the Security Council the adoption of a resolution only, or rules of procedure only, or both. It finally decided by a majority vote to consider first a draft resolution providing for the Security Council to request the assistance of the Trusteeship Council.

The majority of the Committee recommended to the Security Council the adoption of a resolution under the terms of which the Trusteeship Council would be requested to perform, on behalf of the Security Council and subject to the latter's decisions concerning security matters, the functions specified in Articles 87 and 88 of the Charter, to send to the Security Council a copy of its questionnaire one month before forwarding it to the Administering Authority, and to submit to the Security Council its reports and recommendations on pol : al, economic, social and educational matters affecting strategic areas under trusteeship; at the same time, the Secretary-General would be requested to ad· se the Security Council of all reports and petitions received in respect of strategic areas under trusteeship and to send copies thereof to the Trusteeship Council for examination and report to the Security Council.

However, the representatives of Poland and the Union of Soviet Socialist Republics on the Committee opposed the recommendation on the grounds that, generally, it went far beyond the intentions of Article 83, paragraph 3, of the Charter, and, in particular, that it would be contrary to Article 88 of the Charter to give full right to the Trusteeship Council to formulate the questionnaire concerning strategic areas under trusteeship.

Meanwhile, the Trusteeship Council, on 16 December 1947, authorized its President to appoint a committee of three, composed of himself and two other members, to confer with the President of the Security Council or a similar committee of that Council on the question.

The Security Council took up the report of its Committee of Experts on 18 June 1948. After some discussion, it invited the Committee of Three of the Trusteeship Council to confer with a Committee of Three of the Security Council, composed of the President and two other members. The two Committees conferred on 22 June 1948, during the third session of the Trusteeship Council. An exchange of views took place on the responsibilities of the Trusteeship Council in connexion with the political, economic, social and educational advancement of the inhabitants of Trust Territories; and it was agreed that the two Committees would meet again after the President of the Trusteeship Council had ascertained the views of that Council with regard to the draft resolution recommended by the Committee of Experts.

(*c*) Relations between the Trusteeship Council and the Economic and Social Council and Specialized Agencies

The Trusteeship Council at its first session, and the Economic and Social Council at its fifth session, had respectively appointed representatives to a joint committee of both Councils to consider arrangements for co-operation between the two Councils in matters of common concern. The Committee met during August 1947. The questions which it had to consider arose from the fact that, in the economic and social fields, there is some possibility of overlapping of functions between the Economic and Social Council and its Commissions on the one hand, and the Trusteeship Council on the other hand.

In its report to both Councils, the Committee made a number of detailed recommendations regarding methods of co-operation between the two Councils in such fields of common concern, of which the two most important were as follows. First, the Committee, while recognizing that the Economic and Social Council and its Commissions were empowered to make recommendations or studies of general application on matters within their special provinces, and that such recommendations or studies might be made in respect of particular groups of territories, such as those within a given geographical region, or presenting common problems, nevertheless considered that Trust Territories as such should not be singled out for such recommendations or studies without the concurrence of the Trusteeship Council. Secondly, the Committee recommended that, as a matter of principle, all petitions to organs of the United Nations (such as petitions on human rights or the status of women) which emanate from, or relate to conditions in, any Trust Territory, should be dealt with in the first instance by the Trusteeship Council, but that the Trusteeship Council should then seek the assistance of the appropriate Commission of the Economic and Social Council regarding those parts of such petitions which relate to matters with which the Commission is concerned.

The report of the Committee came into effect when it had been approved by both Councils. It was approved by the Economic and Social Council during its fifth session, in August 1947, and by the Trusteeship Council during its second session, in November 1947.

The Trusteeship Council had appointed, during its first session, a committee of two members to join with representatives of the Economic and Social Council in any future negotiations with intergovernmental organizations to be brought into relationship with the United Nations, with respect to such clauses of the agreements as might concern the Trusteeship Council. The Committee participated in the negotiations, held during August 1947, which led to the conclusion of agreements between the United Nations and the World Health Organization, the International Telecommunications Union, the International Bank for Reconstruction and Development, and the International Monetary Fund, and submitted a report to the Trusteeship Council on those aspects of the negotiations with which it was concerned.

B. Extension of the Trusteeship System to new Trust Territories

(a) TRUST TERRITORY OF THE PACIFIC ISLANDS

With the entry into force on 18 July 1947 of the relevant Trusteeship Agreement, the Pacific Islands formerly under Japanese mandate were brought into the international trusteeship system as a strategic area. The Territory consists of the Marshall Islands, the Marianas Islands and the Caroline Islands.

On 2 December 1947, the Security Council was informed by the Government of the United States of America that the latter, for security reasons and in accordance with article 13 of the Trusteeship Agreement, had closed Eniwetok Atoll in the Marshall Islands, and the territorial waters adjacent thereto, for the purpose of conducting experiments relating to nuclear fission. The Security Council took note of the information, but decided to defer further consideration thereof until it had received the report from its Committee of Experts on the functions of the Security Council in relation to strategic areas.

(b) TRUST TERRITORY OF NAURU

In September 1947, the Governments of Australia, New Zealand and the United Kingdom jointly submitted a draft Trusteeship Agreement for the mandated Territory of Nauru. In this draft Trusteeship Agreement, these three Governments were designated as the joint authority which would exercise the administration of the Territory; moreover, in pursuance of an agreement made between the three Governments, and until otherwise decided by them, the Government of Australia would exercise it on their behalf. This interesting provision for an Administering Authority of a Trust Territory consisting of more than one State is the only example of its kind. With one amendment of article 7, offered by the Mandatory Power and designed to show that any military measures taken in the Territory would be taken in discharge of the Administering Authority's duties under Article 84 of the Charter, the draft was approved by the General Assembly on 1 November 1947.

(c) POSSIBLE ADDITIONAL TRUST TERRITORIES

Territories which may be placed under the international trusteeship system fall into three categories (Article 77 of the Charter). In the first category—territories held under mandate—all such territories save Palestine and South West Africa have become independent States or have been placed under the international trusteeship system. In the second category—territories detached from enemy States as a result of the Second World War—are the former Italian colonies of Libya, Eritrea and Italian Somaliland. Of territories in the third category—territories voluntarily placed under the international trusteeship system by States responsible for their administration—none have yet been placed under trusteeship, and there has been no indication so far that any will be placed under it in the near future[1].

(i) *Palestine*

The endeavours of the United Nations concerning the question of the future government of Palestine have been described elsewhere in this report.

(ii) *South West Africa*

By resolution 65 (I) on the future status of South West Africa adopted during its first session, the General Assembly had declared itself unable to accept the proposal by the Government of the Union of South Africa to incorporate the Territory of South West Africa in the Union of South Africa, and had invited the Union Government to propose a Trusteeship Agreement for the Territory.

The Union Government replied that, although it found itself unable to proceed with the invitation of the General Assembly to propose a Trusteeship Agreement for the Territory, it did not intend to proceed with the incorporation of the Territory in the Union; that it would administer the Territory in accordance with the spirit of the Mandate, and would submit annual reports to the United Nations on its administration of the Territory.

The Union Government's reply was considered at the second regular session of the General Assembly, when the Fourth Committee recommended for adoption by the General Assembly a draft resolution stating *inter alia* that it was the clear intention of Chapter XII of the Charter that all territories previously held under mandate, until granted self-government or independence, should be brought under the international trusteeship system, and urging the Union Government to propose a Trusteeship Agreement for South West Africa for consideration by the General Assembly at its third regular session. The General Assembly in plenary meeting adopted a variant of the draft resolution which omitted the reference to Chapter XII of the Charter, and maintained the recommendation that a Trusteeship Agreement should be proposed, without fixing a time-limit. Up to the present, the Secretary-General has received no further communications from the Union Government on the subject.

(iii) *Former Italian colonies*

The question of the final disposal of the former Italian colonies of Libya, Eritrea and

---

[1] See Chapter I.

Italian Somaliland is to be determined jointly by the Governments of France, the Union of Soviet Socialist Republics, the United Kingdom and the United States of America, within one year of the coming into force of the Treaty of Peace with Italy, that is to say by 15 September 1948. It is provided, however, in Annex XI of the Treaty that, should no agreement be reached by that date, the matter shall be referred to the General Assembly for a recommendation, which the four Powers agree to accept.

(iv) *Non-Self-Governing Territories*

At the second regular session of the General Assembly, a draft resolution was presented whereby the General Assembly would have expressed the hope that Members responsible for the administration of Non-Self-Governing Territories would propose Trusteeship Agreements under Article 77, paragraph 1c of the Charter for all or some of them. The draft resolution was approved by the Fourth Committee but failed to secure a majority in plenary meeting.

C. Operation of the trusteeship system

The General Assembly, at its second regular session, considered the first report of the Trusteeship Council and decided to transmit for the consideration of the Council comments on certain of the rules of procedure and on a number of questions in the Provisional Questionnaire.

The Trusteeship Council has carried out a wide variety of its normal functions under Articles 87 and 88 of the Charter in respect of the Trust Territories within the competence of the General Assembly, and a number of specific functions entrusted to it by the General Assembly concerning the City of Jerusalem.

The second session of the Council was held in three parts. The first part began on 20 November 1947 and ended on 16 December 1947; the second part began on 18 February 1948 and ended on 10 March 1948; and the third part began on 20 April 1948 and ended on 5 May 1948. The third session, which is still in progress at the time of writing, began on 16 June 1948. The greater part of the second part, and the whole of the third part of the second session, was occupied with the special problems of the City of Jerusalem.

The deliberations of the Trusteeship Council have led to constructive and co-operative efforts by all members towards attaining the basic objectives of the trusteeship system. In the case of the petition from leaders and representatives of Western Samoa, such co-operation with both the New Zealand Government, as the Administering Authority concerned, and with the local population, was evidenced on the spot; and, as a result, the people of Western Samoa have been securely placed on the road to self-government.

(*a*) CONSIDERATION OF ANNUAL REPORTS SUBMITTED BY ADMINISTERING AUTHORITIES

Rule 72, paragraph 1, of the rules of procedure for the Trusteeship Council provides that the Administering Authorities shall submit their annual reports on Trust Territories within four months from the termination of the year to which the reports relate. The Secretary-General has noted that, so far, several of the Administering Authorities have found themselves unable to transmit their reports within the period prescribed. While the difficulties involved are appreciated, the hope is expressed that, in the future, annual reports may be transmitted in time to permit of their earlier consideration by the Trusteeship Council, and so as to ensure members of the Council adequate time for studying them.

(i) *Western Samoa*

At its second session, the Trusteeship Council had before it a report by the Government of New Zealand on the administration of Western Samoa for the year ended 31 March 1947. The report had been prepared very shortly after the adoption, by the Council at its first session, of the Provisional Questionnaire and was not based upon it. As the report referred mainly to a period before the entry into force of the Trusteeship Agreement, and as more recent information was available from the report of the United Nations Mission to Western Samoa, the Council did not examine it separately but considered it at the same time as the latter report.

(ii) *New Guinea*

The report of the Government of Australia on the administration of New Guinea for the year ended 30 June 1947 had also been prepared very shortly after the adoption of the Provisional Questionnaire, and was not in the precise form required by it.

As a result of a preliminary examination of the report undertaken during the second session, the representative of Australia on the Council furnished supplementary information regarding the Territory. Owing, however, to the inability of the Australian Government at that time to send a special representative to be present during the examination of the report, its further consideration was postponed to the third session.

(iii) *Ruanda-Urundi*

At its third session, the Trusteeship Council has before it the report by the Government of Belgium on the administration of Ruanda-Urundi for the year 1947. While the Council has subjected the report to a detailed examination, it has not yet, at the time of writing, formulated its conclusions regarding the report.

(iv) *Tanganyika*

The Government of the United Kingdom has submitted its annual report on the administration of Tanganyika for the year 1947. At the time of writing, the Trusteeship Council has just commenced its examination of the report.

(v) *Other Trust Territories*

Reports have been received from the Administering Authorities concerned on the administration during 1947 of the Cameroons under British administration and Togoland under British administration. The reports were not, however, received in time for consideration by the Trusteeship Council during its present (third) session. They will therefore be considered at a subsequent session of the Council.

(b) ACCEPTANCE AND EXAMINATION OF PETITIONS

(i) *Petition from the leaders and representatives of Western Samoa*

The Trusteeship Council had before it at its first session a petition from the leaders and representatives of Western Samoa requesting that the Territory be granted self-government, and adopted a proposal by the Government of New Zealand to defer examination of the substance of the petition until a fact-finding mission could go to Western Samoa to investigate its subject-matter.

The Mission which subsequently went to Western Samoa reported to the following effect. While of the opinion that the people of Western Samoa were not then capable of assuming, without outside assistance, full responsibility for their government—a circumstance recognized in some degree by the people themselves—the Mission considered that the political and social stage of development which they had attained was sufficiently advanced to serve as the basis for granting them progressive self-government. It considered, therefore, that the time had come to establish a Government of Western Samoa in which the people would play an important or even dominant role. At the head of the Government there would be a High Commissioner representing the New Zealand Government, and one or more representatives of the people of Western Samoa—the number to be decided eventually by the people themselves, though for the present the three Fautua should fill the role. Sitting together under the presidency of the High Commissioner, the representatives would be known as the Council of State or High Council.

The New Zealand Government would exercise powers commensurate with its responsibilities as the Administering Authority for the Territory. In particular, it would retain control over the adoption and amendment of the constitution, external relations, defence, loans, foreign exchange and audit of public accounts; it would retain the right to initiate and enact legislation for the Territory, and it would appoint the Chief Judge of the High Court as well as the High Commissioner. The latter alone would have power to initiate financial legislation, and he would have power of disallowance over all measures passed by the territorial legislature.

The territorial legislature would consist of a single body with an absolute majority of Samoan representatives. Its President would be chosen from among its members. With the exception of the reserved matters, which would include financial measures, any member of the legislature would have power to initiate legislation on any subject. The legislature would have power to discuss and make recommendations on the annual budget, which would be presented to it by the High Commissioner. For the rest, it would have power to advise the High Commissioner on all matters relating to the government and welfare of the Territory, and would be consulted on the choice of the heads of executive departments.

Since the New Zealand Government, for some time past, had been actively considering the development of measures designed to give the Samoan people a greater voice in the management of their own affairs, the Mission decided to keep both the New Zealand representatives and the Samoan leaders informed of the general trend of its ideas. As a result, shortly before the Mission left Western Samoa at the end of August 1947, in a statement made in the House of Representatives of New Zealand, the Acting Prime Minister announced proposals for a substantial step forward on the road to self-government for the people of Western Samoa. The proposals were closely in line with the Mission's recommendations—a fact which the Mission noted in its report with great satisfaction. In the course of a communication to the Trusteeship Council, dated 21 November 1947, the New Zealand Government announced that the preliminary steps necessary to give effect to its proposals were already being taken, and made it clear that the proposals were to be the first in a series of progressive steps leading ultimately to full self-government for the people of Western Samoa.

The Mission's report, together with the communication from the New Zealand Government referred to, was examined during the first part of the second session of the Trusteeship Council, in consultation with a special representative of the New Zealand Government. The Council adopted the report, expressed satisfaction with the declared policy of the New Zealand Government, and resolved that at the present time the people of Western Samoa should be accorded such measures of self-government as were recommended by the Mission, that they should be encouraged and assisted to assume increasing responsibilities for self-government and that they should be accorded full self-government as soon as they were capable of assuming the responsibilities involved.

(ii) *Petitions concerning the Ewe people*

At the first part of its second session, the Trusteeship Council had before it seven petitions from representatives of the Ewe people, in Togoland under British administration, Togoland under French administration, the Belgian Congo and the Gold Coast, all of which involved a request that Eweland—which, the petitioners stated, was partitioned between Togoland under British administration, Togoland under French administration and the Gold Coast—should be unified under a single administration. One of the petitions, from the All-Ewe Conference at Accra in the Gold Coast, contained also a request for a representative of the petitioners to elaborate their case in person before the Council. The request was granted. The occasion of the hearing of the petitions was noteworthy in that it was the first on which an inhabitant of a Trust Territory was present to plead his cause in person before the Trusteeship Council.

The essential point of all the petitions was a contention that the division of Eweland was an injustice for the Ewe peoples from the social, cultural, economic, political and educational point of view and that the division between two administrations, whose policies, the petitioners maintained, were diametrically opposed, impeded the development of Eweland as a whole and made its progress unbalanced and uncertain.

The petitioners' representations were examined at some length in a memorandum jointly prepared by the Governments of France and of the United Kingdom. While the two Governments did not recognize the force of everything complained of by the petitioners, they agreed that the division of the territory in question was the source of certain difficulties and, in particular, that more uniform progress could be achieved in each sphere if the two Administering Powers were to work out suitable means of co-ordinating their activities in the social, economic, political and cultural spheres. They rejected the two alternative solutions propounded by the petitioners—either the grouping together of all Ewe-people into one territorial unit, or a reunion of the two Togolands—and detailed instead a number of economic, fiscal and cultural measures which they had decided to adopt. All these measures were designed to alleviate any hardships resulting from the division of the people among two administrations.

During the examination of the petitions by the Trusteeship Council, the cause of the Ewe people was pleaded by Mr. Sylvanus E. Olympio, of Togoland under French administration, the representative designated by the All-Ewe Conference. The Council heard also special representatives of the two Administering Authorities concerned, who elaborated the proposed measures which their Governments had outlined in their joint memorandum. Mr. Olympio, however, declared that the measures were inadequate, that they would not, as an administrative union would, provide the Ewe people with a common political organization, economic union and a common educational system.

Having noted all that was said on both sides and the fact that the petitions of the All-Ewe Conference represented the wishes of the majority of the Ewe people, the Trusteeship Council welcomed the measures proposed by the Administering Authorities as an earnest and constructive initial effort to meet the immediate difficulties complained of by the petitioners. The Council went on to recommend that the Administering Authorities should foster the association and co-operation of the Ewe people and assist and encourage them to develop their capacity for self-government, through free discussion among themselves and through progressively increasing opportunities for primary and secondary education. It also invited the Administering Authorities to consult with each other, and with Ewe representatives, with a view to evolving further measures for fulfilling the wishes of the Ewe people. The Council decided also that the first visiting mission to the Trust Territories of Togoland under British administration and Togoland under French administration should devote special attention to the problem set forth in the petitions and to the implementation of measures designed to cope with the problem, and that the problem should be re-examined at the session at which the report of the visiting mission would be considered.

(iii) *Other petitions*

At the first part of its second session, the Trusteeship Council considered thirty-five petitions, other than the seven from the Ewe people.

Petitions concerning the repatriation of ex-enemy nationals from Tanganyika and the Cameroons under British administration

Sixteen petitions were received from German or Italian residents, or former residents, of Tanganyika or the Cameroons under British administration. Some of the petitioners had been, and some were about to be, repatriated to Germany or Italy, and the petitioners' pleas were that they should be permitted either to return to or remain in the Trust Territory concerned.

After having examined the petitions in consultation with a special representative designated by the Administering Authority concerned, the Council decided that the actions complained of by the petitioners were being taken in accordance with the repatriation policy of the Administering Authority, which the Council had approved at its first session. The Council reaffirmed its approval of the policy which, briefly, was to repatriate to their countries of origin persons who had been Axis sympathizers or whose conduct had rendered them liable to deportation under the law of the Trust Territory concerned.

Petitions relating to the draft Convention prepared by the International Labour Office on social policy in non-metropolitan territories

Two petitions relating to the draft Convention concerning social policy in non-metropolitan territories, drawn up by the International Labour Office, had been before the Trusteeship Council at its first session. The petitioners had complained that that part of the draft which related to the prohibition by law of discrimination in employment did not prohibit discrimination on grounds of sex. The petitions had been communicated by the Trusteeship Council to the International Labour Office, which had taken account to some extent of the wishes of the petitioners when the final draft of the Convention had been drawn up. Six petitions before the Council at its second session concerned the same subject. In regard to them the Council could do no more than note the action already taken by the International Labour Office.

Petition concerning the association of women in the work of the Trusteeship Council

A petition from the International Alliance of Women concerned the association of women in the work of the Trusteeship Council, and contained a recommendation that any mission sent by the Council to study conditions in Trust Territories should include a woman member. In reply, the Council authorized the President to inform the petitioners that the Council did not discriminate on the basis of sex in composing its visiting missions, but sought always to secure the services of the most competent and best qualified people.

Miscellaneous Petitions

Eleven petitions before the Trusteeship Council at its second session related to matters in regard to which the Council decided that it could take no action. They contained requests for, or concerned the following:

(*a*) Establishment of a Jewish State in Tanganyika;

(*b*) Internationalization of the Polar regions;

(*c*) Internationalization of strategic areas, both land and water;

(*d*) Internationalization of the production and distribution of strategic raw materials in Non-Self-Governing Territories or Trust Territories;

(*e*) Disposal of some of the former Italian colonies;

(*f*) Establishment of a "universal colonial and mandate trusteeship" under the United Nations;

(*g*) Modification of Articles 73 and 87 of the Charter.

A twelfth petition could not be considered since the matter complained of was not set forth in sufficiently precise terms.

(iv) *Petitions considered by the Trusteeship Council at its third session*

During its third session, the Trusteeship Council, at the time of writing, has considered six petitions and has given preliminary consideration to a seventh.

Petition relating to compulsory marriage and child marriage in the Cameroons under British administration

A petition was received from the St. Joan's Social and Political Alliance concerning the customs of compulsory marriage and child marriage prevalent among the chiefs of the Tikar communities in the Bamenda Division of the Cameroons under British administration. Having examined the petition in consultation with a special representative of the Administering Authority, the Council expressed condemnation of the customs in question, and, noting that it was the policy of the Administering Authority to achieve a modification of the customs expressed its confidence that the Administering Authority would take all appropriate measures to end them. At the same time, the Council requested the Administering Authority to indicate in future annual reports the progress made in achieving the desired end, and noted the matter as one for the attention of the first visiting mission to visit the Territory.

Petition concerning the Trust Territory of Tanganyika

After examination of a petition from Mr. Paul Wamba Kudililwa concerning his deposition from a chieftainship in Tanganyika, the Council decided that no action was called for in regard to it.

Petition concerning the repatriation of ex-enemy nationals from Tanganyika

In regard to four petitions concerning the repatriation of German residents from Tanganyika, the Council reached the same conclusions, already detailed above, as it had reached in regard to the petitions of a similar nature which it had considered at its second session.

Petition concerning the Trust Territory of the Cameroons under British administration

The Council had before it at its third session a petition from the Bakweri Land Committee alleging that it had been deprived of certain lands in the Victoria Division of the Cameroons under Britsh administration. The Council had granted a request for an oral presentation in support of the petition by a representative of the petitioners; the petitioners, however, subsequently notified the Council of their inability to send a representative to Lake Success during its third session, and requested therefore that the hearing of the petition be postponed until a subsequent session. The Council acceded to the petitioners' request, and at the same time pointed out to them that the Administering Authority had notified the Council that an inquiry was being made locally into the matters complained of. While, therefore, the petitioners were informed that their representative would be welcomed if he appeared before the Trusteeship Council at its next regular session, it was stated that he might prefer to defer his appearance until after the Council had been informed by the Administering Authority of the findings of the inquiry.

(c) Periodic visits to Trust Territories

(i) Special Visiting Mission to Western Samoa

The recommendations of the fact-finding Mission sent to Western Samoa to investigate the subject-matter of the petition from the leaders and representatives of the Territory have been described in a preceding section.

The three members of the Mission were Mr. Francis B. Sayre (United States of America), President of the Trusteeship Council, and Chairman of the Mission; Mr. Pierre Ryckmans,

representative of Belgium on the Trusteeship Council; and Senator Eduardo Cruz-Coke, of Chile.

Senator Cruz-Coke arrived at Apia, Western Samoa, on 9 July 1947. The other members of the Mission arrived at Wellington, New Zealand, on 26 June and made contacts with members and officials of the New Zealand Government. They were received by the Prime Minister of New Zealand on 28 June and heard the views of his Government on the question of self-government for the Samoans. They also heard views on the question from several other authorities.

Accompanied by Mr. G. R. Laking, personal representative of the Prime Minister, and Mr. R. T. G. Patrick, Secretary of the Department of Island Territories, the Mission left for Western Samoa on 3 July and arrived in Apia on 4 July. During its stay in the Territory, the Mission held a series of meetings with officials of the New Zealand Administration, representative Samoan leaders, members of the European Citizens' Committee, spokesmen for the religious missions, and other representative groups and individuals; it also visited a number of institutions such as schools and hospitals. The outlying districts of the country were visited. During tours made through the islands of Upolu and Savai'i, meetings and interviews were held with district leaders and the population of the main villages, a number of private individuals were granted hearings, and schools, hospitals and religious missions were visited.

In view of the reference in the petition to the British protectorate of Tonga, the Mission paid a brief visit to its capital to study its system of government.

The last three weeks of its visit were devoted by the Mission to final investigations in Western Samoa. Additional meetings with New Zealand officials and with Samoan and European leaders were held, and the mission's report to the Trusteeship Council was prepared.

The Mission left Western Samoa on 28 August and returned to headquarters in New York, where work on the report was completed.

(ii) Visiting Mission to East Africa

During the first part of its second session, the Trusteeship Council decided to send a visiting mission to the Trust Territories of Ruanda-Urundi and Tanganyika. The visit was timed to take place shortly after the termination of the June 1948 session—a time considered the most suitable from the point of view of both the Administering Authorities concerned and the Trusteeship Council.

During its third session the Council made the following appointments to the Visiting Mission: Mr. Henri Laurentie (France) (Chairman),

Mr. E. W. P. Chinnery (Australia), Dr. Lin Mousheng (China), Mr. R. E. Woodbridge (Costa Rica). The Council fixed 15 July 1948 as the date of the Mission's departure for Ruanda-Urundi, where it would remain some three weeks before proceeding to spend some five to six weeks in Tanganyika. At the time of writing, the terms of reference for the Mission have not yet been drafted, since they will depend to a large extent upon the conclusions still to be reached by the Council on the annual reports on the two Territories concerned.

(d) OTHER ACTIVITIES OF THE TRUSTEESHIP COUNCIL

(i) *Rules of procedure*

During the second session of the Trusteeship Council, certain modifications were made in the rules of procedure, in particular one concerning the oral presentation of petitions. A detailed procedure was drawn up for facilitating the thorough examination of annual reports from Trust Territories.

(ii) *Provisional Questionnaire*

The Provisional Questionnaire adopted by the Trusteeship Council at its first session, for application to each Trust Territory within the competence of the General Assembly, is due to be revised in the light of such suggestions as shall have been received from the Administering Authorities, the Economic and Social Council and the specialized agencies. The matter was reviewed briefly by the Trusteeship Council during its second, and again during its third session. On each occasion it was decided to defer the question of revision so as to allow more time for the receipt of such suggestions.

During its second session, the Trusteeship Council resolved that the Provisional Questionnaire should be transmitted to the Government of Australia, as the Government responsible for the administration of the Trust Territory of Nauru.

(iii) *South West Africa*

In one of the paragraphs of its resolution on the future status of South West Africa, the General Assembly authorized the Trusteeship Council to examine the report on South West Africa for 1946, recently submitted by the Union Government, and to submit its observations thereon to the General Assembly. This question was taken up by the Trusteeship Council during the first part of its second session. Before the report was examined by the Council, the Secretary-General was requested to inform the Union Government that, if it wished to send a representative to be present during the examination of the report, he would be welcome. The Union Government replied that it did not intend to send a representative, but that it would be ready to furnish further information regarding the subject-matter of the report if so requested by the Trusteeship Council. The Council then proceeded to examine the report and, finding that it appeared to be incomplete in certain particulars, appointed a committee of four to formulate for its consideration a list of questions on which further information from the Union Government would be desirable. The list of fifty questions drawn up by the committee, under the seven headings of Government, Financial and Economic, Land and Resources, Labour, Education, Health, and Hereros, was approved by the Council and transmitted to the Union Government.

The Union Government has transmitted replies to the questions which will be considered by the Trusteeship Council during its third session.

(iv) *The City of Jerusalem*

The activities of the Trusteeship Council arising out of the adoption by the General Assembly on 29 November 1947 of resolution 181 (II) concerning the future government of Palestine, and on 26 April 1948 of resolution 185 (S-2) concerning the protection of the City of Jerusalem and its inhabitants, have been described elsewhere in this report.[1]

D. Information from Non-Self-Governing Territories

(a) TRANSMISSION OF INFORMATION UNDER ARTICLE 73 e OF THE CHARTER

The responsibilities of the United Nations in respect of Non-Self-Governing Territories are indicated particularly in Article 73 e of the Charter, under which the Members concerned have undertaken to transmit regularly to the Secretary-General technical information on economic, social and educational conditions in the Territories. By the end of the second regular session of the General Assembly, eight Members of the United Nations had transmitted information in respect of sixty-three Territories. These Members were Australia, Belgium, Denmark, France, the Netherlands, New Zealand, the United Kingdom and the United States of America.

An *ad hoc* Committee on the transmission of information under Article 73 e was appointed by the General Assembly during the second part of its first session (resolution 66 (I) of 14 December 1946). It was composed in equal numbers of representatives of the Members transmitting information and of representatives of Members elected by the General Assembly, the

---

[1] See page 4.

elected Members being Brazil, China, Cuba, Egypt, India, the Philippines, the Union of Soviet Socialist Republics and Uruguay. The Committee met at Lake Success from 28 August to 12 September 1947 and examined the Secretary-General's summaries and analyses of the information transmitted. The General Assembly, at its second regular session, based its own work on the recommendations of the Committee. It established procedures which are operating for the first time this year and which appreciably broaden the scope of the information to be transmitted.

In the *ad hoc* Committee it was generally felt that, while the action taken by the Members responsible for the administration of Non-Self-Governing Territories in transmitting information was appreciated, the information transmitted up to that time did not give a sufficiently clear picture of the conditions of life of the peoples in these Territories. Fuller and more detailed information could be found in official publications of the Administering Members. The General Assembly, acting upon the consensus of opinions expressed in the Committee, adopted resolution 142 (II), which provides a Standard Form for the guidance of Members in the preparation of information to be transmitted under Article 73 e of the Charter. The Standard Form will also serve to guide the Secretariat in preparing the summaries and analyses of information received which the Secretary-General is required to lay before the General Assembly. The first part of the Standard Form relates to general information, certain parts of which are of an administrative and political nature. The transmission of this type of information is optional. The other parts relate to economic, social and educational conditions.

The fact that more detailed information than has hitherto been transmitted under Article 73 e can be found in the official publications of the Administering Members, led to the question of the extent to which the Secretary-General is entitled to use such publications in presenting the summaries and analyses of the information formally transmitted under this Article. This issue, first raised in the *ad hoc* Committee, and later debated in the Fourth Committee of the General Assembly, led to the adoption, on 3 November 1947, of resolution 143 (II). This permits the Secretary-General to use supplemental documents relating to information transmitted under Article 73 e, provided that such documents are official publications of the Members responsible for administration. The resolution further provides that the use of data derived from such official publications shall be limited to subjects covered in Article 73 e; that only such publica-

tions shall be used as are transmitted or notified to the Secretary-General by the Members concerned; that the Secretary-General may also use publications of inter-governmental agencies or scientific bodies on matters relating to Non-Self-Governing Territories as covered by Article 73 e; that supplemental information of this kind shall be communicated to the appropriate specialized agencies; and that, for purposes of comparison, the Secretary-General is authorized to include in his summaries and analyses all relevant and comparable statistical information available in the statistical services of the Secretariat and agreed upon by him and the Members concerned. This last provision relates to statistics from independent countries, and in the discussion interest was shown in obtaining such data from the metropolitan Power concerned and from countries with conditions comparable to those of certain of the Non-Self-Governing Territories.

The Secretary-General, by a letter addressed on 23 January 1948 to the eight Members transmitting information on Non-Self-Governing Territories, drew their particular attention to this resolution. A number of replies have been received.

The United Kingdom Government, in a communication to the Secretary-General of 28 February 1948, expressed its desire to assist in the implementation of resolution 143 (II), and to that end informed the Secretary-General that he was authorized to use, without prior reference in each case, a wide range of publications issued by the United Kingdom and Colonial Governments. Such use it was specified, was for purposes of factual information upon any of the matters mentioned in the Standard Form to the exclusion of those covered in the optional first part.

In a similar communication of 6 April 1948, the Belgian Government informed the Secretary-General that it would transmit, as supplemental documents, a number of official publications on the Belgian Congo. These publications might be used by the Secretary-General in the preparation of his summaries and analyses in respect of subject-matters mentioned in Article 73 e (i.e., economic, social and educational).

The French Government, in a letter dated 19 May 1948, listed official publications which would be sent to the Secretary-General for use in the preparation of summaries and analyses of information transmitted on such subjects as were covered by Article 73 e. The French Government emphasized that extracts from official publications should be used only to the extent that they related to economic, social and educational conditions in Non-Self-Governing Territories, on which the transmission of information was obligatory, and that no use should be made of these publications with regard to Territories on which no information under Article 73 e had been transmitted. In addition, the French Government offered to send to the United Nations Library other publications concerning Non-Self-Governing Territories which, while they did not fall strictly within the framework of resolution 143 (II), seemed to be of particular interest to the Organization as a whole.

By notes of 27 and 28 May 1948, the Government of the United States of America transmitted a number of Government reports on Alaska, Hawaii, Puerto Rico and the Virgin Islands as supplemental documents under the terms of the General Assembly resolution. Certain additional documents will be made available at a later date.

Lastly, the Government of Australia has transmitted certain laws and gazettes in respect of Papua.

The question whether information of a political character should be transmitted to the Secretary-General and in what way such information should be considered arose during the discussions in the *ad hoc* Committee, and was again raised in the Fourth Committee of the General Assembly. Some representatives took the view that Article 73, read in its entirety, required the Administering Members to transmit political information, and that it was unreasonable to limit consideration to the enumeration given in paragraph e of that Article. Other representatives argued that consideration should be limited to paragraph e, since that paragraph set forth the sole terms of the obligation to transmit information. The *ad hoc* Committee finally agreed on the principle of voluntary transmission of information regarding the development of self-governing institutions in Non-Self-Governing Territories, pointing out that some of the Members concerned had already supplied such information. The Fourth Committee substituted a text which differed from the one adopted by the *ad hoc* Committee, asking more explicitly for the transmission of political information.

The General Assembly, however, returned to the text originally proposed by the *ad hoc* Committee which it adopted as resolution 144 (II) on 3 November 1947. In this resolution, the General Assembly noted that some Members had already voluntarily transmitted information on the development of self-governing institutions in Territories under their administration. It considered that the voluntary transmission of such information and its summarizing by the Secretary-General were entirely in conformity with the spirit of Article 73 of the Charter, and

should be duly noted and encouraged. Accordingly, the Secretary-General's summaries will contain data on any political information so transmitted.

(b) Treatment of information

On 3 November 1947, the General Assembly adopted resolution 146 (II), creating a Special Committee on information transmitted under Article 73 e of the Charter. In taking this decision, the General Assembly followed a proposal of the *ad hoc* Committee.

The Special Committee, which is to meet in Geneva on 2 September before the third session of the General Assembly, is to examine the summaries and analyses of information transmitted under Article 73 e of the Charter on conditions in Non-Self-Governing Territories and to submit reports thereon to the General Assembly. These reports may contain procedural recommendations and also substantive recommendations relating to functional fields generally, but not with respect to individual Territories. The Special Committee has been authorized by the General Assembly to avail itself of the counsel and assistance of the specialized agencies, to establish liaison with the Economic and Social Council, and to invite Members to furnish such supplemental information as may be desired within the terms of Article 73 e.

The Fourth Committee, in accordance with the terms of the resolution, elected eight of the sixteen Members on the Special Committee. The composition of this Committee therefore is as follows:

Members transmitting information under Article 73 e of the Charter:

Australia, Belgium, Denmark, France, the Netherlands, New Zealand, the United Kingdom and the United States of America;

Members elected by the Fourth Committee on behalf of the General Assembly:

China, Colombia, Cuba, Egypt, India, Nicaragua, Sweden and the Union of Soviet Socialist Republics.

The Secretary-General will submit to the General Assembly and to the Special Committee summaries and analyses of the information transmitted this year under Article 73 e of the Charter. This will be a continuation of the task begun last year in pursuance of General Assembly resolution 66 (I). As shown above, the Secretary-General is authorized to use, in the preparation of his summaries and analyses, such supplemental documents as are covered by resolution 143 (II).

From the documents which are now beginning to arrive, it is clear that the United Nations will be receiving very extensive official data on economic, social and educational conditions in Non-Self-Governing Territories. The proper use of this data for information purposes will require careful consideration and organization. This year practically no material transmitted under Article 73 e was received prior to 30 June; supplemental information is just beginning to come in. As the Special Committee will convene in Geneva on 2 September, some difficulty will be experienced in preparing adequate summaries and analyses. It may, however, be anticipated that by next year the flow of information will extend over a long period, the Standard Form will have provided a means of achieving greater uniformity of treatment, the Secretary-General will have had the advantage of the commentaries of the Special Committee and, in general, that a broad and balanced account can be given of the technical problems of Non-Self-Governing Territories.

In this the United Nations will be contributing a constructive service to the peoples and the administrative authorities of all those Non-Self-Governing Territories in regard to which the Members responsible for their administration have declared their policy by virtue of Chapter XI.

(c) COLLABORATION WITH THE SPECIALIZED AGENCIES

Any service such as that outlined above would be of limited value if the final result were only the compilation of digests of technical data. Its translation into action is the responsibility of the administrative authorities. In this, assistance may often be provided through other international institutions, in particular through the specialized agencies.

Both the *ad hoc* Committee and the General Assembly paid particular attention to this question of co-operation with the specialized agencies in regard to Non-Self-Governing Territories. General Assembly resolution 145 (II) invited the Secretary-General to enter into relations with the secretariats of the agencies in order to allow them to assist him in preparing analyses of the information required under Article 73 e, and to make recommendations to the General Assembly in respect of the form and content of the information with a view to meeting their own informational needs. The resolution further asked the specialized agencies to communicate to the General Assembly their own conclusions, reached on the basis of information transmitted under Article 73 e as well as of supplemental information, as to conditions in Non-Self-Governing Territories within their own special fields of interest. The specialized agencies were also requested to inform the General Assembly of any special services they might make available to the Administering Members with a view to improving conditions in Non-Self-Governing Territories. Moreover, the Special Committee this year is authorized to avail itself of the counsel and advice of the specialized agencies in such a manner as it may consider necessary or expedient.

Invitations to attend the September meetings of the Special Committee on information transmitted under Article 73 e of the Charter were issued to the specialized agencies. The Secretary-General also communicated to them General Assembly resolution 145 (II) and invited their suggestions. Subsequently, a number of valuable informal conversations have taken place between the secretariats concerned on the best means of avoiding duplication and of ensuring that the information provided by the Governments is used within the proper programmes of international institutions.

The machinery for collaboration is thus being established between the United Nations and the specialized agencies as regards questions relating to Non-Self-Governing Territories. Provision has been made for the exchange of information received, whether under Article 73 e or in the form of supplemental documentation. Secondly, on the basis of resolution 146 (II), the specialized agencies have a convenient means of bringing to the attention of the General Assembly any appropriate commentaries they may have on conditions existing in Non-Self-Governing Territories. Thirdly, by the terms of the same resolution the United Nations has ready access to the assistance of the specialized agencies in matters affecting Non-Self-Governing Territories.

(d) RELATIONS WITH ADVISORY REGIONAL ORGANIZATIONS

The origins of the existing organizations which have been established to advise Governments on the economic and social problems of certain Non-Self-Governing Territories were mentioned in the Secretary-General's report of last year.

The Caribbean Commission is composed of representatives of the Governments of France, the Netherlands, the United Kingdom and the United States of America. Article XVIII of the agreement establishing the Commission states that the Commission, while having no present connexion with the United Nations, shall co-operate as fully as possible with the Organization and with the appropriate specialized agencies on matters of mutual concern. Close liaison has already been established at the secretariat level between the Commission and the United Nations. An illustration of this was offered by the attendance, at the first meeting of the Caribbean Research Council in November-December 1947, of two observers from the Secretariat of the United Nations.

The South Pacific Commission has been established on the same pattern as the Caribbean Commission. The six Member Governments are Australia, France, Netherlands, New Zealand, the United Kingdom and the United States of America. The first meeting of the Commission was held in May 1948. It has been noted that this Commission, like the Caribbean Commission has a purpose in accord with the obligations assumed by the Members of the United Nations under Chapter XI of the Charter. Once again, provision is made for working co-operation with the United Nations and the appropriate specialized agencies.

E. Declaration regarding Non-Self-Governing Territories

The transmission to the Secretary-General of information on economic, social and educational conditions in Non-Self-Governing Territories is an obligation specifically stipulated in the Charter under Article 73 e. The other provisions of Article 73 are of a declaratory character. Their incorporation in the Charter indicates the international importance of principles for the promotion of the well-being of the inhabitants of all Non-Self-Governing Territories.

A resolution adopted at the Ninth International Conference of American States, which convened at Bogota on 30 March 1948, declared that it was the just aspiration of American representatives that an end be put to colonialism and to the occupation of American territories by extra-continental countries. The resolution was considered controversial. Its adoption, however, is a further indication of the value, in the interests of international concord, of positive steps to give the most rapid practical effect to the principles contained in Chapter XI of the Charter. In this sphere, the year under review marked developments which provide evidence of the new spirit and of the passing of old conceptions of colonial rule.

(a) General developments

Chapter XI covers the Territories whose peoples have not yet attained a full measure of self-government. Constitutional changes which are in the direction of establishing self-governing institutions in existing Non-Self-Governing Territories are, therefore, of direct concern to the work of the United Nations since, as a result of them, the peoples may cease to come within the scope of Chapter XI. Furthermore, as recounted

above, the General Assembly, by resolution 144 (II) invited the voluntary transmission of information on the development of self-governing institutions in the Territories.

In this connexion, the following developments may be noted:

A conference was held in the Netherlands from 27 January to 18 March 1948 to consider the relationship of Surinam and Curaçao to the Netherlands, as part of the constitutional reorganization of the Kingdom of the Netherlands as a whole. The major proposals which were accepted included (1) the adoption of a new national constitution defining the spheres of authority of the Kingdom and its component countries; (2) the representation of Curaçao and Surinam in the Netherlands Parliament; (3) permission for the component countries to seek membership in international organizations; and (4) the inclusion of delegates of Curaçao and Surinam whenever the Netherlands Government negotiates matters of interest to their countries.

The relations between the countries of the French Union reached a further stage with the first meeting, at Versailles on 10 December 1947, of the Assembly of the French Union.

On 21 May 1948, the President of the United States of America sent a special message to Congress recommending statehood for the territory of Alaska.

In September 1947, the United Kingdom Government convened a conference at Montego Bay, Jamaica. The conference voted in favour of closer association between the British West Indian territories, and set up a Standing Committee to report on technical problems. On 1 February 1948, a new constitution came into effect for the Federation of Malaya. In East Africa, an East African High Commission came into existence on 1 January 1948, providing for the common administration of specified services which are by their nature held to be interterritorial.

(b) Economic and social developments

Article 73 d of the Charter contains the undertaking by the Members concerned to co-operate with one another and, when and where appropriate, with specialized international bodies with a view to the practical achievement of the social, economic and scientific purposes of the Article.

Following an agreement reached in Paris in May 1947 to hold a series of technical conferences on common problems in British, French and Belgian territories, an Anglo-Belgian-French Labour Conference was held at Jos (Nigeria) in February 1948. In the same month an Anglo-

French Conference was held in Paris on economic and technical co-operation between the West African territories. There have also been discussions on technical questions between officers of the British Colonial Service and the French Ministry of Overseas Territories, and between British and Portuguese colonial officers.

A number of liaison meetings have been held in Singapore attended by representatives of Burma, Ceylon, the Federation of Malaya, Hong Kong, India, Indo-China, Indonesia, North Borneo, Sarawak, Siam and Singapore. Observers representing the Governments of China, the Philippines and the United States of America attended. One of the main tasks of these meetings was to discuss problems relating to the rice supply.

Associate membership in the United Nations Economic Commission for Asia and the Far East has been granted to Hong Kong, British administered territories in South-East Asia, Cambodia and Laos. Provisions permitting Non-Self-Governing Territories to become associate members have been included in the terms of reference of the Economic Commission for Latin America and the proposed Economic Commission for the Middle East.

A conference held at Singapore in August 1947 on social welfare in South-East Asia was attended by representatives or observers from twenty countries and from the United Nations. The International Labour Organisation held a Preparatory Asian Regional Conference in New Delhi in October-November 1947. Among the countries with government, employer and worker representation were Cambodia, Cochin-China, French Establishments in India, New Caledonia, Laos, Malaya and Singapore.

These meetings, and the attention which has been increasingly paid to Non-Self-Governing Territories in many of the discussions under the authority of the Economic and Social Council, further emphasize a point of principle made in the Secretary-General's report of last year. The importance of Chapter XI to the Non-Self-Governing Territories is clear. The fact, however, that the principles concerning these Territories are treated in this Chapter of the Charter in no way indicates the exclusion of non-self-governing peoples from international programmes of co-operation as provided for elsewhere in the Charter. On the contrary, subject to the appropriate constitutional procedures, Non-Self-Governing Territories are, in common with other countries, covered by Article 55 of the Charter by virtue of which the United Nations is required to promote economic and social progress and the observance of fundamental freedoms.

Chapter IV

LEGAL
QUESTIONS

A. International Court of Justice

(a) Jurisdiction of the Court

(i) *Acceptance of compulsory jurisdiction*

Since July 1947, the following States have made declarations of acceptance of the Court's jurisdiction under the terms of Article 36 of the Statute of the Court:

Belgium, Brazil, Honduras, Mexico, Pakistan, Philippines.

(ii) *Instruments conferring jurisdiction on the Court*

Several international agreements concluded during the past year contain provisions conferring jurisdiction upon the Court. Amongst these may be mentioned: the Convention on the privileges and immunities of the specialized agencies, adopted by the General Assembly on 21 November 1947, and the Treaty of Brussels between Belgium, France, Luxembourg, the Netherlands and the United Kingdom of Great Britain and Northern Ireland, signed on 17 March 1948.

(iii) *Requests for advisory opinions*

The following treaties and agreements provide for requests for advisory opinions from the Court to be made, in certain circumstances, by specialized agencies: Havana Charter, signed on 24 March 1948, establishing the International Trade Organization; Convention for the Establishment of an Inter-Governmental Maritime Consultative Organization, Geneva, 6 March 1948; Agreements between the United Nations and the International Bank for Reconstruction and Development, the International Monetary Fund, the World Health Organization and the International Telecommunications Union.

(iv) *Application of Switzerland to become a party to the Statute of the International Court of Justice*

The General Assembly resolution 91 (I) of 11 December 1946, adopting the recommendations of the Security Council on the subject of the conditions under which Switzerland might become a party to the Statute of the International Court, in virtue of Article 93, paragraph 2, of the Charter, was duly communicated to the Swiss Government. As a result, the Swiss Federal Council proposed to the Federal Assembly, in a message dated 8 July 1947, that the Federal Assembly should authorize it to accept the conditions formulated by the United Nations, and to announce the accession of Switzerland to the Statute of the Court. At the same time, Switzerland would recognize the jurisdiction of the Court as compulsory in accordance with Article 36 of the Statute.

On 17 December 1947, the Swiss National Council, by a hundred and two votes to fifteen, adopted a proposal of the Federal Council in favour of the accession of Switzerland to the Court's Statute. As this decision was taken immediately before the adjournment of the session of Parliament, the proposal did not come before the Swiss Council of States until March 1948.

On 13 March 1948, the Swiss Minister at The Hague informed the President of the Court that, by twenty-seven votes to three, the Council of States had passed the proposed decree on the subject of Switzerland's accession to the Court's Statute. Under the terms of the Constitution, the Federal Decree was subject to a demand for a referendum; the latest date for the presentation of such a demand expired in June 1948.

(b) Cases before the Court

(i) *Corfu Channel Case (case for judgment)*

On 9 April 1947, the Security Council adopted a resolution concerning a complaint brought before it by the Government of the United Kingdom against the Government of the

People's Republic of Albania in connexion with an incident in which two British warships were damaged by mines in the Corfu Channel on 22 October 1946. The resolution recommended the two Governments to refer the dispute to the International Court of Justice in accordance with the provisions of the Statute of the Court. Accordingly, the Government of the United Kingdom, in a letter dated 22 May 1947, presented to the Court its application against the Government of the People's Republic of Albania.

On the receipt of a letter from the Government of Albania dated 2 July 1947, the President of the Court consulted both parties and, in an Order dated 31 July 1947, fixed the time-limits for the filing of the memorial and counter-memorial. Within the time fixed for the deposit of its counter-memorial (10 December 1947), the Government of Albania raised a preliminary objection to the admissibility of the application. It asked the Court to place on record that, in accepting the Security Council's recommendation, the Government of Albania was only obliged to submit the above-mentioned dispute to the Court in accordance with the provisions of the Statute of the Court; and to give judgment that the application addressed to the Court by the Government of the United Kingdom against the Government of the People's Republic of Albania was inadmissible, the United Kingdom Government having submitted the said application contrary to the provisions of Article 40, paragraph 1, and of Article 36, paragraph 1, of the Statute of the Court.

By an Order of 10 December 1947, the President of the Court fixed a time-limit for the presentation by the Government of the United Kingdom of a written statement of its observations and submissions in regard to the preliminary objection. In its statement, this Government made submissions contesting those of the Albanian Government.

The Government of the United Kingdom submitted to the Court: (*a*) that the preliminary objection of the Government of Albania should be dismissed; and (*b*) that the Government of Albania should be directed to comply with the terms of the President's Order of 31 July 1947, and to deliver without further delay a counter-memorial on the merits of the dispute.

The Court held public sittings from 26 February to 5 March 1948, to hear the agents and counsel of the parties. On 25 March 1948, it delivered judgment on the Albanian Government's objection.

The Court placed on record the declaration contained in the first submission of the Government of Albania, but subject to the explicit reservation of the obligations assumed by that Government in its letter of 2 July 1947. By fifteen votes to one, it rejected the preliminary objection submitted on 9 December 1947 by the Government of Albania, and decided that proceedings on the merits should continue. It fixed the time-limits for the filing of subsequent pleadings as follows:

(*a*) For the counter-memorial of the Government of Albania, Tuesday, 15 June 1948;

(*b*) For the reply of the Government of the United Kingdom, Monday, 2 August 1948; and

(*c*) For the rejoinder of the Government of Albania, Monday, 20 September 1948.

Judges Basdevant, Alvarez, Winiarski, Zoricic, de Visscher, Badawi Pasha and Krylov, whilst concurring in the judgment of the Court, availed themselves of the right conferred on them by Article 57 of the Statute and appended to the judgment a statement of their separate opinion.

Mr. Daxner, judge *ad hoc,* declaring that he was unable to concur in the Court's judgment, availed himself of the right conferred on him by Article 57 of the Statute and appended to the judgment a statement of his individual opinion.

Immediately after the delivery of the judgment, the agents for the Governments of Albania and the United Kingdom announced to the Court the conclusion between their respective Governments of a special agreement, drawn up as a result of the resolution of Security Council of 9 April 1947, for the purpose of submitting to the Court for decision the following questions:

"1. Is Albania responsible under international law for the explosions which occurred on 22 October 1946 in Albanian waters and for the damage and loss of human life which resulted from them, and is there any duty to pay compensation?

"2. Has the United Kingdom, under international law, violated the sovereignty of the People's Republic of Albania by reason of the acts of the Royal Navy in Albanian waters on 22 October and on 12 and 13 November 1946, and is there any duty to give satisfaction?"

The Court, in an Order of 26 March 1948, stated that this special agreement now forms the basis of further proceedings before the Court in this case.

The United Kingdom Government's memorial having been filed on 1 October 1947, the parties, who had been consulted by the President, agreed in requesting that the time-limits for the filing of subsequent pleadings be maintained as fixed in the Court's judgment.

The Court's Order of 26 March 1948 confirmed these time-limits.

(ii) *Conditions of admission of a State to membership in the United Nations: Article 4 of the Charter (case for advisory opinion)*

In resolution 113 (II) of 17 November 1947, the General Assembly, considering Articles 4 and 96 of the Charter and the views exchanged in the Security Council on the subject of the admission of certain States to membership in the United Nations, requested the Court to give an advisory opinion on the following question:

"Is a Member of the United Nations which is called upon, in virtue of Article 4 of the Charter, to pronounce itself by its vote, either in the Security Council or in the General Assembly, on the admission of a State to membership in the United Nations, juridically entitled to make its consent to the admission dependent on conditions not expressly provided by paragraph 1 of the said Article? In particular, can such a Member, while it recognizes the conditions set forth in that provision to be fulfilled by the State concerned, subject its affirmative vote to the additional condition that other States be admitted to membership in the United Nations together with that State?"

Notice of the request was given, in accordance with the Statute, to all States entitled to appear before the Court. Further, as the question put mentioned Article 4 of the Charter, the Registrar informed the Governments of Members of the United Nations, by means of a special and direct communication as provided in Article 66 of the Statute, that the Court was prepared to receive from them written statements before a date fixed by an Order of the President of the Court.

Written statements were received from the following States: China, El Salvador, Guatemala, Honduras, India, Canada, United States of America, Greece, Yugoslavia, Belgium, Iraq, Ukrainian Soviet Socialist Republic, Union of Soviet Socialist Republics and Australia. These statements were communicated to all Members of the United Nations, which were informed that the President had fixed 15 April 1948 as the opening date of the oral proceedings. A statement from the Government of Siam, dated 30 January 1948, which was received in the Registry on 14 February, that is, after the expiration of the time-limit, was accepted by decision of the President and was also transmitted to the other Members of the United Nations. The Secretary-General of the United Nations sent to the Registry the appropriate documents and designated a representative authorized to present any written and oral statements which might facilitate the Court's task. The French, Yugoslav, Belgian, Czechoslovak and Polish

Governments appointed representatives to present oral statements before the Court.

After the hearing, which took place on 22 to 24 April, the Court deliberated in private. It gave its opinion on 28 May. By nine votes to six, it replied in the negative to the two questions put to it by the General Assembly's resolution.

Judges Alvarez and Azevedo, whilst concurring in the opinion of the Court, availed themselves of the right conferred on them by Article 57 of the Statute and appended a statement of their individual opinions.

Judges Basdevant, Winiarski, McNair, Read, Zoricic and Krylov, declaring that they were unable to concur in the opinion of the Court and availing themselves of the right conferred on them by Article 57 of the Statute, appended to the opinion a statement of their dissent.

(*c*) PRIVILEGES AND IMMUNITIES OF THE COURT

In a letter of 24 May 1948, the Swiss Minister to the Netherlands informed the Court, through the intermediary of the Registrar, that on 30 April 1948, the Swiss Federal Council had decided that the recommendations made by the General Assembly of the United Nations on 11 December 1946 on the subject of the privileges and immunities of the Court would henceforth be applicable in Switzerland.

(*d*) COMPOSITION OF THE COURT AND OF THE CHAMBER FOR SUMMARY PROCEDURE

The terms of office of five judges who were chosen by lot at the time of the first elections to the Court, will end at the expiration of three years from 6 February 1946. These judges are: Messrs. Winiarski, Zoricic, Badawi Pasha, Read and Hsu Mo.

Article 21 of the Statute provides that the Court shall elect its President and Vice-President for three years; they may be re-elected. The period of office of the present President and Vice-President, MM. Guerrero and Basdevant, will expire in April 1949. An election to these two offices must, in accordance with article 9 of the Rules of Court, be held by the Court within a month of the taking up of their duties by the judges who are elected at the partial renewal of the Court.

On 21 April 1948, the following judges were elected for the year 1948-1949 as members of the Chamber for Summary Procedure (Statute, Article 29). Their period of office began on 3 May 1948 and will end on 2 May 1949:

Members:
    Mr. Guerrero, *President,*
    Mr. Basdevant, *Vice-President,*
    Sir Arnold McNair,
    Mr. Krylov,
    Mr. Hsu Mo;

Substitute members:
Mr. Hackworth,
Mr. de Visscher.

(e) MEETINGS OF THE COURT

The Court met from 24 February to 28 May 1948 with a short interval at the beginning of April, to deal with the two cases mentioned above. It also adopted its budget for 1948 and considered certain administrative questions, in particular, that of its publications. The Court decided that the President and the Registrar or Deputy-Registrar should represent it at the third session of the General Assembly in 1948.

B. Development and codification of international law

(a) ESTABLISHMENT OF THE INTERNATIONAL LAW COMMISSION

The Committee on the Progressive Development of International Law and its Codification, which met from 12 May to 17 June 1947, submitted a report to the second regular session of the General Assembly, in which the establishment of an international law commission of fifteen experts was recommended.

After study of this report, the General Assembly, by resolution 174 (II) of 21 November 1947, decided to establish the "International Law Commission" which will be elected at the third regular session, and which will exercise its functions in accordance with the Statute of the Commission. The members of the Commission, as laid down in article 3 of the Statute, shall be elected by the General Assembly from a list of candidates nominated by the Governments of Members of the United Nations. In accordance with article 6, the Secretary-General has communicated to all Members the names of candidates nominated, together with statements of their qualifications.

By resolution 175 (II) adopted by the General Assembly on the same date, the Secretary-General was instructed to take up the "necessary preparatory work for the beginning of the activity of the Commission".

The Secretariat has consequently engaged in preliminary studies, not only of the particular subjects referred to the Commission by the General Assembly (see (b) and (c) below), but also of problems of a more general character which will confront the Commission when it takes up its functions as defined in its Statute. Consideration has been given to a survey of the entire field of international law for the purpose of selecting topics for codification (article 18 of the Statute) and to the method and programme

of work which the Commission may eventually wish to adopt. Attention has also been given to that aspect of the work of the Commission mentioned in article 24 of the Statute which has to do with the consideration of ways and means of making the evidence of customary international law more readily available. In connexion with this work, steps have already been taken for the publication by the United Nations of a compilation of international law cases, covering arbitral awards from 1920 to 1940. This compilation is now being prepared by the Registry of the International Court of Justice. Further, in order to facilitate the preparation, under Article 26 of the Statute, of a complete list of organizations with which the International Law Commission may consult, the Secretary-General has requested all Members of the United Nations to submit the names of organizations concerned with questions of international law.

(b) DRAFT DECLARATION ON THE RIGHTS AND DUTIES OF STATES

By resolution 178 (II) of 21 November 1947, the General Assembly decided to entrust further study of this problem to the International Law Commission, which was instructed to prepare a draft declaration on the rights and duties of States. By the same resolution, the Secretary-General was requested in the first place to draw the attention of the Members of the United Nations to the desirability of submitting comments and observations on the draft declaration originally presented by Panama, and in the second place, to undertake the necessary preparatory work on this subject.

In accordance with this resolution, the Secretary-General has once more requested the Members of the United Nations to forward their comments and observations on the draft declaration presented by Panama. Substantive comments and observations on this declaration have been received from the following Members: Denmark, Dominican Republic, Ecuador, Greece, Mexico, Philippines and Venezuela. The Secretary-General has furthermore, as requested by the resolution, undertaken a preliminary study of the question of the rights and duties of States and has prepared a commentary on the draft declaration presented by Panama, which commentary is to serve as a basis for the work of the International Law Commission on this subject.

(c) FORMULATION OF THE PRINCIPLES RECOGNIZED IN THE CHARTER OF THE NÜRNBERG TRIBUNAL AND IN THE JUDGMENT OF THE TRIBUNAL

By resolution 177 (II) of 21 November 1947, the General Assembly decided to entrust the International Law Commission with the formulation of the principles of international law recognized in the Charter of the Nürnberg Tribunal and with the preparation of a draft code of offences against the peace and security of mankind.

In accordance with the request of the General Assembly regarding preparatory work for the activity of the International Law Commission, the Secretariat has engaged in a preliminary study of and preparation of comments on both the Charter of the Nürnberg Tribunal and the judgment of the Tribunal. Consideration has also been given to the problems which will arise in connexion with the preparation of the draft code of offences against the peace and security of mankind.

(d) TEACHING OF INTERNATIONAL LAW

By a circular letter of 20 January 1948, the Secretary-General drew the attention of all Member States to resolution 176 (II), adopted by the General Assembly on 21 November 1947, whereby the Members were requested, in the first place, to extend the teaching of international law in all its phases, including its development and codification; in the second place, to promote similar teaching regarding the aims, purposes, structure and operation of the United Nations; and, finally, to give the Secretary-General the fullest possible co-operation in the preparatory work on the development and codification of international law. A number of replies have been received by the Secretary-General from Member States in response to the above-mentioned letter.

(e) INTERNATIONAL LEGISLATION UNDER THE AUSPICES OF THE UNITED NATIONS

For the extension of international law into new fields of international activities, the conclusion of multilateral conventions is acknowledged to be the most effective method. A brief reference might therefore be made here to the most important law-making conventions which have been concluded during the past year under the auspices of the United Nations. The substance of these conventions is discussed in detail in other parts of this report.

In the field of international trade, conferences on trade and employment held at Geneva and Havana have resulted in particularly important multilateral agreements. The second session of the Preparatory Committee of the United Nations Conference on Trade and Employment, which met at Geneva from 10 April to 30 October 1947, adopted the General Agreement on Tariffs and Trade and the Protocol of Provisional Application of the Agreement. The Ha-

vana Conference, which met from 21 November 1947 to 24 March 1948, drew up the charter for the International Trade Organization which, in addition to establishing this organization, lays down a number of important principles for the purpose of promoting, on an international basis, the expansion of the production, exchange and consumption of goods.[1]

In the related field of international maritime commerce, the United Nations Maritime Conference, which met at Geneva from 19 February to 6 March 1948, adopted a multilateral convention providing for the establishment of an Inter-Governmental Maritime Consultative Organization.[2]

Mention should also be made of the proposed law-making conventions which have been or are being prepared by the specialized agencies in their respective fields. Two notable examples are the draft convention on the recognition of rights in aircraft prepared under the auspices of the International Civil Aviation Organization, and the draft convention on copyright prepared under the auspices of the United Nations Educational, Scientific and Cultural Organization.

Studies have also been made in the further development of the system and instrumentalities of pacific settlement treaties. The Interim Committee of the General Assembly, in accordance with paragraph 2 (c) of resolution 111 (II) of 13 November 1947, is studying different methods which might be adopted to promote political co-operation in the maintenance of international peace and security. These methods include the conclusion of a multilateral convention for the pacific settlement of international disputes. Thus, preliminary steps are being taken with a view to the strengthening of the system of peace and security provided by the Charter.

(f) APPLICATION AND INTERPRETATION OF THE CHARTER AND PRINCIPLES OF INTERNATIONAL LAW

Particular importance attaches to the development of those rules of international law which have found expression in the Charter, and to the legal precedents which are constantly being built up in the practice of the various organs of the United Nations. Hardly any problem comes before the United Nations which does not raise questions of a legal character and does not require a study of the previous application and interpretation of the Articles of the Charter and of the practice and precedents in the various organs. With the increasing activities of the United Nations, a strong need has thus been felt for a

---

[1] See page 59.
[2] See page 61.

systematic collection of practices and precedents with respect to the application of the provisions of the Charter. To meet this need, the Secretariat has engaged in the preparation of a systematic annotation of the Articles of the Charter as they have been interpreted or applied by the various organs of the United Nations.

In addition, apart from the Charter, rules of international law are constantly being applied and interpreted in the organs of the United Nations and by the Secretariat. The widespread activities of the Organization are a fertile source of questions which require legal analysis and opinions, and the legal precedents thus established in the day-to-day work of the Organization are an important part of the process of developing international law under the auspices of the United Nations. At present these precedents are scattered through various records of meetings and Secretariat memoranda, but the Legal Department of the Secretariat has begun a systematic collection and arrangement of the legal opinions so as to make more readily available the principles of international law followed in the Organization.

C. Privileges and immunities

(*a*) AGREEMENT BETWEEN THE UNITED NATIONS AND THE UNITED STATES OF AMERICA REGARDING THE HEADQUARTERS OF THE UNITED NATIONS

By resolution 169 (II), the General Assembly of the United Nations approved, on 31 October 1947, the "Agreement between the United Nations and the United States of America regarding the Headquarters of the United Nations", which had been signed by the Secretary-General of the United Nations and the Secretary of State of the United States of America on 26 June 1947. The General Assembly authorized the Secretary-General to bring the Agreement into force in conformity with its terms, and to perform, on behalf of the United Nations, such acts or functions as might be required. The Agreement had been previously approved by a Joint Resolution of the Eightieth Congress of the United States; and U.S. Public Law 357, containing its text, was signed by the President of the United States on 4 August 1947.

In accordance with section 28, the Headquarters Agreement was brought into effect by an exchange of notes between the Secretary-General and Mr. Warren R. Austin, permanent representative of the United States at the seat of the United Nations, on 21 November 1947.

On 18 December 1947, the relevant provisions of the Agreement were extended to the interim headquarters of the United Nations. The interim headquarters comprises the land and buildings occupied by the United Nations for its official activities at Lake Success and at Flushing Meadow, Long Island, New York, and such other land and buildings occupied by the United Nations as may be defined from time to time by agreement between the United Nations and the United States of America, after consultation with the proper state and local authorities.

By a letter of 2 December 1947, the Secretary-General informed the Members of the United Nations that the Headquarters Agreement had come into effect. The letter drew the attention of the Governments concerned to the provisions of section 15, in conformity with which the same privileges and immunities are granted to certain categories of representatives of Members as are accorded to diplomatic envoys accredited to the Government of the United States. The Secretary-General requested that lists of persons covered by sub-sections 1 and 2 of section 15 be transmitted to him. Procedures have been agreed upon by which the United States Government is informed of the names of persons entitled to full diplomatic privileges and immunities, and complete lists are published monthly.

Arrangements have been made with the competent United States authorities—federal, state and local—in order to put into application the provisions of section 15 with respect to such matters as exemptions from certain excise taxes, including taxes on luxury items, taxes on telegraph, cable, telephone and radio communications, on transportation, on certain transfers of property, insurance, etc. Arrangements have similarly been made for exemption from taxation on gasoline, hotel tax and sales tax, and exemption from customs duties on goods imported for the personal use of the representatives.

In accordance with section 11 of the Headquarters Agreement, an understanding has been reached with the competent United States authorities as to the accreditation of representatives of the Press, radio, film and other information agencies. All names of persons proposed for accreditation are forwarded to the United States Government for comment, but final accreditation rests with the United Nations two weeks after the notification to the United States authorities.

In order to facilitate the speedy granting of visas to representatives of non-governmental organizations who are entitled to freedom of transit to and from the headquarters district under section 11, sub-section 4, a procedure has been established by which a panel of names of potential representatives is set up by these organizations and forwarded to the United States authorities through the Secretariat of the United Nations. It has also been established that persons invited to the headquarters district by the United Nations would be considered as duly entitled to the privileges of section 11, subsection 5, of the Agreement when notice has been received by the appropriate United States authorities from the Secretary-General that such invitation has been issued.

In the course of the negotiations at which these arrangements were made, United States authorities extended the fullest co-operation, making every effort to implement as quickly as possible the terms of the Headquarters Agreement.

(*b*) GENERAL CONVENTION ON THE PRIVILEGES AND IMMUNITIES OF THE UNITED NATIONS

From the time of the drafting of the General Convention and of the various drafts of the Agreement concerning the headquarters district, the General Assembly considered that these two instruments formed an organic whole defining the status of the Organization in the country where its headquarters were located. The Agreement on the headquarters district expressly refers to the General Convention, to which it forms the natural complement. Because of this relation of interdependence, the accession of the United States to the General Convention was considered necessary in order that the Agreement on the headquarters district might become fully effective. By resolutions 93 (I) and 99 (I), the United States was formally invited to accede to the Convention; by resolution 93 (I), the General Assembly also laid particular stress on the importance of the accession to the Convention of all other Members of the United Nations and urged them to accede at as early a date as possible.

Accessions. In his last annual report, the Secretary-General drew attention to the fact that the number of accessions to the Convention had been disappointing. On 12 March 1948, he sent a further letter to all Member Governments, drawing attention to the recommendations of the General Assembly and requesting them to accede to the Convention as soon as possible. The Secretary-General re-emphasized that it was essential for the efficient exercise of the functions of the Organization and the fulfilment of its purposes that the implementation of Article 105 of the Charter, through the bringing into force of the General Convention, be secured as early as possible.

To date, the following States have deposited their instruments of accession:

	Date of accession
United Kingdom	17 September 1946
Dominican Republic	7 March 1947
Liberia	14 March 1947
Iran	8 May 1947
Honduras	16 May 1947
Panama	27 May 1947
Guatemala	7 July 1947
El Salvador	9 July 1947
Ethiopia	22 July 1947
Haiti	6 August 1947
France	18 August 1947
Norway	18 August 1947
Sweden	28 August 1947
Afghanistan	5 September 1947
Philippines	28 October 1947
Nicaragua	29 November 1947
New Zealand	10 December 1947
Greece	29 December 1947
Poland	8 January 1948
Canada	22 January 1948
Iceland	10 March 1948
Netherlands	19 April 1948
India	13 May 1948
Denmark	10 June 1948

The Secretary-General has also received notice that the instrument of accession of Bolivia will shortly be transmitted to him.

The accession of Canada contained a reservation concerning the application, to Canadian citizens residing or ordinarily resident in Canada, of section 18 (*b*) of the General Convention relating to the immunity from taxation on salaries and emoluments paid by the United Nations to its officials. The accession of New Zealand also contained a reservation on the application, to British subjects domiciled and employed in New Zealand, of section 18 (*b*) of the General Convention.

Information has been received of various legislative steps initiated by a number of other Governments, which will ultimately result in their accession to the Convention. A law authorizing accession has been presented to the Parliament of Egypt. The Government of Pakistan has expressed the expectation that an instrument of accession will be deposited before the third regular session of the General Assembly. A draft Act providing for accession by Turkey has been drawn up and is under consideration by different Committees of the Grand National Assembly and will be submitted to the latter for approval in the immediate future. The Government of the Union of South Africa has notified the Secretary-General that it will have to defer its accession to the Convention pending approval by Parliament of a Bill which has been drafted to replace the existing Diplomatic Immunities Act of 1932.

The General Assembly was informed at its second regular session of the passage on 17 July 1947 by the Senate of the United States of America of a Joint Resolution authorizing acceptance by the United States of the Convention on Privileges and Immunities of the United Nations. The Joint Resolution was forwarded to the United States House of Representatives, which referred it to its Committee on Foreign Affairs. The Committee gave full consideration to the Convention between 18 May and 3 June 1948. It decided to recommend that the Senate resolution on the Convention be considered by the House of Representatives together with certain other proposals relating to the United Nations: resolutions relating to the functioning of the United Nations, the strengthening of United States participation in United Nations organs, the United Nations headquarters loan, etc. The House Committee reported favourably on these proposals, and recommended unanimously the approval of the Joint Resolution on the privileges and immunities of the United Nations. In its report, the Committee, while concurring with the Senate's views as to the desirability of United States reservation with respect to the immunity from national service obligations of officials who are United States citizens, recommended that the reservation regarding exemption from taxation on the salaries and emoluments paid to United States nationals by the United Nations, which was also favoured by the Senate, should not be maintained. On 19 June 1948, the Congress of the United States adjourned without having finally acted upon the Convention.

Temporary arrangements have been made with certain Governments when the need for such arrangements has arisen in connexion with United Nations missions, meetings of commissions, etc.

An agreement complementary to the General Convention, which was acceded to by France, has been negotiated with the French Government for the period of the third session of the General Assembly which is to be held in Paris.

Reservations. In the course of the discussions on the General Convention at the first part of the first session of the General Assembly, some Members indicated that they wished to reserve the attitude of their Governments concerning certain sections of the Conventions, especially as to the taxation of their own nationals and also in relation to the obligations of their nationals relating to military service.

During the second regular session, the question of reservations to the General Convention was raised again on the basis of a report by the Secretary-General, in which reference was made to the action taken by the Senate of the United States of America with regard to the Convention.

The question of exemption from taxation on salaries and emoluments paid by the Organization to its officials is dealt with elsewhere in this report.[1] With regard to the reservation contemplated by the United States to section 18 (*c*) concerning immunity of officials from national service obligations, the opinion was expressed by the Sixth Committee that it was extremely important to avoid the risk of the work of the United Nations being hampered by the calling up of officials; and this point was commended for further discussion between the Secretary-General and the appropriate authorities of the United States. In this connexion, conversations have been held between representatives of the United States and of the Secretary-General, and assurances have been obtained that, in any military service law or act which might be approved by the United States, consideration would be given to the matter of exempting from such national service, essential officials of the United Nations who were United States nationals. The opinion was expressed that such officials could receive the same type of exemption as United States Government officials.

In its report to the Assembly on the Headquarters Agreement, the Sixth Committee also indicated that "the United States Government was disposed to put upon the provisions of article VII relating to the United Nations *laissez-passer* an interpretation which would greatly diminish the value of the *laissez-passer* and might, in a purely hypothetical case, mean that movements of officials in and out of the United States might be impeded although they were being sent abroad on official duties and United Nations business". In this connexion, the Committee noted that from the point of view of the United States this was not a matter of legislation but administration, and expressed the hope that further discussions on this point between the Secretary-General and the appropriate authorities of the United States might lead to a modification of the views of the United States Government as hitherto expressed to the Secretary-General, with the result that the provisions of article VII relating to the *laissez-passer* might produce the full effects which they were designed to secure. As a result, the Secretary-General communicated at length with the Government of the United States, and in meetings held between the representatives of the Secretary-General and of the United States, the general view has been expressed that, under the interpretation given to article VII by the United States, it might be possible that administrative

[1] See page 135.

arrangements could be arrived at by which the *laissez-passer* could be recognized by the United States as a valid travel document and a document of nationality.

(c) CONVENTION ON THE PRIVILEGES AND IMMUNITIES OF THE SPECIALIZED AGENCIES

On 21 November 1947, the General Assembly approved a Convention on the privileges and immunities of the specialized agencies, and proposed it for acceptance by the specialized agencies and for accession by all Members of the United Nations and by any other State member of a specialized agency. The Convention comprises two parts: a general part defining the standard privileges and immunities considered by the General Assembly as necessary for all specialized agencies; and a set of draft annexes, each relating to one specialized agency, the purpose of the annexes being to take into account the particular functions of each specialized agency requiring privileges of a special nature. The two parts of the Convention—standard clauses and annexes—form a complete body of provisions defining the privileges and immunities of each of the specialized agencies. But whereas the first part constitutes a definitive text submitted for final adoption by the General Assembly, the annexes contained in the second part are merely recommendations addressed to each of the specialized agencies.

The question of the acceptance of the standard clauses of the Convention and of the adoption of a final text of the relevant annex has been put on the agenda of the thirty-first session of the International Labour Conference, of the twenty-second Assembly of the International Civil Aviation Organization and of the first World Health Assembly. It may be expected that notification of the acceptance of the standard clauses and of a final text of the annex will soon be received from these specialized agencies. After notification by the Secretary-General and the communication of the texts of the annexes to the Member Governments and to the members of the specialized agencies which are not members of the United Nations, these States will be in a position to accede to the Convention.

Following the action taken by the General Assembly with respect to the privileges and immunities of the specialized agencies, the Economic and Social Council approved, on 25 February 1948, a resolution requesting the Secretary-General:

"(a) To conclude with any specialized agency which may so desire a supplementary agreement to extend to the officials of that agency the provisions of article VII of the Convention on the Privileges and Immunities of the United Nations, and to submit such supplementary agreement to the General Assembly for approval; and

"(b) Pending the entry into force of such agreement, to make arrangements for the use of the United Nations *laissez-passer* by officials of the specialized agency concerned, such *laissez-passer* to be issued on a provisional basis for use only in those countries which have previously undertaken to recognize the validity of *laissez-passer* so issued."

As a result, the Secretary-General, in May 1948, entered into a supplementary agreement with the International Civil Aviation Organization to add to the agreement between that organization and the United Nations a clause extending to the officials of that agency the right to use the *laissez-passer* of the United Nations in accordance with special arrangements to be negotiated between him and the competent authority of the agency, such clause to be submitted to the General Assembly and to the Assembly of the ICAO for approval. The Secretary-General has also entered into arrangements for the use of the United Nations *laissez-passer* by officials of the ICAO on a provisional basis, in accordance with section (*b*) of the above resolution.

The United Nations Educational, Scientific and Cultural Organization has also expressed its intention to enter into negotiations for such a supplementary agreement and such special arrangements.

At the present time, Australia, Guatemala, Luxembourg, Iceland, India, Dominican Republic, Canada (in so far as the officials of the ICAO are concerned) and Lebanon (in so far as the third conference of UNESCO is concerned) have undertaken to recognize the validity of the *laissez-passer* issued under such conditions.

In accordance with a clause which has been included in the agreements between the United Nations and the International Bank for Reconstruction and Development, the International Monetary Fund and the International Telecommunications Union, special arrangements are about to be made for the use of the United Nations *laissez-passer* by the officials of these agencies.

The Secretary-General has also communicated with the World Health Organization and the Universal Postal Union, indicating to these agencies that when they have approved their agreements entered into with the United Nations under Article 63 of the Charter, and containing the above-mentioned clauses, he will be pleased to enter into similar special arrangements with them.

D. Registration and publication of treaties and international agreements

During the past year, the Secretary-General has endeavoured to give progressive effect to the provisions of the regulations approved by the General Assembly on 14 December 1946 (resolution 97 (I)).

Considerable difficulties have had to be overcome. These relate to the practical execution of the provisions of the regulations as regards translation into the languages contemplated by those regulations and as regards the time-limit required for ensuring adequate publication. There were also difficulties in connexion with the time required for the governmental services of Member States to adapt themselves to the new system.

Treaties and international agreements in increasing numbers have been reaching the Secretariat for registration or recording and publication. The monthly statements called for under article 13 of the regulations have been communicated to the Members of the Organization. Six hundred and fourteen treaties or international agreements submitted by twenty-two Governments and two specialized agencies have, up to the present, been received by the Secretary-General. Six hundred and two certificates have been sent to signatories and contracting parties of registered treaties and international agreements.

E. Protection of the name "United Nations", of the emblem of the United Nations and of the United Nations flag

(a) THE NAME "UNITED NATIONS" AND THE UNITED NATIONS EMBLEM

By resolution 92 (I), adopted on 7 December 1946, the General Assembly approved the United Nations emblem and recommended that the Members of the United Nations "should take such legislative or other appropriate measures as are necessary to prevent the use, without authorization by the Secretary-General . . . of the emblem, the official seal and the name of the United Nations".

A letter, dated 14 July 1947, drawing attention to this resolution was sent to all the Members of the United Nations. Replies have been received from thirty-three. Sixteen States indicated that the necessary action had already been taken or that existing laws provided sufficient protection to make further action unnecessary. Thirteen States indicated they were taking action. In the remaining four cases, acknowledgments were received from the United Nations delegations of the countries concerned, and such acknowledgments stated that the matter was being referred to their Governments for attention.

A Bill making the use of the name, official seal and emblem of the United Nations illegal without authorization by the Secretary-General has been passed by the House of Representatives of the United States but has not yet been acted upon by the Senate.

(b) THE UNITED NATIONS FLAG

By resolution 167 (II), dated 20 October 1947, the General Assembly resolved that the flag of the United Nations should be the official emblem of the United Nations and directed the Secretary-General to draw up regulations concerning the dimensions and proportions of the flag.

It also authorized the Secretary-General to adopt a flag code, having in mind the desirability of a regulated use of the flag and the protection of its dignity.

In accordance with this resolution, the Secretary-General has adopted a flag code setting out the conditions under which the United Nations flag can be used, and a system of regulations setting out the dimensions and proportions of the flag and amplifying the provisions of the code. In drafting the flag code and the regulations, it was considered that the use of the United Nations flag should be restricted to purposes closely connected with the aims and ideals of the United Nations, since the view was taken that only by this means could the full meaning of the flag be preserved.

Chapter V

DEVELOPMENT OF PUBLIC UNDERSTANDING

(a) GENERAL CONSIDERATIONS

The authority of the United Nations, of its assemblies and councils, stems ultimately from the peoples it represents. The United Nations can only be effective to the extent that the peoples understand its functions, its possibilities and its limitations, and in so far as with that knowledge, they implement and support its decisions. Bearing these principles in mind, the recommendations of the Preparatory Commission adopted by the General Assembly at the first part of its first session, in London, made public information one of the major functions of the Secretariat; and the General Assembly, in this and subsequent acts at its second regular session, recognized that the development of an informed understanding of the work and purposes of the United Nations among the peoples of the world would be a determining factor in the success or failure of the Organization.

Progress in the evolution of the necessary enlightened public support of the United Nations has been difficult during the past year. Even in the most favourable political climate, progress would inevitably have been slow, for the pull of competing special and national interests is powerful: national loyalties are many centuries old, and the idea of world organization is comparatively new.

It need hardly be said that the political climate in which the United Nations has had to operate during the last two years has not been favourable. It has created public confusion and scepticism as to the role which the United Nations could and should play in the working together of the peoples of the world. It has unleashed baseless attacks and propaganda of all kinds aimed at the very existence of the Organization.

Such propaganda can only be countered by adequate positive information concerning the purposes and activities of the United Nations.

There are, however, well-known economic, financial and technical difficulties which operate in varying degrees of effect in different areas of the world and impede the flow of adequate and sufficient information about the Organization and which have led to distorted public understanding of its powers and work.

In general the Press and radio, in spite of such difficulties, have done and are continuing to do an increasingly effective job with the assistance of the United Nations information services.

But the actual dissemination of information does not in itself develop enlightened public opinion as long as there are great numbers of people who lack the background necessary to understand the reports of the day-to-day work of the Organization which they receive through Press and radio. They have not learned about the United Nations in schools, nor have they lived with it for a sufficient length of time to be able to view and evaluate events with the proper perspective, nor have they learned to discriminate between matters which are within the scope of the Charter and those which are the direct responsibility of the great Powers and other Members acting outside the jurisdiction of the Organization.

In times of exaltation and victory, like that immediately following the San Francisco Conference, people tended to expect immediately more than could possibly be achieved in a millennium; in the recent times of stress, they tend to take an attitude of indifference and even scepticism.

Furthermore, the ordinary newspaper reader or radio listener rarely reads or hears about the constructive work of the United Nations in the economic and social fields, for such information is not as "newsworthy" as are the political clashes within and without the Organization.

Nevertheless, in spite of all obstacles, political and otherwise, recent opinion surveys have shown an increasing number of persons in the various parts of the world who know about the United Nations. According to one opinion poll, conducted by a leading private agency this spring, from 80 to 95 per cent of persons in Brazil, Great Britain, France, Canada, Mexico, Sweden, Switzerland and the United States of America, when asked whether they had "read or heard about an organization called the United Nations" replied in the affirmative. Of those who did know something about the United Nations, however, from 25 to 48 per cent thought that, on the basis of information so far available to them, the Organization had only a poor chance of being able to maintain world peace. Those in Western European countries were the most sceptical. Those in the United States, where 67 per cent thought the United Nations had "either a fair chance or a good chance" of preventing another war, were particularly hopeful.

One of the most interesting features of the poll mentioned above was the unusually small number of persons who answered that they did not know what they thought. This number varied from a high of only 17 per cent in France to a low of 7 per cent in Mexico and Great Britain and 8 per cent in the United States and Canada.

In a public opinion survey made by the same agency six months earlier, in which people were asked whether they were satisfied or dissatisfied with the progress made by the United Nations, the proportion of those who did not know was much higher. It varied from a high of 66 per cent in Sweden to a low of 16 per cent in the United States. The great disparity between the two results, after making due allowance for the different questions answered and for the frailties of all opinion polls, indicates considerable progress in spreading knowledge of the United Nations in the countries concerned.

The fears of the peoples for the future of the United Nations and the peace of the world arise in part from undeniable political facts as well as from information shortcomings due to economic, financial and technical factors. These considerations tend to obstruct or distort knowledge of the United Nations. The resultant ignorance and misinformation in turn only make the political situation worse. A vicious circle of suspicion, ignorance and fear has thus been created which it must be the constant effort of all concerned to break. So long as it continues to exist, the United Nations will lack that measure of public support which is essential to the success of its work.

In so far as action in the field of public information can help to break this vicious circle, the main responsibility has rested, and will continue to rest, with the Member Governments and the existing public and private information

agencies. These agencies, taken together, have vast resources with which to operate, and their financial capacity is measured in hundreds of millions of dollars. It is through these agencies, therefore, that the information services of the Secretariat primarily work.

The Secretariat's task of developing enlightened understanding and support of the United Nations has immediate and long-range aspects. The most compelling and immediate needs can be met through mass media—Press, radio, films and photographs. These reach great numbers of people quickly. At the same time, however, it is essential that the slower processes of education about the United Nations, as distinct from news, should be put to work more fully in respect of both children and adults.

The General Assembly recognized both these aspects in two separate resolutions that were unanimously adopted at the second regular session in 1947. One of these, resolution 110 (II) on war propaganda, requested the Governments to promote friendly relations among nations based on the purposes and principles of the Charter by all available means of publicity and propaganda and to encourage the spread of all information designed to give expression to the undoubted desire of all peoples for peace. This resolution was unanimously endorsed by the Conference on Freedom of Information held at Geneva in the spring of 1948.[1]

The other (resolution 137 (II)) called on Member Governments to encourage teaching of the Charter, structure and activities of the United Nations in schools and institutes throughout the world and to inform the Secretary-General of the steps taken to implement the recommendation.[2]

In further implementation of these two resolutions, the Department of Public Information of the Secretariat has also been concerned with the development of a better balanced picture of the United Nations both through mass media and through schools and institutions of adult education. In this connexion, attention is drawn to significant recommendations as to content and emphasis in this flow of information made by an Advisory Committee of Information Experts called in accordance with resolution 13 (I), II, on public information adopted by the General Assembly on 13 February 1946. This Committee, which met from 25 May to 3 June 1948, noted in its report to the Secretary-General:

"That this scepticism would be lessened and a more effective understanding of the work and purposes of the United Nations achieved if, in

[1] See page 72.
[2] See (c) below.

addition to present activities, more emphasis were placed on information work on:

"(*a*) Constructive economic, social and humanitarian achievements of the United Nations and related agencies;

"(*b*) Public clarification of the functions and limitations of the United Nations and the Charter;

"(*c*) The fact that under present circumstances the United Nations is the only form of world-wide international machinery that the Governments have agreed to use and that the workability of the Organization has been evidenced by recent developments."

During discussions in Committee on the activities of the Department of Public Information at the last regular session of the General Assembly, it was remarked on several occasions that "actions speak louder than words". It was suggested that as and when the United Nations achieves spectacular successes in its endeavours the world will quickly learn of them and confidence will be re-established, but that during these critical years of grappling with unsolved problems the less said about them the better. Experience shows that exactly the opposite is the right policy. At this time, when unsolved problems are so much in the public eye, it is the responsibility of the information services of the United Nations to bring before the peoples of the world the very considerable, if unspectacular, advances in co-operation between nations which have been achieved, for the good of all, in the economic and social and even in the political fields. It is possible to increase the support of public opinion everywhere by presenting a balanced and objective picture of the activities of the United Nations, not now available to the people. Such is the main task of the Organization's public information services.

(*b*) Work of the Department of Public Information

It is with the foregoing factors constantly in mind that the work of the Department of Public Information has been conducted during the past year.

The principal developments during the year under review include the following:

(i) *Accreditation of correspondents*

The Headquarters Agreement negotiated between the United Nations and the Government of the United States of America grants, for the first time in such an international agreement, a special status to representatives of the Press, radio, films and other information agencies. Under this Agreement, the United States Government has agreed not to impede transit to or

from the United Nations headquarters district of all such representatives accredited by the United Nations in accordance with the terms of the Agreement, regardless of laws and regulations that might otherwise be applicable to those who are not citizens of the United States.

The policy of the United Nations on accreditation is to encourage as many professionally qualified people from as many countries as possible to come to the United Nations, wherever its meetings may be held, in order to write or speak about its work. Accreditation is determined solely by two governing factors: (1) that the applicant is a *bona fide* representative of a recognized information medium, and (2) that he is or will be actively engaged in covering the work of the United Nations. The accreditation policy of the Organization permits no distinction among representatives of information agencies on the grounds of political or religious opinion, language, race, nationality or sex.

Agreed procedures for consultation between the United Nations and the United States in order to carry out the terms of the Headquarters Agreement so far as it relates to information representatives have been in effect since 1 March 1948 and have worked satisfactorily.

Special treaty rights have not been accorded up to the present to correspondents wishing to cover the activities of the United Nations at places other than the headquarters district, but the spirit of the General Convention on the Privileges and Immunities of the United Nations, which has now been ratified by twenty-two Member States, together with the General Assembly's resolutions, imposes a strong moral obligation upon Members to avoid interference with reporting on United Nations activities wherever they may take place.

(ii) *Open meetings*

The United Nations has continued its policy of holding open rather than closed meetings of all its organs so that representatives of information agencies may be able to observe and report directly on all that occurs. During the past two years, it has gone far in bringing the conduct of international relations as fully into the open as the conduct of national and local government. Closed meetings have become the rare exception even when issues of the utmost difficulty are under consideration, and sub-committees and small drafting groups often meet in public rather than in closed session. There are occasions, of course, when closed or private meetings may be highly desirable or useful, but it is the policy of the Organization to support the practice of open meetings.

(iii) *Press*

Over two hundred news agencies, newspapers and periodicals from thirty-seven Member countries have accredited correspondents at United Nations headquarters, but most countries are not adequately represented because of the dollar costs involved. Plans are therefore under consideration for the provision of travelling fellowships which may help correspondents to visit the United Nations. Efforts are being made to find other ways by which part of the cost of sending and maintaining correspondents could be met in the currency of the Member nations sending them rather than in dollars.

(iv) *Radio*

As of 30 June 1948, approximately twenty-five countries were rebroadcasting daily, Monday through Friday, over their local stations, radio programme material provided by the Department of Public Information at Lake Success. Many other countries take United Nations programmes on a regular though not a daily basis. Twenty languages are now regularly used in United Nations transmissions. Most of this extended service was initiated during May and June, and it is difficult at this time to assess the full impact. It may be expected, however, that these programmes, reaching as they do an audience of millions of people daily in a large number of countries, will have a significant effect on public opinion since they give a completely neutral and balanced account of the activities of United Nations organs and agencies.

Under a special "Guest Commentator Plan", radio systems of countries not covered by the five official languages have been invited to send to Lake Success, at their own expense, a commentator of their own choosing. In addition to his own interpretative commentaries, the commentator is engaged by the United Nations Radio Division on a free-lance basis to give in his own language United Nations news broadcasts for an agreed number of minutes per week, provided that his radio system undertakes to relay the material locally.

(v) *Telecommunications*

At the present time, the United Nations depends on the generosity of the United States and Canadian short-wave broadcasting services for the provision of transmission time. Without such generous co-operation, nothing could have been done in this field; but operations have now reached a point where nationally-controlled facilities are inevitably seriously inadequate. In this connexion, the Advisory Committee of Information Experts has strongly recommended, in its report to the Secretary-General, the provision of a minimum unit of short-wave transmitters to be operated by the United Nations and to be entirely under its own jurisdiction and control.

United Nations representatives will be attending the next International High Frequency Broadcasting Conference in Mexico City in October 1948. It is essential that they should be in a position at that time to outline the plans of the United Nations for setting up its own radio services. Unless they can do so, they will have difficulties in defending the requirements of the Organization for frequencies in the international high frequency band, since this portion of the radio spectrum is already extremely congested. Requisitions which have been submitted to the Planning Committee in Geneva by national administrations already show that it will be impossible to fulfil these requests from the number of international frequencies available. Once frequencies have been allocated to Member States at the Conference, it is unrealistic to expect that any of them at some future date would be in a position to relinquish frequencies already assigned to existing national services. It will be recalled that the League of Nations recognized the need for having its own radio broadcasting facilities and, at an early period in its history, obtained and operated under League control adequate facilities with excellent results.

(vi) *Publications*

More than 1,000,000 copies of basic leaflets and pamphlets on the United Nations have been published in thirteen different languages. Two periodicals are published. The *United Nations Bulletin,* now a semi-monthly, is the only complete impartial periodical record published anywhere of all the activities of the United Nations and the specialized agencies. It is intended particularly to serve editors, writers, radio commentators, Government officials, teachers and others who are in a position to influence national and world opinion. The second, the *United Nations Newsletter,* is a four-page monthly printed letter specifically designed for members of non-governmental organizations and student groups.

In addition to these two periodicals, the United Nations issues two annuals—the *Yearbook of the United Nations,* which is expected to become the authoritative reference work on the United Nations and the specialized agencies, and a more popular and much briefer annual, an *Every Man's Guide to the United Nations.*

Currency and customs regulations and the difficulties of developing, except at great expense, an effective sales and free distribution system on a world-wide basis, continue to make distribution of all United Nations publications a serious problem. One possible answer was suggested by the Advisory Committee of Information Experts, which recommended to the Secretary-General that the United Nations should consider the establishment of a separately owned or endowed United Nations press, with which the United Nations would have contractual relations similar to those between author and publisher. Through such an arrangement, extensive outside resources for production and distribution could be enlisted, and increased circulation could be obtained without additional expense to the Organization. The United Nations would, of course, have to retain full editorial and policy control over all its publications under such an arrangement.

(vii) *Libraries and reference centres*

Fundamental to the development of enlightened public understanding is the establishment, at as many accessible points as possible, of places to which the public can turn for documents and background information when they want to know exactly what has been said or proposed. Thus, in addition to developing a central library and reference service at headquarters, the Department has been co-operating in the setting up of a network of deposit libraries and centres of international study in all Member countries, to which copies of all documentation and information publications are sent to meet the needs of research workers and leaders of public opinion, and a further network of libraries to which are sent less extensive but sufficient documentary and information publications to meet the needs of the general public.

(viii) *Films and visual services*

Four films, authorized in 1947, have been completed, as follows: (1) *The People's Charter,* edited by the United Nations film unit, using footage from seventeen countries and dealing with the birth of the United Nations, its aims and its relationship to the peoples of the world; (2) *Searchlight on the Nations,* a United States contract production dealing with the new significance of "freedom of information" and the part played by the communications systems of the world in bringing the work of the United Nations to the people; (3) *Maps We Live By,* a Canadian contract production dealing with the development of world mapping and the role maps play in international affairs; and (4) *Clearing the Way,* a United Nations film unit production dealing with the selection and clearing of the site for the permanent United Nations headquarters in New York and the work of the international group of architects in designing the buildings.

The following films, for which contracts were made in 1947, are in production and are to be completed in 1948 on a contractual basis by outstanding documentary film producers. (The country to which the production of each film has been assigned is indicated in parentheses after the title.) *The Fight against Illiteracy* (Mexico); *The United Nations in Action* (Poland); *Young Ideas* (Czechoslovakia); *Common Ground* (United Kingdom); *Juvenile Delinquency* (Belgium); *In Every Port* (Netherlands); *In the Long Run* (United States); *The Eternal Fight* (United States, France); *Lighthouses* (France); *Timber* (Sweden); and *What is the United Nations?* (France).

Arrangements for the exhibition of United Nations films have been made in thirty-three Member countries and negotiations are under way for distribution in others.

Apart from the above programme of production, the Social Affairs Department of the United Nations includes as one of its functions the production of motion pictures on social welfare work. These are also produced under the supervision of the Department of Public Information. Four have already been made: (1) *First Steps,* a one-reel picture produced in the United States, showing the latest techniques in the rehabilitation of children crippled by paralysis (this film won the United States Motion Picture Academy Award as the outstanding documentary short of 1947); and (2) a series of three films, *Mother, Child* and *Community,* produced in India. These three films show the work of a village health visitor in improving conditions of health, welfare and sanitation, especially for mothers, infants and children.

The following films have been produced by outside agencies with the encouragement of the United Nations: *To the Ends of the Earth* (Columbia), on international narcotics control; and *The Search* (MGM), on the international care of displaced children. Documentary films include: *In our Hands* (United Nations Association in the United Kingdom); *Charter of the United Nations* (British Central Office of Information); *Look at Greece,* based on the report of the Food and Agriculture Organization on Greece (Panorama Productions); *Hungry Minds* (National Film Board of Canada).

Film projects under discussion or approved, for which sponsorship is assured, include: two films on cancer and one on epilepsy for the World Health Organization; one film on international amateur radio; one on breaking down international racial and social prejudices; one on international aviation; one on resistance to "war mongering"; one on the Universal Postal Union; one on the operations of the International Children's Emergency Fund; one on the international phases of producer and consumer co-operative work; one on international technical standards.

With regard to photography, a shift of emphasis was effected in the spring of this year from the routine coverage of spot-news events and short-lived activities of the United Nations organs to the recording of their positive and long-term accomplishments. Staff photographers were assigned to accompany important field missions in Indonesia, Kashmir and Palestine; and the production of news pictures, in the generally accepted sense of the term, was superseded by the creation of photographic features and travelling exhibits of durable informational and instructional value.

(ix) *Information Centres*

Twelve information centres are now fully functioning and are located in the following cities:

Copenhagen: for Denmark, Iceland, Norway and Sweden;

Geneva: (at the United Nations European Office);

London: for the United Kingdom, Ireland and Netherlands;

Moscow: for the Union of Soviet Socialist Republics, Byelorussian Soviet Socialist Republic and the Ukrainian Soviet Socialist Republic;

Mexico City: for Mexico and Central America;

New Delhi: for India, Burma and Ceylon;

Paris: for France, Belgium, Luxembourg and the French Commonwealth;

Prague: for Czechoslovakia and Yugoslavia;

Rio de Janeiro: for Brazil;

Shanghai: for China, Philippines and Siam;

Warsaw: for Poland;

Washington: for United States of America.

One more information centre and three correspondent information centres will be established in the course of 1948: namely, an information centre for the Near East (the location of which is still to be determined), and correspondent information centres in:

Buenos Aires: for Argentina, Bolivia, Paraguay and Uruguay;

Teheran: for Iran, Afghanistan and Pakistan;

Sydney: for Australia and New Zealand.

With the exception of the office at Geneva, information centres are divided into three categories according to whether their substantive staffs consist of six, four or two persons. The Geneva Information Centre, in view of special responsibilities covering extensive activities of the United Nations and the specialized agencies, has a larger staff.

The centres maintain all possible contacts with all information media; prepare releases for the use of the press and other information media, in the languages of their area; disseminate background and feature articles produced by headquarters and by the specialized agencies; organize, whenever necessary, press conferences, report on the United Nations activities and conferences in their area; act for the United Nations radio in maintaining contacts, supplying material to and reporting on the activities of the national broadcasting systems as regards the United Nations; in the field of visual information, assist in the production and distribution of United Nations films, organize film shows, exhibits, supply photographic and film material on United Nations activities, distribute posters and other visual information material; work with the division of Special Services in developing contacts and servicing non-governmental organizations, etc., in the organization of lecture services, and in developing contacts for headquarters with schools and educational agencies for experiments and services in connexion with teaching about the United Nations.

(c) GENERAL ASSEMBLY RESOLUTION ON TEACHING ABOUT THE UNITED NATIONS: WORK WITH SCHOOLS AND NON-GOVERNMENTAL ORGANIZATIONS

Progress in the implementation of General Assembly resolution 137 (II) has already been reported.[1] There remains to be described the part played by the information services of the United Nations, in co-operation with the United Nations Educational, Scientific and Cultural Organization, in the implementation of this resolution and of the complementary resolution passed by the UNESCO General Conference in Mexico City.

The main responsibility for developing teaching about the United Nations in schools must, of course, rest with the national authorities, leaders and institutions of Member States. However, the United Nations, in co-operation with UNESCO, has made a modest start in providing certain facilities and assistance where required, and every effort will be made to develop further contacts.

Efforts to date have been concentrated on creating networks of (a) reference units at colleges and public libraries and (b) volunteer groups at teacher-training institutes, which will help teachers in arranging courses on the United Nations, provide educational aids and answer questions raised both by teachers and pupils. After one year of operation, some 1,205 refer-

[1] See page 79.

ence units have been set up in various libraries in thirty-eight Member nations and nine dependencies; in addition, some 596 key officials, leading educators and volunteer groups at training colleges are developing facilities for assisting teachers in some forty Member nations and six dependencies.

In the second place, the United Nations has been working, in consultation with UNESCO, on the planning of "model" courses together with kits of illustrative material, textbooks and other educational aids. Limited editions of model kits will be produced in as many languages as possible to be tried out experimentally in schools of Member nations; each country, in its turn, will then be able to adapt these for national use. Side by side with this project, groups of educators have come to headquarters in order to plan educational "units" to include aspects of United Nations activities in various normal courses of the school curricula. In addition, writers of textbooks and articles for periodicals have worked at headquarters on parallel plans; and special services are being developed for working with both teachers' periodicals and children's newspapers on long-term plans for further aids to teaching about the United Nations in schools.

Thirdly, parallel activities have been developed in the adult education field through lecture services and public assemblies. People unable to visit headquarters and obtain for themselves a balanced picture of the aims and activities of the United Nations may often be able to obtain a clear understanding if they can listen to lectures by persons directly associated with the United Nations Secretariat and delegations who can talk with first hand knowledge. Although places near headquarters naturally have certain advantages, every effort has been made to utilize

personnel on home leave or travelling on official business, and to organize a parallel service of unofficial correspondent speakers to give lectures, on as wide a geographical basis as possible. Through such means, members of delegations and of the Secretariat, or p .ons from the network of correspondent speakers, have during the past year participated in discussion groups in forty-seven Member States.

Finally, attention is drawn to the important role of non-governmental organizations in the field of adult education and in working with Governments for the implementation of United Nations recommendations. Representatives attending meetings of United Nations organs, the specialized agencies and other official international agencies can, in general, make recommendations to their Governments. The implementation of decisions therefore depends on action by Governments, which in turn depends upon the influence of public opinion. It is exactly in this task that non-governmental organizations are in a position to help; they can "follow through" recommendations of the United Nations and the specialized agencies, in the general political field and in specialized fields and, through organized enlightened and interested public opinion, can support Governments in ratifying and implementing resolutions and recommendations. Some idea of the number of people involved in the activities of these non-governmental organizations may be gathered from the fact that the membership represented by accredited observers of organizations in the United States alone is estimated at more than 40,000,000, and that four of the largest international organizations, with the bulk of their membership outside the United States, by themselves comprise over 276,000,000 members.

Chapter VI

ORGANIZATION, ADMINISTRATION AND FINANCE

A. Organization and structure of the Secretariat

The progress noted in the Secretary-General's report of last year in the field of organization and administration has continued steadily throughout the ensuing twelve months. Though known weaknesses have not in all cases been fully repaired and new problems are constantly arising, evidence is not lacking of the increased efficiency with which the Secretariat, within the limits imposed by available personnel and budgetary resources, has been able to cope with the manifold and difficult tasks that have been laid upon it. The results of the improvements recently effected on the basis of the findings of the Management Survey and of recommendations of the Advisory Committee on Administrative and Budgetary Questions will not be fully apparent for some time to come; but it is hoped that the organizational and administrative framework which has now emerged will be well adapted to the future needs of the Organization though, of course, continued improvement in organization and administration will still be sought.

Since the close of the second regular session of the General Assembly, particular attention has been given to the question of administrative procedures, with a view to the simplification and clarification of financial and administrative controls throughout the Secretariat, at headquarters and in the overseas offices.

In the matter of financial control, full responsibility for the administration of its own allotments has been placed with each department, within which certifying officers, appointed by the Assistant Secretary-General for Administrative and Financial Services on the recommendation of the Assistant Secretary-General concerned, assume responsibility for ensuring that proposed transactions or services are in accord with existing rules and regulations; that funds are available within allotments; and that expenditures are reasonable and are readily identified with the purpose of original appropriations. Issuance of allotments follows a simplified pattern; allotments are made on an annual basis for more stable and fixed charges and on a six-monthly basis for other continuing charges.

Control, in its budgetary and administrative aspects, has been tightened in the matter of employment of consultants, official travel and research project grants. Allotments for these three items are issued separately after a review of departmental requirements, submitted monthly.

In matters of administration, procedures supporting this decentralization of financial control in the administration of budget appropriations and budget allotments have been progressively developed. The printing programme of the Organization has been consolidated to facilitate review and approval by the Publications Board prior to the expenditure of United Nations funds under this heading.

Property and stores systems have been partially reorganized along lines recommended by the Board of External Auditors and the Management Engineering Division; certain expendable stocks, formerly maintained by the departments, have been consolidated with the main stores. The centralized registry system is in process of decentralization; departmental branch registries are being established to provide registry service for each department. Local transport has been stabilized through the continued operation of a carpool and the chartering of buses to run between Lake Success and public transportation facilities.

A simplification has been made of all personnel actions relating to appointment, promotion, transfer, assignment to special mission duties and separation, supplemented by review through inter-departmental committees of classification and description of posts; a codification of staff rules has been issued in accordance

제2부 유엔총회 회의록(1948)

with resolution 161 (II) of the General Assembly. Conditions of employment and payment of staff members recruited to temporary posts have been further reviewed to ensure the most effective and economical arrangements suitable for temporary assignments.

Simplification of procedures affecting the payment of salaries and all allowances has been effected, with a corresponding reorganization of the Staff Accounts Division of the Bureau of the Comptroller, enabling a substantial reduction to be made in the total number of staff employed in these operations.

A comprehensive review of personnel, budgetary and financial questions concerning the United Nations and the specialized agencies has been undertaken by the Consultative Committee on Administrative Questions of the Co-ordination Committee, leading to the formulation of standard procedures and practices in these questions and to the simplification of procedure for securing reimbursement for goods and services provided by the United Nations.

Special arrangements have been made to serve various commissions and committees such as the United Nations Temporary Commission on Korea, the United Nations Special Committee on the Balkans, the Palestine missions, the Trusteeship Visiting Mission, and the Committee of Good Offices on the Indonesian Question. The organization and administration of these missions have given rise to many special problems, but rapid progress is being made in coping with them.

During the period covered by this report, a detailed survey of all departments was made by the Management Engineering Division of the Bureau of Administrative Management and Budget. The results of this survey formed the basis for organizational changes in a number of departments and for consequential adjustments in the budget for 1948. The more important changes that have occurred in the responsibilities and functions of the main units of the Secretariat during this period are briefly outlined in the following paragraphs.

EXECUTIVE OFFICE OF THE SECRETARY-GENERAL

An important development in the organization of this Office and its relations with the other departments and services of the Secretariat was the establishment early in 1948 of an additional post of Assistant Secretary-General with the following broad duties:

(i) To assist the Secretary-General as necessary, and to reduce to a minimum the burden of day-to-day work falling on him;

(ii) In co-operation with departments, to co-ordinate the internal work of the United Nations and the execution of agreed policy;

(iii) To co-ordinate the work of the United Nations and specialized agencies and overseas operations.

Consequent on the establishment of this new post, the organization and functions of the Executive Office are now being reviewed.

DEPARTMENT OF ECONOMIC AFFAIRS

Some changes have occurred in the structure of the Department of Economic Affairs. A unit has been established on a temporary basis in the Office of the Assistant Secretary-General to serve as the secretariat of the Interim Co-ordinating Committee for International Commodity Arrangements, pending the establishment of the International Trade Organization. The Division of Economic Stability and Development, created in 1947, has been organized into an Office of the Director, three functional sections dealing respectively with economic stability, economic development, international financial and commercial relations, and a geographical area units section. Finally, the organization of the Statistical Office has been completed to enable it to cope with the responsibilities placed upon it by the Statistical Commission, the Population Commission and the Economic and Social Council in the fields of collection, analysis and publication of statistics, of research and promotion of internationally comparable statistics, and of co-ordination of the statistical activities of the United Nations and specialized agencies.

The principal development in the economic field has been the establishment and organization of the staffs of the regional economic commissions: the Economic Commission for Europe, the organization of which was virtually completed by the end of 1947; the Economic Commission for Asia and the Far East, established during 1947; and the Economic Commission for Latin America, established during 1948. In anticipation of favourable action by the Economic and Social Council at its seventh session, preparatory work is under way for the establishment of a fourth regional body—an Economic Commission for the Middle East.

DEPARTMENT OF SOCIAL AFFAIRS

The only significant change in the structural organization of the Department of Social Affairs has been the merging of the Section on Studies and Research and the Section on Education, Science and Culture into a Section of Cultural Activities, and the abolition of the two sections dealing with public health and refugees in the Division of Social Activities. Matters pertaining to these activities are being dealt with by the Office of the Director of the Division.

DEPARTMENT OF TRUSTEESHIP AND INFORMATION FROM NON-SELF-GOVERNING TERRITORIES

The organizational structure of the Department of Trusteeship and Information from Non-Self-Governing Territories remains, practically unchanged. The only new development in this Department was the establishment of a section for Jerusalem in the Division of Trusteeship, in order to assist the Trusteeship Council in the discharge of the responsibilities entrusted to it by resolution 181 (II), adopted by the General Assembly of 29 November 1947 (part III of the Plan of Partition with Economic Union).

DEPARTMENT OF PUBLIC INFORMATION

During 1948, the Library was reorganized and all existing library and reference services, except the language reference services and those related to the Geneva Office, were centralized for the time being in the Department of Public Information. This reorganized service comprises the Library and the Documents Index Unit, formerly under Conference and General Services, the reference and related services previously performed by the Reference and Publications Division of the Department of Public Information, and certain library and reference activities transferred from other departments. It is responsible for maintaining all library and reference collections of the Secretariat (except those in Geneva) for use by all organs of the United Nations; for indexing all United Nations documents, furnishing background information about the United Nations, the specialized agencies and their activities; and compiling periodic opinion surveys. The editorial responsibilities which the former Reference and Publications Division carried out with regard to the *Bulletin*, pamphlets and similar publications have been combined with the services performed by the former Press Division in a consolidated Press and Publications Office. Sales of all publications of the United Nations, as well as the technical operations connected with the printing of publications of the Department of Public Information were transferred from Conference and General Services to the former Department, and are now performed by a section attached to the Office of the Assistant Secretary-General.

GENEVA OFFICE

Reorganization of the Geneva Office has been completed during 1948 in accordance with the suggestion, made by the Advisory Committee on Administrative and Budgetary Questions in its report on the 1948 budget, that both the system of control by headquarters and the internal organization of the Office could be simplified. As a result of a clarification of responsibilities and lines of communication with headquarters, the delegation of a considerable measure of local authority in matters of administration and finance, and the regrouping of certain services, substantially greater flexibility and speed of operation have been secured. In particular, Conference and General Services in the Geneva Office now cover the same group of services as those under the control of the corresponding Department at headquarters, while the Assistant Director for Administrative and Financial Services at Geneva has been given an overall responsibility for all matters relating to personnel, budget and finance. At the same time, the functions of the Geneva Office have been clearly defined. They may be briefly described as follows:

(i) To provide office accommodation and services for units of the United Nations Secretariat located in Geneva (the staff of the Economic Commission for Europe, the joint secretariat of the Permanent Central Opium Board and Narcotic Drugs Supervisory Body, a unit of the Department of Social Affairs, representatives of the Department of Trusteeship and of the Joint Division of Co-ordination and Liaison, and the Information Centre);

(ii) To act as a European centre for the holding of conferences, both of the United Nations and of specialized agencies;

(iii) To provide facilities of a temporary character for United Nations commissions operating in Europe;

(iv) To provide, on a reimbursable basis, office space and certain services for specialized agencies with secretariats in Geneva.

ADMINISTRATIVE AND FINANCIAL SERVICES

The work of this Department has continued, up to the present, to be carried out through three main Bureaux: the Bureau of Administrative Management and Budget, the Bureau of the Comptroller and the Bureau of Personnel. Plans for the reorganization of the Department have, however, been prepared and are reflected in the budget estimates for 1949. In formulating these plans, consideration has been given to the various suggestions and proposals made by the Preparatory Commission of the United Nations, the Advisory Committee, and the Fifth Committee of the General Assembly. The basic consideration in the reorganization scheme is that the Assistant Secretary-General for Administrative and Financial Services has been delegated the responsibility, vested in the Secretary-General, of exercising administrative and financial control over the entire operations of the Secretariat. The scheme drawn up is, therefore, primarily concerned with the most effective organization of these control functions.

Specifically, it is proposed under the scheme to merge the Bureau of Administrative Management and Budget and the Bureau of the Comptroller, and to regroup the functions presently performed by these two Bureaux into four divisions as follows:

(1) Accounting Division, designed to achieve a closer control over all accounting activities;

(2) Treasury Division, which would consolidate all functions relating to the receipt, custody and actual disbursement of funds, together with activities relating to investments, insurance and taxation;

(3) Organization and Budget Division, which would be responsible for the functions now located in the Organization and Estimates Division of the Bureau of Administrative Management and Budget, as well as for the overall financial control of the budget and its complete preparation;

(4) Policy Division, concerned with policy and procedural questions affecting salaries and allowances, administrative instructions, liaison with specialized agencies in administrative and financial matters, and financial rules and regulations.

The second important feature of the reorganization plan is the proposed establishment of an Inspection Service, comprising the present Internal Audit Division of the Comptroller's Office and the Management Engineering Division of the Bureau of Administrative Management and Budget. This Service would be responsible for the periodic review and examination of all administrative actions of the Secretariat having financial implications, to ensure conformity with financial rules and regulations and the economical use of funds. In addition, the Inspection Service would systematically review operating procedures, work records, and standards of performance in order to obtain maximum utilization of staff and equipment.

No fundamental reorganization of the Bureau of Personnel is immediately envisaged, although its internal functions and procedures are being improved and simplified.

It is not proposed that the reorganization plan outlined above should be fully operative until 1 January 1949.

OTHER DEPARTMENTS

In the Department of Conference and General Services, a thorough reorganization of the structure and operations of the former Bureau of Technical Services, which has now become the Bureau of Documents, has recently been completed and is described in section B below. The remaining departments of the Secretariat remain relatively unchanged though in some cases, notably the Department of Security Council Affairs, special arrangements have had to be made to cope with a constantly increasing workload.

B. Conference Services

Although the preparations for and conduct of the second regular session of the General Assembly showed a clear improvement when compared with the previous year's performance, certain shortcomings in the technical services had nevertheless been observed by the Advisory Committee on Administrative and Budgetary Questions and were frequently apparent in the results obtained. With the co-operation of the Bureau of Technical Services, a thorough study of its organization and operations was accordingly undertaken by the Management Survey. On the basis of this study, agreement was eventually reached on a detailed plan of reorganization to be put into effect as of 1 April 1948.

The principal element of the reorganization consisted in the integration of the services responsible for producing the official records of meetings in such a way that the manuscript of those records would be completed in the working languages within a single administrative unit. Secondly, a Documents Control Staff was established to review all documents submitted for issue and to record the statistics of all divisions of the Bureau of Documents, as it was renamed. Finally, with the transfer of the Library and certain minor functions from the Bureau to other departments, the Bureau now presents a well-integrated pattern of related services.

An appreciation of the efficiency of the new Bureau of Documents is scarcely possible at this time. Its inauguration coincided with a sharp increase of work which inevitably hindered its settling down, so that the experience of only four to six weeks is available for evaluation. The results will be more apparent during the third regular session of the Assembly, although, of course, conditioned by the special circumstances which will prevail in Paris.

Reference has often been made in meetings of the Fifth Committee and of the Advisory Committee to the backlog of translation, editorial and printing work not accomplished. It was decided at the time of the reorganization that the only method of giving the new Bureau a chance to keep abreast of the current work was to put to one side the whole of this backlog and to liquidate it only as current work allowed.

Finally, emphasis must once more be laid on the problem of flexibility. The number of staff is rigidly controlled throughout the year by budgetary limitations. The Secretary-General is continually seeking the most flexible use of the number of staff members available by promoting dual functions, particularly in the realm of translation, editing and précis-writing; but there is a limit to adaptability. Nor does temporary employment solve the problem of emergency stresses. Skilled technicians are not available at short notice, nor are they willing to leave their homes and occupations for assignments which may last no more than a month. The persistent fluctuation of demand upon the fixed resources of the Secretariat, (as exemplified by the assignment of a numerous staff to Commissions abroad or by the coincidence of the second special session of the General Assembly with previously scheduled meetings of Commissions and Councils), gives rise to constant difficulties in providing the necessary services, to the occasional prolongation of sessions, and to an undesirable delay in granting leave.

This condition, it would seem, can only be remedied by the imposition of a discipline over the demand for conference services comparable to the discipline controlling the resources.

A summary of the progress of the component units of the Bureau of Documents follows.

INTERPRETATION DIVISION

The integration of both types of interpreters (simultaneous and consecutive) has enabled a large degree of flexibility to be achieved, a considerable number of interpreters now being able to use both techniques. Three main committee rooms and one sub-committee room are equipped for telephonic simultaneous interpretation; the remaining committee room and both Council chambers, as well as the General Assembly Hall at Flushing Meadow, are equipped for wireless interpretation. Wireless interpretation was, moreover, used at the Havana Conference, and will be used in Geneva for the seventh session of the Economic and Social Council and in Paris for the third session of the General Assembly. The present staff of interpreters totals seventy-three, including eight in Geneva, three with the Special Committee on the Balkans, and one in India. The staff in 1947 comprised eighty-one interpreters.

OFFICIAL RECORDS DIVISION

This Division comprises verbatim reporters, translators and revisers, and a reconstituted précis-writing service. Records in the working languages are now produced in final manuscript form entirely within the Division, eliminating the administrative control which was necessary when more than one division was involved. At its second regular session, the General Assembly provided for verbatim records only for the meetings of the Security Council and its Commissions, for the meetings of the General Assembly itself, and for one of its Main Committees. As a result, the staff of verbatim reporters had to be reduced to one team. Moreover, the Fifth Committee requested the Secretary-General to approach the Economic and Social Council and the Trusteeship Council to see whether they would be disposed, in view of financial stringencies, to agree f   he present to dispense with written verbatim   ords of their meetings.

During their sessions held in the first half of 1948, members of both Councils, expressing their dissatisfaction with summary records, requested the Secretary-General to provide verbatim reporting services. After the financial and personnel position had been explained, neither Council formally requested the provision of verbatim records; but the Trusteeship Council informed the Secretary-General of its need for such records for meetings at which hearings and certain other forms of testimony were taken. To overcome this difficulty, attempts have been made to avoid simultaneous meetings of the Trusteeship Council and the Security Council; however, owing to the pressure of business of both organs, this has not always been possible.

The production of summary records has suffered from an inadequate number of fully-qualified précis-writers conversant with both working languages. It is hoped, however, that the intensive training provided by continuous service will improve both the quality and the promptness of such records. Nevertheless, the present staff is calculated to cover only six meetings daily, a figure which represents merely the intervals of comparative inactivity. It should be added that interchangeability of staff between the various functions of the Official Records Division is a goal which will be reached only after considerable training.

TRANSLATION DIVISION

This Division represents the former Languages Division, which has, however, been relieved of responsibility for interpretation and for the translation of official records into the working languages. It thus remains responsible for translating all documents other than records and for translating the official records into the three official non-working languages, Chinese,

Russian and Spanish. Translation of the Treaty Series is a responsibility of the Division for which special arrangements have had to be made.

The number of languages from which translations must be made (documents were received in thirty-three languages in the period under review) and the diversity of technical subject-matter combine to make the specialized grouping of translators a matter of some complexity. A Terminology Section has been formed to compile bulletins on special subjects, and to maintain a terminology card-index, which is proving increasingly valuable in economizing the time and ensuring the accuracy of translations.

REPRODUCTION AND DISTRIBUTION DIVISION

This Division represents the former Documents Division less the Printing, Sales and Index Sections. The last two and a part of the first-named were transferred to the Department of Public Information, while the remainder of the Printing Section was re-formed into the Printing Liaison Division. Increased use of the photo-offset printing presses has led to an appreciable economy in contractual letterpress printing.

PRINTING LIAISON DIVISION

Effective management of printing funds requires careful planning and strict collaboration with the Comptroller, the Bureau of Administrative Management and Budget, and the Publications Board. In view of this, and of the fact that a sizeable portion of the annual budget is allocated to printing, it was decided to transform the former Printing Section into a Division. This change in status did not, however, entail an increase in staff, and in the largest Section, Copy Preparation, a reduction of nine posts was effected.

During the twelve months from 1 June 1947 to 31 May 1948, the monthly average of output, both as regards composition and printing, was three times as great as that of the seven preceding months covered in the Secretary-General's annual report of 1947.

DOCUMENTS CONTROL STAFF

This unit, already briefly mentioned, is organized to perform three separate functions aimed at controlling the receipt of documents in the Bureau, co-ordinating their dispersal for the necessary action and recording the working statistics of their progress through the different services. The control of the inflow of documents is the responsibility of the Chief of Editorial Control, whose duty it is to scrutinize all documents for unnecessary duplication, unnecessary length and faulty presentation. A staff of editorial control officers is assigned to work closely with De-

partments submitting documents, in order to deal at the source with many of the problems which might otherwise cause additional work at a later stage. Experience has shown that such pre-editing can be of the greatest value and can be efficiently performed with a minimum of interference with documentary substance.

HEADQUARTERS CONFERENCE SERVICES STATISTICAL SUMMARY

	Headquarters	United Nations Conference on Trade and Employment (Havana)
1. Number of meetings forecast	2,102	222
Number of meetings held	2,398	848
Average number of daily meetings forecast	8.6	
Average number of daily meetings held	9.8	

Average duration of meetings: 2 hours 30 minutes.

2. Number of meetings with: simultaneous interpretation, 1,140; consecutive interpretation, 1,068; verbatim reports, 584; summary records, 1,285

3. Number of pages translated (30 March 1947 to 1 April 1948), 130,086.
   Percentage of translations into: Chinese, 9; English, 16; French, 44; Russian, 18; Spanish, 13.

4. Documents production

	Internal	External printing
Number of jobs	27,567	1,112
Number of pages	255,826	40,487
Number of impressions	219,722,885	237,321,100

EUROPEAN OFFICE, GENEVA

Conferences held in the European Office during the past twelve months comprised 1,837 meetings (not including those of the thirtieth session of the International Labour Conference which met in the premises of the European Office but was not serviced by it). Of this total 1,149 meetings were held by United Nations bodies and 688 by specialized agencies.

Specially noteworthy among conferences held in the European Office were the second session of the Preparatory Commission of the United Nations Conference on Trade and Employment; two sessions of the Economic Commission for Europe; two sessions of the Interim Commission of the World Health Organization; five sessions of the Preparatory Commission for the International Refugee Organization; the third session of the Assembly of the Food and Agriculture Organization; the United Nations Conference on Freedom of Information; the United Nations Maritime Conference; and the second Assembly of the International Civil Aviation Organization.

United Nations Commissions which have been provided with a temporary base in the European Office for periods up to two months include the Special Committee on Palestine, the Special Committee on Balkans, and the Committee of Good Offices on Kashmir.

The specialized agencies with growing secretariats in the European Office are the World Health Organization (111 staff members) and the International Refugee Organization (98 staff members).

On 30 June, the United Nations Secretariat in the European Office totalled 640 staff members. The premises were being used to almost their full capacity.

C. General Services

With the expansion of United Nations interests throughout the world and the concomitant increases in the size and number of United Nations missions, commissions and other conferences meeting abroad, the demand upon the Bureau of General Services has constantly increased during the period under review. The volume of freight moving abroad from headquarters has required the establishment of specialized packing and shipping facilities. A total of 11,801 pieces of freight were shipped during the past twelve months; for the International Trade Conference in Havana, a round-trip movement of 450 persons and 100 tons of equipment and supplies was required. A corresponding increase affected the Transportation Service during the eleven months to 31 May 1948, during which period 7,370 travel reservations, 5,792 hotel reservations, and 4,798 passport, visa and *laissez-passer* transactions were executed. Approximately 930 *laissez-passer* have been issued. United Nations vehicles during the same period travelled 1,012,303 miles carrying 72,108 passengers. Aeroplanes have been obtained on charter for the United Nations Mediator in Palestine and for the Committee of Good Offices on Kashmir.

Communications between headquarters, the European Office, regional offices and special missions and conferences abroad have been improved by the institution of a diplomatic pouch service, based on the General Convention on the Privileges and Immunities of the United Nations. At the request of the General Assembly at its second regular session, studies are being conducted with regard to the feasibility of establishing a United Nations postal service.

While the establishment and operation of United Nations offices and commissions abroad have required an expansion in certain phases of General Services, the emphasis at headquarters has been placed upon consolidating and stabilizing existing programmes. The problem of office space has been resolved to a considerable extent by the acquisition of the Manhattan Office Building at the permanent site, the centralization of United Nations metropolitan offices in that building, the utilization of 43,000 square feet of additional space at Lake Success, and the discontinuance of leases in three widely separated buildings in the metropolitan area. A programme for improving existing working conditions at headquarters is now under way; as a first step an allotment of $50,000 has been granted for this work. The safety and fire protection programme instituted in 1946 brought down the insurance rates, effective 1 June 1947, to 25 per cent of the former rate.

D. Staff Administration

(a) RECRUITMENT AND APPOINTMENTS

Recruitment from outside the United States of America has continued, principally through recruitment representatives who have covered the European area and twenty-three countries in other regions of the world. Recently, a special recruitment trip was made to the Middle East.

Progress in the system of recruitment and promotion by competitive tests has been achieved in three main directions:

(i) Plans for recruiting by examination about twenty young trainees from India and Latin America have been formulated. It is hoped that, by this means, candidates of high calibre will be added to the permanent cadre of the Secretariat;

(ii) Three competitions for linguistic candidates have been held. It has been found possible to use joint examinations for translators and précis-writers to be attached to the Translation and the Official Records Divisions respectively, and to arrive at a common principle of devising and administering these examinations;

(iii) A series of tests has been organized within the Secretariat to find young people well fitted for advancement to junior administrative posts. From those whose promise is high enough to suggest a bright future, it is hoped to select a few individuals and to place them in the same category as the trainees. The trainee scheme is thereby opened to internal as well as to external competition.

One special problem has been the staffing of missions. Partly by transfer of existing staff members and partly by initial recruitment, 180 persons have been sent (as of 30 June 1948) on mission assignments with the United Nations Special Committee on the Balkans; the Committee of Good Offices on the Indonesian Question; the Committee of Good Offices on Kashmir; the United Nations Temporary Commission on Korea; the United Nations Truce Commission for Palestine; and the Visiting Mission to East Africa.

The Personnel Selection Committee, established by the Secretary-General in the summer of 1946 for the purpose of considering and reviewing the qualifications of personnel recommended by department heads for permanent appointment in the Secretariat, had held 104 meetings by 15 June of this year and had considered 1,129 nominations. The position, as of 30 June, was that out of 2,865 established posts of all grades at headquarters (excluding purely temporary groups of personnel), indeterminate appointments had been given to or recommended by the Committee for 865 members of the staff. Of these totals, the corresponding figures for established posts of grade 8 and above (i.e. for other than secretarial, clerical and manual workers) were 1,368 and 539 respectively.

(b) Geographical distribution

Within the provisions of the Charter establishing efficiency, competence and integrity as the first considerations, the entire recruitment and placement programme has been directed to the improvement of geographical distribution. In this connexion, the Secretary-General has established the policy that, within the high standards required by the Charter, and until a more balanced distribution is achieved, in every appointment to the Secretariat above grade 7 consideration will be given to the improvement, both in number and rank, of the geographical distribution of the staff. The policy provides also that, for the time being, no further appointments are to be made from over-represented countries unless it is demonstrated that suitably qualified candidates from under-represented countries are not available, and (save where the need for filling the post is urgent and could not have been foreseen) that sufficient time has been allowed for reasonable local inquiry in the under-represented countries if the records available at headquarters do not include those of qualified candidates from such countries.

These principles are also to be taken fully into account whenever the contracts of existing staff members are under review. The Bureau of Personnel, in accordance with the recommendations of the Advisory Committee on Administrative and Budgetary Questions, as endorsed by the General Assembly at its second regular session, has conducted an extensive review of the qualifications and experience of the present members of the staff with a view to replacing those who do not reach the high standards necessary. As a result of this concentrated effort, there has been a slow but steady improvement in the geographical distribution picture, on which the Secretary-General will present a special and more detailed report to the General Assembly at its next session.

(c) Salaries and allowances

Salary schedules

The schedule of annual *net* (i.e. tax-exempt) salaries, adopted in the present form as of 16 June 1947, includes nineteen grades. The lowest grades represent the best salaries paid in the headquarters area for clerical and secretarial work (converted from a gross to net basis); the highest grades represent the rate adopted by the General Assembly for the post of top-ranking director ($11,000). Grades are divided into a series of seven step rates in order to provide for a system of periodical salary increments in recognition of satisfactory service. The schedule of *gross* rates for manual workers engaged at headquarters was developed after considering the best rates paid in the locality for similar work and, in order to conform with local practices, was fixed on an hourly basis. The wages of manual workers engaged at offices away from headquarters are also fixed in accordance with local customs and practices.

The salary and wage rates at headquarters were developed on the basis of conditions prevailing in the area in May 1946. Subsequently, a system of cost-of-living adjustments was adopted as a flexible means of meeting changing conditions in the area without having to change base salary rates. The revised cost-of-living adjustments instituted on 16 June 1947 for staff members in the New York and Washington, D. C. areas have remained in effect during the past year: namely, $240 for all staff members without dependants at $6,700 and below; $450 for staff members with dependants below $6,700; and $300 for those at $6,700. No allowance is paid to staff members receiving salaries of more than $6,700. Comparable cost-of-living adjustments are provided for workers paid on an hourly basis. The necessity for an increase in these rates is under study and, should a decision be made to alter the present rates, a supplementary estimate will be submitted as indicated in the foreword to the 1949 budget estimates.

At offices away from headquarters, salary differentials (i.e. percentage differences ranging from plus 30 to minus 25) from United Nations headquarters rates to cover differences in living costs and other conditions, have been established and are reviewed from time to time. A committee of cost-of-living experts, appointed by the United Nations and certain of the specialized agencies, has been working during the past year to develop more accurate methods of measuring cost-of-living differences between countries, as a basis for fixing differentials.

Classification of posts

Basically, the classification plan included in the provisional salary and wage administration plan of 1946 has remained unchanged. During the past year, however, efforts have been made to simplify this plan by establishing standard post descriptions written in concise terms in lieu of detailed individual job descriptions; by reducing to a minimum the number of categories necessary to cover the various types of posts within the Secretariat; and by assigning within each category only the number of grades justified by substantial differences as to duties, responsibilities and authorities. This plan, which is to be introduced in the form of a manual of standard post descriptions, is now well advanced.

Allowances and grants

The system of special allowances and grants for regular members of the staff, which was installed as of 16 June 1947, has been continued during the past year with very few changes. These allowances may be divided into three broad categories: namely, those applying to any staff member under particular circumstances; those applying to staff recruited from outside the local area; and those applying to staff recruited from outside the country as well as from outside the local area. Allowances and grants currently in force are as follows:

Travel. The schedule of travel subsistence allowance rates established in February 1947 is still in effect for any staff member who may be in official travel status. It has, however, been found desirable in some cases to establish special rates (some higher and some lower than the standard rates) for members of the staff assigned to missions and conferences, in order to provide allowances commensurate with actual living expenses. A policy has also been adopted of requiring staff below the rank of director to travel wherever possible in cabin class or in comparable accommodations on steamers rather than by first class. Such staff members are required to travel on home leave by cabin class or its equivalent;

Children's allowances and education grants. In accordance with resolution 161 (II) adopted by the General Assembly on 20 November 1947, children's allowances and education grants were increased from $144 to $200 per year for each eligible child, effective 1 January 1948. Adjustments (both upward and downward from $200) have been made in the children's allowance at duty stations where the salary scales are subject to a plus or minus differential;

Installation allowances. Provision is made for assisting in meeting the installation costs of staff members recruited from outside the local area of the duty station, by payments in the form of daily living allowances and installation grants. There has been no change in these allowances during the past year. The daily living allowance, which is payable at rates from $5 to $7 per day for the first sixty days, with graduated additions for dependants, is designed to compensate each of these staff members for the initial extraordinary living costs incurred during the period immediately following his entry on duty. The purpose of the lump sum installation grant, which is payable to staff members with contracts of one year or longer, and amounts to $125 for single staff members and $200 for those with dependants, is to help each of these staff members to meet the costs of equipping a new home;

Rental allowance. The rental allowance which, subject to certain limitations, amounts on the average to about 25 per cent of the rent a staff member is required to pay and is payable to headquarters staff recruited from outside the area is, in effect, a special cost-of-living adjustment. Housing conditions in the New York area following the war period were such that residents of the area normally residing in rent-controlled housing had the advantage of rentals more than 25 per cent lower than those available to persons coming from outside the area, since the newcomer usually had to accept accommodations in housing which had not been under rent control or housing which had been newly constructed and the rates for which were substantially higher. This situation has not changed appreciably during the past year;

Expatriation allowance. The expatriation allowance, instituted on 16 June 1947 as an integral part of the allowance system, is payable (at $250 per year for single staff members and $500 per year for those with dependants) to staff recruited from outside the country of their duty station, and is designed to compensate for the added costs and disadvantages of living away from home. In order to implement the decision of the General Assembly during its second regular session, action has been taken to discontinue payment of the allowance to staff members on their completion of two years of service away from the home country. It is felt, however, that payment of this allowance to eligible staff members on a continuing basis is fully justified. A recommendation to this effect is embodied in the budget estimates for 1949.

Home leave

The home leave provisions were revised on 15 April 1948 to grant home leave at any time during the calendar year in which the staff member's two years of service would be completed. A maximum travel time of thirty days for the round-trip journey was established, with time in excess of thirty days being chargeable to annual leave. If home leave is postponed for two years, because of the exigencies of the service or at the staff member's request when travel time would exceed thirty days, the period of leave is increased to four working weeks and the travel time is increased to a maximum of sixty days. Advance home leave will be granted only in exceptional circumstances after a minimum of twelve months of service.

(d) Joint Staff Pension Scheme

Since the Joint Staff Pension Scheme was inaugurated on 27 January 1947, the Staff Benefit Committee, which was entrusted by the General Assembly with the administration of the scheme, has held numerous meetings for the purpose of admitting new members and authorizing the payment of benefits. At 31 May 1948, the membership in the scheme exceeded 1,500.

In accordance with resolution 162 (II) adopted by the General Assembly at its second regular session, the Staff Benefit Committee has reconsidered the proposals for a permanent pension scheme presented to that session. The new proposals prepared by the Committee were submitted to the Advisory Committee on Administrative and Budgetary Questions at its first session in 1948, and the Advisory Committee presented its observations thereon in its first report for 1948. In the light of these observations, the Staff Benefit Committee again revised its proposals for a permanent scheme, and these, in their final form, will be presented to the third session of the General Assembly.

Those features of the United Nations Pension Scheme of special interest to the specialized agencies were also considered by the Secretary-General's Committee on Co-ordination.

The first balance sheet and report on the operations of the Pension Fund will be presented to the third session of the Assembly.

(e) International Civil Service Advisory Board

During the past year, further consideration has been given by the Co-ordination Committee and its Consultative Committee on Administrative Questions to the functions and composition of the International Civil Service Advisory Board. As a result, the Board's terms of reference were slightly revised and agreement was reached on a list of persons to be appointed as Board members. Letters of appointment are to be sent by the Secretary-General in July, and the first meeting of the Board is tentatively scheduled for January or February 1949.

The Board's purpose will be to contribute to the improvement of recruitment and related phases of personnel administration in all the international organizations through:

(i) Advice and the interchange of information on methods of recruitment and on the means by which appropriate standards of recruitment in the Secretariat and the specialized agencies may be ensured;

(ii) Consideration, at the request of the Co-ordination Committee, of related phases of personnel administration, and developing and making recommendations for guiding principles and appropriate policies arising from the consideration of such problems.

(f) Staff training and welfare activities

The programme of training and information for members of the staff has emphasized special orientation for newcomers, language training and general orientation lectures. Eleven hundred staff members participated in this year's language courses. The lectures included a series on American life, given in co-operation with Columbia University, a series on United Nations activities for staff going on home leave, and an informational series for staff going to Paris. *Secretariat News,* a house organ, published semi-monthly, includes information of general interest to the staff.

An eight-week internship programme, enabling students to receive a close insight into the workings of an international organization, was conducted from 15 January to 5 March 1948. A similar programme will commence on 12 July 1948, with forty-three students from thirty-three countries and eleven internes who have received scholarships sponsored by philanthropic and educational institutions. The internes for the international programme, who were chosen from candidates nominated by Member Governments, will receive a living allowance through the financial support of the Rotary International, the Carnegie Endowment for International Peace and the Hugh Moore Memorial Fund. Internes are assigned to posts throughout the Secretariat and work a regular workweek, without pay.

Staff medical and housing programmes

During the past twelve months, 17,360 visits were made to the health clinic for first aid or general medical treatment. The largest number of visits for any single illness was for upper respiratory infections. There were 6,980 visits for health education and preventive medicine, which included two chest X-ray surveys covering 2,477 members of the Secretariat, delegations, cafeteria staff and contractors. In addition, immunization and physical examinations have been given to all staff members going abroad. The clinic has taken over the liaison work with the Health Insurance Plan of Greater New York, Blue Cross and United Medical Service, as well as all medical insurance reporting and filing of compensation reports. Health regulations and standards for the United Nations nursery school were set up by the clinic, which is responsible for health supervision and routine inspection of the children in the school.

The housing difficulties of the staff have been alleviated as a result of the availability of some 400 apartments in the second United Nations housing project, at Parkway Village. When completed this project will have over 600 apartments as compared with 143 apartments in the first housing project at Great Neck.

Staff activities

Through the Carnegie Endowment for International Peace, the Volunteer Services Office has been established to take over the work of the Staff Activities Section, which was abolished at the end of 1947. These services are under the guidance of a director, paid by the Carnegie Endowment, and a group of thirty-five to forty volunteers donate their time one or two days a week. The services include supervisory duties in connexion with various invitations extended to staff members and their families, and a staff information desk providing facilities on travel, vacations, shopping, education, entertainment and the arts. These services are also available to members of the delegations and their families in so far as possible. A recreation committee was established to stimulate and encourage the formation and growth of United Nations clubs. The international nursery school began operations this year, and a parents' association was created for the purpose of establishing an international school at both elementary and secondary grade levels.

(g) Appeals

From the date of the constitution of the Appeals Board, 3 April 1947, up to 30 June 1948, sixteen separate Boards, with the Chairman and Secretary as the only permanent members, have held sixty-five meetings, three preliminary meetings having been devoted to the adoption of rules of procedure. Of the issues dealt with by the Board, ten involved appeals against termination, including disciplinary action; five concerned allowances; one an advisory opinion; and three, decisions of principle. During this period, six appeals were withdrawn after favourable action by the Administration; twelve were held to be non-receivable for non-observance of procedure; approximately thirty did not materialize after the preliminary notices were given. To date, the Board has sent ten texts of advices to the Secretary-General, five of which have been accepted. In two other cases, the Secretary-General partially accepted the Board's advices; in one case, he accepted the minority advice. As of 30 June, the Secretary-General's decision was pending in the remaining two cases.

(h) Staff Committee

Close relations have been maintained with the Staff Committee, which has continued during the past twelve months to play an active role in making known to the Administration the views of the staff in matters affecting its general interests. In particular, the Administration has found it helpful to continue the policy initiated in 1947 of communicating to the Staff Committee, for its comments and suggestions, all proposed actions relating to such questions as salaries and allowances, appointments, promotions, housing, transport, welfare, discipline and general conditions of work.

E. Headquarters of the United Nations

Preparations for building the permanent headquarters on the site in New York City selected by the General Assembly at its first session have progressed materially during the year. Unfortunately, however, the beginning of actual construction was delayed for the reasons outlined below.

The basic design for the permanent headquarters was established by a Board of Design Consultants, composed of prominent architects and engineers from different parts of the world who served under the leadership of the Director of Planning. The plan was composed of the following main elements: the General Assembly Hall, a Secretariat office building, a conference area for Council chambers and committee rooms, and underground garages, with appropriate landscaping of the entire site. The plan also incorporated the programme of the City of New York for the development of adjacent areas and approaches to the site.

Construction cost estimates for the project, according to the original plan, indicated that approximately $84,000,000 would be required for its execution. In view of prevailing world economic conditions, this expenditure was considered to be somewhat higher than was justified for the Organization's immediate needs. After consultation with the Headquarters Advisory Committee, the plans were accordingly readjusted, as a result of which the estimated cost was reduced to $65,000,000.

After all possible methods of financing the construction programme had been fully explored, the conclusion was reached that a loan from one or more of the Member Governments offered the only feasible solution of the problem. During the second regular session of the General Assembly, the United States delegation informed the Secretary-General that the Government of the United States of America would be prepared to enter into negotiations with a view to concluding a loan agreement whereby an interest-free United States Government loan would be made available for the purpose of financing all or part of the cost of constructing the headquarters. It was understood that such a loan would be subject to Congressional approval, and that it would be for an amount not to exceed $65,000,000, repayable in annual instalments from the ordinary budget of the United Nations over a period to be determined by negotiations. The President of the United States signified his willingness to request such an approval by the Congress on the conclusion of the negotiations between the Secretary-General and the United States Government.

The General Assembly, by resolution 182 (II) on 20 November 1947, unanimously approved the design as set forth in a report presented by the Secretary-General; and authorization was given to him to negotiate and conclude, on behalf of the United Nations, an agreement with the Government of the United States of America for an interest-free loan not to exceed $65,000,000. On receipt of the loan, the Secretary-General was further authorized to proceed with the construction and furnishing of the headquarters, together with appropriate site development. In carrying out this responsibility, he was to be assisted by a Headquarters Advisory Committee consisting of the representatives of sixteen Member Governments.

After several months of negotiations with the United States Government, a general understanding was reached on the terms of the proposed loan. A draft of the agreement was submitted to the Headquarters Advisory Committee and considered by that committee on 25 February 1948. With the approval of the Committee, further negotiations were held with the United States Government, and the agreement was signed on 23 March 1948. The loan agreement provides for repayment of the loan over a period of thirty-one years in annual instalments ranging from $1,000,000 to $2,500,000, the payments to begin on 1 July 1951 and continue through 1 July 1982.

The United States Senate unanimously approved the agreement during the summer of 1948. The House of Representatives, whose approval was also required, failed to bring the proposal to a vote before adjournment, although its Committee on Foreign Affairs had unanimously reported in favour of it. The situation as of 30 June was, therefore, that the actual beginning of construction was awaiting the completion of Congressional approval to make available the money provided for under the agreement.

The General Assembly resolution of 20 November 1947 authorized as an interim measure the immediate expenditure of $1,000,000 from the Working Capital Fund for the continuation of planning work and the preparation of detailed drawings and specifications. Early in 1948, the Headquarters Planning Office began the task of preparing detailed construction plans. Research studies were also undertaken to explore the most advanced techniques and methods covering the field of mechanical installations, building materials, lighting, acoustics, ventilation, communications and circulation.

As the planning has progressed, cost estimates have been periodically rechecked in order to ensure that the cost of the project will not exceed the $65,000,000. This has necessitated certain minor revisions and readjustments, in view of the rise in building costs and the need for conforming to fluctuations in the programme of requirements. Such changes were adopted after discussion with the Headquarters Advisory Committee.

While some design problems of a non-structural character are still in the developmental stage, final working drawings needed to award excavation and construction contracts will be completed in August 1948. Ninety-five per cent of all demolition work is finished and arrangements have been made for the relocation of residential tenants occupying the few remaining buildings on the site. The area on which buildings are to be constructed has been cleared; it is expected that the entire site clearance programme will be finished in August 1948.

The Manhattan Office Building, which is located on the permanent site, was acquired from the City of New York on a lease-purchase arrangement in August 1947. This seven-story office building has been in use since September 1947. It serves as the Manhattan headquarters for the Organization, housing several delegations and Secretariat offices.

F. Finance

(a) WORKING CAPITAL FUND

By resolution 166 (II) adopted by the General Assembly at its second regular session, the Working Capital Fund was maintained at $20,000,000. Under the authorities established in that resolution, there had been advanced, as at 31 May 1948, the following amounts from the Working Capital Fund:

	$ US
(i) To finance budgetary expenditures pending the receipt of contributions	7,779,476.67
(ii) Loans to specialized agencies	2,823,691.55

(iii) Advances for staff housing, motor vehicle purchases, etc.......	511,608.70
(iv) Advances for unforeseen and extraordinary expenses.......	201,180.19
(v) Other (including permanent headquarters site, $2,093,073.28)..	2,292,553.13

TOTAL 13,608,510.24

In addition to the outstanding advances shown above, authorizations issued under resolution 166 (II) for which funds have not yet been disbursed amounted to $2,465,362.50, leaving a balance of $3,926,127.26 in the Working Capital Fund. Under the terms of the resolution, Member Governments were to make advances to the Working Capital Fund in accordance with the scale adopted for contributions to the third annual budget (1948).

(b) CONTRIBUTIONS TO THE 1946, 1947 AND 1948 BUDGETS

The status of contributions to the 1946, 1947 and 1948 budgets, up to 30 June 1948, was as follows:

	Total amount	Paid (In $US)	Balance due
Assessments for the year 1946..........	19,386,378.36[1]	19,379,494.36 (99.9 per cent)	6,884.00
Assessments for the year 1947..........	27,450,000.00[2]	27,383,009.87 (99.8 per cent)	66,990.13
Assessments for the year 1948..........	34,775,775.00[3]	9,219,482.03 (26.5 per cent)	25,556,292.97
Working Capital Fund................	20,000,000.00	19,938,000.00 (99.7 per cent)	62,000.00
	101,612,153.36	75,919,986.26	25,692,167.10

[1] Appropriations, $19,390,000, less estimated miscellaneous income, $160,000, plus assessments for Afghanistan, Iceland and Sweden, $156,378.36.

[2] Appropriations, $27,740,000, less estimated miscellaneous income, $133,621.64 and assessments for new Members entering during 1946 as noted in [1] above, $156,378.36.

[3] Appropriations, $34,825,195, less estimated miscellaneous income for 1948, $761,727, less increase in estimated miscellaneous income for 1947, $191,998.08, less excess of appropriations for 1946 over obligations incurred, $59,712.52; plus supplementary appropriations in respect of 1947, $876,568, plus excess of estimated over actual miscellaneous revenue received during 1946, $87,449.60.

In effect, the 1947 scale of assessments was continued in 1948 with certain minor adjustments. The assessment of 3.9 per cent previously established for India was continued for India and Pakistan, subject to an inter-governmental adjustment between the two States. The assessment for Sweden was reduced from 3.25 per cent to 2.04 per cent, while assessments were established for Siam and Yemen, consequent on their admission to membership, at 0.27 per cent and 0.04 per cent respectively.

Under the authority granted the Secretary-General by resolution 163 (II) of 20 November 1947 to accept a portion of the contributions of Member States for the financial year 1948 in currencies other than United States dollars, and after consultation with the Chairman of the Committee on Contributions, the Secretary-General advised the Member States of the percentages of their 1948 contributions which could be paid in the currencies of France, the Netherlands and Switzerland. These percentages were based on estimated 1948 United Nations expenditures in those countries in respect of the third session of the General Assembly, the International Court of Justice and the European Office, respectively.

The total percentage which could be accepted in currencies other than U.S. dollars was 20.5 per cent of the 1948 assessments on Member States other than the United States of America, as follows:

	Per cent
French francs	5.5
Netherlands guilders	2.5
Swiss francs	12.5

Under this arrangement Members, other than the United States could have elected to pay in the above currencies approximately the equivalent of $4,300,000. Seventeen Member States availed themselves of this opportunity, to the amount of $3,860,000.

(c) Status of the 1947 Budget

As required by regulation 33 of the Provisional Financial Regulations of the United Nations, the financial report and accounts of the United Nations for the year ending 31 December 1947 were submitted to the Board of Auditors for audit early in 1948. The financial report and the report of the Board of Auditors have been prepared for distribution to Members. Copies were made available to the Advisory Committee on Administrative and Budgetary Questions in accordance with the provisions of regulation 34 (e) of the Provisional Financial Regulations.

The financial report for the year 1947, duly certified by the Board of Auditors, shows that total obligations for the year amounted to $27,290,241.21 against appropriations of $28,616,568 voted by the General Assembly, leaving an unobligated balance of appropriations of $1,326,326.79.

Under the terms of General Assembly resolution 74 (I) of 7 December 1946, the period of office of the "Auditor-General (or officer holding equivalent title)" of the Ukrainian Soviet Socialist Republic was to expire on 30 June 1948. The General Assembly, at its second regular session, appointed the "Auditor-General (or officer holding equivalent title)" of Colombia to the forthcoming vacancy for a three-year term commencing 1 July 1948 (resolution 150 (II) of 1 November 1947).

(d) Status of the 1948 Budget

At its second regular session, the General Assembly approved a budget of $34,825,195 for the expenses of the Organization during the financial year 1948 (resolution 166 (II), part A, 20 November 1947). As at 31 May 1948, obligations and expenditures under these appropriations amounted to $12,437,971, leaving a balance of $22,387,224 for expenses during the last seven months of the year, including the expenses of the General Assembly in Paris.

Under part B of resolution 166 (II) (unforeseen and extraordinary expenses), the General Assembly authorized the Secretary-General, with the prior concurrence of the Advisory Committee on Administrative and Budgetary Questions, to enter into commitments to meet unforeseen and extraordinary expenses for which no provision had been made in the budget; provision was made that the concurrence of the Advisory Committee would not be necessary for commitments not exceeding $2,000,000, provided that they were certified by the Secretary-General as relating to the maintenance of peace and security, or to economic rehabilitation. As at 20 June 1948, commitments under this authorization amounted to $977,040, and covered expenses in connexion with the Committee of Good Offices on the Indonesian Question, with Palestine and the City of Jerusalem, the Economic Commission for Latin America, and the second special session of the General Assembly.

Authority was also given under part B of the resolution for such commitments as might be necessary, not exceeding $75,000, for hearing cases of the International Court of Justice away from The Hague, under Article 22 of the Statute of the International Court of Justice. As at 31 May 1948, no commitments of this nature had been entered into.

In accordance with the terms of the resolution relating to unforeseen and extraordinary expenses, the Secretary-General will submit to the third session of the General Assembly a report on all commitments entered into under this resolution, together with supplementary estimates in respect thereof. A review of budget expenses is now in course of completion, to determine to what extent it may be possible to absorb unforeseen expenses within the main budget appropriations for 1948 without supplementary appropriations.

By part B of resolution 181 (II) of 29 November 1947, the Secretary-General was given authority by the General Assembly to draw upon the Working Capital Fund in amounts not exceeding $2,000,000 for expenses in connexion with the United Nations Commission for Palestine. Expenses of the Commission incurred in the early part of the year amounted to about $130,000. The Commission was relieved from the further exercise of its responsibilities by resolution 186 (S-2), III, adopted by the General Assembly at its second special session on 14 May 1948.

At its second regular session, the General Assembly, by resolution 182 (II) of 20 November 1947, also authorized the Secretary-General, subject to the prior concurrence of the Advisory Committee, to obligate Working Capital Fund resources in amounts not exceeding $1,000,000 for the purpose of continuing in 1948 necessary work in connexion with the permanent headquarters of the United Nations. Commitments in this connexion to the amount of $755,000 have been authorized with the concurrence of the Advisory Committee.

(e) THE 1949 BUDGET ESTIMATES

The Budget Estimates for the financial year 1949, which are being presented to the General Assembly in a separate document, amount to $33,469,587 as compared with $34,825,195 for the financial year 1948, a decrease of $1,355,608. The main elements involved in the decrease are:

(a) Reduced cost of the General Assembly in 1949. In 1948 the General Assembly is being held in Europe, thus necessitating a larger outlay of funds;

(b) No provision is made in the 1949 estimates for the continuation of missions to Greece and Korea.

The budget document for 1949 has been developed to include various detailed schedules and tables of comparison, in accordance with the requests made by the Advisory Committee on Administrative and Budgetary Questions.

(f) TAX EQUALIZATION

The Convention on the Privileges and Immunities of the United Nations has been commented upon elsewhere in this report.[1] The relation of the Convention to the question of tax equalization was considered by the General Assembly at its second regular session. At that session the Assembly adopted, on 20 November 1947, resolution 160 (II) again requesting all Members which had not yet fully acceded to the Convention to take the necessary legislative action to do so in order to exempt their nationals employed by the United Nations from national income taxation; and, pending such action, to grant relief from double taxation to their nationals employed by the United Nations.

By the same resolution the Secretary-General was requested to prepare and submit to the next regular session of the General Assembly a Staff Contributions Plan in accordance with the recommendations of the Advisory Committee. This Staff Contributions (or Assessment) Plan has been prepared and was submitted to the Advisory Committee for consideration at its June session.

Further, in accordance with resolution 160

[1] See page 110.

(II), the Secretary-General has omitted from personnel contracts any clause which binds the Organization to refund national income taxation in the absence of annual authorization by the General Assembly. The programme for reimbursement of national income taxation has, in the meatime, been continued under the authorization of the General Assembly in respect of the years 1946, 1947 and 1948.

(g) INVESTMENTS

The Investments Committee, appointed under General Assembly resolution 155 (II), held its first session in April 1948 to consider, principally, the investment of the Pension and Provident Funds. Its recommendations have been accepted by the Secretary-General, and steps have been taken, in accordance with those recommendations, with the object of obtaining the 2½ per cent interest required by the Pension Scheme.

(h) TRANSFER OF THE ASSETS OF THE LEAGUE OF NATIONS

In accordance with the terms of the "Common Plan" (General Assembly resolution 24 (I) of 12 February 1946), the material assets of the League of Nations were transferred to the United Nations in 1946. The valuation of the assets was established at $10,809,529.21; credits to the equivalent amount have been recorded on the books of the United Nations.

Under the provisions of the Common Plan, the United Nations agreed that the credits arising from the transfer would be distributed in accordance with percentages laid down by the League of Nations, and that the General Assembly would decide on the purposes to which, and the dates on which, these credits should be applied, provided that, in any case, the credits should begin to be available not later than 31 December 1948.

The Fifth Committee, in its report to the General Assembly at the second part of the first session, took note of the intention of certain Members to arrange for discussions to consider an arrangement under which all former members of the League of Nations now Members of the United Nations could be allocated a share in the credit on a basis comparable with that applicable to members of the League of Nations as set out in the League of Nations scheme of distribution. Up to this time, the Secretary-General has received no indication that the discussions referred to have taken place.

SALES AGENTS OF THE UNITED NATIONS PUBLICATIONS

ARGENTINA
Editorial Sudamericana·S.A.
Alsina 500
BUENOS AIRES

AUSTRALIA
H. A. Goddard Pty. Ltd.
255a George Street
SYDNEY, N. S. W.

BELGIUM
Agence et Messageries de la
Presse, S. A.
14-22 rue du Persil
BRUXELLES

BOLIVIA
Librería Científica y Literaria
Avenida 16 de Julio, 216
Casilla 972
LA PAZ

CANADA
The Ryerson Press
299 Queen Street West
TORONTO

CHILE
Edmundo Pizarro
Merced 846
SANTIAGO

CHINA
The Commercial Press Ltd.
211 Honan Road
SHANGHAI

COLOMBIA
Librería Latina Ltda.
Apartado Aéreo 4011
BOGOTA

COSTA RICA
Trejos Hermanos
Apartado 1313
SAN JOSÉ

CUBA
La Casa Belga ·
René de Smedt
O'Reilly 455
LA HABANA

CZECHOSLOVAKIA
F. Topic
Narodni Trida 9
PRAHA 1

DENMARK
Einar Munksgaard
Nørregade 6
KøBENHAVN

DOMINICAN REPUBLIC
Librería Dominicana
Calle Mercedes No. 49
Apartado 656
CIUDAD TRUJILLO

ECUADOR
Muñoz Hermanos y Cía.
Nueve de Octubre 703
Casilla 10-24
GUAYAQUIL

EGYPT
Librairie "La Renaissance d'Egypte"
9 Sh. Adly Pasha
CAIRO

FINLAND
Akateeminen Kirjakauppa
2, Keskuskatu
HELSINKI

FRANCE
Editions A. Pedone
13, rue Soufflot
PARIS, Vᵉ

GREECE
"Eleftheroudakis"
Librairie internationale
Place de la Constitution
ATHÈNES

GUATEMALA
José Goubaud
Goubaud & Cía. Ltda.
Sucesor
5a Av. Sur No. 6 y 9a C. P.
GUATEMALA

HAITI
Max Bouchereau
Librairie "A la Caravelle"
Boîte postale 111-B
PORT-AU-PRINCE

INDIA
Oxford Book & Stationery Company
Scindia House
NEW DELHI

IRAN
Bongahe Piaderow
731 Shah Avenue
TEHERAN

IRAQ
Mackenzie & Mackenzie
The Bookshop
BAGHDAD

LEBANON
Librairie universelle
BEYROUTH

LUXEMBOURG
Librairie J. Schummer
Place Guillaume
LUXEMBOURG

NETHERLANDS
N. V. Martinus Nijhoff
Lange Voorhout 9
s'GRAVENHAGE

NEW ZEALAND
Gordon & Gotch, Ltd.
Waring Taylor Street
WELLINGTON

NICARAGUA
Ramiro Ramírez V.
Agencia de Publicaciones
MANAGUA, D. N.

NORWAY
Johan Grundt Tanum Forlag
Kr. Augustgt. 7A
OSLO

PHILIPPINES
D. P. Pérez Co.
132 Riverside
SAN JUAN

SWEDEN
A.-B. C. E. Fritzes Kungl.
Hofbokhandel
Fredsgatan 2
STOCKHOLM

SWITZERLAND
Librairie Payot S. A.
LAUSANNE, GENÈVE, VEVEY,
MONTREUX, NEUCHÂTEL,
BERNE, BASEL
Hans Raunhardt
Kirchgasse 17
ZURICH I

SYRIA
Librairie universelle
DAMAS

TURKEY
Librairie Hachette
469 Istiklal Caddesi
BEYOGLU-ISTANBUL

UNION OF SOUTH AFRICA
Central News Agency
Commissioner & Rissik Sts.
JOHANNESBURG and at CAPETOWN
and DURBAN

UNITED KINGDOM
H. M. Stationery Office
P. O. Box 569
LONDON, S.E. 1
and at H.M.S.O. Shops in
LONDON, EDINBURGH, MANCHESTER,
CARDIFF, BELFAST and BRISTOL

UNITED STATES OF AMERICA
International Documents Service
Columbia University Press
2960 Broadway
NEW YORK 27, N. Y.

URUGUAY
Oficina de Representación de
Editoriales
Av. 18 de Julio 1333 Esc. 1
MONTEVIDEO

VENEZUELA
Escritoría Pérez Machado
Conde a Piñango 11
CARACAS

YUGOSLAVIA
Drzavno Preduzece
Jugoslovenska Knjiga
Moskovska Ul. 36
BEOGRAD   [48E3]

Printed in France.   Price in the United States: $1.50   5 September 1948

355

제3부 | 유엔한국위원단 보고서 (1949)

1. 유엔한국위원단 보고서 제1권

해제문서 19 : A/936 (Report of the United Nations Commission on Korea, Volume I)

문서명	Report of the United Nations Commission on Korea, Volume I		
	유엔한국위원단 보고서 제1권		
발신	유엔한국위원단	생성일시	
		발신일시	1949년 8월
수신	유엔총회	수신일시	
		문서번호	Official Records: Fourth Session Supplement No.9 (A/936)
문서형태	보고서	문서분량	41쪽
주제명	1. 유엔한국위원단의 창설 : 권한, 구성과 조직 2. 유엔한국위원단 및 부속기관의 주요활동 개요 3. 정치 · 경제 · 사회 발전과 한국의 독립 및 통일 문제에 영향을 주는 요인들 4. 요약 분석 그리고 결론		
주요내용	본 문서는 1948년 12월 12일, 유엔총회 결의 195(III)에 의하여 창설된 유엔한 국위원단이 도착한 1949년 1월 30일부터 1949년 7월 28일까지의 활동을 기록한 보고서 제1권에 해당하는 것으로 제2권 부속 문서(A.936.Add.1)와 함께 총 2권의 보고서로 구성됨. 상세한 내용은 본문 참조.		
검색어	최고인민회의(Supreme People's Assembly), 남로당(South Korea Labour Party), 민족자주연맹(National Independence Federation), 민족청년단(National Youth Corps), 민족청년방위단(National Youth Defence Corps), 조국통일민주주의전선(Democratic Front for the Attainment of Unification for the Fatherland), 민주국민당(Democratic Nationalist Party), 전국애국단체연합회(National Federation of Patriotic Organization), 한국국방군(Korean Security Force), 한국독립당(Korean Independence Party), 한국민주당(Hankook Democratice Party), 조선민주주의인민공화국, (미)경제협조처(Economic Cooperation Administration, ECA), 조선경비대(Korean Constabulary), 주한미군 군사고문단(Korean Military Advisory Group, KMAG), 서북청년단(Northwest Youth Corps) 공진항, 김구, 김규식, 김동원, 김성수, 김약수, 김병회, 김일성, 모윤숙, 백남훈, 변영태, 신익희, 이춘호, 장면, 장기영, 조병옥, 지대형, 윤치창, 정한경, 정환범, 최창순, 리우위안(Liu Yu-Wan), 슈튜(Ting T. Ssutu), 코스티유(Henry Costilhes), 무기르(Yasin Mughir), 씽(Anup Singh), 루나(Rufino Luna), 쇼(Patrick Shaw), 제이미슨(A. B. Jamieson), 마가냐(Miguel Angel Magaña), 에르난데스(Captain Sánchez Hernández), 번(Patrick Byrne), 샤오 유 린(Shao Yu Lin)		

〈목차〉

제1장

유엔한국위원단의 창설
: 권한, 구성과 조직

A. 창설

1. 임시위원단 총회에 대한 보고와 제3차 정기총회 의제에 한국문제 상정

1947년 11월 14일, 유엔한국임시위원단이 유엔총회 결의 112(II) A 및 B에서 규정된 바대로 한국 독립문제에 대한 보고서를 유엔총회 제3차 정기총회에 제출함. 1948년 9월 22일과 23일 개최된 회의에서 운영위원회(General Committee)[1]가 제3차 정기총회의 임시의제를 검토하여 한국독립 문제를 의제 16항목으로 상정하기를 권고하는 결정을 함. 이에 대해 소련 및 폴란드 대표단이 유엔총회에 의해 설치된 임시위원단이 "불법기구"임을 주장하며 의제에서 삭제하기를 요구하였으나 47대 6(기권 없음)으로 부결되었고 한국독립문제는 제1위원회의 검토 및 보고 사항으로 회부됨.

2. 제1위원회에서의 토의

한국문제가 제1위원회에서 다루어지기 전에 대한민국과 조선민주주의인민공화국은 각각 총회의 한국문제 토의에 참가할 것을 요청함. 대한민국 대표단

---

[1] 총회를 운영하기 위한 절차위원회(Procedural Committees)에 해당하는 위원회로, 본회의에 대해 의제포함 여부를 권고하고 의제의 순위를 결정하는 역할을 한다(유엔개황, 외교부, 2008)

장은 유엔 사무총장에게 보내는 1948년 10월 1일자 서한에서 한국대표단이 제3차 정기총회에 참석하는 것은 1947년 11월 14일 채택된 결의안에 대한 한국의 응답이라고 말했고, 1948년 10월 8일자로 유엔 사무총장에게 보내는 전보에서 북한 외무상은 1948년 8월 남북한에 걸쳐 실시된 총선거에 따라 '최고인민회의(Supreme People's Assembly)'와 '조선민주주의인민공화국' 통일정부가 수립되었음을 주장하며, 한국문제는 합법적인 대표들이 참가하여 검토되고 해결되어야 한다고 주장함. 유엔 사무총장은 제1위원회에서 한국문제가 상정될 때 위원회 위원들 모두에게 남북한 각각의 통신문을 회람시키겠다고 답변함.

1948년 11월 6일 제229차 및 제230차 제1위원회 회의에서 체코슬로바키아의 '민주인민공화국정부의 요청을 받아들여 한국문제에 대한 토의에 북한 대표를 초청하자'는 결의안과 '장면을 수석으로 하는 한국대표단을 투표권 없이 한국문제에 대한 제1위원회 토론에 초대하자'는 결의안이 동시에 상정됨. 체코슬로바키아가 상정한 북한대표 초청안은 30 대 6, 기권 6으로 부결되었고 한국대표단 초청안은 39 대 6, 기권 1로 통과됨. 제1위원회는 또한 다음 회의에서 임시위원단의 보고관이 보고서를 제출하도록 초청할 것을 결의함.

1948년 12월 7일, 제231차 회의에서 한국정부 대표의 진술을 청취한 후 두 개의 결의안, (a) 한국임시위원단의 보고서 결론을 승인하고 새로운 한국위원단을 설치하자는 오스트리아, 중국, 미국이 제출한 공동결의안 (b) 유엔한국임시위원단의 종료를 제안하는 소련의 결의안이 각각 상정되었고, 1948년 12월 8일, 제236차 회의에서 공동결의안은 41 대 6, 기권 2로 채택되었고, 소련의 결의안은 42 대 6, 기권 3으로 부결됨.

3. 유엔총회에서의 토의

1948년 12월 11일 개최된 제186차 전원회의(plenary meeting)에서 유엔총회는 제1위원회가 결의하여 채택을 권고한 '한국의 독립문제에 대한 제1위원회 보고서'에 대한 심의를 시작함. 기존 임시위원단의 활동이 그 임무를 완전히 수행하지 못하였으나 남북한의 접촉을 증진시키는 데에 중요한 역할을 할 수 있다는 점에 대해 인식을 공유하였고, 추가적으로 위원단을 파견하는 것에 동의하였지만 기존의 유엔한국임시위원단을 구성한 회원국을 그대로 보내지 않고, 그 대신 '오스트리아, 중국, 엘살바도르, 프랑스, 인도, 필리핀, 시리아'를 파견하자는 캐나다 대표단의 제안을 40 대 0, 기권 3으로 채택함.

B. 권한

1948년 12월 12일 유엔총회 결의 제195(III)에 유엔한국위원단의 권한이 규정되어 있으며, 주요내용은 다음과 같음. 1947년 11월 14일자 총회결의에 명시된 목표를 완전히 달성하기 위한 방법으로 호주, 중국, 엘살바도르, 프랑스, 인도, 필리핀 및 시리아로 구성된 한국위원단을 설치하여 임시위원단의 사업을 계승하여 수행하고 본 결의에 명시된 한국정부의 지위에 유의하여 다음의 임무를 수행함.

- 1947년 11월 14일자 결의에서 총회가 설정한 제 원칙에 의거하여 한국의 통일과 전 한국 국방군(Korean Security Force)의 통합을 실현하도록 주선하고, 한국의 분단으로 인하여 발생한 경제적, 사회적 및 기타 우호적 교류에 대한 장벽의 제거가 용이하도록 방법을 강구함.

- 자유롭게 표현된 국민들의 의사에 기초한 의회정치가 더욱 발전하도록 감시와 협의를 수행하며 점령국의 실제 철수를 감시하며 철수가 이행되었을 때 동 철수 사실을 확인하고 목적을 위하여 필요하다면 양 점령국 전문가의 협조를 요청함.

이상의 임무수행을 위해 구체적으로 다음과 같이 결의함.

- 본 결의가 채택된 날로부터 30일 이내에 한국으로 출발하여 그 본부를 설치하고, 1947년 11월 14일 결의에 의하여 설치된 임시위원단을 대체한 것으로 간주함.

- 한국 전역을 순회하며 협의하고 시찰할 권한이 있으며, 자체의 사무 절차를 정하고 사태의 진전에 따라 또한 본 결의 조항의 범위 내에서 동 위원단 임무 수행에 관하여 총회 소총회(Interim Committee)와 협의할 수 있으며, 유엔 총회의 차기 정기회기 또는 본 결의안 주제를 토의하기 위해 정기총회 이전에 소집될 수도 있는 특별회기에 보고서를 제출하며, 또한 필요하다고 판단되는 경우에는 회원국에 배포할 목적으로 사무총장에게 중간보고서를 제출함.

C. 유엔 사무총장이 보낸 서한 및 전문(電文)

1949년 1월 6일자로 유엔 사무총장이 유엔한국위원단을 구성하는 7개국 정부에 보내는 서한에서 위원단에 파견될 대표명단을 최대한 신속히 제출해 줄 것을 요청함.

D. 위원단 구성

총회 결의에 따라 오스트레일리아, 중국, 엘살바도르, 프랑스, 인도, 필리핀과 시리아의 대표들로 위원단을 구성할 예정이었으나, 1949년 1월 말, 중국 대표 리우위안(Liu Yu-Wan)과 교체대표 슈튜(Ting T. Ssutu), 프랑스의 임시대표 코스티유(Henri Costilhes)가 서울에 도착하고 이어 시리아 대표 무기르(Yasin Mughir)가 1949년 1월 30일 도착하였으며, 인도대표 씽(Anup Singh)과 필리핀 대표 루나(Rufino Luna)가 1949년 2월 1일 도착함. 오스트레일리아 대표 쇼(Patrick Shaw)와 교체대표 제이미슨(A. B. Jamieson)이 사무국 본진(main body)과 함께 2월 5일에 서울에 도착함. 쇼(Patrick Shaw)는 1949년 2월 23일 도쿄 임지로 복귀하고 교체대표 제이미슨(A. B. Jamieson)이 대표직을 승계함. 엘살바도르 대표 마가냐(Miguel Angel Magaña)가 1949년 3월 26일에 도착함. 같은 날 시리아 대표 무기르(Yasin Mughir)가 떠나고 교체대표로 에르난데스(Captain Sánchez Hernández)가 5월 14일 서울에 도착함. 엘살바도르 대표단이 정부의 지시로 7월 20일 철수하였다가 7월 26일에 다시 합류함.

위원단 사무국은 사무국장(principal secretary) 아래 10명의 현지 채용인력을 포함하여 총 27명으로 구성되었으며, 그 외에 사무부국장(deputy principal secretary) 1명, 비서(assistant secretaries) 3명, 행정관(administrative officer) 1명, 행정보좌관(assistant administrative officer) 1명, 통역(interpreters) 2명, 개요기록자(precis writer) 2명, 비서 겸 타자원 6명을 둠.

번호	국적	총인원	성명	직명
1	호주 (Australia)	2	쇼(Patrick Shaw)	대표
			제이미슨(A. B. Jamieson)	교체대표 (1949.2.23부)
2	중국 (China)	2	리우위안(Liu Yu-Wan)	대표
			슈튜(Ting T. Ssutu)	제1 교체대표
3	엘살바도르 (El Salvador)	2	마가냐(Miguel Angel Magaña)	대표
			에르난데스(Sánchez Hernández)	교체대표 (1949.4.29부)
4	프랑스 (France)	1	코스티유(Henry Costilhes)	임시대표[2]
5	인도 (India)	1	씽(Anup Singh)	대표
6	필리핀 (Philippines)	1	루나(Rufino Luna)	대표
7	시리아 (Syria)	1	무기르(Yasin Mughir)	대표
	계	10		

E. 조직

1949년 2월 2일부터 7월 28일까지 위원단은 서울에서 공개회의 1회, 비공개회의 50회를 개최하였음.

1. 의장

위원단 첫 회의는 오스트레일리아와 엘살바도르 대표의 불참으로, 리우 위안(Liu Yu-Wan, 중국대표), 코스티유(Henri Costilhes, 프랑스대표), 씽(Anup

---

2 기존 유엔한국임시위원단에서 쇼, 코스티유, 씽이 교체된 인물이다.
3 유엔한국임시위원단에서 고문역할을 수행하였음.

Singh, 인도대표), 루나(Rufino Luna, 필리핀대표), 무기르(Yasin Mughir, 시리아대표)만이 참석한 채 진행됨. 상임의장을 결정할 때까지 15일씩 번갈아 임시의장을 맡기로 함. 제6차 회의에서 참가국의 알파벳순으로 30일씩 교대로 의장을 맡기로 결정함.

2. 보고관(office of rapporteur)

제6차 회의에서 종전에 임시위원단이 사용하던 절차규칙을 일부 개정하여 채택하였고 만장일치로 리우위안(Liu Yu-Wan, 중국)이 보고관으로 선출됨.

3. 분과위원회 및 특별위원회

1948년 12월 12일 유엔총회 결의에 규정된 권한을 행사하기 위하여 위원단은 3개의 상설 분과위원회와 2개의 특별위원회를 설치함.

(a) 분과위원회

■ 제1분과위원회(오스트레일리아, 인도, 시리아)

한국의 분단으로 야기된 현재의 경제·사회적 장벽의 성격과 그 정도를 연구하고 남북한의 경제·사회적 협력과 정치적 통일을 촉진함.

■ 제2분과위원회(중국, 프랑스, 필리핀)

의회정치의 발전 문제를 연구하고 의회정치에 관한 전문가 및 단체의 견해와 의견을 수집하며, 문제에 대한 정부당국의 자문에 응함.

■ 제3분과위원회

한국을 점령한 미군의 철수를 감시하고 검증하는 절차를 연구하고 보고하는 것에서, 한반도 전체의 점령군 철수를 실제로 감시하고 검증하는 것으로 분과위원회 권한이 확대됨.

(b) 특별위원회

- 1949년 2월 21일, 제13차 위원단 회의에서 한국인들의 위원단 접근 문제
의 기술적 측면을 조사하고 보고하기 위하여 오스트레일리아, 시리아 대표로
구성된 특별위원회를 설치함.

- 1949년 5월 26일, 제31차 위원단 회의에서 감시반 문제를 다룰 전원특별
위원회를 설치함.

- 위의 두 특별위원회는 각각 1회만 회의를 개최되고 위원단에 보고한 후 무
기한 휴회함.

제2장

위원단 및 부속기구의
주요활동 개요

A. 위원단의 활동과 결정

1. 제1·제2분과위원회 설치

- 1948년 12월 12일 유엔총회 결의 제4항에 기술된 임무 수행을 위해 업무 분담 작업에 박차를 가하여 1949년 2월 9일 제5차 위원단 회의에서 제1, 제2 분과위원회 설치 결의를 채택함.

- 결의에 따라 제1분과위원회에 대해서는 통일을 촉진하는 데에 방해가 되는 한국 내 현존하는 장애물들을 제거하려는 위원단의 열정을 한국민이 인식할 수 있도록 하고 장애물 제거를 위해 필요한 정보를 수집하고 방법을 강구하며 북한과의 즉각적인 접촉을 시도하는 임무가 부여됨.

- 제2분과위원회는 한국의 의회정치 발전문제를 연구하고 정부당국의 자문에 응하며 의회정치를 더욱 발전시키기 위한 전문가 및 단체의 의견과 견해를 수집함.

2. 정부, 대중 및 언론과의 관계

(a) 정부

위원단과 정부 간의 주요 의사소통 경로는 다음의 네 가지임.

(1) 가끔씩 이루어지는 대통령과 위원단 위원과의 직접적인 접촉

(2) 1949년 2월 16일 위원단 위원과 정부에 의해 임명된 연락위원회 위원들 간의 첫 면담

　　조병옥 국회연락위원회 위원장, 장기영 교체대표, 이춘호 연락관, 장기영과 모윤숙이 뒤이어 위원장이 됨.

(3) 제1, 제2분과위원회가 위원단의 임무에 대한 견해와 정보를 얻기 위하여 정부 구성원과 관료들을 대상으로 실시한 청취의 내용은 본장 "B. 분과위원회"에서 다룸.

(4) 빈번한 서신교환

- 위원단과 정부의 관계에서 위원단의 업무수행에 영향을 미칠 수 있는 문제들이 노정됨. 북한과의 접촉문제 및 개인 및 단체와의 협의(자문) 등에 관한 것인데, 1949년 3월 2일 제17차 위원단회의에서 채택된 제1분과위원회 보고서에 적시되어 있음. 한국정부는 위원단이 소련을 통하지 않고 북한 정부나 지도자와 직접 접촉하는 것을 인정하지 않으며 협조하지 않을 것이라는 것과, 북한과의 경제·사회적 교류도 원하지 않는다는 것을 분명히 한다는 내용.

- 위원단은 1949년 2월 9일 결의와 1949년 2월 18일 채택된 제1분과위원회의 보고서에서 북한과의 경제·사회적 장벽을 제거할 방법으로 북한과의 즉각적인 접촉 및 북한지역으로의 여행방법을 모색하겠다고 밝힘.

- 위원단은 대한민국 정부가 유일한 합법정부임을 승인하며, 북한지역 정부와 소통을 제안한 것이 아니라는 데에 만장일치로 합의하고 있음.

- 개인 및 단체와의 면담과 관련하여 한국 정부는 정부 밖의 사람들이 정부의 동의 없이 면담하는 것에 대해 반대하고 위원단에 접촉하려는 사람들이 있

으면 연락위원회를 통해야 한다는 것을 분명히 밝힘.

- 대통령과 연락위원회는 김구와 김규식과 같은 인물들을 면담할 경우, 국민들을 혼란에 빠뜨릴 수 있고 심각한 결과를 낳을 수 있다고 하면서 국회의원들과 만남을 주선해 주겠다고 제안함.

- 1949년 2월 16일 결의에서 위원단은 한국 저명인사들이 위원단이나 위원들에게 진정한 목적을 가지고 접촉하려고 할 경우 자유롭게 할 수 있도록 하겠다고 선언함.

- 위원단 의장이 이승만대통령에게 위원단의 임무수행이 한국정부의 비협조와 반대로 인해 방해받고 있음을 알리고 업무수행이 효과적으로 진행될 수 있도록 정부에서 받아들일 수 없는 견해를 가진 사람들과의 면담에 대해서도 위원단에게 활동의 자유를 보장해 줄 것을 요청함.

- 유엔총회 결의에서 정의한 업무수행과 관련하여 위원단의 기본방침을 재고해야 할 추가적인 상황은 발생하지 않음.

- 1949년 6월 30일 한국 외무부장관 임병직이 위원단에게 임무가 아직 완료되지 않은 위원단이 1년간 더 한국에 남아서 임무를 수행해 주길 희망한다는 서한을 보냈으며, 위원단은 7월 20일 제41차 회의에서 유엔총회에 제출하는 보고서에 외무장관의 요청내용을 반영하겠다고 회신함.

(b) 대중

위원단은 평판이 좋은 한국시민들이 자유롭게 위원단에 접근할 수 있도록

1949년 2월 21일, 특별위원회에 대해 정부연락위원회의 선별을 거치지 않고 면담을 신청할 수 있는 위원단 출입사무소 설치 가능성에 대한 검토를 지시함. 1949년 2월 23일, 제14차 회의를 앞두고 특별위원회가 출입사무소 설치를 권고하는 보고서를 제출했으나 한국정부와 위원단의 관계에 대한 기본적인 양해가 합의되기 전까지 보류를 결정함.

- 위원단은 한국인들이 위원단과 소통할 수 있는 다른 조치를 취하지는 않았으나 정부 외의 특정 인물들과의 접촉에 착수하였고 제1, 제2분과위원회가 위원단의 승인을 얻어 다양한 대표들을 초청하여 의견을 청취하였으며 한국정부는 이에 대해 반대하지 않음.

- 위원단은 김구, 김규식과 같은 논란이 되는 인물의 경우에는 청문을 실시하기 전에 공공의 안전에 미치는 영향 등에 관한 정부 의견을 청취하여 초대여부를 결정함.

- 1949년 6월 13일, 위원단이 대중들과 소통하기 위해 보낸 초청을 알리는 보도 자료에서 제1분과위원회가 앞으로 공식적인 청취는 중단하되 개별적으로는 계속해서 의견을 듣겠다고 공표함.

- 1949년 7월 4일, 남북한의 대중들과 소통하기 위한 방법으로 라디오방송을 실시하기로 결정하였으나 검열 등의 문제가 불거져서 7월 20일, 방송을 그만두기로 결정함.

- 국회의원 5명과 함께 와서 청원서를 제출한 김약수가 후에 국가보안법 (National Security Law) 위반 혐의로 체포됨. 국회부의장 김약수는 국회의원 김병회와 함께 제1분과위원회의 청문에 참석했던 인물로, 위원단은 7월 12일

제40차 회의에서 이 소식을 인지함. 국회의원들에 대해 공개된 혐의는 국회의원들이 국회 내에서 남로당(South Korea Labour Party)의 하수인으로 활동했고, 그들의 청원 제출은 당으로부터의 명령에 의한 것이라고 함. 이 문제에 대해서는 위원단에 청원 제출을 한 것이 범죄로 간주되는 행위라는 증거가 없어서 당분간 관여하지 않기로 결정함.

(c) 언론

- 위원단과 언론과의 관계는 1949년 2월 10일 제6차 회의에서 채택된 위원단 절차규정 제20조 "공식보도 서한은 위원단 의장의 사전 승인을 받아야 한다. 위원단에 의한 반대 지시가 없으면 보도자료와 구두브리핑은 사무국에 의해 이루어질 수 있다"에 의거하여 규정됨.

- 위원단 정책의 언론을 통한 보도에서 발생하는 왜곡을 방지하기 위하여 한국어 번역의 정확성을 보장하기 위한 예방조치들을 취하고 브리핑자료를 보관하기로 결정함.

- 1949년 3월 31일, 한국 기자그룹이 위원단의 임무·태도·정책 등에 대한 20가지 질의사항을 보내왔고, 4월 22일 제26차 회의에서 답변내용을 채택함. 같은 회의에서 한국 기자그룹이 1949년 4월 21일, 위원단 의장에게 위원단의 "관심과 진실성"에 대해 의구심을 갖고 기자단 질의를 철회하는 서한을 보낸 것에 대해 토의하였으며 4월 23일자 보도자료를 통해 이를 부인하고 과거에도 그랬던 것처럼 언론과의 협력을 계속해 나갈 것임을 밝힘.

- 위원단은 7월 20일과 22일 제41차, 제42차 회의에서 기자회견에 참석했던 5명의 한국기자들이 체제전복적 정당(subversive party)의 당원이었다는 혐의

로 체포되었다는 정보를 검토하였고, 이에 대응하여 언론관계 업무를 변경하여 모든 기자회견을 추후 공지가 있을 때까지 중단하고 당분간 보도자료 만을 배포한다고 밝힘.

3. 북한과의 접촉

- 위원단은 소련을 통해 북한과 접촉하기로 결정하고 제1분과위원회에 통신문 초안을 작성하게 하여 1949년 2월 18일, 유엔한국위원단 쇼(Patrick Shaw) 의장 명의로 유엔사무총장이 소련측에 전달해 줄 것을 요청함. 위원단의 임무를 수행하기 위하여 북한을 방문하고자 하나 남북한의 직접적인 교류가 불가능해, 소련으로 하여금 위원단이 북한측 지도자들과 접촉할 수 있도록 주선하여 주기를 요청한다는 내용임.

- 1949년 3월 18일 제21차 위원단 회의에서 북한과의 접촉에 있어 문제점을 분석한 제1분과위원회의 보고서를 검토하고, 북한과의 접촉방법에 관하여 검토한 사무국보고서에 대하여 토의한 후 5 대 1로 사무국장(principal secretary)을 통해 김일성에게 서한을 보내기로 한 결정을 채택함. 분단된 남북한의 통일 및 그 장애물 제거를 위하여 위원단이 최선의 노력을 기울이고 있으며, 임무수행을 위해 북한과 접촉해야 하는데 그동안 소련을 통해 접촉노력을 하였으나 성사되지 않았다는 것과 북한과의 소통을 희망하며 서한에 대한 회신을 요청한다는 내용임.

- 1949년 6월 11일, 서한이 김일성에게 전달되지 않았다는 전보가 홍콩으로부터 수신되었으며, 위원단은 6월 13일 북한에 대한 방송을 승인함. 6월 29일 위원단 의장인 씽(Anup Singh)이 영어로 방송하고 한국어로 번역하는 방식으로 수차에 걸쳐 이루어짐.

- 1949년 7월 12일, 제40차 회의에서 북한으로부터 온 정기우편을 통해 조국통일민주주의전선(Democratic Front for the Attainment of Unification for the Fatherland) 성명서가 사무국에 접수되었음을 주목하고, 과거에 홍콩을 통해 보냈으나 전달하지 못했던 서한을 다시 보내기로 결정함.

- 1949년 7월 8일 제39차 회의에서 제1분과위원회의 최종보고서를 채택하고 보고서에 담긴 권고내용을 즉시 공개하기로 결정함(보도자료 30호). 위원단이 남북한 대표들 간의 통일을 위한 토의를 돕기 위한 의지와 준비가 되어 있음을 알리고, 시험삼아 남북한 간의 무역재개를 원조하고 남북 상호간의 악의적인 비방전을 중지할 것을 권고한다는 내용임.

4. 의회정치의 발전

- 1949년 2월 10일, 위원단 의장이 공개회의 석상에서 위원단의 전신인 임시위원단이 작년 총선거 감시에 나타난 국민들의 자유의사 표시에 입각한 의회정치 기구들이 발전할 수 있도록 유엔회원국들의 경험을 살려 최선을 다해 임무를 수행할 것임을 밝힘.

5. 점령군의 철수

- 1949년 3월 25일 제23차 회의에서 김약수 국회부의장과 61명의 국회의원이 서명하여 제출한, 한반도 통일을 위해 위원단이 대한민국 정부를 도와 외국군대 철수를 감독해달라는 청원을 심의함.

- 1949년 4월 22일, 위원단은 1949년 4월 14일자로 주한 미 대사가 위원단 의장에게 보낸 통신문을 심의함. 통신문에는 주한 미 대사가 대한민국 대통령

에게 보낸 서한이 첨부되어 있고 특히 제4항에 주한미군이 위원단과 협의를 거쳐 수개월 내에 철수할 것이라는 내용이 담겨 있음.

- 1949년 5월 2일 주한미국대사가 대한민국 대통령에게 발송한 주한 미 군 사고문단(Korean military advisory group) 설치에 관한 서한 사본을 위원단에 송부함.

- 1949년 5월 23일, 북한지역 점령군인 소련군의 철수를 한국위원단이 시찰할 수 없다는 사실을 확인하며, 한국통일의 문제가 1947년 이래로 유엔의 소관 사항으로 남아 있는 현실에서 점령군 철수에 관한 시기나 철수 촉진 문제와 관련하여 위원단이 이 문제에 대한 책임이 없음을 확인하는 결의를 채택함.

- 1949년 6월 9일, 제33차 회의에서 미군 철수문제와 관련하여 위원단과 주한미군사령관 로버츠 준장을 동반한 미국대사 무초와 회담을 가졌으며 이 자리에서 미국대사가 미군철수와 관련하여 주요 내용을 전달함. 미군이 그동안 점진적인 철수작업을 진행 중이었고 6월말 경에 철수가 완료될 것으로 예상하고 있으며, 미군이 사용하던 시설 및 장비는 한국정부에 인도하고 철수 완료 후에도 승인받은 500명과 주한미군사고문단이 남을 것이며, 미군철수와 관련하여 한국정부와 이미 회담을 가졌다는 내용임. 아울러 미군철수와 관련하여 미국정부는 위원단의 감시와 검증에 충분히 협조할 것이나 여기에 소련군사전문가의 도움을 받는 것에 대해 미국이 반대하지는 않으나 미국이 북한지역의 소련군 철수에 참여하는 것을 조건으로 해야 하며, 나아가 한국정부와도 협의하여야 함을 밝힘.

- 1949년 6월 13일, 제34차 회의에서 1948년 12월 12일 유엔총회결의 제4항 (c)에 의해 부여된 점령군의 한국철수 감시 및 검증 임무를 유념하고 나머지 주

한미군의 철수를 감시하고 검증할 것과 이를 감시하고 위원단에 보고할 분과 위원회(오스트레일리아, 중국, 엘살바도르, 인도로 구성)를 설치하기로 결의함.

- 1949년 6월 20일, 제35차 회의에서 제3분과위원회의 보고서를 승인하고, 제3분과위원회에 점령군철수의 감시 및 검증 권한을 부여하고, 업무진행상황을 수시로 위원단에 보고하도록 함. 아울러 1949년 6월 13일 위원단 결의내용을 미국정부 및 한국정부에 통지하고, 1948년 12월 12일 유엔총회 결의 제4항 (d)의 이행을 위해 점령군 철수 감시 및 검증에 필요한 정보를 미국 및 한국 정부에 요청하되, 군사전문가의 원조는 요청하지 않기로 함.

- 1949년 7월 27일 제48차 회의에서 제3분과위원회가 제출한 2차 중간보고서를 승인하고, 민간행정업무 정리를 위해 김포공항에 일시적으로 남아있는 50명 미만의 공군 병력을 제외하고는 1949년 6월 29일에 주한 미군의 철수가 완료되었으며, 대한민국 대통령과 주한미군사령관 간에 체결된 과도기에 시행될 잠정적 군사안전에 관한 행정협정이 1949년 6월 30일부로 효력이 소멸되면서, 한국국방군에 대한 미국정부 또는 주한 미 군사고문단의 통제권도 소멸되었음을 선언함. 아울러 미군이 한국 내에 보유하고 있던 모든 군사물자는 군 병력과 함께 철수된 물자를 제외하고는 전부 철수완료일을 기준으로 한국 국방군에 인도하였음을 확인함.

- 주한미군 철수작업이 진행되는 동안 철수 전에 한국의 안전보장을 위하여 위원단에 보다 광범위하고 강력한 권한을 부여할 것을 요구하는 시위가 전국애국단체협의회(National Federation of Patriotic Organization) 등의 단체에 의해 수차례 개최되었으며, 위원단 방문, 시위 및 항의가 발생함.

- 1949년 6월 17일, 국회부의장 김약수와 5명의 국회의원이 위원단 사무

국장(principal secretary)을 방문하고 점령군철수에 관한 1949년 5월 24일 위원단 결의를 비난하는 한편, 한국에서 미국과 소련의 군사 파견단(military mission)을 폐지시켜줄 것을 요청하는 청원서를 제출함. 6월 20일에는 국회부의장 김동원이 141명의 국회의원이 서명한 미국 군사파견단 설치를 환영하는 '한국에 대한 미국 군사원조(United States Military Aid to Korea)에 관한 공동선언문'을 제출함.

6. 감시반(observer team)

-1949년 4월 29일 제27차 회의에서 엘살바도르 대표가 한국의 평화와 안전을 유지하고 점령군의 철수에 관한 위원단의 책임을 수행하는 수단으로 감시반(observer team) 설치를 제안했으나, 이 문제에 대해 특별위원회의 검토 후 부정적 견해를 담은 리포트가 제출되자 6월 6일 제32차 회의에서 채택됨.

- 1949년 7월 11일자 대한민국 외교부장관의 서한이 위원단의 주목을 끌었는데 내용은 북한 인민군이 38선 이남 지역의 마을과 국방군을 공격하였다는 것이며, UN군사감시단(Unit of United Nations Military Observers)이 한국에 주둔한다면 이러한 불법적인 공격을 지연시키거나 막을 수 있다고 주장하며 위원단이 이러한 권고를 유엔총회에 해줄 것을 요청하였으나 위원단은 이와 관련한 어떠한 권고도 하지 않기로 결정함. 다만 외교부장관의 제안을 위원단이 유엔총회에 제출하는 보고서에는 기록할 것이라고 확인함.

7. 현지시찰 및 순회

본 보고서 작성기간 동안 위원단의 현지시찰 및 방문이 이루어졌으며 가장 광범위하게 이루어진 것은 전라남도와 제주도임.

B. 분과위원회 활동과 결정

1. 제1분과위원회

(a) 권한, 조직 및 연표

1949년 2월 9일 채택된 결의에 따라 제1분과위원회를 설치하였으며, 초기에는 오스트레일리아, 인도, 시리아 대표로 구성됨. 제1분과위원회는 1949년 2월 9일부터 6월 24일까지 총 36회의 회의를 개최하였고 그 중 14회는 회담, 22회는 업무회의임. 서울의 다양한 산업 및 상업 중심지를 방문하였고 38선 지역 상황을 수차례 점검함.

(i) 북한과의 접촉

- 2월 10일 북한과 접촉할 방법을 모색하는 것으로 업무를 개시하여 첫 단계로 대통령 및 내각을 예방하였고 제3차 회의에서 북한과의 통신 및 교통수단에 대해 조사할 것을 사무국에 지시함.

- 2월 15일 제9차 회의에서 대통령 면담결과를 위원단에 보고하였으며 소련을 통해 북한과 첫 접촉을 하기로 결정함. 이에 따라 제1분과위원회는 2월 16일과 17일의 제4차와 제5차 회의에서 소련에 대해 북한과의 접촉을 주선해 줄 것을 요청하는 전문을 작성하였으며 1949년 2월 18일 제11차 회의에서 이를 채택함. 이와는 별개로 분과위원회는 항공, 해상, 철도, 또는 육로를 통해 북한으로 이동할 수 있는 현실적으로 가능한 방법을 지속적으로 모색하라는 지시를 받음.

- 3월 12일 제14차 회의에서 홍콩을 경유하여 김일성에게 서한을 전달하기로 합의하였으며, 3월 18일의 제21차 회의에서는 김일성에게 전달할 편지내용을 최종 확정함. 4월 12일의 제25차 회의에서는 4월 8일, 북한에 전달할 편지를 홍콩선박의 선장에게 전달하였다는 보고를 받음. 그러나 북한으로부터 일체의 회신이 없자 위원단은 6월 13일 제34차 회의에서, 분과위원회가 김일성에게 보낸 편지 내용을 포함하여 방송내용을 확정짓고, 6월 29일부터 수차에 걸쳐서 한국어 및 영어로 대북 라디오방송을 실시함.

(ii) 경제적 장벽의 제거

- 4월 11일 제21차 분과위원회 회의에서는 경제적 장벽의 문제를 연구하기 위하여 서울 및 지방의 산업 및 상업 중심지를 방문하기로 결정하여 5월 2일부터 5일 사이에 17차례에 걸쳐 방문하였고, 6월 8일 제33차 분과위원회 회의에서 남북한 간의 무역거래에 관한 정확한 자료를 정부와 비정부기관에 요청하기로 함.

(iii) 기타 활동

- 7월 15일과 17일, 제38차와 제39차 분과위원회 회의에서 북한으로부터 우편을 통해 수령한 조국통일민주주의전선(Democratic Front for the Attainment of Unification for the Fatherland)의 성명서를 심의함.

- 제1분과위원회는 위원단의 계획과 목표를 설명하는 대북 라디오방송을 실시할 것을 권고함. 7월 20일 제41차 위원단 회의에 방송원고가 제출되었으나 한국정부의 라디오시설 이용에 문제가 발생하여 연기하기로 결정함.

(b) 정보 및 의견 검토(조사)

- 1949년 2월 24일과 3월 1일, 제7차, 제9차 회의에서 제1분과위원회가 면담 시에 적용할 정책을 결정하고 면담 대상 인물을 선정하였으며, 선정된 인물에 대해서는 사전에 대한민국 정부로부터 사전승인을 받지 않기로 2월 28일 제8차 분과위원회 회의에서 결정하였고 이를 위원단에 보고하여 3월 2일 제17차 회의에서 승인을 받음.

- 분과위원회는 1949년 3월 9일부터 6월 2일까지 총 14명에 대해 면담을 진행하였으며 이 가운데 5명은 정부의 고위직 대변인, 3명은 국회의원, 3명은 유력 정치인이었고 주한 미 경제협조처(ECA)처장 1명, 신문발행인 1명, 감리교 종교지도자 1명이 포함됨.

- 제1분과위원회의 면담 대상자에 대한 질문 내용은 다음과 같음.
(i) 통일문제에 대한 귀하의 의견은 무엇입니까?
(ii) 대한민국 정부수립 이래로 통일을 촉진하기 위해 취해진 조치가 있다면 무엇이며, 어떠한 조치가 취해져야 합니까?
(iii) 한국의 경제적, 사회적 그리고 기타 장벽을 제거하는 것이 어느 정도까지 가능하다고 생각합니까?

- '통일을 위한 조건', '경제·사회·문화적 장벽의 제거'에 대하여 정부측, 비정부측, 일반의견 등으로 구분하여 회담에서 제시된 의견을 정리함.

(c) 조사결과 및 권고

- 6월 22일과 24일의 제35차 및 제36차 회의에서 위원단에 제출할 조사결과

및 권고내용을 포함한 최종보고서 초안 작성에 착수함. 공식면담과 일반 시찰에 의거하여 최종보고서를 작성하고 조사결과를 바탕으로 권고내용도 작성하여 위원단에 제출하였으며, 1949년 7월 8일 제39차 회의에서 이를 채택함.

2. 제2분과위원회

(a) 권한, 조직 및 연표

- 유엔총회 결의 제195호(Ⅲ)의 제4항(c)을 이행하기 위하여 1949년 2월 9일 위원단 제5차 회의에서 설치된 제2분과위원회는 중국, 프랑스, 필리핀 대표로 구성되며 다음의 권한을 가짐.
 (i) 한국의 의회정치 발전을 연구하고
 (ii) 정부당국의 자문에 응하여 요청한 정보와 조언을 제공하며
 (iii) 한국의 의회정치 발전에 관한 전문가 및 단체의 의견 및 견해를 수집함.

- 제2분과위원회는 1949년 2월 11일부터 6월 24일까지의 기간 동안 25차례의 회의를 개최함. 분과위원회 제2차 회의에서 위원단에 정보 및 참고사항을 제공할 목적으로, 중국, 프랑스 대표와 위원단 사무국으로 구성된 작업반을 만들어 대한민국 정부 수립 이후 연표를 작성하기로 함.

- 제2분과위원회의 다른 주요활동은 한국의 공무원 및 주요 인사들을 면담하며 반란이 일어난 전라남도와 제주도 두 중요 지역을 방문하고 광범위한 시찰을 실시하여 의회정치 발전에 관한 보완적 연구를 하는 것임.

- 제2분과위원회의 최종 보고서는 6월 22일 제35차 위원단 회의에 제출되었으며, 일부 수정을 거쳐 6월 28일 제37차 회의에서 채택됨.

(b) 정보 및 의견 검토(조사)

- 제2분과위원회는 1949년 2월 20일부터 4월 14일까지 11차례의 면담을 실시했으며, 면담에 참여한 사람은 장관급 3명, 국회의원 2명, 정치지도자 2명, 사회·교육·종교단체 지도자 4명임.

- 의회정치 문제에 관한 2가지 포괄적인 측면(1. 대한민국 정부수립 이후 의회정치의 발전/ 2. 의회정치와 통일문제의 관계)에 대한 설문이 이루어졌음.

(c) 결론과 권고

- 대한민국 정부수립 후 단시일 내에 의회정치가 발전하고, 전라남도와 제주도 등에서 발생한 반란으로 인해 약간의 혼란이 있었으나 잘 극복하고 있는 것으로 보이며 한국에서 민주주의가 성장해가는 과정에 좋은 징조를 보이고 있다고 판단됨. 대한민국의 안전이 확보되고 법과 질서가 전 지역에 걸쳐 확립되면 의회정치의 비약적 발전을 이뤄낼 것으로 믿음.

3. 제3분과위원회

(a) 권한, 조직

- 한국에서의 점령군 철수 감시와 검증에 관한 1948년 12월 12일 유엔총회 결의 제4항(d)을 이행하기 위하여 1949년 6월 13일, 제34차 위원단 회의에서 오스트레일리아, 중국, 엘살바도르, 인도 대표로 구성된 제3분과위원회를 설치함.

(b) 미합중국 점령군대의 철수 시찰 및 검증

- 1949년 6월 16일, 미군철수 감시 및 검증을 목적으로 제3분과위원회가 설치되었다는 사실과 미군철수 감시 및 검증 업무에 필요한 병력 및 장비, 주한 미 군사고문단의 현황자료를 위원단에 제출할 것을 통지하는 내용을 담은 보고서를 제출함. 1949년 6월 20일 제35차 위원단 회의에서 제3분과위원회의 보고서를 승인하고 제3분과위원회에 점령군의 한국철수를 감시하고 검증할 권한을 부여함.

- 제3분과위원회는 6월 21일과 29일 인천항에서 잔류 미군의 마지막 출국을 확인하였고, 7월 27일 제2차 업무진행보고서를 통해 6월 30일 기준으로 한국에 잔류하고 있는 유일한 미군부대는 민간행정협정이 체결될 때까지 김포공항에 주둔하고 있는 약 50명의 공군과 승인 받은 500명을 보유한 주한 미 군사고문단이 전부임을 보고함.

- 제3분과위원회는 1949년 6월 29일자로 김포공항에 체류 중인 50명을 제외한 미군 전원이 철수하였다는 것과 대한민국 대통령과 주한미군사령관 간에 체결된 과도기에 시행될 잠정적 군사안전에 관한 행정협정이 1949년 6월 30일부로 효력이 소멸되며 한국국방군에 대한 미국정부 또는 주한 미 군사고문단의 통제권도 소멸되었음을 확인함. 아울러 미군이 한국 내에 보유하고 있던 모든 군수물자는 군 병력과 함께 철수된 물자를 제외하고는 철수완료일을 기준으로 모두 한국국방군에 인도하였음을 확인함. 이러한 내용의 보고서가 1949년 7월 27일 제48차 위원단 회의에서 승인됨.

(c) 1948년 12월 12일 유엔총회 결의 제4항 (d)의 소련점령군대에의 적용

- 점령군의 철수 및 감시 권한을 부여받은 제3분과위원회는 소련점령군에 대해서도 그 임무를 수행하고자 위원단에 보고서를 제출하였고 1949년 7월 4일 위원단회의에서 동 보고서를 승인하였으며, 유엔사무총장에 대해 소련정부에 이 사실을 알려줄 것을 요청함.

4. 위원단에 대한 한국인의 접근 문제에 관한 특별위원회

- 1949년 2월 21일 제13차 위원단 회의에서는 2월 16일자 위원단 결의에 따라 한국의 저명인사들이 위원단에 자유롭게 접근할 수 있도록 접근의 기술적 측면을 검토할 특별위원회를 오스트레일리아 및 시리아 대표로 구성함. 특별위원회는 위원단을 방문하기 위해 출입증을 신청할 수 있는 출입증 교부사무소를 설치할 것을 건의하였으나 건의사항에 대한 검토가 연기됨.

5. 감시반에 대한 특별위원회

엘살바도르 대표가 한국의 대외적 평화와 안전에 기여할 수단으로 감시반 설치를 권고하여 이에 대한 필요성 여부를 검토하기 위해 특별위원회(Ad Hoc Committee of the Whole)를 구성하였으며, 그 기능과 유용성에 대하여 검토한 후 설치하지 않기로 결정함.

제3장

정치·경제·사회적 발전 및
한국의 독립과 통일문제에 영향을 주는 요소

A. 대한민국

1. 관할권 이양의 완료

(a) 재정협정

- 1948년 9월 11일 서명된 대한민국과 미국 간의 임시 재정 및 재산처리 협정을 9월 18일 국회에서 비준하였으며 9월 20일 미국에 통지함으로써 발효됨.

(b) 재산의 양도

- 1948년 12월 초까지 한국 당국에 재산 및 운영시설에 대한 행정통제권이 인계되었으며, 귀속재산(vested property, 과거 일본인이 소유했던 재산)의 양도도 같은 달에 완료됨.

2. 주한미군의 철수

(a) 철수의 완료

- 주한 미군의 점령이 종료되는 1949년 6월 30일 자정까지 김포공항의 운영을 위해 잔류하고 있던 공군병력 50명을 제외한 모든 주한미군의 철수가 완료되었고 미군이 점유하고 있던 군사시설이 한국정부에 양도됨.

(b) 주한미군사고문단

- 대한민국 정부의 요청에 따라 한국에 남은 주한 미 군사고문단 500명의 승인병력이 한국국방군(Korean security forces)의 발전과 훈련을 위해 자문과 협력을 제공함.

3. 대외관계

(a) 정치적 대외관계

- 대한민국은 지금까지 12개 국가와 바티칸으로부터 외교적 승인(diplomatic recognition)을 받음. 대한민국은 워싱턴, 파리와 도쿄에 외교사절단을 파견했을 뿐만 아니라 뉴욕, 로스앤젤레스, 샌프란시스코, 호놀룰루, 상하이와 홍콩에 영사관을 설치함.

- 1949년 1월 1일, 중국이 대한민국에 법률상 국가승인(de jure recognition, 정식국가 승인)을 부여함. 리우위안(Liu Yu-Wan)이 최초의 중국대사로, 이어서 샤오 유 린(Shao Yu Lin)이 중국대사로 임명을 받아 7월 25일 서울에 도착함.

- 프랑스와는 1949년 2월 5일 외교관계를 수립하였으며 필리핀은 1949년 3월 2일에 대한민국에 대해 정식으로 국가 승인을 함. 영국정부는 1949년 1월

19일에, 1949년 1월 1일에는 미국정부가 대한민국을 정식으로 승인함. 바티칸 (로마 교황청)이 1949년 4월 12일 한국으로 파견할 교황사절단을 구성하였으며 1949년 7월 15일 번 주교(Monsignor Patrick Byrne)가 정식 신임장을 제출함. 칠레는 1949년 5월 27일에, 뉴질랜드는 6월 21일에 대한민국을 정식으로 승인함. 도미니카공화국과 쿠바가 7월 13일, 19일에 차례로, 브라질이 6월 4일에 정식으로 대한민국을 승인함. 7월 17일에는 캐나다가 한국을 독립 주권국가로서 정식 승인하였음을 알림. 1949년 7월 22일에 네덜란드가 대한민국을 정식으로 승인함.

 - 1949년 2월 2일 대한민국 정부는 장면을 워싱턴 주재 한국대사로 임명하였고, 3월 25일에 신임장을 제출함. 2월 10일에는 변영태를 마닐라에 특별대표로 파견하였고, 5월 31일에는 공진항이 파리주재 한국공사로 부임하였으며 영국정부는 윤지창을 런던주재 한국공사로 접수함.

 - 1948년 12월 24일 도쿄에 위치한 연합군총사령부에 파견할 외교사절단을 구성하였고 1949년 2월 10일, 정환범을 특별대표로 임명하여 주한 미군정 실시 이후 일본에서 한국을 대표하던 정한경을 승계하도록 함.

 - 1949년 1월 5일에 로스엔젤레스, 1월 24일에 상하이, 3월 15일에 뉴욕, 4월 10일에 호놀룰루, 5월 4일에 홍콩, 그리고 6월 10일에 샌프란시스코에 각각 영사관을 설치하였으며 1949년 늦여름에 대만 타이페이에 영사관을 설치할 예 정임.

 - 대한민국은 유엔의 한 특별기구에 가입되어 있으며, 그 외에도 몇몇 기관에 회원가입 또는 참석을 신청함. 세계보건기구(WHO)는 최창순박사가 옵저버로 참석한 1949년 6월 30일 로마 회의에서 투표로 한국의 가입을 승인하였고 회원가입은 대한민국이 세계보건기구헌장 비준서를 유엔사무총장에게 제

출하면 최종 확정하도록 함. 그 외, 유엔식량농업기구(FAO), 아시아극동경제위원회(ECAFE)에 가입을 신청하였으며, 유엔교육과학문화기구(UNESCO) 회원가입 준비를 마침.

(b) 경제적 대외관계

(i) 미국경제협조처(ECA)

- 미군정 출범과 더불어 대한 원조 및 부흥 사업이 개시되어 1945년 11월부터 1949년 3월까지의 기간 동안 주한미군이 정부 및 점령지역 원조예산으로 총 191,754,000달러에 달하는 민간물자를 구입하였으며, 이러한 원조 및 부흥 사업은 1948년 가을 한국에 진출한 주한 미 경제협조처가 1949년 1월 1일 공식적으로 미육군부로부터 진행 중인 사업관리에 대한 책임을 위임받아 계속 진행됨.

(ii) 일본과의 무역

- 1949년 4월, 대한민국은 1950년 회계연도 기간 동안 일본으로 2,900만 달러의 상품(주로 쌀과 해산물)을 수출하고 약 4900만 달러의 상품(주로 석탄, 기계, 제조품)을 수입한다는 내용의 무역협정에 서명함. 미국 경제협조처(ECA) 호프만(Paul C. Hoffman) 처장의 평가에 따르면, 한국의 대외무역관계가 주로 한국을 식민지로 이용하려는 일본의 정책에 의하여 형성되었기 때문에 일본과의 무역관계는 상호보완적인 성격을 갖게 되었고 이로 인해 한국의 무역은 계속해서 일본에 치우친 채로 이루어질 수밖에 없는 사정이 있으며, 장차 일본을 제외한 극동지역에서 정치·경제적으로 안정적인 시장 확보가 여의치 않을 것으로 예상되므로 한국의 독립과 주권을 침해하지 않는 범위 내에서 일본과의

무역을 최대한 늘려가는 것이 바람직하다고 평가하고 동시에 한국이 다자간 무역협정에 적극 참여할 것을 권유함.

4. 한국국방군(Korean Security Forces)의 조직과 기능

(a) 육군, 해군 그리고 예비군

- 1948년 12월 12일 유엔총회결의 제4항 (a)는 위원단으로 하여금 모든 한국국방군을 통합하도록 하였으나 위원단이 정치적 통일 차원의 임무를 수행하는데 있어서 진전을 보지 못했기 때문에 일부 몇몇 군사시설과 부대를 조사하는 모습을 보여주는데 그쳤으며 육군, 해군과 경찰의 통합문제를 체계적으로 다루지는 못함.

- 북한정권의 국방기능을 담당하는 상당한 규모의 군 병력의 훈련소식을 입수하였는가 하면, 소련 및 중국 군대와 군사적 성격의 협정을 체결하였다는 소식이 전해지는 등, 대한민국 정부가 군사적인 대비를 갖출 필요성이 증대되고 있는 상황임.

- 1945년 11월 13일, 군정명령 제28호에 의하여 한국국방군이 공식적으로 창설되고 주한미군정 국방지휘부(Office of the Director of National Defence of the Military Government of Korea)가 설치되어 산하에 육군 및 해군부서와 함께 군사국이 설치되었으며, 국방지휘부는 경찰에 대한 전반적 지휘권도 보유함.

- 군정 명령이 반포된 날부터 1947년 후반까지 조선경비대(Korean con-stabulary)가 창설되어 육군으로 전환되었으며, 1947년 말 조선경비대의 공식 규모는 약 2만 명이었으며, 같은 기간 동안 3천 명 규모의 해안경비대가 창설됨.

- 최초 계획은 38선 이남의 8개 도에 각각 적어도 한 개 연대를 편성하는 것으로 과거 중국 혹은 일본 육군에서 훈련받은 약 60명의 장교들로 지휘부를 구성함.

- 한국국방군 편성의 두 번째 단계는 1947년 말에 시작되었는데 이 때 미국 군사자문관들이 투입되면서 훈련시설의 조직이 발전되었고 1948년 3월부터 7월 사이에 약 5만여 명 분의 무기와 장비가 도착했으며, 1948년 가을에 미군 병력으로 구성된 임시군사자문단이 구성됨. 로버츠(W. L. Roberts) 준장 지휘 아래 임시군사자문단을 계승한 주한 미 군사고문단(Korean Military Advisory Group)이 500여명의 인가병력을 보유함.

- 미군정이 거의 마지막으로 설치한 조직이 한국 육군이어서 어쩔 수 없이 일제치하로부터 계속된 경찰이 국방 기능도 담당하게 되고 그러다 보니 양 조직 사이에 갈등이 촉발될 수밖에 없는 형편이었으나 후에 내무부 아래에 경찰 조직을 두고 국방부 아래에 육군과 해군을 두는 것으로 조직을 개편하여 문제가 해결됨. 초기에 국방부는 총리의 지휘를 받음.

- 1948년 11월, 국방군 편성에 관한 법률이 국회에서 통과되고 대통령이 국방군의 최고사령관으로서 헌법상의 책임을 지게 되었으며 대통령을 보좌하는 군사자문위원회(War Council)를 두고 그 밑에 국방위원회(National Defence Committee)와 중앙정보부(Central Intelligence Bureau), 국방자원통제위원회(National Defence Resources Control Committee), 군사회의(Military Council)를 둠. 국방부가 국방행정을 담당함.

- 국방군은 현재까지 부분적 지원 형식(반모병제)으로 병력을 확보하였으나 최근 정부가 징병제 법안을 제출하여 1949년 7월 15일 통과되었고 1948년 말에 발표된 육군 병력은 약 5만 명에 달함. 정부가 목표로 하는 육군 병력은 20

만 명이며 대한민국 정부가 미국에 대해 예비군 20만 명을 포함하여 40만 명분의 무기와 장비를 요청하였다는 보고가 있음.

- 육군의 거의 모든 장비는 미국으로부터 도입된 것이고 미 당국은 이를 순전히 방어적 성격의 것이라고 밝힘.

- 국방군은 약 7천 명의 해군병력과 80척의 선박을 보유하고 있으며 선박은 소해정(minesweeper, 기뢰제거용 선박)과 연안경비정(coast guard cutters)으로 구성되어 있음.

- 1949년/1950년 예산에서는 국방부에 대한 약 140억 원의 지출을 승인함.

(b) 경찰

- 경찰은 내무부장관의 직접 지휘 하에 있으며 약 6만여 명의 인원인데, 약 1만여 명 이상이 대도시(수도) 경찰이고 나머지는 8개 도에 분산되어 있음.

- 1949년/1950년 예산에서 내무부에 약 150억 원 이상이 배정됨.

- 경찰의 역할은 법과 질서의 유지를 담당하는 것이고 최근까지도 38선 이남의 치안유지를 전담하여 남한 전역 및 제주도에서 발생한 대규모 소요와 혼란을 진압하는데 주된 역할을 하였으며, 최근에 와서는 육군이 38선 주변 지역과 대규모 폭동(disturbance) 진압에 대한 더 큰 책임을 맡게 됨.

- 전라남도 지역에서 발생한 육군부대 내의 반란은 육군에 의해 진압되었고 제주도의 평화를 확보하는 일도 궁극적으로 육군이 맡아서 1949년 5월에 작전

을 완료함.

　(c) 준군사조직

　- 연 초에 모든 청년단체가 대통령이 명예단장으로 있는 민족청년단
(National Youth Corps)으로 통합되면서 청년단체가 독립적이고 통제되지 않
는 자경단으로 변질할 우려가 해소되었고 청년단체의 에너지를 치수사업이나
간척사업에 집중되도록 유도함. 일부 자발적으로 경찰활동을 하는 청년단체가
있기는 하지만 감소 추세에 있으며 어떤 경우든 현재는 중앙통제 하에 있음. 민
족청년방위단(National Youth Defence Corps)이 1949년 6월 창설됨.

5. 의회정치의 발전

　- 1948년 12월 12일 유엔총회 결의 제4항 (c)는 위원단에게 장차 의회정치
의 발전을 위해 감시와 자문을 맡도록 지시하였고, 위원단은 이를 38선 이남과
이북 모두에 적용되는 것으로 해석했으나, 위원단이 북한 시찰을 허락받지 못
했기 때문에 38선 이남지역에 국한됨.

　- 1948년 7월 12일의 대한민국 헌법 채택과 1948년 7월 17일의 헌법 공포는
정부 수립의 출발이었으나, 보완해야 할 점들이 적지 않음. 해결되지 않은 근본
적인 문제들은 일제 부역자의 숙청, 과거 일본이 보유한 귀속재산의 처리, 토지
개혁과 지방행정 문제 등임.

　- 대한민국 헌법에 의거한 의회정치의 발전은 공정하지 못했고 불안정했으
며, 1년간의 헌법시행은 다른 대부분의 기본법들처럼 의회정치의 현실 문제에
불완전한 답을 제공하였고 해석의 문제점을 해결하기 위하여 명확한 개정 또

는 지속적인 헌법 시행을 필요로 하고 있음.

　(a) 행정부의 권한

　- 대통령이 국가원수 및 총사령관으로서 국무회의를 구성하는 각부 장관과 육군 및 해군의 주요 장교를 임명함. 국무총리를 임명할 때에는 국회의 동의가 필요함. 헌법에 따르면 국무총리는 대통령의 지시에 따라 내각 국무위원들의 활동을 감독하고 조정하며, 참모기능을 하는 총무처, 공보처, 법제처 및 기획처를 직속으로 둠.

　- 헌법과 같은 날 공포된 정부조직법에 따라 수립된 정부는 내무부, 외무부, 국방부, 재무부, 법무부, 문교부, 농림부, 상공부, 사회부, 보건부, 교통부, 체신부로 구성되고, 대통령 산하의 직속기관으로 인사위원회, 감독위원회 및 회계감사원을 설치함.

　- 대통령에 의한 행정 각부 통제 및 통솔이 성공적으로 이루어지고 있는 듯이 보이지만, 대한민국이 매일 같이 당면하고 있는 긴급한 문제들을 해결하기 위해서는 정부에 대한 대중적 지지가 너무 부족하기 때문에 '이상적인' 내각 구성을 좀 더 '실용적인' 것으로 변모시킬 필요가 있다는 지적이 제기되고 있고 내각에 야당 인사를 포함시키라는 압력도 커지고 있음.

　(b) 국회

　- 1948년 5월 10일 유엔한국임시위원단의 감시 하에 실시된 총선거에서 선출된 국회의원으로 구성된 국회는 개원 이래 지금까지 약 200회의 회의를 개최하였고, 현재 제4특별회기 중에 있음.

- 1948년 9월 14일 통과된 법령 제5호에 따라 8개의 상임위원회가 설치되었고, 1949년 7월 교섭위원회가 추가됨. 국회는 최근까지 약 35건의 법률을 제정하였을 뿐 아니라 다수의 결의안을 채택함.

- 최근까지 국회는 독립적으로 국회의원 각자가 독자성을 유지한 채 활동하였으며, 이러한 환경은 헌법이 입법부의 독립을 보장하고 뚜렷하게 정의할 수 있는 정치세력이나 정당에 의한 통제가 없었기에 가능했던 것임.

(c) 정당

- 한국에서 민주국민당(Democratic Nationalist Party)과 한국독립당(Korean Independence Party)을 제외한 정치단체들은 조직과 자금이 없고 따라서 입법과정에서 이들 정당들이 소속 국회의원에 대해 효과적인 통제를 못하고 있는 상황이지만 변화의 조짐이 보임.

- 현재 국회 내에서 가장 강력한 정당은 1949년 2월 10일에 설립된 민주국민당으로, 한국민주당(Hankook Democratice Party, 한민당)과 국민당(Nationality Party)의 합당으로 설립되었으며 김성수, 지대형, 신익희, 백남훈으로 구성된 위원회가 이끌고 있음. 80만 명의 당원을 보유하고 있다고 주장하고 있으며 약 85명의 국회의원의 지지를 모을 수 있는 가장 단합된 정당임.

- 민주국민당과 다소 대립적인 정당은 고(故) 김구의 한국독립당으로 1922년 5월 설립되었고 1948년 10월에 재편됨. 90만 명의 당원을 보유하고 있다고 주장하고 있으며 전국에 걸쳐 존재하는 조직을 보유하고 있다고 함. 한국독립당은 1948년 5월 10일 총선거와 선거결과에 대하여 반대하는 입장을 유지함. 김구의 사망 이후 독립된 단체로서의 앞날에 대해 의문이 제기됨.

- 김구의 한국독립당의 목표와는 밀접하게 연결되어 있지만 지지세력이 완전히 다른 단체를 김규식이 이끌고 있는데, 민족자주연맹(National Independence Federation)이라고 불리는 이 단체는 50만 명의 당원을 보유하고 있다고 함.

- 공산당에 대응하기 위해 단합해야 한다는 민족적 열망과 국회법 개정으로 인해 국회의원의 정당 변경이 어려워지자 유사한 입장에 있는 정치단체들이 통합하는 경향이 나타남.

(d) 행정부와 입법부의 관계

- 행정부와 입법부의 권한 행사에서 발생되는 문제는 주로 행정 각부의 책임, 충돌하는 정책의 결정, 대통령의 거부권행사와 관련이 있음.

- 권력분립이론에 입각한 헌법은 대통령의 권한범위 내에서 국정에 관한 기본 계획 및 정책수립을 내각에 일임하고 입법권을 국회에 부여하였으나, 행정 각부의 의회에 대한 책임을 묻고 통제하는 규정이 없기 때문에 행정부와 입법부간의 정책 충돌이 교착상태에 빠져 헌법상 행정부와 입법부 간에 유지되는 견제와 균형을 무너뜨리는 결과를 초래함.

(e) 신문과 언론의 자유

- 남한의 신문사들은 영세하고 주된 관심 분야를 길게 보도하는 경향이 있으며 유엔한국위원단의 활동도 보도하고 있음. 서울에만 30개가 넘는 일간지와 주간지가 있고 각 도에도 신문이 있지만 수도권 신문들에 비해 영향력이 약함. 어떤 신문사도 발행부수나 광고로 자립하기가 어려운 형편임.

- 1907년도부터 시행된 신문법이 일반적으로 쓸모없고 억압적이라고 여겨지지만 여전히 발효 중이고 1949년 6월까지 적용됨.

- 총리실 부속기관이지만 대통령과 더욱 밀접한 공보실에서 다음의 내용들에 대해 발행을 금지함. (1) 대한민국의 국책에 반(反)하는 기사 (2) 대한민국에 피해를 입히는 기사 (3) 공산당이나 북한을 인정하거나 옹호하는 기사 (4) 선동을 목적으로 허위사실을 보도하는 기사 (5) 대한민국과 우방국의 관계와 국가위신을 손상시키는 기사 (6) 민심을 자극하기 쉬운 기사와 나아가 민심에 영향을 끼치는 기사 (7) 국가 기밀을 누설하는 기사

(f) 법과 질서의 유지

- 대한민국의 짧은 역사에서 최대의 난제는 국가안보를 지키는 것이고 행정부와 국회는 다른 모든 문제에서는 서로 다른 생각을 갖고 있지만 이 문제에서만은 한 마음이었음. 1948년 11월 국회에서 국가보안법이 제정된 것은 이러한 사실을 잘 증명함.

- 외교부장관이 위원단 의장에게 보낸 서신에 따르면, 1948년 9월 4일부터 1949년 4월 30일 사이에 33,347사건이 국가보안법에 따라 처리되었으며 89,710명이 체포됨. 28,404명이 석방되고 21,606명이 검찰에 송치되었으며 29,284명이 보안대(security office)로, 6,985명이 헌병으로 인계되고 1,187명에 대해 재판이 진행 중임.

- 대한민국 정부가 수립된 지 얼마 지나지 않은 1948년 10월 19일, 전라남도 여수와 순천에서 반란이 일어나 1948년 10월 20일부터 1949년 4월 15일까지 9,536명의 반란자들이 살상되거나 체포되었고 504명의 군인과 경찰이 사망

했으며 345명이 부상을 당함. 11,000건의 수사 및 검거 사건이 있었고 23,000명 이상이 사건에 연루되었으며, 관련자의 80퍼센트 이상이 유죄판결을 받았고 재산상 피해가 50억 원을 넘는 것으로 추산됨.

- 전략적인 위치, 가난, 전통적인 고립 및 건전한 지방행정의 부재와 맞물려 제주도는 해방이후 남로당(South Korea Labour Party)활동의 중심지인 것처럼 되어버렸고 1948년 4월 경찰과 서북청년단(Northwest Youth Corps)의 공산주의 혐의자에 대한 검거와 탄압으로 인해 폭동 현장이 됨. 소요는 제주도 전 지역으로 확산되었고 이를 진압하기 위해 많은 병력이 파견되었으나 1949년 5월까지 진압작전이 종료되지 못함. 공식적인 통계에 따르면 1만 명이상이 이 반란에 가담하였으며 그 중 2,000여명이 사살되고 6,000명 이상이 체포됨.

6. 경제적 분단이 남한에 미친 영향

- 1948년 5월 전력공급이 중단되었음에도 불구하고 남북한 간의 경제적 교류는 1949년 4월 1일 대한민국 정부에 의해 상거래가 금지될 때까지 지속되었으며, 한국 정부의 통상국에 따르면, 남한은 1948년에 북한으로부터 1,206,786,250원에 달하는 물품을 수입하였고, 같은 기간 466,515,644원에 달하는 물품을 북한에 수출하였음. 1949년 1/4분기 중 북한으로부터의 수입은 531,558,700원, 대북 수출은 302,721,500원에 달함.

제4장 요약, 분석 그리고 결론

A. 1948년 12월 12일 유엔총회 결의를 이행하기 위한
위원단의 노력

1. 통일

(a) 위원단의 방북 허가를 얻기 위한 노력

- 유엔한국위원단이 설치된 이후 북한에 접근할 수 있는 방법을 모색하는 과정에서 소련에 주선을 요청하고 다양한 경로를 통해 김일성에게 서한을 발송하여 위원단의 방북을 허가해 줄 것을 요청하였으며, 수차례 반복한 대북방송을 통해서도 방문허락을 요청하였으나 모든 노력은 실패하였고 북한과의 접촉을 위한 위원단의 이러한 노력에 대해 아무런 대답도 얻지 못함.

(b) 한국의 통일을 위한 제안

- 대한민국 정부는 북한에서 소련군대를 철수시키고 북한정권과 보안대를 해체하여 대한민국 정부가 북한지역에 관할권을 행사할 수 있도록 위원단이 소련정부에 촉구해줄 것을 제청하였으나 이는 위원단 감시 하에 북한에서 선거가 실시됨으로써 달성될 수 있는 것임.

- 정부 바깥에 있는 인사들은 위원단에 대해 통일 방안을 모색하기 위해 남북한 대표자 간에 다양한 형태의 협의를 시작할 것을 제안하였으나 한국 정부

는 이러한 방식의 협의에 대해 반대함. 위원단은 의미 있는 토론이라면 어떠한 형태의 협의도 지원할 용의가 있다고 밝힘.

- 북한이 제안한 모든 통일방안은 1947년 11월 14일 및 1948년 12월 12일의 유엔 총회의 결의에 부합되지 않는 것으로 이들의 제안에 대해 위원단은 어떠한 행동도 취하지 않음.

2. 국방군(security forces)의 통합

- 위원단은 정치적인 차원에서의 임무수행이 불가능하였기 때문에 남북한 군대의 통합을 이끌어낼 수 없음.

3. 38선 : 우호적 교류의 장애물

- 남북한 상호간의 불신으로 인해 위원단은 남북한 간의 상품 및 서비스의 우호적 거래에 방해가 되는 장벽을 쉽사리 제거하는 조치를 취할 수 없음.

- 국경지대는 38선을 따라 잦은 교전과 무장 침입의 전장이 되었으며, 미군 정보당국에 따르면 일부 공격은 대한민국 내에 공작원을 침투시키기 위한 목적으로 이루어진다고 함.

- 북한은 외교관계를 유지하고 있는 소련으로부터 승인을 받았으며 김일성의 모스크바 방문이 많은 언론의 주목을 받았고 방문기간 동안 소련의 원조와 북한과 소련의 문화교류에 관한 협정이 체결되었다고 보도됨.

4. 의회정치 발전의 심화

- 위원단은 의회정치의 추가적인 발전을 위하여 대한민국 정부의 자문요청에 응할 준비가 되어 있었으나 한국정부는 이러한 문제는 북한에만 해당되며 남한에는 해당되지 않는다는 견해를 가지고 있었으므로 위원단에 대해 이와 관련된 요청을 하지 않음. 그러나 위원단은 이 문제와 정부관료, 전문가, 사회단체의 견해를 청취하였고 북한지역의 정부구조와 북한지역에 의회정치를 확대하는 방안에 대한 조사를 실시함.

5. 점령군의 철수

- 위원단은 1948년 12월 12일 유엔총회 결의 제4항 (d)에 따라 위원단에 부과된 주한 미 점령군의 철수감시 임무를 완수하였으며 주한 미 점령군의 철수는 위원단의 감시 하에 1949년 6월 29일 완료됨.

B. 1948년 12월 12일의 유엔총회 결의 이행에 영향을 미치는 요소들

- 유엔한국임시위원단은 총회에 제출한 보고서 제2부에서 1947년 11월 14일 한국문제에 관한 최초의 총회결의가 채택되었던 당시와 임시위원단이 권고안을 내놓은 1948년 2월 26일 사이에 진전이 있었는지에 대해 의구심을 갖고 있었으며, 그 중 특별한 내용은 분단된 한반도의 남과 북에 경쟁적 정치체제가 수립되었고 세계도처에서 격화되고 있는 두 개의 이데올로기 대립이 여기에서도 나타났다고 하는 것으로, 위원단은 유엔총회가 이러한 근본적인 어려움을 해결해주기를 기대함.

- 임시위원단은 보고서 제1부에서 남한지역의 총선거 실시는 한국독립을 재확립하는 계기가 될 것이라는 결론을 내렸다고 밝히고 전체 한국인의 3분의 2가 거주하는 남한에서 실시된 5·10 선거는 임시위원단의 감시 하에 유권자들의 자유의지가 타당하게 반영된 선거였다고 보고함.

- 유엔총회는 임시위원단의 보고서 제1부와 제2부의 내용을 모두 승인하였고 전체 한국인의 대다수가 거주하는 남한에서 총선거가 실시되어 유권자의 자유의지가 타당하게 표명된 선거에 기초하여 정부가 구성되었으며, 남한을 실효적으로 통제하고 관할권을 행사하고 있는 유일한 합법적인 정부가 수립되었음을 확인하고 이 모든 과정이 임시위원단의 감시 하에 이루어졌음을 선언하는 보고서를 승인함.

- 총회는 임시위원단의 결론에 기초하여 유엔한국위원단을 설치하였으며 위원단에 대해 유엔총회에 의하여 규정된 한국정부의 지위를 명심하여 한국의 통일을 위해 주선하라는 임무를 부여함.

- 임시위원단 임무가 끝날 무렵 대한민국 정부가 수립되었으나 현재 위원단은 대한민국 정부가 독립된 주권국가로서 영토를 관리하고 있음을 확인하였으며, 위원단이 한국에 도착하기 전에 이미 파리에서 열린 제3차 유엔총회에서 한국정부 대표의 주장을 인정하는 결의를 했다는 것을 국민들에게 알린 상태임. 위원단은 유엔총회가 한국정부를 한반도 전체에 대한 합법정부로 인정한 것인지 아니면 38선 이남의 남한지역에 대한 합법정부로 인정한 것인지의 여부에 대해 한국정부와 논할 필요성이 없다고 판단함.

- 남한정부는 유엔총회에 의해 북한정권이 불법화되었다는 입장을 견지하며 위원단도 남한정부와 입장을 같이하여 북한을 상대하는 것을 자제하고 소

련을 설득하여 북한정권을 해체하고 대한민국 정부가 북한지역에서 위원단의 감시 하에 선거를 실시하도록 해야 한다고 주장함.

- 정부에 대한 위원단의 권한을 묘사하는 서식이 정부에 대한 지위를 강화한 것은 아니므로 위원단이 수요자의 요청 없이 임무수행을 하는 데에는 한계가 있으며, 이는 한국정부가 유엔총회결의 제4항 (c)가 한국에도 적용되는 것을 인정하지 않고 있고 의회정치의 발전과 관련해서 위원단의 협력을 원하지 않는 등, 위원단에 부여된 권한을 제대로 수행하는 기회를 갖지 못하고 있는 것과 관련이 있음.

- 위원단은 한반도의 통일정부 수립을 위해 북한 지도자들과 협의할 필요가 있다는 생각을 가지고 있지만 한국정부는 이를 반대하고 위원단의 유일한 파견목적이 한국정부의 권리주장을 옹호하기 위한 것이라는 입장을 표명함. 이러한 입장은 대립적인 두 정권 간의 협상 기회를 만드는 것을 불가능하게 할 것이고 남한정부와 다른 이러한 견해는 위원단이 북한과 접촉할 수 없었기 때문에 실현되지 못함.

- 위원단은 북한지역 방문 승인과 통일에 관한 예비적이고 임시적인 검토를 할 수 있게 해달라는 요청을 다양한 경로를 통해 북한에 전달하고 대북방송을 하였으나 어떠한 대답도 얻지 못하고 실패로 귀결됨.

C. 한국문제의 현황

1. 평화통일에 대한 열망

- 한국정부는 통일문제에 대한 북한과의 공식 토론에 참가하지 않을 것을 분명히 밝혔을 뿐 아니라 이를 위한 비공식적 노력에도 불쾌감을 드러냄. 아울러 이러한 노력을 배신행위로 받아들이는 분위기에서 위원단은 정부 바깥의 인사들을 접촉하는 것이 자유롭지 않다는 것을 느낌.

- 김구, 김규식이 이끄는 원외야당에 의해 주장되는 남북협상 제의에 대해 정부는 국민의 분열과 혼란을 획책하는 공산주의자들의 간계라고 간주함. 남한 정부는 남북한의 지도자들이 한 자리에 모여서 공통의 문제에 대한 해결책을 모색함으로써 한국문제의 난관을 극복할 수 있을 것이라는 국민의 생각을 과소평가하고 있는 것으로 보임.

- 대한민국은 여전히 5·10 선거문제에 관한 견해차에서 비롯된 정치적 분단이라는 약점을 안고 힘겹게 움직이고 있으며, 정부는 이러한 분단을 시정하려는 노력을 하지 않고 있음.

2. 타협정신의 부족

- 한반도 통일을 위한 위원단의 노력에 대해 북한정권은 무시와 비협조로 일관하였으며, 한국을 사랑한다거나 통일을 희망한다는 말은 많았지만 행동은 늘 그와 상반되게 나타나서 신뢰할 수 없음. 38선에서 발생하는 무력충돌은 불법행위이며 양쪽 모두 한국 국민이기 때문에 불행한 일이기도 함.

- 남북한 간의 상호 적대적인 불신이 굳어지면서 남북한의 무역 등 경제 교류가 재개될 수 없었으며 한국정부의 반대로 북한에 교류 재개를 제안할 기회조차 갖지 못했다는 사실을 보고하지 않을 수 없음.

3. 남북한에서 확대되는 군사력

- 38선 양쪽에 군사 태세가 증가하였고, 이것은 공개적인 군사적 충돌을 자극할만한 심각한 위험을 안고 있음을 의미함.

- 북한은 최근 소련과 조약을 체결하고 중공군과 군사원조에 관한 협정을 체결하였으며 남한정부는 군비준비를 서두르고 있고 미국정부에 대해 이미 받은 군사원조보다 더 많은 군사원조를 요청하고 있으며, 남한은 미군으로부터, 북한은 소련으로부터 군사 훈련 및 자문 지원을 받고 있음.

- 의견 대립과 전복 활동(subversion)등의 선전전이 증가하고 있음.

4. 국제정치 정세

- 한국문제 해결과 관련하여 위원단이 청취한 다양한 의견을 살펴보면, 일반적으로 소련과 미국이 현재의 곤경에 대한 책임이 있다고 믿고 있으며, 이와 동등하게 소련과 미국이 38선의 장애물을 공동으로 제거하고 1945년 12월 모스크바 삼상회의에서 약속한 한국의 독립 및 통일을 회복하지 않는 한 문제는 해결되지 못할 것이라는 의견이 일반적임.

- 대한민국 정부는 소련이 여전히 북한 지역에 대해 결정적인 통제권을 행사하고 있다고 주장하며 소련이 북한정권을 보호하는 것을 중지하고 북한사람

들이 대한민국에 대한 충성심을 표현하는 것을 허락한다면 한국문제는 해결될 것이라고 함. 한국정부는 북한에 의한 침략과 침입 위협을 방지하기 위해 미국은 군사 및 경제 원조를 할 의무가 있다고 기대하고 있음.

- 대한민국의 방위에 대한 미국의 책임을 주장하는 목소리와 한국정부가 미국에 군사적인 원조를 요청했다는 소식이 자주 보도되었으며, 한국 대통령이 수차에 걸쳐 미국은 한국의 미래에 대한 책임을 지고 있고 태평양 안보를 위협하는 위험에 맞서 태평양안전보장조약을 체결하고 결속을 강화해야 한다고 주장함.

- 미국과 소련 간의 합의가 없이는 한국 문제가 해결될 수 없다는 일반적 견해에 입각하여 위원단의 한국문제 해결능력을 의문시하는 경향이 있으나, 위원단은 자신들에게 부여된 임무를 수행하지 못하는 까닭를 평가함에 있어 미소 관계가 남한과 북한 사이의 관계 악화에 계속해서 결정적인 요인으로 작용할 것이라고 판단함.

D. 결론

- 한국 국민은 단일민족으로서 인종적·문화적으로도 동일하며 남북한의 평화통일과 독립을 강력하게 희망하고 있음. 통일이 되었다면 좀 더 높은 수준에서 경제를 안정화시켰을 것이며 원조 또한 현재 수준 정도로까지는 필요하지 않았을 것임.

- 한국의 분단은 제2차 세계대전의 전략상 필요했기 때문이며 국가를 두 부분으로 분리하여야할 정당한 이유는 없음.

- 한국정부는 어떤 면에서는 유엔에 의해 수립되었다고 생각되기 때문에 많은 문제에 대한 해결방법을 유엔에 기대하고 있으며, 위원단의 체류를 1년 더 연장해달라고 요청하고 있는 것에서도 알 수 있는 것처럼, 위원단의 존재가 한반도를 안정화시키는 요소가 되고 있다고 평가하고 있음.

- 한국문제에 대한 철저한 검토 결과 다음과 같은 결론을 제출함.

(1) 현재 남북관계의 적대적인 선전전과 행동은 남북관계를 더욱 악화시키고 통일전망을 더욱 어둡게 할 것으로 보임.

(2) 1948년 12월 12일 유엔총회 결의의 목적을 달성하기 위한 한국위원단의 노력에 대한 소련정부의 반대가 계속되는 한, 적대적인 선전전을 완화시키는 것은 물론이고 통일을 달성하는 데에 필요한 상당한 정도의 진전을 용이하게 할 조치도 불가능할 것으로 보임.

(3) 전 세계에 걸친 미국과 소련간의 적대 행위는 현재의 곤란한 문제를 해결해나가는 데에 근본적인 문제로 작용할 것이고 양국이 한국문제에 관해 합의에 도달하려는 새로운 노력을 기울이지 않는 한, 유엔총회가 인정한 원칙에 의거하여 통일을 향한 뚜렷한 진전을 이루지 못할 것으로 보임.

(4) 새로 수립된 대한민국 정부는 내부의 혼란과 38선에서 계속되는 충돌 등 초반부터 다양한 어려움에 직면하고 있음. 이러한 난관 속에서도 한국정부는 정치적 토대를 넓히고 어려움에 더욱 성공적으로 대처해 나가고 있으며 통일을 달성하기 위해 더욱 효과적인 역할을 할 수 있을 것이라고 믿고 있음.

(5) 앞서 존재한 임시위원단과 마찬가지로 현재의 유엔한국위원단도 한국의 상황이 처음보다 더 나아진 것은 없다고 인정할 수밖에 없다는 것, 그리고 유엔총회가 정한 목적 달성을 용이하게 할 수 없었다는 사실을 기록하지 않을 수 없음.

－이상의 내용에 대해 유엔한국위원단의 루나((Rufino Luna, 필리핀대표), 리우위안(Liu Yu-Wan, 중국대표), 제이미슨(A. B. Jamieson, 호주대표), 마가냐(Miguel Angel Magaña, 엘살바도르대표), 코스티유(Henry Costilhes, 프랑스대표), 씽(Anup Singh, 인도대표)이 서명함.

UNITED NATIONS

REPORT OF THE UNITED NATIONS COMMISSION ON KOREA

Volume I

GENERAL ASSEMBLY

OFFICIAL RECORDS : FOURTH SESSION

SUPPLEMENT No. 9 (A/936)

LAKE SUCCESS

New York

1949

This document constitutes volume I of the Report of the United Nations Commission on Korea. A second volume containing the annexes is also being published.

Only a certain number of the documents issued by the United Nations Commission on Korea (series A/AC.26/1 et seq.) to which reference is made in the footnotes to the present report have been included in the annexes published in volume II. In each case the number of the annex has been given in the footnote. The remaining documents are available for consultation in the Archives Section of the Secretariat at Headquarters.

REPORT OF THE
UNITED NATIONS
COMMISSION ON KOREA

VOLUME I

GENERAL ASSEMBLY

OFFICIAL RECORDS : FOURTH SESSION

SUPPLEMENT No. 9 (A/936)

LAKE SUCCESS
New York
1949

A/936
August 1949

제3부 유엔한국위원단 보고서(1949)

412

TABLE OF CONTENTS

iii

제3부 유엔한국위원단 보고서(1949)

INTRODUCTION

The United Nations Commission on Korea was created by General Assembly resolution 195 (III) of 12 December 1948. It held its first meeting on 2 February 1949 in Seoul, Korea. Between that date and 28 July 1949, the Commission held fifty meetings, all in Seoul.

The present report covers the period from the arrival of members of the Commission in Seoul on 30 January 1949 to 28 July 1949. The report is divided into two parts. Part II consists of annexes of relevant documents. Part I is divided into four chapters.

Chapter I (paragraphs 1 to 24) deals with the creation and organization of the Commission and its terms of reference.

Chapter II (paragraphs 1 to 92) summarizes the main activities of the Commission and its subsidiary bodies.

Chapter III (paragraphs 1 to 104) presents an account of the political, economic and social developments and factors affecting the problem of the independence and unification of Korea.

Chapter IV (paragraphs 1 to 35) contains a summary and analysis of the efforts of the Commission to implement the General Assembly resolution of 12 December 1948; the factors affecting the implementation of that resolution; an analysis of the present status of the Korean problem; and the conclusions reached by the Commission.

The complete report was adopted unanimously on 28 July 1949. The representative of Syria was not present when the report was drafted nor when it was adopted.

Chapter I

CREATION OF THE UNITED NATIONS COMMISSION ON KOREA: ITS TERMS OF REFERENCE, COMPOSITION AND ORGANIZATION

A. Creation

1. REPORT OF THE TEMPORARY COMMISSION TO THE GENERAL ASSEMBLY AND INCLUSION OF THE PROBLEM OF KOREA IN THE AGENDA OF THE THIRD REGULAR SESSION

1. The United Nations Temporary Commission on Korea submitted its report to the General Assembly at its third regular session, as provided in General Assembly resolution 112 (II) A and B of 14 November 1947, on the problem of the independence of Korea. The report[1] of the Temporary Commission was made in two parts: the first part of the report, concerned with the observation of elections and covering the Commission's work from 12 January 1948 to 24 May 1948, was transmitted to the Secretary-General on 21 July 1948 from Korea; and the second part, dealing with developments following the 10 May elections, was completed at Lake Success and dispatched to the Secretary-General in Paris on 15 October 1948.

2. At meetings held on 22 and 23 September 1948, the General Committee considered the provisional agenda of the third regular session of the General Assembly and decided to recommend the inclusion of the problem of the independence of Korea as item 16 on the agenda.[2] At its 142nd plenary meeting, on 24 September 1948, the General Assembly considered the recommendations of the General Committee regarding the agenda. The delegation of the Union of Soviet Socialist Republics, supported by the delegation of Poland, proposed that item 16 should be deleted from the agenda, on the ground that the Temporary Commission established by the General Assembly was an "illegal body". The proposal of the Union of Soviet Socialist Republics was rejected by 47 votes to 6, with no abstentions.[3] The problem of the independence of Korea was then referred to the First Committee for consideration and report.

2. DISCUSSION IN THE FIRST COMMITTEE

3. Before the First Committee took up the question of Korea, the representatives of the Government of the Republic of Korea and of the "Government of the Democratic People's Republic of Korea" requested participation in the discussion of the problem of Korea at the meetings of the General Assembly. By a letter[4] dated 1 October 1948 to the Secretary-General, the chief of the delegation of the Government of the Republic of Korea further stated that the presence of his delegation at the third regular session of the General Assembly was responsive to the reso-

lution adopted on 14 November 1947 while, in a cable[5] to the Secretary-General dated 8 October 1948, the Minister of Foreign Affairs of the "Democratic People's Republic of Korea" asserted that, following general elections held in August 1948 throughout North and South Korea, the "Supreme People's Assembly" and the "United Government of the Democratic People's Republic of Korea" had been established and that the problem of Korea must be considered and settled with the "participation of lawful representatives". The Secretary-General replied that these communications would be circulated to the members of the First Committee at the time when the Korean question came up for discussion in that Committee.

4. On 4 November 1948, the delegation of Czechoslovakia submitted a draft resolution[6] to the Chairman of the First Committee proposing that the First Committee should consider the request of the "Government of the Democratic People's Republic of Korea" and invite its delegation to participate in the debate on the Korean question. At its 200th meeting, on 15 November 1948, the First Committee considered the question proposed by the Czechoslovak delegation. The delegations of the Union of Soviet Socialist Republics, the Byelorussian Soviet Socialist Republic, the Ukrainian Soviet Socialist Republic and Poland supported the draft resolution, while delegations of China, El Salvador, Haiti and the United States of America expressed the view that it was inappropriate to discuss the procedural question of issuing an invitation before the report of the Temporary Commission had been examined and the legal status of the Government of the Republic of Korea had been decided. By 38 votes to 6, with 6 abstentions, the First Committee postponed consideration of the Czechoslovak draft resolution.

5. At its 229th and 230th meetings, on 6 December 1948, the First Committee resumed discussion of the Czechoslovak draft resolution, together with a draft resolution[7] presented by China proposing to invite the delegation of Korea, under the chairmanship of Mr. John M. Chang, to participate, without the right to vote, in the debate in the First Committee on the Korean problem. The delegations of the USSR, the Byelorussian SSR, Poland, the Ukrainian SSR and Yugoslavia supported the Czechoslovak resolution and the delegations of Canada, Egypt, El Salvador, New Zealand, Norway, the Philippines, Syria, the United Kingdom and Uruguay supported the Chinese draft resolution. After considerable debate the First Committee, at its 230th meeting, rejected the Czechoslovak draft resolution by 30 votes to 6, with 8 abstentions. Before the Chinese draft resolution was put to a vote, the representa-

---

[1] A/575 and A/575/Add.1 to Add.4, *Official Records of the third regular session of the General Assembly, Supplement No. 9.*
[2] A/653.
[3] *Official Records of the third regular session of the General Assembly, plenary meetings,* pages 92 to 94, 104 to 105.
[4] A/C.1/365.

[5] A/C.1/366.
[6] A/C.1/367.
[7] A/C.1/395.

tive of Australia suggested, and the representative of China accepted, an amendment inserting the words "of the Government of the Republic" between "the delegation" and "of Korea". The amended Chinese proposal was adopted by 39 votes to 6, with 1 abstention. The First Committee also decided to invite the Rapporteur of the Temporary Commission to submit his report at the next meeting.

6. After hearing the statement of the Rapporteur at the 231st meeting of the First Committee, and the statement of the representative of the Government of the Republic of Korea at the 232nd meeting, on 7 December 1948, a general debate took place in which the representatives of Australia, Brazil, Burma, the Byelorussian SSR, Canada, China, Czechoslovakia, the Dominican Republic, El Salvador, France, India, Iraq, the Netherlands, New Zealand, the Philippines, Poland, Syria, the Ukrainian SSR, the United Kingdom, the United States of America, the USSR and Yugoslavia participated. The Committee had before it two draft resolutions:

(a) A draft resolution submitted jointly by Australia, China and the United States of America (A/C.1/426), approving the conclusions of the report of the Temporary Commission on Korea and establishing a new Commission on Korea;

(b) A draft resolution presented by the USSR (A/C.1/474/Corr.1) proposing the termination of the Temporary Commission on Korea.

The representatives of the Byelorussian SSR, Czechoslovakia, Poland, the Ukrainian SSR, the USSR and Yugoslavia stated that their delegations could not approve the report of the Temporary Commission, on the ground that it did not reflect the wishes of the Korean people, and that they could not accept the joint draft resolution of Australia, China and the United States of America, on the ground that it was contrary to the decision of the Korean people. They stated further that the Temporary Commission had put new obstacles in the way of the restoration of Korea's independence and should therefore be abolished. The representatives of all other delegations who took part in the debate accepted the conclusions of the report of the Temporary Commission and supported the joint draft resolution. Toward the end of the general debate, the representative of Canada proposed the closure of the debate under rule 106 of the Assembly's rules of procedure. The Canadian proposal was adopted at the 235th meeting of the First Committee, by 30 votes to 6, with 3 abstentions.

7. At the 236th meeting, on 8 December 1948, the joint draft resolution and the draft resolution of the USSR were put to a vote. The joint draft resolution was adopted by 41 votes to 6, with 2 abstentions. To fill the blank in paragraph 4 of the joint draft resolution concerning the membership of the Commission, the representative of the United States of America proposed the insertion of the words "the same Member States which composed the United Nations Temporary Commission on Korea". The proposal was adopted by 41 votes to none, with 1 abstention. The representatives of the Byelorussian SSR, Czechoslovakia, Poland, the Ukrainian SSR, the USSR and Yugoslavia did not take part in the voting on this proposal. The representative of the Ukrainian

SSR declared that his Government would take no part in any activities of any Korean Commission which might be set up.

8. By 42 votes to 6, with 3 abstentions, the First Committee rejected the draft resolution submitted by the delegation of the USSR.

3. DISCUSSION IN THE GENERAL ASSEMBLY

9. At its 186th plenary meeting on 11 December 1948, the General Assembly began its consideration of the report of the First Committee on the problem of the independence of Korea, which recommended adoption of the resolution voted by the First Committee.[8] The General Assembly also considered the USSR draft resolution, which was re-presented in the plenary meeting.[9] Following the statement of the Rapporteur of the First Committee, a general debate took place at the 186th and 187th meetings in which only the representatives of Australia, the Byelorussian SSR, Canada, China, Czechoslovakia, Poland, the Ukrainian SSR, the USSR and Yugoslavia participated. The representatives of the Byelorussian SSR, Czechoslovakia, Poland, the Ukrainian SSR, the USSR and Yugoslavia reiterated the position expressed by them in the First Committee.

In supporting the resolution recommended by the First Committee, the representative of China stated that the work of the Temporary Commission remained half done and it was necessary to establish a new Commission to carry out the objectives of the General Assembly resolution of 1947. Urging the adoption of the resolution, the representative of Australia remarked "even if it does not immediately bring about unity, it can perform a valuable service in increasing the contacts between south and north". Also speaking in favour of the resolution, the delegation of Canada submitted an amendment which read as follows: "In paragraph 4, delete words consisting of 'the same Member States which composed the United Nations Temporary Commission on Korea' and substitute therefore words 'consisting of the following States: Australia, China, El Salvador, France, India, the Philippines and Syria'". Before the Canadian amendment was put to a vote, the representative of the USSR stated that his delegation would not take part in voting on any amendment bearing upon membership or other aspects of a new commission. The amendment was adopted by 40 votes to none, with 3 abstentions. By a roll-call vote, the General Assembly, at the 187th plenary meeting on 12 December 1948, adopted the resolution, as amended, by 48 votes to 6, with 1 abstention.

At the request of the representative of the USSR, the President of the General Assembly put to the vote the USSR draft resolution, which proposed the termination of the United Nations Temporary Commission on Korea; it was rejected by 46 votes to 6, with no abstentions.

B. Terms of reference

10. The terms of reference of the United Nations Commission on Korea are contained in General Assembly resolution 195 (III) of 12 December 1948, the text of which follows:

---

[8] A/788.
[9] A/790.

"*The General Assembly,*

"*Having regard* to its resolution 112 (II) of 14 November 1947 concerning the problem of the independence of Korea,

"*Having considered* the report of the United Nations Temporary Commission on Korea (hereinafter referred to as the 'Temporary Commission'), and the report of the Interim Committee of the General Assembly regarding its consultation with the Temporary Commission,

"*Mindful* of the fact that, due to difficulties referred to in the report of the Temporary Commission, the objectives set forth in the resolution of 14 November 1947 have not been fully accomplished, and in particular that unification of Korea has not yet been achieved,

"1. *Approves* the conclusions of the reports of the Temporary Commission;

"2. *Declares* that there has been established a lawful government (the Government of the Republic of Korea) having effective control and jurisdiction over that part of Korea where the Temporary Commission was able to observe and consult and in which the great majority of the people of all Korea reside; that this Government is based on elections which were a valid expression of the free will of the electorate of that part of Korea and which were observed by the Temporary Commission; and that this is the only such Government in Korea;

"3. *Recommends* that the occupying Powers should withdraw their occupation forces from Korea as early as practicable;

"4. *Resolves* that, as a means to the full accomplishment of the objectives set forth in the resolution of 14 November 1947, a Commission on Korea, consisting of Australia, China, El Salvador, France, India, the Philippines and Syria should be established to continue the work of the Temporary Commission and carry out the provisions of the present resolution, having in mind the status of the Government of Korea as herein defined, and in particular to:

"(*a*) Lend its good offices to bring about the unification of Korea and the integration of all Korean security forces in accordance with the principles laid down by the General Assembly in the resolution of 14 November 1947;

"(*b*) Seek to facilitate the removal of barriers to economic, social and other friendly intercourse caused by the division of Korea;

"(*c*) Be available for observation and consultation in the further development of representative government based on the freely-expressed will of the people;

"(*d*) Observe the actual withdrawal of the occupying forces and verify the fact of withdrawal when such has occurred; and for this purpose, if it so desires, request the assistance of military experts of the two occupying Powers;

"5. *Decides* that the Commission:

"(*a*) Shall, within thirty days of the adoption of the present resolution, proceed to Korea, where it shall maintain its seat;

"(*b*) Shall be regarded as having superseded the Temporary Commission established by the resolution of 14 November 1947;

"(*c*) Is authorized to travel, consult and observe throughout Korea;

"(*d*) Shall determine its own procedures;

"(*e*) May consult with the Interim Committee with respect to the discharge of its duties in the light of developments, and within the terms of the present resolution;

"(*f*) Shall render a report to the next regular session of the General Assembly and to any prior special session which might be called to consider the subject-matter of the present resolution, and shall render such interim reports as it may deem appropriate to the Secretary-General for distribution to Members;

"6. *Requests* that the Secretary-General shall provide the Commission with adequate staff and facilities, including technical advisers as required; and authorizes the Secretary-General to pay the expenses and *per diem* of a representative and an alternate from each of the States members of the Commission;

"7. *Calls upon* the Member States concerned, the Government of the Republic of Korea, and all Koreans to afford every assistance and facility to the Commission in the fulfilment of its responsibilities;

"8. *Calls upon* Member States to refrain from any acts derogatory to the results achieved and to be achieved by the United Nations in bringing about the complete independence and unity of Korea;

"9. *Recommends* that Member States and other nations, in establishing their relations with the Government of the Republic of Korea, take into consideration the facts set out in paragraph 2 of the present resolution."

C. Letters and telegrams from the Secretary-General

11. In a letter, dated 6 January 1949, to the Governments of the seven members composing the United Nations Commission on Korea, the Secretary-General requested that the names of their representatives on the Commission be communicated to him as soon as possible. All the Governments concerned except El Salvador announced the appointment of their representatives to the Commission in the latter part of January. In a telegram dated 17 January 1949, the Secretary-General informed the Governments represented on the Commission that it was scheduled to meet in Seoul on 31 January 1949.

D. Composition of the Commission

12. According to the resolution of the General Assembly, the Commission was to consist of the representatives of Australia, China, El Salvador, France, India, the Philippines and Syria. At the end of January 1949, the representative and alternate representative of China, Mr. Liu Yu-Wan and Mr. T. T. Ssutu, and the temporary representative of France, Mr. Henri Costilhes, were present in Seoul. The representative of Syria, Mr. Yasin Mughir, arrived in Seoul on 30 January 1949 and the representative of India, Mr. Anup Singh, and the representative of the Philippines, Mr. Rufino Luna, arrived on 1 February 1949. The representatives of Australia, Mr. Patrick Shaw and Mr. A. B. Jamieson, then alternate, together with the main body of the secretariat, arrived in Seoul on 5 February. Mr. Patrick Shaw returned to his post in Tokyo on 23 February and was succeeded by Mr. A. B. Jamieson. The for-

mer returned to Seoul on 2 July 1949 and departed for Tokyo again on 12 July. The notification of the appointment to the Commission of Mr. Miguel Angel Magaña as representative of El Salvador was received on 11 March 1949, and Mr. Magaña arrived in Seoul on 26 March 1949, the same day that the representative of Syria, Mr. Yasin Mughir, left Seoul. On April 29, it was announced that an alternate representative of El Salvador, Captain Sánchez Hernández, had been appointed; he arrived in Seoul on 14 May. Upon the instructions of its Government, the delegation of El Salvador withdrew from the Commission on 20 July, but rejoined it on 26 July.

13. The secretariat of the Commission, totalling twenty-seven members including ten locally recruited personnel, was headed by a principal secretary. In addition, the secretariat included a deputy principal secretary, three assistant secretaries, an administrative officer, an assistant administrative officer, two interpreters, two précis-writers and six secretary-typists.

14. At its 49th meeting on 27 July 1949, the Commission unanimously decided to add, at the end of section D of chapter I of the present report, the following paragraph expressing appreciation of the work of the secretariat:

"The Commission wishes to pay tribute to the untiring work and devotion to duty shown by all the members of the Secretariat under the able guidance and leadership of the principal secretary, Mr. Egon Ranshofen-Wertheimer. Very few in number and working under difficult material conditions, they have performed their required tasks with distinction."

15. Mr. Costilhes (France) regretted that the documents of the Commission had not been available in French, due to the lack of translators, and pointed out that this fact should in no way constitute a precedent.

E. Organization

16. During the period 2 February to 28 July 1949, the Commission held one public meeting and fifty closed meetings, all in Seoul.

1. OFFICE OF CHAIRMAN

17. At the first meeting of the Commission the following representatives were present: Mr. Liu Yu-Wan (China), Mr. Henri Costilhes (France), Mr. Anup Singh (India), Mr. Rufino Luna (Philippines) and Mr. Yasin Mughir (Syria). Due to the absence of the delegations of Australia and El Salvador, it was decided to elect a temporary Chairman for a fifteen-day period, to be succeeded by the representatives in rotation in the English alphabetical order of the countries represented until such time as the Commission decided upon a permanent system of chairmanship. Mr. Liu Yu-Wan was elected temporary Chairman. At the 6th meeting, the Commission formally adopted the system of rotation of Chairmen. It was decided that the chairmanship should rotate every thirty days in the English alphabetical order of the countries represented, and that the Chairman should assume office immediately. Accordingly, Mr. Patrick Shaw (Australia) became the first Chairman of the Commission.

18. In accordance with the decision of the Commission, the following representatives have assumed the chairmanship for periods of thirty days each:

Mr. Patrick Shaw, succeeded by Mr. A. B. Jamieson after 23 February (Australia), 10 February-11 March 1949;

Mr. Liu Yu-Wan, alternate Mr. T. T. Ssutu acting during his absence (China), 12 March-10 April 1949;

Mr. Miguel A. Magaña (El Salvador), 11 April-10 May 1949;

Mr. Henri Costilhes (France), 11 May-9 June 1949;

Mr. Anup Singh (India), 10 June-9 July 1949;

Mr. Rufino Luna (Philippines), 10 July-9 August 1949.

2. OFFICE OF RAPPORTEUR

19. At its 6th meeting the Commission adopted, with some amendments, the rules of procedure formerly employed by the Temporary Commission and Mr. Liu Yu-Wan (China), was unanimously elected Rapporteur.

3. SUB-COMMITTEES AND *ad hoc* COMMITTEES

20. To implement its terms of reference as provided in the General Assembly resolution of 12 December 1948, the Commission at various times established three standing sub-committees and two *ad hoc* committees.

(a) *Sub-committees*

21. Sub-Committee I, composed of the representatives of Australia, India and Syria, was established by a resolution adopted at the 5th meeting of the Commission, on 9 February 1949, to study the nature and extent of the existing economic and social barriers caused by the division of Korea, and to promote economic and social co-operation and political unification between north and south. Mr. Anup Singh, representative of India, was elected Chairman at the 2nd meeting of the Sub-Committee. At its 24th meeting, on 5 April 1949, the Commission unanimously elected Mr. Miguel A. Magaña, representative of El Salvador, to Sub-Committee I.

22. Sub-Committee II, composed of the representatives of China, France and the Philippines, was established by a resolution adopted at the 5th meeting of the Commission, to study the development of representative government and to gather views and opinions from experts and organizations on the problem of representative government, and to be available for consultation with governmental authorities on the problem. Mr. Henri Costilhes, temporary representative of France, was elected Chairman at the 1st meeting of the Sub-Committee, and Mr. Rufino Luna, representative of the Philippines, agreed to preside over the hearings of the Sub-Committee.

23. Sub-Committee III, composed of the representatives of Australia, China, El Salvador and India, was established by a resolution adopted at the 34th meeting of the Commission on 10 June 1949. At the 35th meeting of the Commission on 20 June 1949, the powers of the Sub-Committee were increased from authority to study and report on procedures to be employed in the observation and verification of the withdrawal of American occupation forces from Korea, to authority actually to observe and verify the withdrawal of occupation forces from all Korea. Mr.

Jamieson, representative of Australia, was elected Chairman at the 1st meeting of the Sub-Committee.

(b) Ad hoc *committees*

24. In the course of its work, the Commission established two *ad hoc* committees. At the 13th meeting on 21 February 1949, the Commission appointed an *Ad Hoc* Committee composed of the representatives of Australia and Syria, to investigate and report on the technical aspect of the question of the access of Koreans to the Commission. The *Ad Hoc* Committee of the Whole on the question of observer teams was established at the 31st meeting of the Commission on 26 May 1949. These two *Ad Hoc* Committees held only one meeting each and, following their reports to the Commission, adjourned *sine die*.

Chapter II

SUMMARY OF THE MAIN ACTIVITIES OF THE COMMISSION AND OF ITS SUBSIDIARY BODIES

A. Activities and decisions of the Commission

1. ESTABLISHMENT OF SUB-COMMITTEES I AND II

1. During the initial stages of its proceedings, the Commission devoted itself to organizing the work of carrying out the tasks outlined in paragraph 4 of the General Assembly resolution of 12 December 1948.

2. Sub-Committees I and II were established by a resolution[10] adopted at the 5th meeting of the Commission on 9 February 1949.

Under this resolution, Sub-Committee I was to:

"1. . . . impress upon the people throughout Korea the Commission's . . . desire to extend its good offices to remove existing barriers in Korea with a view to promoting unification;

"2. Study the . . . existing . . . barriers . . .; obtain . . . information . . . concerning efforts to remove such barriers; and recommend methods for further improvement;

"3. Explore means for promoting social and cultural relations among the people throughout Korea; and . . .

"4. Make immediate contact with North Korea . . ."

In entrusting these tasks to Sub-Committee I, the Commission sought to initiate the implementation of paragraphs 4 (*a*) and 4 (*b*) of the General Assembly resolution.

3. Sub-Committee II, established with a view to carrying out paragraph 4 (*c*) of the General Assembly resolution, was directed to study the development of representative government in Korea, to be ready for consultation with governmental authorities, and to gather from experts and organizations opinions and views bearing on the further development of representative government.

4. The provisions of paragraph 4 (*d*) of the General Assembly resolution pertaining to the observation and verification of the withdrawal of occupation forces were left to be dealt with at a later stage.

2. RELATIONS WITH THE GOVERNMENT, THE PUBLIC AND THE PRESS

(a) *The Government*

5. The main channels of communication used in the relations between the Commission and the Government were the following:

(i) Direct contacts between the President of the Republic of Korea and members of the Commission, which took place from time to time.

(ii) The Liaison Committee appointed by the Government had its first interview with members of the Commission on 16 February 1949. It was composed originally of Mr. Chough Pyong Ok, Chairman, Mr. Chang Lee Yung, alternate representative, and Mr. Lee Choon Ho, liaison officer. Subsequently, Mr. Chang, and then Miss Moh Youn Sook, became Chairman. Contacts between this Committee and the Commission were continuous.

(iii) Hearings of members and officials of the Government were held by Sub-Committees I and II for the purpose of eliciting views and information bearing on the tasks of the Commission. They are dealt with below in the present chapter under "B. Sub-Committees".

(iv) There was a frequent exchange of written communications.

6. As the Commission and its Sub-Committees proceeded with the development of their working programmes, certain problems concerning the relation of the Government with the Commission, and affecting the latter's work, emerged. These problems turned on the questions of contact with the north and consultation with individuals and organizations. As stated in a report of Sub-Committee I[11] adopted by the Commission at its 17th meeting on 2 March 1949, the respective positions were as follows:

"In respect to contact with North Korea, the Government of Korea has declared that it disapproved of any approach except through the Soviet Union, and it would adopt a non-co-operative attitude in any efforts which the Commission might make in seeking to establish direct contact with the Government or leaders of the north. However, in the course of the Chairman's discussion with the President, the latter stated that

---

[10] A/822, annex I.

[11] A/AC.26/SC.1/4/Rev.1.

he would guarantee the receipt, by leaders in the north, of a communication from the Commission.

"The Government has further indicated that, in its opinion, economic and social intercourse between the north and the south does not exist, and the Government does not intend that there should be any. Assuming that a contact were to be made with the north, the Government of Korea might be unwilling to co-operate in efforts of the Commission to remove existing barriers.

"The Commission has declared, in its resolution of 9 February 1949, and in the report of Sub-Committee I adopted on 18 February 1949, that it sought to make immediate contact with North Korea as a means of seeking to remove economic, social and other barriers, and that it would continue to explore practical means of travelling to North Korea.

"The Commission, in requesting the USSR Government to lend its good offices to establish contact with leading personalities in North Korea, has taken this as a first step, and in the meantime will explore other avenues of approach to the north.

"The Commission has been unanimous in its agreement that it does not propose to communicate with a government in North Korea, recognizing that the Government of the Republic of Korea is the only lawful government in the country.

"In respect to consultation with individuals and organizations, the Korean Government has made it clear that it disapproved of the Commission consulting personalities outside the Government without its consent. The Government, through its Liaison Committee, has suggested that if any person desired to approach the Commission for purposes of consultation, his references should be cleared with the Liaison Committee.

"The President and the Liaison Committee have indicated that consultation with certain personalities such as Mr. Kim Koo and Mr. Kimm Kiusic would throw the public into confusion and would result in grave consequences. However, the President offered to arrange contacts for the Commission with members of the National Assembly.

"By its resolution of 16 February 1949, the Commission has declared that reputable Koreans wishing to approach the Commission or its members for *bona fide* purposes should be freely permitted to do so.

"The Chairman informed President Rhee that the Commission was disturbed by the implied desire of the Korean Government to restrict its work, and regarded as an unjustifiable limitation the Government's attitude of disapproval of interviews with unofficial persons. In order to carry out its work effectively, the Commission required freedom of operation, even involving consulting people whose views were not acceptable to the Government.

"The Commission is, however, cognizant of the status of the Government of the Republic of Korea as defined in the General Assembly's resolution.

"Having examined the record of the Government's position and the Commission's policy summarized above, Sub-Committee I is of the opinion that no change in the basic policy of the Commission is required unless or until there is

concrete evidence that the Government is restricting it in its work."

7. The dual principle of maintaining its freedom of operation while remaining mindful of the status of the Government of the Republic of Korea as defined in the General Assembly resolution was adhered to by the Commission throughout its work. No occasion for the Commission to reconsider its basic policy arose.

8. In a letter,[12] dated 30 June 1949, the Minister of Foreign Affairs of the Republic of Korea, Mr. B. C. Limb, informed the Commission that the people and the Government were deeply appreciative of its efforts, and acknowledged the goodwill and prestige of the United Nations. He expressed the hope that the Commission would remain in Korea, where its tasks were not yet completed, for at least another year, and requested it to "communicate this matter to the United Nations General Assembly and obtain its concurrences".

At the 41st meeting, on 20 July, the Commission decided to inform the Foreign Minister that his communication would be recorded in its report to the General Assembly. The letter to be addressed to him, however, was not to commit the Commission to any recommendations in this connexion.

(b) *The public*

9. Having placed on record, in its resolution of 16 February 1949,[13] its desire that any reputable Korean citizen be freely permitted to approach it for *bona fide* purposes, the Commission, at its 13th meeting on 21 February 1949, instructed an *Ad Hoc* Committee to investigate the possibility of opening a Commission pass office to which Koreans could apply as an alternative to the screening by the Government's Liaison Committee.

The report of the *Ad Hoc* Committee, recommending the establishment of a pass office, came before the Commission at its 14th meeting on 23 February 1949. It was agreed that no decision on technical arrangements should be made until an understanding with the Government on the basic issue of the Commission's relations with the Government was reached, and the question was not re-opened during the subsequent period of the Commission's activities.

10. While the Commission took no other steps to enable Koreans to communicate with it, it took the initiative itself in approaching certain personalities outside the Government. With the approval of the Commission, Sub-Committees I and II invited various representative Koreans to appear for hearings before them. The invitations were accepted by most of the individuals so chosen and no objection was made by the Government. A system of passes for distribution by members of the Commission and secretariat was instituted with the approval of the Commission and has been useful.

11. Among the persons heard were such controversial figures as Mr. Kim Koo[14] and Mr. Kimm Kiusic. The practice followed by the Commission in such cases was to sound out, prior to the scheduling of a hearing, the opinion of the Government concerning the possible effects of the

[12] A/AC.26/36 (see volume II, annex IV, A.3).
[13] A/AC.26/3.
[14] Mr. Kim Koo was assassinated on 26 June 1949.

hearing on public security, that opinion being considered along with other factors in determining whether to invite persons to appear before it. In no case did the Commission reject any of the names proposed by the Sub-Committees.

12. An invitation to the public to communicate with an organ of the Commission was reiterated in Press release No. 21 on 13 June 1949, authorized by the Commission at its 34th meeting on the same date.[15] The release announced that Sub-Committee I had decided to call a halt to its formal hearings, but that it was not "closing its doors or shutting its ears". It was stated that the Chairman of Sub-Committee I welcomed communications or calls from Koreans who felt that they had suggestions for the unification of Korea.

13. As a means of communicating with the public of South and North Korea, the Commission approved, at its 38th meeting on 4 July, a programme of broadcasts to be made by its members over the Seoul radio station of the Republic of Korea. An invitation to make such broadcasts had been extended by the Director of the Office of Public Information on the occasion of the Commission's broadcast to North Korea (see paragraph 24 below). The programme, however, was abandoned before the first broadcast had been made. At the 41st meeting, on 20 July, the Commission noted that a disagreement which had arisen over the text of a proposed broadcast constituted an attempt at censorship on the part of the Office of Public Information, and decided not to carry out the programme.[16]

14. During the period covered by this report, the Commission received many written communications, although the number of these was not so great as those addressed to the Temporary Commission during the corresponding period of the preceding year. However, there were many communications from mass meetings, each of which bore many signatures. Messages from unknown individuals were not given specific individual consideration. Several petitions dealt with basic issues under consideration by the Commission and emanated from organizations or groups of members of the National Assembly.

15. The author of one petition, Mr. Kim Yak Soo, and five National Assemblymen who accompanied him when he presented the petition, were later arrested on charges of violation of the National Security Law. Mr. Kim Yak Soo, a Vice-President of the National Assembly, and Mr. Kim Pyung Hoi, a member of the latter, had previously appeared at hearings of Sub-Committee I. The Commission, at its 40th meeting on 12 July, took cognizance of these arrests. The published charges against the Assembly members were that they had acted as instruments of the South Korea Labour Party in the National Assembly and that their petition to the Commission had been presented in the discharge of orders received from that party. It was decided not to pursue this matter for the time being as there was no evidence that the charge was to be construed as meaning that the act of addressing a petition to the Commission was regarded as a crime.

(c) The Press

16. The Press relations of the Commission were governed by rule 20 of its rules of proce-

dure adopted at the 6th meeting on 10 February 1949, as follows:

"Official Press communiqués shall be previously approved by the Chairman of the Commission. Press releases and verbal briefings may be issued by the secretariat, unless instructions to the contrary are given by the Commission."

As a result of distorted accounts concerning the Commission which had appeared in the local Press, a discussion of Press relations took place at the 18th meeting of the Commission. It was decided that briefings concerned with the policy of the Commission should first be cleared by it. Precautions were also taken to assure the correct translation into Korean of Press releases, while a record of the briefings was also kept. Regular contact with the Press was maintained by the Press officer of the Secretariat. Statements to the Press were made from time to time by the Chairman of the Commission and by individual representatives in their own behalf.

17. On 31 March 1949, the Korean Press group assigned to the Commission submitted twenty questions pertaining to the mission, attitudes and policies of the Commission. A draft memorandum of suggested replies submitted to the Commission at its 25th meeting on 12 April 1949 was referred to a drafting group.

At its 26th meeting on 22 April, the Commission considered the drafting group's recommended replies to the Press questionnaire. The recommendations as amended were unanimously adopted by the Commission.[17] At the same meeting, the Commission discussed a letter addressed to the Chairman of the Commission by the Korean Press group on 21 April 1949, withdrawing the questionnaire and casting doubt upon the "interest and sincerity" of the Commission. The Commission, in a Press release (No. 11, dated 23 April) rejected the implications contained in the letter, and stated that it would continue to co-operate with the Press as it had sought to do in the past.

18. At its 41st and 42nd meetings, on 20 and 22 July, the Commission considered information which had become available on the arrest, on charges of being members of a subversive party, of five of the Korean journalists who had been attending its Press conferences. The Commission decided, at its 42nd meeting, to meet this development with a modification of its Press relations practices, and issued the following Press release (No. 33 of 22 July):

"The Commission, having taken note of the recent arrest of five of the newspapermen assigned to it, and being anxious to avoid any further repercussions which might affect correspondents assigned to cover activities of the Commission, has decided to suspend all Press conferences until further notice. For the time being only Press releases will be issued."

3. Contact with North Korea

19. After an exchange of views at its 7th and 9th meetings concerning methods of approach to North Korea, the Commission agreed that one such approach should be made through the Government of the Union of Soviet Socialist Republics. Sub-Committee I was requested to draft a communication to that Government for consideration at the 10th meeting of the Commission.

---

[15] A/931, annex 4, appendix II.
[16] A/AC.26/W.16/Rev.1/Add.1.

[17] A/905, annex 2.

8

20. At the 10th and 11th meetings of the Commission, the recommendations of Sub-Committee I concerning contact with North Korea, which included the text of a proposed telegram to the Government of the USSR, were discussed. The Commission adopted the Sub-Committee's recommendations, with amendments to the text and, on 18 February 1949, requested the Secretary-General of the United Nations to transmit the following message to the Government of the USSR:

"The United Nations Commission on Korea, established by resolution of the General Assembly of 12 December 1948 to lend its good offices to bring about the unification and complete independence of Korea, is now meeting at Seoul. On 9 February 1949 the Commission established a Sub-Committee specifically charged with the task of making immediate contact with North Korea to arrange visits there for the Commission, its subsidiary bodies or individual members with a view to breaking down existing barriers between North and South Korea. The Commission wishes to ensure transmission of its aims and purposes by every possible means. Owing to the lack of normal communication between North and South Korea, the Sub-Committee is exploring various means of making contact with leading personalities in North Korea and as one such means requests the Government of the USSR to lend its good offices to establishment of the desired contact for the purpose stated above. — SHAW, Chairman UNCOK"

21. At its 19th meeting on 10 March 1949, the Commission began consideration of a report of Sub-Committee I recommending that a letter be forwarded to a leading personality in North Korea at the earliest possible date with the request that a visit of the Commission be facilitated. The Chairman of Sub-Committe I informed the Commission that, as a result of enquiries in Hong Kong, a channel of communication and transportation had been found to be available via ship between that port and North Korea.

22. At its 21st meeting on 18 March 1949, the Commission considered a new report of Sub-Committee I analysing the problems confronting the Commission in respect to making contact with North Korea. A secretariat report on technical enquiries at Seoul, Shanghai and Hong Kong concerning possible communication and transportation links with North Korea was annexed to the Sub-Committee's report.

Following a discussion of the recommendations of Sub-Committee I, the Commission, by a roll-call vote of 5 to 1,[18] instructed the principal secretary to dispatch, over his signature, the following letter to General Kim Il Sung, it being understood that the channel of communication suggested by the Sub-Committee was to be utilized in forwarding the letter:

"As you are aware, the United Nations Commission on Korea established by the General Assembly of the United Nations under a resolution adopted on 12 December 1948 (copy attached), has been desirous since its inception of making contact with the north. It gave expression to this desire in a resolution adopted on 9 February 1949 establishing two Sub-Committees (copy attached). Having been charged to lend its good offices in bringing about the unification of Korea

[18] In favour: Australia, China, France, India, Syria; opposed: Philippines.

and to seek to facilitate the removal of barriers to economic, social and other friendly intercourse caused by the division of Korea, as well as to be available for observation and consultation in the further development of representative government based on the freely expressed will of the people, and to observe the actual withdrawal of the occupying forces and verify the fact of withdrawal when such has occurred, etc., the Commission felt that it could not implement these instructions without being in a position to inform itself of the situation north of the 38th parallel. As a first step in the implementation of the instructions received from the General Assembly, the Commission, on 18 February 1949, through the Secretary-General of the United Nations, requested the Government of the USSR to lend its good offices for the establishment of the desired contact.

"In view of the lack of normal communications, including the impossibility of getting in touch with you directly by mail or cable, I am choosing rather reluctantly this way of approaching you with the request to facilitate such a visit. This visit should take place at the earliest possible date. The Commission is informed that there are practical means of travel to North Korea via ship from Hong Kong without undue delay. However, it feels that you might suggest a more direct means of access.

"For your information, I am attaching a list of the Commission, with indications of the membership of Sub-Committees I and II, as well as a list of names of the members of the secretariat who might accompany them. The latter are international officials who have sworn their allegiance exclusively to the United Nations and who are not allowed to accept any instructions from their own or from any other Government.

"In view of the absence of normal means of communication, your reply may be sent through the same channels as this letter is forwarded in its original. The necessary arrangements have been made in Hong Kong for any message of yours to be transmitted to me without delay. I shall, however, be glad to receive any authentic reply from you in any other manner you might prefer."

23. At the time of dispatch, that fact and the contents of the letter were withheld from publication pending receipt of a reply or until a reasonable lapse of time should have justified the assumption that no answer was to be forthcoming.

At its 28th and 29th meetings, on 18 and 19 May 1949, respectively, the Commission considered the steps to be taken in view of incorrect Press comments and speculations occasioned by the journeys of a member of the secretariat to Hong Kong, which in turn had provoked some concern in the minds of members of the Government of the Republic of Korea. To avoid further misinterpretation, the Commission issued a Press release giving the full text of the letter and explaining the manner in which it had been transmitted.

24. At its 28th meeting on 18 May 1949, the Commission adopted the recommendation of Sub-Committee I that, pending receipt of a reply to the letter, the Sub-Committee should look into other possible means of communication with the north, including the use of broadcasting facilities.

On 11 June 1949, a cable was received from Hong Kong stating that the letter to General Kim Il Sung had not been delivered.

The text of a broadcast to North Korea was approved by the Commission at its 34th meeting on 13 June 1949.[19] The broadcast was made on 29 June 1949 by Mr. Anup Singh, the Chairman, in English and translated into Korean. The broadcast was repeated several times. The radio facilities were provided by the Government of the Republic of Korea.

25. At its 40th meeting on 12 July the Commission took note of the fact that copies of a "Manifesto" of the Democratic Front for the attainment of unification for the Fatherland had been received by regular mail from North Korea by members of the Commission and the secretariat. The practicability of the mail channel having thus been demonstrated, the Commission decided to use it and to mail to General Kim Il Sung a copy of the letter previously sent via Hong Kong. A covering note was attached to explain the technical reason for this step and to make clear that the letter was not a reply or acknowledgment of the "Manifesto".

26. At its 39th meeting on 8 July the Commission adopted the final report of Sub-Committee I (see paragraphs of chapter II below). It was decided that the following recommendations contained in the report should be made public at once (Press release No. 30):

"... That the Commission should:

"1. Make known its willingness and readiness to assist in any discussions between representatives of the north and the south to consider plans and possibilities for the unification of Korea;

Note: This recommendation was adopted in the presence of five members of the Commission by 3 votes to 1, with 1 abstention.

"2. Offer its assistance for the purpose of resumption of legitimate trade between north and south on a trial basis;

"3. Recommend the cessation of all propaganda—emanating from within or outside of Korea—designed to inflame ill-feeling between the two zones of Korea, as being highly detrimental to the prospects of unification.

"In connexion with the first of the decisions quoted above, the Commission would be prepared to assist in discussions and deliberations between leaders of the north and south. The Commission would lend its assistance only if there was a reasonable prospect of both sections allowing the participation of representatives of all shades of opinions. There must be a sincere desire for conciliation and understanding. The initiative must come from the Koreans themselves. The Commission will help in any constructive negotiations between the north and the south."

The first of the recommendations quoted above provoked adverse criticism on the part of certain members of the National Assembly which necessitated the issuance of a Press release by the Commission.

4. DEVELOPMENT OF REPRESENTATIVE GOVERNMENT

27. When drafting the terms of reference of Sub-Committee II, the Commission interpreted the directions concerning "further development

of representative government" contained in paragraph 4 (*c*) of the General Assembly resolution 195 (III) to apply to both South and North Korea.

28. In his statement of policy, read at the public meeting on 13 February 1949, the Chairman defined the attitude of the Commission in the following terms:

"After the long interval between the suppression of Korean independence and its rebirth, Korea stands in need of help in the further development of representative institutions. The tasks of modern government are difficult and complex, its practical problem of democracy is that they should be carried out through institutions truly representative of the popular will so as to ensure both freedom and efficiency. The experience of Members of the United Nations may be invaluable to a newly liberated people. The Commission has been charged by the United Nations to make such experience available. It stands ready to consult with governmental authorities in Korea and to provide such information and advice as they may ask for. The Commission will observe with keen interest and active solicitude the efforts of the people of Korea to improve the representative institutions so happily established on the basis of their will freely expressed in the elections observed last year by the Commission's predecessor."

29. The position taken by the Commission was at variance with that of the Government of the Republic of Korea as expressed by its representative at the third regular session of the General Assembly. The Government construed paragraph 4 (*c*) of the resolution of 12 December 1948 as requiring to be implemented only north of the 38th parallel.

30. At its 37th meeting on 28 June 1949 the Commission, by 4 votes to 2, adopted the final report of Sub-Committee II[20] which had been submitted to the Commission on 22 June 1949 (see section B, 2, paragraphs 70 to 75 below).

31. The activities of the Commission in respect of "the further development of representative government" are set forth in the part of this report dealing with Sub-Committee II.

5. WITHDRAWAL OF OCCUPATION FORCES

32. At its 23rd meeting on 25 March 1949, the Commission considered a petition submitted by Mr. Kim Yak Soo, a Vice-President of the National Assembly, and signed by himself and sixty-one members of the Assembly. The petition requested the Commission to assist the Republic of Korea in unifying the country by supervising the withdrawal of foreign troops.[21]

Since the question of troop withdrawals had not yet been formally considered, it was agreed at that meeting that the Vice-President of the Assembly should be informed that the subject would be placed on the Commission's agenda at an early date.

33. At its 26th meeting on 22 April, the Commission began consideration of a communication dated 14 April 1949 from the United States Ambassador in Korea to the Chairman of the Commission.[22] The communication referred to a

[19] A/931, annex 4.
[20] A/AC.26/34 (see volume II, annex II, A.1)
[21] A/AC.26/NC.2 (*ibid.*, annex III, C, 1).
[22] A/AC.26/14 (*ibid.*, annex III, B, 1).

letter[23] from the Ambassador, a copy of which was attached thereto, addressed to the President of the Republic of Korea, paragraph 4 of which stated, *inter alia*, that United States forces "will be withdrawn 'as early as practicable', hopefully in a *matter of months*, subject to consultation with the United Nations Commission". In his communication to the Chairman, the Ambassador stated that it was the policy of his Government to keep the Commission fully informed of all steps taken that might affect its activities, and that he would therefore keep the Commission currently informed of developments relating to the subject.

Following a discussion, the Commission decided that its members would consult informally with the United States Ambassador at an early date.

On 2 May 1949, the United States Ambassador transmitted to the Chairman of the Commission a copy of a letter addressed to the President of the Republic of Korea regarding the establishment by the United States of a Korean military advisory group.[24]

34. At its 29th meeting on 19 May 1949, the representative of the Philippines introduced a draft resolution to the effect that, as long as the Commission had been unable to observe the withdrawal of USSR occupation forces, and while the problem of troop withdrawals "remains a problem of the United Nations, the United States may not withdraw unilaterally its troops in South Korea without previous consultation with the General Assembly or its Interim Committee". In the discussions which followed, the question was raised whether, under the General Assembly resolution of 12 December 1948, the Commission had any responsibility for either the timing or the facilitating of the withdrawal of troops, and both positive and negative views found expression.

35. The debate was continued at the 30th meeting on 23 May 1949, when the representative of the Philippines presented a revised draft resolution designed to meet the views stated by other members of the Commission. The resolution was adopted, with some changes offered by the representatives of China and El Salvador, and accepted by the representative of the Philippines, by 3 votes to 1 with 2 abstentions. Members who abstained felt that there was no need for such a resolution, while the dissenting member did not agree that the Commission could be absolved of all responsibility in the matter of withdrawal or non-withdrawal of troops. The text of the resolution[25] follows:

"*The United Nations Commission on Korea*,

"*Having in mind* the provisions of section 3 of the resolution of the General Assembly of 12 December 1948, recommending to the occupying Powers to withdraw their occupation forces from Korea as early as practicable;

"*Mindful* of the fact that this Commission has not as yet been able to observe the actual withdrawal of the USSR occupation force from its zone as announced to the world by radio from Moscow and Pyongyang and by the USSR delegation in the General Assembly,

"*Considering* that said section 3 of the resolution of the General Assembly contemplates the withdrawal by both Powers of their occupation forces from Korea and thus bring about the unification of Korea as a natural sequel of the abandonment of the 38th parallel by the occupation forces, and

"*Considering* that the problem of the independence of Korea has been a problem of the United Nations since 1947, when the United States referred this international question to the United Nations,

"*Resolves* that, while this problem remains a problem of the United Nations, it is the opinion of this Commission that under the General Assembly resolution of 12 December 1948 this Commission assumes no responsibility regarding either the timing or the facilitating of the withdrawal of the forces of the occupying Powers."

36. The question of troop withdrawal was again discussed at the 32nd meeting on 2 June, in connexion with unofficial reports of withdrawals of United States forces. It was agreed that a meeting between the Commission and the Ambassador of the United States of America was desirable.

A hearing of Ambassador Muccio of the United States, accompanied by Brigadier-General Roberts, then commanding the United States Army Forces in Korea, was held at the 33rd meeting on 9 June 1949. The following were the main points regarding the withdrawal of American troops made by the Ambassador:

(1) Gradual withdrawal had been proceeding for some time and completion of the withdrawal was expected by the end of June 1949.

(2) The major portion of the supplies and equipment of the United States occupation forces would be turned over to the Government of the Republic of Korea prior to completion of withdrawal.

(3) A Korean military advisory group, with an authorized strength of five hundred United States officers and men, would remain after completion of the withdrawal.

(4) There was a meeting of minds between the Governments of the United States and of the Republic of Korea concerning the withdrawal.

(5) The United States would not object to the Commission's obtaining the assistance of military experts of the Union of Soviet Socialist Republics in the observation and verification of the withdrawal of United States forces, subject to reciprocal rights being granted American experts in North Korea. Moreover, the Government of the Republic of Korea would have to be consulted.

(6) The United States would co-operate fully with the Commission in respect of its observation duties and extend all facilities to it.

The latter assurance was confirmed in a letter from the Ambassador to the Chairman of the Commission on 11 June 1949 stating that "The Commanding General USAFIK will be glad to furnish the Commission with the services of any US military experts which the Commission may feel that it requires and, in addition, will make available full details of the troop withdrawal operation".

[23] A copy of this letter was also sent to the Commission for its information by the Government of the Republic of Korea.
[24] A/AC.26/14/Add.1 (see volume II, annex III, B, 2).
[25] A/AC.26/25 (A/928, annex 4).

37. At its 34th meeting on 13 June 1949, the Commission adopted the following resolution:[26]

"The Commission

"*Mindful* of the duty entrusted to it by paragraph 4 (*c*) of the General Assembly resolution of 12 December 1948 to observe the withdrawal from Korea of the forces of the occupying Powers and to verify the fact of withdrawal when such has occurred,

"*Decides*:

"1. To observe the withdrawal of the remaining occupation forces of the United States of America and to verify the fact of withdrawal when such has occurred;

"2. To establish a Sub-Committee, composed of the representatives of Australia, China, El Salvador and India, to examine and report to the Commission on the procedures to be employed in observing the withdrawal of the occupation forces of the United States."

38. A report of Sub-Committee III[27] was approved by the Commission at its 35th meeting on 20 June 1949, when the following resolution was adopted:

"*The Commission*,

"*Consequent* on its resolution of 13 June 1949,

"1. *Approves* the report of the Sub-Committee established by that resolution;

"2. *Empowers* the said Sub-Committee, hereafter to be known as Sub-Committee III, to observe and verify the withdrawal of occupation forces from Korea;

"3. *Directs* Sub-Committee III to report to the Commission from time to time on the progress of its work."

In approving the report of the Sub-Committee, the Commission agreed:

1. To notify the Governments of the United States of America and of the Republic of Korea of the decisions taken by the Commission in its resolution of 13 June 1949.

2. To ask those Governments for certain information required to implement paragraph 4 (*d*) of the General Assembly resolution of 12 December 1948, which it interpreted as requiring observation and verification of the withdrawal of occupation forces in respect of both personnel and *matériel*.

3. To ask no assistance of military experts, which it was authorized to request under paragraph 4 (*d*) of the General Assembly resolution.

39. At the 48th meeting on 27 July, the second progress report of Sub-Committee III was submitted to the Commission and approved. At the same meeting the Commission adopted the following resolution:

"*The Commission*,

"*Having been charged* by the General Assembly resolution of 12 December 1948 with the task of observing the actual withdrawal of occupying forces and of verifying the fact of withdrawal when such has occurred, and having been able to discharge this task in that part of Korea south of the 38th parallel,

"*Declares that*:

"(*a*) The withdrawal of the United States occupation forces in Korea was completed on 29 June 1949, with the exception of not more than 50 Air Force personnel stationed temporarily at Kimpo Airport pending completion of arrangements for civilian administration;

"(*b*) With the lapse on 30 June of the executive agreement relating to interim and security matters between the President of the Republic of Korea and the Commanding General, USAFIK, of 24 August 1948, the right of the Government of the United States and the authority of the Commanding General, USAFIK, to assume control of the Korean security forces lapsed and no such right or authority now exists in the Government of the United States or the Chief of the Korean Military Advisory Group;

"(*c*) The United States Government no longer possesses or controls any military equipment in Korea except the side-arms and motor vehicles remaining in the possession of the Korean Military Advisory Group. As of the date of completion of United States troop withdrawal, the United States had transferred all its military *matériel* in Korea to the Korean security forces, except for such *matériel* as had been withdrawn with the troops."[28]

The activities of the Commission in observing and verifying the withdrawal of United States forces are treated in the part of this report dealing with Sub-Committee III (see section B, 3, paragraphs 76 to 86 below).

40. During the period of the Commission's deliberations concerning the withdrawal of United States forces, the latter was the subject of political agitation throughout the territory of the Republic of Korea. A mass meeting at the Seoul Stadium, sponsored by the National Federation of Patriotic Organizations, on 11 June 1949, after adopting a resolution requesting, *inter alia*, that the United States fulfil its obligation in respect of the protection of Korea prior to withdrawing its troops, addressed a message to the United Nations General Assembly. In it the Assembly was requested to grant "more extensive authority and strong power" to the Commission and to take new measures to ensure the security of the Republic of Korea.

After the meeting, the Chairman of the Commission was presented with a "memorial" by a group of demonstrators before Duk Soo Palace, and was requested to address the group. The "memorial" called on the Commission to enter North Korea, disband the "puppet armed forces" and hold general elections there. Members of the Commission met informally with some Koreans, who wished to impress such desires upon the Commission, on 13 June 1949.

41. Several similar mass meetings were held during the weeks which followed. On two occasions, on 30 June and 16 July 1949, mass demonstrations held at the Seoul Stadium wound up at the entrance to the grounds of Duk Soo Palace (the headquarters of the Commission) in order to present petitions to the Commission.[29]

42. On 17 June 1949, a Vice-President of the National Assembly, Mr. Kim Yak Soo, accompanied by five members of the Assembly, called on the principal secretary of the Commission. They submitted a petition,[30] signed by Mr. Kim Yak Soo, criticizing the Commission for its reso-

[26] A/AC.26/29 (A/931, annex 2).
[27] A/AC.26/SC.4/1.

[28] A/AC.26/29/Add.1 (A/931, annex 3).
[29] A/AC.26/NC.11 and A/AC.26/NC.13.
[30] A/931, annex 6 A.

lution of 24 May 1949 on the withdrawal of occupation forces, and requesting it to abolish military missions of the United States and of the Union of Soviet Socialist Republics in Korea.

43. On 20 June 1949, a Joint Declaration for United States Military Aid to Korea[31] welcoming the establishment of the United States military mission, was submitted by Mr. Kim Dong Won, a Vice-President of the Assembly, over the signature of 141 members.

6. Observer teams

44. At the 27th meeting, on 29 April 1949, the representative of El Salvador read a statement[32] to the Commission proposing that it study the question of the establishment of observer teams as a means of contributing to the peace and security of the Republic of Korea and of facilitating the discharge of the Commission's responsibility in connexion with the withdrawal of occupation forces. Discussion of the proposal was begun at that meeting and was resumed at the 31st meeting on 26 May. It was decided to establish an *Ad Hoc* Committee of the Whole, under the chairmanship of the representative of El Salvador, to study and report to the Commission within two weeks whether observer teams were authorized under the resolution of 12 December 1948, and what their functions and usefulness would be.

45. At its 32nd meeting on 2 June, the Commission adopted the report of the *Ad Hoc* Committee of the Whole on the question of observer teams[33] which expressed the view that "it would not be useful at the present time to continue the consideration of the question".

46. In a letter, dated 11 July 1949,[34] the Foreign Minister of the Republic of Korea drew the Commission's attention to "a record of some of the more flagrant examples of attack by the so-called 'People's Army' of North Korea upon the communities and security forces south of the 38th parallel". Believing that these attacks were likely "to produce conditions which will be dangerous to the peace of the Orient", the Foreign Minister suggested that if a unit of United Nations military observers were stationed in Korea it could "retard and stop these unlawful attacks". He requested the Commission to transmit the suggestion to the General Assembly and to recommend favourable action.

At its 41st meeting on 20 July, the Commission decided, as in the case of a previous letter (*cf.* paragraph 8 of chapter II above), not to commit itself to making any recommendations, but to assure the Foreign Minister that his suggestion would be recorded in the Commission's report to the General Assembly.

7. Observation trips and visits

47. The following observation trips and visits were undertaken by the Commission during the period covered by this report, the most extensive being one to Cholla Namdo Province and one to Cheju Do:

(i) Kaesong and along the 38th parallel, 19 February 1949, 9 March 1949 (Chunchon) 15 June 1949 (Ongjin) 26-27 June 1949.

(ii) Korean National Assembly, 23 February 1949, 21 May 1949.

(iii) Public mass meetings at Seoul Stadium, in honour of the Commission, 12 February 1949, commemorating Rebellion of 1919, 1 March 1949, Kim Koo funeral ceremony, 5 July 1949.

(iv) American Army installations in Seoul and Ascom City, 24 February 1949.

(v) Korean Military Academy, 3 March 1949.

(vi) Korean military installations in and around Seoul, 7 March 1949.

(vii) Ceremony at Capitol Buildings, first anniversary of elections and open-air mass meeting, 10 May 1949.

(viii) Cholla Namdo Province, 25-28 April 1949.

(ix) Cheju Do, 8-13 May 1949.

(x) Chonan (by-elections), 6 June 1949.

Other visits and trips were undertaken by the Sub-Committees of the Commission and are reported on separately.

B. Activities and decisions of Sub-Committees

1. Sub-Committee I

(a) *Terms of reference, organization and chronology*

48. In establishing Sub-Committee I by a resolution[35] adopted on 9 February 1949, the Commission instructed it to:

"1. Utilize every available medium such as the Press, radio, public meetings and personal contact in order to impress upon the people throughout Korea the Commission's earnest desire to extend its good offices to remove existing barriers in Korea with a view to promoting unification;

"2. Study the nature and extent of existing economic, social and other barriers in Korea; obtain full information from official as well as from unofficial sources concerning efforts to remove such barriers; and recommend methods for further improvement;

"3. Explore means for promoting social and cultural relations among the people throughout Korea;

"And, as a means of discharging the tasks enumerated in paragraphs 1, 2 and 3,

"4. Make immediate contact with North Korea with a view to arranging visits there for the Commission, its subsidiary bodies or individual members;"

49. The Sub-Committee consisted at first of the representatives of Australia, India and Syria. The Syrian representative left Korea on 26 March. At the 24th meeting of the Commission on 5 April 1949, the representative of El Salvador was appointed to the Sub-Committee. The permanent Chairman was the representative of India, who was elected at the 2nd meeting.

50. The Sub-Committee held thirty-six meetings, of which fourteen were hearings and twenty-two business meetings, between 9 February and 24 June 1949. In addition, it made visits to various industrial and commercial centres in Seoul and in the provinces and made several trips to inspect conditions along the 38th parallel.

[31] A/931, annex 6 B.
[32] A/906, annex 1.
[33] A/928, annex 5.
[34] A/AC.26/40 (see volume II, annex IV, A, 4).

[35] A/822, annex 1.

(i) *Contact with the north*

51. Work was begun on 10 February with a consideration of means of establishing contact with North Korea. As a first step, the views of officials, political leaders and other personalities were to be sought, and for this purpose a visit was made to the President of the Republic and members of his Cabinet. A recommendation was also presented to the Commission to send a letter to a leading political figure in the north, proposing a meeting with important personalities there. At its 3rd meeting, on 15 February, the Sub-Committee instructed the Secretariat to make enquiries regarding means of transportation to and communication with North Korea.

52. The result of the interview with the President was reported to the Commission at its 9th. meeting, on 15 February, when it was decided to make the first approach to North Korea through the Union of Soviet Socialist Republics. Pursuant to that decision, Sub-Committee I, at its 4th and 5th meetings on 16 and 17 February, drafted a telegram requesting the USSR to lend its good offices in establishing contact with the north, which was adopted by the Commission at the 11th meeting on 18 February 1949. The Sub-Committee was also instructed to continue its exploration of practical means of travel to North Korea by air, sea, rail or road, independently of the results of the telegram addressed to the USSR.

53. At the 14th meeting on 12 March, agreement was reached to recommend transmission of a letter to General Kim Il Sung via Hong Kong. A revised version of this letter was approved by the Commission at its 21st meeting on 18 March, for transmission over the signature of the principal secretary. At its 25th meeting, on 12 April, the Commission was informed that the letter had been entrusted by a member of the secretariat to the captain of a vessel in Hong Kong on 8 April for delivery to the addressee.

54. Pending the receipt of a reply to the letter to Kim Il Sung, the Sub-Committee was authorized to explore other means of contact with North Korea, including radio broadcasts. A Sub-Committee draft of a radio broadcast, which included the text of the letter to General Kim Il Sung,[36] was approved by the Commission, with minor changes, at its 34th meeting on 13 June. The radio message to North Korea was broadcast on 29 June from Station HLKA in English and Korean, and was re-broadcast several times during the following days.

(ii) *Removal of economic barriers*

55. At the 21st meeting of the Sub-Committee, on 11 April, plans were made to visit industrial and commercial centres in Seoul and in the provinces, in May, as a preliminary step in the study of the problem of economic barriers. After approval of these plans by the Commission at its 25th meeting, on 12 April, seventeen industrial plants and other facilities were visited from 2 to 5 May.

56. At the Sub-Committee's 33rd meeting, on 8 June, it authorized requests to official and non-official sources for information concerning the exact situation regarding trade between North and South Korea. A secretariat report on these enquiries was submitted at the 34th meeting, on 17 June, but action w deferred pending receipt of a reply from the Ministry of Commerce.

(iii) *Other activities*

57. At its 38th and 39th meetings, on 15 and 18 July, the Sub-Committee discussed a "Manifesto" of the Democratic Front for the Attainment of Unification for the Fatherland received by members of the Commission and of the secretariat individually by mail from North Korea.[37] Addressed to "countrymen" and "members of political parties and social organizations", it announced a programme of "simultaneous elections throughout Korea for a unified legislative organ" in September 1949. Together with attacks against the Republic of Korea and the United States of America, it contained a demand that the Commission withdraw from Korea.

Sub-Committee I decided to recommend that a radio broadcast explaining the programme and the objectives of the Commission should be beamed to the north. The text of the broadcast was submitted to the Commission at its 41st meeting on 20 July, but it was decided to defer action as difficulties had arisen in connexion with the use of radio facilities of the Government of the Republic of Korea (see chapter II, paragraph 13 above).

(b) *Survey of information and opinions*

58. The policy to be followed in selecting personalities to be heard by Sub-Committee I was discussed at its 7th and 9th meetings on 24 February and 1 March; at the latter a tentative list of personalities to be heard and a statement of the chief topics to be discussed were drawn up. While taking the view that changes in either of these respects did not require the approval of the Commission, the Sub-Committee undertook to submit them to Commission members for comment. This position was appproved by the Commission at its 17th meeting on 2 March. In practice, however, all lists have been submitted in the form of reports which the Commission has approved.

59. It was decided not to obtain prior clearance from the Government of the Republic of Korea of persons selected, and to convey this position officially to the Government. A statement on the position of the Commission *vis-à-vis* the Government bearing on this and other questions was prepared at the 8th meeting of the Sub-Committee, on 28 February, and approved by the Commission at its 17th meeting on 2 March (see chapter II, paragraph 6 above).

60. In the course of the hearings, which began on 9 March 1949 and concluded on 2 June, the Sub-Committee heard fourteen persons. Of these, five were Government spokesmen holding high office, three were members of the National Assembly, three were influential political personalities, one was the head of the United States Economic Co-operation Administration in Korea, and the others were a newspaper publisher and a Protestant religious leader.

61. The following questions constituted the general framework for enquiries addressed to persons appearing before Sub-Committee I:

"(i) What are your views concerning the problem of unification?

"(ii) What steps, if any, have been taken to promote unification since the establishment of the

---

[36] Sub-Committee I was informed on 11 June that the letter addressed to Kim Il Sung had not been delivered. No reasons were given.

[37] A/AC.26/W.17 (see volume II, annex IV, C).

Government of the Republic of Korea, and what steps should be taken in this direction?

"(iii) To what extent is it possible to remove economic, social and other barriers in Korea?"

62. The following is a résumé of opinions expressed at the hearings of Sub-Committee I:[38]

Conditions for unification

The Government view. Government spokesmen expressed the view that any negotiations required to unify Korea by peaceful means could be conducted only with the Union of Soviet Socialist Republics and not with the North Korean régime, which they considered to be illegal. They held the view that all international agreements and administrative policies adopted by that régime were to be regarded as null and void unless approved by the Government of the Republic of Korea. They also opposed any suggestion of a conference between leaders of north and south. It was urged that the Commission should persuade the USSR to dissolve the North Korean "puppet" government as well as all North Korean political parties. Demand was made for the release of all political prisoners held in the north and safe-conducts to enable them to cross the 38th parallel. It was proposed that the Commission should take steps to obtain the immediate withdrawal, under its supervision, of the Soviet Union's army, Chinese communist forces, guerrilla troops and other military groups and the dissolution of the People's Army and security forces. A wish was expressed for American arms, as a means of resisting any aggression from the north, and for a continued stay of United States troops until the security forces of the Republic were strong. It was held that once the foregoing conditions had been satisfied the Government of the Republic of Korea would be able to hold general elections in the north under United Nations observation.

Non-governmental views. There was no uniformity of view among members of the National Assembly or persons unconnected with the Government. The following are ideas expressed by one or more of them:

Two members of the National Assembly took the view that the withdrawal of all foreign troops from Korea was a prerequisite to unification.[39] Most persons in this group, including two members of the National Assembly, held that an understanding between the USSR and the United States of America was a prerequisite to a solution of the Korean problem.

The view was expressed by some that efforts should be made to convene a north-south conference. There was a difference within this group over whether this should be unofficial, with officials limited to participation as observers, or whether it should be an official conference.

One member of the National Assembly, who felt that there was no likelihood that the north and south would agree to a conference, urged the Commission to negotiate directly with each

side. Another member of the National Assembly proposed that the Commission should formulate a plan to make Korea a neutral Asiatic Switzerland.

A proposal was also made that a meeting should be arranged between a non-official or semi-official representative of the Commission and a personal representative of Kim Il Sung.

It was felt by some that the creation of vested political interests in the north and south had prejudiced the chances of unification.

Criticism of the Government's policies in the light of their effect on the prospects of unification was also heard. The Government was reproached with passivity in the matter of unification. It was viewed by one witness as too pro-American. Suggestions were made by some persons for improvements in the Government's policy in the matter of respect for freedom of speech, protection of human rights and equality in economic, educational and cultural fields. Expression was also given to a desire for political reforms and for a broadening of the Government with a view to obtaining greater popular support.

Some persons thought that the elections of 10 May 1948 were the necessary point of departure for efforts of unification. They proposed that elections be held in the north with a view to filling the 100 seats to which the people of the north were entitled under the Constitution and the Election Law.

Others proposed nation-wide elections, to be held at the expiration of the term of the present Assembly in 1950 without regard to the legal situation created as a consequence of the May 1948 elections and post-election events.

Removal of economic, social and cultural barriers

The Government view. Spokesmen for the Government insisted that barriers to exchange of any kind between north and south must be maintained while an unco-operative and illegal régime existed in the north.

Non-governmental views. There was some difference of view on this matter. Two members of the National Assembly maintained that existing economic exchange should be legalized and increased. This view was shared by some others. One political leader expressed the opinion that unification must precede a removal of barriers.

On the other hand, a member of the National Assembly, and a religious leader, thought a removal of economic barriers inadvisable. The chief of ECA thought it unlikely.

Re-establishment of cultural intercourse was thought by one member of the National Assembly to be difficult because of its political implications.

General suggestions

A proposal was made by one political leader that the Commission should name a group of Koreans to constitute an advisory body with whom to consult on all problems affecting the Commission's work.

63. At its 32nd meeting, on 3 June, the Sub-Committee decided to close its formal hearings, to prepare a general survey of the results of the hearings, and to recommend that the Commission issue a Press release regarding these decisions, informing the public at the same time that Sub-Committee I was open to receive further constructive suggestions for the unification of Korea.

---

[38] A complete survey of opinions expressed is contained in annex I to the present report (see volume II, annex I, A, 2 (b)).

[39] A petition taking the same view and bearing the signature of sixty-three members of the National Assembly was presented to the Commission on 18 March 1949. In this connexion it should be noted, however, that a proposal to demand the withdrawal of United States troops was defeated in the National Assembly on 20 November 1948 by 88 votes to 3 out of 113.

This was approved by the Commission at its 34th meeting on 13 June.

64. In addition to the information gathered at its hearings and at the hearings of Sub-Committee II, the Sub-Committee made several trips to inspect conditions in various fighting areas along the 38th parallel. It visited Kaesong and Paekchong on 19 February and Tang Ham Ni on 25 May. Refugee camps and a military installation were inspected on 15 June near Chunchon where, on arriving at the parallel, the party came under fire from the north. Visits were also made to Korean Army headquarters in Seoul on 23 June and to the Ongjin Peninsula on 26 and 27 June.

(c) Findings and recommendations

65. The 35th and 36th meetings, on 22 and 24 June, were devoted to drafting the final report together with findings and recommendations to be made to the Commission.

66. On the basis of its formal hearings and general observations, the Sub-Committee made the following findings in its final report to the Commission:[40]

(1) "There is an overwhelming desire for unification among Koreans.

(2) "The division of the nation has generated a feeling of political frustration, bitterness and restlessness. Despite isolated and indirect references to the possibility of unification by the use of force, the desire for unification by peaceful means remains preponderant. Many Koreans in the south look to the United Nations Commission for the solution of their problems. Tension, however, has been exacerbated by the violence of propaganda.

(3) "Despite the failure of the north-south conference of April 1948, the idea of a renewed attempt in this direction still persists and remains the subject of strong disagreement between the Government on the one hand and some members of the National Assembly and other political leaders on the other hand.

(4) "The division of Korea has resulted in adverse economic consequences for the south, where the Committee observed the economic conditions. The existing ban on normal trade between the two zones is a serious impediment in the way of the unification of the country.

(5) "The divergence of views between the Government and leaders outside it on the problem of unification has caused a deterioration of mutual confidence between them which may prejudice the prospects of unification. This increase in political tension is evidenced by the recent arrest of eleven members of the National Assembly and the assassination of Mr. Kim Koo, a leading political figure and eminent patriot, on 26 June 1949. Improvement in the political atmosphere would enhance the possibilities of unification.

(6) "The political relationship between the United States of America and the Union of Soviet Socialist Republics has a direct and vital bearing upon the fundamental problems of Korea."

67. In submitting these findings, the Sub-Committee made the following preliminary statement:

"The difficulty in establishing direct contact with North Korea constituted a major obstacle for the Committee in its attempt to implement its terms of reference. In view of the existing tension at the 38th parallel, and the persistently hostile attitude of North Korea towards the Commission as reflected in the Pyongyang broadcasts, the Committee discounted the possibility of direct physical penetration into the northern zone without prior clearance from the authorities."

68. On the basis of the foregoing findings, the Sub-Committee recommended that the Commission should:

(1) "*Authorize* the Committee to continue exploring all possible means of effecting unification;

(2) "*Report* to the General Assembly its view that an important means of contributing to the prospect of unification would be the achievement of a broader basis of popular support for the Government of the Republic;

(3) "*Make known* its willingness and readiness to assist in any discussions between representatives of the north and the south to consider plans and possibilities for the unification of Korea;

(4) "*Offer* its assistance for the purpose of a resumption of legitimate trade between north and south on a trial basis;

(5) "*Recommend* the cessation of all propaganda — emanating from within or outside of Korea — designed to inflame ill-feeling between the two zones of Korea as being highly detrimental to the prospects of unification;

(6) "*Bring* to the attention of the Governments of the United States and the Union of Soviet Socialist Republics through the General Assembly, their original responsibility for the present division of Korea and urgently exhort them continually to use their good offices in furthering the unification of Korea on the basis of independence and the principles approved by the United Nations."

69. The report of the Sub-Committee, including its findings and recommendations, was adopted by the Commission at the 39th meeting on 8 July 1949.[41]

2. Sub-Committee II

(a) *Terms of reference, organization and chronology*

70. To implement paragraph 4 (c) of General Assembly resolution 195 (III), the Commission, at its 5th meeting on 9 February 1949, established Sub-Committee II, composed of the representatives of China, France and the Philippines, with the following terms of reference:

(1) To study the development of representative government in Korea;

(2) To be available for consultation with Government authorities and to provide such information and advice as may be requested;

(3) To gather from experts and organizations opinions and views which have a bearing on the further development of representative government in Korea.

71. The Sub-Committee held twenty-five meetings altogether during the period 11 February-24 June 1949. At the 1st meeting, Mr. Henri Costilhes, temporary representative of France, was elected Chairman, and Mr. Rufino Luna, representative of the Philippines, agreed to pre-

---

[40] A/AC.26/37 (see volume II, annex I, A, 1).

[41] The third recommendation was adopted by 3 votes to 1, with 1 abstention.

side at the hearings of the Sub-Committee. At the 2nd meeting, the Sub-Committee appointed a working group, consisting of the representatives of China and France, together with the Secretary, to prepare a chronology of events since the establishment of the Government of the Republic of Korea, for the purposes of information and reference by the Commission.[42] The other major activities of the Sub-Committee were: (1) hearings of Korean officials and personalities; (2) trips to Cholla Namdo and Cheju Do.

72. The Sub-Committee, having heard a number of officials, personalities and representatives of religious and social organizations, decided, at its 11th meeting, to supplement its study of the development of representative government by making extensive observation trips to Cheju Do and Cholla Namdo, the two important areas affected by recent revolts. At its 14th meeting, the Sub-Committee decided upon the dates of 18-21 April for the Cheju Do trip, and of 25-28 April for the Cholla Namdo trip. The report and the recommendations of the Sub-Committee on making these trips were adopted by the Commission at its 22nd meeting. Because of bad weather, the trip to Cheju Do was postponed and re-scheduled to 8 May in connexion with the decision of the Commission to be present during the election of 10 May 1949 in North Cheju Gun. The trip to Cholla Namdo took place according to the original schedule. A detailed report of these trips and their evaluation is included in annex II of the final report of the Sub-Committee to the Commission.[43]

The Sub-Committee completed its final report on 17 June 1949 and submitted it to the Commission at its 35th meeting on 22 June. Up to that time, the Sub-Committee had not received any requests from governmental authorities either for consultation or for information and advice. The report, with some amendment, was adopted at the 37th meeting of the Commission on 28 June 1949.[44]

(b) *Survey of information and opinion*

73. The Sub-Committee conducted eleven hearings from 20 February to 14 April 1949. The persons who appeared before the Sub-Committee included three officials of ministerial rank, two members of the National Assembly, two political leaders and four leaders of social, educational and religious organizations. Although spokesmen of the Government had expressed the view that the phrase "further development of representative government" in paragraph 4 (*c*) of the General Assembly resolution of 12 December 1948, applied only to North Korea, the three officials who were invited to give their views answered the questions asked concerning representative government in the south.

74. The questionnaire dealt with two broad aspects of the problem of representative government: A. the development of representative government in Korea since the establishment of the Government of the Republic of Korea; B. its relation to the problem of unification. The detailed views of these eleven officials and personalities were recorded in the summary records of the Sub-Committee and a summary of these views is contained in annex I of the final report of the

Sub-Committee to the Commission.[45] The following is a résumé of the views on the development of representative government in Korea expressed in the hearings of the Sub-Committee:

A. *Development of representative government in Korea*

(i) *Steps taken in the development of representative government since the establishment of the Republic of Korea*

All those heard maintained that concrete steps had been taken toward the development of representative government. Generally speaking, those steps were preservation of peace and order; establishment and reorganization of administrative machinery; and enactment of laws and regulations. However, one person thought that the Government had not fully implemented its pledges to democratize its policy and to guarantee civil rights. He also expressed a pessimistic view regarding the further development of representative government.

(ii) *Problems confronting the Government and the people in their efforts for the development of representative government*

The consensus of opinion was that the geographic, political and ideological division of Korea and the resulting economic and social conditions and unrest were the main obstacles to the development of representative government. In addition, one person stressed the gulf between the Government and the people as a major factor which hampered the development of representative government. Still another believed that the failure to adopt a cabinet system of government had slowed the development of representative government. Friction between the Executive and the National Assembly, however, was regarded as an encouraging mark of such growth.

(iii) *Specific views and proposals on the further development of representative government*

All eleven persons had concrete suggestions to offer. The wide range of such suggestions reflected the differences in political outlook. They included removal of the 38th parallel; strengthening the Government by increasing the strength of the security forces; adoption of a cabinet system of government; creation of an upper house and of a supreme advisory council to the President; appointment of the most competent persons to important offices and purge of corrupt officials; repeal of laws and regulations inherited from the Japanese régime; establishment of a planned economy to solve the present economic difficulties; increase in production; moral and spiritual training; educational reforms to raise the intellectual and cultural level of the people.

B. *Development of representative government in relation to the problem of unification*

(i) *Political bases for unification*

All eleven stressed the importance of the racial, cultural and linguistic homogeneity and geographic and economic unity of Korea. All of them took the Government of the Republic of Korea as a basis or starting-point for bringing about unification, and most of them urged that the United Nations Commission should observe general elections in North Korea for the purpose of filling the 100 seats in the National Assembly left vacant for the representatives of North Korea.

---

[42] A/AC.26/SC.2/5.
[43] See volume II, annex II, A, 2 (b).
[44] A/AC.26/34 (*ibid*, annex II, A, 1).

[45] See volume II, annex II, A, 2 (a).

(ii) Comments on the structure of government and conditions in North Korea

All of them looked on the régime in North Korea as a communist dictatorship under the control of the North Korean Labour Party.

(iii) Possibilities of extending representative government within North Korea

Doubt or pessimism concerning the chances of a growth of representative government within North Korea was expressed by all except two persons, who counted on a strong loyalty of northern Koreans to the Government of the Republic of Korea and felt that the democratic elements in North Korea, though hidden, were not inconsiderable.

(iv) Representation and participation of all Koreans in a unified Korea

Most of the eleven persons heard were vague in their statements on this question. However, several of them believed that a general election in North Korea, under the observation of the United Nations Commission on Korea, would help solve this problem. Two of the eleven emphasized that the problem of unification should be solved before the question of participation or representation could be considered.

(c) *Conclusions and recommendations*

75. On the basis of the opinions expressed at its hearings and the impressions gathered by the Sub-Committee in the course of its observations, the Sub-Committee arrived at the following conclusions:

"Since the establishment of the Government of the Republic of Korea, many concrete steps have been taken and progress has been made in the development of representative government, particularly in view of the short period of time which has elapsed and the tremendous problems confronting the young Republic. However, the growth of representative government has been frequently hampered by disturbances in several areas, notably in Cholla Namdo and Cheju Do. Although sporadic guerrilla activities continue in some mountain areas, the Government, which was faced with the necessity of declaring martial law in some areas for a short time and curfew hours in almost all cities, towns and villages, seems to have succeeded in crushing the main rebellion and in restoring peace and order. The divergences of view continue between the Executive and the National Assembly regarding the implementation of the Constitution and the enactment of such important bills as the Anti-Traitors Law, Land Reform Bill and Local Administration Bill. This is, however, a wholesome sign for the growth of democracy in Korea.

"It is believed that, once the security of the Republic is completely assured and law and order established throughout the country, greater strides can be made toward the further development of representative government."[46]

3. SUB-COMMITTEE III

(a) *Terms of reference, organization*

76. To implement paragraph 4 (*d*) of the General Assembly resolution of 12 December 1948 concerning observation and verification of the withdrawal of occupation forces from Korea, a sub-committee, composed of the representatives of Australia, China, El Salvador and India, was

established by the Commission at the 34th meeting on 13 June 1949 under the terms of the following resolution:

"*The Commission,*

"*Mindful* of the duty entrusted to it by paragraph 4 (*d*) of the General Assembly resolution of 12 December 1948 to observe the withdrawal from Korea of the forces of the occupying Powers and to verify the fact of withdrawal when such has occurred,

"*Decides:*

"1. To observe the withdrawal of the remaining occupation forces of the United States of America and to verify the fact of withdrawal when such has occurred.

"2. To establish a Sub-Committee composed of the representatives of Australia, China, El Salvador and India, to examine and report to the Commission on the procedures to be employed in observing the withdrawal of the occupation forces of the United States."

(b) *Observation and verification of withdrawal of United States occupation forces*

77. The Sub-Committee met on 14 and 16 June. On 16 June 1949, it submitted a report to the Commission[47] recommending: (1) notification to the Governments of the United States of America and of the Republic of Korea of the decisions taken by the Commission in its resolution of 13 June 1949 quoted above; (2) that requests should be made of the two Governments for certain information concerning personnel and *matériel* of the United States occupation forces and concerning the status of the Korean Military Advisory Group which was necessary to enable the Commission to discharge its duty under paragraph 4 (*d*) of the General Assembly resolution of 12 December 1948; and (3) that the assistance of military experts of the two occupying Powers should not be requested by the Commission.

78. The report was approved by the Commission at its 35th meeting on 20 June 1949 when it adopted the following resolution:

"*The Commission,*

"*Consequent* on its resolution of 13 June 1949,

"1. *Approves* the report of the Sub-Committee established by that resolution;

"2. *Empowers* the said Sub-Committee, hereafter to be known as Sub-Committee III, to observe and verify the withdrawal of occupation forces from Korea;

"3. *Directs* Sub-Committee III to report to the Commission from time to time on the progress of its work."

79. Sub-Committee III at once began the discharge of the tasks assigned to it. On 21 June and 29 June it witnessed the last scheduled embarkation of United States occupation forces in Korea at Port Inchon.

80. In connexion with the verification of withdrawal, the Sub-Committee had recommended to the Commission in the report approved on 20 June that requests for information be addressed to the Governments of the United States and of the Republic of Korea. Such requests were made of the Governments named on 23 June 1949.

81. On 30 June and 1 July the Sub-Committee made visits to the Camp Sobingo Youngsan area, Ascom City and Inchon, the sites of former

46 A/AC.26/34 (see volume II, annex II, A, 1).

47 A/AC.26/SC.4/1.

major United States military establishments, for the purpose of verifying the withdrawal of United States occupation forces. On 9 and 10 July 1949, the Sub-Committee visited Pusan for the same purpose.

82. On 27 July the Sub-Committee submitted its second progress report, which presented for approval the following findings:

"As of 30 June 1949, the only United States troops remaining in Korea were some 50 Air Force personnel, who will be stationed at Kimpo Airport until arrangements for civilian administration can be instituted, and the personnel of the Korean Military Advisory Group, which has an authorized strength of 500 men.

"The Sub-Committee has not been able to verify the disposition made of United States military *matériel* in Korea because the information requested in this connexion has not been supplied to it. The Sub-Committee has not, however, considered that it was essential to press for such information. The Ambassador of the United States has adduced considerations of military security affecting the Republic of Korea which appear to the Sub-Committee to be cogent."

83. The Sub-Committee expressed itself as satisfied, on the basis of its observations and of the information which it had obtained, that the following were the facts concerning the withdrawal of United States occupation forces from Korea:

(*a*) The withdrawal of the United States occupation forces in Korea was completed on 29 June 1949, with the exception of the fifty-odd Air Force personnel referred to above;

(*b*) With the lapse on 30 June 1949 of the executive agreement relating to interim military and security matters between the President of the Republic of Korea and the Commanding General, USAFIK, of 24 August 1948, the right of the Government of the United States and the authority of the Commanding General, USAFIK, to assume control of the Korean security forces lapsed and no such right or authority now exists in the Government of the United States or the Chief of the Korean Military Advisory Group;

(*c*) The United States Government no longer possesses or controls any military equipment in Korea except the side-arms and motor vehicles remaining in the possession of the Korean Military Advisory Group. As of the date of completion of United States troop withdrawal, the United States had transferred all its military *matériel* in Korea to the Korean security forces, except for such *matériel* as had been withdrawn with the troops. Such transfers were made under the provisions of the United States Surplus Property Act of 1944 as amended. Deliveries of *matériel* other than those referred to above would have to be made under legislative authorization in effect at the time.

84. The report[48] was approved by the Commission at its 48th meeting on 27 July 1949.

(c) *Application to the occupation forces of the Union of Soviet Socialist Republics of paragraph 4 (d) of the General Assembly resolution of 12 December 1948*

85. Paragraph 2 of the Commission's resolution of 20 June 1949 (see paragraph 78 above)

---

had empowered Sub-Committee III to "observe and verify the withdrawal of occupation forces from Korea". Accordingly, the Sub-Committee at its 3rd, 4th and 5th meetings, considered the application of the resolution to the other occupying Power, the Union of Soviet Socialist Republics. It agreed to recommend to the Commission transmission to the Secretary-General of a request that the Government of the USSR be informed: (1) of the action taken by the Commission in respect of the observation and verification of the withdrawal from Korea of the forces of the occupying Powers; and (2) of the readiness of the Sub-Committee to carry out its duties in respect of the occupation forces of the USSR.

86. The report of the Sub-Committee was approved by the Commission on 4 July 1949, and the request to the Secretary-General was made the same day.

4. *Ad Hoc* COMMITTEE ON THE QUESTION OF ACCESS OF KOREANS TO THE COMMISSION

87. At its 13th meeting on 21 February 1949, the Commission, consequent on its resolution of 16 February 1949,[49] concerning free access to it of reputable Koreans, established an *Ad Hoc* Committee, composed of the representatives of Australia and Syria, to investigate the technical aspects of access of Koreans to the Commission.

88. The *Ad Hoc* Committee met on 22 February 1949. It recommended to the Commission[50] establishment of a Commission pass office, manned by a Secretariat member, to which Koreans could apply for a pass to visit the Commission. The Committee pointed out that it had limited itself to a technical examination of the problem, other aspects of which were for the Commission and the standing sub-committees to consider.

89. At the 14th meeting of the Commission on 23 February 1949, it was agreed to defer action on the Committee's recommendation.

5. *Ad Hoc* COMMITTEE OF THE WHOLE ON OBSERVER TEAMS

90. At the 27th meeting of the Commission on 29 April 1949, the representative of El Salvador read a statement recommending that the Commission study the question of establishing a scheme of observer teams as a means of contributing to the external peace and security of the Republic of Korea.[51] At the 31st meeting of Commission on 26 May, it was decided to establish an *Ad Hoc* Committee of the Whole, under the chairmanship of the representative of El Salvador, to study and report to the Commission within two weeks: (1) whether the Commission possessed authority to establish such observer teams, and (2) on the functions and usefulness of such observer teams.

91. The *Ad Hoc* Committee of the Whole met on 31 May. After discussion, the Committee decided to adjourn *sine die* and report to the Commission that in the view of the Committee it would not be useful at that time to continue consideration of the question.

92. The report of the Committee[52] was adopted by the Commission at its 32nd meeting on 2 June 1949.

---

[48] A/AC.26/SC.4/1.
[49] A/AC.26/3.
[50] A/AC.26/SC.3/1 (A/830, annex 7).
[51] A/906, annex 1.
[52] A/928, annex 5.

Chapter III

POLITICAL, ECONOMIC AND SOCIAL DEVELOPMENTS AND FACTORS AFFECTING THE PROBLEM OF THE INDEPENDENCE AND UNIFICATION OF KOREA

A. The Republic of Korea

INTRODUCTORY

1. Events in Korea have not waited on the achievement of unification. Into the vacuum created by the disappearance of military government on both sides of the parallel, powerful indigenous political forces have rushed and quickly thrown up new political and socio-economic structures. Unfortunately, it is possible to give here a detailed picture only of developments south of the 38th parallel. What is going on in North Korea could not be seen by the Commission and remains a subject of rumour and unverified reports.

2. In the territory of the Republic of Korea the transfer of jurisdiction and the settlement of financial and property accounts between the former military occupant and the new Government—begun while the Temporary Commission was still on the scene—are substantially complete. The occupation forces of the United States of America have been withdrawn. The Republic is building its own security forces with American help. The structure of government has been further elaborated. Programmes of economic development and economic and social reform are under way. The Republic of Korea is substantially master in its own house and has already been recognized as such by a number of countries.

1. COMPLETION OF TRANSFER OF JURISDICTION

(a) *Financial agreement*

3. The Initial Financial and Property Settlement between the Republic of Korea and the United States of America, signed on 11 September 1948 and ratified by the National Assembly on 18 September 1948, became effective with notification of the ratification to the United States on 20 September 1948.[53] Its provisions in respect of transfers of goods and assets to the Republic had been substantially carried out by June 1949.

4. Article VII, under which the two Governments were to collaborate in arranging a satisfactory settlement of any unpaid debt owing to the Soviet authorities in Korea for power furnished for the Korean economy from 9 September 1945 to 14 May 1948, could not be carried out. It was replaced by an Electric Power Agreement signed on 10 June 1949, under which the United States would release to the Republic the goods that had been stockpiled under a special United States Army allocation to pay this power bill, while the Republic in return assumed liability for the bill if and when a settlement could be arranged. The goods were to have been transferred upon ratification of the Agreement by the National Assembly. In anticipation of this, they have already been placed in the custody of the Government. They consist principally of heavy electrical equipment valued at $9,519,859.66,

goods *en route* from the United States valued at $710,937.08, and goods *en route* from Japan valued at $29,200. In addition, the United States turned over $1,372,528 in unobligated funds and $142,120 in proceeds from sales of materials on hand. Materials worth $1,044,004.73 had already been delivered to North Korea.

5. An initial payment was made by the United States of $23 million as the fair dollar value of goods and services procured by United States Army Forces in the period up to 1 July 1948 from the Korean economy with *won* drawn from a Military Government overdraft account at the Bank of Chosen. A later settlement covered the period up to 31 December 1948 and a bill will be due for goods and services used by United States troops until their withdrawal at the end of June 1949.

6. Payment of the first instalment, due on 1 July 1949, of the Korean Government's indebtedness for property furnished through the United States Foreign Liquidation Commissioner and Military Government is awaiting the results of current discussions of the dollar-*won* rate of exchange. The payments received by the United States are to be expended in Korea, partly on educational programmes and partly on the acquisition of property in Korea, principally the buildings which house the American Mission in Korea and its dependent personnel.

(b) *Turning over of property*

7. Administrative control over accounts, properties and operating facilities had been assumed by Korean authorities by early December 1948. The transfer of vested[54] property was completed in the same month. Such United States Army control of transportation, communication and other facilities as remained ceased with completion of withdrawal at the end of June 1949.

2. WITHDRAWAL OF UNITED STATES TROOPS

(a) *Completion of withdrawal*

8. The withdrawal of the United States occupation forces had been completed, with the exception of some 50 Air Force personnel temporarily required to operate Kimpo Airfield, by midnight of 30 June 1949, when the United States occupation of Korea came to an end. At the same time, the Executive Agreement of 24 August 1948, relating to interim military and security matters, automatically lapsed. The military installations occupied by American troops had been turned over to the Korean Government as the withdrawal progressed over a period of months. The last installations at the port of Inchon were transferred at midnight of 29 June 1949, when American guards were replaced by Korean military personnel. Except for the side-arms and carbines which the withdrawing troops carried and a small quantity of special combat equipment, all weapons and most ordnance equipment were transferred to the Republic of Korea for the use of its security forces. Some civilian engineering equipment

---

[53] For the text of the settlement, see the second part of the report of the United Nations Temporary Commission on Korea to the General Assembly, A/575, volume II, page 17.

[54] Formerly Japanese-owned.

and vehicles were transferred as logistical support for the large American Mission in Korea.

(b) *Korean Military Advisory Group*

9. A Korean Military Advisory Group with an authorized strength of 500 United States officers and enlisted men, which had been established previously, remains in Korea at the request of the Government of the Republic and is now advising and assisting the Government in the development and training of the Korean security forces. These services are being rendered on the basis of an informal understanding, which is to be replaced by a formal agreement now under negotiation. According to the Chief of the Group, Brigadier General W. L. Roberts, the officer personnel under his command carry only side-arms and the enlisted men 30-calibre carbines and none has combat equipment. While possessing some motor vehicles, they are dependent for transportation to a considerable degree on the Korean security forces. The Group is supplied through the American Mission in Korea.

3. EXTERNAL RELATIONS

(a) *Political*

10. To date, the Republic of Korea has been accorded diplomatic recognition by twelve Governments and by the Vatican. It has diplomatic missions in Washington, Paris and Tokyo, as well as consulates in New York, Los Angeles, San Francisco, Honolulu, Shanghai and Hong Kong.

11. On 1 January 1949, China accorded *de jure* recognition to the Republic of Korea. Mr. Liu Yu-Wan was the first diplomatic representative of China with the rank of Ambassador. Subsequently, Mr. Shao Yu Lin was appointed Chinese Ambassador, arriving in Seoul on 25 July.

12. The Government of France announced its decision to establish diplomatic relations with the Republic of Korea on 5 February 1949. Mr. Henri Costilhes, French Consul in Seoul, became *Chargé d'Affaires*. He presented his credentials on 13 April.

13. On 2 March 1949, the Philippine Government extended *de jure* recognition to the Republic of Korea, and on 21 March sent Mr. Manuel Gallego on a brief good-will mission to Seoul, with the rank of Ambassador Extraordinary and Plenipotentiary.

14. Recognition was extended by the United Kingdom on 19 January 1949, on which date Mr. Vyvyan Holt, British Consul-General in Seoul, became *Chargé d'Affaires*. On 17 March, Mr. Holt presented his credentials as Minister Plenipotentiary and Envoy Extraordinary.

The United Kingdom's notice of recognition read in part: "His Majesty's Government in the United Kingdom, having regard to the terms of a resolution adopted by the General Assembly of the United Nations on 12 December 1948, recognize the Republic of Korea as an independent, sovereign State, whose territory is that part of the Korean Peninsula in which free elections were held under the observation of the United Nations Temporary Commission, and recognize the Government, which Your Excellency represents, as being the lawful Government of that State."

15. On 1 January 1949, the Government of the United States announced that, in the light of the General Assembly resolution of 12 December 1948, it had decided to extend full recognition to the Government of the Republic of Korea. On 20 April 1949, Mr. John J. Muccio, hitherto Special Representative in Seoul, presented his credentials as Ambassador to the Republic of Korea.

16. On 12 April 1949, the Vatican established an apostolic delegation to Korea and appointed Monsignor Patrick Byrne, Apostolic Visitor in Seoul since October 1947, as Apostolic Delegate and titular Bishop Gazerensis. Bishop Byrne presented his credentials on 15 July 1949.

17. Chile accorded *de jure* recognition to the Republic of Korea on 27 May 1949, and New Zealand on 21 June. The Dominican Republic and Cuba extended recognition on 13 and 19 July respectively. Brazil accorded *de jure* recognition on 4 June. On 17 July, the Canadian Ambassador in Washington informed the Korean Ambassador there that Canada regarded its vote for Korean membership on the United Nations as full recognition of the Republic's status as an independent sovereign State. It was announced on 22 July 1949, that the Netherlands had also recognized the Republic.

18. On 2 February 1949, the Republic of Korea named Mr. Chang Myun (John M. Chang), as Ambassador to Washington. He presented his credentials on 25 March. On 10 February, the President of the Republic sent Mr. Pyen Yong Tai to Manila as Special Representative. On 31 May, Mr. Gong Jin Hang was appointed *Chargé d'Affaires* of the Republic of Korea in Paris. The United Kingdom has accepted the Republic's nomination of Mr. Yun Tchi Chang as Minister to London.

19. On 24 December 1948, the Republic inaugurated its own diplomatic mission to the Supreme Commander for the Allied Powers in Tokyo and, on 10 February 1949, named Chung Han Bum as Special Envoy to succeed Henry de Young (Chung Han Kyung), who had represented Korea in Japan during and after the period of the United States Military Government in Korea.

20. Consulates were opened in Los Angeles on 5 January 1949, in Shanghai on 24 January, in New York on 15 March, in Honolulu on 10 April, in Hong Kong on 4 May and in San Francisco on 10 June. A Consulate was to be opened in Taipeh, Formosa in the late summer of 1949.

21. The Republic has been admitted to membership in one specialized agency of the United Nations and has applied for membership in or participated in meetings of several others. The World Health Organization voted to admit the Republic on 30 June 1949 at its Rome meeting, which Dr. Choi Chang Soon attended as an observer. The membership will not become final until the Republic deposits its ratification of the Constitution of WHO with the Secretary-General of the United Nations.

The Republic has applied for membership in the Food and Agriculture Organization and has been invited to join its Rice Committee. It has also applied for membership on the Economic Commission for Asia and the Far East, which is to consider the application at its September meeting in Singapore. Preparations are being made to apply for membership in the United Nations Educational, Scientific and Cultural Organization.

FAO invited the Republic to send an observer to the Indo-Pacific Fisheries Conference at Singapore on 24 March 1949 and Mr. Whang Sung Soo and Mr. Chung Moon Ki attended. Mr. Pak Cho Uk and Mr. Han Duk Bong attended the meeting of the International Telecommunications Union in Geneva on 18 May as observers.

(b) *Economic*

(i) *United States Economic Co-operation Administration in Korea*

22. A Korean relief and rehabilitation programme had been initiated with the beginning of military government. Civilian supplies in a total value of $191,754,000 were procured by the United States Army under appropriations for the government and relief of occupied areas in the period from November 1945 to March 1949. The appropriation for the fiscal year 1949 was $95 million. These sums were spent mostly for such essential items as foodstuffs, clothing, shoes and textiles, coal and petroleum products, transportation and communication equipment, utility and industrial repair equipment and supplies, agricultural supplies and equipment, and medical and sanitary supplies.

23. The ECA entered the Korean scene in the fall of 1948 and, on 1 January 1949, officially took over from the Department of the Army responsibility for the administration of the foregoing programme.

24. On 10 December 1948, the United States and the Republic of Korea signed an Agreement on Aid at Seoul,[55] the preamble of which expressed the belief of the parties that the Agreement would "help to achieve the basic objectives of the Charter of the United Nations and the United Nations General Assembly resolution of 14 November 1947". In return for the aid furnished by the United States, the Government of the Republic of Korea promised to make the most advantageous use of all available Korean resources and of the aid furnished by the United States. It was to exercise economy in governmental expenditures and increase governmental revenue in order to balance the budget, seek economic stability through currency and credit controls, ensure a maximum contribution of its foreign exchange resources to Korean recovery and welfare through foreign exchange and trade controls, make every effort for maximum production, collection and equitable distribution of locally-produced supplies, facilitate private foreign investments subject to constitutional and statutory restrictions, develop export industries as rapidly as possible, and further maximum production by its management or disposition of Government-owned productive facilities and properties.

The Government of the United States was to appoint a representative to assist the Government of the Republic to make the most effective use of Korean resources and of the aid furnished by the United States. Mr. Arthur C. Bunce, who had been appointed Chief of the ECA Mission in Korea on 24 September 1948, is the United States representative under the Korean Aid Agreement.

25. The ECA budget request of $150 million for Korea for the fiscal year 1950, the first such ECA request, marks the change-over from a relief programme to a capital development programme. In explaining the budget request to the United

States Congress, Mr. Paul C. Hoffman expressed the hope that by 1952 the need of the Republic of Korea for outside assistance would have been reduced to approximately $35 million. He stated further:

"The ECA programme is designed, first, to increase Korea's production of exportable commodities and, second, to reduce the Republic's needs for imports so that it will be able to finance the imports of commodities which it cannot produce itself. Pending the achievement of these objectives, Korea will continue to require United States assistance in financing the imports of essential commodities, such as fertilizer, petroleum products, and industrial raw materials. Thus, approximately $110 million of the fiscal year 1950 programme represents the cost of fertilizer, feed and industrial raw materials which Korea must have during the next year . . .

"The capital development programme for the fiscal year 1950 is estimated at approximately $32 million. This is roughly only one-fifth of the programme; but it is the key 20 per cent. It represents the start of a programme which, if carried forward, would give the Republic of Korea greatly increased coal production, increased thermal power generating capacity, fertilizer plants, cement plants, an expanded fishing fleet, and other industries necessary to enable South Korea to approach economic independence.

"The three basic areas of capital development contemplated for South Korea are coal production, electric power and fertilizer. These three fields are closely interconnected. Korea's greatest import need is fertilizer; but it is impracticable to undertake the construction of fertilizer plants in South Korea until adequate electric power is available. Increased electric power is, in turn, dependent chiefly on increased coal production. Therefore, the order of development must be first, coal; second, electric power; and third, fertilizer."

The capital development programme for 1950 includes extensive work on the Korean tungsten mines, rehabilitation and expansion of silk mills, additions of over a hundred small fishing vessels to the South Korean fleet, and a cement plant-building programme. Rehabilitation of the railroad and communication systems and necessary improvements in the road network, together with several irrigation projects, are also part of the 1950 programme.

26. At the end of his presentation of the ECA capital development programme, Mr. Hoffman added:

"I wish to emphasize that new capital installations have been planned with unification as a hoped-for goal, so as not to duplicate facilities in North Korea, except to a minor extent which is unavoidable if we are to progress towards a balanced economy in South Korea. In some instances, the planned installations would supplement these in the north, whereas in other cases they represent normal additions to plants made necessary by the growth of population and by advantages of geographical location."

(ii) *Trade with Japan*

27. In April 1949 the Republic signed a trade agreement with Japan by the terms of which $29 million of goods, mainly rice and marine products, were to be exported to Japan during the 1950 fiscal year and Korea was to import from Japan approximately $49 million of goods, consisting

---

[55] A/AC.26/W.3 (see volume II, annex I, C). The Agreement was ratified by the National Assembly on 13 December 1948.

chiefly of coal, machinery and manufactures. Concerning this Agreement and the problem of Korean foreign trade, Mr. Hoffman, in the statement from which quotation has already been made, said: "Because Korea's historical foreign trade relationships were to a very large degree molded by the Japanese policy of exploiting Korea as a colonial possession, the economies of the two countries are in many respects complementary. This will necessarily cause the continuation of Korea's trade orientation toward Japan. Additional factors contributing to this trend are the present disruption in China and the division of Korea. But, aside from these factors, Korea's economy tends to be competitive with, rather than complementary to, that of most of the Far Eastern countries other than Japan.

"Even assuming future conditions of relative economic and political stability, Far Eastern markets for Korean exports, other than Japan, will be limited. Our plans therefore call for the maximum trade—in so far as such trade is consistent with Korea's independence and sovereignty—between Korea and Japan. Of course, all possible avenues for otherwise expanding Korea's foreign trade will be exploited and Korea will be encouraged in every way to participate in multilateral trade agreements."

4. ORGANIZATION AND FUNCTION OF THE KOREAN SECURITY FORCES

(a) *Army, Navy and Reserves*

28. Paragraph 4 (a) of the General Assembly resolution of 12 December 1948 instructs the Commission, among other things, to lend its good offices to facilitate the integration of all Korean security forces. While the Commission has made some enquiries concerning the Korean security forces, and has been shown over several Korean military installations and camps, it has not systematically dealt with the question of integration of the Korean Army, Navy and Police because of its inability to make progress in the discharge of its duties on the level of political unification.

29. Reports from across the parallel indicate that the northern régime is training and equipping men in considerable numbers to carry out the so-called function of national defence. It is reported that agreements of a military character have been concluded with the Union of Soviet Socialist Republics and Chinese communist forces. In the south, the Government of the Republic has likewise stepped up the pace of its armed preparations by continued recruitment and training of its armed forces. It has acquired arms and equipment from the United States occupation forces and is vigorously seeking further supplies of arms and equipment from the United States.

30. The building of the Korean security forces was formally initiated with Military Government Ordinance No. 28 of 13 November 1945, which established the office of the Director of National Defence of the Military Government of Korea and established thereunder a Bureau of Armed Forces, with an Army and Navy Department. The Director of National Defence was also charged with over-all direction of the Bureau of Police. From the date of that Ordinance up to the latter part of 1947 a Korean constabulary was created and transformed into a recognized army. The authorized strength of the Korean constabulary at the end of 1947 was 20,000 men. In addi-

tion, a Coast Guard, 3,000 men strong, was established during that period.

31. The goal of this first programme was the organization of at least one regiment in each of the eight provinces south of the 38th parallel. The Korean command was composed initially of about sixty officers, who had previously been trained in the Chinese or Japanese armies. The training of additional officer personnel was handicapped by language difficulties and the lack of advisers, supplies and equipment. These difficulties were eventually overcome by the institution of English language courses and later of a Korean military academy.

32. The second period in the organization of the Korean security forces began at the end of 1947, at which time there was an influx of United States advisers and an improvement in the organization of training facilities. Between March 1948 and July 1948, arms and equipment for an estimated strength of 50,000 men arrived. A provisional military advisory group, composed of American military personnel, was established in the fall of 1948. Its successor, the Korean Military Advisory Group, under the command of Brigadier General W. L. Roberts, has an authorized strength of 500 officers and enlisted men.

33. Since the Korean Army was almost the last organization to be established by Military Government, it was inevitable that the Police, which carried over from the Japanese régime, should have exercised national defence functions. This duplication was attended by a certain rivalry and friction between the two branches of the armed services. Difficulties were eventually overcome as a result of administrative reorganization, which placed the Police under the direction of the Ministry of Home Affairs and the Army and Navy under the Ministry of Defence. After the establishment of the Republic, the Ministry of Defence was at first directed by the Prime Minister who, however, resigned the post early in the year.

34. The law for the organization of the national armed forces was passed by the National Assembly in November 1948. Building on the constitutional responsibility of the President, as the Commander in Chief of the national armed forces, it provides for a War Council to assist him, and under that Council, for a National Defence Committee with a Central Intelligence Bureau, a National Defence Resources Control Committee and a Military Council. The Ministry of National Defence is charged with duties of military administration. In the Ministry of National Defence are an Army General Staff and a Navy General Staff acting under the direction of the Minister of National Defence. As of March 1949, the Army was composed of six brigades (now renamed divisions), each of which included three infantry regiments and a cavalry battalion, artillery battalion, engineers battalion, transport battalion and one special troops company. Eventually, each division is to number 15,000 men, but the complements are not yet full and the cavalry, engineers, artillery and special troop units are not yet fully organized. In addition to the six infantry divisions already mentioned, the Army includes an armoured regiment, a 105-millimetre howitzer regiment, an anti-tank regiment, an engineers regiment, a transport regiment and four reserve brigades consisting of two infantry battalions each. It is reported that the

reserve brigades were recently re-grouped into two divisions and that two more divisions may soon be organized. The Korean Military Academy is now training about 1,000 officers in various camps.

35. The security forces have until now been recruited on a semi-voluntary basis, but the Government has recently submitted a conscription bill to the Legislature, which passed it on 15 July 1949. The strength of the Army was publicly stated at the end of 1948 to be about 50,000 men. Training has been proceeding rapidly since. The goal at which the Government aims is an army of 200,000 men.[56] There are reports that the Government has asked the United States for arms and equipment for 400,000 men, of whom 200,000 would constitute a reserve. In addition to the standing army, the law for the organization of the armed forces provides for a national defence corps composed of persons who have completed prescribed courses of military training and constitute the reserve. The strength of this group is set by law at the same number as that of the standing army.

36. Almost all the equipment of the Army has been obtained from the United States and is said by American authorities to be of a purely defensive character.

37. The security forces also include a naval force of about 7,000 men and eighty vessels. The latter consist of minesweepers and coast guard cutters.

38. The 1949/50 budget authorizes an expenditure of about 14 billion *won* by the Ministry of National Defence.

(b) *Police*

39. The Police is under the direct control of the Department of National Police in the Ministry of Home Affairs.

40. The estimated strength of the Police force of the Republic is about 60,000 men. The metropolitan police number a little more than 10,000 and the rest are distributed in the eight provinces. The Police are armed with carbines, tommy guns, light and heavy machine guns, most of which are of American origin. The 1949/50 budget allocates to the Ministry of Home Affairs a little more than 15 billion *won*.

41. The role of the Police in the maintenance of law and order is dealt with in another place in this report. Almost the entire burden of maintaining security along the 38th parallel has until recently fallen on the Police, who at first also played a primary role in the suppression of large-scale disorders in the southern provinces and on Cheju Do. The Army, however, has recently taken over larger responsibilities along the parallel and in dealing with large-scale disturbances. The outbreak in Cholla Namdo, which began with the mutiny of an Army unit, was suppressed by the Army, and the pacification of Cheju Do had finally to be entrusted to the Army, which completed the operation in May 1949.

(c) *Para-military organizations*

42. At the beginning of the year, all youth organizations were merged into the National Youth Corps, of which the President of the Republic is

[56] United Press dispatch, Washington, D.C., 13 July, 1949, in the *Seoul Sinmun*, 14 July 1949.

the honorary head. This merger appears to have settled a problem which for some time had caused anxiety: that youth groups might become independent and uncontrolled *vigilante* organizations. A programme has gradually been developed to train the Youth Corps along military lines. At the same time, arrangements are being made to direct the energy of the Youth Corps into constructive channels, such as irrigation and reclamation projects. For this purpose, an American with considerable experience in the Civilian Conservation Corps in the United States has been employed recently as advisor to the Corps. Some voluntary police activities by the Youth Corps still continue, but appear to be decreasing, and in any case are now under central control. A National Youth Defence Corps was established in June 1949.

5. Development of representative government

43. Paragraph 4 (*c*) of the General Assembly resolution of 12 December 1948 instructs the Commission to be available for observation and consultation in the further development of representative government. The Commission has interpreted this to apply to the parts of Korea lying north and south of the 38th parallel. Since, however, the Commission has not been permitted to see North Korea for itself, the following account is confined to developments south of the parallel.

44. The adoption of the Constitution of the Republic on 12 July 1948 and its promulgation on 17 July marked merely the initiation of the process of building a structure of government. The Constitution is in many respects a programme, the details of which, and in many cases, the principles, have still to be fixed. Among the fundamental problems left unsettled were the purge of collaborators, the disposition of former Japanese property, land reform and local administration. In respect of formal structure, the Constitution has required supplementing by detailed laws for the organization of the Government and of the National Assembly. A civil service is in process of creation as are other State services.

45. The development of representative government under the Constitution of the Republic has been both uneven and uneasy. A year's experience of the Constitution in practice has shown that, like most other fundamental laws, it answers only imperfectly the practical problems of representative government and requires express amendment or sustained constitutional practice to resolve difficulties of interpretation.

(a) *The executive power*

46. Limitations of space forbid a detailed survey of the executive branch of the Government. The President, as Chief of State and Commander in Chief of the Armed Forces, appoints the Ministers of State who form the State Council, and the principal officers of the Army and Navy. Only the appointment of the Prime Minister requires the approval of the Legislature. According to the Constitution, the Prime Minister, under the direction of the President, supervises and co-ordinates the activities of his Cabinet colleagues. He also has under his direct control an Office of General Affairs (administration), an Office of Public Information, an Office of Legislation and an Office of Planning, all of which perform staff functions.

47. The further framework of the Government is established by the Law for the Organization of the Government, which was promulgated on the same day as the Constitution. The departments of the Government are: Home Affairs, Foreign Affairs, National Defence, Finance, Justice, Education, Agriculture and Forestry, Commerce and Industry, Social Affairs, Health, Transportation and Communications. Directly subordinate to the President are a Civil Service Committee, an Inspection Committee and a Board of Audit.

48. The first year of operation of the Executive Branch saw fairly frequent changes by the President in the composition of the Cabinet in response to the exigencies of efficiency and politics. Administration, which has come to be the key to efficient democratic government, is an art still new to the people of Korea; problems of pay, tenure and status present great difficulties and the organization of the public services is still a long way from being complete or satisfactory.

49. The policies of the Executive Branch appear to emanate directly from the President, who has thus far succeeded in maintaining effective control over the composition and policies of the Government. There is great pressure, however, for a change from this basis of government, which is described by one of the heads of the leading Democratic Nationalist Party as "idealistic", to what is termed a more "practical" basis of formation of the Cabinet by the majority party which would hold office as long as it had popular support.[57] The President must also meet pressure from many quarters to include members of the opposition in his Cabinet. This demand is made on the ground that the Government's basis in popular support is too narrow at a time when the problems facing the Republic are daily becoming more urgent.

(b) The National Assembly

50. The present National Assembly is the one which was elected under the observation of the Temporary Commission on 10 May 1948. Since that date, it has held about two hundred meetings in its constituent phase and its legislative character. The present session of the Assembly is the fourth special session.

51. Eight standing committees were established by Law No. 5, passed on 14 September 1948. In July 1949, a Negotiations Committee was added, and appears to mark the beginning of an attempt to meet the need for machinery to budget legislative time.

52. The National Assembly has enacted about thirty-five laws as well as many resolutions. Among the more important ones, in addition to the Government Organization Law and Law No. 5 already mentioned, are a National Traitors Law (22 September 1948), a Law on the Organization of the National Army (30 November 1948), a National Security Law (1 December 1948), a Local Administration Law (4 July 1949), a Land Reform Law (22 June 1949) and a Military Service Law (enacted on 15 July 1949, but not yet promulgated). It has considered and passed three Government budgets and, in the exercise of its constitutional power in respect of treaties, has approved the Aid Agreement with the United States and the Trade Agreement with Japan.

53. The National Assembly has been marked by great independence of spirit until recently.[58] Procedurally, this has been made possible by the constitutional independence of the Legislature, the absence of clearly defined political groups in its midst, the lack of party control and discipline, and the parliamentary latitude allowed individual members by the Assembly rules.

(c) Political parties

54. With the possible exception of the Democratic Nationalist Party and the Korean Independence Party, political groupings in Korea lack organization and funds. While parties and political groups are many, most of them are small personal followings of individuals of greater or lesser political prominence. Public favour is wooed with manifesto and slogan. The most vigorously stated element of party programmes is the nationalist. The familiar classification of parties into right and left has hardly any application in Korea, where groups tagged with a rightist appellation are found to call for a planned economy, and is of little help in the analysis of current political issues.

55. The lack of party organization is particularly evident in the halls of the Legislature. The parties have little effective control over their nominal representatives in the National Assembly. There are, however, signs of change in this respect.

56. The strongest party at present in the National Assembly is the Democratic Nationalist Party, founded on 10 February 1949 by a merger of the Hankook Democratic Party and the Nationalist Party, and directed by a committee composed of Kim Sung Soo, Chi Tae Hyung, Shin Ik Hi and Paek Nam Hoon. It claims a membership of 800,000 and can muster the support of about eighty-five members of the Legislature, in which it is the most cohesive group. Despite the fact that it has the largest single representation in the Cabinet, the President has not always had its support in the National Assembly. As with most other parties, the nationalist plank is the strongest in its platform. In the social and economic fields it stresses the principles of equal economic opportunity.

57. More or less opposed to the Democratic Nationalist Party is the Korean Independence Party of the late Kim Koo, founded in May 1922 and re-organized in October 1948, which claims 900,000 members, and is said to have a well-developed organization throughout the country. The Korean Independence Party has played a significant role by standing apart in the 10 May 1948 elections and by maintaining a certain opposition to the consequences of those elections since. The recent death of Kim Koo raises the question of the future of his party as an independent unit. Closely associated with Kim Koo's party in aims, though deriving its support from entirely different sources, has been the group headed by Kimm Kiusic. This organization, which goes by the name of the National Independence Federation, comprises a number of groups and parties, which together claim a membership of 500,000. One constituent of the National Independence Federation for a while was the Socialist Party, founded in December 1948 by Cho So Ang.

---

[57] See hearing of Kim Song Soo by Sub-Committee II, 30 March 1949, A/AC.26/SC.2/10.

[58] See chapter III. paragraph 65 et seq.

58. A Women's Nationalist Party also exists and a Taehan Labour-Farmer Party was established in October 1948.

59. Before the establishment of the Republic of Korea, the major political organizations of the left which had been active included: the South Korea Labour Party, the People's Republican Party, the Labouring People's Party, the Chundo Kyo Young Friends Party and the front organization of the South Korea Labour Party, namely, the Democratic National Front.

The South Korea Labour Party, formerly the Korean Communist Party, was officially formed late in November 1946 with Huhr Hun as the Chairman. In 1947 it claimed to have a membership of 800,000. Following the disturbances of August 1947, many of the leaders of the South Korea Labour Party were arrested. In February 1948 the so-called South Korean All-Out Strike Committee, under the direction of the South Korea Labour Party, issued a declaration of strike against the activities of the United Nations Temporary Commission on Korea. This movement was accompanied by outbreaks of violence in six provinces of South Korea.[59]

The South Korea Labour Party went underground definitively with the promulgation of the National Security Law on 1 December 1948. Those of its affiliate and front organizations which have not followed it underground have led a precarious existence. The South Korea Labour Party is said by the Government to have been at the bottom of the serious disturbances in Cheju Do and in Cholla Namdo.

60. In all political camps there is evidence of a tendency to unite with others whose positions are allied. Two things strengthen the tendency toward union. One is the inability to resist the growing nationalist fervour in the Republic with its imperative demand for unity against the Communists. A practical consideration is the fact that the recent amendment to the National Assembly rules, which established the Negotiations Committee already mentioned, effectively penalizes a failure to close ranks within the Legislature. The adoption of those rules should make more difficult the shifting of members from one political camp to another on different issues, which has been such a marked feature of the Assembly's history until now.

61. The Democratic Nationalist Party, which is a result of the merger of two parties in February, continues to seek to draw related groups to itself. It is the group which is likely to derive the greatest advantage from the new Assembly rules and from its dominant position in the Government. It has about sixty registered members in the Legislature, of which it forms the most cohesive group. It can count on the frequent support of others not formally affiliated with it. Next to the Democratic Nationalists stands the Il Min Hoi, a group of about forty, whose name indicates support for the President's "one people" principle and on which the President has been able to rely for more consistent support than he could obtain from any other group. Opposed to the foregoing groups in the Legislature were the Dong Sung Hoi and Echung Hoi which claimed a membership of more than fifty before the recent arrest of the most prominent members of the for-

mer group. Since the arrests, several members of Echung Hoi have transferred to Il Min Hoi. A buffer group is the Shin Chung Hoi, with about thirty members, who follow the Prime Minister, Lee Bum Suk. Their ability to maintain themselves seems doubtful. A new group, more or less allied with the Democratic Nationalist Party, is the Dong Ji Hoi, which claims about twenty-five members. The leader of this group is Lee Yung Young, Minister of Social Affairs and a member of the Chosun Democratic Party, whose nominal leader, Cho Man Sik, is reported under arrest in North Korea. Otherwise unaffiliated members of the National Assembly are seeking to join together in order not to be put at entire disadvantage under the new Assembly rules. The Independent Club has not yet succeeded in obtaining the necessary minimum of twenty members. The Labour-Farmer Party, which has often been found in the Government camp, has about ten members.

62. Before leaving the subject of political organization, it is necessary to say something about the political role of the nation's youth. Strenuous efforts are being made by the Government to mobilize the youth for purposes of nationalist self-assertion and defence. As already noted, the Government was also concerned over the tendency of the youth to engage in anti-social *vigilante* activities. The National Youth Corps was founded on 19 December 1948 under the chairmanship of President Syngman Rhee by a merger of all previously existing youth groups, one of which had been founded by the Prime Minister. The platform of the National Youth Corps expresses fervent devotion to the Republic and professes allegiance to its President. Since the organization includes nominally the 6,000,000 youth of the Republic, it serves as a recruiting agency for the Army. It is said that 70 per cent of the Army recruits are members of the Youth Corps. The organization is financed through the sale and operation of Government property. Recently a subsidiary organization, the National Youth Defence Corps, has been formed. The National Youth Corps has held numerous mass demonstrations in support of the demands for military aid made by the Government of the Republic.

63. In addition to the youth, various women's organizations, Christian organizations and others have held mass demonstrations to support the political demands of the Government.

(d) *Relations of the Executive and the Legislature*

64. The principal problems thrust up by the play of forces between the Executive and the Legislature have to do with Executive responsibility, the resolution of conflicts of policy and the nature and exercise of the presidential veto. The Constitution, which purports to be based on the theory of separation of powers, in fact entrusts to the Cabinet, within the framework of the powers of the President, the leadership in the formulation of fundamental plans and policies concerning national affairs (article 72:1). The law-making power is entrusted to the National Assembly. The Constitution, however, makes no workable provision for enforcing Executive responsibility to the Legislature, nor, within the limits of such responsibility, for assuring a reasonable degree of Executive control of the Legislature. Consequently, conflicts of policy between the two branches of Government have

---

[59] See first part of the report of the United Nations Temporary Commission on Korea, A/575, volume I, paragraphs 63 to 65.

either resulted in a deadlock or, in some instances, have been broken in ways which may affect the continued maintenance of the constitutional checks and balances between the Executive and the Legislature.

The National Traitors Law

65. Article 101 of the Constitution provided that:

"The National Assembly which enacted the Constitution may establish a special law dealing with the punishment of malicious anti-national acts committed prior to 15 August 1945."

One of the first acts of the National Assembly was to pass such legislation, which became law on 22 September 1948. On 7 December, two additional laws established a special investigation committee composed of members of the National Assembly and subsidiary organs of the Special Court for the trial of offenders.

66. The implementation of the National Traitors Law provoked the longest sustained and most serious difficulties between the two branches of the Government. In February 1949, the President was reported in the Press (*Chosun Choong* and *Ilbo*, 16 February) to have said that enforcement of the law was the prerogative of the Executive and to have deplored arrests of suspected persons by the Special Investigators and their police. The President was quoted as declaring that if the law threatened public security it was appropriate to suspend it temporarily.

67. In the National Assembly, members of the Special Investigation Committee declared that the arrangement for special police had been made as a matter of administrative convenience with the approval of the Minister of the Interior and other officers of the Government, since the Special Investigation Committee had been empowered by the law to call on the police for assistance and to give them orders. On 17 February, the Assembly voted to ask the President to retract his statement.

68. Under date of 16 February 1949, however, the Executive had transmitted to the National Assembly a proposed amendment to the law which would have reduced the liability to prosecution of police officials who had served under the Japanese. It was also proposed to put the appointment of members of the Special Investigation Committee in the hands of the President and to limit its functions to investigating and reporting to the Procurator General, who would have had the power to decide finally whether to prosecute. At the National Assembly meeting of 24 February 1949, the amendments were denied a second reading and were accordingly rejected.

69. In the following months disputes over the enforcement of the law flared up from time to time, but the differences were left unresolved. Other difficulties arose which added fuel to the fire. The Government's grain collection programme was severely criticized in February 1949 when the Legislature banned compulsory purchase over the Government's protests. Even the Government's budget could only be passed with difficulty and with drastic cuts at the end of March, after many stormy meetings which were marked by charges of waste of funds.

Local administration and land reform laws

70. Disagreement over two other basic items of legislation, land reform and local administration,

was soon added to the foregoing differences. The second reading of a local administration bill which would have provided for the election of provincial governors, municipal and village officials was initiated at the 41st meeting of the regular session of the National Assembly on 26 February and completed at the 49th meeting on 9 March. It was provided that the law should become effective six months after promulgation. The law was transmitted to the President on 17 March. On 31 March, the law was returned to the National Assembly by the Prime Minister with a proposal that the date of promulgation be left to the President. By way of justification, the Prime Minister stated his opinion that the law was of minor importance compared with the problem of unification and that implementation of the law might aggravate the situation in the disturbed areas and endanger the security of the nation.

71. In the course of the debate which followed, the Government was taunted with not trusting the people, with believing that threats to security were to be rooted out only by means of mass arrests, torture, detention, theft and suppression, with being out of touch with the people, their misery and wants, and with seeking to control local affairs through pro-Japanese officials. The Minister of Home Affairs expressed plaintively his feeling that "the Assembly is apt to distrust the Executive".

72. At the 71st meeting on 4 April 1949, the question of maintaining the original date when the law was to have become effective came to a vote. The provision was sustained by a vote of 81 to 31 out of 167. A secret ballot resulted in a vote for retention of 82 to 80, with 5 absentions, out of 167.

73. The question then arose of the effect of this vote. Those who supported the original provision took the view that the return of the bill with a suggested modification was not a veto; that the Assembly, having voted the suggestion down, needed only to send the bill back. The effect of this would have been to make the bill law, the fifteen-day period for a veto having expired. On the other side, members of the Hankook Democratic Party argued that a two-thirds vote was necessary to sustain the original provision. The law was returned to the President, who returned it again toward the end of April. By a vote of 88 to 13 out of 145, the National Assembly declared the second return of the law illegal and sent it back to the President on 30 April. It then adjourned.

74. The law was again returned unsigned with a declaration that it was to be considered as abrogated under article 40 of the Constitution, since no final action had been taken on it at the session which enacted it. The effect of this would have been to require the Assembly to enact the law *de novo* and to give the President another opportunity to consider it. The Speaker of the National Assembly, Mr. Shin Ik Hi, stepped down from the rostrum on 30 May to attack the Government's procedure as a "cheap, ready-made veto".

75. The Land Reform Bill, which had been adopted by acclamation on 27 April, was returned by the President on 16 May with a notice that it had been abrogated for the same procedural reason as the Local Administration Law. The notice of abrogation was accompanied by a request for modification of some of its provisions.

The second special session of the Legislature had adjourned in the meantime. On 15 June, the third special session returned the bill unaltered by a vote of 97 to 19 out of 153, not quite a two-thirds vote. No further question was raised by the Executive, which promulgated the law on 22 June. At the same session presidential vetoes of an Emergency Food Law and of a Temporary Vested Properties Law were over-ridden by huge majorities, 128 to 1 and 132 to 3.

76. The Government in the meantime had offered to implement the Local Administration Law within the stipulated time if it were altered to give the President authority to appoint provincial governors and the mayor of Seoul. The National Assembly unexpectedly conceded this request by a vote of 79 to 55 out of 149 on 17 June. The law was promulgated on 4 July by the Government and is to become effective on 15 August 1949.

Third special session of the National Assembly

77. A series of incidents inflamed relations between the Government and the National Assembly in June. On 31 May, the Vice Minister of Home Affairs was questioned on the reasons for the continued forced exaction of contributions from the population of the provinces by the provincial governments and police. This illegal practice had grown to the dimensions of an important source of local public revenue. The Vice Minister, while agreeing that the practice was illegal and declaring that it had been ordered stopped, though without result, observed that the National Assembly had made no budgetary provision for the public obligations which these exactions were used to meet. On the following day, there was excited debate over the failure of the police to stop a mob which had beaten up a National Assembly member. On 2 June discussion of forced contributions was resumed. When word was received that the mob responsible for the previous day's outrage was seeking entrance to the National Assembly, a motion was made and carried by 82 votes to 61 to demand resignation of the entire Cabinet. The next day the same mob attacked the offices of the Special Investigating Committee. On 4 June 1949, there was severe legislative criticism of the Government's action in closing down the *Seoul Shinmun*, the largest metropolitan daily, for failing to follow Government directives.

78. A crisis stage was reached on 6 June, when the offices of the Special Investigating Committee were entered by the police "on superior order", the files seized and the special police disarmed, arrested and (so it was charged in the National Assembly) beaten. A motion renewing the demand for the resignation of the entire Cabinet and declaring that no Government measure would be considered until the demand had been met was carried by 89 to 59 votes. As already noted, the Assembly did, however, subsequently compromise with the Government on the Local Administration Law. On 21 June it adjourned.

79. It was in the light of the foregoing that Sub-Committee II of the Commission felt justified in reporting to the Commission on 18 June, and the Commission approved on 28 June, the conclusion that the continuing divergences of view between the Executive and the National Assembly regarding the implementation of the Constitution and the enactment of such important bills as the Anti-Traitors Law, Land Reform Bill and Local Administration Bill were "a wholesome sign for the growth of democracy in Korea".

Fourth special session of the National Assembly

80. When the Assembly reconvened on 1 July 1949, some of the leaders of the opposition to the Government were no longer present. Three members of the National Assembly had already been arrested in May on charges of violation of the National Security Law. After the close of the third special session, seven other members, including Vice-President Kim Yak Soo, were arrested for the same reason.

81. The resignation of Vice-President Kim Yak Soo was accepted on 2 July by 99 to 0 out of 124. On the same day, a resolution to withhold for the time being application of the decision not to consider Government-initiated measures until the Cabinet resigned was carried by 103 to 1 out of 135.

82. In his speech at the opening meeting the President declared plainly that the Special Investigation Committee must depend on the Government to make arrests and added that, if the previous practices continued, he might set up another investigation committee. This declaration was followed the very next day by the resignation of almost all the members of the Special Investigation Committee and its staff. Newly elected members expressed reluctance to take up their duties and four of them soon resigned.

83. At the same time the National Assembly, by 74 to 9 out of 136, shortened the period for the initiation of prosecutions to 31 August.

Amendment of the National Assembly rules

84. Discussion of amendments to the National Assembly rules (Law No. 5), which had been submitted by the Government on 25 June 1949, was begun on 8 July 1949, and completed the following day, when the entire bill was passed.

85. The procedural dispute over the Government's handling of the Local Administration Bill appears to have been settled by two provisions in the new rules, one permitting the Government to submit amendments to a bill proposed by members of the National Assembly, the second providing that discussion of bills which have been returned to the National Assembly pursuant to article 40 of the Constitution shall continue at the next session so long as the tenure of the members lasts.

86. The amendments also establish a Negotiations Committee for the purpose of negotiating important issues regarding procedure. The Committee is to be composed of representatives of each party in the National Assembly in proportion to party numbers, which are determined on the basis of lists of affiliated members to be submitted by the parties. The Negotiations Committee may nominate members who want to speak on the floor and notify the Chairman of the National Assembly of its nominees. They are to be heard first. Closure of debate cannot be moved until all the persons so nominated have been heard. Each party is to elect members to standing committees in proportion to its numbers. For the purpose of disposing of special issues not within the purview of the standing committees, special committees are to be established with parties represented in proportion to numbers. Election to standing or special committees of

members without party affiliation appears not to be possible under the rules. It appears that no group with less than twenty members will be able to obtain representation in committees.

(e) *The Press and freedom of speech*

87. South Korean newspapers make up in vigour for their somewhat crude technical standards and immature journalistic practices. They report the news and comment at length on issues of interest. Coverage includes the activities of the United Nations Commission on Korea. In Seoul alone there are about thirty dailies and many weeklies. The provinces also have their own newspapers, but these have considerably less influence than the newspapers of the capital. None of the newspapers derives enough revenue from circulation or advertising to be self-sustaining.

88. A Press Law, dating from the year 1907 and generally regarded as obsolete and repressive, is still in force and was applied up to June 1949.[60] This Law has not yet been replaced by more suitable legislation, though the question of replacing it has been raised several times by members of the National Assembly.

89. In addition, the newspapers operate under the following directives issued by the Office of Public Information, an adjunct of the Prime Minister's office which, however, works closely with the President.[61]

"It is forbidden to print:

"(1) Articles contrary to the policy of the Republic of Korea;

"(2) Articles detrimental to the Republic of Korea;

"(3) Articles approving or protecting the Communist Party and the North Korean 'puppet' régime;

"(4) Articles reporting false facts for purposes of agitation;

"(5) Articles reflecting upon the relations of the Republic of Korea with friendly Powers and hurting the national prestige;

"(6) Articles agitating the public mind with an excitable tenor and news and, moreover, having a detrimental influence upon the public mind;

"(7) Articles betraying national secrets."

90. The Government has been somewhat nervous over the effect of critical Press reports and comments on the maintenance of law and order. The Government has closed seven important newspapers and one news agency in the period from September 1948 to May 1949; it is reported in all cases but one to have arrested the members of the respective editorial staffs.[62] The best known of these newspapers was the *Seoul Shinmun*, the largest daily in South Korea, which was closed by Government order on 3 May 1949, on the ground that it had failed to follow Government directives and to print Government releases in sufficient numbers. This action of the Government was sharply questioned in the National Assembly on 2 June and following.

(f) *Maintenance of law and order*

91. In the brief history of the Republic, its most besetting problem has been the safeguarding of national security. In this, the Executive and the National Assembly, despite all other differences, have been of one mind. Perhaps the best evidence of this is the enactment of the National Security Law[63] in November 1948 by the National Assembly, the concession made to the Government in respect of local administration, and the acquiescence of the Legislature in the arrests of those of its members who had been charged with offences against the National Security Law.

92. The National Security Law makes it a crime to betray the Constitution by posing as a government or, "in collusion with a betrayer", to seek to consolidate or group together with the object of disturbing the tranquillity of the State. Propaganda or deliberate incitement to achieve the aim of such organizations is punishable, as is the giving of weapons, money, supplies or promises, voluntarily and with knowledge of the hostile nature of such organizations and groups.

93. According to a communication to the Chairman of the Commission from the Ministry of Foreign Affairs,[64] in the period from 4 September 1948 to 30 April 1949, 33,347 cases were handled under this Law and 89,710 persons were arrested. 28,404 persons were released, 21,606 were turned over to the Prosecutor's Office for further proceedings, 29,284 were transferred to a "security office", 6,985 were transferred to the Military Police, and action in the case of 1,187 was pending.

94. Mention has already been made of the arrest of ten Assembly members who, according to the communication from the Ministry of Foreign Affairs already mentioned, are charged with having organized a cell in the National Assembly under the direction of members of the South Korea Labour Party. It is also charged that large sums of money were received by some of these members of the National Assembly from the South Korea Labour Party for purposes of agitation.

Cholla Namdo insurrection

95. Shortly after the establishment of the Government of the Republic, a major insurrection took place in Cholla Namdo, one of the largest and richest provinces in Korea, located on the tip of the peninsula. The uprising started in Yosu and Soonchon on 19 October 1948. Led by some officers of the 14th Regiment of Korean constabulary, 2,000 soldiers scheduled for duty on the island of Cheju were joined by several thousand civilians in a revolt against the Government. The rebels occupied Yosu for three days and Soonchon for about a week before they were dislodged. They established people's committees and tribunals, which tried and executed about 500 government officials, soldiers, and other persons. The rumour was spread by the rebels that the north had invaded the south and that the Government of the Republic had fled from Korea. In the meantime, the riots spread to such other important counties as Kurye, Posong, Kwangyang, Hadong and Kokson. The Government used a large force to crush the rebellion and, in early Novem-

---

[60] A/AC.26/W.14 (see volume II, annex II, B).
[61] As reported to the National Assembly on 4 June 1949 by Mr. Kim Hyung Sun, Vice-Director of the Office of Public Information. On 17 June 1949, the newly appointed Director of Public Information issued a directive that the North Korean "People's Army" was to be referred to as the "Insurgent Army".
[62] These facts were reported by the Press when they occurred. See in particular: *Chosun Ilbo* of 14, 16, 19 September 1948 and 5 May 1949; *Seoul Shinmun* of 14, 15 October 1948 and 14 January and 6 March 1949.

[63] A/AC.26/W.15 (see volume II, annex II, C).
[64] A/AC.26/39.

ber, announced that the main rebel force in Yosu and Soonchon had been annihilated. Guerrilla activities continued in southern Cholla Namdo until early 1949, when the last remnant of rebels was driven into the Chiri mountains. Official figures of the number of persons who participated in the rebellion or the number of troops used against them are not available. Official estimates of casualties and property damage show the scale of the uprising. From 20 October 1948 to 15 April 1949, 9,536 rebels were killed, wounded and captured; 504 soldiers and police were killed and 345 wounded. There were 11,000 investigations and arrests involving more than 23,000 persons; more than 80 per cent of those involved were found guilty. Property damage was estimated as over five billion *won*.

Uprising in Cheju Do

96. Strategic location, poverty, a traditional isolation and lack of sound local administration combined to make Cheju Island a likely centre for the activities of the South Korea Labour Party after liberation. The island, which is about 120 square miles in area and has a population of 300,000, became the scene of riots in April 1948 following the arrest and beating of persons suspected of being communists by police and members of the Northwest Youth Corps. Disturbances spread throughout the island and continued until early 1949, when the Government sent in a large force to pacify it. The operation was not completed until May 1949. Official figures indicate that more than 10,000 people took part. Nearly 2,000 were killed and more than 6,000 were captured. Casualties on the Government side are not available. Destruction was on a vast scale. Village after village was burned down and the damage to houses, livestock and crops was estimated at many billion *won*. Eighty police stations were attacked, burned down or damaged, fifteen Government offices and about twenty schools were burned down or partly destroyed The police seemed to have been a particular object of attack; over one hundred of them were killed or wounded.

6. EFFECT OF THE ECONOMIC DIVISION OF THE COUNTRY ON THE SOUTH

97. Despite the cut-off of electric power in May 1948, economic exchange between north and south continued until April 1949. According to the Bureau of Foreign Commerce of the Government of the Republic of Korea, South Korea imported from North Korea, in the year 1948, goods in the value of 1,206,786,250 *won*. In the same period, South Korea exported to North Korea goods to the value of 466,515,644 *won*. In the first three months of 1949, imports from North Korea were 531,558,700 *won* and exports were 302,721,500 *won*.

98. On 1 April, trade with North Korea was prohibited by the Government of the Republic. The reasons given were, first, that the North Korean régime was using the channels of trade for the introduction of subversive propaganda, and secondly, that the North Korean régime had confiscated a ship and cargo coming from a South Korean port to Pyongyang for purposes of barter in December 1948, and that the northern régime could not, on the basis of this experience, be trusted not to confiscate other goods that might be sent. In addition to the legitimate trade cut off at the beginning of April, there has also been a certain amount of illegitimate trade, much of which was carried on and continues to be carried on via the costly and roundabout route through Hong Kong.

99. The effects of the division of the country and of the loss to the Republic of its natural supplier of power, coal and fertilizer are evident on every side. It has had the effect of requiring the diversion of a substantial part of the national revenue (nearly 15 per cent in the fiscal year 1949-50) to increased expenditures for national defence and internal security. It has meant the expenditure of a significant portion of ECA aid on the production of power, the purchase of equipment and construction of facilities to increase coal production for use in thermal power plants and industry, the import of nitrogenous fertilizer, of chemicals and of sulphite pulp for paper manufacture, the building of an oil refinery which duplicates one in the north, and the like.

100. Without the aid granted by the United States through ECA, the Republic could not make ends meet for a number of years to come. With that aid, it hopes to be on a self-sustaining basis by 1952, but its standard of life at that time will be lower than it might enjoy if the country were united. It is estimated that if the country were not divided, exports and imports could in a short time be balanced at about $80 million annually.

101. The all-out struggle to increase production, which is necessary if the Republic is to survive the division of the country, has to be made in the face of serious inflation, insufficient and seriously depleted capital plant, worn-down transportation equipment, shortages of consumer goods, and a general nervousness concerning the future. Wages have not kept pace with prices, and the latter have risen substantially, particularly in respect of rice. Agriculture remains the major occupation of the country and absorbs the activities of 80 per cent of the population. While the institution of the last phase of land reform should quiet farmer discontent to a degree, the failure of the Government's grain collection programme indicates a certain tension between town and country which a greater abundance of consumer goods might relieve. The general economic stringency under which the Government has to plan the economic development of the country, however, makes the satisfaction of this want difficult, although the importation of cotton textiles is in some measure an attempt to meet this demand. The rural areas could probably supply a larger industrial labour force with profit to town and country alike, but as yet industry is not sufficiently developed to absorb any large number of migrants from the farms. The shortage of fuel caused by the division of the country has resulted in overcutting of timber resources. In seeking to correct this, the Government must allocate a substantial portion of the proceeds of private export trade to finance the import of bituminous coal and of wood. A united Korea would be on an export basis in respect of coal. The fishing industry, which once provided an important part of the national food consumption and some export revenue, suffered badly as a result of the war and is only being rehabilitated slowly because of lack of fishing vessels. Paper production is one-tenth of what it was before liberation. Transportation facilities are in serious need of repair and extension.

102. Despite enormous obstacles, the Republic has, however, made significant increases in basic

production, notably in coal and electric power. Anthracite mined in Government-financed mines in 1946 was about 250,000 metric tons. Production thus far in 1949 gives ground for belief that 1,200,000 tons will be produced this year. The goal for 1950 is 2 million tons. This increase in coal production has been accompanied by a significant growth of power production. From a monthly production of little over 18,000 kilowatts in 1945, power generated in South Korea increased to more than 78,000 kilowatts in March 1949 and was going up rapidly.

103. Korea's foreign trade has been principally with Hong Kong, which accounted for over 75 per cent of total imports and the greater part of total exports. This trade shows a tendency to decline, however, while exchange between Hong Kong and North Korea is increasing. The recently concluded trade agreement with Japan signifies the renewal of an old established trade connexion. While most imports are financed through ECA funds, the Government will use the proceeds of private export trade to finance imports of bituminous coal itself.

104. The revenue side of the Government budget of 211 billion *won* for the 1949-50 fiscal year exhibits some of the difficulties under which the development of a viable economy in the South labours. The principal income of the Government will be derived from governmental enterprises and public services rather than from the taxation system, which will yield only about 11 billion *won* and needs drastic reform to provide additional revenue and to check inflationary pressure, much of which comes from within the Government itself.[65] Payments of nearly 15 billion *won* to Government personnel mark an increase in 1949 of about 50 per cent over 1948, though the number of Government officials had been reduced from 134,000 in the latter year to 116,000 in 1949. Currency in circulation is over 40 billion *won* and this year is likely to increase since the budgetary deficit of nearly 30 billion *won* will have to be met by further borrowings from the central bank.

Chapter IV

SUMMARY, ANALYSIS AND CONCLUSIONS

A. Efforts of the Commission to implement the General Assembly resolution of 12 December 1948

1. UNIFICATION

(a) *Efforts of the Commission to gain access to the north*

1. The Commission was no sooner established in Seoul than it began to consider means of obtaining access to the north. For that purpose, it sought to obtain the good offices of the Union of Soviet Socialist Republics; it addressed a letter to General Kim Il Sung by various routes; it made repeated broadcast appeals to the north for facilities to permit a visit. All its efforts have met with failure, because until now there has been no response to these attempts of the Commission to contact the north.

(b) *Korean proposals for unification*

2. The Government of the Republic has proposed that the Commission approach the USSR to urge it to withdraw its troops from North Korea, to disband the North Korean régime and security forces, and to allow the Government of the Republic to assert jurisdiction in the northern zone. The accomplishment of the foregoing would be followed by elections in North Korea under the observation of the Commission.

Persons outside the Government have presented to the Commission suggestions in various forms for the initiation of discussions between representatives of north and south looking to unification. No suggestions for the solution of the practical questions involved in the initiation of such discussions have been put forward. Moreover, all such suggestions have been opposed by the Government of the Republic. The Commission has limited itself to a public expression of its readiness to assist in any discussions initiated by representatives of north and south under conditions offering assurance that they would be meaningful.

3. All proposals emanating from the north concerning ways of achieving the unification of Korea have been based on principles inconsistent with the General Assembly resolutions of 14 November 1947 and 12 December 1948 and, procedurally, have involved the exclusion of the United Nations from any part in their realization. The question of action by the Commission in respect of such suggestions has not arisen.

2. INTEGRATION OF SECURITY FORCES

4. In view of the inability of the Commission to make progress in the performance of its duties on the political level, it has not been possible to seek to bring about accord in respect of the integration of the security forces of north and south.

3. THE 38TH PARALLEL — A BARRIER TO FRIENDLY INTERCOURSE

5. The Commission has been unable to set on foot measures to facilitate a reduction of barriers to the beneficial exchange of goods and services and to other friendly intercourse between north and south because of the suspicion which prevails between their respective régimes. The Government of the Republic has now outlawed trade as an instrument of subversive propaganda and an exchange of views with the north on this or any other subject has not been possible.

6. The border is becoming the scene of increasingly frequent exchanges of fire and of armed raids along the 38th parallel. According to infor-

---

[65] An income tax law was enacted on 12 July 1949 and promulgated on 15 July. A law for the establishment of local revenue offices was enacted on 19 July.

mation received from United States military authorities, some of the raids from the north were set on foot for the purpose of introducing groups of trained *saboteurs* into the territory of the Republic.

7. The People's Republic has been recognized by the USSR with which it maintains diplomatic relations. Much publicity has been given to a recent visit of General Kim Il Sung to Moscow and to the evidences of esteem shown him. It is reported that an agreement for economic aid and cultural exchange was concluded in the course of this visit.

8. All these events have tended to fortify the 38th parallel in its character as a barrier to the friendly intercourse of the people of Korea with each other.

4. FURTHER DEVELOPMENT OF REPRESENTATIVE GOVERNMENT

9. The Commission has held itself available to the Government of the Republic of Korea for consultation in the further development of representative government. The Government of the Republic, which takes the view that the Commission's functions in this regard have relevance only north of the 38th parallel, has not required the Commission's services in this respect in the south. The Commission has, however, studied the problems of representative government in the Republic and has heard the views of Government officials, experts and organizations on the subject. It has also made enquiries concerning the structure of government in the north and the means of extending representative government there.

5. WITHDRAWAL OF OCCUPATION FORCES

10. The Commission has fulfilled, in respect of the occupation forces of the United States of America, the duty laid upon it by paragraph 4 (*d*) of the General Assembly resolution of 12 December 1948, to observe the withdrawal of the occupation forces of the occupying Powers. The withdrawal of United States occupation troops was completed on 29 June 1949, under the observation of the Commission, which has since verified the fact of their withdrawal. While unable to verify the disposition made of the military equipment belonging to the United States, which was not withdrawn with its troops, the Commission is satisfied that all of this has been transferred to the Korean security forces and that none of it remains under the control of the United States.

11. The Commission has signified to the USSR, through the Secretary-General of the United Nations, its readiness to carry out in respect of the occupation forces of that Power the duties imposed by paragraph 4 (*d*) of the General Assembly resolution of 12 December 1948. The Commission has received no reply to the message transmitted to the USSR on its behalf.

B. Factors affecting the implementation of the General Assembly resolution of 12 December 1948

12. The Temporary Commission, in the second part of its report to the General Assembly, had expressed a doubt whether the developments which it reported constituted a progress in the situation which existed on 14 November 1947, when the General Assembly adopted its first resolution on the Korean problem, and on 26 February 1948, when the Interim Committee made its recommendations. Of these developments, the chief one was the establishment of rival political régimes in the two zones into which Korea is divided. The Temporary Commission had stressed the urgent need for setting up some procedure for peaceful negotiations before military evacuation of the occupying forces had abandoned Korea to the arbitrary rule of rival political régimes whose military forces might find themselves driven to internecine warfare. The Commission had refrained from going further and defining methods for peaceful relations between the governments of North and South Korea, because that task was believed to be futile so long as the opposing ideologies and policies to which those governments subscribed continued in opposition to each other with ever-increasing violence in all parts of the world where they confronted each other. The Commission looked to the General Assembly for an answer to this basic difficulty.

13. The Temporary Commission, in the first part of its report, declared that it had concluded that the holding of elections in the southern zone of Korea would be a step in the re-establishment of the independence of Korea, and reported that the elections held on 10 May were a valid expression of the free will of the electorate in those parts of Korea which were accessible to the Commission and in which the inhabitants constituted approximately two-thirds of the people of all Korea.

14. The General Assembly approved the conclusions of the Temporary Commission, both those offered in the first part and those stated in the second part of the report. It recorded its concurrence in the conclusions stated in the first part of the report by declaring that there had been established a lawful government (the Government of the Republic of Korea), having effective control and jurisdiction over that part of Korea where the Temporary Commission was able to observe and consult and in which the great majority of the people of all Korea resided; that this Government was based on elections which were a valid expression of the free will of the electorate of that part of Korea and which were observed by the Temporary Commission; and that this was the only such government in Korea (paragraph 2 of the resolution of the General Assembly of 12 December 1948).

15. The General Assembly gave effect to the conclusions stated in the second part of the report by establishing the present Commission. It charged the Commission to "have in mind the status of the Government of the Republic of Korea as defined by the General Assembly"; at the same time that it was to "lend its good offices to bring about the unification of Korea".

16. In the opinion of the present Commission, its predecessor had not misread the omens. The problem of Korean independence and unification has been increasingly prejudiced by the consolidation of the rival political régimes which had emerged when the Temporary Commission reported last year.

17. The Government of the Republic of Korea had just come into being when the Temporary Commission finished its principal labours in Korea. The present Commission, however, found

a Government actively administering its territory in full awareness of its independent sovereign status.

18. That Government had informed the Korean public, even before the Commission came to Seoul, that the resolution represented an acknowledgment of the claims made by the Government's representative at the first part of the third regular session of the General Assembly in Paris. The Commission saw no need to engage in discussion with the Government over the question whether the General Assembly had approved the claim of the Government to be the lawful authority of all Korea, or of only that part lying south of the 38th parallel. This could only have added to the difficulties of the Government, without evident advantage to the cause in which the Commission was labouring.

The Government has not abated in any respect the claims which it put forward at Paris. It has maintained inflexibly the contention that the northern régime has been outlawed by the General Assembly and that the Commission, like the Government, ought therefore to refrain from dealing with it. It has insisted that the Commission was authorized to deal only with the USSR in respect of North Korea in order to persuade the Soviet Union to dissolve the northern régime and to permit the Government of the Republic to hold elections in the northern zone under the supervision of the Commission.

19. The form in which the Commission's powers were cast did not strengthen its position *vis-à-vis* the Government. The Commission was "to lend its good offices" : it was "to be available for observation and consultation" ; it was to "seek to facilitate" : all attributes of an intermediary, who cannot function in the absence of demands for the services authorized to be performed. It has been noted elsewhere in the present report that the Government of the Republic has not recognized that paragraph 4 (c) of the General Assembly resolution had any application to itself, and for that reason has not called on the Commission for help of any kind in meeting the developing problems of representative government. It has not called on the Commission for assistance in initiating or conducting negotiations or, indeed, any preliminary exchange of views with North Korean leaders. It has not required the services of the Commission for the purpose of exploring the practical possibilities of a reduction of other than political barriers. In the absence of an initiative from the Government, the Commission has had no opportunity to open the armoury of its own powers.

20. In barring *ab initio* any idea of discussion with northern leaders of the basis for the creation of an all-Korean régime, the Government has indicated that in its view the Commission had been sent to Korea for the sole purpose of lending its good offices to the Government of the Republic of Korea in vindication of the latter's claims. Acceptance of that view would have made it impossible for the Commission to have undertaken the role which the Temporary Commission had in mind in pressing urgently for the institution by the General Assembly of machinery of negotiation between the rival political régimes, and which the General Assembly assigned to the Commission in December 1948.

The differences with the Government have not alone, or even chiefly, been at the root of the lack of achievement which the Commission is obliged to report. The problems created by the differences between the Government and the Commission never became real, because the Commission was unable to establish contact with the north.

21. From north of the parallel the Commission has been a target of defamation and inflammatory attacks, which have not been without effect and counterpart in the south. The most courteous appeals for facilities that would permit a visit to the north and allow the initiation of preliminary and tentative exploration of the subject of unification have been ignored. Every channel of communication has been employed without avail. The USSR, requested through the Secretary-General to lend its good offices to establish contact between the Commission and the north, has not acknowledged the communication. Transmission of a message directly to General Kim Il Sung through shipping channels via Hong Kong has been without result. Transmission of the Commission's request through a weekly mail exchange between north and south has elicited no response. Repeated radio broadcast appeals have been equally without reply, unless the systematic vituperation of the Pyongyang radio was such.

C. Present status of the Korean problem

1. Fervent desire for peaceful unification

22. The Government has not only made clear that it would not participate in official discussions with the north looking to unification, but has also indicated that it frowned on unofficial efforts in this behalf. It has made clear that it views any suggestions for north-south discussion, even of an unofficial and most tentative kind, as a form of disloyalty. In the face of this attitude, the Commission has not felt free to encourage extra-governmental efforts of contact.

23. The Commission, moreover, has not felt that the proposals of the extra-legislative opposition to the Government led by Mr. Kim Koo and Mr. Kimm Kiusic for the initiation of north-south discussions in a conference, or by some other means, merited encouragement. Consistently with the view they took when the question of participation in the 10 May 1948 elections was under consideration, the leaders of the opposition are not deterred by the results of these elections from favouring new elections in the north and south. The Government has always regarded the conference proposal as a communist trick designed to bring about public discord and confusion. The experience of the so-called "North-South Conference" of last year certainly goes far to confirm this belief. The suggestions which the Commission has heard from those who favour a new conference have impressed it as vague and wishful. The difficult questions involved in such a conference have either not been faced or have found no answer. The means of making such a conference truly representative, the status of the participants, the questions with which they would deal, the procedure to be employed for giving effect to any agreement that might be reached, all these problems have been evaded by those who advocated such a conference.

24. Despite the failure of the "North-South Conference" of April 1948, the idea of a renewed attempt in this direction still persists in some quarters. The Government appears to have underestimated the hold on the imagination of the people of Korea of the idea that Korea's difficulties could be overcome if leaders of north and south would sit down together and seek a common answer to its problems. The propaganda agencies of the northern régime have been able to make much political capital by appropriating the idea of a conference. It is they who have been able to make play with the slogans of the "people's democracy", the "fatherland front", a "conference" of delegates from political parties and social organizations of South and North Korea. The latest move in that direction from the north has been a "Manifesto" of the Democratic Front for the Attainment of Unification for the Fatherland.[66]

25. The Republic still labours under the disadvantage of political division, which began with the difference of view over the question of the 10 May 1948 elections. The Government has made no effort to heal this breach. Instead of mobilizing the strength of the patriotic opposition behind itself and presenting to the north the spectacle of a vigorous and united Republic, it faces the 38th parallel at the head of a divided people.

2. LACK OF A SPIRIT OF COMPROMISE

26. The Republic is a result of free elections and the expression of a people's will. Psychologically, if not materially, the activities of the north have compelled the Republic to go on a war footing, and this spiritual mobilization has to some extent brutalized the conduct of government and engendered suspicion of those who remain independent and critical of spirit. This comes at a time when the feeling for freedom in the sense of the association of liberty with responsibility has hardly broken through the millennial tradition of government from above, or else has not advanced beyond the level of license. The north has troubled the relative calm which is needed for the psychological and social translation of the laws of liberty into the practice of freedom through a careful nurture of procedural and institutional growth.

27. The failure of the north to respond to the Commission's appeals is only one sign of its contempt for the international community's efforts to obtain a peaceful solution of the Korean problem on the basis of the principles announced in the two General Assembly resolutions.

The northern régime is the creature of a military occupant and rule, by right of a mere transfer of power from that Government. It has never been willing to give its subjects an unfettered opportunity, under the scrutiny of an impartial international agency, to pass upon its claim to rule. The claims to be a "people's democracy" and its expressions of concern for the general welfare are falsified by this unwillingness to account for the exercise of power to those against whom it is employed.

Professions of devotion to Korea and of a desire for unity are many, but are belied in action. The cutting-off of electric power had grave effects on the morale and economy of the south. The armed attacks along the border serve no legitimate purpose and are unfortunate, since the people on both sides of the parallel are Korean.

[66] See volume II, annex IV, C.

The activities of the north reach deep into the territory of the Republic to mislead those whose grievances are legitimate enough into struggling for ends which they do not understand and which have nothing in common with their own purposes. To provoke small groups of harassed people into taking up hopelessly crude arms against those in authority in the hope of ending their troubles is utterly irresponsible.

28. The suspicion engendered by mutual rivalry and conflicting claims to supremacy has not only pinioned the spiritual freedom of the Korean people, it has also resulted in the blocking up of the normal channels of trade for fear that previous experience would be repeated and that along them would flow not only goods, but propaganda. In this respect, also, the objectives of the General Assembly have been defeated. The Commission must report that until now it has met opposition from the Government of the Republic to suggestions for a renewal of economic exchange, while it has never been given an opportunity of making proposals to that end to the north. Hence, it has been able only to make public an expression of its readiness to assist in a resumption of legitimate trade on a trial basis.

3. GROWING MILITARY STRENGTH IN NORTH AND SOUTH

29. There is much military posturing on both sides of the parallel. This holds a serious danger of provoking open military conflict. Military conflict in Korea would mean the most barbarous civil war. The USSR continues to refuse to have any dealings with the Commission; it lends countenance to northern leaders in bellicose utterances and in a refusal to consider ways of adjusting existing differences on any plane of relations between north and south. In this connexion, note should be taken of the fact that the North Korean régime has recently concluded a treaty with the USSR. It is reported that an agreement for military aid has been concluded between North Korea and the Chinese communist forces in Manchuria.

Border raids from the north are frequently reported and are said to be increasing in intensity. The Commission, on one occasion, has itself seen a contest for hills in the vicinity of the parallel. The scale of such conflicts is small. The Commission is not in a position to judge what they portend, though it can testify that they upset the peaceful routine of the countryside and cause unnecessary loss of life. The propaganda efforts of dissension and subversion have been stepped up.

30. All this induces equal and opposite reactions in the south. The Government is hastening the pace of its military preparations and is pressing the United States for military aid beyond that already received. United States military personnel advise and assist in the training of the Republic's forces, as on the other side of the parallel military personnel of the USSR reportedly perform like services for the northern forces.

4. INTERNATIONAL POLITICAL CLIMATE

31. Running through the diverse opinions concerning the solution of the problem of Korea which the Commission has heard is a general belief that the USSR and the United States are responsible for the present plight of the country and have left it in the lurch. An equally general

opinion is that the problem cannot be solved until the two Powers take steps in concert to lift the barrier at the 38th parallel and restore to Korea the independence and unity which were promised at the Moscow Conference of Foreign Ministers in December 1945.

The Government of the Republic claims that the USSR still exercises decisive control over the régime in the north. It has expressed the opinion that the problem of Korea can be solved if the USSR will withdraw its protection from the northern régime and allow the people of North Korea to give expression to their hidden loyalty to the Republic. From the United States, the Government of the Republic expects, as a matter of obligation, military and economic aid for defence against the menace of aggression and invasion from the north.

32. Recent events in Asia have induced nervousness in the territory of the Republic, and emboldened propaganda from the north. These events have been cited by the Government of the Republic as a reason why the defence of the Republic should become a United States commitment. The Korean Press carries frequent reports from Washington of requests by the Government of the Republic for arms and other military aid from the United States. In June and July many mass meetings and parades were held to protest against the withdrawal of American troops and to demand arms for defence. The President of the Republic has on several recent occasions insisted that the United States had a responsibility for the future of the Republic and should assist the countries of the Pacific to close ranks in a Pacific Pact against the dangers that threaten them.

33. Underlying the prevalent belief that the Korean problem cannot be solved without prior accord between the USSR and the United States is a general scepticism concerning the ability of the United Nations to find a solution to the Korean problem, although this by no means signifies that the presence of the Commission is not found useful in other respects. In appraising the reasons for its own failure to accomplish the task with which it had been charged, the Commission may take note of factors having a decisive bearing on that lack of success. Among these, the relations between the USSR and the United States continue to be the largest single, and perhaps decisive, factor contributing to the growing hardening of relations between north and south.

D. Conclusions

34. The people of Korea are remarkably homogeneous. Ethnically and culturally they are one. They have a passionate longing for unity and independence and have a profound desire for the peaceful unification of their country.

The division of Korea has resulted in adverse economic consequences in the south, the only part of Korea to which the Commission has had access. The aftermath of the Second World War would have made the need for outside aid urgent in any case. But if the country were united, the south would not require such aid in the same degree and would be able to stabilize its economy more easily and at a higher level.

The division of Korea has caused bitterness, frustration and mutual distrust among its people.

The frequent raids along the 38th parallel have further accentuated these feelings. The division of Korea was caused by the exigencies of the Second World War. There is no justification for the continued separation of the two parts of the country.

The Republic of Korea looks to the United Nations for the solution of many of its problems, for it feels that the Republic is in some sense a creation of the United Nations. In the opinion of the Government, as evidenced by its request that the stay of the Commission in Korea be prolonged for another year, the presence of the Commission has been a stabilizing factor in the situation.

35. Bearing in mind these fundamental considerations underlying the Korean problem, the United Nations Commission on Korea has reached the following conclusions:

(1) The embittered propaganda and hostile activities which now mark the relations between the two parts of Korea render the prospect of unification more and more remote.

(2) As long as the opposition of the Union of Soviet Socialist Republics to the efforts of the United Nations Commission to achieve the objectives of the General Assembly resolution of 12 December 1948 continues, neither a relaxation of hostile propaganda nor any other measure can facilitate to a substantial degree the achievement of unification.

(3) The world-wide antagonism between the Union of Soviet Socialist Republics and the United States of America continues to be, as it was when the Temporary Commission was in Korea, one of the basic factors underlying the present difficulties. Without a new effort by those Powers to reach agreement on the question of Korea, no substantial progress toward the achievement of unification on the basis of the principles approved by the General Assembly can be made.

(4) From its very inception, the newly formed Republic of Korea has been confronted with many difficulties. It faced insurgent uprisings from within and was menaced by continuous clashes on the 38th parallel. While making due allowance for these factors, the Commission believes that a broadening of the Government's political base would allow it to meet these difficulties more successfully and so enable it to play a more effective part in achieving unification.

(5) The present Commission, like its predecessor, must place on record an acknowledgment that the situation in Korea is now no better than it was at the beginning, and that it has not been able to facilitate the achievement of the objectives set by the General Assembly.

Done in a single copy in the English language at the Duk Soo Palace, Seoul, Korea, this twenty-eighth day of July in the year nineteen hundred forty-nine.

Representative of:	(*Signed*)
The Philippines (Chairman)	Rufino LUNA
China (Rapporteur)	LIU Yu Wan
Australia	A. B. JAMIESON
El Salvador	Miguel A. MAGAÑA
France	Henri COSTILHES
India	Anup SINGH

SALES AGENTS OF THE UNITED NATIONS PUBLICATIONS

ARGENTINA
Editorial Sudamericana S.A.
Alsina 500
Buenos Aires

AUSTRALIA
H. A. Goddard Pty. Ltd.
255a George Street
Sydney, N. S. W.

BELGIUM
Agence et Messageries de la
Presse. S. A.
14-22 rue du Persil
Bruxelles

BOLIVIA
Librería Científica y Literaria
Avenida 16 de Julio. 216
Casilla 972
La Paz

CANADA
The Ryerson Press
299 Queen Street West
Toronto

CHILE
Edmundo Pizarro
Merced 816
Santiago

CHINA
The Commercial Press Ltd.
211 Honan Road
Shanghai

COLOMBIA
Librería Latina Ltda.
Apartado Aéreo 4011
Bogotá

COSTA RICA
Trejos Hermanos
Apartado 1313
San José

CUBA
La Casa Belga
René de Smedt
O'Reilly 455
La Habana

CZECHOSLOVAKIA
F. Topic
Narodni Trida 9
Praha 1

DENMARK
Einar Munksgaard
Nørregade 6
København

DOMINICAN REPUBLIC
Librería Dominicana
Calle Mercedes No. 49
Apartado 656
Ciudad Trujillo

ECUADOR
Muñoz Hermanos y Cía.
Nueve de Octubre 703
Casilla 10-24
Guayaquil

EGYPT
Librairie "La Renaissance d'Egypte"
9 Sh. Adly Pasha
Cairo

FINLAND
Akateeminen Kirjakauppa
2. Keskuskatu
Helsinki

FRANCE
Editions A. Pedone
13. rue Soufflot
Paris, Vᵉ

GREECE
"Eleftheroudakis"
Librairie internationale
Place de la Constitution
Athènes

GUATEMALA
José Goubaud
Goubaud & Cía. Ltda.
Sucesor
5a Av. Sur No. 6 y 9a C. P.
Guatemala

HAITI
Max Bouchereau
Librairie "A la Caravelle"
Boîte postale 111-B
Port-au-Prince

INDIA
Oxford Book & Stationery Company
Scindia House
New Delhi

IRAN
Bongahe Piaderow
731 Shah Avenue
Teheran

IRAQ
Mackenzie & Mackenzie
The Bookshop
Baghdad

LEBANON
Librairie universelle
Beyrouth

LUXEMBOURG
Librairie J. Schummer
Place Guillaume
Luxembourg

NETHERLANDS
N. V. Martinus Nijhoff
Lange Voorhout 9
s'Gravenhage

NEW ZEALAND
Gordon & Gotch. Ltd.
Waring Taylor Street
Wellington

NICARAGUA
Ramiro Ramírez V.
Agencia de Publicaciones
Managua, D. N.

NORWAY
Johan Grundt Tanum Forlag
Kr. Augustgt. 7A
Oslo

PHILIPPINES
D. P. Pérez Co.
132 Riverside
San Juan

SWEDEN
A.-B. C. E. Fritzes Kungl.
Hofbokhandel
Fredsgatan 2
Stockholm

SWITZERLAND
Librairie Payot S. A.
Lausanne, Genève, Vevey,
Montreux, Neuchâtel,
Berne, Basel
Hans Raunhardt
Kirchgasse 17
Zurich I

SYRIA
Librairie universelle
Damas

TURKEY
Librairie Hachette
469 Istiklal Caddesi
Beyoglu-Istanbul

UNION OF SOUTH AFRICA
Central News Agency
Commissioner & Rissik Sts.
Johannesburg and at Capetown
and Durban

UNITED KINGDOM
H M. Stationery Office
P. O. Box 569
London, S.E. 1
and at H.M.S.O. Shops in
London, Edinburgh, Manchester,
Cardiff, Belfast and Bristol

UNITED STATES OF AMERICA
International Documents Service
Columbia University Press
2960 Broadway
New York 27, N. Y.

URUGUAY
Oficina de Representación de
Editoriales
Av. 18 de Julio 1333 Esc. 1
Montevideo

VENEZUELA
Escritoría Pérez Machado
Conde a Piñango 11
Caracas

YUGOSLAVIA
Drzavno Preduzece
Jugoslovenska Knjiga
Moskovska Ul. 36
Beograd

Printed in France.   Price in the United States : 40 cents.   12 November 1948.

제3부 유엔한국위원단 보고서(1949)

2. 유엔한국위원단 보고서 제2권 : 부속문서

해제문서 20 : A/936/Add.1 (Report of The United Nations Commission on Korea, Volume II - Annexes)

문서명	Report of the United Nations Commission on Korea, Volume II - Annexes		
	유엔한국위원단 보고서 제2권 : 부속문서		
발신	유엔한국위원단	생성일시	
		발신일시	1949년 8월
수신	유엔총회	수신일시	
		문서번호	Official Records: Fourth Session Supplement No.9 (A/936/Add.1)
문서형태	보고서	문서분량	67쪽
주제명	1. 통일을 위한 활동 및 경제적 · 사회적 장벽 제거에 있어서 위원단의 노력에 관한 주요 문서 2. 의회정치 발전에 관한 주요 문서 3. 주한미군 철수 및 주한미군사고문단 설치에 관한 주요 문서 4. 위원단의 위임사항 이행에 관한 위원단, 대한민국 정부, 그리고 북한의 입장 및 태도에 관한 주요 문서 5. 위원단 및 사무국 대표단 목록 6. 문서목록		
주요내용	본 문서는 1948년 12월 12일, 유엔총회 결의 195(III)에 의하여 창설된 유엔한국위원단이 도착한 1949년 1월 30일부터 1949년 7월 28일까지의 활동을 기록한 유엔한국위원단 보고서 제1권에 이은 제2권 부속문서로, 보고서 관련 서류 원문을 모은 것임. 상세한 내용은 본문 참조.		
검색어	한국신문법, 국가보안법, 한국국방군(Korean Security Forces), 주한 미 군사고문단(Korean Military Advisory Group), 김구, 김규식, 김동원, 김약수, 김일성, 이승만, 이철원, 임병직, 조병옥, 씽(Anup Singh), 번스(Arthur C. Bunce), 제이미슨(A. B. Jamieson), 무쵸(John J. Muccio), 리우위안(Liu Yu-Wan), 마가냐(Miguel Angel Magaña), 로버츠(W. L. Roberts), 루나(Rufino Luna), 베르트하이머(Egon Ranshofen-Wertheimer), 슈와츠(Sanford Schwarz), 루카스(Graham Lucas), 샤바스(Arsen Shahbaz), 주홍티(朱鴻題, Hung-Ti Chu), 카츠(Alfred Katz), 페이마스터(Jehangir Paymaster), 류(Harry Liao), 프리스맨(Mark Priceman), 로브(Marian Robb), 리들(Harold Riddle), 류(C. C. Liu)		

〈목차〉

V. 위원단 및 사무국 대표단 목록

    1. 유엔한국위원단에 파견된 대표단

    2. 위원단 사무국 조직

    3. 현지 채용 직원

VI. 문서목록

    A. 한국 독립문제에 관한 유엔 문서

    B. 유엔한국위원단의 문서 전체목록

부속문서 I

통일을 위한 활동 및 경제적·사회적 장벽을
제거하기 위한 위원단의 노력에 관한 주요 문서

A. 제1분과위원회 최종보고서 및 부록(A/AC.26/37)

1. 제1분과위원회 보고서 본문

- 조직구성, 제1분과위원회의 위임사항(권한), 진행한 회의 및 시찰지역에 관하여 서술하고 있으며, 위임사항의 이행, 제안 및 수집된 의견, 위원단 및 정부의 정책에 관하여 검토하였으며, 남북 간 장벽의 제거방안에 대하여 검토하였고, 38도선을 둘러싼 상황을 분석함.

- 제1분과위원회에서 표명된 견해들을 요약하고 제1분과위원회의 조사결과를 서술한 후, 위원단에 대한 '권고'로 마무리하고 있음.

2. 부록

(a) 북한에 대한 접촉

   (i) 소련정부에 전달하기 위해 유엔사무총장에게 전송한 전보
      (원문은 위원단 보고서[A/936, 제1권] 제2장 제20단락에 수록되어 있음)

(ii) 김일성장군에게 보낸 서한

(원문은 위원단 보고서(A/936, 제1권) 제2장 제22단락에 수록되어 있음)

(b) 통일문제에 관한 정보 및 의견 조사

- 1949년 3월 2일 위원단이 제1분과위원회의 보고서를 채택하고 위원회가 선정한 인물들을 대상으로 한 면담 및 구술청취를 승인하였으며, 다음 세 가지 사항에 대해 의견을 청취함.

(i) 통일문제에 관한 당신의 견해는 무엇인가?

(ii) 대한민국 정부수립 이래로 통일을 촉진할 만한 조치가 있었다면 무엇이며 통일을 향해 어떠한 조치가 취해야 하는가?

(iii) 한반도에서 경제적, 사회적, 기타 장벽을 제거하는 것이 어느 정도로 가능한가?

- 1949년 3월 3일부터 6월 2일에 걸쳐 위원단은 아래의 행정관료, 국회의원, 민간인을 대상으로 실시함.

이범석(국무총리 겸 국방부장관)

김약수(국회부의장)

박건웅(전 과도입법의회 의원)

임영신(상공부장관)

번스(A. C. Bunce, 미국 경제협조처[ECA] 한국대표단장)

이응준(육군 참모총장)

김도연(재무부장관)

김규식(민족자주연맹 의장)

김병회(국회의원)

설의식(새한민보 사장)

김병연(평안남도 도지사, 대한민국 정부 임명)

김구(한독당 당수)

권윤호(기독교 지도자)

이청천(장군, 국회의원)

통일문제에 관해 자문을 구한 인물들

신익희(국회의장)

백 L. G.(조선기독교대학 학장)

윤치영(전 내무부장관)

노기남(서울교구 주교)

김법린(동국대 학장)

조소앙(사회당 당수)

임병직(외무부 장관)

김효석(내무부 장관)

- 1949년 2월 11일 위원단은 이승만 대통령 및 정부와 인터뷰를 실시함.

- 위원단의 인터뷰는 남한지역에 한정되어 있었고 그것도 주로 지식인층을 대상으로 함. 접근이 불가능한 북한지역의 사정에 관해서는 북한의 라디오방송을 청취하였으나, 주로 위원단의 활동을 반대하는 내용으로 구성됨.

- 제1분과위원회는 위의 인터뷰 대상 인물들을 각각 (a) 한국인 행정관료 (b) 국회의원 (c) 민간 지식층의 범주로 나누고 이들이 제1분과위원회의 세 가지 설문 사항인 (ㄱ) '정부가 통일을 촉진시키기 위해 취한 조치' (ㄴ) 통일방안 제안 (ㄷ) 경제적, 사회적, 기타 장벽의 제거 가능성 문제에 대해 언급한 내용을 보고함.

B. 미국 경제협조처 한국대표단장 번스(Arthur C. Bunce)의
청문에서의 발언요지와
번스가 제출한 경제발전에 관한 보고서(A/AC.26/SC.1/13)

1. 번스(Arthur C. Bunce)의 청문회 발언요지

위원단 의장의 질문에 대한 번스(Arthur C. Bunce)의 주요 답변 내용은 다음과 같음.

- 남북한의 생활수준의 차이에 대한 질문에서 양곡이 수출되지 않는 한 1인당 소득은 북한이 더 많을 것이라는 견해를 피력함.

- 북한 주민이 남한으로 내려오는 주된 이유가 정치적인 동기에 있는가라는 질문에 대해, 정치적 동기 외에, 종교의 자유, 상업의 제한 등의 이유가 있으며 북한의 토지개혁에 불만을 품은 사람들도 있다고 답변함.

- 북한에서 소련의 경제정책이 북한을 위한 것인지 소련을 위해 고안된 것인가의 여부에 대해, 외부에서 일부 숙련된 기술자들을 데려와서 북한의 재건과 산업 발전을 지원했다고 함.

- 남북 분단이 지속되고 있는 한, 미국의 원조 없이 얼마나 빨리 현재의 경제 수준을 유지할 수 있게 되겠는지에 대한 질문에 대해, 만약 차기년도에 미국이 원조를 중단한다면 일 년 내에 생산과 생활수준의 어려움을 겪으며 식량폭동이 일어날 것이라고 전망함.

- 미국이 한국에 대해 얼마나 오랫동안 원조를 계속할 것인지에 대한 질문에, ECA의 계획은 장기지원이지만, 국회의 세출예산에 의존하고 있기 때문에 한 번에 일 년 이상의 기간을 약속할 수는 없다고 답변함.

- 남북이 분단되어 있는 동안 남북한의 통상거래 전망은 어떠한가라는 질문에 대해, 교역은 어려울 것이라고 부정적으로 답함.

- 한국예산의 몇 %를 군대와 경찰에 지출하고 있는지의 질문에 대해,

1949~1950년 회계연도 예산총액 1,960억 원의 예산 가운데 국방부가 120억 원, 치안국을 포함한 내무부 예산이 약 50억 원에 달한다고 밝힘. 단일 항목으로 가장 고액의 지출은 230억 원을 초과한 교통세출비이며 이는 석탄 생산과 운송을 증가시키기 위해 새로운 지선(spur railroad)을 가설하는 비용을 포함한 것이라고 답변함.

- 곡물판매실적이 저조한 원인이 서울과 같은 도시에서 배급미가 중단된 것 때문인가라는 질문에 대해 직접적인 관련이 있다고 응답함.

- 한국에 대한 외국인의 자본투자 규모에 관한 질의에 대해, 몇몇 유류저장과 기타 시설을 제외하고는 실제로 투자는 거의 없다고 답변함.

- 한국 정부의 재정 상태에 대한 질문에 대해, 재정 상태는 매우 양호하다고 답변함.

- 한국경제를 일본경제와 통합시키기 위하여 어떤 조치를 취했는가에 대한 질문에 대해, 과거 한국의 수출의 80~90퍼센트가 일본을 대상으로 한 것이었으나 지금은 대일 수출 규모는 소액에 불과하다고 함.

- 한국정부가 주한 미국사절단의 활동과 관련하여 어떠한 재정상의 책임을 부담하고 있는가에 대한 질문에 대해, ECA는 한국정부와 긴밀히 협의하여 부흥계획을 입안하고 있고 ECA예산을 심의하기 위해 설치한 기획실에 적어도 30명 이상의 한국인 관료가 협의에 참여하고 있다고 밝힘.

- 한국정부가 미국으로부터 많은 군수장비를 매입하고 있는데 이것이 한국의 경제사정에 비추어 적절한가에 대한 질의에 대해, 안전보장 없이는 경제 원조가 성공할 수 없다고 하면서 군사비용은 경제부흥과 함께 같이 고려해야 하는 필수적 요소라는 견해를 밝힘.

- 이외에도 사무국장으로부터, 엄청난 규모의 북한 월남민을 수용하는 것이 남한경제에 어떠한 영향을 미쳤는가에 대한 질문에 대해, 급격한 인구증가와 극심한 주택부족 등 심각한 문제를 야기했다고 답함. 북한, 중국, 만주 등지로부터 보이지 않는 자본의 유입이 있었는가에 대한 질문에 대해, 소수의 개인소지

품 외에 실제로 대단한 자본의 유입은 없었다고 답변함. 남한지역의 비료공장 설립가능성에 대한 질문에 대해, 지방의 석탄 매장량을 충분히 조사한 후에 가능할 것이라고 답변함. 450환 대 1달러의 환율이 수입을 용이하게 하려는 목적에서 책정된 것인가하는 질문에 대해, 환율이 15환 대 1달러에서 50환 대 1달러, 450환 대 1달러로 점차 인상되었다고 말하고 미국의 입장에서는 더 올리고 싶지만 현재의 물가와 임금을 고려하여 책정된 것이라고 답함.

2. 번스(Arthur C. Bunce)가 제출한 보고서(1949.4.4)

(1) 한국에서 미국과 소련의 경제 협상의 내력

    (a) 서론

    (b) 미·소 공동위원회

    (c) 1946년의 공동위원회

    (d) 1947년 공동위원회의 후속 국면

    (e) 선거권 문제

(2) 분단의 경제적 영향

3. 미군정기 남한의 주요한 발전

(a) 농업

    (i) 농업생산

    (ii) 식량 수집과 배급

    (iii) 농민과 토지

(b) 공업과 광업

(c) 교육과 기술훈련

C. 미국과 대한민국 간의
원조에 관한 협정(1948.12.10) (A.AC.26/W.3)

- 전문과 12개 조문으로 구성되어 있으며 각 조문의 주요 사항은 아래와 같음.

전문

대한민국 정부는 경제적 위기를 방지하고 국력 부흥을 촉진하고 국내 안정을 확보하기 위해 미국정부에 대해 재정적, 물질적, 기술적 지원을 요청하였으며 미국 의회는 대통령에게 대한민국에 원조를 제공할 권한을 부여함.

제1조

1948년 6월 28일 미 의회에서 통과된 법률(공법 793호, 제80차 회의)에 의거하여 대통령에게 허용된 범위 내에서 한국에 대해 원조를 제공함.

제2조

한국정부는 한국의 모든 자원을 가장 이로운 방법으로 이용하고 미국정부가 한국에 제공하는 원조도 마찬가지의 방법으로 이용하기로 하며, 균형재정을 도모하는 한편, 경제안정을 위해 통화량과 신용을 통제하며, 외국환이 한국경제에 최대한 공헌할 수 있도록 외국환 거래와 무역을 규제하고 환율을 최대한 신속하게 책정함. 아울러 식량수급을 포함한 국내생산물을 적절히 관리하고 외국인의 사적 투자 및 무역을 허용하고 수출산업을 발전시키며 생산을 극대화하기 위하여 정부소유의 생산시설 및 재산을 운용하거나 처분함.

제3조

한국정부는 미국원조 대표단이 임무를 수행하는 데에 필요한 모든 편의를 제공하고 원조와 관련된 모든 사항에 대해 미국대표와 협의함.

제4조

한국정부는 한국경제를 안정시키기 위하여 전반적인 경제부흥계획을 수행하며 외국환의 정기적 사용을 위해 미국의 원조대표단과 협의하고 동의하에 진행함.

제5조

한국정부는 미국이 제공한 물자와 자금을 국내에 공급할 때 적정가격으로 공정하게 공급하도록 보장하고 본 협정에 따라 미국정부가 증여로 제공한 상품, 서비스, 기술정보에 대한 달러가격을 통보하며, 한국정부는 그 가격에 따라 한국은행 특별계정에 예치하고 미국 원조대표단의 허가 없이 이를 수출할 수 없음. 이 협정에 따른 모든 원조물자가 미국이 제공한 것임을 표시해야 함.

제6조

한국정부와 타 국가 간의 상품 및 서비스 교역을 권장하되, 다른 제3국과의 무역에 부여하는 것과 동일한 대우를 곧바로 미국과의 상품교역에도 부여함 (최혜국대우 규정).

제7조

상업, 제조업, 해운 및 기타 영업상의 행위에 관하여 현재 또는 장래에 모든 제3국 국민에게 부여하는 대우와 동일한 대우를 미국 국민(자연인 및 법인)에게 부여함(즉, 최혜국대우를 규정).

제8조

한국정부는 내수 및 수출용으로 필요한 한국산 물자의 적정량을 고려한 후에, 미국이 자국 내의 자원부족이나 부족 가능성으로 인해 동일한 한국산 물자를 저장하거나 기타 목적으로 매매, 교역, 물물교환 등의 적절한 조건으로 미국으로 이송할 경우, 편의 제공과 동시에 제반 장애를 제거하는 구체적 조치를 취하며 필요할 시에는 양국 간 교섭에 나설 것.

제9조

미국이 한국에 지원하는 상품과 기술지원에 관하여 양국 국민들이 모든 정보를 알 수 있도록 협조할 것, 언론이 이를 취재하고 자유롭게 보도할 수 있도록 보장하며, 미국 의회의 의원들이 원조과정을 시찰하고 조언할 수 있도록 보장함.

제10조

대한민국 정부의 요청이나 유엔의 원조 등으로 인해 본 협정에 따른 원조가 필요하지 않다고 유엔이 인정할 경우, 대한민국 정부가 협정 조건을 준수하지 않거나 사정의 변경 등으로 인해 미국 대통령이 중지를 결정할 경우, 원조가 중단됨.

제11조

한국 국회가 본 협정에 동의하였음을 미국에 정식 통보함으로써 효력이 발생하며 어느 한쪽이 상대방에게 협정 종료를 통보할 경우 3개월이 지나기 전까지는 협정의 효력이 유지되며 본 협정은 양국 간 교섭에 의해 언제든지 개정될 수 있음.

제12조

본 협정은 유엔에 등록하고 한국어와 영문으로 2통을 작성하며 동등한 효력을 가지나 서로 간에 상이한 점이 있을 경우에는 영문 협정문이 우선함.

부속문서 II

의회정치 발전에 관한 주요 문서

A. 제2분과위원회 최종보고서 및 부록(A/AC.26/37)

1. 제2분과위원회의 최종보고서

- 대한민국의 중요한 발전을 연대순으로 서술하고 한국정부 관료 및 주요 인사들에 대한 청문, 최근 소요가 발생한 전라남도와 제주도 지방에 대한 순시 등에 관해 서술함.

2. 부록

(a) 의회정치 발전에 관한 청문의 개요와 분석

- 제2분과위원회의 권고 및 위원단의 결정, 한국정부 관료의 견해, 국회의원 및 정치지도자의 견해, 전문가와 종교 및 사회단체 대표자의 견해, 결론으로 구분하여 기술함.
- 직업과 지위를 기준으로 해서 다음의 세 부류로 청문 대상 인물들을 선정함.
  (a) 장관급 고위 관료 3명
  　　김효석(내무부장관)
  　　임병직(외무부장관)

유진오(법무부 국장)

(b) 국회의원 및 정치가

신익희(국회의장, 민주국민당 최고위원)

윤치영(국회의원, 전 내무부장관)

조소앙(사회당 당수)

김성수(전 한민당 당수, 민주국민당 최고위원)

(c) 전문가, 사회·종교지도자

안재홍(남조선과도입법의원 민정장관, 신생활협회 회장)

김법린(불교학자, 검사위원회 위원)

백 L. G.(조선기독교대학 학장)

Rao Paul M(천주교 신부)

- 청문에 참석하기 전 사전에 주어진 주제

(a) 한국에서 의회정치의 발전

대한민국 정부수립이래 현재까지 의회정치 발전을 위해 취해진 조치

의회정치 발전을 향한 정부 및 국민이 직면하는 문제들

장래의 의회정치 발전을 위한 구체적 견해 및 제안

(b) 통일문제와 관련된 의회정치의 발전

통일을 위한 정치적 기초

북한의 현 상황과 정치구조에 대한 견해

북한 내부에 의회정치가 파급될 가능성

통일 한국에서 모든 한국인의 대표와 참여 문제

(b) 최근 발생한 소요의 영향을 받은 지역들에 관한 시찰 보고서

- 제2분과위원회의 권고 및 위원단의 결정, 전라남도 시찰, 제주도 시찰(제주도는 두 그룹으로 나누어 시찰함), 제주도 폭동의 원인과 결과, 시찰의 결과

로 구분하여 기술함.

B. 한국 신문법(A/AC.26/W.14)
(1907년[광무 11년] 공포, 1909년[광무 12년] 개정)

- 총 41개 조문으로 구성되어 있음. 1949년 6월 14일 공보처장에 취임한 이 철원(Lee Chul Wun) 신임처장이 국회에서 취임사를 전하며 앞으로 본법(광무 신문법)을 적용하지 않을 것임을 천명함.

C. 국가보안법(A/AC.26/W.15)
(1948년 12월 1일, 법률 제10호)

- 총 6개 조문으로 구성,

- 제1조에서 국헌을 위배하여 정부를 참칭하거나 그에 부수하여 국가를 변란할 목적으로 결사 또는 집단을 구성하는 자를 처벌함을 규정함(수괴와 간부는 3년 이상의 징역 또는 금고, 주도적 역할을 수행한 자는 1년 이상 10년 이하의 징역 또는 금고, 그 정을 알고 결사 또는 집단에 가입한 자는 3년 이하의 징역에 처함).

- 제2조에서는 살인, 방화, 또는 운수, 통신기관 건조물 기타 중요한 시설의 파괴 등의 범죄행위를 목적으로 하는 결사나 집단을 조직한 자나 그 간부의 직에 있는 자는 10년 이하의 징역에 처하고 그에 가입한 자는 3년 이하의 징역에 처함을 규정함.

- 제3조에서는 전 2조의 목적 또는 그 결사, 집단의 지령으로서 그 목적한 사항의 실행을 협의선동 또는 선전을 한 자는 10년 이하의 징역에 처함을 규정함.

- 제4조에서는 본법의 죄를 범하게 하거나 그 내용을 알고 총포, 탄약, 도검 또는 금품을 공급, 약속 기타의 방법으로 방조한 자는 7년 이하의 징역에 처함을 규정함.

- 제5조에서는 본법의 죄를 범한 자가 자수를 한 때에는 그 형을 경감 또는 면제할 수 있음을 규정함.

- 제6조에서는 타인을 모함할 목적으로 본법에 규정한 범죄에 관하여 허위의 고발, 위증 또는 직권을 남용하여 범죄사실을 날조한 자는 해당 내용의 규정으로 처벌함을 규정함.

- 부칙에서 공포한 날로부터 시행함을 규정하고 있음.

부속문서 Ⅲ

주한미군 철수 및
주한 미 군사고문단(KMAG) 설치 관련 주요 문서

A. 제3분과위원회 보고서

1. 제3분과위원회 제1차 경과보고[4]

(1) 미군 점령부대의 한국철수 감시 및 검증

- 김포비행장에 잔류하고 있는 약간의 공군병력을 제외하고는 미군이 남한에서 완전히 철수하였으며, 주한미군사고문단에 구성되어 있는 장교와 병력은 점령군의 범위에 들어가지 않음. 미군이 지금까지 주둔하고 있던 서빙고 캠프(Camp Sobingo)와 인천지역의 에스캄 캠프(Camp Ascom)를 시찰하였으며 부산과 광주를 방문하게 되면 마무리될 예정임.

(2) 소련 점령군의 한국철수 감시 및 검증

- 제3분과위원회는 위원단에 다음의 절차를 진행하도록 권고함. 즉 유엔사무총장에게 위원단 의장 명의로 소련정부에 대해 위원단의 임무수행에 협조를 요청하는 내용의 각서를 전달해 줄 것을 요청함.

---

4 Document A/AC.26/SC.4/2.

부록

(a) 제이미슨(A. B. Jamieson) 제3분과위원회 위원장이 미국 대사에게 보낸 서한(1949.6.23)

－ 군수물자, 병력, 주한 미 군사고문단에 관한 정보를 요청함.

(b) 제3분과위원회 위원장이 대한민국 외교부에 보낸 서한(1949.6.23)

－ 군수물자, 주한 미 군사고문단에 관한 정보를 요청함.

(c) 위원단 의장이 유엔사무총장에게 외교각서와 함께 보낸 서한(1949.6)

－ 유엔사무총장에게 본 문서에 첨부한 외교각서(위원단의 임무수행에 협조를 요청하는 내용)를 소련정부에 전달해 줄 것을 요청함.

2. 제3분과위원회의 제2차 경과보고[5]

－ 제3분과위원회의 제1차 경과보고서 제출 이후 미군 점령부대의 철수를 검증하며, 기존의 미군 주둔지를 방문하여 철수작업을 확인하고 한국국방군(Korean Security Forces)으로 이전작업이 진행되는 것을 확인하였으며, 일부 미 공군병력의 김포공항 잔류를 제외하고는 미군의 철수작업이 1949년 6월 29일자로 완료되었음을 확인함.

---

5 Document A/AC.26/SC.4/3. 제목번호가 본문(p.35)에는 8번으로 되어 있으나 제목번호가 목차에선 2로 되어 있고 내용상 순서로 2번이 맞으므로 2번으로 표기함.

부록

　(a) 무쵸(John J. Muccio) 미국대사가 제3분과위원회 위원장에게 보낸 서한 (1949.7.8)

　- 1949년 6월 29일자로 주한미군 철수작업이 완료되었음을 알리고 주한 미군사고문단의 인원이 500명 이하이며 승인된 병력을 제외하고는 전부 철수하였음을 확인함.

　(b) 무쵸(John J. Muccio) 미국대사가 제3분과위원회 위원장에게 보낸 서한 (1949.7.25)

　- 1949년 6월 29일자로 주한미군철수작업이 완료되었음을 재확인하고 대한민국 대통령과 주한 미군사령관 사이에 체결된 군사 및 안전문제에 관한 잠정 행정협정이 1948년 8월 24일부로 실효되었음을 재확인함. 김포공항의 안정적인 운영을 위해 최소한의 공군병력인 7명의 장교와 52명의 병력이 잔류하고 있음을 알리며 잔류 병력 또한 김포공항으로부터 1949년 9월 1일까지 철수할 것을 희망하고 있음을 알림.

　(c) 로버츠(W. L. Roberts) 주한 미 군사고문단 단장이 제3분과위원회 위원장에게 보낸 서한(1949.7.16)

　- 한국에 주둔중인 미군의 부대별 해체일자와 철수선박 승선일자 등 전체 철수계획 일정과 단계별 철수인원을 상세하게 재확인하고 1949년 6월 29일부로 철수작업이 완료되었음을 재확인함.

B. 미국대사가 위원단에 보낸 서한 및 위원단 면담에서의 발언

1. 무초(John J. Muccio) 미국대사가 군대철수문제와 관련하여 대한민국 대통령에게 발송한 서한(복사본)을 첨부하여 위원단 단장에게 보낸 서한(1949.4.14)[6]

- 유엔이 한국 국민의 자유와 독립을 회복시키는 데에 상당한 기여를 하였고 미국은 12월 12일의 유엔총회결의를 지지함을 확인하며, 준비가 되는 대로 위원단과 협의하면서 수개월 내로 철수할 것임을 알림. 미군철수와는 별도로 한국의 경제적, 정치적 안정에 필요한 경제적, 기술적, 군사적 원조를 계속 제공할 것임을 약속함.

2. 무초(John J. Muccio) 미국대사가 주한 미 군사고문단 설치와 관련하여 대한민국 대통령에게 발송한 서한(사본)을 동봉하여 위원단 단장에게 보낸 서한(1949.5.2)[7]

- 한국의 요청을 수용하여 주한 미 군사고문단을 설치하기로 결정하였다는 내용.

3. 군대 철수와 관련한 주한 미 대사의 청문회 발언 발췌문[8]

- 미국은 가능한 한 최대한 신속하게 미군을 철수시키려 하고 있으며, 가능하다면 90일 이내로 철수하겠다는 의사를 밝히고 철수과정에서 위원단의 감시

---

6 Document A/AC.26/14.
7 Document A/AC.26/14/Add.1.
8 Document A/AC.26/SR.33.

와 검증이 원활히 이루어질 수 있도록 최대한 협조할 것이며, 한국을 위해 향후 주한 미 군사고문단의 설치를 검토하고 있음을 밝힘.

4. 주한 미 대사가 위원단 앞에서 한 발언을 확인하며 위원단 의장에게 보낸 서한(1949.6.11)[9]

- 1948년 12월 12일의 결의에 따라 주한미군의 철수를 진행하며 그 과정에 위원단이 감시 및 검증할 수 있도록 최대한 협조할 것임을 재확인함.

C. 한국에서의 외국군대 철수 및 군사대표단 설치에 관한 국회의원 및 애국단체의 서한

1. 김약수 국회부의장과 국회의원들이 제출한 외국군대의 철수를 촉구하는 청원(1949.3. 18)[10]

- 남북분단 및 고착화가 외국군대의 장기 점령으로 인한 것임을 주장하며, 한국으로부터 외세의 배제를 희망하는 여론이 높음을 주장하며, 위원단의 목적 달성을 위해서도 외국군대가 완전히 철수하여야 함을 주장하며, 국회부의장 김약수를 포함하여 국회의원 62명이 연서함.

---

9 Document A/AC.26/14/Add.2.
10 Document A/AC.26/NC.2.

2. 김약수 국회부의장이 미국 및 소련 군사 대표단의 한국 내 설치를 반대하는 성명서 및 청원[11]

- 소련이 북한 지역에 군사고문단을 주재시키고 있는 것처럼 미국도 남한에 동일하게 군사고문단을 주재시키려 하는 것을 비난하면서 유엔에 대해 한국 내 미국 및 소련의 군사사절단의 주재를 할 수 없게 해 달라고 요청함.

3. 김동원 국회부의장 및 국회의원들이 한국 내 미국 군사대표단 설치를 지지하는 성명 및 청원[12]

- 김약수 국회부의장 및 국회의원 62명이 연서하여 제출한 청원서가 국회를 대표하여 제출된 것이 아니라고 주장하면서 현재 대한민국의 국방상황이 국가의 안전을 보장하는 데에 충분하지 않다는 사실을 고려하여 한국의 우방인 미국의 군사원조가 절실히 필요하고 미국 군사사절단의 설치를 환영한다는 내용으로, 김동원 국회부의장을 포함한 국회의원 141명이 연서함.

4. 한국의 정당 및 사회단체가 미군 철수 감시에 앞서 북한의 소련군 철수의 확인을 요청하는 위원단 의장 앞으로 보낸 서한(1949.6.22)[13]

- 북한지역에서 소련군이 철수하였는지 확인도 되지 않는 상황에서 미군이 1947년 11월 14일 유엔총회 결의에 따라 철수하고 있다는 사실을 지적하는 한편, 김약수 국회부의장이 국회의원 62명과 함께 제출한 청원은 한국의 실정을 무시한, 한국을 위태롭게 하는 반민족적 행위라고 주장하면서 미군 철수를 감

---

11 Document A/AC.26/NC.7.
12 Document A/AC.26/NC.7.Add.1.
13 Document A/AC.26/NC.8.

시하기 전에 북한지역의 소련군 철수를 검증해달라고 요청함. 28개 정당 및 사회단체가 연서함(국민회, 민족통일총본부, 대한부인회, 한국청년단, 민주국민당, 조선민주당, 대한국민당, 사회당, 여자국민당, 대한노동자연합회, 한국농민연합회, 한국노농당, 한국상공회의소, 전국학생연맹, 한국학도호국단, 한국반공연맹, 기독교협회, YMCA, 천도교본부, 불교신자협회본부, 대종교본부, 유교연맹본부, 전국문화단체총연맹, 우국노인회, 한국외교관지원협회, 전국작가협회, 북한대표단).

부속문서 Ⅳ

위원단의 위임사항 이행에 대한 위원단, 대한민국 정부, 북한의 입장 및 태도에 관한 주요문서

A. 대한민국 정부의 태도

1. **임병직 외무부장관이 위원단 의장에게 보낸 서한으로, 대한민국이 한반도 전체에 대해 완전한 주권을 행사하기 위해 위원단이 실시해야할 특별조치들을 제안함(1949.3.3).[14]**

   - 정치, 군사, 안보, 외교, 경제 분야로 나누어 위원단이 취해야할 조치로서, 북한지역에서 소련이 정당 및 사회단체를 해산하고 남북한의 자유로운 통행을 확보하여 자유로운 분위기에서 유엔한국위원단의 감시 하에 총선거를 실시할 것, 한반도에서 소련군 및 중공군과 유사 군대를 철수시켜 줄 것, 대한민국 정부가 남북한 지역에서 국가의 안녕과 질서를 유지할 전적인 책임을 질 것, 북한 내에 유통 중인 통화에 대해서는 소련이 책임을 질 것, 한국에서 생산되는 모든 전력은 한국 내에서만 사용하게 할 것 등을 제안함.

2. **임병직 외무부장관이 대북 접촉 노력과 관련하여 위원단 의장에게 보낸 서한(1949.5.19)[15]**

   - 위원단이 북한과 협상 또는 회담을 추진하고 있다는 보도에 우려를 표명

---

14 Document A/AC.26/9.
15 Document A/AC.26/23.

하고 그동안 한국정부가 위원단에 협조하여 북한과 접촉을 시도하였으나 완전히 실패하였음을 상기시키면서 대 북한 접촉에 반대한다는 분명한 입장을 전달함.

3. 임병직 외무부장관이 위원단 활동 지속에 관해 위원단 의장에게 보낸 서한(1949.6.30)[16]

– 유엔한국위원단의 활동에 감사를 표하며 앞으로 최소한 1년 이상 동안 위원단이 임무를 계속 수행해 줄 것을 요청함.

4. 임병직 외무부장관이 위원단 의장에게 유엔 군사감시단의 설치를 제안하는 서한(1949.7.11)[17]

– 북한 인민군의 38선 부근 불법남침 사례들을 동봉하여 북한의 불법적인 공격을 저지하고 중지시키기 위해 유엔군사감시단을 설치해 줄 것을 요청함.

5. 위원단 임무 해석에 관한 위원단 대표들과 대한민국 정부연락위원회의 간담(1949.2.16)[18]

– 연락위원회 의장인 조병옥 박사가 통일은 남한의 정부수립에 의해 마련된 기반 위에서 이루어져야 하며 위원단은 북한 지역 총선거 실시를 참관하고 북한정권을 인정하는 행동은 삼가야 한다고 주장함. 남북한의 경제적, 사회적, 기타 교류에 반대하는 입장을 분명히 하고 김구, 김규식 등에 대해서도 강한 반감

---

16 Document A/AC.26/36.
17 Document A/AC.26/40.
18 Document A/AC.26/W.6.

을 드러냄.

B. 대한민국 정부에 대한 위원단의 입장

제1분과위원회의 보고서[19]

– 원문은 위원단 보고서 제2장 6번째 단락에 수록되어 있음.

C. 북한의 태도

위원단의 남한에서의 철수를 요구하고 1949년 9월의 한반도 전체의 총선거 실시를 알리는 조국통일민주주의전선의 "성명서"[20]

– 미제국주의자들 및 그 추종자들이 조국통일 달성을 방해하고 있다고 주장하고 미군의 즉각적인 철수, 남북한 동시선거 실시, 자유로운 분위기에서의 선거 실시, 총선거에 의해 구성되는 최고입법기관을 통해 조선민주주의인민공화국 헌법을 제정하고 동 헌법에 기초하여 신정부를 수립하며 남북한의 현 정부로부터 통치권을 인수받고 기존 정부는 해산시켜 조국통일을 평화롭게 달성하자고 주장함.

---

19 Document A/AC.26/SC.1/4/Rev.1.
20 A/AC.26/W.17.

부속문서 V

위원단 및 사무국 대표단 목록

1. 유엔한국위원단에 파견된 대표단

번호	국적	인원(명)	성명	직명
1	호주 (Australia)	4	쇼(Patrick Shaw)	대표 (Representative)
			제이미슨(A. B. Jamieson)	교체대표 (Representative) (1949.2.23부)
			가레트(Claire Garrett)	비서겸 타자원 (Secretary-typist)
			풀라르(Joan Fullard)	비서겸 타자원 (Secretary-typist)
2	중국 (China)	3	리우위안(Liu Yu-Wan)	대표 (Representative)
			슈튜(Ssutu Ting The)	제1 교체대표 (Alternate)
			Loo W. D.	비서 (Secretary)
3	엘살바도르 (El Salvador)	2	마가냐(Miguel Angel Magaña)	대표 (Representative)
			에르난데스(Sánchez Hernández)	교체대표 (Alternate) (1949.4.29부)
4	프랑스 (France)	3	코스티유(Henry Costilhes)	임시대표 (Temporary Representative)
			바르테레미(Marcel Barthelemy)	비서 (Secretary)
			마르텔(Charles Martel)	비서 (Secretary)
5	인도 (India)	1	씽(Anup Singh)	대표 (Representative)

6	필리핀 (Philippines)	3	루나(Rufino Luna)	대표 (Representative)
			루나(Norberto Luna)	비서(Secretary)
			페레르(Antonio Ferrer)	비서(Secretary)
7	시리아 (Syria)	1	무기르(Yasin Mughir)	대표 (Representative)
	계	17		

2. 위원단 사무국 조직

번호	직명	성명	인원(명)
1	사무국장 (Principal Secretary)	베르트하이머 (Egon Ranshofen-Wertheimer)	1
2	사무부국장 (Deputy Principal Secretary)	슈와츠(Sanford Schwarz)	1
3	비서 (Assistant Secretaries)	루카스(Graham Lucas) 샤바스(Arsen Shahbaz) 주홍티(朱鴻題, Hung-Ti Chu)	3
4	행정관 (Administrative Officer)	카츠(Alfred Katz)	1
5	행정관보 (Assistant Administrative Officer)	페이마스터(Jehangir Paymaster)	1
6	통역 (Interpreters)	류(Harry Liao) 프리스맨(Mark Priceman)	2
7	개요기록자 (Précis-Writers)	로브(Marian Robb) 리들(Harold Riddle)	2
8	비서 겸 타자원 (Secretary-Typist)	콤튼(Dorothy Compton) 위베르트(Anne Marie Hubert) 류(Barbara Liu) 쉬한(Ann D. Sheehan) 우드(Marion Wood) 위맨(Cora Wyman)	6
9	군사전문고문 (Military Technical Adviser)	류(C. C. Liu)	1
		계	18

3. 현지 채용 직원

번호	직명	성명	인원(명)
1	통역 (Interpreter)	이묘묵(Myo-Mook Lee)	1
2	번역-통역 (Translator-Interpreters)	김용원(Yong Won Kim) 이규용(Kyu Yong Lee) 로버트 박(Robert T. Park)	3
3	서한 담당비서 (Correspondent- Secretaries)	리디아 고(Lydia C. Koh) 이은자(Unja Lee)	2
4	서기 겸 전령 (Clerk-Messenger)	이종대(Chong Dea Lee)	1
5	사무기기 기사 (Office Machine Operator)	전윤상(Chun, Yun Sang)	1
6	운전기사 (Dispatchers)	전기붕(Chun Ki Poong) 김ㅁㅁ(J. H. Kim)	2
7	접수담당자 (Receptionist)	이소영(So Young Lee) 조순예(Soon Yeh Cho) 리히(Flory Leigh)	3
		계	13

부속문서 Ⅵ

문서목록

A. 한국의 독립문제에 관한 유엔 문서

1. 유엔한국임시위원단의 총회 보고서

2. 유엔총회 소총회 보고서

3. 유엔총회 어젠다로 한국독립문제를 항목에 포함시키는 문제

4. '제1위원회'의 토의

      (a) 문서(Documents)

      (b) 개요기록(Summary Records)

5. '제5위원회'의 토의

6. '제1위원회' 및 '제5위원회' 보고서에 관한 총회의 토의

B. 유엔한국위원단 문서 전체목록

1. 위원단 어젠다(Agenda)

2. 위원단 회의 개요기록(Summary Records of the Meeting of the Commission)

3. 일반문서(General Documents)

4. 조사보고서(Working Papers)

5. 개인 및 단체로부터 수령한 서신

6. 정보보고서

7. 분과위원회 문서(Sub-Committee Documents)

제1분과위원회/제2분과위원회/제3분과위원회

8. 신문발표

UNITED NATIONS

REPORT OF THE UNITED NATIONS COMMISSION ON KOREA

Volume II — Annexes

GENERAL ASSEMBLY

OFFICIAL RECORDS : FOURTH SESSION

SUPPLEMENT No. 9 (A/936/Add. 1)

LAKE SUCCESS
New York
1949

(67 p.)

REPORT OF THE
UNITED NATIONS
COMMISSION ON KOREA

VOLUME II – Annexes

GENERAL ASSEMBLY

OFFICIAL RECORDS : FOURTH SESSION

SUPPLEMENT No. 9 (A/936/Add. 1)

LAKE SUCCESS
New York
1949

NOTE

All United Nations documents are designated by symbols, i.e., capital letters combined with figures. Mention of such a symbol indicates a reference to a United Nations document.

A/936/Add.1
August 1949

TABLE OF CONTENTS

ANNEXES

제3부 유엔한국위원단 보고서(1949)

iv

TEXTS OF MAIN DOCUMENTS CONCERNING THE COMMISSION'S EFFORTS IN LENDING ITS GOOD OFFICES TO BRING ABOUT UNIFICATION AND IN SEEKING TO REMOVE ECONOMIC AND SOCIAL BARRIERS

A. Final report of Sub-Committee I and selected appendices (A/AC.26/37)

1. MAIN BODY OF THE REPORT OF SUB-COMMITTEE I

Organization

1. Sub-Committee I was established by a resolution[1] of the Commission at its 5th meeting on 9 February.

The Sub-Committee originally consisted of the representatives of Australia, India and Syria. The Syrian representative departed from Seoul on 26 March. The representative of El Salvador was appointed to the Sub-Committee on 5 April. At its 2nd meeting the representative of India was elected Chairman of the Sub-Committee.

Terms of reference

2. At its 5th meeting, the Commission laid down the following terms of reference for Sub-Committee I:

(i) To utilize every available medium such as the Press, radio, public meetings and personal contact in order to impress upon the people throughout Korea the Commission's earnest desire to extend its good offices to remove existing barriers in Korea with a view to promoting unification;

(ii) To study the nature and extent of existing economic, social and other barriers in Korea; obtain full information from official as well as from unofficial sources concerning efforts to remove such barriers; and recommend methods for further improvement;

(iii) To explore means for promoting social and cultural relations among the people throughout Korea;

And, as a means of discharging the tasks enumerated in paragraphs (i), (ii) and (iii),

(iv) To make immediate contact with North Korea with a view to arranging visits there for the Commission, its subsidiary bodies or individual members.

Meetings and visits

3. The Committee held 36 meetings, comprising 14 hearings and 22 regular meetings. It exchanged views with the President of the Republic of Korea and members of his Cabinet on 11 February 1949.[2]

The Committee visited the following points near the 38th parallel to study prevailing conditions along the parallel:

Kaesong and Paekchon on 19 February 1949; Iang Nam Ni, north of Tongduch, On-ni, on 25 May 1949; Chunchon on 15 June 1949; Ongjin on 26/27 June 1949.

A visit was made to the headquarters of the Korean Army and to a military hospital in Seoul on 23 June 1949, where captured prisoners and wounded soldiers were questioned regarding their political views, military training, etc.

The Committee inspected industrial establishments in and around Seoul between 5 and 8 May, to study the economic situation created by the division of the country at the 38th parallel.

Implementation of terms of reference

4. In its endeavour to promote the unification of Korea, the Committee undertook the following tasks:

(a) Attempted to contact North Korea with a view to arranging a visit of the Commission, subsidiary bodies, or individual members thereof through the following means:

A cable was sent to Lake Success requesting the good offices of the Government of the Union of Soviet Socialist Republics for establishing contact with the north (appendix (a) (i)). Subsequently, a letter was dispatched to Kim Il Sung via Hong Kong (appendix (a) (ii)). On 29 June 1949, Mr. Singh (India), as Chairman of Sub-Committee I, made a broadcast to the north explaining the objectives of the Commission and stressing its desire for contact.

(b) Gathered information and opinions from representative Koreans on the existing political, economic and social problems resulting particularly from the division of Korea.

(c) Solicited suggestions regarding possible means of eliminating existing barriers in Korea and effecting the unification of the country.

Suggestions and opinions gathered

5. To ascertain views regarding the problem of unification, the Committee interviewed a number of Koreans, officials[3] as well as non-officials, and also talked with United States representatives in Seoul.

The Committee also took note of the deliberations of the National Assembly and studied local Press reports.

On completing its formal hearings on 3 June 1949, the Committee issued a Press statement[4] inviting the general public to submit views regarding unification.

Policies of the Commission and the Government

6. Contact with North Korea; hearings before the Committee:

The Committee called upon the President of the Republic and his Cabinet on 20 February 1949 to find out what the Government expected of the Commission, and was informed that it

---

[1] A/AC.26/1.
[2] A/AC.26/SC.1/1.

[3] The word "officials" in the present report refers to members of the Cabinet.
[4] A/AC.26/30.

should seek contact with the north only through USSR channels.

Subsequently the Government expressed the view that the names of all persons to appear before the Commission should first be cleared by the Government. The Committee recommended to the Commission the rejection of both these propositions, and the Commission agreed.

Removal of barriers

7. The Committee visited a number of industrial establishments in South Korea.

The Ministry of Foreign Affairs informed the Commission, on 28 May 1949, that legal trade between North and South Korea was officially banned as from 1 April 1949, but that mail was regularly exchanged between the two zones.[5] The Committee learned, however, that some trade was being transacted between north and south via the port of Hong Kong. This method naturally resulted in excessively high costs to the consumer.

The Committee obtained impressive evidence of the economic inter-dependence of North and South Korea, and discovered that many firms operating in the south were suffering acutely from the lack of basic materials formerly obtained from the north. At present, supplies obtained from the Economic Co-operation Administration tend to alleviate this situation to a certain extent.

Situation on the 38th parallel

8. The Committee visited the principle points on the southern side of the 38th parallel,[6] where fighting between the north and south had been reported. These points included Kaesong, Paekchon, Iang Nam Ni, Choon Chun and Ongjin.

Tension was evident at all these places, and on 15 June, during the visit to Choon Chun, the party that included two members of the Committee and two members of the Secretariat, accompanied by Korean military and police officials, was fired upon from the north and had to take cover. The Committee saw damage to a greater or lesser extent at all the points which it visited. At Paekchong it saw a police station which had been burnt down, at Iang Nam Ni it saw a police post which had been destroyed by mortar fire and in the distance nine burnt houses in a village. North of Chunchon it saw a village which had been completely evacuated.

On 26 June, the Committee went to Ongjin, near the western extremity of the parallel, reported to have been, for the previous two weeks, the scene of severe fighting. A visit was made to a nearby village, where more than half the dwellings had been burned to the ground. A number of people were said to have been kidnapped from that village, by raiders from the north.

Later, the Committee witnessed artillery fire by the opposing armies fighting on Gahchi Hill.

A military hospital was inspected, and two young soldiers who had surrendered from the north were interviewed.

Information gathered from a few North Korean soldiers at Ongjin indicated that they were generally ignorant about the situation in both North and South Korea. According to them, the Government of the Republic of Korea and the Commission were "tools of American imperialism". They had also been told by their officers that their brethren in South Korea were yearning for the northern army to come down and liberate them from that yoke.

Summary of views expressed before the Committee

9. The United States of America and the USSR are primarily responsible for the division of the country, and should therefore be called upon to lend their good offices for the unification.

Officials in South Korea have advocated the holding of general elections in North Korea under United Nations supervision to elect one hundred representatives from North Korea to join the present National Assembly in Seoul.

A number of people recommended a conference between representatives of north and south. Some advocated a conference on an official level between the regimes of north and south, while others suggested a conference of non-officials, representatives of various political parties in both zones, in which officials might participate but only as observers. Such a conference might seek to arrive at basic agreements on unification, and might recommend a general election throughout Korea on the expiration of the term of office of the present National Assembly (May 1950). It was also proposed that a conference of political leaders in the south should be held in order to strengthen the basic political structure of the Government of the Republic, prior to convening a north-south conference.

With regard to economic intercourse between the north and the south the Government expressed the view that economic channels between the two zones had been exploited by the north for subversive political purposes. The Government of the Republic had therefore officially banned any economic intercourse between north and south. This view, however, was not shared by non-officials, who felt the desirability and indeed the urgent necessity, of the resumption of trade between the two zones.

The United Nations should take control of all the police and armed forces now in the service of North and South Korean authorities until a unified security force is set up by a central national government.[7]

A Korean advisory group might be established to assist the Commission in the solution of Korea's problems.

Findings

10. The difficulty in establishing direct contact with North Korea constituted a major obstacle for the Committee in its attempt to implement its terms of reference. In view of the existing tension at the 38th parallel, and the persistently hostile attitude of North Korea towards the Commission as reflected in the Pyongyang broadcasts,[8]

---

[5] A/AC.26/SC.1/23.
[6] For reports on these trips see A/AC.26/37, appendix V.

[7] A/AC.26/SC.2/5, annex 2.
[8] For a specimen Pyongyang broadcast regarding the Commission, see A/AC.26/37, annex VI, appendix I.

the Committee discounted the possibility of direct physical penetration into the northern zone without prior clearance from the authorities.

On the basis of its formal hearings and general observations, the Committee has made the following findings:

(1) "There is an overwhelming desire for unification among Koreans.

(2) "The division of the nation has generated a feeling of political frustration, bitterness and restlessness. Despite isolated and indirect references to the possibility of unification by the use of force, the desire for unification by peaceful means remains preponderant. Many Koreans in the south look to the United Nations Commission for the solution of their problems. Tension however has been exacerbated by the violence of propaganda.

(3) "Despite the failure of the north-south conference of April 1948, the idea of a renewed attempt in this direction still persists and remains the subject of strong disagreement between the Government on the one hand and some members of the National Assembly and other political leaders on the other hand.

(4) "The division of Korea has resulted in adverse economic consequences for the south, where the Committee observed the economic conditions. The existing ban on normal trade between the two zones is a serious impediment in the way of the unification of the country.

(5) "The divergence of views between the Government and leaders outside it on the problem of unification has caused a deterioration of mutual confidence between them which may prejudice the prospects of unification. This increase in political tension is evidenced by the recent arrest of eleven members of the National Assembly and the assassination of Mr. Kim Koo—a leading political figure and eminent patriot—on 26 June 1949. Improvement in the political atmosphere would enhance the possibilities of unification.

(6) "The political relationship between the United States and the USSR has a direct and vital bearing upon the fundamental problems of Korea."

Recommendations

11. The Commission should:

(1) "*Authorize* the Committee to continue exploring all possible means of effecting unification;

(2) "*Report* to the General Assembly its view that an important means of contributing to the prospect of unification would be the achievement of a broader basis of popular support for the Government of the Republic;

(3) "*Make known* its willingness and readiness to assist in any discussions between representatives of the north and the south to consider plans and possibilities for the unification of Korea;

(4) "*Offer* its assistance for the purpose of a resumption of legitimate trade between north and south on a trial basis;

(5) "*Recommend* the cessation of all propaganda—emanating from within or outside of Korea—designed to inflame ill-feeling between the two zones of Korea, as being highly detrimental to the prospects of unification;

(6) "*Bring* to the attention of the Governments of the United States and the USSR, through the General Assembly, their original responsibility for the present division of Korea and urgently exhort them continually to use their good offices in furthering the unification of Korea on the basis of independence and the principles approved by the United Nations."

2. Appendices

(a) contact with north korea

(i) *Telegram to the Secretary-General for transmittal to the Government of the Union of Soviet Socialist Republics*

(The text appears in chapter II, paragraph 20, of the report of the Commission: A/936, vol. I.)

(ii) *Letter to General Kim Il Sung*

(The text appears in chapter II, paragraph 22, of the report of the Commission: A/936, vol. I.)

(b) survey of information and opinions on the problem of unification

1. On 2 March 1949, the Commission adopted the report of the Sub-Committee.

Paragraph 1 of this report[9] authorizes the Committee "to gather information from and obtain the opinions of personalities on problems arising out of the division of Korea and on possible methods for removing existing economic, social and other barriers, with a view to promoting unification".

Paragraph 2 listed the names of the first group of persons to be interviewed at Committee hearings and paragraph 3 set forth the following general questions to be asked at the hearings:

(i) What are your views concerning the problem of unification?

(ii) What steps, if any, have been taken to promote unification since the establishment of the Government of the Republic of Korea, and what steps should be taken in this direction?

(iii) To what extent is it possible to remove economic, social and other barriers in Korea?

2. From 3 March to 2 June 1949, the Committee interviewed the following officials and non-officials:

Lee Bum Suk, Prime Minister and Minister of National Defense,

Kim Yak Soo, Vice-Chairman of the National Assembly,

Pak Kun Oong, Former member of the Interim Legislative Assembly,

Yim Louise, Minister of Commerce and Industry,

A. C. Bunce, Chief of the Korean Mission, US Economic Co-operation Administration,

Lee Eung Jun, Major-General, Chief of Staff, Korean Army,

Kim To Yeun, Minister of Finance,

---

[9] A/AC.26/7.

Kimm Kiusic, Chairman, National Independence Federation,

Kim Pyung Hoi, Member of the National Assembly,

Sul Eui Sik, Publisher of the *Sai Han Minbo*,

Kim Pyung Yon,[10] Governor of the Pyongan Namdo Province (North Korea),

Kim Koo, Chairman, Korean Independence Party,

Kwon Yun Ho, Protestant leader,

Lee Chung Chun, General, Member of the National Assembly.

At hearings of Sub-Committee II members of Sub-Committee I consulted the following persons regarding their views on the problem of unification:

Sin Ik Hi, Chairman of the National Assembly,

Paik L. G., President, Chosen Christian College,

Yun Chi Yung, Former Minister of the Interior,

Bishop Ro, Vicar Apostolic of Seoul,

Kim Bup Rin, President of Dong Kook University,

Cho So Ang, Chairman of the Socialist Party,

Limb B. C., Minister of Foreign Affairs,

Kim Hyo Suk, Minister of the Interior.

3. On 11 February 1949, the Committee exchanged views with President Syngman Rhee and his Cabinet.[11]

4. For background material the Committee used the National Assembly debates and pertinent articles in the local Press.

5. Since the Committee has not been able to visit North Korea, its activities have been necessarily confined to the south; and even in the south it was able to interview only a small number of people representing mainly the intelligentsia. However, the Committee has regularly examined the intercepts of radio broadcasts from Pyongyang (North Korea), which definitely reveal a non-co-operative and hostile attitude toward the Commission.

Views concerning the problem of unification

(a) *Korean officials, Executive Branch*

1. The USSR was primarily responsible for the establishment of the 38th parallel, and in sponsoring a puppet regime in violation of the General Assembly's resolutions of 14 November 1947 and 12 December 1948, it jeopardized all chances for the unification of Korea.

2. The real source of authority in the north was exercised by the USSR and not by the Korean regime. Therefore, any attempt to unify Korea by peaceful means must be made by negotiating with the Soviet Union and not with the regime in the north.[12]

3. However, the United States was partly responsible for the unfortunate situation in Korea

at the present time because it had failed in the past to check communist infiltration and had even encouraged compromises with the communists.[13]

All previous attempts for unification made by the United States had ended in failure.[14] The Government of the Republic refused to negotiate with the northern regime as it considered it illegal.

4. The Korean Government sought unification by peaceful means. Since, however, it was faced with a menace of communism from the north, it might have to meet force with force; and for defensive purposes it needed an adequate supply of weapons.[15]

5. The Korean Government favored the retention of American armed forces in Korea until its own security forces were adequate to resist aggression from the north.[16]

(b) *Members of the National Assembly*

1. Two members of the National Assembly maintained that the presence of foreign troops in Korea retarded unification, and subsequently this view was also supported by 63 members of the National Assembly in a petition addressed to the Commission on 18 March 1949.[17]

Mr. Kim Yak Soo believed that the 38th parallel constituted a demarcation line in the rival struggles of the United States and the USSR. Both he and General Lee Chung Chun held the view that an understanding between the United States and the USSR was an indispensable prerequisite in attempting to solve the problems of Korea. Meanwhile, Koreans themselves should exert their own efforts toward unification.[18]

2. Mr. Kim Pyung Hoi believed in unification without the participation of foreign Powers although their co-operation with the United Nations in achieving unification was desirable. He advocated the complete withdrawal of foreign troops from Korea.[19]

(c) *Non-official persons*

1. The majority of persons consulted expressed the view that the problem of unification stemmed from the differences which existed between the United States and the USSR and that unification depended largely upon an understanding between these nations.

2. The Powers that originally created the division of Korea must assume moral responsibility for the removal of the barriers. They had further accentuated the differences by instituting their two respective economic, political and military systems.

3. Mr. Kimm Kiusic held the view that the existence of an illegal *de facto* regime in the north with which neither the United Nations nor the Government of the Republic was prepared to negotiate formally further added to the difficul-

[10] Appointed by the Government of the Republic of Korea.
[11] A/AC.26/SC.1/1.
[12] A/AC.26/SC.1/1, A/AC.26/23.
[13] A/AC.26/SR.13, page 3; Press release 2A, 7 May 1949, Office of Public Information, Seoul; A/AC.26/23.
[14] A/AC.26/23.
[15] Statement of President Rhee, Press release 2A, 7 May 1949, Office of Public Information, Seoul.
[16] *Ibid.*
[17] A/AC.26/NC.2.
[18] A/AC.26/SC.1/8 and A/AC.26/SC.1/26.
[19] A/AC.26/SC.1/18.

ties.[20] He advocated a conference between non-official leaders of north and south, under the supervision of the Commission, in which officials from both sides could participate as mere observers. He did not appear too sanguine about the prospect of such a conference but thought the attempt well worthwhile.

4. Mr. Kim Koo and Mr. Kwon Yun Ho shared in substance Mr. Kimm Kiusic's views and added that the assistance of the Commission would be necessary to ensure the security of such a conference.

5. General Lee Chung Chun did not advocate a north-south conference. He looked to the Commission for a solution to the problem of unification.

Steps taken by the Government to promote unification

(a) *Korean officials, Executive Branch*

1. The Government has kept 100 seats vacant in the National Assembly to be filled by representatives from the north. It has appointed governors for the five provinces in the north.[21] These officials however had not been able to assume their posts in North Korea.

2. Until December 1948, the Government sought to engage in direct legal barter trade with the north. The North Korean authorities had confiscated a ship (Yang Do Whan) which had proceeded to the north under a barter trade agreement. The north exploited commercial channels for subversive propaganda. Trade between the south and the north was officially banned by the Korean Government and it did not intend to lift its ban.[22][23]

3. The Government had appealed to Koreans in the north for their support for unification.[24]

4. Colonel B. C. Limb, Minister of Foreign Affairs, stated that the removal of the 38th parallel as a barrier was possible only through the co-operation of north and south. Since such co-operation was impossible in view of the non-co-operative attitude of the north, unification must precede co-operation between the two zones.[25]

5. Mr. Lee Bum Suk, Prime Minister, stated that the Government did not wish to have any dealings with the communists since in the first place, no compromise with communism was possible. Furthermore, it would be detrimental to the growth of democracy in the south. The Government preferred to contact the people in the north rather than their leaders.[26]

(b) *Members of the National Assembly*

1. Mr. Kim Pyung Hoi maintained that the Government had done nothing to promote Korean unification. On the contrary the Government had retarded unification by concluding an economic pact with the United States and by requesting the retention of American troops in Korea.[27]

(c) *Non-official persons*

1. In the opinion of the majority of non-officials no significant steps had been taken by the Government to promote unification. Mr. Pak Kum Oong felt that since the establishment of the Republic of Korea and of a regime in the north, differences had become intensified. He attributed these differences largely to personal rivalries and to a desire for political power among the leaders.[28]

2. Mr. Sul Eui Sik also thought that the Government had made no real efforts to attain unification. The Government had constantly pursued an ultra-pro-American policy, and it was not disposed to deal with the Soviet Union or the North Korean regime which it persistently ignored.[29]

3. Mr. Kimm Kiusic stated, that as a step toward unification, the three major political parties[30] had recently merged, and efforts were being made to bring other parties into this group. In his view it was of primary importance to consolidate the "non-left" political parties *vis-à-vis* the left.[31]

Proposed plans for unification

(a) *Korean officials, Executive Branch*

1. On 3 March 1949, Colonel B. C. Limb. Minister of Foreign Affairs,[32] suggested that the Commission should take the following steps:

(i) Persuade the Soviet Union to dissolve the North Korean "puppet" government, as well as all political parties and social organizations thereof, release political prisoners held in the north and guarantee safe conduct across the parallel, thus enabling the Korean Government to conduct general elections in North Korea under the supervision of the United Nations Commission.

(ii) Supervise the immediate and complete withdrawal of the Soviet Army, the Chinese Communist Army, guerrilla troops and other similar military units or groups from North Korea.

(iii) Lend its good offices for the immediate dissolution of the "People's Army" and security forces of the north.

2. The Government also stated than any international agreement or treaties concluded by the north and any subsequent administrative policies adopted without the approval of the Korean Government should be declared null and void.

All assets removed from Korea by the Soviet Army should be returned or reimbursement made therefor.

3. In general, the Government was opposed to any proposal for unification except its own. It even indicated its disapproval of the plans made by some of the members of the National Assembly.

---

[20] A/AC.26/SC.1/17.
[21] A/AC./26/SC.1/16, page 4.
[22] A/AC./26/SC.1/1, page 4; A/AC.26/SC.1/10; A/AC./26/W.6.
[23] There is a weekly exchange of mail across the 38th parallel (A/AC.26/SC.2/12, page 12).
[24] A/AC.26/SC.2/12, page 12.
[25] A/AC.26/SC.2/12, page 13.
[26] A/AC.26/SC.1/6.

[27] A/AC.26/SC.1/18.
[28] A/AC.26/SC.1/9.
[29] A/AC.26/SC.1/20.
[30] The National Independence Federation, the Korean Independence Party had recently merged to form the "society for the acceleration of unified independence," A/AC.26/SC.1/17 page 6.
[31] AC/AC.26/SC.1/17, page 6.
[32] A/AC.26/9.

제3부 유엔한국위원단 보고서(1949)

The Government has indicated its disapproval of certain proposals recommended by certain members of the National Assembly and other political leaders.

4. President Rhee was opposed to any attempts by the Commission to make direct contact with the authorities in the north since in his view it would imply recognition of the regime. Instead the Commission should request the USSR for facilities to visit the north. The Commission should verify the alleged withdrawal of the USSR troops and subsequently demand the dissolution of the northern regime on grounds of its illegality.[33]

5. Mr. Lee Bum Sak, the Prime Minister, advocated strengthening the military forces of the Republic for parity with the north.[34] This view, however, was not shared by other officials, who felt that the south was in a position to defend itself against any possible attack from the north.

All officials, however, favoured the retention of United States troops in South Korea, until its security forces were strengthened and adequate.

6. The Government was specially opposed to the following proposals made to the Commission:

(a) Conference of leaders of the north and south

The Government felt that no useful purpose would be served even if a conference could be convened. In the light of past experience such a conference would not only fail to achieve constructive results but would actually strengthen the Communists and weaken democratic government in Korea.[35]

(b) Withdrawal of United States troops

Dr. Chough Pyong Ok of the Korean Government Liaison Committee expressed dissatisfaction with a recent proposal made by a group of National Assembly representatives demanding the immediate withdrawal of foreign troops,[36] on the grounds that their action was calculated to cause unrest in the south.[37]

"On 7 February 1949, President Rhee appeared before the National Assembly, and again expressed his strong disapproval of the proposed resolution demanding the withdrawal of foreign troops. In the course of his speech, he said: 'if you (the National Assembly) insist on adhering to the so-called simultaneous and immediate withdrawal of foreign troops it will surely result in nothing but destruction.' He added that if United States troops left Korea, the way would be paved for the penetration of Soviet troops into the south."[38]

(b) Members of the National Assembly

1. According to Mr. Shin Ik Hi, Chairman of the National Assembly, the overwhelming majority of the Assembly representatives believed that the only means of unification was to fill the vacant seats in the National Assembly for representatives of the north.[39]

2. Mr. Kim Pyung Hoi suggested that the Commission should prepare a plan to make Korea the "Switzerland of Asia," and submit this plan to the United States and to the USSR. Troop withdrawal, however, was a primary prerequisite to such a plan.

The Commission might also request the United States and the USSR to sponsor a north-south conference, or alternatively the United Nations Commission might convene a conference of representatives of the Republic of Korea and the North Korean People's Government.

3. If it proved impossible to negotiate with the north, then the people of South Korea should prepare the political basis for unification. Steps should be taken for protection of human rights and partisan favouritism should be abolished. Improved conditions in the south would attract the people of the north. Korea could not be unified without negotiations with the "communists" of North Korea.[40]

(c) Non-official persons

1. Mr. Kimm Kiusic advocated a conference between north and south and suggested the establishment of a small advisory or consultative group to assist the Commission in its work.[41]

2. Mr. Sul Eui Sik recommended that the Korean Government and the northern regime should appoint an election committee to be composed of representatives including non-officials of both zones. This committee would organize a nation-wide election to establish a national government.

Failing this he favoured the conference plan, as well as the proposal to establish an advisory group[42] or consultative group proposed by Mr. Kimm Kiusic.

3. Mr. Cho So Ang suggested that the Commission should request the United States and the USSR to arrange a north-south conference. Both he and Mr. Sul believed that a prerequisite to unification was an understanding between the United States and the USSR in respect to the Korean problem.[43]

4. Mr. Pak Kun Oong favored a plan for unification giving due consideration to the legal aspect of the Korean problem and safeguarding the prestige of the leaders of the south and north as well as of the United States and USSR Governments.[44]

5. Mr. Kim Koo supported the idea of a north-south conference. He also made the following alternative proposals:

The Commission should:

(i) Supervise elections in the north to fill the 100 seats set aside by the National Assembly;

[33] A/AC.26/SC.1/1.
[34] A/AC.26/SC.1/6.
[35] A/AC.26/SC.1/1, A/AC.26/SC.1/16, page 5, A/AC.26/23.
[36] Resolution introduced at the 22nd session of the National Assembly, 4 February 1949. In this connexion also see A/AC.26/NC.2, petition to the Commission from sixty-two National Assembly members concerning the withdrawal of foreign troops from Korea.
[37] A/AC.26/W.6.
[38] Report of the 24th session, National Assembly, 7 February 1949.
[39] A/AC.26/SC.2/2, page 6.
[40] A/AC.26/SC.1/18.
[41] A/AC.26/SC.1/17.
[42] A/AC.26/SC.1/20.
[43] A/AC.26/SC.2/11.
[44] A/AC.26/SC.1/9.

(ii) Or supervise elections in the whole country without disturbing the Government of the Republic;

(iii) Or revert to the resolution of the General Assembly of 14 November 1947 and hold general elections in the whole country.

However, he believed that a preliminary north-south conference should precede any general elections.

Removal of economic, social, and other barriers

In the present circumstances, the Government disfavoured and prohibited economic intercourse between the north and the south.

(a) *Members of the National Assembly*

1. Mr. Kim Yak Soo stated that illegal commerce between the south and the north was carried on via Hong Kong and he advocated legalization and extension of trade between the two zones. In his judgment cultural intercourse was more difficult because of its political implications.[45]

(c) *Non-official persons*

1. The general view was that while the removal of economic, social and other barriers would constitute a major step toward unification, the present political situation almost precluded any possibility of the elimination of such barriers in the foreseeable future.

2. Dr. A. C. Bunce, Chief of the United States Economic Co-operation Administration in Korea, pointed out that previous attempts to promote economic intercourse with the north had failed, and he saw no likelihood of an improvement in the present situation.[46]

3. Mr. Kimm Kiusic foresaw no possibility of economic, social or cultural intercourse without the removal of the barrier of the 38th parallel.[47]

4. Mr. Cho So Ang suggested that barriers could be removed by legalizing trade and encouraging contacts between families split between the south and the north.[48]

5. Mr. Kim Koo did not know why the Government had prohibited trade between the two zones. He thought that north-south trade should be encouraged rather than halted.

6. Mr. Kwon Yun Ho had little hope of improving cultural and economic relations between the two zones.

A summary of this survey is contained in document A/AC.26/SC.1/28.

B. Excerpts from the hearing of Mr. Arthur C. Bunce, Chief of the Korean Mission, United States Economic Co-operation Administration, and report on important economic developments submitted by him (A/AC.26/SC.1/13)

1. EXCERPTS FROM THE HEARING OF MR. ARTHUR C. BUNCE

The CHAIRMAN introduced Dr. A. C. Bunce, Chief of the Korean Mission of the United States Economic Co-operation Administration, who was accompanied by Mr. R. A. Kinney, his Special Assistant.

In connexion with section 3 (2) of his report (see appendix), Dr. Bunce pointed out that the cost of cereal imports into South Korea had declined from $50 million in the fiscal year 1947 to $40 million in the fiscal year 1948, and to $15 million in the fiscal year 1949. It was hoped that next year South Korea would be on an export basis in rice.

The CHAIRMAN asked for Dr. Bunce's opinion on whether the standard of living might be higher in North Korea than in South Korea, since most of the basic industries were located in the north.

Dr. BUNCE replied that it was difficult to answer yes or no. Unless food was being exported, the amount *per capita* should be higher in the north. That area also possessed most of the electric power, coal, iron and steel and fertilizer industries. But South Korea had more consumers' goods, such as textiles, rubber shoes, light bulbs and small machine tools.

The CHAIRMAN wondered whether the main ca se for refugees coming to the south was a political one.

Dr. BUNCE said he had met a large number of refugees, of whom he had known many previously during his stay of six years in North Korea. The refugees could be divided into several categories. First, there were those who felt politically oppressed, including ministers and other Christians who believed they were losing religious freedom, and a large group who were antagonistic to Russian occupation and were unwilling to co-operate with the USSR Command.

A second group consisted of middle-class merchants who had found themselves unable to make a living because of trade restrictions, and who came south because of pressure of economic circumstances.

A third group was composed of farmers dissatisfied with land reforms in the north.

Dr. Bunce explained that, prior to the end of the war, farm tenancy was much more extensive in South Korea than in North Korea, where it probably did not exceed 50 per cent. All land in the north, including that formerly farmed by tenants and that operated by the owners, had reverted to the Central Committee of the so-called government, to be re-distributed to farmers. The tenants had not been charged for the land but had found that taxes, which were supposed to be 23 to 27 per cent of output, actually ranged from 33 to 50 per cent of production. The tax rates were based on a year of good crops rather than on actual current production. Despite widespread floods in 1946, which destroyed a portion of the crops, taxes in that year were assessed on the basis of the previous year's crops. Consequently many farmers, including farmers who had formerly owned their farms, had become destitute through the winter. Having been landowners before, they felt a certain antagonism toward the n regime and many had come to South Korea.

The CHAIRMAN inquired whether Dr. Bunce considered that the USSR economic administration in North Korea had been designed to benefit the zone itself or the USSR.

[45] A/AC.26/SC.1/8, page 3.
[46] A/AC.26/SC.1/13.
[47] A/AC.26/SC.1/17, page 11.
[48] A/AC.26/SC.2/11, page 3.

Dr. BUNCE said the Russians during their occupation had brought some good technicians into North Korea, to help re-establish and develop the industries of that area. Mr. Pauley, United States representative who had investigated removals of plants and equipment from North Korea, had found that in general the reports of such removals were exaggerated. Machine tools and some power equipment had been removed, but there had been nothing like the stripping of industrial machinery which had occurred in Manchuria.

There had been reports from North Korea that the People's Republic had founded USSR-Korean joint stock companies and the Russians and Koreans were operating them as joint enterprises on a fifty-fifty ownership basis.

The CHAIRMAN asked how soon South Korea would be able to maintain its present economic level without United States aid, as long as the country remained divided.

Dr. BUNCE replied that if South Korea were deprived of American aid in the next fiscal year, it would suffer an extreme set-back in production and living standards within a year, and food riots would probably result. Without imported fertilizer, South Korea could not possibly grow enough cereals to meet its food needs.

The CHAIRMAN asked how long the United States proposed to continue its assistance to Korea.

Dr. BUNCE replied that the ECA plans were based on a long-range programme, but that commitments could not be made for more than a year at a time because they were dependent upon Congressional appropriations. Objective estimates indicated that if the rehabilitation programme could be carried on for an additional three years, South Korea could not only maintain but improve its standard of living within five years, though its foreign exchange balance might continue to show an annual shortage of 30 to 40 million dollars. For the thirty-five years prior to Japan's surrender in 1945, Korea had usually imported more than it exported, and the Japanese had made up the balance of payments by taking over ownership of an even larger portion of Korea's basic resources.

If Korea were united, imports and exports could be balanced at a figure of about $80 million each year, and Korea would not have to go into debt or be economically dependent upon any other country.

The CHAIRMAN asked what were the prospects of commercial intercourse between North and South Korea as long as the country remained divided.

Dr. BUNCE said such exchange was very difficult. In its one attempt to promote such trade, the Military Government had deposited money in an escrow account in Japan and had released goods to a private trader. This trader had obtained a ship and taken the goods north to Hungnam. There the goods had been taken off and the ship loaded with fertilizer, but before the ship left port, the crew was seized and jailed and the ship itself confiscated. Ten of the crew had made their way to South Korea within three or four weeks, and others later.

Since the ship had been confiscated two days after the recognition of the Republic of Korea by the United Nations General Assembly, it might have been done in retaliation, but this was not certain.

The CHAIRMAN asked if Dr. Bunce felt that the present Government in South Korea was carrying out economic reforms energetically enough to satisfy the people.

Dr. BUNCE said he had been frankly amazed at the tremendous progress made since the Government came to power. When he had left Korea last year for a short period, he had not believed that it was possible to attain such increases in production of coal and electric power. Since his return the attitude displayed by the Korean people in attempting to solve their problems had increased his confidence.

The CHAIRMAN inquired what per cent of the Korean budget was spent on military and police forces.

Dr. BUNCE referred to the proposed budget for the fiscal year 1949-50, which had just been released. Out of a total budget of over 196 thousand million *won*, the Ministry of National Defence was to be allotted some 12 thousand million *won* (for ordinary expenses, plus 1,666,533,800 *won* for extraordinary expenses), and the Ministry of Home Affairs, which included the police department, was to receive some 5 thousand million *won* for ordinary expenses, plus 10,026,- 004,588 *won* for extraordinary expenses.

In reply to another question by the Chairman, he said that the largest single item in the budget was an appropriation of over 23 billion *won* for transportation. This included the cost of building a new spur railroad to increase production and distribution of coal.

Dr. LIU (China) asked what were the causes of the poor rice collections in the current year, which were reported to be only 50 per cent of the amount to be collected.

Dr. BUNCE said that the Military Government had carried on a series of unpopular but successful compulsory collection programmes.

The Korean Government, on the other hand, had adopted a programme of voluntary grain contributions, on the ground that a democracy should not force people to sell their produce. No quotas were allocated, and farmers were told that they might sell all they could above their own needs. The Government had appealed for contributions, but these had been low on account of its failure to establish quotas. The Prime Minister had commented on the results by saying to the Americans: "You taught us too much democracy".

The CHAIRMAN asked whether the poor rice and grain collections were responsible for the impending stoppage of rations in cities like Seoul.

Dr. BUNCE replied that they were directly responsible.

The CHAIRMAN asked if serious consequences might be expected.

Dr. BUNCE said this would depend on whether rice had been smuggled out or was still on hand. Indications were that prices might not rise too much unless profiteers got hold of the rice and held it off the market; if that were allowed to happen the price would rise and they would reap billions in profits. The Government had promised to take strong action against grain speculators. On the other hand, if the rice were held by a large number of small dealers, prices would be kept within bounds and people would not suffer too much.

The CHAIRMAN inquired as to the extent of tenancy and the average size of farm holdings.

Mr. KINNEY said that tenant farmers constituted only about 40 per cent of the farm population of South Korea at present. The average holding per farm household was one *chungbo,* or about two and a half acres, per farm.

Dr. BUNCE observed that accurate figures on farm tenancy were hard to obtain, but those available indicated that tenancy had been reduced from 73 per cent of the cultivated area in 1945 to between 40 and 45 per cent at present.

The CHAIRMAN asked if it were being progressively reduced.

Mr. KINNEY replied that at present most large landlords were anxious to sell because of the imminence of enactment of a land reform programme, whereas tenants wished to wait until such a programme was in force. The National Assembly at present had under consideration a measure whereby the cost of land purchased by farmers would be approximately the value of three annual crops; but there was strong sentiment in the Assembly to aid the farmers by reducing this price. It was expected that the bill would be passed in the current month, and undoubtedly its terms would be generally favourable to farm tenants.

The CHAIRMAN inquired as to the extent of foreign capital investments in Korea.

Dr. BUNCE replied that there were practically none at present, except for a few oil storage and other facilities. The Chinese had the largest remaining holdings. There had been some capital investment by British and Americans, but the Japanese had liquidated practically all foreign holdings but their own. There was no ownership by foreign capital of any of the country's basic resources in South Korea.

The Military Government had found that 80 percent of the total industrial corporate wealth of the country was in Japanese hands. It had declared that this wealth must be held in trust for the Korean people, and had prohibited sale of large industrial properties to private investors, even to Koreans.

The Korean Government itself would have to decide whether to socialize or to sell such large industries.

The CHAIRMAN asked what was the financial status of the Korean Government, and whether it had a large public debt.

Dr. BUNCE replied that its financial status was very sound. It had no public debt, but only an internal debt to itself. Inflation was much abated. He believed that after a year and a half of constructive effort, production might be stabilized, the national economy balanced, and a permanent foreign exchange rate established.

The Japanese had increased the circulation of currency to a tremendous degree (from 4 to 8 thousand million *won* in one month following surrender in August-September 1945). Terrified lest law enforcement break down and the Koreans attack them, many Japanese employers had paid their workers a year's salary as insurance for their own safety, and this practice might have been a significant factor in preventing widespread attacks upon the Japanese immediately following Japan's surrender.

The whole system of taxation and law enforcement had been dominated by the Japanese, and had broken down when they were ordered to leave Korea. Industries almost without exception had come to a complete standstill, all mills had closed, and the workers were celebrating their liberation. There were no tax collection agencies, and the only way to finance the administration was to increase the circulation of currency. The Korean Government's Bank of Chosun currency issue was almost 39 thousand million *won* at present.

The United States authorities had settled with the Korean Government in US dollars for occupation costs of the United States Army in *won.* $25 million had been turned over to the Korean Government and at present it had a reserve of 28 million US dollars, while it had no foreign debts payable in "hard currencies".

The Government now had the problem of balancing its budget so as to stop the increase in the circulation of currency. As the programme of ECA imports was accomplished, and the imported commodities sold by the Korean Government, the Korean Government was to set up a counterpart fund from the *won* proceeds of the sale of ECA goods. This counterpart fund could not be used without the authority of the ECA. To the extent that it would collect from the Korean people for these imported supplies, the Korean Government could bring in a tremendous quantity of *won.* Collections for imported goods had been poor in the past but they were expected to improve.

The CHAIRMAN wondered if anything had been done to integrate the economy of Korea with that of Japan.

Dr. BUNCE cited the recent trade agreement with the occupation authorities in Japan. In the past, 80 to 90 per cent of all Korean exports had gone to Japan, but now Japan imported little from Korea, largely because it was trying to build up its own foreign exchange. It was hoped that in the future many of the goods which Korea needed could be obtained from Japan. If ECA dollars went to Japan for machinery, Korea would get more for its money, and Japan would be helped toward recovery; there would be mutual advantages.

The CHAIRMAN asked if the Korean Government had assumed any financial responsibility in connexion with activities of the American Mission in Korea.

Dr. BUNCE said the ECA had worked in close co-operation with the Korean Government, which had drafted its rehabilitation programme with the aid of American consultants. The new Government had established an Office of Planning which had considered the preliminary ECA budget, and at least thirty Korean officials had consulted ECA officials in revising it. The programme of aid was essentially a joint Korean-American project.

The CHAIRMAN said he understood that the Government was anxious to buy more military equipment, especially from the United States. Did this seem warranted in view of Korea's economic situation?

Dr. BUNCE said this was a difficult problem. Without security in South Korea the programme of economic aid could not possibly succeed. At the same time excessive military expenditures would defeat the objectives of the economic aid programme. It must be recognized that certain essential military needs must be met, but also that military expenditures would do nothing to rebuild industry and increase production. The two needs must be considered together.

In reply to a question by Mr. MAGAÑA (El Salvador), Dr. BUNCE said the Korean Government was empowered to open trade with any country; it already had considerable trade with Japan, the Netherlands East Indies, Hong Kong, the United States, China and the Philippines, and the objective was to expand its total volume of trade. The policy of ECA was to purchase goods from any country which offered the lowest price.

The CHAIRMAN asked if Dr. Bunce would suggest any steps the Commission might take to break down economic barriers between North and South Korea.

Dr. BUNCE said he had prepared his detailed report in order to give the Commission the background of the repeated unsuccessful attempts made by United States authorities to lessen economic barriers. Whether the Commission might succeed would depend on the extent to which the People's Committee in Pyongyang, representing the people of North Korea, would feel free to work with the Commission toward attainment of a truly independent Korea.

The PRINCIPAL SECRETARY had four questions. First, how had the enormous number of northern 'refugees been absorbed into the economy of South Korea?

Dr. BUNCE said their absorption had created a serious problem. The original tendency for most of them to settle in Seoul had brought a sharp population increase and an acute housing shortage in the past few years. To offset this trend, a policy had been developed of lodging them temporarily in camps, where they were vaccinated and inoculated, then moving them to rural areas where they had relatives.

A consistent attempt had been made to distribute refugees throughout rural areas and small towns, but in spite of it the population of Seoul had increased tremendously.

The PRINCIPAL SECRETARY'S second question was whether there had been any invisible import of capital from North Korea, China or Manchuria.

Dr. BUNCE said most of the refugees had brought practically nothing with them except a few personal belongings. Refugees from Japan had been limited as to amount of baggage. The result had been an influx of population but not of capital.

The PRINCIPAL SECRETARY wondered what hope there was of establishing fertilizer production in the south.

Dr. BUNCE said it was hoped this would be possible after a more thorough survey of the extent of local coal deposits. If sufficient coal were available, thermal electric power plants could be developed to provide power for fertilizer manufacture, though it was not likely that this could be done in the next fiscal year. If the aid programme continued, there was hope of financing the erection of factories for fertilizer production.

The PRINCIPAL SECRETARY wondered whether the exchange rate of 450 *won* to one dollar had been established in order to facilitate imports.

Dr. BUNCE said the rate had been something of a compromise. The original rate of 15 to $US1 for occupation forces had later been raised to 50 to $US1, then to 450. The United States authorities would have liked to raise it still more, but in view of prices and wages prevailing at the time, they had been unwilling to establish a rate which might have appeared to enable Americans to exploit Korean labour through their *won* purchases. Recent calculations showed that the present price of Korean rice on the open market approximated the world price and indicated that in this regard at least the dollar-*won* rate was not too inequitable.

2. REPORT PRESENTED BY MR. ARTHUR C. BUNCE
April 4, 1949

(1) *History of United States economic negotiations with the USSR in Korea*

(a) *Introduction*

It was never the intention of the Government of the United States that the dividing line between the Soviet and American occupation zones along the 38th parallel north latitude should become a barrier severing the normal economic relationships between the two halves of the economically interrelated Korean peninsula. During the early days of the occupation of Korea, the American Command initiated negotiations with the Soviet Command to try to obtain Soviet co-operation in unifying the economy of Korea. Rebuffed in these attempts in Korea, (and at least in one instance told by the Soviet Commander that even the matter of securing chlorine to meet an emergency in water purification would have to be discussed at a higher level), the Commanding General of the United States forces in Korea recommended that this problem be handled at a higher level.

(b) *The Joint Conference*

In December, 1945, the Foreign Ministers of the United States of America, the United Kingdom, and the Union of Soviet Socialist Republics met at Moscow and agreed, with China's adherence, to set up a US-USSR Joint Commission which would assist in creation of a Korean Provisional Government. Paragraph 4 of the Moscow Agreement provided for the convening of a US-USSR conference "for the consideration of urgent problems affecting both southern and northern Korea and for the elaboration of measures establishing permanent co-ordination in administrative-economic matters" between the respective Commands in Korea. In this Joint Conference, held in Seoul from 16 January to 5 February 1946, the United States representatives attempted to reach an agreement to remove the 38th parallel as a barrier and to provide for the consideration of Korea as an economic and administrative whole. The Soviet Command, however, viewed the problem as one of exchange and co-ordination between the two adjoining zones of military responsibility. They insisted that administrative-economic integration of the two zones must await formation of the provisional government provided for in the Moscow Agreement. As a result, the American Command was unable to reach an agreement providing for economic unification. The Joint Conference did provide the basis for several agreements, including the allocation of broadcast bands for radio stations in North and South Korea, provisions for periodic and restricted exchange of mail between the two zones, and continuation of the flow of electricity across the 38th parallel into South Korea during 1946.

(c) *The Joint Commission, 1946*

The US-USSR Joint Commission met in Seoul from 20 March to 6 May 1946. During these sessions of the Commission the American delegation made repeated efforts to reach an agreement with the Soviets regarding economic and administrative unification of the two occupation zones prior to the formation of the Korean Provisional Government. The Americans several times attempted to place on the Commission's agenda a series of proposals to effect economic co-ordination between the zones concurrently with the negotiations regarding establishment of the Korean Provisional Government. The Soviet delegation rejected these proposals, contending that no such discussions could take place before the Koreans had actually taken over operation of the Government and could participate in such planning from the beginning. As a result of this Soviet attitude, the economic sub-committee of the Joint Commission, headed by Dr. A. C. Bunce of the American delegation and Chancellor Balasanov of the USSR, was unable to proceed with any pre-planning or with discussion of any economic topics other than the wording of the questionnaires regarding the economic platform of a future Korean Government. During a subsequent deadlock in the Joint Commission over freedom of expression, the American delegation again sought to discuss (under paragraph 2 of the Moscow Decision) integration of the country's economy and administration. The Soviet delegation refused also to consider these questions, and the Commission adjourned *sine die* on 6 May 1946.

(d) *Subsequent developments. The Joint Commission, 1947*

Between the time the Joint Commission adjourned on 6 May 1946 and reconvened on 21 May 1947, the American Command made several attempts to negotiate an over-all economic agreement with the Soviet Command. Thus, on 2 July 1946, the American Commander proposed that a conference between economic specialists of the two Commands be held in Seoul. Such a conference, to be convened in accordance with one of the decisions reached by the Joint Conference in February 1946, would, in the words of the US

Commanding General, "confine itself to economic matters which are of importance to our immediate situation". The proposals for such a conference were repeated by the American Commander on 26 July and 31 August 1946, without avail. During the second meeting of the Joint Commission, the efforts of the American delegation to implement its objective of political and economic unification of Korea were blocked for essentially the same reason as in 1946—failure to agree upon what Koreans were to be consulted in the formation of a Korean Provisional Government, and Soviet unwillingness to discuss measures for economic unification of Korea before political unification was achieved. During the entire period from the end of the war until the present, there has been limited barter trade between North and South Korea, with officials in both zones attempting to supervise such trade. Several American attempts to arrange for large scale purchase of fertilizer from North Korea, with payment either in US dollars or goods, proved fruitless.

(e) *Electric power problems*

The Korean power system, developed by the Japanese, constituted a well-integrated unit based almost entirely upon the dependable water supply of North Korea, with a few standby thermal plants for use mainly in case of an emergency. Well over 90 per cent of Korea's hydro-electric power capacity is located north of the 38th parallel, and prior to and during the war had become the source of almost all of South Korea's power. After the Japanese surrender of 15 August 1945, electric power continued to flow south across the 38th parallel, although at a rate substantially below that of the pre-Japanese surrender period.

The problem of electric power was discussed at the Joint Conference in January-February 1946. The initial American position was that the hydro-electric power generated in Korea should be made available to the Korean people as a whole, that each zone should bear the costs of generation and transmission in proportion to the amount of power consumed, and that stocks and production of maintenance materials should be divided in proportion to needs. A "Joint Control Plan" was submitted by the American Command to the Soviets on 22 January 1946. This plan envisaged the formation of a special joint Soviet-American commission controlling "by use of technical observers" the entire Korean electric power system, which was to be operated by Korean technicians from the five electric power companies functioning in Korea at the time of the Japanese surrender.

However, the Soviets insisted that there were two separate power systems, one in each zone, and that relations between the two systems should be conducted as if they were entirely independent of each other. The Soviets agreed to supply the minimum amounts of power requested by the Americans for the period through December 1946. Payment was to be in electrical equipment, foodstuffs, and other specified materials. The Soviets at first insisted that two-thirds of all power deliveries to South Korea be paid for in rice, which the Americans declared was not possible at that time, in view of the growing food shortage in South Korea.

The question of method and amount of payment for the electric power furnished South

Korea was a continuing source of misunderstanding from January 1946 until the power from North Korea was finally cut off on 14 May 1948. The payments from South Korea were rendered more difficult by the Soviet insistence upon receiving largely goods and equipment in short supply and difficult to obtain. However, the United States Congress appropriated $5 million for the use of South Korean authorities to help them in purchasing goods to pay the Soviets. All indications are that the cutoff of power from North Korea, four days after the successful South Korea elections of 10 May 1948, was motivated mainly by political considerations. On 14 May 1948, at the time of the power cutoff, over $2 million worth of critical materials, purchased according to Soviet specifications, were in Seoul awaiting pick-up by Soviet representatives, and sufficient quantities of the materials requested by the Soviets in payment for past delivery of power were *en route* to Korea to enable South Korea to pay its power bill to North Korea in full.

(2) *Economic effects of the division of Korea*

The peninsula of Korea is an economically interrelated unit, and the rigid division of the country at the 38th parallel has disrupted the normal functioning of the Korean economy.

Before the Japanese surrender, approximately 64 per cent of the population of Korea lived south of the 38th parallel, and 36 per cent north of this parallel. In the post-war period, over two million Koreans who had been living in Japan, China (especially Manchuria), and other parts of the Far East repatriated to South Korea. In addition, at least two million Koreans living in the Soviet occupation zone fled south across the 38th parallel into the American occupation zone. The result of this influx, coupled with the continuation of the traditional high rate of natural increase, was to increase the population of South Korea from 1945 to the present by over 25 per cent, or from slightly over 16 million in 1945 to over 20.5 million. Since the outflow of population from the Soviet occupation zone in the post-war period is estimated to have approximately equalled the combined total of inflow of population plus natural increase, the population of North Korea has remained relatively stationary during the past four years and totals slightly over 9 million. As a result, the traditional balance of population of Korea has been upset, and at present about 70 per cent of the total population of Korea lives south of the 38th parallel, and only about 30 per cent in North Korea.

This marked concentration of the population in South Korea is especially significant in relation to the production of foodstuffs in the two zones of Korea. In the period 1940 to 1944, when 64 percent of the population lived in South Korea, slightly less than 64 per cent of the country's food, measured in calories, was produced in South Korea. Although South Korea produced more rice *per capita* than did North Korea, the north grew more millet, corn, and other cereals *per capita,* with the result that, prior to the end of the war, the *per capita* food production was almost equal in the two areas. At present, however, North Korea has exclusive access to almost all of Korea's large commercial fertilizer facilities, with the result that the task of trying to

maintain or to increase the level of agricultural production has been relatively easier in the north than in South Korea. It is estimated that South Korea, with 70 per cent of the population at present, still produces about 64 per cent of the total foodstuffs, and conversely that North Korea, with 30 per cent of the population, produces 36 per cent of the total foodstuffs.

Undoubtedly the most serious economic unbalance stemming from the division of Korea is the resulting acute shortage of electric power and fuels in South Korea. Over 90 per cent of Korea's ample electric power production facilities, including almost all of Korea's dependable, year-around hydro plants, are located in North Korea. Therefore, while South Korea has been acutely short of electric power, North Korea has electric power substantially in excess of its requirements and, according to some reports, is sending North Korea power not only into Manchuria, but also into the Maritime Provinces of the USSR.

During the years prior to Japanese surrender, over 75 per cent of Korea's coal was produced in North Korea, where almost all of Korea's best deposits of coal are located. In addition, North Korean forests were the source of over two-thirds of Korea's lumber and fuel wood. The accumulated effect of the acute shortage of electric power, coal, and fuel wood in South Korea as a result of the division of Korea, has resulted in severe over-cutting of South Korea's forest resources.

The major portion of Korea's heavy industries and mines is located in North Korea. Over 95 per cent of Korea's iron ore production facilities, and over 90 per cent of Korea's iron and steel production facilities, are located north of the 38th parallel. Korea has one of Asia's largest and most efficient concentrations of chemical industries located in the Hungnam-Hamhung area in North Korea. Korea's only petroleum processing plant is a major installation, designed to serve the needs of all Korea, located at Wonsan in North Korea. Seven of the eight major cement plants in Korea are located in North Korea. South Korea has the bulk of Korea's textile, food processing, and light chemicals plants, but many of these plants were built to process raw materials from North Korea.

The economic results of the post-war division of this economically interrelated peninsula have been serious, and would have been disastrous for South Korea and its people if the United States had not provided substantial economic assistance. The United States Government has supplied South Korea with over $350 million worth of foodstuffs, fertilizer, raw materials for industry, electrical supplies, transportation and communications equipment, medical supplies, automotive equipment, etc, since the end of the war.

The American Government, working through the Economic Co-operation Administration and in close co-operation with the Government of the Republic of Korea, has developed a broad long-range programme for the economic rehabilitation of South Korea, beginning 1 January 1949, subject, of course, to Congressional appropriations on an annual basis. The basic emphasis of this programme is on expansion of production of coal, electric power, cereals, marine products and exportable minerals. The objective of the programme is to get South Korea on as sound and stable an economic footing as possible, as rapidly as possible. Although the goal of the programme is a united Korea, independent both politically and economically, it is recognized that the development of an economically self-sustaining Korea presents tremendous difficulties as long as Korea remains divided along the 38th parallel. As far as possible, the developments in South Korea are designed to supplement the needs of a united Korean nation.

3. *Major developments in South Korea during the period of Military Government*

(a) *Agriculture*

Agriculture is the backbone of the Korean economy and over two-thirds of the population of Korea, both north and south of the 38th parallel, are engaged in agricultural pursuits. Therefore, during the period of United States Military Government control of South Korea from September 1945 to August 1948, primary emphasis was placed upon trying to help solve the most pressing problems of agriculture. These problems include expansion of agricultural production, elevation of of the status of the farm population, and providing an adequate supply of foodstuffs for all Koreans, both producers and non-self-suppliers.

(i) *Agricultural production*

Planted acreage and agricultural production declined during the years 1940 to 1946, largely as a result of a reduction in the amount of commercial fertilizer applied to Korea's depleted soils, Since almost all land suitable for cultivation in South Korea is already being tilled and any extension of cultivated area can only be accomplished gradually, future increases in agricultural production must come more as a result of expanded double cropping and greater yield per acre, than from an extension of arable acreage. The key to increased yields from Korea's depleted soils is the increased application of farm-produced and commercial fertilizers. Yields of rice and other cereals in Japan (which traditionally has utilized almost twice as much commercial fertilizer per planted acre as Korea) generally average about 50 per cent above Korean yields. In early 1947, the United States Military Government in Korea developed a five-year plan to increase applications of commercial fertilizer in South Korea to the highest levels in Korean history. Since almost all Korea's chemical fertilizer plants are situated north of the 38th parallel, the post-war division of Korea has severed South Korea from its normal source of supply, and has rendered it almost entirely dependent upon fertilizer imports. The American Government purchased and brought into South Korea over 150,000 metric tons of commercial fertilizer in the period 1 July 1946 to 30 June 1947, and stepped imports up to 400,000 metric tons for the period 1 July 1947 to 30 June 1948. Present indications are that imports for the period 1 July 1948 to 30 June 1949 will exceed 600,000 metric tons. That this programme, plus other factors favourable to agriculture, has greatly improved agricultural production is shown by the following table:

TREND OF AGRICULTURAL PRODUCTION IN SOUTH KOREA
(1935-1939 annual average imports index 100)

	Planted average	Production
1940-1944	97	94
1945	86	74
1946	79	71
1947	84	80
1948	97	103
1949 (goal)	101	108

(ii) *Food collection and distribution*

The compulsory grain collection and rationing programme conducted by the Japanese from 1938 to 1945 broke down at the end of the war, and a free market in rice and other cereals was authorized in October 1945. However, lowered agricultural production coupled with the influx of over three million Koreans into South Korea from Japan, Manchuria, and the Soviet occupation zone of North Korea, resulted in a growing shortage of foodstuffs during the first half of 1946.

In order to assure adequate stocks of food to meet the minimum needs of the population, the Military Government re-established controls over food, and instituted plans for compulsory collection of cereals from the farmers, beginning in the summer of 1946. During the period from July 1946 until August 1948, the Military Government conducted five grain collection programmes which succeeded in collecting from the farmers the bulk of the cereals produced which were surplus to their needs. These collected grains, in turn, were rationed to the non-self-suppliers in the cities and towns at fixed low prices. The result of these successful grain collection programmes, plus the American financed imports of cereals to make up for deficits (180,848 metric tons were imported in 1946, 448,962 metric tons in 1947, and slightly over 250,000 in 1948) was the relatively equitable distribution of available foodstuffs in Korea, with the result that the food situation was stabilized. Reflecting this relative stability of the food situation, the open market price of rice increased only about 50 per cent (from 10,000 *won* to 15,000 *won* per *suk*) from September 1946 to the present time.

(iii) *The farmers and their land*

The lot of the generally capable Korean farmers deteriorated during the period of Japanese rule, as the sharp increase in farm tenancy evidences. Farm tenancy in South Korea increased from 40 per cent of the cultivated area in 1910 to about 73 per cent in 1945. During the period of Military Government rule, however, the following developments greatly improved the position and general well-being of the farm population:

(1) Military Government Ordinance No. 9, of 5 October 1945, provided that farm rentals must not exceed one-third of production, whereas previously the tenant farmers paid an average of 60 per cent of their production as rent, in addition to high taxes and water fees.

(2) The Military Government sale to tenant farmers of formerly Japanese-owned farmland, which comprised 15.3 per cent of the total farm acreage in South Korea, enabled over 500,000 tenant farmers to become the owners of all or part of the land they tilled. Payments were set

at the relatively low figure of 20 per cent of production for fifteen years. The post-war inflation had the effect of sharply reducing the farmers' burden of accumulated debts, and this factor, coupled with the sharp increase in the income of tenant farmers as a result of reduction of farm rentals, afforded many farmers the opportunity to buy the farms they tilled. Such purchases were facilitated by the general eagerness of absentee landholders to sell their farmland because the reduction in farm rentals made farmland a much less profitable investment than formerly. In addition, the apparent inevitability of an over-all land reform program which will redistribute the lands of absentee landlords, rendered these holdings less secure. As a result of all these factors, the per cent of farm tenancy dropped from 73 to 40 per cent of the total cultivated farmland between the end of the war and August 1948. At present the National Assembly is considering a land reform law providing for the purchase and distribution of the holdings of Korean absentee landlords to tenant farmers.

(b) *Industry and mining*

The adverse effects of Korea's division into two military occupation zones is nowhere more marked than in the industry of South Korea. The basic military directives to the American occupation forces called for the re-activation of industry and the stimulation of production, but the division of Korea made this most difficult. Other adverse factors include the economic dislocation resulting from the disintegration of the Japanese Empire economy (of which Korea was an integral part) and the shortage of technicians following the repatriation of the Japanese (who had monopolized control and direction of Korean industry prior to Japan's surrender).

Reflecting the gradual expansion of industrial output in South Korea, total coal production in South Korea was increased from approximately 270,000 metric tons in 1946, to 450,000 metric tons in 1947, and 760,000 metric tons in 1948. The cotton textile industry has been rehabilitated and expanded, and there are over 275,000 spindles now operatable. Shortage of electric power has been the main factor limiting production in the textile, as well as most other, industries.

(c) *Education and technological training*

During the period of the Japanese rule of Korea, Korean educational facilities underwent some expansion, but they were far short of actual needs. Also, Japanese students were usually given preferential status in educational institutions in Korea, and as a result a substantial part of the total school enrolment, especially in high schools and colleges, was Japanese. In 1945 the Military Government launched a major expansion of educational activities with the following results:

(1) An expansion of Korean primary school enrolment from approximately 1,500,000 in 1945 to 2,500 000 in 1948; an expansion in the number of Korean primary school teachers from 13,782 in 1945 to 34,757 in 1948; and in number of primary schools from 2,694 in 1945 to 3,442 in 1948;

(2) An increase in the number of middle schools from 252 in 1945 to 423 in 1948, with Korean enrolment increasing from 62,136 in 1945 in 226,960 in 1948;

(3) Expansion of institutions of higher learning from 19 in number in 1945 to 29 in 1948, with student enrolment increasing from 3,039 Koreans in 1945 to 21,250 students in 1948;

(4) Adult education programmes with primary emphasis on development of a literate population. The very substantial results of these programmes are reflected in the rapid increase in the per cent of the population able to read the Korean script, Hangul, from less than one-third of the population in 1945 to an estimated 83 per cent of the population in 1948.

(5) Under the Japanese rule positions of engineering and technical leadership in Korean industry, mining, transportation and communications were largely monopolized by the Japanese, with the result that the Korean population was seriously deficient in the technical skills necessary to operate the Korean economy. In order to help increase the skill of the Korean population, a broad programme of vocational and technical training was undertaken and a separate Technological Training Board was established to supervise this activity. This programme for the expansion of technological training has hardly more than started but it is planned that it will be pushed vigorously under the industrial rehabilitation programme being developed by the Korean Government, in co-operation with the Economic Co-operation Administration.

C. Agreement on Aid concluded between the United States of America and the Republic of Korea (signed at Seoul on 10 December 1948) (A/AC.26/W.3)

Preamble

The Government of the Republic of Korea having requested the Government of the United States of America for financial, material and technical assistance to avert economic crisis, promote national recovery, and insure domestic tranquillity in the Republic of Korea, and

The Congress of the United States of America, in the Act approved June 28, 1948 (Public Law 793, 80th Congress), having authorized the President of the United States of America to furnish assistance to the people of the Republic of Korea and:

The Government of the United States of America and the Government of the Republic of Korea, believing that the furnishing of such assistance, on terms consonant with the independence and security of the Government of the Republic of Korea, will help to achieve the basic objectives of the Charter of the United Nations and the United Nations General Assembly resolution of November 14, 1947, and will further strengthen the ties of friendship between the American and Korean peoples:

The undersigned, being duly authorized by their respective Governments for that purpose, have agreed as follows:

Article I

The Government of the United States of America will furnish the Government of the

Republic of Korea such assistance as the President of the United States of America may authorize to be provided in accordance with the Act of Congress approved June 28, 1948, (Public Law 793, 80th Congress), and any Acts amendatory or supplementary thereto.

Article II

The Government of the Republic of Korea in addition to making the most advantageous use of all available Korean resources, will make similarly effective use of the aid furnished to the Government of the Republic of Korea by the Government of the United States of America. In order further to strengthen and stabilize the economy of Korea as soon as possible, the Government of the Republic of Korea hereby undertakes to effectuate, among others, the following measures:

(*a*) The balancing of the budget through the exercise of economy in governmental expenditures and the increase of governmental revenues by all practicable means;

(*b*) The maintenance of such controls over the issuance of currency and the use of private and governmental credit as are essential to the attainment of economic stability;

(*c*) The regulation of all foreign exchange transactions and the establishment of foreign trade controls, including an export and import licensing system, in order to insure that all foreign exchange resources make a maximum contribution to the welfare of the Korean people and recovery of the Korean economy;

(*d*) The establishment of a rate of exchange for the Korean currency as soon as economic conditions in Korea warrant such action;

(*e*) The exertion of all possible efforts to attain maximum production, collection and equitable distribution of locally-produced supplies, including the continuance of a program of collection and distribution of indigenously-produced cereal grains designed to,

(1) Assure a minimum adequate staple ration at controlled prices for all non-self-suppliers, and where necessary to distribute to indigent and needy persons their fair share of available food supplies; and,

(2) Obtain foreign exchange;

(*f*) The facilitation of private foreign investment in Korea together with the admittance of private foreign traders to transact business in Korea subject to such restrictions as are prescribed in the Constitution and the Laws of the Government of the Republic of Korea;

(*g*) The development of Korean export industries as rapidly as practicable;

(*h*) The management or disposition of government-owned productive facilities and properties in such a manner as will insure, in the general welfare, the furtherance of maximum production.

Article III

1. The Government of the United States of America will appoint an official (hereinafter referred to as the United States Aid Representative) to discharge the responsibilities in Korea of the Government of the United States of America under the terms of this Agreement. Within the terms of this Agreement, the United States Aid Representative and his staff will assist the Government of the Republic of Korea to make the most effective use of Korea's own resources and of aid furnished to the Government of the Republic of Korea by the Government of the United States of America, thereby to advance reconstruction and promote economic recovery in Korea as soon as possible.

2. The Government of the Republic of Korea agrees to extend diplomatic privileges and immunities to the United States Aid Representative and members of his mission.

3. The Government of the Republic of Korea will furnish all practicable assistance to the United States Aid Representative in order to enable him to discharge his responsibilities. The Government of the Republic of Korea will permit the free movement of employees of the Government of the United States of America engaged in carrying out the provisions of this Agreement to, in or from Korea; facilitate the employment of Korean nationals and residents; authorize the acquisition of facilities and services at reasonable prices; and in other ways assist the United States Aid Representative in the performance of his necessary duties. The Government of the Republic of Korea, in consultation with the United States Aid Representative, will effectuate such mutually acceptable arrangements as are necessary for the utilization of the petroleum storage and distribution facilities, and other facilities which are required to carry out the objectives of this Agreement.

4. The Government of the Republic of Korea will permit the United States Aid Representative and his staff to travel and to observe freely the utilization of assistance furnished to Korea by the Government of the United States of America, and will recognize his right to make such recommendations in respect thereto as he deems necessary for the effective discharge of his responsibilities under this Agreement. The Government of the Republic of Korea will maintain such accounts and records pertaining to the Aid Program, and will furnish the United States Aid Representative such reports and information as he may request.

5. In the event the United States Aid Representative ascertains the existence of abuses or violations of this Agreement, he will so inform the Government of the Republic of Korea. The Government of the Republic of Korea will promptly take such action as is necessary to correct such abuses or violations as are found to exist and inform the United States Aid Representative of action taken. If, in the opinion of the United States Aid Representative, appropriate corrective action is not taken by the Government of the Republic of Korea, he may take such steps as may be appropriate and proper and may recommend to the Government of the United States of America the termination of further assistance.

6. The Government of the Republic of Korea will establish an operating agency to develop and administer a program relating to requirements, procurement, allocation, distribution, pricing, and accounting for supplies obtained under this agreement. In the development and execution of such

a program the operating agency will consult with the United States Aid Representative.

Article IV

1. The Government of the Republic of Korea will develop an over-all economic recovery plan designed to stabilize the Korean economy. An integral part of this economic recovery plan will be an import-export program to be agreed upon by the United States Aid Representative and the Government of the Republic of Korea. In consonance with this agreement upon the import-export program, the Government of the Republic of Korea will transmit to the United States Aid Representative fully justified import requirements, together with estimates of export availabilities, this information to be transmitted at such times and in such form as may be desired by the United States Aid Representative.

2. The Government of the Republic of Korea will insure that the periodic allocation of foreign exchange by categories of use will be made in consultation with and with the concurrence of the United States Aid Representative, and that expenditures of foreign exchange will be made in accordance with such allocations.

3. Where it is deemed necessary, the Government of the Republic of Korea will employ foreign consultants and technicians to assure the effective utilization of domestic resources and of equipment and materials brought into Korea under the import-export program. The Government of the Republic of Korea will in each case inform the United States Aid Representative of its intention to employ such individuals.

Article V

1. The Government of the Republic of Korea will take all appropriate steps regarding the distribution within Korea of goods provided by the Government of the United States of America pursuant to this Agreement, and of similar goods imported through the use of other funds or produced locally, to insure a fair and equitable distribution of these supplies at reasonable prices consistent with local economic conditions within the Republic of Korea, and to insure that all such goods are used for the purpose envisaged by this Agreement.

2. The Government of the United States of America shall from time to time notify the Government of the Republic of Korea of the indicated dollar cost of commodities, services, and technical information (including any cost of processing, storing, transporting, repairing or other services incident thereto) made available to Korea on a grant basis pursuant to this Agreement. The Government of the Republic of Korea, upon notification of such indicated dollar costs, shall thereupon deposit in a special account in its name at the Bank of Chosen a commensurate amount in *won*, computed at a *won*-dollar ratio which shall be agreed to at such time between the Government of the Republic of Korea and the United States Aid Representative. The Government of the Republic of Korea will use any balance in the special account to pay the United States Aid Representative such funds as he may require from time to time to meet the *won* expenses incurred in the discharge of his responsibilities within Korea

under this Agreement. The remaining sums in the special account may be used only for such other purposes as may be agreed upon from time to time between the Government of the Republic of Korea and the United States Aid Representative.

3. The Government of the Republic of Korea will not permit the re-export of goods provided by the Government of the United States of America pursuant to this Agreement or the export or re-export of commodities of the same character produced locally or otherwise procured, without the concurrence of the United States Aid Representative.

4. The Government of the Republic of Korea will insure that all commodities made available under this Agreement or the containers of such commodities shall, to the extent practicable, be marked, stamped, branded, or labeled in a conspicuous place as legibly, indelibly, and permanently as the nature of such commodities or containers will permit, in such a manner as to indicate to the people of Korea that such commodities have been furnished or made available by the United States of America.

Article VI

1. The Government of the Republic of Korea will undertake to use its best endeavor to cooperate with other countries in facilitating and stimulating and increasing interchange of goods and services with other countries and in reducing public and private barriers to trade with other countries.

2. Pending the entry into force of a Treaty of Amity and Commerce between the Government of the United States of America and the Government of the Republic of Korea, the Government of the United States of America shall accord, immediately and unconditionally, to the merchandise trade of the Republic of Korea treatment no less favorable than that accorded to the merchandise trade of any third country. Similarly, treatment no less favorable than that accorded to the merchandise trade of any third country shall be accorded, immediately and unconditionally, within the Republic of Korea, to the merchandise trade of the United States of America.

3. Departures from the application of the most-favored-nation treatment provided for in paragraph 2 of this article shall be permitted to the extent that they are in accord with the exceptions recognized under the General Agreement on Tariffs and Trade, dated October 30, 1947 concluded at the Second Session of the Preparatory Committee of the United Nations Conference on Trade and Employment, as now or hereafter amended. The provisions of this paragraph shall not be construed to require compliance with the procedures specified in the General Agreement with regard to the application of such exceptions.

4. The provisions of paragraphs 2 and 3 of this article shall apply, with respect to the United States of America, to all territory under its sovereignty or authority.

5. The Government of the Republic of Korea shall accord most-favored-nation treatment to the merchandise trade of any area in the free territory of Trieste, Japan or Western Germany in the occupation or control of which the Government of the United States participates, for such time and to such extent as such area accords most-favored-

nation treatment to the merchandise trade of the Republic of Korea.

6. The provisions of paragraphs 2 and 3 of this article shall not derogate from such other obligations concerning the matters contained in this Agreement as may at any time be in effect between the Government of the United States of America and the Government of the Republic of Korea.

7. The Government of the Republic of Korea will take the measures which it deems appropriate to prevent, on the part of private or public commercial enterprises, business practices or business arrangements affecting international trade which have the effect of interfering with the purposes and policies of this Agreement.

8. The provisions of this article and of article VII shall apply during such period as the Government of the United States of America extends aid to the Government of the Republic of Korea under the terms of this Agreement, unless superseded by a Treaty of Amity and Commerce.

Article VII

The Government of the Republic of Korea shall, with respect to commercial, industrial, shipping and other business activities, accord to the nationals of the United States of America treatment no less favorable than that now or hereafter accorded by the Republic of Korea to nationals of any third country. As used in this paragraph, the word "nationals" shall be understood to include natural and juridical persons.

Article VIII

The Government of the Republic of Korea will facilitate the transfer to the United States of America, for stock-piling or other purposes, of materials originating in the Republic of Korea which are required by the United States of America as a result of deficiencies or potential deficiencies in its own resources, upon such reasonable terms of sale, exchange, barter or otherwise, and in such quantities, and for such period of time, as may be agreed to between the Governments of the United States of America and the Republic of Korea after due regard for the reasonable requirements of the Republic of Korea for domestic use and commercial export of such materials. The Government of the Republic of Korea will take such specific measures within the intent of this Agreement as may be necessary to carry out the provisions of this paragraph, including the promotion of the increased production of such materials within the Republic of Korea, and the removal of any hindrances to the transfer of such materials to the United States of America. The Government of the Republic of Korea will, when so requested by the Government of the United States of America, enter into negotiations for detailed arrangements necessary to carry out the provisions of this paragraph.

Article IX

1. The Government of the Republic of Korea and the Government of the United States of America will co-operate in assuring the peoples of the United States of America and of Korea full information concerning the goods and technical assistance furnished to the Government of the Republic of Korea by the Government of the United States of America.

2. The Government of the Republic of Korea will permit representatives of the Press and radio of the United States of America to travel and to observe freely and to report fully regarding the receipt and utilization of American aid.

3. The Government of the Republic of Korea will permit representatives of the Government of the United States of America, including such committees of the Congress as may be authorized by their respective houses to observe, advise, and report on the distribution among the people of commodities made available under this Agreement.

4. The Government of the Republic of Korea will co-operate with the United States Aid Representative in providing full and continuous publicity in Korea on the purpose, source, character, scope, amounts and progress of the economic and technical aid provided to the Government of the Republic of Korea by the Government of the United States of America under the provisions of this Aid Agreement.

Article X

1. Any or all assistance authorized to be provided pursuant to this Agreement will be terminated:

(a) If requested by the Government of the Republic of Korea;

(b) If the United Nations finds that action taken or assistance furnished by the United Nations makes the continuance of assistance by the Government of the United States of America pursuant to this Agreement unnecessary or undesirable.

(c) If the President of the United States of America determines that the Government of the Republic of Korea is not adhering to the terms of this Agreement; or whenever he finds, by reason of changed conditions, that aid provided under this Agreement is no longer necessary or desirable; or whenever he finds that, because of changed conditions, aid under this Agreement is no longer consistent with the national interests of the United States of America.

Article XI

This Agreement shall become effective with the formal notification to the Government of the United States of America that the Korean National Assembly has consented to this Agreement. It shall remain in force until three (3) months after the day on which either Government shall have given to the other notice of intention to terminate.

This Agreement may be amended at any time by agreement between the two Governments.

Article XII

This Agreement shall be registered with the United Nations.

DONE in duplicate, in the English and Korean languages at Seoul, Korea, this 10th day of December 1948. The English and Korean texts shall have equal force, but in the case of divergence the English text shall prevail.

For the Government of the United States of America
John J. MUCCIO

For the Government of the Republic of Korea
LEE Bum Suk
KIM Do Yun

Annex II

TEXTS OF MAIN DOCUMENTS RELATING TO THE DEVELOPMENT OF REPRESENTATIVE GOVERNMENT

A. Final report of Sub-Committee II and appendices (A/AC.26/34)

1. MAIN BODY OF THE REPORT OF SUB-COMMITTEE II

1. To implement the resolution of the General Assembly of 12 December 1948, the Commission, at its 2nd and 3rd meetings, discussed the question of setting up subsidiary bodies. It was agreed that the representatives of China, France and Syria should form a working group to draw up the terms of reference of Sub-Committee II to carry out paragraph 4 (*c*) of resolution 195(III) of the General Assembly.[49] At its 5th meeting on 9 February 1949, the Commission adopted the draft resolution of the working group and established Sub-Committee II. consisting of the representatives of China, France and the Philippines.[50] At the first meeting of the Sub-Committee, Mr. Henri Costilhes, representative of France, was elected Chairman. Mr. Rufino Luna, representative of the Philippines, agreed to preside over all the hearings of the Sub-Committee.

2. The terms of reference of the Sub-Committee were defined by the Commission at its 5th meeting as follows:

(*a*) To study the development of representative government in Korea;

(*b*) To be ready for consultation with governmental authorities and to provide such information and advice as may be requested;

(*c*) To gather from experts and organizations opinions and views which have a bearing on the further development of representative government in Korea.

3. From 11 February to 24 June 1949, the Sub-Committee held twenty-five meetings altogether, including ten meetings devoted to hearings. Summary records of all these hearings were distributed to members of the Commission. The major decisions and activities of the Sub-Committee are recorded in documents A/AC.26/5, A/AC.26/11, A/AC.26/SC.2/14 and A/AC.26/SC.2/15.

Chronology of important developments in Korea

4. At the initial meetings of the Commission, a desire was expressed to have a survey made of political events in Korea, and it was felt that members of the Chinese and French delegations to the Temporary Commission, who had constituted the Main Committee left in Seoul, might be best qualified to prepare a resume on important political developments from August 1948 to January 1949. At its first meeting, the Sub-Committee decided to request the representatives of China and France, together with the Secretary of the Sub-Committee, to prepare such a resume. The working group recommended that, instead of a report, a chronology of important events with commentaries should be prepared. The Sub-Committee, at its 2nd meeting, adopted the recommendation of its working group. This decision was incorporated in the Sub-Committee's first report and recommendations, adopted by the Commission at its 14th meeting. At its 7th meeting, the Sub-Committee approved the *Chronology of important developments in Korea from 15 August 1948 to 31 January 1949* (A/AC.26/SC.2/5). It was circulated for the information and reference of the members of the Commission.

Hearings of Korean officials and personalities

5. The desire that the Sub-Committee should soon proceed with hearings was expressed by the Chairman of the Commission at its 11th meeting. The Sub-Committee, at its 3rd meeting, decided on the first list of persons to be heard. The Sub-Committee gave careful consideration to the selection of officials and experts, since views had been expressed by some officials of the Government of the Republic of Korea that paragraph 4 (*c*) of the resolution of the General Assembly of 12 December 1948 applied to North Korea only and that it would be unnecessary for the Commission to consult non-official Koreans, especially those who are regarded as undesirable elements. In preparing its first report on the persons to be heard and the topics to be discussed at the hearings, one consideration by which the Sub-Committee was guided was that, while it upheld the Commission's right to hear or consult any Koreans, it would try to avoid any unnecessary misunderstanding and controversy with the Korean Government.

6. Following the submission of the Sub-Committee's report and recommendations, the Commission discussed the question of consulting Korean personalities together with that of the attitude of the Government in this matter. In adopting the report of the Sub-Committee at its 14th meeting, the Commission established certain principles and procedure concerning the hearing of Korean personalities:

(*a*) The Sub-Committee had the right to select any Koreans for hearings and the view expressed by Korean authorities should not alter the independent position of the Commission in this regard;

(*b*) In order to avoid unnecessary misunderstandings and controversy with the Korean Government, and to test its reaction, the Sub-Committee should proceed gradually, but not too slowly, with its interviews;

(*c*) The Sub-Committees should submit the list of persons to be heard to the Commission for review.

This procedure was followed by both Sub-Committees in their hearings. Sub-Committee II's second list of persons to be heard was adopted at the 22nd meeting of the Commission.

7. The eleven persons consulted by Sub-Committee II were carefully selected. They repre-

---

[49] Paragraph 4(*c*) states: "Be available for observation and consultation in the further development of representative government based on the freely-expressed will of the people".
[50] A/AC.26/SR.5.

sented the Government, political parties and educational, social and religious organizations. Their views on the development of representative government reflected sufficiently the attitude of the Government and the main trends of public opinion on this question. A summary and analysis together with a conclusion of the hearings is appended to this report as appendix (a).

Trips to the provinces affected by recent disturbances

8. The work of the Sub-Committee in gathering views and opinions concerning the further development of representative government in Korea was not limited to its hearings. The Sub-Committee was of the opinion that conditions in local areas, particularly in those provinces affected by recent disturbances, had a bearing on the question. To observe general conditions in those areas and to gather views and opinions on the spot, the Sub-Committee organized trips to Cholla Namdo (25-28 April) and Cheju Do (8-14 May). The trip to Cheju Do was planned with a view to observing the elections of 10 May at the same time. A detailed report of these trips is contained in appendix (b).

9. Before going on to the general conclusions, it should be pointed out that in relation to its second term of reference, namely, "be ready for consultation with governmental authorities and provide such information and advice as may be requested", the Sub-Committee has not received any requests of that nature.

General conclusions

10. On the basis of the views expressed by Korean officials and personalities, the observation trips undertaken by the Sub-Committee, and its deliberations, the Sub-Committee is of the opinion that, since the establishment of the Government of the Republic of Korea, many concrete steps have been taken and progress has been made in the development of representative government, particularly in view of the short period of time which has elapsed and the tremendous problems confronting the young Republic. However, the growth of representative government has been frequently hampered by disturbances in several areas, notably in Cholla Namdo and Cheju Do. Although sporadic guerrilla activities continue in some mountain areas, the Government, which was faced with the necessity of declaring martial law in some areas for a short time and curfew hours in almost all cities, towns and villages, seems to have succeeded in crushing the main rebellion and restoring peace and order. The divergences of view continue between the Executive and the National Assembly regarding the implementation of the Constitution and the enactment of such important bills as the Anti-Traitors Law, Land Reform Bill and Local Administration Bill. This is, however, a wholesome sign for the growth of democracy in Korea.

11. It is believed that once the security of the Republic is completely assured and law and order established throughout the country, greater strides can be made toward the further development of representative government.

2. Appendices

(a) SUMMARY AND ANALYSIS OF HEARINGS REGARDING THE DEVELOPMENT OF REPRESENTATIVE GOVERNMENT

Recommendations of the Sub-Committee and decisions of the Commission

1. In accordance with the terms of reference of Sub-Committee II laid down by the first resolution of the Commission establishing the Sub-Committee, which directed it to "3. Gather from experts and organizations opinions and views which have a bearing on the further development of representative government in Korea . . ."[51] Sub-Committee II, at its 2nd meeting, decided to conduct hearings with officials and experts on the question of the development of representative government. For this purpose a questionnaire dealing with the problem of representative government and its related subjects was prepared.

2. At its 4th meeting, the Sub-Committee agreed that the first group of people to be heard should consist of not more than six persons. It approved the main topics for discussion at the hearings. The names of those to be heard and the topics for the hearings were incorporated into the Sub-Committee's first report and recommendations to the Commission.[52] The Commission, at its 4th meeting, adopted the Sub-Committee's report. The first group of hearings, when five persons were heard, took place between 28 February and 15 March 1949 inclusive.

3. Having completed the hearings of the first group of persons, Sub-Committee II, at its 10th meeting, decided to hear six more people. The report of the Sub-Committee on further persons to be heard is contained in document A/AC.26/SC.2/7, which was adopted by the Commission at its 22nd meeting. These hearings were held between 30 March and 14 April 1949 inclusive.

4. Since the General Assembly resolution of 12 December 1948 called upon "all Koreans to afford every assistance and facility to the Commission in the fulfilment of its responsibilities", the Sub-Committee did not overlook the importance of hearing the views of Koreans from the north. Under the present circumstances, however, it was not possible to hear the views of northern Koreans directly. The Pyongyang radio intercepts remain the only channel of news from the north. Secondly, no attempt was made to invite members of the South Korea Labour Party (communist party) for hearings, since they have been driven underground and are regarded by the Korean authorities as subversive elements. With regard to the position of the Korean Government on the question of the access of Koreans to the Commission, the Sub-Committee maintained that, while the Commission still upholds the principle underlying the resolution of the Commission adopted at its 10th meeting, the Sub-Committee, in making up the list for the hearings, should give due consideration to the wishes of the Korean Government concerning certain persons who might be regarded as undesirable elements.

5. In order to attain a balanced representation of views held by high officials and of the main

---

[51] A/AC.26/1.
[52] A/AC.26/SC.2/1 and A/AC.26/SC.2/1/Rev.1.

trends of opinion held by private citizens concerning the problem, the following individuals were invited for hearings. On the basis of their professions and positions, they can be classified as follows:

(a) Three high officials with ministerial rank: Kim Hyo Suk, Minister of Internal Affairs; Limb, B. C., Minister of Foreign Affairs; Yoo Chin O, Director of the Office of Legislation;

(b) Members of the National Assembly and political leaders:

(i) Members of the National Asesmbly: Shin Ik Hi, Chairman of the National Assembly and member of the Supreme Council of the Democratic Nationalist Party; Yun Chi Yung, Member of the National Assembly and former Minister of Internal Affairs;

(ii) Leaders of political parties: Cho So Ang, leader of the Socialist Party; Kim Soong Soo, leader of the former Hankook Democratic Party and member of the Supreme Council of the Democratic Nationalist Party;

(c) Experts, social and religious leaders: An Chai Hong, civil administrator of the defunct Interim Government and leader of the New Life Association; Kim Bup Rin, Buddhist scholar and member of the Inspection Committee; Park, L. G., President of Chosen Christian College; Rao, Paul M., Vicar Apostolic.

6. Topics for discussion at the hearings were given in advance to the persons invited. In addition to extemporaneous questions and answers at the hearings, the people heard all followed the outline given below in presenting their views:

(a) The development of representative government in Korea:

(1) Steps taken in the development of representative government from the establishment of the Republic of Korea to the present,

(2) Problems confronting the Government and the people in their efforts for the development of representative government,

(3) Specific views and proposals on the further development of representative government;

(b) The development of representative government in relation to the problem of unification:

(1) Political basis for unification,

(2) Comments on the structure of government and conditions in North Korea,

(3) Possibilities of extending representative government within North Korea,

(4) Representation and participation of all Koreans in a unified Korea.

Views of officials

7. The views of the three Ministers (Minister of Foreign Affairs, Minister of Internal Affairs and Director of the Office of Legislation), with reference to the question of the development of representative government in Korea, reflected the attitude of the Government.

Both Minister Kim and Minister Limb emphasized the suppression of all communist activities, whether inspired in the north or in the south, and measures for an increase in production and for bringing about land reform as concrete steps taken in the development of representative government since the establishment of the Republic of Korea.

The Foreign Minister seemed to regard recognition of the Government of the Republic of Korea by friendly Powers as an indication in itself of the representative character of the Government.

The Director of the Office of Legislation, who had an important part in the drafting of the Constitution of the Republic, pointed out that the Government did not actually begin to function until three months after its establishment. He listed the following as concrete steps taken toward the development of representative government: (a) preservation of peace and order; (b) reorganization of administrative machinery of the Government in order to reduce costs of administration and number of government employees; (c) absorption of the Police Department by the Ministry of Internal Affairs, in order to put it under the control of a civilian; (d) placement of the national defence force under the Ministry of Defence, a post held by a civilian as provided in the Constitution; (e) establishment of the Inspection Committee and of the Board of Audit to investigate any misbehaviour of officials; (f) establishment of the Office of Planning in order to organize economic recovery; (g) establishment of the Office of Legislation and of the Law Drafting Committee in order to complete the work of drafting civil and criminal laws; (h) implementation of the constitutional provision regarding the arrest of civilians without a warrant.

8. With regard to the problems confronting the Government, the three Ministers unanimously stressed the division of Korea by the 38th parallel, terrorism by the communists and economic difficulties as the greatest obstacles to the development of representative government.

Minister Limb stated that "in the light of the present situation one cannot expect representative government to develop smoothly and without reverses".[53] He added further "when economic reconstruction is accomplished and law and order again prevail, South Korea will experience a marked development toward democracy and representative government".[54]

9. As for specific views and proposals on the further development of representative government, Minister Kim maintained that removal of the 38th parallel through the agreement of the Powers concerned should be a prerequisite, and the Director of the Office of Legislation believed that an increase in production by carrying out the five-year plan and the establishment of a strong military force were the most urgent measures to be put into effect.

10. All these officials believed that the strongest foundation existing for unification was the racial, cultural and linguistic homogeneity of Korea. They felt that the 100 seats in the National Assembly reserved for North Korea constituted a political basis for unification. They all claimed that the Government of the Republic of Korea was the only Government which had jurisdiction

[53] A/AC.26/SC.2/12, page 5.
[54] Ibid, page 6.

over the zone north of the 38th parallel and the moral force to govern a united Korea.

Admitting the responsibility of Koreans in a divided Korea, Mr. Yoo stated that the division had not been effected by the Koreans, and that the responsibility for the resulting situation had been transferred to the United Nations. He could not see any possibility of unification through consultation with the north until the communist party changed its policy. The appointment of the five exiled leaders from the north as governors of the northern provinces had had a profound psychological effect on North Korea in favour of unification. However, under the circumstances, a strong force in South Korea was necessary for a peaceful solution of the problem of Korean unification and independence.

11. All the ministers condemned the northern regime as a one party dictatorship modelled on the Soviet pattern which, they said, disrespects and disregards fundamental human rights and freedoms. In their view, there was no possibility of extending representative government within North Korea until Korea was united under the leadership of the Government of the Republic of Korea.

Views of the members of the National Assembly and political leaders

(i) *Members of the National Assembly*

12. Mr. Shin, who was once a prominent member of both the Korean Independence Party and the National Society for the Acceleration of Korean Independence, and the leader of the short-lived Nationalist Party, was elected Chairman of the National Assembly, succeeding Dr. Rhee when the latter was elected President of the Republic of Korea. Following the establishment of the Government of the Republic of Korea, the Hankook Democratic Party and the Nationalist Party were amalgamated to form the Democratic Nationalist Party. Mr. Shin became one of the five members of its Supreme Council. As Chairman of the National Assembly, Mr. Shin tries to play the role of a moderator. On the whole he supports the Government.

Mr. Yun, once a member of the former Hankook Democratic Party and former Minister of Internal Affairs, is considered an outstanding supporter of the Government's policy.

While Mr. Shin was evasive in his statements and replies to questions, Mr. Yun was emphatic on the legal status of the Government of the Republic of Korea and its sovereign right in recovering the territory north of the 38th parallel. Neither of these gentlemen elaborated on the steps which had been taken in the development of representative government. However, Mr. Yun asserted, on the one hand, that the Koreans were capable of managing their own affairs and, on the other hand, stated that Korea could not afford to do without American occupation forces.

13. Mr. Shin, speaking in general and vague terms, mentioned external pressure and internal division as major problems confronting the Government of the Republic of Korea and spoke of the need of bringing the Government and all the people into a union as a concrete suggestion for the further development of representative government.

Taking into consideration the economic distress of the people, Mr. Yun believed that the Government of the Republic of Korea, with the assistance of the United States and the United Nations Commission, could overcome all the obstacles with which it was faced.

In reply to a question, Mr. Shin thought certain constitutional amendments regarding the power of the President and the creation of an upper house might be necessary measures for the further development of representative government.

14. Cultural homogeneity, the existence of the Government based on its present Constitution, and filling the vacancies of the 100 seats in the National Assembly for the northern representatives, were regarded by Messrs. Shin and Yun as important bases for unification. They referred to the northern regime as a class dictatorship under the control of the USSR. Mr. Yun, especially, saw no solution in a compromise between the right and the left and was convinced that any coalition would always lead to communist domination and thus to the self-destruction of Korea. Emphasizing the sovereignty of the Korean Government, he protested against the idea of having a conference between the north and south. He further curtly remarked that Korea was not a laboratory for such experiments.

15. Mr. Shin thought extension of representative government into North Korea was possible since the people in the north desired to come under the jurisdiction of the Government in the south. Mr. Yun believed that the only way of extending representative government to the north was for the Commission to conduct and supervise a general election there in order to select the 100 representatives for the vacant seats in the National Assembly. Furthermore, he urged the Commission to give full support to the Government of the Republic of Korea and observe its legal status. He believed that the Commission should "arouse world opinion to condemn the country which is violating international laws and treaties by continuing its illegal occupation of Korean territory".[55]

(ii) *Leaders of political parties*

16. Messrs. Kim Soong Soo and Cho So An, two outstanding political leaders, have followers in the National Assembly. Mr. Kim was a leader of the former Hankook Democratic Party (extreme right) which played a prominent role during the elections of 10 May 1948 and in the election of Dr. Rhee as President, and which after the establishment of the Government became a component part of the Democratic Nationalist Party, the dominant political party in the National Assembly. Although he has held no government office, Mr. Kim, though not a member of the National Assembly, is regarded as a party whip of the Democratic Nationalist Party. Mr. Cho, formerly a close associate of Mr. Kim Koo and leading member of the Korean Independence Party, broke away from this group after the establishment of the Government and subsequently organized the Socialist Party (moderate), which claims to have a number of members in the National Assembly. Mr. Cho holds no office in the Government and regarded the enactment of land reform and local self-government bills and

---

[55] A/AC.26/SC.2/4, page 6.

제3부 유엔한국위원단 보고서(1949)

the National Traitors' Act as evidences of the development of representative government. He believed that the full implementation of those laws would greatly improve the situation in South Korea. Mr. Kim maintained that, while the Chief Executive had failed to follow the usual practice of selecting members of the party which had won a majority in forming the Cabinet, the Government of the Republic of Korea was a representative one. It was weakened by the inclusion of certain minority and left-wing leaders in the Cabinet. He considered this type of idealism a major problem standing in the way of the development of representative government. For the further development of representative government, he urged that a parliamentary form of government be completed and perfected.

Mr. Cho offered three suggestions for the further development of representative government: (a) politically, the Government should appoint the most competent men to hold office. Many laws and regulations inherited from the Japanese regime must be eliminated and the fundamental rights and freedoms must be respected; (b) economically, he suggested a planned economy to solve the economic problem confronting Korea and to serve as a basis for representative government; (c) culturally, he emphasized the need for free primary education and exchange of ideas.

17. Referring to political bases for unification, Mr. Kim felt that Koreans were a united people and that unification would automatically be achieved by getting rid of a handful of communist leaders. Mr. Cho maintained that Koreans desired neither class dictatorship nor a monopoly of political power, but instead wished to have a a democratic or socialist regime which would guarantee equal rights and opportunity for all.

While Mr. Kim condemned the régime in the north as an illegal government, Mr. Cho pointed out that there was no freedom of elections in North Korea. He believed that a strong and democratic government in South Korea would help bring about unification. Mr. Kim felt that "the only way to extend representative government within North Korea would be for the Commission to supervise and observe an election there."[56] Unless the Commission saw some way to gain access to the north and carry out a general election there, there would be no hope of peaceful unification. "The only effective method of uniting Korea is to bring strong pressure upon Russia through world public opinion."[57] Furthermore, he believed that there were democratic elements in the north which would play a prominent role in the movement to unify the country.

Views of experts and representatives of religious and social organizations

18. The four personalities who appeared before the Sub-Committee, also represented four religious or social organizations: the Catholic, Protestant, Buddhist religions and a New Life Association. With the exception of Mr. Kim Bup Rin, the Buddhist professor who is concurrently a member of the Inspection Committee, the experts held no official positions in the Government. The four of them supported the

Government but with varying degrees of criticism and apology.

19. Bishop Ro and Mr. Kim believed that the Government had been doing its utmost to improve its internal organization and the public welfare, and that accomplishments in this direction indicated definite progress in the development of representative government.

In listing some of the steps taken in the development of representative government, Dr. Paik, President of Chosen Christian College, was somewhat apologetic in saying that "of course, there is room for improvement, for no government is perfect; everything depends upon how the man in authority exercises his powers",[58] and Mr. An, who was the highest civil administrator during the Military Government and who is regarded as a "middle-of-the-roader", was positive in stating that the Government had not fully implemented its pledge to democratize the police force and to guarantee civil rights. However, he regarded the friction between the executive and the legislative bodies as a healthy sign in the development of representative government, since it meant that the chief executive could not do things as he pleased when the National Assembly tried to overrule him. Furthermore, he gave credit to the Government for maintaining law and order, although disturbances continued.

20. With regard to the problems confronting the Government, all of the experts emphasized the economic difficulties resulting from the division of the country, differences in ideologies and the menace of communism. This situation, intensified by the inability of the Government to improve Korean economy in order to meet the primary needs of the people, had created confusion and unrest which in turn caused the people to be easily persuaded to listen to irresponsible and communist propaganda and the promises of demagogues.

While Dr. Paik considered an uneducated and uninformed electorate an important major problem confronting the Government in its efforts for the development of representative government, Mr. An mentioned the gulf existing between the Government and the people as a major obstacle to this development. He believed that the Chief Executive would have to be responsible for such a situation.

21. These four experts were all specific in offering suggestions toward the further development of representative government.

Bishop Ro emphasized the importance of moral and spiritual education and the appointment of persons of integrity and ability to government posts as specific measures for the further development of representative government, while Dr. Paik stressed the necessity of raising the intellectual and cultural level of the people. Mr. Kim made the following specific proposals: (a) the Government must win the people to a high patriotism; (b) an upper house as a means to facilitate the expression of the popular will and a supreme advisory council to the president to give advice on policy, should be created; (c) a purge of corrupt officials should be thoroughly carried out. Mr. An believed that the development of representative government in Korea could only be

---

[56] A/AC.26/SC.2/10, page 6.
[57] *Ibid.*, page 7.

[58] A/AC.26/SC.2/3, page 7.

achieved through the free expression of the will of the people and that at present "free expression of the will of the people is practically impossible because of the nervousness and the sensitiveness of the Government".[59] It was also his opinion that fear of communism had driven the Government to resort to persecution and to arrest as communists those who happened to disagree with it. Mr. An expressed the fear that "if the next election has to be held before the unification of the country, the Government will intervene in it to a marked extent".[60]

22. Bishop Ro, Dr. Paik and Mr. An all shared the view that the Government of the Republic of Korea, with the full support of the people, should be the rallying point for all Koreans and a potent force for unification. To do so, this Government should not only become more tolerant and inclusive, but also should be strengthened. This is what Dr. Paik called the policy of attraction backed by a big stick. They all regarded the northern regime as controlled by a few men dictated to from Moscow, and one which allowed no freedom. They saw no prospect of compromise and agreement with the north and no immediate hope for extending representative government there. Bishop Ro urged that the Government with the full support of the United Nations should extend its jurisdiction to the north. They all felt that the solution of the Korean problem required definite agreement between the two great Powers. When the unification could be achieved, the question of representation would be easily solved. Emphasizing that unification must precede the participation of all Koreans in a unified Korea, Mr. An warned that "this is perhaps the last chance to solve the Korean problem through an international organization. If it fails, there is no telling what might happen . . ."[61]

Conclusions

23. From the views expressed by the eleven persons who appeared before the Sub-Committee, the following general conclusions are drawn on each of the topics in the questionnaire:

(*a*) Officials and private individuals alike raised no question regarding the representative character of the structure of the Government set up in accordance with the Constitution of the Republic of Korea, adopted on 12 July 1948, and promulgated on 19 July 1948 by the National Assembly.

They all agreed that the Government of the Republic of Korea should be the rallying point for solving the problem of Korean independence and unification, and that it should be strengthened.

Some believed the Government should be strengthened by the creation of a strong military force. Others felt it could be strengthened by winning greater confidence and support from the people and by appointing men of integrity and ability to important government posts.

(*b*) All except one, who regretted that the Government had not fully implemented its pledges to democratize its policy and to guarantee civil rights,[62] seemed to agree that the Government has been trying its best to further the development of representative government by completing the government structure, enacting new laws and increasing production. In view of the short period of time which has elapsed and the difficult problems confronting the Government, it has made noticeable progress in the growth of representative government. Without exception, all gave full credit to the Government for maintaining peace and order, which is essential to the growth of any democracy.

(*c*) It was the consensus of opinion of all the persons heard by the Sub-Committee that the geographic and ideological division of Korea and the resulting economic conditions and unrest were the main obstacles to the development of representative government. In this connexion, it should be pointed out that Mr. An stressed the gulf between the Government and the people as a major obstacle, while Mr. Kim Soong Soo felt that the development of representative government had been hampered by the failure to adopt a cabinet system of government.

(*d*) Numerous and concrete proposals made by these persons regarding the further development of representative government indicated their concern with this problem. Their views are naturally varying because of the difference in their positions and points of view.

(*e*) They agreed unanimously that racial, cultural and linguistic homogeneity and geographic and economic unity are the strongest bases for unification. However, they differed in political approach to the problem of unification. While the majority believed that political bases for unification had been firmly established in the structure of the Government and in the provision for reserving 100 seats in the Assembly for the representatives from the north, a minority felt that the Government must reform itself by being more tolerant and inclusive in order to be the rallying point for unification. Thus they all agreed that the Government of the Republic of Korea is a starting point for bringing about unification.

(*f*) Regarding the structure of government and conditions in North Korea, the consensus of opinion was that the regime in North Korea is a dictatorship under the control of one party—the North Korea Labour Party (former communist party). According to the religious leaders who appeared before the Sub-Committee, there had been religious persecution in North Korea, and there is still little freedom of worship.

(*g*) The overwhelming majority were not optimistic regarding the extension of representative government within North Korea. However, two persons believed that the desire of the northern people to live under the jurisdiction of the Republic of Korea and the existence of hidden democratic elements in North Korea are important factors in the further development of representative government.

(*h*) The majority were very vague in expressing their views on the question of representation and participation of all Koreans in a united Korea. The more definite view was that a general

[59] A/AC.26/SC.2/6, page 6.
[60] *Ibid.*, page 19.
[61] A/AC.26/SC.2/6, page 13.
[62] A/AC.26/SC.2/6, page 2.

election in North Korea under the observation of the United Nations Commission on Korea should be the natural solution to this problem. Two of the eleven persons emphasized the point that unification should precede participation of all Koreans in a unified government, and that with unification the problem of representation would be automatically solved.

(b) REPORT ON TRIPS TO THE PROVINCES AFFECTED BY RECENT DISTURBANCES

Recommendation of the Sub-Committee and decisions of the Commission

1. The provisions of paragraph 4 of the resolution of the General Assembly of 12 December 1948 required the Commission among other things to be available for consultation and observation in regard to the further development of representative government based on the freely expressed will of the people. The Commission, at its 5th meeting, established, therefore, two sub-committees and entrusted Sub-Committee II with the task of studying the development of representative government in Korea and gathering from experts and organizations opinions and views which have a bearing on the matter.[63]

2. After having heard a number of officials, experts and representatives of organizations at the hearings, the Sub-Committee, at its 10th meeting, discussed the question of observation trips in the provinces in order to gather views and observe conditions at first hand. It was felt that the study of the development of representative government should be supplemented by making observation trips to such places as Yosu, Soon Chun and Cheju Island, where revolts and disturbances had recently taken place.

3. At its 11th meeting, the Sub-Committee agreed on a report and recommendations concerning the trips to Cholla Namdo and Cheju Do. The report was adopted by the Commission at its 22nd meeting. The Commission authorized the Sub-Committee to organize these trips for the purposes of observing general conditions and it was understood that the other members of the Commission would be invited to participate.[64]

4. The Sub-Committee discussed the detailed preparations for these trips at its 14th and 18th meetings, and fixed a date for the trip to Cheju Do, from 18 to 21 April, and for the trip to Cholla Namdo from 25 to 28 April. It requested the Secretariat to make the necessary arrangements.

5. On 18 April, the representatives of China, France and India and six members of the secretariat flew to Cheju Island, in accordance with the original schedule, but because of bad weather, the party was unable to land. The trip to that area was therefore postponed. However, the trip to Cholla Namdo was made according to the original schedule.

6. Before the Sub-Committee set another date for the trip to Cheju Do, it was informed that the Government of the Republic of Korea might invite the Commission to observe the elections in North Cheju on 10 May 1949. At its 20th meet-

ing, the Sub-Committee decided that, if a written invitation from the Government were extended to the Commission to observe the said elections, the visiting group should leave Seoul on 8 May 1949.

7. The question of observing the election on Cheju Island was brought to the attention of the Commission which, at its 24th meeting, reviewed the history of the elections on Cheju Do in 1948. It was agreed to observe the elections if a written invitation were extended to the Commission from the Government of the Republic of Korea.

8. In a letter dated 22 April, Colonel Limb, Minister of Foreign Affairs, expressed the desire of the Government for the Commission to observe "the by-elections" on Cheju Do. At its 27th meeting, the Commission reaffirmed its decision with the understanding that the Commission would merely be present during the elections without assuming any responsibility for the results of such elections.

Trip to Cholla Namdo

9. The Sub-Committee, having completed a series of hearings, embarked on the second phase of its programme by organizing observation trips to areas affected by recent disturbances, in order to study present conditions in those areas and the problems confronting the Government.

Cholla Namdo, one of the richest and largest provinces of Korea, is located on the tip of the peninsula. The southern part of Cholla Namdo became the centre of an uprising on the mainland on 19-20 October 1948, when some of the officers of the 14th Regiment of the Korean Constabulary, together with some of the two thousand soldiers scheduled for duty on the Island of Cheju, and an equal number of civilians under the influence of the communists, revolted against the Government and took control of Yosu on 19 October and of Soon Chun on the following day. Riots spread to other counties—Kurye, Posong, Kwangyang, Hadong and Koksong. The Government mobilized land and sea forces to subdue the revolt on the peninsula of Yosu and, on 4 November, it announced the complete annihilation of the rebellion. However, a number of rebel bands escaped into the Chiri Mountains, north-east of Soon Chun, and to several small islands off the peninsula, to continue guerrilla activities.

In order to have an over-all picture of the conditions in Cholla Province, the Sub-Committee selected Kurye, Yosu and Soon Chun, three counties seriously affected by the rebellion, Kwangju, the capital city of Cholla Namdo, and Hwasun, an important coal mining centre, as the main places of interest. To get an impression of Cholla Pukto, the party also stopped at its capital, Chonju, for a few hours, on its way back to Seoul.

10. The observation group, under the auspices of Sub-Committee II, consisted of Mr. Costilhes, representative of France, Mr. Jamieson, representative of Australia, Mr. Ssutu, alternate representative of China, Mr. Magaña representative of El Salvador, and Mr. Singh, representative of India, together with six members of the secretariat, including two Korean interpreters. Two representatives of the Korean Government, Dr.

---

[63] A/AC.26/1.
[64] A/AC.26/11; A/AC.26/SR.22, pages 4-5.

Chyung Kyoo Hong, Director of the Office of General Affairs, and Mr. Chang Ku Yung, member of the Liaison Committee, and one American Liaison Officer, Mr. John Gardiner, accompanied the party.

The group left Seoul in a special train early on the morning of 25 April. It visited Kurye, Soon Chun, Yosu, Kwangju, Hwasun and Chonju in accordance with its original schedule. It spent two nights on the train and one night in Kwangju, and returned to Seoul late on the evening of the 28 of April.

11. The first area to be inspected was Kurye in Cholla Namdo. It is about eight hours by train from Seoul and located at the foot of the Chiri Mountains, where the guerrillas took refuge.

Following a short reception, the party drove through the town and neighbouring villages to the base of the Chiri Mountains.

The population of the county of Kurye was estimated at over 60,000, and that of the town itself at about 14,000. The first major raid by the rebels on Kurye took place on 26 October 1948 and the second was made by over 300 rebels on 19 November. The group was told that there had been a great deal of looting during the raids; some signs of destruction were still visible. The Buddhist Temple which the party visited, built in the fifth century A.D. and located on the hillside, had been raided, and occupied for a short time, twice by guerrillas, once in December 1948, and again in January 1949. The entire population of the village on the hill near the temple fled during the raids and had not returned when the observation party was there.

According to official statistics, 900 inhabitants were either killed or missing and over 3,000 houses were destroyed in the county of Kurye from the time of the uprising to March 1949. In terms of *won*, the destruction amounted to almost 500,000,000. Over 2,000 families were in need of relief.

After the tour of Kurye, the group proceeded to Soon Chun. In order to take every possible measure for the safety of the members of the Commission, the Korean authorities advised that the group should travel only by day in this region. The party, therefore, spent the night on the train in the station at Soon Chun.

12. On the morning of 26 April, the group proceeded to Yosu, a fishing centre, an important port and naval base during Japanese domination, and the spring-board for the October revolt. The county of Yosu has an estimated population of over 160,000, and the inhabitants of the city itself number over 60,000. As in Kurye, thousands of the townspeople lined up on the streets to greet the members of the Commission when they entered. After an official reception and a tour of the city by automobile, the party scattered to see the devastation caused by the rebels at closer range. Yosu was occupied by the rebels for three days before national troops dislodged them. When the defeated rebels fled to the nearby islands, many young people followed them. According to reports obtained on the spot, the missionaries in Yosu succeeded in arranging an amnesty and consequently a large number of these young people returned to the city. The ruins in the city of Yosu were widespread. Entire

blocks had been razed to the ground and hastily constructed tents and shacks were scattered in different sections of the city. It was very apparent that many people were living in dire conditions. According to official statistics, the persons killed or missing in Yosu county from the uprising to March 1949 numbered over 1,000 and nearly 3,000 homes were destroyed. The destruction was estimated to amount to over 6 billion *won*, and the number of families in need of relief was put at over 2,000.

13. Having visited Yosu, the group returned to Soon Chun to observe general conditions there.

When the train had stopped overnight in Soon Chun station, the first night of the trip, the Chairman of the Sub-Committee and three members of the secretariat, including the secretary of Sub-Committee II, walked into town from the station in order to see it and to gather information from the local residents unobtrusively.

The county of Soon Chun has an estimated population of over 170,000 and the town of Soon Chun has nearly 50,000 inhabitants. It was occupied by the rebels at the time of the insurrection for about a week before national troops drove them out on 27 October. The fighting and killing there, during that period, was more severe than at Yosu, but the destruction seemed less visible. As a result of the uprising and subsequent disturbances, nearly 2,500 persons were killed or missing and about an equal number of homes were destroyed according to official statistics. In terms of *won*, the value of the destruction was placed at over 1,700,000. It was estimated that over 4,200 families were in need of relief.

At the official reception given to the group at the Girls' Middle School, speeches of welcome by the mayor and student representatives and speeches by the Chairman of the Commission and the Chairman of the Sub-Committee in response were delivered. Then the students entertained the group with a programme of songs and dances. There was also an exhibit of student art and craft work. All this illustrated the rich culture of Korea and the development of education.

14. After the visit to Soon Chun, the group proceeded to Kwangju, capital of the province of Cholla Namdo, which has a population of 100,000. There the members spent the night at the Korean hotel and in army billets. Early the following morning the party gathered at the provincial government building to meet with leading dignitaries and the Press, before making a tour through the city to see hospitals, schools and factories. The group visited first the medical school—with a student body of about 300—college hospital and medical library, and then a large high school for girls. All school buildings in Kwangju appeared to be well constructed and equipped, and it was apparent that stress was laid upon medical education and physical culture.

The Chonnam Spinning Mills—one of the important vested properties operated now by the Government—which the party visited, manufactures 40,000 roles of cotton sheeting monthly. Most of the machinery is of Japanese origin, installed during their domination. There are over 1,000 looms operated by 3,400 workers. The mill is dependent upon the ECA for raw cotton.

At the conclusion of its visit to the factory, the group proceeded to the auditorium of the

Agricultural Vocational School for an official reception. A colourful programme of songs and formal dances was presented by the students and speeches of welcome and response were delivered.

15. On its way back to Soon Chun, the group stopped over a few hours to inspect the Hwasun coal mine, located about half way between Kwangju and Soon Chun. This coal mine was reorganized in 1934 by the Japanese, who consolidated several pits. When Japan surrendered, the Koreans, in August 1945, organized a self-governing committee to continue the operation of the mine. In 1946 it was put under the control of the Military Government. It was said that in 1946 many clashes occurred among the workers. After the establishment of the Government of the Republic of Korea, the Hwasun coal mine came under the direct control of the Department of Commerce and Industry. The deposits of this mine are estimated at about 9 million tons and it produces approximately 15,000 tons per month, roughly 20 per cent of the coal needed in South Korea. At present the mine employs about 2,300 men; 20 to 30 per cent of the miners came from the north. Production has been hampered by lack of power and modern equipment. For efficient production, the mine would require electric power of 400 kilowatts. Since the current has been cut off by North Korea, it has to generate its own power but it can only generate about one third of the electricity it requires.

16. The group spent another night on the train in Soon Chun Station. On its way back to Seoul it stopped at Chonju, capital of Cholla Pukto, in order to gather an impression of Cholla Namdo's neighbouring province. An informal reception was given to the party at the provincial government building and the local Press interviewed the delegates. Afterwards the party visited a tobacco factory, which produces cigarettes under the control of the Monopoly Bureau of the Department of Finance. This factory employs 1,000 workers and produces 7 million cigarettes and 6,000 kilogrammes of tobacco daily. A visit to a silk mill, established by the Japanese twenty-seven years ago, was also included in the itinerary.

Chonju appeared to be more prosperous than any other city visited in the Cholla provinces. According to the Vice-Governor, the communists were active in Cholla Pukto after the liberation; however, the situation has now improved greatly and there have been no serious disturbances lately.

17. From this brief visit to the troubled areas, a few conclusions can be drawn. The revolt in Yosu and Soon Chun appears to have been a locally well-planned uprising, judging by its swiftness and the organized way in which control of the cities was taken. The rebels first captured ammunition dumps and then took over police headquarters and administrative and financial services. They organized the People's Committee with the help of local citizens. It was said that they committed all kinds of cruel acts, including plundering, killing and arson. While the uprising was directed by the leaders of the South Korea Labour Party, not all the participants were its members. According to an investigation by eleven religious organizations, conflicts between the national army and the police had some influence on the riots in Cholla Namdo. It should be stated that the causes of the revolt were manifold.

Contrary to certain reports in the metropolitan Press, peace and order in these troubled areas have been restored. However, the task of rehabilitation is tremendous, since it involves over 16,000 families, totalling 87,000 people in all the troubled areas of Cholla Namdo. It was estimated that nearly two thousand million *won* was needed for rehabilitation.

Trip to Cheju Do

18. For the purpose of studying the general conditions, and at the same time being present at the elections in North Cheju Gun on 10 May 1949, the Sub-Committee organized a second major observation trip, to Cheju Island, situated about thirty miles from the tip of the peninsula. This island, over 120 square miles in area, known also as Quelpart, became a part of Korea some 900 years ago. Located south of Korea Strait and half way between South Japan and the northern coast of China, Cheju Island's strategic importance is evident and it was an important Japanese military base during the Second World War. The latest estimate of its population is placed at nearly 300,000, with about 30,000 living in its capital, Cheju City. The principal occupations of the inhabitants of the island are agriculture, fishing and the raising of livestock. The people are noticeably industrious and self-reliant. However, because of its insular position and the consequent lack of cultural exchange with the outside world, the local system of economy and indigenous culture are prominent and strong provincialism is apparent.

19. Following liberation from Japanese domination, Peoples' Committees were set up on Cheju Island, presumably under the influence of the communist leaders. It was said that the belated arrival of United States troops and inefficient administration on the island during the Military Government gave an opportunity to the communists to attempt to dominate the whole territory. Belated strict measures to curb communist activities led to open defiance of the Government authorities on 3 April 1948. Disturbances became more widespread and violent during the registration for the 10 May elections and on Election Day itself. Since less than 50 per cent of the registered voters cast their ballots, the elections in North Cheju Gun were invalidated. Disturbances continued in many areas and the major activities of the rebels were not crushed until April 1949, a few weeks before the Sub-Committee went there.

20. The group, consisting of Mr. Costilhes, representative of France, Mr. Singh, representative of India, and six members of the secretariat, including two Korean interpreters, and accompanied by Chang Kee Yung, a member of the Liaison Committee, left Seoul on a transport plane on the morning of 8 May. The representatives of China and the Philippines had been recalled by their Governments for consultations and were not able to participate. The Chinese alternate representative, who had joined the group in its unsuccessful attempt to land on Cheju in April, could not participate because of his health. Due to bad weather, the party could not return by air on 12 May as scheduled. Instead, it came back by water and rail and reached Seoul on 14 May.

Upon arrival at Cheju Airport, the group was greeted by the Governor, the Army Commander, the Police Chief and other officials and a cheering crowd. The Governor's residence became the living quarters for the group. In the late afternoon a large mass meeting was held in the main square of the city to welcome the members of the Commission, and was followed by a public dinner. The Governor and the representative of the Women's Patriotic Association delivered welcoming addresses and the representatives of both France and India responded.

On the morning of 9 May, the observation group divided into two groups for the purpose of observing the elections and general conditions in various areas.

Group One

21. In order to observe the elections in Cheju City and its neighbouring areas, and to observe conditions around this city, Group One, headed by the representative of India with three members of the secretariat, remained in Cheju City.

On the day preceding the election, Group One visited the island of Chuja, an important fishing centre, with a population of 4,800. The members of the group were told by the mayor and some of the inhabitants, of the people's fervent desire for unification. In this connexion they emphasized the urgent demand for and acute shortage of carbide for night fishing, which is important to the livelihood of the populace. Three hundred drums of carbide a year are needed. The main source of carbide, however, is north of the 38th parallel, and due to the division of Korea, this supply has been severely limited.

22. On Election Day, Group One, accompanied by the Governor and the Chief of Police, made a tour of the polling stations in and around the capital. There were eleven such booths in electoral district A and they were open from 7 a.m. to 4 p.m. The populace seemed to be taking the election seriously; 60 per cent of the registered voters had visited the polls by noon. The voting took place in an orderly manner.

23. The following day, Group One visited an internment camp and the Cheju alcohol plant. At the former place, 2,000 prisoners were found to be living in an old warehouse. The women outnumbered the men by roughly three to one and there were many babies in arms and young children. These people had been in hiding in the hills with the rebels. According to the director of the camp, 90 per cent of the prisoners had surrendered and the remainder had been captured by the Korean Army. Questions were addressed to a group of rebels who had been captured just a few days previously. Two persons gave the reasons why they had joined the rebels. A young boy said that he had joined the South Korea Labour Party under duress and without realizing what he was doing. Mr. Lee Doo Won, an outspoken individual over thirty years of age, said that, being dissatisfied with the conditions prevailing after the liberation, he became a member of the South Korea Labour Party in Inchon before he came to Cheju Do and joined the rebels in the mountains in June 1948. He emphatically stated that he was not a communist and that only his party could solve the Korean problem. Criticizing the police and the army, he said that

if those forces had sincerely worked for the welfare of the people and if the Government had genuinely advocated the complete sovereignty of Korea, then there would have been no rebellions against it. In answer to a question by the group, an aged prisoner told how he had found himself in a tragic situation, having to flee to the hills with the rebels after they had attacked his village. This might be the case with many of the other prisoners who had run away and subsequently returned.

The Cheju alcohol plant was constructed by the Japanese shortly before Pearl Harbor and at that time maintained a monthly output of about 1,000 *suk*. After the liberation, and upon the establishment of the Government of the Republic of Korea, the plant became a vested property and came under the control of the Department of Commerce and Industry. Production had decreased due to the shortage of coal and skilled technicians, and is only about 50 per cent of the pre-war figure at present. The basic raw material used in the making of alcohol is the sweet potato, grown on the island, but the plant has been faced with a shortage of its coal supply, which originally came from North Korea. In addition to the manufacture of alcohol, this plant produced about two-thirds of the electric current consumed in Cheju City. The manager of the plant told the group that if the unification of North and South Korea could be achieved, the plant would be able to secure an adequate supply of high quality coal and could produce more electricity.

In order to gather further information on the operation of the Korean Army in Cheju, Group One visited Colonel Yu's staff headquarters and his operations headquarters in the mountains. Colonel Yu, who had been sent down from Seoul in March 1949 to complete the "mop-up" operation and returned later to Seoul with the members of the Commission, stated that, during the period 25 March to 12 April, the casualties of the rebels were 2,345 and the Army captured 3,600. The total loss of the civilian population during this period was 1,668. Asked whether the basic causes of communism had been eliminated in Cheju Do, Colonel Yu said that he was unable to give a reliable answer. However, he observed that if the insurgents who had now repented and surrendered were left with nothing to do the way might be paved for further trouble. Although he realized the grave financial difficulties facing the infant Republic, Colonel Yu nevertheless emphasized the responsibility of the Government in the work of rehabilitation.

24. Before the group returned to Seoul, the election results in North Cheju Gun were announced. According to these returns, 97 per cent of the registered voters went to the polls in district A, and in district B 99 per cent of the registered voters cast their ballots. There were seven candidates in each district. Mr. Hong Sun Yong, a member of the *Kook Min Whei*,[65] representative-elect of district A and Mr. Yang Pyung Chik, former member of the Korean Independence Party, representative-elect of district B, ran as independents. Both Messrs. Hong and Yang, who were born in Cheju Do and have lived

[65] Nationalist Society, affiliated with the National Association for the Rapid Realization of Korean Independence, headed by President Rhee.

there all their lives, came to visit the members of the Commission on the evening of 12 May. Mr. Hong, a college graduate and the principal of the Girls' School in Cheju City for over ten years, emphasized the major problem of rehabilitation. He pointed out that, due to the riots, the impossibility of farming in many areas, the burning down of a large quantity of barley and the lack of fertilizer, which came mostly from the north, there was a great shortage of food on the island. Unless 60,000 *suk* of rice could be brought to the island to feed the needy, many people would face starvation before the October harvest. Mr. Yang, who has been interested in the youth movement and local affairs, claimed that he belonged to no political party at present. He said the communists had been active before the riots in April. Due to the nervousness of the police, many villages and houses were left unguarded when the raids commenced. The rebels compelled people to follow them to the mountains and, in most cases, the whole family chose to accompany the father, fearing arrest by the police. He thought that although people respected the police, some of them were secretly helping the rebels. He believed that while there was comparative safety on the island, there were still over 500 rebels hiding in the mountains. He emphasized the responsibility of the Government in the reconstruction of Cheju Do and the importance of revising and developing the educational system as a preventive measure against communism.

Group Two

25. In accordance with the decision of the Sub-Committee, its Chairman, secretary and two other members of the secretariat constituting Group Two of the visiting party to Cheju Do, traveled by jeep around the circumference of the island.

In spite of repeated requests to the Minister of Internal Affairs and the local authorities in Cheju for only a minimum of police escort and for dispensing with official receptions, Group Two was heralded by a truckload of police and followed by a jeep carrying the police escort agreed upon. Whenever the group approached a village, it was greeted by seemingly all the inhabitants of that place, lined up along the road, waving flags and cheering. The gates of all the villages were decorated with identical posters of welcome and slogans regarding the unification of Korea. Policemen, alternating with spear-carrying guards, were posted all along the roads. The enthusiasm and hospitality of the Korean officials and the detailed security measures made it difficult for the group to have complete freedom of movement and a flexible itinerary.

At Aewol Li, a small port about thirty miles from Cheju City, the group made its first stop in order to wait for a stalled police jeep. The opportunity was used to visit the harbour and local polling centre. The party was greeted by the Chairman of the Election Committee, and reminiscences about last year's elections as well as information concerning the present elections were exchanged.

In the early afternoon, the group reached Mosul Po, which has a good harbour and a large airdrome built by the Japanese. The Mayor, Chief of Police and other dignitaries entertained the group at a luncheon party. The plight of this

town and the possibility of developing it into a trading centre were the two points stressed by the Korean officials in their conversations with the members of the group.

On its way to Sogwi Po, located roughly in the centre of the south coast of Cheju Island, the group observed an increasing number of partially destroyed villages, some of which were totally burned down and abandoned. All inhabited places are now enclosed by protecting walls made of the loosely piled up volcanic rocks and stones for which Cheju Island is known. The gates are guarded and closed at night. The most striking feature was the village of Kang Jung Ni, in which every house had been burned to the ground and the rebuilding had been undertaken by old and young of both sexes.

The party arrived at Sogwi Po before dusk and, because of the poor accommodations in the hotel and at the insistence of the *gun* chief, the party was quartered in his house for the two nights it was in that area. The first evening, the members attended a dinner and reception at which all the local officials and prominent citizens were present. The *gun* chief delivered a welcoming speech and Mr. Costilhes responded on behalf of the group.

26. The following morning the party devoted most of its time to a trip in the Sogwi Po area. According to the *gun* chief, the city of Sogwi 'Po suffered its first attack by the rebels in October 1948 and again in November 1948. During the fighting, 190 houses were burned down; the ruins are still to be seen. The casualties among civilians, police and rebels amounted to several hundred. First the group visited an internment camp. Men, women and children, a few hundred of them, were crowded into two separate small houses: in one were those already screened; in the second those still under examination.

The party drove some miles inland to a more mountainous region in order to visit a number of villages. The pattern of the previous day's journey was repeated, the people everywhere were gathered for the usual mass welcome. Hahya Ri, most prosperous village of this area, situated on the dividing line between seaboard and mountains, had remained immune to rebel attacks. The group visited the school, the most prominent structure in the community, as is the case in most of the villages. In greeting the party, the principal of the school took pride in pointing out that not one of his teachers had joined the rebels or become one of their ringleaders, as had been the case in many other places.

On its way back to Sogwi Po, the group stopped to watch a large number of women divers—about 100 of them—diving for seafood and seaweeds. Both of these are important products in the economy of Cheju Island.

27. On its return trip to Cheju City, on 11 May, the party stopped at Song San Ni, formerly a Japanese naval base. It visited what had been the Japanese ammunition dump along the coast and inspected a canning factory in operation and an iodine plant now shut down due to the shortage of materials and technicians. The chief of the district, in discussing local conditions, presented a gloomy picture of the prevailing scarcity of food there and throughout the whole island. A second stop was made at Tong

Hong Ni, on the northern coast about thirty miles from Cheju City, a town which had been completely destroyed on 5 January. The destruction of villages on the north-eastern and central southern coasts seems to have been greater than in any other part of the island. All the way from Segwi Po, the party was greeted by cheering crowds whenever it entered or passed through a village. In the afternoon the party reached Cheju City and rejoined Group One.

Causes and effects of the riots on Cheju Do

28. Only a first hand observation of the destruction and ruin conveys an adequate picture of the magnitude of the problem of rehabilitation confronting the Government. The impression of the entire group was deepened by the official figures on the destruction caused by the rebels. There were no statistics on the casualties and property damage from 25 March to 12 May 1949. During this period, the Army intensified its programme of pacification. Up to 25 March, the total civilian casualty list, excluding the rebels, reached over 3,560. Houses, together with their furniture, either completely destroyed or damaged, numbered 33,489. The value of this destruction was placed at over 1,000 million *won*. The loss in livestock due to the uprising was equally great; over some 46,000 head of cattle, horses, hogs and sheep, valued at over 1,000 million *won*. The year of disturbances on Cheju Island reduced the number of its primary schools from ninety-six to fifty-one and the enrolment from 35,701 to 27,205. Two of the eleven middle schools were completely burned down and the enrolment in the middle schools dropped from 3,359 to 3,258. Seventeen teachers joined and led the rioters and over 283 students followed them. It will require more than 55 million *won* to restore the schools to their original condition.

29. The primary causes for the riots and disturbances on Cheju Do are manifold. The following reasons are generally accepted as important:

(*a*) Because of the strategic, as well as the remote, location of Cheju Island, the South Korea Labour Party chose to concentrate its activities there following liberation;

(*b*) Poor economic conditions on the island provided a breeding place for the political activities of extremists;

(*c*) Lack of close contact with the mainland resulted in strong provincialism, which in turn fostered dissension against the Government and caused disorder;

(*d*) Undiscriminatory measures applied by the authorities to punish the people who fled with the rebels either of their own volition or under compulsion, gave rebel leaders the opportunity to gather larger forces against the Government.

30. The trouble started when the North-west Youth Group made its appearance on Cheju Do and co-operated with the police in searching for communists and communist suspects. In doing so, members of the North-west Youth Group overstepped their authority. It was said that communists and communist suspects had been subjected to severe beatings by them.

Fighting and destruction in the villages followed more or less the same pattern; first it was a struggle between the rebels and the police, and gradually the Army as well as the population was drawn into it. The people joined the rebels either under duress or in order to escape reprisals and punitive action by the authorities. Destruction was caused and cruelty exhibited by both sides.

31. The trip to Cheju Do provided the members of the Commission with evidence that the villages which had been burned or deserted were in the process of being rebuilt, and that conditions in those places had gradually become normal again. The tremendous problem of rehabilitation had to be seen in order to be realized and appreciated.

Evaluation of the observation trips

32. By visiting the two main areas of recent disturbances, the Commission not only had an opportunity to see at first hand the seriousness of the destruction and the urgency of the problem of rehabilitation and the extent to which the foundation of the Government has been affected by the riots, but also had a good chance to study the degree to which the division of Korea by the 38th parallel has affected the recovery of industries and the livelihood of the people.

33. The presence of the Commission in those areas far from Seoul helped to spread the idea of the United Nations among the common people and to enable them to understand and appreciate the work of the United Nations in general and the task of the Commission in particular.

34. The members of the Commission who participated in the observation trips were impressed by the zeal of the large crowds gathered along roads and streets to greet and cheer them. The Korean authorities did their best in arranging transportation and accommodation for the groups, and the members of the Commission encountered no difficulties in their travels. The pattern of the receptions by local authorities and people indicated plainly the existence of a centralized administration and its relatively efficient operation.

35. The observation group verified that peace and order had been restored in the disturbed areas, and that life in the villages and towns had returned to normal. The small number of rebels still hiding in the mountains constitutes no immediate and serious menace to the security of the two provinces and no challenge to governmental authority.

36. A well planned programme of rehabilitation, to be carried out by an efficient local administration and greater opportunity for the people to take part in the government, should eliminate most of the causes for a repetition of such riots.

37. In all the places visited by the observation groups, the people uniformly expressed their urgent desire for the unification of Korea and their great reliance on the Commission for bringing about that unification.

B. Korean Press Law (A/AC.26/W.14)

Promulgated in 1907
(Korean Régime, Kwang-mu, 11th year)

Revised in 1909
(Korean Régime, Ryung-hui, 2nd year)

Article 1

Any person desiring to publish a newspaper shall first obtain permission for its publication by presenting an application to the Minister of Home Affairs through the Provincial Governor, in Seoul, through the Director of the Police Bureau.

Article 2

In the said application the following information shall be given:

(1) Name of paper;

(2) Classification of items to be printed;

(3) Date of publication;

(4) Offices of publication and printing;

(5) Names, residence and age of publisher, editor and printer.

Article 3

No one except males above the age of 20, and resident in Korea, shall be eligible as publisher, editor, or printer of such paper.

Article 4

A publisher shall deposit a sum of 300 yen as security at the time of sending in the application to the Bureau of Home Affairs.

Payment of deposit required can be made by a bank certificate of deposit.

Article 5

A newspaper printing items relating to prices of goods and articles on science and art only shall be exempt from security deposit.

Article 6

Permission shall first be obtained in case of making change in items 1, 2 and 5 of article 2. Change in other items shall be reported within a week of being made. In case of the death of a publisher, editor, or printer, or the loss by any one of them of the qualifications described under article 3, application shall be made for permission to appoint a lawful successor within a week following such event, but publication may be continued by appointing a temporary successor pending decision on the application.

Article 7

In case of temporary suspension of publication, report shall be made as to its duration, but such suspension shall not continue for more than one year.

Article 8

Application and reports regarding the two previous articles shall be forwarded as in article 1.

Article 9

In cases of non-publication within two months of the date of permission being granted, the license is thereby cancelled; so too in the case of non-issue of publication the day after the expiring of the term granted for temporary suspension.

Article 10

Two copies of each issue of a newspaper shall be forwarded prior to circulation to both the Bureau of Home Affairs and the District Office.

Article 11

The publication is prohibited of any article reflecting on the dignity of the Royal Family, contravening the national constitution, or destructive of international friendship.

Article 12

Publication is prohibited of any article regarding confidential proceedings of official meetings and confidential documents, details, or abstracts. This clause also applies to those special matters prohibited publication.

Article 13

Publication is prohibited of those articles favouring an offender or protecting or praising the accused or the prisoner.

Article 14

Publication is prohibited of judicial cases awaiting trial or of those cases debarred a public hearing.

Article 15

It is prohibited to print fictitious articles of a defamatory nature.

Article 16

It is prohibited to pay or to receive compensation for publishing a certain item, or for correcting or withdrawing an item or not.

Article 17

Publication shall bear on every issue the name of the paper, date of issue, publishing office, printing office, and name of publisher, editor and printer.

Article 18

In case of a newspaper undergoing trial on account of any article appearing in it, the sentence pronounced by the Court shall appear in its entirety in the issue of that paper following the day of pronouncement.

Article 19

In case of items reproduced from the *Official Gazette*, should errata have been made in the original and later corrected, the corrections shall appear in the paper reproducing the items in its following issue.

Article 20

In case request is made for correction of any article or for publication of a correction or refutation by any person involved in the matter published, it shall appear in the following issue of the paper concerned.

In case of a letter of correction or refutation exceeding the original article by more than twice its length, matter in excess may be charged for at the same rate as that charged for ordinary advertisements.

Requests framed in language and ideas prohibited by the Press Law and not bearing the name and address of the writer may be refused.

Article 21

The Minister of Home Affairs may prohibit the circulation of a newspaper, confiscate any issue of it, or order temporary or permanent suspension of a paper should he find its contents prejudicial to the peace and order of the country or to the morale of society.

Article 22

The sum deposited as security shall be returned should a paper suspend issue, forfeit its licence, or be prohibited publication.

Article 23

The sum deposited as security shall be used to meet the expenses of the trial or to discharge a fine inflicted remaining unpaid for one week following the day judgment is pronounced; in case the amount deposited is not sufficient to meet such expenses or fine, the balance shall be collected in accordance with the Act for Enforced Payment as in criminal cases.

Article 24

In case of Court expenses or a fine being met by the deposit made the publisher shall supplement the deposit within a week from the day notice has been given, and publication of the paper shall be discontinued until the deficit in deposit has been made good.

Article 25

In case of an offence against article 11, the publisher, editor and printer shall be liable to imprisonment for a period not exceeding three years, and the machinery used in committing the offence shall be confiscated.

Article 26

The publisher and editor of a paper committing an offence against the public peace and order or morality shall be liable to imprisonment for a period not exceeding 10 months, or a fine of 50 to 300 yen.

Article 27

In case of offences against article 12 and article 16, the editor of the paper shall be liable to imprisonment for a period not exceeding 10 months, or a fine of 50 to 300 yen.

Article 28

In case of an offence against an order given under article 21, the publisher, editor and printer shall be liable to a fine of 50 to 300 yen.

Article 29

In case of an offence against articles 13 and 14, the editor shall be liable to a fine of 20 to 200 yen.

Article 30

In case a newspaper is published without first obtaining permission as required by article 1, or continues publication contrary to article 23, or not having deposited security prints articles other than those specified in article 5, the publisher shall be liable to a fine of 40 to 100 yen.

Article 31

In case of an offence against articles 18, 19 and 20 (1) the editor shall be liable to a fine of 10 to 100 yen.

Article 32

In case of an offence against articles 3, 6, 10 and 17, the publisher shall be liable to a fine of 10 to 50 yen.

Article 33

In case of an offence against article 15, it shall be considered one of fraud and come under the criminal law provided an appeal has been made by the injured party or by a party specially interested in matter.

Article 34

Newspapers published in foreign countries in the Korean language, in Chinese, or in mixed script, coming in to Korea, or published in Korea by foreigners, may be prohibited circulation or confiscated by the Minister of Home Affairs should their contents be deemed prejudicial to public peace and order or to public morality.

Article 35

Any Korean subject offending against article 34 shall be liable to a fine not exceeding 300 yen.

Article 36

Any Korean knowingly circulating or forwarding a paper prohibited distribution under article 34 shall be liable to a fine not exceeding 50 yen.

Article 37

In the case of those articles rendering the editor liable to punishment being signed by another person, he, too, shall be held equally responsible with the editor.

Article 38

This law shall not apply to offenders against it mitigating their acts by self-surrender, or to those punishable on more than two counts, or for bribery.

Supplementary Law

Article 39

The regulations of this law apply correspondingly to printed matter of every description whatsoever.

Article 40

This law shall be in force from the day of promulgation.

Article 41

Any newspaper published previous to the promulgation of this law shall bring itself into conformity with the regulations of this law within two months following the day of promulgation.

제3부 주엔한국위원단 보고서(1949)

Note: Lee Chul Wun (Dr. Clarence Rhee), the new Director of the Office of Public Information, made the following statement to the Assembly on the occasion of the assumption of his new office, 14 June 1949:

"I want to express my sincere gratitude for the kindness you showed me during my office as Secretary-General (of the National Assembly), and as the new Director of the Office of Public Information I solicit your closest co-operation and intelligent enlightenment.

"Now our Republic faces a most critical moment. I, as Director of the Office of Public Information, will not spare any effort in attempting to solve the problems before me. This can only be done by the unified effort of both officials and citizens. I believe the primary duty of the Director of the Office of Public Information is to convey the will of the Government thoroughly to the people and thus to enable the people to understand and support the Government. This in itself will pave the way to the whole nation to overcome its difficulties.

"Speaking of the freedom of speech, the Office of Public Information is supposed to be concerned with helping the freedom of speech of the people toward a sound and constructive trend. It is not supposed to suppress the freedom of speech. However, there must be a certain limit beyond which no published remark or speech should go. I shall not allow any such vicious, distorted, false or agitative speeches under any circumstances. I will leave the door wide open for constructive criticism.

"I hope you will give me advice any time, and I shall be very grateful for it. Please do not feel that I have left you. I am hoping to make the office a good agent for both the Government and the National Assembly.

"Speaking of the Kwang Moo newspaper law, I will not use this law any more."

C. National Security Law (Law No. 10 of 1 December 1948) (A/AC.26/W.15)

Article I

Those who betray the Constitution by posing as a government, and those who, in collusion with the betrayers, seek to consolidate or group together with the object of disturbing the tranquility of the State, shall be punished in accordance with the following provisions:

1. Leaders and officers of the organizations or groups shall be sentenced to life imprisonment or hard labour for life, or to no less than three years imprisonment or hard labour.

2. Those who played leading roles shall be sentenced to imprisonment or hard labour for from one to ten years.

3. Those who, with knowledge of the hostile nature of any organizations or groups, have joined the same or taken part in their activities shall be punished with imprisonment for not more than three years.

Article II

Those who group themselves or form an organization with the aim of murder or of incendiary action and destruction of communication or transportation facilities, together with the officers of the said organization, shall be punished by imprisonment for not more than ten years, and those affiliated with such organization shall be punished by imprisonment for not more than three years.

Though the original object of the organization or group is not criminal in intent, if members of such organizations or groups commit murder, arson, or destruction collectively on the instructions, or with the knowledge of the officers of the organization or group, the latter may be dissolved by the President.

Article III

Those persons who deliberately incite or indulge in propaganda to attain the aims of the organizations or groups mentioned in the two previous articles shall be punished with imprisonment or hard labour for not more than ten years.

Article IV

Those who of their own free will and with knowledge of the hostile nature of such organizations and groups deliberately give weapons, money, supplies, promises, and other things for the purpose of inducing anyone to violate this law shall be punished by hard labour for not more than seven years.

Article V

Those who have committed a crime as specified in this law, but have confessed voluntarily shall have their punishment mitigated or shall be entirely exonerated.

Article VI

Those who bear false witness or give false testimony or abuse their official position with intent to distort the facts concerning the crimes enumerated above shall be punished in accordance with the laws governing such offences.

Addendum

This law shall be effective from the date of its promulgation.

33

Annex III

TEXTS OF MAIN DOCUMENTS CONCERNING THE WITHDRAWAL OF THE UNITED STATES MILITARY FORCES IN KOREA AND THE ESTABLISHMENT OF THE KOREAN MILITARY ADVISORY GROUP

A: Reports of Sub-Committee III

1. FIRST PROGRESS REPORT OF SUB-COMMITTEE III AND APPENDICES (A/AC.26/SC.4/2)

(1) *Observation and verification of the withdrawal from Korea of United States occupation forces*

In accordance with paragraph 2 of the resolution of the Commission of 20 June 1949, Sub-Committee III has engaged in the observation and verification of the withdrawal of United States occupation forces from Korea. It has witnessed the last scheduled embarkations of United States troops at the port of Inchon, 21 June and 29 June. Except for some military personnel still stationed at Kimpo Airport, but soon to be withdrawn, all United States occupation forces appear now to have been withdrawn from Korea. The officers and men comprised in the Korean Military Advisory Group are stated not to fall in the category of occupation forces.

The Sub-Committee is now engaged in verifying the fact of withdrawal of United States occupation forces. In that connexion, it has taken the following steps:

(a) Under date of 23 June 1949, the Sub-Committee addressed to the Ambassador of the United States and the Minister of Foreign Affairs of the Republic of Korea requests for information required to enable it to verify the fact of withdrawal. The requests for information correspond to information requirements set forth in the report of Sub-Committee III of 16 June 1949[66] approved by the Commission on 20 June 1949. The texts of these requests are annexed (appendices (a) and (b))

(b) The Sub-Committee is presently engaged in visiting the sites of former major military establishments where United States occupation forces had been stationed. It has already visited the Camp Sobingo and Ascom City-Inchon areas. Visits to Pusan and Kwang-ju will conclude this aspect of its work.

(2) *Observation and verification of the withdrawal from Korea of the occupation forces of the Union of Soviet Socialist Republics*

Sub-Committee III has considered the question of the application of the Commission's resolution of 20 June 1949 to the occupation forces of the Union of Soviet Socialist Republics. In discussions at the 3rd, 4th and 5th meetings of the Sub-Committee, it was agreed to recommend to the Commission the employment of the following procedure for this purpose: transmission to the Secretary-General of the United Nations, over the signature of the Chairman of the Commission, of a request to convey to the Government of the Union of Soviet Socialist Republics the information contained in the attached *aide-mémoire* (appendix (c)).

[66] A/AC.26/SC.4/1

APPENDICES

(a) LETTER TO THE AMBASSADOR OF THE UNITED STATES OF AMERICA FROM THE CHAIRMAN OF SUB-COMMITTEE III

Seoul, 23 June 1949

I have the honour to transmit herewith the text of a resolution concerning the observation and verification of the withdrawal of occupation forces from Korea, adopted by the Commission at its 35th meeting on 20 June 1949. You will observe from a reading of the second paragraph of the resolution in question that the Commission has charged Sub-Committee III, of which I am Chairman, with the actual task of observation and verification of the withdrawal of occupation forces.

Sub-Committee III has studied and reported to the Commission on the question of the information which will be required in order to permit observation and verification of the withdrawal of the occupation forces of the United States now in progress. That report has been approved by the Commission.

The following is the information which the Sub-Committee seeks to obtain:

A. *Matériel*

In respect of *matériel*, the task of the Commission will be to ascertain whether military equipment subject to the control of the United States is being retained in Korea. In view of the short interval of time remaining before completion of withdrawal operations of the United States, only verification and not observation of this aspect of the withdrawal will be possible.

It is believed that a verification sufficient to enable the Commission to report, on information and belief, that military *matérial* of the United States occupation forces had been withdrawn from Korea and that, as to the remaining *matériel*, the United States had divested itself of control, can be made on the basis of the following information: a statement, supported by documentary evidence such as inventories, military orders, bills of lading, and evidences of transfer of title from the United States to the Republic of Korea for the period 1 January 1949 to the completion of withdrawal, of stocks on hand, in-shipments, out-shipments, and transfers to the Korean security forces of the numbers and quantities of *matériel* broken down by military and non-military types.

The Sub-Committee, accordingly, requests that the foregoing information be furnished by the Government of the United States. A request for information concerning transfers of United States *matériel* to the Korean security forces is being addressed simultaneously to the Government of the Republic of Korea.

The Sub-Committee is aware that considerations of military security must be taken into account in determining the procedures governing the disclosure, transmission and publication of the required information. For that reason, it is suggested that there be an exchange of views concerning means of making a complete dis-

520

closure, while meeting the necessary security requirements at the same time.

B. *Personnel*

The Sub-Committee will observe such out-shipments of personnel of United States occupation forces as are still to take place. For purposes of verification, the Sub-Committee desires to have the following information: copies of the orders directing the out-movements of United States military personnel from 1 January 1949 to the completion of the withdrawal, together with the necessary rosters and such other evidence as will show definitive departure from Korea. As a further step toward verification of the withdrawal of military personnel, the Commission desires to visit the sites of the major military establishments where the occupation forces have been stationed after 1 January 1949 in order to determine that no occupation forces still remain there. Your assistance in providing facilities for such visits would be appreciated.

C. *Korean Military Advisory Group*

The Sub-Committee desires to have a detailed statement concerning the status of the Korean Military Advisory Group and its functions and powers, particularly in respect of any formal rights or *de facto* exercise of control over: (1) the disposition of *matériel* transferred to the Korean security forces; and (2) the activities of those forces themselves. In this connexion, the Sub-Committee would require copies of the agreement or agreements between the Government of the United States and the Government of the Republic of Korea affecting the status, functions, and powers of the Korean Military Advisory Group. A similiar request for information is being addressed to the Government of the Republic of Korea.

(Signed) A. B. JAMIESON,
Chairman, Sub-Committee III,
United Nations Commission on Korea

(*b*) LETTER TO THE MINISTER OF FOREIGN AFFAIRS OF THE REPUBLIC OF KOREA FROM THE CHAIRMAN OF SUB-COMMITTEE III

Seoul, 23 June 1949

I have the honour to transmit herewith the text of a resolution concerning the observation and verification of the withdrawal of occupation forces from Korea, adopted by the Commission at its 35th meeting on 20 June 1949. You will observe from a reading of the second paragraph of the resolution in question that the Commission has charged Sub-Committee III, of which I am Chairman, with the actual task of observation and verification of the withdrawal of occupation forces.

Sub-Committee III has studied and reported to the Commission on the question of the information which will be required in order to permit observation and verification of the withdrawal of the occupation forces of the United States now in progress. That report has been approved by the Commission.

The following is the information which the Sub-Committee seeks to obtain:

A. *Matériel*

In respect of *matériel*, the task of the Commission will be to ascertain whether military equipment subject to the control of the United States is being retained in Korea. In view of the short interval of time remaining before completion of the withdrawal operations of the United States only verification and not observation of this aspect of the withdrawal will be possible.

It is believed that a verification sufficient to enable the Commission to report, on information and belief, that military *matériel* of the United States occupation forces had been withdrawn from Korea and that, as to the remaining *matériel*, the United States had divested itself of control, can be made on the basis of the following information: a statement, supported by documentary evidence such as inventories, military orders, bills of lading, and evidences of transfers of title from the United States to the Republic of Korea for the period 1 January 1949 to the completion of withdrawal, of stocks on hand, in-shipments, out-shipments, and transfers to the Korean security forces of the numbers and quantities of *matériel* broken down by military and non-military types.

The Sub-Committee, accordingly, has addressed a request to the Government of the United States for the foregoing information. As a means of making independent verification of the information to be supplied by the United States concerning transfers of United States *matériel* to the Korean security forces, the Sub-Committee desires to obtain from the Government of the Republic of Korea a documented statement in the same terms as that requested from the Government of the United States concerning transfers of military *matériel* from the United States to the Korean security forces for the period 1 January 1949 to the date of completion of the withdrawal.

The Sub-Committee is aware that considerations of military security must be taken into account in determining the procedures governing the disclosure, transmission and publication of the required information. For that reason, it is suggested that there be an exchange of views concerning means of making a complete disclosure, while meeting the necessary security requirements at the same time.

B. *Korean Military Advisory Group*

The Sub-Committee desires to have from your Government a detailed statement concerning the status of the Korean Military Advisory Group and its functions and powers, particularly in respect of any formal rights or *de facto* exercise of control over: (1) the disposition of *matérial* transferred to the Korean security forces; and (2) the activities of those forces themselves. In this connexion, the Sub-Committee wishes to obtain from your Government copies of the agreement or agreements between the Government of the United States and the Government of the Republic of Korea affecting the status, functions and powers of the Korean Military Advisory Group. A similar request for information is being addressed to the Government of the United States.

(Signed) A. B. JAMIESON,
Chairman, Sub-Committee III,
United Nations Commission on Korea

(c) COMMUNICATION TO THE SECRETARY-GENERAL OF THE UNITED NATIONS, FROM THE CHAIRMAN OF THE COMMISSION TOGETHER WITH AN AIDE-MEMOIRE

Seoul, June 1949

On the instructions of the United Nations Commission on Korea, I have the honour to request you to convey the information contained in the attached *aide-mémoire* to the Government of the Union of Soviet Socialist Republics.

(Signed) Anup SINGH, *Chairman, United Nations Commission on Korea*

AIDE-MEMOIRE

The United Nations Commission on Korea, by resolution adopted at its 33rd meeting on 13 June 1949, established Sub-Committee III, charged it to examine and report to the Commission procedures to be employed in the observation and verification of the withdrawal of United States occupation forces from Korea. By resolution adopted at its 35th meeting on 20 June 1949, the Commission charged Sub-Committee III with the task of actual observation and verification of the withdrawal of occupation forces from Korea. The texts of both resolutions are attached.

In accordance with the directions contained in the resolution of 20 June 1949, Sub-Committee III has completed its observation of the withdrawal of United States occupation forces from Korea and is now engaged in a verification of the fact of such withdrawal.

Sub-Committee III now stands ready, in respect of the occupation forces of the Union of Soviet Socialist Republics, whenever proper facilities are afforded for the purpose, to carry out on behalf of the Commission the duties laid upon the latter by paragraph 4 *(d)* of the General Assembly resolution of 12 December 1948.

8. SECOND PROGRESS REPORT OF SUB-COMMITTEE III AND APPENDICES (A/AC.26/SC.4/13)

1. Since the date of the first progress report of Sub-Committee III, the Sub-Committee has been engaged in verification of the fact of withdrawal of United States occupation forces from Korea. In that connexion, it has taken the following steps in addition to those previously reported :

(a) One of its members, Captain F. Sánchez-Hernández, alternate representative of El Salvador, accompanied by three members of the secretariat, inspected the former United States military installations at Pusan from 9 to 10 July 1949 and verified that no United States military personnel remained there, except for a number of officers forming part of the Korean Military Advisory group and not considered to fall in the category of occupation forces. A visit to Kwang-ju was cancelled as it was considered to be unnecessary.

(b) As stated in the first progress report, similar visits of verification had already been made to the Camp Sobingo and Ascom City-Inchon areas.

(c) On 5 July 1949, a meeting took place between members of Sub-Committee III and the Ambassador of the United States of America for the purpose of an exchange of views on means of making a complete disclosure of information concerning transfer of United States military *matériel* to the Korean security forces, as suggested in the letter of 23 June to the Ambassador from the Chairman of the Sub-Committee. Other questions were also discussed. As a result of that exchange of views,[67] it was agreed that the Ambassador of the United States would furnish the Sub-Committee with the following :

(i) Information on the exact function and status of the Korean Military Advisory Group and a copy of any agreement to be concluded between the Governments of the United States and of the Republic of Korea relating thereto ;

(ii) A statement that troop withdrawal had been completed, together with a chart showing the stages of withdrawal ;

(iii) A statement that United States military occupation of Korea had ceased as of midnight on 30 June 1949.

On 21 July 1949, the Chairman addressed a request to the Ambassador of the United States for additional information on the following points :

(iv) The lapse of the right previously possessed by the Government of the United States to take control of the Korean Army in any specified area ;

(v) The authority under which the transfer of military *matériel* had been made to the Korean security forces before the completion of troop withdrawals and the authority under which such transfers would be made after that time ;

(vi) The arrangement under which United States Air Force personnel continued to be maintained at Kimpo Airport.

(d) The foregoing information has now been furnished to the Sub-Committee. It is contained in two communications to the Chairman of the Sub-Committee from the Ambassador of the United States under dates of 8 July 1949 (appendix *(a)* and 25 July 1949 (appendix *(b)*) and in a communication made on behalf of the Ambassador of the United States by Brigadier General W. L. Roberts, Chief, United States Military Advisory Group to the Republic of Korea, under date of 16 July 1949 (appendix *(c)*).

(e) The Sub-Committee has had no reply to its letter to the Minister of Foreign Affairs of the Republic of Korea on 23 June 1949 in which it requested information concerning the transfer of *matériel* from the United States to the Republic of Korea.

(f) The Sub-Committee met on 27 July 1949 to consider the findings to be reported to the Commission in respect of the verification of the withdrawal from Korea of the United States occupation forces.

2. The Sub-Committee has the honour to report to the Commission that it has completed its task in respect of verification of the withdrawal of United States occupation troops from Korea, and presents the following findings for approval :

---

[67] A/AC.26/SC.4/14.

As of 30 June 1949 the only United States troops remaining in Korea were some fifty Air Force personnel who will be stationed at Kimpo Airport until arrangements for civilian administration can be instituted, and the personnel of the Korean Military Advisory Group, which has an authorized strength of 500 men.

The Sub-Committee has not been able to verify the disposition made of United States military *matériel* in Korea because the information requested in this connexion has not been supplied to it. The Sub-Committee has not, however, considered that it was essential to press for such information. The Ambassador of the United States has adduced considerations of military security affecting the Republic of Korea which appear to the Sub-Committee to be cogent.

3. The Sub-Committee is satisfied, on the basis of its observations and of the information which it has obtained, that the following are the facts concerning the withdrawal of United States occupation forces from Korea.

(*a*) The withdrawal of the United States occupation forces in Korea was completed on 29 June 1949, with the exception of the fifty-odd Air Force personnel referred to above;

(*b*) With the lapse on 30 June 1949 of the executive agreement relating to interim military and security matters between the President of the Republic of Korea and the Commanding General, USAFIK, of 24 August 1948, the right of the Government of the United States and the authority of the Commanding General, USAFIK, to assume control of the Korean security forces lapsed and no such right or authority now exists in the Government of the United States or the Chief of the Korean Military Advisory Group;

(*c*) The United States Government no longer possesses or controls any military equipment in Korea except the side-arms and motor vehicles remaining in the possession of the Korean Military Advisory Group. As of the date of completion of United States troop withdrawal, the United States had transferred all its military *matériel* in Korea to the Korean security forces, except for such *matériel* as had been withdrawn with the troops. Such transfers were made under the provisions of the United States Surplus Property Act of 1944 as amended. Deliveries of *matériel* other than those referred to above would have to be made under legislative authorization in effect at the time.

APPENDICES

(*a*) COMMUNICATION TO THE CHAIRMAN OF SUB-COMMITTEE III FROM THE AMBASSADOR OF THE UNITED STATES OF AMERICA

Seoul, 8 July 1949

I have the honour to refer to your letter of 23 June 1949, and to the exchange of views which I had with your Committee on 5 July 1949 on the subject of the observation and verification of the withdrawal of occupation forces from Korea.

I should like to confirm that the withdrawal of the United States military forces in Korea was completed on 29 June 1949, and the United States military occupation organization, known as "USAFIK," was deactivated as of midnight, 30 June 1949. At the same time, the executive agree-

ment relating to interim military and security matters entered into between the President of the Republic of Korea and the Commanding General, USAFIK, on 24 August 1948, automatically lapsed.

The United States Government no longer possesses or controls any military equipment in Korea except the side-arms and motor vehicles remaining in the possession of the Korean Military Advisory Group.

The Korean Military Advisory Group is remaining in Korea at the request of the Government of the Republic of Korea for the purpose of advising and assisting the Korean Government in the development and training of the Korean security forces. The Korean Military Advisory Group is a constituent element of the American Mission in Korea and has an authorized strength of not more than 500 military personnel. The Korean Military Advisory Group is now carrying on its functions on the basis of an informal understanding with the Korean Government. The Government of the United States proposes to negotiate a formal agreement with the Korean Government at an early date pertaining to the organization and functioning of the Advisory Group.

As soon as such an agreement is concluded, I shall be glad to make a copy of the signed agreement available to your Committee.

(*Signed*) John J. MUCCIO
Ambassador

(*b*) COMMUNICATION TO THE CHAIRMAN OF SUB-COMMITTEE III FROM THE AMBASSADOR OF THE UNITED STATES OF AMERICA

Seoul, 25 July 1949

I have the honour to refer to your letter of 21 July 1949, in which you requested written confirmation of certain points pertaining to verification by the United Nations Commission on Korea of the withdrawal of the United States occupation forces from Korea. I am glad to take up below, seriatim, the points raised in your letter under reference:

1. In my letter to you of 8 July 1949, I confirmed that the "withdrawal of the United States Military forces in Korea was completed on 29 June 1949, and the United States military occupation organization, known as 'USAFIK,' was deactivated as of midnight, 30 June 1949. At the same time, the executive agreement relating to interim military and security matters entered into between the President of the Republic of Korea and the Commanding General, USAFIK, on 24 August 1948, automatically lapsed". The authority of the Commanding General, USAFIK, to assume control of the Korean security forces, under certain conditions, stemmed from that executive agreement. With the lapsing of that agreement and the deactivation of USAFIK, neither the Government of the United States nor the Chief, KMAG, has any authority to take control of the Korean security forces.

2. All *matériel* transferred to the Korean security forces before the completion of troop withdrawal, plus a small quantity still in transit, was made available to the Korean Government under the provisions of the Surplus Property Act of

1944 as amended. Any deliveries of *matériel*, apart from those referred to above, would have to be made under legislative authorization in effect at the time.

3. United States Air Force personnel continue to be stationed at Kimpo Airport pursuant to informal arrangement with the Korean Government for the purpose of insuring the uninterrupted operation of the Airport pending completion of more formal arrangements respecting the future operation of the Airport. The strength of the United States Air Force unit at Kimpo is being progressively reduced and now comprises seven officers and fifty-two men. Subject to agreement with the Korean Government and the appropriation of funds by the United States Congress, it is contemplated that the Civil Aeronautics Authority will assume operation of the Airport at an early date. It is hoped that withdrawal of United States Air Force personnel from the Airport will be completed by 1 September 1949.

I wish further to confirm that the chart transmitted by General Roberts to you showing stages of withdrawal of United States occupation forces from Korea was sent in my behalf.

(*Signed*) John J. Muccio
Ambassador

(*c*) Communication to the Chairman of Sub-Committee III from the Chief of the United States Advisory Group to the Republic of Korea

San Francisco, 16 July 1949

In accordance with your request, I have the honour to transmit herewith a report showing the progressive outshipment of tactical troops of the United States Army from the Republic of Korea.

The tabulation appended hereto as inclosure No. 1 is self explanatory. It shows in the left hand column the unit concerned, in the next two columns the date of inactivation or outshipment. The authorized strength together with progressive reductions are shown in the next columns. It should be noted that all USAFIK personnel remaining in Korea on 13 June 1949 were on that date transferred to Headquarters and Headquarters Company USAFIK, which thereupon had a personnel strength of 1,703.

All 5th Regimental Combat Team personnel remained assigned to the Regimental Combat Team which on that date had a strength of 2,162. By 20 June 1949, air and surface outshipments including those on USAT *Munimori* which sailed that date had reduced the personnel to 1,703 and 1,600 respectively; and by 29 June, air and surface transportation to include the USAT *Beaudoin* and the USAT *Brewster* had reduced tactical troop strength in Korea to zero except for Captain Gregory of the Adjutant General Department and one assistant who stayed behind to verify the count; these two left by air 1 July 1949.

I trust that the attached tabulation and the explanation given above will meet your needs and will show that the withdrawal of United States Army tactical units from the Republic of Korea was completed on 29 June 1949.

(*Signed*) W. L. Roberts
Brigadier General, USA
Chief, United States
Advisory Group to the
Republic of Korea

HQ USAFIK

Unit	Date of inactivation June	Date of shipment	Authorized strength OFF	EM	May 2	9	16	23	30	June 6	13	20	23	29
HQ USAFIK	28		69	107	206	205	199	199	131	131	185	1,703	1,000	0
HQ CO USAFIK	28		7	105	104	114	112	112	86	86				
235 APU	18		1	15	15	15	15	15	5	5	4	0	0	0
360 DENT PROS		May 20	2	6	7	7	7	7	0	0	0	0	0	0
152 FIN DISB SEC		June 22	3	24	37	20	22	22	9	9	6	0	0	0
249 MED DET		May 20	2	8	8	8	18	18	0	0	0	0	0	0
971 CIC DET		20	5	1	9	9	9	9	0	0	0	0	0	0

5th RCT

Unit	Date of inactivation	Date of shipment	Authorized strength	May 2	9	16	23	30	June 6	13	20	23	29
5th INF REGT	(Compl date)	June 29	152	2,898	3,167	2,973	2,951	2,951	2,354	2,354	2,162	1,600	800	0
555 FA BN		May 27	36	473	539	468	469	469	0	0	0	0	0	0
72 ENGR (C) CO		27	5	162	173	161	161	161	0	0	0	0	0	0
58 CAV RCN TRP		27	6	151	167	162	161	161	0	0	0	0	0	0
12 MED COLL CO		27	5	130	95	93	93	93	0	0	0	0	0	0
317 HID		May 20	7	35	21	20	20	0	0	0	0	0	0	0
517 EUD		June 25	9	139	197	183	184	184	140	140	134	0	0	0
282 ARMY BAND		May 20	1	28	35	35	35	35	0	0	0	0	0	0

USAFIK SPECIAL TROOPS

Unit	Date of inactiva-tion	Date of shipment	Authorized strength		Actual Strength									
					May					June				
	June		OFF	EM	2	9	16	23	30	6	13	20	23	29
HQ & HQ DET...	28		25	92	153	142	138	138	179	179	148	0	0	0
4 ORD MM CO	12		9	186	219	194	191	191	88	88	14	0	0	0
371 ORD AMMO SUP	12		1	22	23	20	18	18	12	12	6	0	0	0
510 EUD	20		12	214	232	223	222	222	175	175	87	0	0	0
514 ORD DET	28		1	17	33	22	21	21	28	28	29	0	0	0
35 TC TRK CO	25		5	103	121	124	124	124	121	121	91	0	0	0
536 TC TRK CO	25		4	78	69	88	86	86	89	89	53	0	0	0
90 TC HAR CFT CO	4		29	56	84	79	73	73	69	69	0	0	0	0
3 MED PORT	28		19	168	194	180	178	178	163	163	136	0	0	0
76 SIG SVBN	3		38	457	483	416	412	412	135	135	0	0	0	0
55 MP CO	25		4	97	128	123	119	119	79	79	76	0	0	0
207 MP SV CO	15		13	196	191	161	149	199	86	86	15	0	0	0
25 CID	15		9	2	12	11	11	11	10	10	10	0	0	0
576 QM SV CO	10		7	162	182	168	159	159	106	106	0	0	0	0
594 QM DEP SUP CO	25		8	178	186	165	162	162	105	105	93	0	0	0
382 STA HOSP	22		47	162	212	184	183	183	110	110	64	0	0	0
	May													
874 OPT RPR TM	20		1	6	3	4	4	4	0	0	0	0	0	0
535 MED SUP DET	22		1	13	11	10	10	10	0	0	0	0	0	0
143 VET FD INSP	20		1	4	5	5	5	5	0	0	0	0	0	0
		June												
1st BN, 5th INF		29	35	825										
2nd BN, 5th INF		21	35	825										
3rd BN, 5th INF		20	35	825										

B. Communications from the Ambassador of the United States of America to the Commission, and his hearing before the Commission

1. LETTER TO THE CHAIRMAN OF THE COMMISSION FROM THE SPECIAL REPRESENTATIVE OF THE UNITED STATES OF AMERICA, TRANSMITTING A COPY OF HIS LETTER TO THE PRESIDENT OF THE REPUBLIC OF KOREA CONCERNING THE QUESTION OF TROOP WITHDRAWAL (A/AC.26/14)

Seoul, 14 April 1949

I have the honour to transmit a copy of a letter which I have addressed today to the President of the Republic of Korea, paragraph 4 of which relates specifically to the question of troop withdrawal.

It is the policy of my Government to keep the Commission fully informed of all steps taken that may affect its activities, and I shall therefore keep the Commission currently informed of developments relating to this subject.

(Signed) John J. MUCCIO
Special Representative

(Text of the letter)

Seoul, 14 April 1949

I have the honour to confirm the statements I made to you this afternoon that American diplomatic officers have been authorized to communicate to Governments to which they are accredited that the present position of the United States Government with respect to Korea is as follows:

1. It is the United States view that the United Nations has already made substantial progress toward restoring freedom and independence of the Korean people and that in the General Assembly resolution of 12 December it has a formula for pursuing that progress to fruition.

2. The United States believes consolidation of existing gains and success of further United Nations efforts in Korea will depend in large measure on firm and unwavering support by United Nations Member States of the 12 December resolution and endorsement of Government of Republic of Korea contained therein.

3. In this connexion the United States feels every assistance and facility should be afforded the new United Nations Commission on Korea established under the 12 December resolution in its efforts to help the Korean people and their lawful government to achieve goal of free and united Korea, a goal to which the United States is convinced an overwhelming majority of Koreans of both north and south wholeheartedly aspire.

4. United States position on troop withdrawal is based on the view that to withdraw its occupation forces prematurely or to permit their retention on Korean soil for any longer than is necessary would in either case be to jeopardize attainment of United Nations objectives in Korea. Accordingly, and in keeping with the spirit of the General Assembly resolutions on Korea, the United States has during the past several months effected substantial reduction of its occupation forces in Korea. Such United States forces as still remain do so at the request of the Korean Government pending further development of its own rapidly improving security forces and, in accordance with the 12 December resolution, will be withdrawn "as early as practicable", hopefully in matter of months, subject to consultation with the United Nations Commission.

5. In addition to supporting procedures set forth in the 12 December resolution, and quite apart from question of troop withdrawal, it is the United States intention to continue to provide economic, technical, military and other assistance regarded as essential to economic and political stability of the newborn Republic.

6. The United States is convinced the main burden of responsibility for the failure of United

Nations efforts so far to achieve final solution of Korean problem must be placed on the Soviet Union and its evident determination to subordinate legitimate aspirations and welfare of the Korean people to its own objective of communist domination of the entire Korean peninsula. The United States believes further this obstacle can be overcome only through united support of United Nations decision as envisaged in paragraph 2 above.

I would appreciate an expression of your Excellency's views regarding the United States position on troop withdrawal as outlined in paragraph four above.

I may add that as the United States regards the Korean problem as one of international concern, and in line with the general policy of keeping the United Nations Commission on Korea fully informed of any action that may affect its activities, I am furnishing that Commission with a copy of this letter.

(*Signed*)   John J. Muccio
Special Representative

2. Letter to the Chairman of the Commission from the Ambassador of the United States of America, transmitting a copy of his letter to the President of the Republic of Korea regarding the establishment of the Korean Military Advisory Group (A/AC.26/14/Add.1)

Seoul, 2 May 1949

In accordance with the second paragraph of my letter of 14 April 1949, I have the honour to transmit herewith a copy of a letter which I have addressed as of this date to the President of the Republic of Korea regarding the establishment of a Korean Military Advisory Group.

(*Signed*)   John J. Muccio
Ambassador

(*Text of the letter*)

Seoul, 2 May 1949

I have the honour to refer to your request for a United States military and naval mission and to recent references thereto in our discussions looking towards setting a date for the early withdrawal of United States occupation forces.

As you know there has been in existence on a provisional basis for more than eight months a United States military mission known as the Provisional Military Advisory Group whose function it has been to advise and assist the Korean Government in the development and training of its own security forces. It is the judgment of my Government that, due in no small part to the spirit of eager co-operation which has been shown by the Korean Government and its responsible officials, the work of the Provisional Military Advisory Group has contributed significantly to raising the capabilities of the security forces of the Republic of Korea. This judgment would seem to be substantiated by your own recent statement to the effect that Korean defense forces "are now rapidly approaching the point at which our security can be assured, provided the Republic of Korea is not called upon to face attack from foreign sources".

In order to assure the continuance of this progress without further dependence upon the presence of United States occupation forces in Korea, my Government has decided to establish an augmented Korean Military Advisory Group to function as a part of the American Mission in Korea, with responsibility for the training mission heretofore undertaken by the Provisional Military Advisory Group. Under my over-all direction as Ambassador, the Korean Military Advisory Group will be headed by Brigadier General William L. Roberts, presently Commanding General, United States Army Forces in Korea, and Commanding Officer of the Provisional Military Advisory Group. Further details concerning the composition of the new military advisory group will be discussed at an appropriate time with the proper officials of your Government.

(*Signed*)   John J. Muccio
Ambassador

3. Excerpts from the hearing of the Ambassador of the United States of America concerning troop withdrawal (A/AC.26/SR.33)

The Chairman stated that he and the Principal Secretary, in accordance with a decision made at the previous meeting, had visited the United States Ambassador (Mr. Muccio) and invited him to meet with the Commission to review the question of the withdrawal of United States troops from Korea. The Commission was also interested in learning how the Ambassador and General Roberts envisaged the technical process of co-operation with the Commission in its observation of withdrawal.

Mr. Muccio had accepted the invitation immediately and was now present with General Roberts, Commanding General of United States Army Forces in Korea. The Ambassador was invited to make a general statement concerning the background of the withdrawal. Members might then ask questions which he could answer or not as he chose, either on or off the record.

Mr. Muccio expressed pleasure at the opportunity to meet with the Commission, and recalled the informal exchange of views he had had with some members of the Commission on 15 May. Other members had not been present, and clarification might be required as to certain points raised in that discussion.

The General Assembly resolution of 14 November 1947 had provided for withdrawal by the occupying Powers of their armed forces "as early as practicable and if possible within ninety days". But in view of the delay in considering the Korean problem at the Paris session of the General Assembly, the matter of troop withdrawal had not actually been considered until some time later than had at first been anticipated.

On 6 and 7 February 1949, United States Secretary of the Army Royall and General Wedemeyer had spent some time in Seoul and had reviewed with President Rhee and Prime Minister and Minister of Defence Lee Bum Suk the question of providing the Korean Army with equipment, arms and ammunition. Secretary Royall had outlined certain plans which had been formulated by the best American military talent in Korea and referred to General MacArthur's headquarters and to Washington for further study. The need to continue the task force then in being and the then provisional United States Military Advisory Group had been discussed in the light of plans to continue the programme of equipping and training Korean security forces which were growing in strength.

Later Mr. Muccio had been called to Washington for consultations on the matter with appropriate officials of his Government. Immediately upon returning to Korea, he had discussed the question of troop withdrawal with President Rhee. As a result of this exchange of views, President Rhee had stated on 19 April that the time was fast approaching when Korean security forces would be equal to coping with the situation.

In a further conference between American and Korean authorities the previous Monday, President Rhee had expressed the view that retention of United States military forces in Korea would not "mean much". He was more interested in a statement by American authorities that the United States would stand by Korea; such a statement would have a more salutary effect than retention of a small task force.

Withdrawal of United States forces from Korea had in effect been under way for some time, during which the large number of troop originally present had been gradually reduced, in pace with the increasing capabilities of the Korean security forces. The question now was not one of withdrawal, but of the time of its completion. The bulk of United States combat forces would leave Korea between the 21st and 30th of the current month. Mr. Muccio assured the Commission that he and General Roberts, commanding United States Army Forces in Korea and Chief of the Korean Military Advisory Group, would be glad to do everything possible to facilitate the Commission's observation and verification of the completion of the withdrawals.

The exact technique to be employed in observation and verification was a matter for the Commission to decide, but the United States authorities were prepared to extend whatever co-operation was requested. Mr. Muccio did not know to what extent the Commission might have discussed the matter with the Korean authorities, but was confident that the latter would have no hesitancy in providing full facilities to the Commission during the final period of troop withdrawal.

Mr. Muccio offered to leave with the Commission a copy of a policy statement on Korea issued that morning by the State Department in Washington. In the minds of many people in Korea, withdrawal of the United States task force was associated with a fear that the United States was abandoning Korea. The main purpose of the statement was to assure the Korean people that the United States was not abandoning Korea, but considered the withdrawal as merely a further step in normalizing relations between the Governments of the United States and Korea.

The CHAIRMAN asked whether any request for military aid for Korea had been submitted to Congress.

Mr. Muccio replied that no Congressional authorization had been required for transfers to Korean security forces so far of arms, equipment and ammunition, which had been supplied directly by the United States Army under the Surplus Property Act. Most of the United States military equipment in Korea had already been turned over to Korean authorities, and the rest would be transferred before the troop withdrawals were completed.

Congressional authorization would be required for continued support of Korean combat forces in future. Korean requirements for the future would be subject to the general programme of military assistance to other countries which was now before Congress.

Mr. LUNA (Philippines) asked for clarification of a slight legal point on which he had doubts. The General Assembly resolution of 14 November 1947 recommended that Korea's future national government should arrange with the occupying Powers for troop withdrawal. It thus appeared that the Government of Korea should take the initiative in the matter. Yet the decision seemed to have been made already by the United States State Department without regard for the role of the Korean Government.

Mr. Muccio thought there was a meeting of minds between the Korean and United States Governments, as a result of his own discussions with Korean authorities as well as those of Army Secretary Royall and General Wedemeyer.

Mr. SINGH (India) asked Mr. Muccio's opinion as to whether the Korean Government was actually reconciled to the idea of United States troop withdrawal or was likely to make further protests, in view of public controversy concerning the issue. For example, a public meeting scheduled for 11 June to protest the withdrawal was ostensibly inspired by the Ministry of Foreign Affairs.

Mr. Muccio said the main concern of the Korean Government had always been not to prevent the withdrawal, but to be assured of an adequate supply of equipment and ammunition before it took place.

In reply to a question by the CHAIRMAN, Mr. Muccio stated that the authorized strength of the Korean Military Advisory Group to be retained in Korea was 500 officers and men. Upon completion of the withdrawal, no other United States military personnel would remain in Korea, except for a few temporary residual groups such as that at Kimpo Airport. Discussions were under way concerning arrangements to replace such personnel, who would remain for a few weeks at most.

Mr. SINGH (India) pointed out that the Commission was obliged to report on military as well as other developments which had occurred during its stay in Korea, and asked whether it would receive details of withdrawal movements effected during that period.

Mr. Muccio said he would be glad to furnish the Commission with full details of such movements, including dates and numbers of troops involved.

Mr. MAGAÑA (El Salvador) hoped General Roberts would clarify the manner in which the Commission could observe and verify the final withdrawals. He had prepared a list of seven questions; the answers to some might be deleted from the record as constituting military secrets.

His first question concerned the total number of personnel in each occupation force.

General ROBERTS said the United States occupation forces numbered approximately 8,000.

Mr. MUCCIO said he could make the general statement that United States troops were distributed principally in the areas of Inchon, Ascom City and Seoul. He would be glad to furnish full details in reply to certain other questions. Korean security forces had received a good portion of the supplies intended for them; others were being turned over to them, and all would have been delivered before the United States forces left.

He thought the Korean Government should be asked to furnish information as to where the supply depots were located, if the Commission found it essential. Relations between the Korean Government and the United States Korean Military Advisory Group were now under consideration.

Mr. JAMIESON (Australia) wished, without prejudice to whatever position the Commission might take in future, to hear Mr. Muccio's comment on section 4 (d) of the General Assembly resolution, which empowered the Commission to request the assistance of military experts of the two occupying Powers.

Mr. MUCCIO said he had discussed the point with General Roberts, who would be glad to furnish any personnel for this purpose which the Commission felt that it desired or required.

General ROBERTS confirmed that he would furnish full data on troop dispositions and sailings, and invited the Commission to watch the actual embarkations.

Mr. JAMIESON (Australia) wondered if the United States authorities interpreted section 4 (d) of the resolution to mean that their Government would furnish experts to observe withdrawal of USSR forces and vice versa.

The CHAIRMAN observed that the real question would be what the drafters of the resolution sponsored by the United States delegation at the Paris Assembly had in mind.

Mr. MUCCIO said United States authorities were prepared to furnish the Commission with full facilities for observation; it was for the Commission to ascertain what the Soviets would do in the north.

He did not know how the United States delegation in Paris had interpreted section 4 (c).

Mr. LUNA (Philippines) recalled that the Commission had received copies of two letters addressed by the Ambassador to President Rhee. Did the Ambassador care to inform the Commission as to whether the President had replied to these letters?

Mr. MUCCIO said the first letter, dated 14 April, had been mainly an outline or clarification of the position of the United States vis-à-vis Korea and the United Nations; it had not called for a reply. The second letter, dated 2 May, announcing establishment of the Korean Military Advisory Group, had been itself a reply to a request advanced by the Korean Government on several occasions, particularly at the time of Secretary Royall's visit. Details of the relationship between the Military Advisory Group and the Korean Army were now under consideration. Relations so far had been highly satisfactory, and no difficulty was anticipated.

Mr. Muccio wished to correct an impression prevalent in some quarters that his letter had been sent to the Commission for its information only.

The position of his Government had been that the Commission was an international body, and that questions as to interpretation of its terms of reference were not proper subjects for United States intervention. Clarification of its duties and responsibilities under the General Assembly resolution of 12 December 1948 appeared to be reserved to the competence of the Commission, of which the United States was not a member.

He had therefore phrased his letter carefully to avoid any indication as to what the United States expected the Commission to do or not to do. Such decisions rested entirely with the Commission.

Mr. LIU (China) wished to put a hypothetical case in connexion with the question asked by the Australian representative. If the Commission should so interpret the resolution as to invite Russian experts to observe the United States withdrawals from South Korea, and if the Russians accepted the invitation, would United States military officials in South Korea object?

Mr. MUCCIO replied that Korean authorities had not been consulted and that this was their country, but that as far as the United States was concerned, there would be no objection, provided of course that American experts were given reciprocal rights in North Korea.

The CHAIRMAN thanked the Ambassador for his explanations and for the good will with which he had replied to questions.

4. LETTER TO THE CHAIRMAN OF THE COMMISSION FROM THE AMBASSADOR OF THE UNITED STATES OF AMERICA, CONFIRMING HIS STATEMENT BEFORE THE COMMISSION (A/AC.26/14/Add.2)

Seoul, 11 June 1949

I have the honour to refer to the appearance of myself and the Commanding General USAFIK before the Commission on 9 June 1949, and to confirm herewith my verbal statement that my Government was prepared to co-operate to the fullest with the Commission in order to assist it in observing and verifying the withdrawal of United States troops from Korea in accordance with paragraph 4 of the General Assembly resolution of 12 December 1948.

The Commanding General USAFIK will be glad to furnish the Commission with the services of any United States military experts which the Commission may feel that it requires, and in addition will make available full details of the troop withdrawal operation.

(Signed)   John J. MUCCIO
Ambassador

C. **Communications from members of the National Assembly and patriotic organizations regarding the withdrawal of foreign troops from Korea and the establishment of military missions in Korea**

1. PETITION FROM MR. KIM YAK SOO, VICE-PRESIDENT OF THE NATIONAL ASSEMBLY, AND OTHER MEMBERS, URGING THE WITHDRAWAL OF FOREIGN TROOPS FROM KOREA (A/AC.26/NC.2)

Seoul, 18 March 1949

The whole people of Korea is grateful to you for having come to this country to accelerate the democratic development of this country. Needless to say that the Republic of Korea is confronted with a grave national crisis at present a .d this crisis can be got through only by giving solution to those basic problems which now lie before the whole nation. From this standpoint and by way of facilitating your work in Korea, we desire to have the privilege of making a few suggestions. Your responsibility for this country is indeed great, because you are expected not only to make the foreign forces evacuate this country but to put this evacuation under strict supervision so that the peaceful unification of our fatherland may be effected and the democratic development may be carried out. Were this responsibility to be successfully fulfilled on your part, the spontaneous expression of the national opinion should first of all be respected. This respect for the national opinion means the exclusion from Korea of foreign influences and of the pressures from outside quarters, and therefore is in accordance with the United Nations Charter. The territorial division of Korea between south and north and the consequent split of thirty million people in the divided zones are caused by the long-term occupation of Korea by foreign forces.

Accordingly the origin of all those difficult problems which now beset the nation is not in the Korean people themselves but is in the fact that the self-det   ining power of the Korean people is now abse..t because of the prevailing foreign influences in this country. As is well known, the Korean people is highly civilized and is very proud of its long historical background spreading over more than 5,000 years. They love peace and do not desire war. Moreover, in settling our present national crisis, the idea of the nation is very far from such an undertaking as military conquest of north by south or vice versa. What the people of Korea most earnestly desire to do is to effect the peaceful unification of our fatherland and to .eject the idea of Korea's repeating the undesirable example of Greece. This is the most earnest and prevalent opinion of the whole Korean people and it is specially requested that you would kindly assist the Republic of Korea so that its Government may effect the unification of Korea by the peaceful method referred to above. Lastly it cannot be too strongly stressed that unless foreign influences are completely withdrawn from this country, the objective for which you have come to this country will be entirely frustrated.

(Signed by)

Representative:

Kim Yak Soo	Ree Moon Won
Kang Wock Choong	Baik Hyung Nam
Pak Yun Won	Seu Yong Kill
Whang Byung Kyu	Kim Yong Chai
Ro Il Whan	Son Chai Hak
Whang Yun Ho	Rym Suk Kyu
Kim Byung Hoi	Kim Wok Chyu
Choi Tai Kyu	Ree Koo Soo
Kim Dong Choon	Kang Sun Myung
Cho Wok Hyun	Kwun Tai Wook
Kim Bong Doo	Kim Ick Ro
Chung Chin Keun	Kim Ki Chul
Pak Ki Woom	Shin Sung Kyun
Ryu Chun Sang	Kim Yung Ki
Kim Choong Ki	Heu Yung Ho
Ryu Kong Kyun	Bai Chung Hyuk
Wong Chang Kill	Bai Heun
Ree Seung Woo	Kim Kyung Bak

Hong Soon Wok	Kang Dall Soo
Oh Taik Kwan	Kim Ik Ki
Chya Kyung Mo	Chang Hong Yum
Choi Bum Sool	Shin Kwang Kyun
Kim Myung Tong	Pak Chan Hun
Kim Yong Hyun	Cho Kuk Hyun
Ree Chong Keun	Ree Chong Soon
Kim Yung Dong	Ree Man Keun
Cho Kyu Kap	Chung Hai Chun
Cho Chong Seung	Yun Byung Koo
Kim Chang Ryul	Ryu Hong Ryul
Ree Chin Soo	Oh Ki Ryul
Kim In Sik	Pak Chong Nam

2. STATEMENT AND PETITION PRESENTED BY MR. KIM YAK SOO, VICE-PRESIDENT OF THE NATIONAL ASSEMBLY, OBJECTING TO THE ESTABLISHMENT OF UNITED STATES AND SOVIET MILITARY MISSIONS IN KOREA (A/AC.26/NC.7)

In submitting the petition, Mr. Kim stated:

We are very happy to see that the United Nations Commission on Korea members are very busy in observing the withdrawal of the US troops from South Korea. But we have learned that the Soviet Union left a military advisory group in North Korea and that the USA is going to do the same in South Korea. If that is the case, the form of occupation is merely changed into the establishment of military missions and, in essence, the foreign troops, though small in number, will be staying on Korean soil just the same. So long as the foreign troops remain in Korea, the international aspect of the Korean problem is still retained. We, therefore, request the United Nations to do away with the US-USSR military missions in Korea.

(Text of the Petition)

Dear members of the United Nations Commission on Korea,

We pray for your good health. Under date of 18 March 1949 we submitted to you a petition signed by sixty-two members of the National Assembly requesting withdrawal of the foreign troops from Korea. We regret that we have not yet received any reply to this petition from you.

We were also surprised to see the resolution of 24 May as reported in the United Nations Commission on Korea News Release No. 18. While adopting this resolution, the delegates of France and Australia abstained, the Syrian delegate was absent, and the Indian delegate opposed it. How could the UNCOK pass the resolution in that manner? We Koreans are very much disappointed in the Commission, and we fear that the Commission lost its prestige.

On the other hand, we express our heart-felt gratitude to the Commission for the fulfilment of one of its tasks by observing the US troops' withdrawal from Korea. The establishment of the US-USSR military missions in Korea may make a second Greece out of Korea; and we oppose it. For the sake of international obligation and prestige we request the UNCOK to abolish the two nations' military missions.

Humbly submitted by

KIM YAK SOO   *(Seal)*

3. Statement by and petition from Mr. Kim Dong Won, Vice-President of the National Assembly, and other members, supporting the establishment of the United States Military Mission in Korea (A/AC.26/NC.7/Add.1)

When submitting the petition, Mr. Kim Dong Won made these remarks:

We, the members of the National Assembly, were surprised to read the petition submitted to the United Nations Commission on Korea by Mr. Kim Yak Soo, requesting the Commission to abolish the United States Military Mission in Korea.

Although yesterday (19 June) was Sunday, all the patriotic Assembly members, considering the importance of the issue, got together and drafted this petition and signed it. It should be made known clearly that there were 150 members present in the National Assembly this morning, of whom 141 signed this petition.

We want to make it clear that Mr. Kim Yak Soo's petition does not reflect the will of the National Assembly and that it is purely his personal view. Even at the end of the adjourning ceremony of the National Assembly this morning he admitted this fact and added that there had been five other Assembly members who accompanied him while presenting his petition.

(Joint declaration for United States military aid to Korea)

The undersigned representatives of the National Assembly, considering the existing conditions of the national defence of the Republic of Korea which are not sufficient to guarantee the security of the nation,

Recognize the absolute need for military aid of the friendly United States who has the responsibility of developing and protecting the Republic of Korea,

And welcome the establishment of the United States Military Mission.

Signed by

Chong To Young
Cho Han Paek
Chang Hong Tam
Kim Jun Yon
Park Hae Chung
Ch'oe Suk Hwa
Kim Moon Pyong
Suh Sang Il
Song P'il Man
Suh Woo Suk
Yoo Chin Hong
Lee Ho Suk
An Chun Sang
Lah Yong Gyoon
Kim Sang Sun
Cho Yung Kyu
Paek Nam Ch'ae
Lee Man Kun
Shin Pang Hyun
Chung Chun
Lee Chung Iae
Chu Ki Yong
Hong Hi Chong
Ch'oe Pong Sik
Cho Kook Hyon

Hong Soon Nyong
Park Chun
Oh Suk Choo
Kim Pong Cho
Lee Suk
Kim Kyong Do
Kim I-Soo
Won Yong Han
Kim Chong Son
Chong Kwang Ho
Kim Ik Ki
Hong Sung Ha
Lee Pyong Kwan
Kim Sang Ho
Kim Ung Chin
Yoon Pyong Koo
Yoo Sung Kap
Won Yong Gyun
Ch'oe Un Kyo
Hwang Ho Hyun
Song Pong Hae
Ch'oe Kyu Kak
Lee Chong Soon
Lee Yoo Sun
Yoo Hong Yol

Signed by (continued)

Suh Sung Dal
Hong Ik Pyo
Kim Chin Koo
Yoo Chun Sang
Lee Suk Choo
Suh Chong Hi
Chong Hae Chun
Lee Chong Gun
Yang Pyong Chik
Koo Chung Hoe
Kim Chik Hyon
Kwak Sang Hoon
Kim Ch'ul
Hwang Doo Hyon
Cho Chae Myon
Kim Myong Dong
Kim Kyong Pae
Kim Ik No
Kim Chung Ki
Lee Chong Rin
Cho Hon Young
Kim Chong Moon
Shin Hyon Mo
Lee In
Kim Chae Hak
Yoo Rai Won
Chung Koo Sam
Suh I Hwan
Park Hae Kuk
Park Sang Young
Kim Kyo Chung
Han Suk Pong
Lee Pum Kyo
Park Kwan Soo
Oh Tae Yol
Park Woo Kyung
Cho Chong Sung
Lee I-Sang
Kim Kyo Hyon
Chong Kyun Sik
Park I'Woon
Kim Yong Jai
Lee I-Ki
Chong Chin Kun
Kim Yong Dong
Yun Ch'i Young

Hong Pom Hi
Kim Ung Kwon
Ch'oe Kook Hyon
Park Ch'an Hyon
Shin Ik Hi
Lee Ch'ong Ch'on
Yoon Chae Woo
Kim Tong Won
Lee Yong Chun
Park Soon Suk
Lee Sung Hak
Shin Kwang Kyun
Lee Yo Han
Kang Dal Soo
Lee Kang Woo
Chong Woo Il
Kwong Pyong Ro
Cho Pyong Han
Han Am Kook
Ch'oe Hon Kil
Lee Hang Pal
Chin Hon Sik
Chang Pyong Man
Lee Sung Duk
Lee Chu Hyong
Kwon T'ae Hi
Kwon T'ae Wook
Ch'oe Ch'ang Sup
Cho Kyu Kap
P'yo Hyon T'ae
Ch'oe Suk Hong
Kang I-Moon
Kim Woo Sik
Huh Chung
Chang Ki Young
Kim To Yon
Park Chong Hwan
Min Kyong Sik
Song Chang Sik
Shin Sang Hak
Suh Soon Young
Yim Young Sin
Kim Sang Ton
Ch'oe Yoon Dong
Kim Yong Hwa

4. Letter to the Chairman of the Commission from political and social organizations, appealing to the Commission to verify the withdrawal of Soviet forces from North Korea before observing the evacuation of the United States military forces (A/AC.26/NC.8)

Seoul, 22 June 1949

We wish to express our sincere gratitude to the United Nations Commission on Korea for its great effort to strengthen and unify Korea, it is an honour for us to send you this letter.

As you know, the communist army in the north is raiding South Korea every day and there is no way to verify whether the Soviet occupation troops in North Korea have evacuated or not. There is also news that the three big ports of North Korea—Wonsan, Najin and Chungjin —have been leased to the USSR. These facts indicate that the ominous hands of the aggressive and imperialistic Soviet Union are moving toward the Far East. In this situation the US troops are withdrawing in conformity with the United Nations General Assembly resolution of 14 November 1947, without taking any adequate defensive measures for Korea. This withdrawal of the US troops is bringing louder and louder cries from the Korean people in Seoul as well as in the provinces, imploring the USA not to withdraw its troops before the strengthening of Korean defence forces and calling for arms so as to secure the peace of Korea, which is a bulwark of world democracy.

Despite this present internal and external situation, Kim Yak Soo and sixty-two other members of the National Assembly had in the past petitioned your Commission requesting the withdrawal of the US troops; and again recently Kim Yak Soo and five other members of the National Assembly, pretending to represent the above-mentioned sixty-two members, called on your Commission to oppose the establishment of the United States Military Mission. It was an anti-national act ignoring the Korean situation. The traitorous nature of their act is clearly depicted by the resolutions of the Mass Meetings for Strengthening National Defence which are now being held throughout the nation and by the increasing indignation of the people. We believe that the members of the Commission know that the Soviet Union is turning a covetous eye on Korea and that its sinister ambition is being revealed day by day. However, your Commission, though it is the envoy of international peace, has approved and is observing unilateral withdrawal of the US troops. Such an attitude on the part of the UNCOK may help to intensify the tragedy already caused by murder, arson and pillage on the part of the North Korean Army. And that is definitely not what your Commission intends.

Thus on behalf of the whole nation we appeal to you to verify the withdrawal of the Soviet Union troops from North Korea before observing

the evacuation of the US forces. We also wish to request you to study measures for realizing a free election in North Korea and at the same time to take new measures for Korean unification.

Nationalist Society
General Headquarters National Unification
Taihan Women's Society
Korean Youth Corps
Democratic Nationalist Party
Chosun Democratic Party
Taehan Nationalist Party
Socialist Party
Women's Nationalist Party
Korean Labourers Federation
Korean Farmers Federation
Korean Labourers and Farmers Party
Korean Chamber of Commerce
Hankook Labourers and Farmers Party
National Students Federation
Korean Students Patriotic Corps
Korean Anti-Communist Federation
Christian Association
YMCA
Headquarters, Ch'undo-Kyo
Headquarters Buddhist Association
Headquarters Tai Chong Kyo
Headquarters Confucius Association
Federation of All Korea Cultural Organizations
Patriotic Old Men's Society
Supporting Association for Korean Diplomats
All Korea Writers Association
Northern Representatives Group

Annex IV

TEXTS OF MAIN DOCUMENTS REGARDING THE POSITIONS AND ATTITUDES OF THE COMMISSION, THE GOVERNMENT OF THE REPUBLIC OF KOREA, AND NORTH KOREA IN RESPECT TO THE IMPLEMENTATION OF THE TERMS OF REFERENCE OF THE COMMISSION

A. Attitude of the Government of the Republic of Korea

1. LETTER TO THE CHAIRMAN OF THE COMMISSION FROM THE MINISTER OF FOREIGN AFFAIRS OF THE REPUBLIC OF KOREA, SUGGESTING CERTAIN MEASURES TO BE PUT INTO EFFECT BY THE COMMISSION TO EXERCISE FULL SOVEREIGNTY OVER ALL ITS TERRITORY (A/AC.26/9)

3 March 1949

I have the honour to forward herewith a message from the Government of the Republic of Korea to the United Nations Commission on Korea.

(*Signed*) B. C. LIMB
Minister of Foreign Affairs

(*Text of message*)

The Government of the Republic of Korea takes this opportunity to express its hope that

the United Nations Commission on Korea, which has undertaken the task of realization of complete unity of Korea, will eventually through consecutive measures enable the Republic of Korea to exercise full sovereignty over the entire territory of Korea as provided for in the Constitution, in reality as well as in name.

This hope on the part of the Government of the Republic of Korea is believed to be self-explanatory in view of the history of its birth and international commitments thereon.

Moreover, in the light of the unanimous support of all Korean people in the south of 38 parallel and the long cherished desire as demonstrated in the recent uprisings of the Koreans in the north, it is firmly believed that this hope will prove to be the will of the thirty million population of the entire Korea, which will surely be ascertained through the free election as proposed hereunder.

Therefore the Government of the Republic of Korea has the honour to suggest to the United

Nations Commission on Korea that the following measures be put into effect as soon as possible.

I. *Political measures*

It is hoped that the United Nations Commission on Korea will persuade the Soviet Union to dissolve the North Korean puppet government as well as all the political parties and social organizations thereof, release the political prisoners in the north and ensure free passage through south and north, so that the Government of the Republic of Korea can conduct the general elections under the supervision of the United Nations Commission on Korea in North Korea under such free atmosphere as in the 10 May election in the south.

II. *Military measures*

Korea will never tolerate any foreign Powers or any internal armed forces organized as the instrument of aggression of foreign Power. The following measures are suggested in this connexion:

(*a*) A thorough supervision of the immediate and complete withdrawal from Korea of the Soviet Army, Chinese Communist Army, the guerrilla troops and any other similar military units or groupings;

(*b*) Lending good offices for the immediate dissolution of the so-called People's Army and security force that have obviously been organized for aggressive purposes.

III. *Security measures*

The Government of the Republic of Korea is willing to take the full responsibility for state security order in case of social emergency or unrest throughout Korea that might follow as a result of the measures proposed in the preceding two paragraphs.

IV. *Diplomatic measures*

(*a*) Any international agreement or treaty concluded and subsequent administrative policies adopted without the approval of the Government of Republic of Korea should be declared null and void;

(*b*) All the assets removed by the Soviet Army from Korea should be either returned or reimbursed.

V. *Economic measures*

(*a*) To make the Soviets take full responsibility for the existing monetary currency in North Korea and check additional increase of circulation;

(*b*) All electricity produced in Korea should be used in Korea exclusively.

2. LETTER TO THE CHAIRMAN OF THE COMMISSION FROM THE MINISTER OF FOREIGN AFFAIRS OF THE REPUBLIC OF KOREA, CONCERNING ITS EFFORTS TO CONTACT NORTH KOREA (A/AC.26/23)

Seoul, 19 May 1949

There is considerable speculation over the recurrent reports that the United Nations Com-

mission is planning to negotiate or confer with certain representatives of the communist organization in northern Korea regarding the re-unification of Korea. In order to put this speculation to rest, this Government desires to know directly from you whether or not such reports have a foundation in fact; and, if so, whether this plan has been officially approved by the Commission. It will be highly appreciated by this Government if you may be so good as to enlighten us on this question at the earliest convenient date, for the consequences from such a plan to open negotiations would be most serious.

You will recall the first conversation held between some of your distinguished members and the Ministers of this Government soon after your arrival in Seoul early this year. The question of the desirability of your dealing with the Korean communist leaders of the north was brought up at that time. As you know, we made clear our feeling that many disadvantages and no advantages would result from any such plan.

The fact is that we are fighting the Korean Communists for the very life and freedom of our country as an independent democratic State, which the Korean Communists are avowedly, deliberately and violently endeavouring to destroy. As we have said before, we had no communist problem in this country before the liberation, but the compromising policy of the Joint Commission encouraged and increased the communist agitators who infiltrated from abroad. Under the handicap of these circumstances, the United States Government did everything it could to remove the dividing line between north and south through negotiations over a period of two years, but the efforts were all in vain.

Later, at the request of the United Nations Temporary Commission on Korea we opened a way for the leaders of north and south to get together for a joint conference. The result was injurious to the cause of freedom and democracy, succeeding only in strengthening the communist position both north and south. We endured all this to satisfy the desires of those who were convinced they should experiment with the possibility of winning reasonable co-operation of the communists. It has been our hope that there would be an end to these attempts since it has been clearly evidenced that such experiments must end in failure and disadvantage to the cause of representative democratic government in Korea.

It is quite a surprise to us that you express a desire to deal with these people once again, in spite of the demonstrated failure of this experiment. Consequently, we remind you of this failure. It was disappointing to us to hear the feeling expressed that the Korean Government was not co-operating with the United Nations Commission. We regret exceedingly if we have appeared unable to co-operate in a manner wholly to your satisfaction. We are fully aware of the role of the United Nations in the re-establishment of Korean sovereignty and we intend to co-operate in the fulfilment of the United Nations' responsibilities in the problems of re-unifying our country and making possible the extension of representative democratic government into the area from which the United Nations Commission has thus far been excluded. We are certain that you gentlemen would not wish us to condone any experiment that endangers the very life of our nation by exposing it to the same dangers we are jointly trying to overcome.

This Government would appreciate an explicit statement from you as to just what you would hope to accomplish by such negotiations. If you tell us how northern and southern Korea might be united as a result of a meeting with the Soviet puppets in the north, we would examine such a proposal closely. Without knowing what methods you intend to pursue, or to what ends they might lead, our sincere efforts toward co-operation are rendered more difficult.

As we have said before, it is not the Koreans in the north who are preventing reunion of northern and southern Korea; it is their Soviet overlords whose orders they obey. These are the real authorities with whom you must deal. We are sure that our position in this matter will be understood by the representatives of all free nations, represented both on the Commission and in the General Assembly of the United Nations, many of whom are themselves confronted with this same problem of survival against communist aggression. We are confident that you will have no disposition to proceed with any plans that would harm our cause rather than helping it.

(*Signed*) B. C. LIMB
Minister of Foreign Affairs

3 LETTER TO THE CHAIRMAN OF THE COMMISSION FROM THE MINISTER OF FOREIGN AFFAIRS OF THE REPUBLIC OF KOREA, RELATING TO THE CONTINUATION OF THE WORK OF THE COMMISSION (A/AC.26/36)

Seoul, 30 June 1949

I have the honour to inform you that the people and the Government of the Republic of Korea are deeply appreciative of the sincere efforts of the United Nations Commission on Korea to fulfil the tasks which were entrusted to them by the United Nations. We fully acknowledge also that the prestige and the goodwill of the United Nations have wrought a tremendous influence upon the minds of the Korean people, and that they are convinced that the good offices of the United Nations extended through the United Nations Commission on Korea will finally enable them to achieve their aspired goal of unification and peace.

We earnestly hope the United Nations Commission on Korea will continue its work in Korea, for its tasks have not been completed. The Commission has much to accomplish. It has not yet witnessed the complete withdrawal of the Russian occupation forces from the north and it has yet to complete the great task of bringing about the unification of Korea.

The continuation of the work of the United Nations Commission on Korea for at least another year will be greatly appreciated by the Government and the people of Korea. Kindly communicate this matter to the United Nations General Assembly and obtain its concurrence on the desire of the people and Government of the Republic of Korea.

(*Signed*) B. C. LIMB
Minister of Foreign Affairs
Republic of Korea

4. LETTER TO THE CHAIRMAN OF THE COMMISSION FROM THE MINISTER OF FOREIGN AFFAIRS OF THE REPUBLIC OF KOREA, SUGGESTING THE ESTABLISHMENT OF A UNIT OF UNITED NATIONS MILITARY OBSERVERS (A/AC.26/40)

Seoul, 11 July 1949

I have the honour to enclose herewith a record of some of the more flagrant examples of attack by the so-called "People's Army" of northern Korea upon the communities and security forces south of the 38th parallel.

These communist attacks, if permitted to continue without proper means of defence and prevention, are likely to produce conditions which will be dangerous to the peace of the Orient.

Mindful of this danger and desiring to be helpful in the peaceful unification of Korea, the United Nations General Assembly, I am sure, will do all in its power to retard and stop these unlawful attacks by the communists from the north.

May I be permitted to suggest that the establishment of a unit of United Nations military observers, composed of officers of sufficiently high rank (to secure for the findings of that observer team the necessary authority and prestige) stationed in Korea, working in conjunction with the United Nations Commission on Korea, will accomplish that purpose.

The Government of the Republic of Korea will welcome such a unit of United Nations military observers. I hope you will be so good as to communicate this matter to the United Nations General Assembly and recommend its favourable action on this subject.

(*Signed*) B. C. LIMB
Minister of Foreign Affairs

5. INTERVIEW BETWEEN MEMBERS OF THE COMMISSION AND THE LIAISON COMMITTEE OF THE GOVERNMENT OF THE REPUBLIC OF KOREA, CONCERNING THE INTERPRETATION OF THE COMMISSION'S TASK (16 FEBRUARY 1949) (A/AC.26/W.6)

After the usual exchange of courtesies Dr. CHOUGH Pyong Ok, Chairman of the Liaison Committee, stated that he would like to outline to the members of the Commission his Government's interpretation of the Commission's task. He began by saying that in the opinion of the Korean Government unification of Korea meant unification on the basis constituted by the establishment of the South Korean Government. In other words his Government felt that the Commission would have to go to North Korea and supervise their elections which would be held to fill the 100 vacant seats reserved for representatives from North Korea in the Assembly.

While expressing his Government's view that the Commission was required to go north in order to carry out its task, Dr. Chough was emphatic in cautioning the Commission concerning the manner in which it should address the North Korean authorities in order to avoid any suggestion of recognition of their régime. It was in this connexion that he expressed great resentment over the cable sent by the Secretary-General of the United Nations to the Foreign Minister of the North Korean régime acknowledging receipt of the application of the latter for membership in the United Nations. He stated that the cable had been intercepted at the RCA station in Seoul and was not being sent on to its destination.

Concerning consideration of paragraph 4 (c) of the General Assembly resolution Dr. Chough gave it as the opinion of his Government that the phrase "further development of representative government" referred to the development of such government above the 38th parallel.

The CHAIRMAN pointed out that the Commission had interpreted this to mean rather the development of representative government throughout the whole of Korea and that members of the Commission would be happy to give any advice they could if called upon to do so.

Dr. CHOUGH replied that this would of course always be borne in mind and that he was sure there could be a useful and beneficial exchange of information. He reverted again immediately, however, to the primary necessity of establishing democratic government in the north. Although Dr. Chough did not refer specifically to the Commission's task of observing the withdrawal of occupying forces he did express himself rather heatedly on the recent motion before the South Korean Assembly in which thirty-odd members had demanded the withdrawal of United States forces. He stated that the supporters of this motion had either been misled or were carrying out Soviet policy. In making such a move their action was calculated to cause unrest in South Korea and was unwarranted. Decisions on so important a point were a prerogative of the Government.

As Dr. Chough made no reference to the removal of barriers to economic, social and other friendly intercourse between the two halves of Korea, this point was brought up by the Chairman of the Commission. Dr. Chough's reaction was very strong. He stated that there was now no economic intercourse between the two parts of Korea and that his Government did not intend that there should be any. The north, he said, would take advantage of any opening in this direction to encourage trade in a direction that would not only benefit only the north but would undermine the economic structure in the south. Moreover, the north could not be trusted to supply only goods. He instanced a comparatively recent case in which a cargo of fish was received from the north and subjected to a check by the police who, he said, found that the fish contained thousands of currency notes which were obviously intended to be used to pay communist agents in the south.

The resolution does not speak specifically of cultural intercourse but Dr. Chough referred excitedly to culture. There was an old culture in the south, he asserted, but in the north there was now only Marxist ideology. To talk of removing cultural and like barriers, therefore, would be to invite the unleashing of a flood of communist propaganda.

Dr. Chough then referred to the statements made at the public meeting of the Commission and particularly to the Commission's resolution of 9 February. The Korean Government was considerably disturbed at the implication that the Commission intended to conduct interviews with persons outside the Government. The lawful governmental body was the most suitable for con-

tact, he continued. In fact, were it to be learned that the Commission was consulting with certain personalities in Seoul public opinion would be confused and thrown into doubt. He implied that the result might be very serious. Asked whether his Government did not see any value in the Commission's consulting with what might be regarded as an opposition party, he began a strong attack on Kim Koo. He referred also to Kimm Kiusic and said that these men and their supporters could not be considered an opposition party at all. They want to overthrow the Government from the bottom up and secure unification on their own terms. He had told Chiang Kai-Shek when he saw him in China on his way to Paris that Kim Koo was finished. Addressing the Commission directly Dr. Chough said: "He is a rebel: he is a traitor". Both Kim Koo and the South Korean Labour Party, he continued, were puppets of the North Korean Government which is in turn a puppet of Soviet Russia. The only terms on which Kim Koo could be accepted would be after he had publicly come forward and stated: "We made a mistake. We will co-operate with the Government and the United Nations".

Mr. COSTILHES, referring to a warning against creating public unrest, asked whether it was not possibly the publicity that might be associated with interviews with personalities outside the Government that was worrying the latter.

Dr. CHOUGH said that of course publicity was especially harmful and repeated his reference to the opening of flood-gates of propaganda. His whole manner implied that whether or not any publicity was given to interviews with such personalities the Korean Government would look on them most unfavourably. The Chairman thanked Dr. Chough for his explanation on this point and stated that the Commission would always bear in mind what he had said but that he would understand no guarantee could be given as to whom the Commission would see.

Dr. Chough referred next to the policy statements read by delegates at the public meeting. He said that his Government was disturbed by Mr. Mughir's statement that if the Commission could not accomplish its purposes he would pack his bags and go home. The Government had every confidence in the ability and eagerness of Commission members to discharge their duties, Dr. Chough added. However there was a feeling in Korea that the Commission might possibly stay say ten months without accomplishing any actual result. But the presence of the Commission would nevertheless be regarded as a symbol of protection and security. The Korean people were in fact hoping for a miracle but even if there were no miracle the presence of the Commission had a historical implication, namely, to protect this young child of democracy on behalf of the United Nations. Statements such as Mr. Mughir's were very discouraging to the Koreans.

Mr. CHANG Kee Yung then spoke a few words. He reverted to the subject of interviewing Korean personalities. He said that doubts had been created among the Korean people when the Temporary Commission had interviewed certain people. Happily, however, the Temporary Commission had made a majority decision to hold the elections and there was now a lawful government with which the Commission could consult.

Asked whether the Government would object to the Commission's consulting opposition members of the National Assembly, Mr. Chang was evasive. He did not indicate that the Government would welcome such a procedure.

B. Position of the Commission in relation to the Government of the Republic of Korea

REPORT OF SUB-COMMITTEE I (A/AC.26/SC. 1/4/Rev.1)

(The text appears in chapter II, paragraph 6, of the report of the Commission)

C. Attitude of North Korea

"MANIFESTO" OF THE DEMOCRATIC FRONT FOR THE ATTAINMENT OF UNIFICATION FOR THE FATHERLAND, DEMANDING THE WITHDRAWAL OF THE COMMISSION FROM KOREA AND ANNOUNCING A GENERAL ELECTION TO BE HELD THROUGHOUT KOREA IN SEPTEMBER 1949 (A/AC.26/W.17)[68]

Dear fellow countrymen:

Dear members of democratic political parties and social organizations of South and North Korea:

Dear brothers and sisters:

Nearly four years have already elapsed since our fatherland was liberated from the yoke of Japanese imperialism. Notwithstanding, our fatherland still remains divided by the artificial demarcation line of the 38th parallel.

During the four years the southern and northern parts of our fatherland have followed diametrically opposed directions.

In the northern half of our fatherland democratic construction has been and is still progressing fruitfully and the centuries' old cherished aspirations of the people are being realized.

In the southern half of our fatherland reactionaries have established their régime and are adopting all sorts of measures to suppress the democratic forces. Both economically and politically, South Korea is more and more being reduced to the servitude of the United States.

Who is obstructing our people in the attainment of unification? For whose interests is the division of our country being perpetuated? The American imperialists are obstructing the attainment of unification for the fatherland; and their hirelings, the pro-Japanese, and national traitors are deceiving the people, selling the interests of the fatherland and the people, and are prepared to ruin the fatherland and the people in order to protect the interests of their American masters and their régime.

The American imperialists have insulted us by saying that our people are ignorant and are incapable of governing and developing our country. They have been for nearly four years and are

still pursuing measures designed to convert South Korea into their military and political base for their anti-democratic struggle in the Far East and to make South Korea a new economic source for the United States of America in order to fatten the bellies of the Wall Street monopolistic capitalists. For four years the diplomacy of the United States and all the efforts of the American authorities have been aimed at carrying on an American imperialist plunder programme in South Korea.

Already at the Moscow Three Foreign Ministers Conference held at the end of 1945, the American delegation proposed that an administrative organ be set up with representatives from the Four Powers including the United States of America, China, the United Kingdom and the Soviet Union, and that the administrative organ exercise its functions for the control of Korea through a high commissioner. This American proposal did not envisage any plan for the formation of a Korean government. According to the draft American proposal, a virtual mandate on our fatherland would have lasted for a period of up to ten years. The acceptance of such a proposal would mean that Korea should be placed under foreign rule for a long period of time without its independent people's régime.

However, this American proposal was rejected.

Accepting the Soviet Union's proposal, the Moscow Three Ministers Conference adopted a plan providing for the creation of conditions for the formation of a democratic Korean government, making Korea an independent State with the facilities of democratic development, and the liquidation of the harmful effects of the long Japanese imperialist rule in Korea.

This decision was in consonance with the interests of all walks of life of the Korean people, while it was against the interests of American imperialists and the national traitors, who, holding the reins of government in their own hands, were trying to prevent the masses from participating in the administration of the country and developing Korea along democratic lines. The interests of American imperialists and the national reactionary elements agreed entirely.

Therefore, the combined forces of the Korean reactionary elements and the American imperialists resorted to all sorts of measures with the object of frustrating the USSR-US Joint Commission which was charged with implementing the Moscow Three Ministers decision.

At this grave juncture for our nation, the Soviet Union, which faithfully upholds the principles of respecting the national independence and sovereignty of other nations, opened the door once again for the attainment of unification for our fatherland, by proposing the simultaneous withdrawal of the Soviet and American troops from Korea so as to give the Korean people the possibility of forming a united, democratic government with their own hands without the assistance and participation of the United States and the Soviet Union.

We Korean people heartily supported this just proposal of the Soviet Union, which agrees with our national interests. However, the Government of the United States rejected this proposal, for the proposal ran counter to the interests of the American imperialists and the Korean reactionary elements.

---

[68] Copies of the original text in Korean were sent to the delegations and secretariat through the exchange of mail service between the north and south. It was also beamed to the south on 28 June 1949 through the Pyongyang Radio and intercepted by the SCAP Radio reception stations in Tokyo. The English version of the Pyongyang radio intercept has been used in making the translation.

The Government of the United States unlawfully insisted that the Korean issue be put before the United Nations General Assembly.

Without hearing the will of the Korean people, and in spite of the opposition of the delegates from the Soviet Union and other democratic nations, the United Nations General Assembly created the so-called United Nations Temporary Commission on Korea under pressure of the United States.

The United Nations Commission on Korea, a tool for the aggressive policy of the United States, completely failed because its activities have been in contradiction to the interests of the Korean people who were indignant at its unlawful activities.

Through the unlawful, so-called United Nations "Little Assembly", in which delegates from true democratic nations did not participate, the Government of the United States had a resolution adopted for the holding of separate elections in South Korea.

An absolute majority of our people rose in unison and launched a movement to boycott the separate elections.

Only with brute force and undisguised armed force were the American authorities and the reactionary elements able to hold the so-called elections in South Korea on 10 May 1948, which were nothing but a fraud and fake. On the basis of this they formed the so-called "National Assembly" and the separate puppet "government" with Syngman Rhee, a vicious enemy of the Korean people and a murderer, as the ringleader.

The so-called National Assembly is a pitiful creature which does not approach anything like a real one. This National Assembly cannot represent the Korean people, for not a single worker or farmer has been elected to it. In other words, it cannot represent the Korean people, for there are no representatives of the absolute majority of the South Korean people. The so-called National Assembly of South Korea is a group consisting of the pro-Japanese, national traitors, and enemies of the people, including large holders, capitalists, and former officials of the Japanese Government-General.

Syngman Rhee and company, who are under the aegis of the American authorities, created the National Assembly simply for the purpose of legalizing their crimes of treason. Syngman Rhee and company imprison any Assemblyman, who dares demand the withdrawal of American troops and the peaceful unification of the fatherland, and ruthlessly suppress any attempt, no matter how slight, by Assemblymen to oppose the traitorous policy of Syngman Rhee and company.

In order to have their aggressive policy approved as a matter of form, the Government of the United States once again took the Korean issue to the United Nations General Assembly.

Under the coercion of the United States delegation, the United Nations General Assembly refused to hear the voice of true representatives of Korean people and resolved to dispatch to Korea the so-called new United Nations Commission on Korea.

American imperialists were afraid that on the rostrum of the United Nations General Assembly the true representatives of the Korean people should expose to the whole world the aggressive policy of the United States of America in Korea by disclosing the real character of the separate elections in South Korea and the actual conditions existing in our fatherland.

Into what have the Americans and national traitors changed the southern half of our fatherland? In the course of the four years under the rule of the American authorities and the Korean reactionary elements South Korea has become a wild arena of terrorism and political suppression against the democratic movement in South Korea.

In South Korea there is no freedom of speech, Press, assembly, association and demonstration. Democratic political parties and social organizations have been driven underground and their Press organs destroyed. Anyone in South Korea who truly expresses the long cherished desire of the people is shot to death without trial, arrested, and tortured unconditionally.

The Americans who came to garrison Korea three weeks after the surrender of Japan did not kill even a single member of the Japanese military personnel. They let them go.

In South Korea, under the direction of the Americans, tens of thousands of patriots who fight the great popular battle for the enforcement of democratic reforms, as well as the attainment of unification, independence and democratization of the fatherland, are being shot to death, imprisoned and tortured.

As a result of the rule by the American authorities and the national traitors, the economy of South Korea continues to be wrecked, while industrial production also continues to go downward. Under the beautiful name of so-called "economic aid" American monopolists are using South Korea as a market for the disposal of their surplus commodities. As a result of such "aid", millions of unemployed and beggars are roaming the streets of South Korea.

The agrarian economy is retrogressing. The people in the southern half, which is a granary of the fatherland, are forced to groan under hunger and starvation.

The Syngman Rhee puppet government and the fellow traitors in it have concluded all sorts of "pacts" and "agreements" with their masters, American imperialists. Through these "pacts" and "agreements" they made South Korea a true slave economically to American capitalists. The people of all Korea are indignant over the traitors' policy which enslaved South Korea.

The Korean People's Supreme Council had submitted a petition to the USSR and the US Governments respectively, asking for the withdrawal of their troops. The Soviet Government gladly complied with the Korean people's request and ordered its troops to withdraw from North Korea. The evacuation of the Soviet troops took place over six months ago. In spite of it, the American troops are still staying in South Korea. The Korean people are further indignant over it.

Now there is no pretext or condition which justifies continued occupation of South Korea by US troops. The Korean people are fighting against it because the US occupation hinders unification and complete independence of our fatherland. The Soviet Union has been giving us unlimited assistance to carry on this just task of Korean people.

Through different stages, the Soviet policy in regard to the solution of the Korean problem has been in perfect consonance with the interests of the Korean people. At the Three Power Foreign Ministers Conference at Moscow in 1945, the Soviet delegate, guarding the interests of the Korean people, refused the proposal made by the US delegate. The Soviet delegate consistently and repeatedly insisted upon the principles of the Moscow decision at the meeting of the US-USSR Joint Commission. When it became clear that the implementation of the Moscow agreement was impossible, the Soviet Government insisted upon the withdrawal of the occupying troops and showed in reality its genuine policy of respecting the sovereignty and rights of our people by taking the initiative in withdrawing its troops from Korea. The Soviet Government was and is still insisting on the right of the Korean people concerning the unification, democracy and independence of our fatherland.

Dear fellow brothers and sisters!

The US imperialists and national traitors are attempting to perpetuate the division of our fatherland for their greedy purpose. The time has come for us to solve with our own hands the question of the unification of our fatherland, because the division of our fatherland which has lasted for four years is causing misery to an extent no longer tolerable to our Korean people.

There is only one plan which will enable the unified, democratic Korea to develop her economy to meet the interests of the Korean people. South Korean economy, which is at the present in the stage of destruction, shall be speedily rehabilitated on the basis of the structure of North Korean economy. Who would be ignorant of the fact that both North and South Korea are economically inter-dependent on each other? The achievement of the North Korean people constitutes a prototype which shows how rapidly the unified, democratic, independent Korea can develop herself.

The reactionary elements who, under the aegis of American imperialists, are carrying the day in the southern half of our fatherland, do not want the peaceful attainment of unification for the fatherland on a democratic basis. Syngman Rhee and company are training troops and are asking their American masters for arms. Syngman Rhee and company are provoking an internecine civil war and are trying to immerse the fighters for the attainment of democratization and unification in a sea of blood. In the southern half of our fatherland terrorism and pursuit are becoming more and more vicious day by day and tens of thousands of persons fighting for the people are being killed.

The American imperialists, who are masters of the national traitors, have rich experience in provoking internecine strife for the purpose of suppressing democratic movements. Under the "aid" of American imperialists, the flames of war are raging in China and Greece. At present they are trying to immerse the Korean people in a sea of blood. They are inciting the Korean reactionary elements to war. No wonder that the so-called "National Defence Army" is almost daily provoking clashes along the 38th parallel.

It is the Americans and their hirelings, Syngman Rhee and his traitor company, who are inciting and organizing the suppression of the people on Cheju Island and the guerrillas in South Cholla Province, as well as the clashes along the 38th parallel. Our people do not want an internecine strife. Our people do not want to shed blood in the interests of American monopolists and their hirelings, the national reactionary elements. The Korean people want and can attain, on our own and by peaceful means, unification for our fatherland. Can the Korean people be divided? Of course not! The Korean people have always been, and will be, one.

At this grave juncture for our fatherland and the people, the true patriots of South and North Korea, as well as members of political parties and social organizations, irrespective of their property or social position, must unite themselves in the struggle for the attainment of unification for the fatherland.

Dear brothers and sisters! The Democratic Front for the Attainment of Unification for the Fatherland calls on all the democratic political parties and social organizations of South and North Korea, as well as all the Korean people, to carry out peaceful unification for the fatherland and proposes the following peaceful means for unification:

1. Let us hold the task of peaceful unification of the fatherland in our own hands and fulfil it.

2. We demand the immediate withdrawal of the American troops from Korea who are obstructing the peaceful unification of the fatherland.

3. We demand the immediate evacuation of the unlawful organ, the so-called "United Nations Commission on Korea", from our soil.

4. We propose to hold simultaneously elections throughout South and North Korea for a united legislative organ.

5. Let us hold the elections under the guidance of a committee consisting of delegates from democratic political parties and social organizations which stand for peaceful unification of the fatherland.

6. For the purpose of discussing a plan for peaceful unification of the fatherland, let us call a conference of delegates from political parties and social organizations of South and North Korea, which in turn will form an Election Guidance Committee.

7. Let us hold the elections for the legislative organ in September 1949 on the principles of universal, equal elections on the basis of the secret ballot. Those who enthusiastically co-operated with the Japanese Empire during the days of the Japanese rule are deprived of the right to vote.

8. In order to ensure the freedom of election let us enforce the following measures without fail:

(a) Discontinue suppression of democratic political parties and social organizations and their leaders;

(b) Legalize all democratic political parties and social organizations and ensure them freedom of activity;

(*c*) Revoke the order for the closing down of the Press organs of democratic political parties and social organizations and ensure the democratic political parties and social organizations the right to have their own Press organs;

(*d*) Ensure freedom of speech, Press, assembly, mass meetings and demonstration;

(*e*) Release immediately all political prisoners.

9. The Election Guidance Committee shall have the following powers:

(*a*) To give the existing governments in South and North Korea and their appropriate organs the necessary directives regarding the preparations and holding of the election;

(*b*) To review the execution of its decisions and directives;

(*c*) To supervise the withdrawal of foreign troops from Korea by a committee to be formed by the Election Guidance Committee.

10. Simultaneously with the formation of the General Election Guidance Committee, the existing police and security forces in South and North Korea shall be placed under the direct control of the Election Guidance Committee. The Election Guidance Committee shall eliminate from the police forces pro-Japanese and those who had served the Japanese police and military police, and disband the police units which participated in the suppression of the people's resistance on Cheju Island and the guerrilla movement in South Korea.

11. The supreme legislative organ, formed by the general elections, shall adopt a constitution for the Republic of Korea and form a government in accordance with the provisions of the constitution, and the government thus formed shall take over government functions from the existing governments in South and North Korea and then dissolve them.

12. The existing troops in south and north shall be combined on a democratic basis by the new government of the Republic of Korea. The units of the South Korea National Defence Army which participated in the suppression of the people's resistance on Cheju Island and other areas, as well as of the partisan movement, shall be disbanded. Those who participated in the suppression of the people's resistance and the partisan movement are banned from serving in the armed forces, and those who incited and organized the suppression shall be punished.

Such is the programme which we propose to democratic political parties and social organizations and all the people for the peaceful attainment of unification for the fatherland. We are convinced that all the Korean people will enthusiastically support our proposal. Anyone who persists in opposition and obstruction of the task for peaceful unification shall not escape punishment by the Korean people. The Korean people, marching forward toward the attainment of unification, democratization and independence for the fatherland, are capable of liquidating all who are standing in our way.

Long live a united, democratic, independent Korea!

Long live the Korean people who will be united forever!

Annex V

LIST OF DELEGATIONS TO THE COMMISSION, AND SECRETARIAT

1. DELEGATIONS TO THE COMMISSION

Australia: Patrick Shaw, Representative;[69] A. B. Jamieson, Representative; Claire Garrett, Secretary-typist; Joan Fullard, Secretary-typist.

China: Liu, Yu-Wan, Representative; Ssutu, T. T., Alternate; Loo, W. D., Secretary.

El Salvador: Miguel Angel Magaña, Representative; Fidel Sanchez-Hernandez, Alternate.[70]

France: Henri Costilhes, Temporary Representative; Marcel Barthelemy, Secretary;[71] Charles Martel, Secretary.

India: Anup Singh, Representative.

Philippines: Rufino Luna, Representative; Norberto Luna, Secretary;[72] Antonio Ferrer, Secretary.

Syria: Yasin Mughir, Representative.[73]

2. SECRETARIAT OF THE COMMISSION

Principal Secretary: Egon Ranshofen-Wertheimer.

Deputy Principal Secretary: Sanford Schwarz.

Assistant Secretaries: Graham Lucas,[74] Arsen Shahbaz, Hung-Ti Chu.

Administrative Officer: Alfred Katz.

Assistant Administrative Officer: Jehangir Paymaster.

Interpreters: Harry Liao, Mark Priceman.

[69] Mr. Shaw and Miss Garrett returned to Tokyo on 23 February. Mr. Shaw accompanied by Miss Fullard returned to Seoul on 2 July. They left again for Tokyo on 12 July.
[70] Mr. Magaña informed the Commission that El Salvador was withdrawing from membership on the Commission on 20 July. On 26 July the delegation of El Salvador rejoined the Commission.
[71] Mr. Barthelemy left Seoul on 12 June.
[72] Mr. Norberto Luna left Seoul on 20 June.
[73] Mr. Mughir left Seoul on 26 March.
[74] Mr. Lucas left Seoul on 30 May.

Précis-writers: Marian Robb, Harold Riddle.

Secretary-typists: Dorothy Compton, Anne-Marie Hubert, Barbara Liu, Ann D. Sheehan, Marion Wood, Cora Wyman.

Military Technical Adviser: Colonel C. C. Liu.[75]

3. LOCALLY RECRUITED STAFF

Interpreter: Myo-Mook Lee.

Translator-Interpreters: Yong Won Kim, Kyu Yong Lee, Robert T. Park.

Correspondent-Secretaries: Lydia C. Koh, Unja Lee.

Clerk-Messenger: Chong Dea Lee.

Office Machine Operator: Chun, Yun Sang.

Dispatchers: Chun, Ki Poong. J. H. Kim.

Receptionists:[76] So Young Lee, Soon Yeh Cho, Flory Leigh.

Annex VI

LIST OF DOCUMENTS

A. United Nations documents concerning the problem of the independence of Korea

1. REPORT OF THE TEMPORARY COMMISSION ON KOREA TO THE GENERAL ASSEMBLY

A/575, A/575/Add.1 and A/575/Add.2, first part of the report of the United Nations Commission on Korea, volumes I to III.

A/575/Add.3 and A/575/Add.4, second part of the report of the United Nations Temporary Commission on Korea, volumes I to II.

2. REPORT OF THE INTERIM COMMITTEE OF THE GENERAL ASSEMBLY

A/583, consultation by the Temporary Commission on Korea with the Interim Committee.

3. INCLUSION OF THE ITEM OF THE PROBLEM OF THE INDEPENDENCE OF KOREA IN THE AGENDA OF THE GENERAL ASSEMBLY

A/653, adoption of the agenda of the third regular session and allocation of items to the Committees (item 16, the problem of the independence of Korea).

4. PROCEEDINGS IN THE FIRST COMMITTEE
(*a*) DOCUMENTS

A/C.1/365, letter from the chief delegate at the General Assembly for the Government of the Republic of Korea to the Secretary-General, dated 1 October 1948.

A/C.1/366, cable from the Minister of Foreign Affairs of "The Democratic People's Republic of Korea" to the Secretary-General, dated 8 October 1948.

A/C.1/367, letter dated 4 November 1948 from the Czechoslovak Delegation to the Chairman of the First Committee transmitting a draft resolution inviting the delegation of "The Democratic People's Republic of Korea" to participate in the examination of the problem of the independence of Korea.

A/C.1/395, draft resolution of China inviting the delegation of the Republic of Korea to participate without the right to vote in the debate of the First Committee on the Korean question.

A/C.1/426, joint draft resolution of Australia, China and the United States of America on the problem of the independence of Korea.

A/C.1/427/Corr.1, draft resolution of the USSR proposing the abolishment of the United Nations Temporary Commission on Korea.[77]

A/C.1/428, draft resolution on the problem of the independence of Korea adopted by the First Committee at its 236th meeting on 8 December 1948.

(b) SUMMARY RECORDS

A/C.1/SR.200, summary record of the 200th meeting, 15 November 1948.

A/C.1/SR.229 to 236 inclusive, summary records of the 229th to the 236th meetings, 6 to 8 December 1948.

5. PROCEEDINGS IN THE FIFTH COMMITTEE

A/C.5/288, United Nations Commission on Korea; report of the Secretary-General on the financial implications of the establishment of the Commission.

A/C.5/289, letter from the President of the General Assembly to the Chairman of the Fifth Committee, dated 9 December 1948.

A/C.5/SR.177, summary record of the 177th meeting, 9 December 1948.

---

[75] Colonel Liu joined the Secretariat on 21 June and completed his duties with the Commission on 16 July 1949.

[76] These served at different periods.
[77] With slight revision this document was issued as A/790 which was again considered by the plenary meeting of the General Assembly.

6. Proceedings of the General Assembly on the Reports of the First and Fifth Committees

(a) documents

A/788, report of the First Committee, 9 December 1948.

A/795, report of the Fifth Committee, 10 December 1948.

(b) verbatim records of the general assembly[78]

A/PV.142, verbatim record of the 142nd meeting, 24 September 1948.

A/PV.186, verbatim record of the 186th meeting, 11 December 1948.

A/PV.187, verbatim record of the 187th meeting, 12 December 1948.

B. Complete list of documents of the United Nations Commission on Korea[79]

1. Agendas of the Commission

A/AC.26/Agenda 1	Provisional agenda for the 1st meeting	2 February 1949
A/AC.26/Agenda 2	Provisional agenda for the 2nd meeting	7 February 1949
A/AC.26/Agenda 3	Provisional agenda for the 3rd meeting	7 February 1949
A/AC.26/Agenda 4	Provisional agenda for the 4th meeting	8 February 1949
A/AC.26/Agenda 5	Provisional agenda for the 5th meeting	9 February 1949
A/AC.26/Agenda 6	Provisional agenda for the 6th meeting	10 February 1949
A/AC.26/Agenda 7	Provisional agenda for the 7th meeting	11 February 1949
A/AC.26/Agenda 8	Provisional agenda for the 8th meeting	12 February 1949
A/AC.26/Agenda 9	Provisional agenda for the 9th meeting	15 February 1949
A/AC.26/Agenda 9/Rev.1	agenda for the 9th meeting	15 February 1949
A/AC.26/Agenda 10	Provisional agenda for the 10th meeting	16 February 1949
A/AC.26/Agenda 11	Provisional agenda for the 11th meeting	18 February 1949
A/AC.26/Agenda 12	Provisional agenda for the 12th meeting	18 February 1949
A/AC.26/Agenda 13	Provisional agenda for the 13th meeting	21 February 1949
A/AC.26/Agenda 14	Provisional agenda for the 14th meeting	23 February 1949
A/AC.26/Agenda 14/Rev.1	agenda for the 14th meeting	23 February 1949
A/AC.26/Agenda 15	Provisional agenda for the 15th meeting	25 February 1949
A/AC.26/Agenda 16	Provisional agenda for the 16th meeting	28 February 1949
A/AC.26/Agenda 16/Rev.1	agenda for the 16th meeting	28 February 1949
A/AC.26/Agenda 17	Provisional agenda for the 17th meeting	2 March 1949
A/AC.26/Agenda 17/Rev.1	agenda for the 17th meeting	2 March 1949
A/AC.26/Agenda 18	Provisional agenda for the 18th meeting	9 March 1949
A/AC.26/Agenda 18/Rev.1	agenda for the 18th meeting	9 March 1949
A/AC.26/Agenda 19	Provisional agenda for the 19th meeting	10 March 1949
A/AC.26/Agenda 19/Rev.1	agenda for the 19th meeting	10 March 1949
A/AC.26/Agenda 20	Provisional agenda for the 20th meeting	17 March 1949
A/AC.26/Agenda 21	Provisional agenda for the 21st meeting	18 March 1949
A/AC.26/Agenda 22	Provisional agenda for the 22nd meeting	19 March 1949
A/AC.26/Agenda 23	Provisional agenda for the 23rd meeting	24 March 1949
A/AC.26/Agenda 23/Rev.1	agenda for the 23rd meeting	24 March 1949
A/AC.26/Agenda 24	Provisional agenda for the 24th meeting	5 April 1949
A/AC.26/Agenda 24/Rev.1	agenda for the 24th meeting	5 April 1949
A/AC.26/Agenda 25	Provisional agenda for the 25th meeting	11 April 1949
A/AC.26/Agenda 25/Rev.1	agenda for the 25th meeting	12 April 1949
A/AC.26/Agenda 26	Provisional agenda for the 26th meeting	20 April 1949
A/AC.26/Agenda 26/Rev.1	agenda for the 26th meeting	22 April 1949
A/AC.26/Agenda 27	Provisional agenda for the 27th meeting	29 April 1949
A/AC.26/Agenda 28	Provisional agenda for the 28th meeting	16 May 1949
A/AC.26/Agenda 28/Add.1	Provisional agenda for the 28th meeting	17 May 1949
A/AC.26/Agenda 29	Provisional agenda for the 29th meeting	18 May 1949
A/AC.26/Agenda 30	Provisional agenda for the 30th meeting	20 May 1949
A/AC.26/Agenda 30/Rev.1	agenda for the 30th meeting	23 May 1949
A/AC.26/Agenda 31	Provisional agenda for the 31st meeting	24 May 1949
A/AC.26/Agenda 32	Provisional agenda for the 32nd meeting	1 June 1949
A/AC.26/Agenda 33	Provisional agenda for the 33rd meeting	8 June 1949
A/AC.26/Agenda 34	Provisional agenda for the 34th meeting	11 June 1949
A/AC.26/Agenda 35	Provisional agenda for the 35th meeting	17 June 1949
A/AC.26/Agenda 36	Provisional agenda for the 36th meeting	21 June 1949
A/AC.26/Agenda 37	Provisional agenda for the 37th meeting	25 June 1949
A/AC.26/Agenda 38	Provisional agenda for the 38th meeting	2 July 1949

[78] See also *Official Records of the third session of the General Assembly, Part I,* pages 95, 104 to 105, 1006 to 1043.

[79] Covering the period up to 28 July 1949.

1. Agendas of the Commission (*continued*)

A/AC.26/Agenda 39	Provisional agenda for the 39th meeting	7 July	1949
A/AC.26/Agenda 39/Rev.1	agenda for the 39th meeting	8 July	1949
A/AC.26/Agenda 40	Provisional agenda for the 40th meeting	11 July	1949
A/AC.26/Agenda 40/Rev.1	agenda for the 40th meeting	13 July	1949
A/AC.26/Agenda 41	Provisional agenda for the 41st meeting	19 July	1949
A/AC.26/Agenda 41/Rev.1	agenda for the 41st meeting	20 July	1949
A/AC.26/Agenda 42	Provisional agenda for the 42nd meeting	21 July	1949
A/AC.26/Agenda 42/Rev.1	agenda for the 42nd meeting	22 July	1949
A/AC.26/Agenda 43	Provisional agenda for the 43rd meeting	22 July	1949
A/AC.26/Agenda 44	Provisional agenda for the 44th meeting	23 July	1949
A/AC.26/Agenda 45	Provisional agenda for the 45th meeting	25 July	1949
A/AC.26/Agenda 46	Provisional agenda for the 46th meeting	25 July	1949
A/AC.26/Agenda 47	Provisional agenda for the 47th meeting	26 July	1949
A/AC.26/Agenda 48	Provisional agenda for the 48th meeting	27 July	1949
A/AC.26/Agenda 49	Provisional agenda for the 49th meeting	27 July	1949
A/AC.26/Agenda 50	Provisional agenda for the 50th meeting	28 July	1949
A/AC.26/Agenda 50/Rev.1	agenda for the 50th meeting	28 July	1949

2. Summary records of the Meetings of the Commission

A/AC.26/SR.1	Summary record of the 1st meeting	2 February	1949
A/AC.26/SR.2	Summary record of the 2nd meeting	9 February	1949
A/AC.26/SR.3	Summary record of the 3rd meeting	7 February	1949
A/AC.26/SR.4	Summary record of the 4th meeting	10 February	1949
A/AC.26/SR.4/Corr.1	Corrigendum to the summary record of the 4th meeting	16 February	1949
A/AC.26/SR.5	Summary record of the 5th meeting	10 February	1949
A/AC.26/SR.6	Summary record of the 6th meeting	13 February	1949
A/AC.26/SR.7	Summary record of the 7th meeting	13 February	1949
A/AC.26/SR.7/Corr.1	Corrigendum to the summary record of the 7th meeting	26 February	1949
A/AC.26/SR.8 with Annexes 1, 2, 3, 4, 5, 6, 7, 8, 9	Summary record of the 8th meeting with various statements made at this meeting	12 February	1949
A/AC.26/SR.9	Summary record of the 9th meeting	16 February	1949
A/AC.26/SR.9/Corr.1	Corrigendum to the summary record of the 9th meeting	26 February	1949
A/AC.26/SR.10	Summary record of the 10th meeting	17 February	1949
A/AC.26/SR.10/Corr.1	Corrigendum to the summary record of the 10th meeting	26 February	1949
A/AC.26/SR.11	Summary record of the 11th meeting	19 February	1949
A/AC.26/SR.11/Corr.1	Corrigendum to the summary record of the 11th meeting	28 February	1949
A/AC.26/SR.12	Summary record of the 12th meeting	21 February	1949
A/AC.26/SR.13	Summary record of the 13th meeting	22 February	1949
A/AC.26/SR.14	Summary record of the 14th meeting	25 February	1949
A/AC.26/SR.15	Summary record of the 15th meeting	4 March	1949
A/AC.26/SR.16	Summary record of the 16th meeting	4 March	1949
A/AC.26/SR.17	Summary record of the 17th meeting	5 March	1949
A/AC.26/SR.18	Summary record of the 18th meeting	11 March	1949
A/AC.26/SR.18/Corr.1	Corrigendum to the summary record of the 18th meeting	18 March	1949
A/AC.26/SR.19	Summary record of the 19th meeting	15 March	1949
A/AC.26/SR.19/Corr.1	Corrigendum to the summary record of the 19th meeting	18 March	1949
A/AC.26/SR.20	Summary record of the 20th meeting	21 March	1949
A/AC.26/SR.21	Summary record of the 21st meeting	25 March	1949
A/AC.26/SR.21/Corr.1	Corrigendum to the summary record of the 21st meeting	31 March	1949
A/AC.26/SR.22	Summary record of the 22nd meeting	28 March	1949
A/AC.26/SR.23	Summary record of the 23rd meeting	26 March	1949
A/AC.26/SR.24	Summary record of the 24th meeting	7 April	1949
A/AC.26/SR.25	Summary record of the 25th meeting	19 April	1949
A/AC.26/SR.26	Summary record of the 26th meeting	16 May	1949
A/AC.26/SR.27	Summary record of the 27th meeting	13 May	1949
A/AC.26/SR.27/Corr.1	Corrigendum to the summary record of the 27th meeting	18 May	1949
A/AC.26/SR.28	Summary record of the 28th meeting	23 May	1949
A/AC.26/SR.29	Summary record of the 29th meeting	24 May	1949
A/AC.26/SR.29/Corr.1	Corrigendum to the summary record of the 29th meeting	27 May	1949

2. Summary records of the Meetings of the Commission (*continued*)

A/AC.26/SR.30	Summary record of the 30th meeting	21 May	1949
A/AC.26/SR.30/Corr.1	Corrigendum to the summary record of the 30th meeting	1 June	1949
A/AC.26/SR.30/Corr.2	Corrigendum to the summary record of the 30th meeting	13 June	1949
A/AC.26/SR.31	Summary record of the 31st meeting	1 June	1949
A/AC.26/SR.32	Summary record of the 32nd meeting	6 June	1949
A/AC.26/SR.33	Summary record of the 33rd meeting	15 June	1949
A/AC.26/SR.34	Summary record of the 34th meeting	17 June	1949
A/AC.26/SR.35	Summary record of the 35th meeting	27 June	1949
A/AC.26/SR.35/Corr.1	Corrigendum to the summary record of the 35th meeting	3 July	1949
A/AC.26/SR.36	Summary record of the 36th meeting	29 June	1949
A/AC.26/SR.36/Corr.1	Corrigendum to the summary record of the 36th meeting	3 July	1949
A/AC.26/SR.37	Summary record of the 37th meeting	6 July	1949
A/AC.26/SR.37/Corr.1	Corrigendum to the summary record of the 37th meeting	8 July	1949
A/AC.26/SR.38	Summary record of the 38th meeting	8 July	1949
A/AC.26/SR.39	Summary record of the 39th meeting	15 July	1949
A/AC.26/SR.40	Summary record of the 40th meeting	15 July	1949
A/AC.26/SR.41	Summary record of the 41st meeting	25 July	1949

3. General documents

A/AC.26/1	Resolution adopted at the 5th meeting concerning the establishment of sub-committees	9 February	1949
A/AC.26/2	Rules of procedure adopted at the 6th meeting	10 February	1949
A/AC.26/3	Resolution adopted at the 10th meeting concerning access of Koreans to the Commission	17 February	1949
A/AC.26/4	Report of Sub-Committee I concerning contact with North Korea, adopted at the 11th meeting	18 February	1949
A/AC.26/5	Report of Sub-Committee II concerning persons and topics for hearings, adopted at the 14th meeting	25 February	1949
A/AC.26/6	Resolution concerning social functions adopted at the 16th meeting	1 March	1949
A/AC.26/7	Report of Sub-Committee I concerning personalities to be heard and main topics of discussion, adopted at the 17th meeting	2 March	1949
A/AC.26/8	First information report (period 1-19 February 1949)	4 March	1949
A/AC.26/9	Message from the Government of the Republic of Korea, letter from B. C. Limb, Minister of Foreign Affairs	9 March	1949
A/AC.26/10	Report of Sub-Committee I concerning contact with North Korea, adopted at the 21st meeting	19 March	1949
A/AC.26/11	Report of Sub-Committee II concerning further list of persons to be heard and trips to the provinces, adopted at the 22nd meeting	21 March	1949
A/AC.26/12	Second information report (period 20 February-12 March 1949)	26 March	1949
A/AC.26/13	Report of Sub-Committee I concerning further list of persons to be heard and visits to industrial areas	12 April	1949
A/AC.26/14	Communication from the Special Representative of the United States, John J. Muccio, to the Chairman of the Commission, Miguel Angel Magaña, regarding troop withdrawal	18 April	1949
A/AC.26/14/Add.1	Communication from the Ambassador of the United States of America, John J. Muccio, to the Chairman of the Commission, Miguel Angel Magaña, regarding the establishment of a Korean Military Advisory Group	4 May	1949
A/AC.26/14/Add.2	Communication from U.S. Ambassador Muccio to the Chairman of the Commission regarding withdrawal of United States troops	13 June	1949

A/AC.26/15	Third information report (period 13 March-2 April 1949)	19 April	1949
A/AC.26/16	Replies to Press questionnaire of 31 March 1949, as approved by the Commission at its 26th meeting	22 April	1949
A/AC.26/17	Communication from the Minister of Foreign Affairs of the Republic of Korea, B. C. Limb, to the Chairman of the Commission concerning the by-election to be held on the island of Cheju Do on 10 May 1949	28 April	1949
A/AC.26/17/Add.1	Communication from the Minister of Foreign Affairs of the Republic of Korea, B. C. Limb, to the Chairman of the Commission, concerning the by-election to be held at Chon-an Gun on 10 June 1949	9 May	1949
A/AC.26/18	Question of observer teams, statement by the representative of El Salvador at the 27th meeting	30 April	1949
A/AC.26/19	Fourth information report (period 3-23 April 1949)	6 May	1949
A/AC.26/20	List of documents issued by the Commission for the period 24 January-11 May 1949	12 May	1949
A/AC.26/20/Add.1	List of documents issued by the Commission period 12 May-12 July 1949	13 July	1949
A/AC.26/21	Resolution adopted at the 28th meeting concerning the composition of the Commission	18 May	1949
A/AC.26/22	Report of Sub-Committee I concerning contact with North Korea, adopted at the 28th meeting	19 May	1949
A/AC.26/23	Letter from the Minister of Foreign Affairs of the Republic of Korea, B. C. Limb, to the Chairman of the Commission, Mr. Henri Costilhes, concerning contact with North Korea	19 May	1949
A/AC.26/24	Draft resolution of the Philippines concerning withdrawal of occupation forces (introduced at the 29th meeting)	19 May	1949
A/AC.26/24/Rev.1	Amended draft resolution of the Philippines concerning withdrawal of occupation forces	19 May	1949
A/AC.26/24/Rev.1/Corr.1	Corrigendum to the amended draft resolution of the Philippines concerning withdrawal of occupation forces	20 May	1949
A/AC.26/25	Resolution adopted at the 30th meeting concerning withdrawal of occupation forces	24 May	1949
A/AC.26/26	Report of Sub-Committee I concerning persons to be heard, adopted at the 30th meeting	23 May	1949
A/AC.26/27	Fifth information report (period 24 April-14 May 1949)	27 May	1949
A/AC.26/28	Sixth information report (period 15 May-4 June 1949)	10 June	1949
A/AC.26/29	Resolution adopted at the 34th meeting concerning observation of withdrawal of occupation forces	13 June	1949
A/AC.26/29/Add.1	Resolution adopted at the 35th meeting concerning observation of withdrawal of occupation forces	20 June	1949
A/AC.26/30	Report of Sub-Committee I concerning broadcast to North Korea and Press release regarding hearings, adopted at the 34th meeting	13 June	1949
A/AC.26/31	Draft outline of the report of UNCOK to the General Assembly	18 June	1949
A/AC.26/32	Report of Sub-Committee I concerning field visits, adopted by the Commission at its 36th meeting	24 June	1949
A/AC.26/33	Draft resolution of El Salvador concerning the problem of Korea	25 June	1949
A/AC.26/33/Rev.1	Draft resolution of El Salvador concerning the problem of Korea	8 July	1949
A/AC.26/33/Rev.2	Draft resolution of El Salvador concerning the problem of Korea	8 July	1949
A/AC.26/34	Final report of Sub-Committee II, adopted at the 37th meeting	29 June	1949

3. General documents (*continued*)

A/AC.26/35	Communication from the Minister of Foreign Affairs of the Republic of Korea, B. C. Limb, to the Chairman of the Commission concerning observation of withdrawal of occupation forces	1 July	1949
A/AC.26/36	Communication from the Minister of Foreign Affairs of the Republic of Korea, B. C. Limb, to the Chairman of the Commission, Anup Singh, concerning continuation of the work of the Commission	1 July	1949
A/AC.26/37	Final report of Sub-Committee I, adopted at the 39th meeting	8 July	1949
A/AC.26/38	Seventh information report (period 5 June-2 July 1949)	9 July	1949
A/AC.26/39	Communication from the Ministry of Foreign Affairs to the Commission concerning arrest of members of the National Assembly	11 July	1949
A/AC.26/40	Communication from the Minister of Foreign Affairs of the Republic of Korea, B. C. Limb, to the Chairman of the Commission, concerning United Nations military observers	11 July	1949
A/AC.26/41	Withdrawal of the Delegation of El Salvador from the Commission, resolution adopted at the 41st meeting	21 July	1949
A/AC.26/41/Corr.1	Corrigendum to the resolution concerning the withdrawal of the Delegation of El Salvador from the Commission	21 July	1949
A/AC.26/42	Report to the General Assembly	27 July	1949
A/AC.26/43	Annexes to the report to the General Assembly	28 July	1949

4. Working papers

A/AC.26/W.1	Resolution 195 (III) of the General Assembly adopted 12 December 1948	24 January	1949
A/AC.26/W.2	Provisional rules of procedure	7 February	1949
A/AC.26/W.3	Korean-Aid Agreement, agreement on aid between the United States of America and the Republic of Korea	7 February	1949
A/AC.26/W.4	Application of the Republic of Korea for admission to membership	8 February	1949
A/AC.26/W.5	Texts of messages and address delivered on the occasion of the mass meeting for welcoming the members of the Commission	14 February	1949
A/AC.26/W.6	Notes on interview between members of the Commission and the Liaison Committee appointed by the Korean Government	17 February	1949
A/AC.26/W.7	Text of speech of Mr. Jamieson, Chairman of the Commission, before the Korean National Assembly	22 February	1949
A/AC.26/W.8	Addresses of welcome by Mr. Sin Ik Hi, Chairman of Korean National Assembly	25 February	1949
A/AC.26/W.9	Letter from Chairman of the Liaison Committee to the Principal Secretary	25 February	1949
A/AC.26/W.10	Terms of office of the Chairmen	9 March	1949
A/AC.26/W.10/Rev.1	Terms of office of the Chairmen	31 March	1949
A/AC.26/W.11	Materials bearing on the interpretation of the General Assembly resolution of 12 December 1948	23 March	1949
A/AC.26/W.12	Report of the drafting group on the Press questionnaire	21 April	1949
A/AC 26/W.13	Communications from Dr. Chough Pyung Ok, Personal Representative of President Rhee, to the heads of certain Permanent Delegations to the United Nations	4 May	1949
A/AC.26/W.14	Korean Press Law	23 June	1949
A/AC.26/W.15	National Security Law—Law No. 10 of 1 December 1948	24 June	1949
A/AC.26/W.16	Korean broadcasts by the Commission (note by the Secretariat)	2 July	1949

4. WORKING PAPERS (*continued*)

A/AC.26/W.16/Rev.1	Korean broadcasts by the Commission, draft of broadcast	7 July	1949
A/AC.26/W.16/Rev.1/Add.1	Korean broadcasts by the Commission, exchange of communications between the Principal Secretary and Clarence Ryee, Director of the Office of Public Information of the Republic of Korea	26 July	1949
A/AC.26/W.17	Text of the Manifesto of "The Democratic Front for the Attainment of Unification for the Fatherland"	12 July	1949
A/AC.26/W.18	Press interview with a former lieutenant of the "People's Army of North Korea"	18 July	1949
A/AC.26/W.19	Arrest of newspapermen covering the Commission activities, communication from Dr. Anup Singh, Representative of India	19 July	1949
A/AC.26/W.19/Add.1	Arrest of newspapermen covering the Commission activities, communication from Miss Moh Youn Sook, Chief Liaison Committee to the United Nations Commission	20 July	1949
A/AC.26/W.19/Add.2	Arrest of newspapermen covering the Commission activities, communication from Mr. Clarence C. Ryee, Director, Office of Public Information	21 July	1949

5. COMMUNICATIONS RECEIVED FROM INDIVIDUALS AND ORGANIZATIONS

A/AC.26/NC.1	Communication from the Chairman of the Han Kook Independence Party to the Commission	10 February	1949
A/AC.26/NC.2	Communication from Kim Yak Soo, Vice-President of the National Assembly, and members of the Assembly to the Commission	19 March	1949
A/AC.26/NC.3	Communication from the Korean Labour and Farmer Party to the Commission, statement regarding unification	22 March	1949
A/AC.26/NC.4	Communication from the Tai Han Chung Nyon Tan (Korean Youth Corps) to the Commission	22 March	1949
A/AC.26/NC.5	List of communications from organizations and individuals (received during the period 1 February-31 March 1949)	7 April	1949
A/AC.26/NC.5/Add.1	List of communications from organizations and individuals (received during the period 1 April-30 June 1949)	7 July	1949
A/AC.26/NC.6	Communication from Shin Haing Sik, Representative of Korea Public Opinion Investigation Association, to the Chairman of the Commission	7 May	1949
A/AC.26/NC.7	Communication from Kim Yak Soo, Vice-President of the National Assembly, concerning establishment of military missions in Korea	21 June	1949
A/AC.26/NC.7/Add.1	Communication from Kim Dong Won, Vice-President of the National Assembly, concerning establishment of military missions in Korea	22 June	1949
A/AC.26/NC.8	Communication to the Chairman of the Commission, Mr. Anup Singh, from political and social organizations, concerning withdrawal of occupation forces	24 June	1949
A/AC.26/NC.9	Communication from the mass meeting of northerners in South Korea to the Commission presenting a resolution adopted at the mass meeting	30 June	1949
A/AC.26/NC.10	Communication to the Commission from the mass meeting held on 1 July 1949 under the auspices of the Korean Labourers Federation and the Korean Farmers Federation presenting a message and resolution adopted at that meeting	4 July	1949

5. COMMUNICATIONS RECEIVED FROM INDIVIDUALS AND ORGANIZATIONS (*continued*)

A/AC.26/NC.11	Communication to the Commission from the mass meeting of Korean Christians concerned with the national safety	15 July	1949
A/AC.26/NC.12	Arrest of newspapermen covering the Commission activities, communication from Lee Insoo, editor in chief of the *Seoul Times* to the Commission	20 July	1949
A/AC.26/NC.13	Communications to the Commission from the Korean Youth Corps and the Korean Students mass meeting for strengthening national defence	20 July	1949

6. INFORMATION PAPERS

A/AC.26/Inf.1	Korean officials	4 February	1949
A/AC.26/Inf.2	Delegations to the Commission	8 February	1949
A/AC.26/Inf.2/Rev.1	Delegations to the Commission	31 March	1949
A/AC.26/Inf.3	Secretariat of the Commission	8 February	1949
A/AC.26/Inf.3/Rev.1	Secretariat of the Commission	16 February	1949
A/AC.26/Inf.3/Rev.2	Secretariat of the Commission	12 March	1949
A/AC.26/Inf.3/Rev.3	Secretariat of the Commission	12 March	1949
A/AC.26/Inf.3/Rev.4	Secretariat of the Commission	31 March	1949
A/AC.26/Inf.2/Rev.2	Delegations to the Commission	16 May	1949
A/AC.26/Inf.2/Rev.2/Corr.1	Delegations to the Commission	17 May	1949
A/AC.26/Inf.2/Rev.3	Delegations to the Commission	6 July	1949
A/AC.26/Inf.3/Rev.5	Secretariat of the Commission	6 July	1949

7. SUB-COMMITTEE DOCUMENTS

(a) SUB-COMMITTEE I

A/AC.26/SC.1/1	Summary record of interview with the President of the Republic of Korea and Cabinet members	11 February	1949
A/AC.26/SC.1/2	Report and recommendations	16 February	1949
A/AC.26/SC.1/2/Rev.1	Report and recommendations, contact with North Korea	17 February	1949
A/AC.26/SC.1/3	Report and recommendations	25 February	1949
A/AC.26/SC.1/4	Report of Sub-Committee I, position of the Commission in relation to the Government of Korea	28 February	1949
A/AC.26/SC.1/4/Rev.1	Position of the Commission in relation to the Government of Korea	2 March	1949
A/AC.26/SC.1/5	Personalities to be heard and main topics of discussion	2 March	1949
A/AC.26/SC.1/6	Hearing of Lee Bum Suk, Prime Minister and Minister of National Defence	10 March	1949
A/AC.26/SC.1/6/Corr.1	Corrigendum to A/AC.26/SC.1/6	19 March	1949
A/AC.26/SC.1/7	Communication with North Korea	9 March	1949
A/AC.26/SC.1/8	Hearing of Kim Yak Soo, Vice-Chairman of the National Assembly	11 March	1949
A/AC.26/SC.1/9	Hearing of Pak Kun Oong, former member of the Interim Legislative Assembly	16 March.	1949
A/AC.26/SC.1/10	Hearing of Miss Louise Yim, Minister of Commerce and Industry	17 March	1949
A/AC.26/SC.1/11	Suggested course of action in contacting North Korea	17 March	1949
A/AC.26/SC.1/11/Corr.1	Corrigendum to A/AC.26/SC.1/11	19 March	1949
A/AC.26/SC.1/12	Further list of persons to be heard	21 March	1949
A/AC.26/SC.1/13	Hearing of Dr. A. C. Bunce, Chief of Korean Mission, United States Economic Co-operation Administration	11 April	1949
A/AC.26/SC.1/14	Further list of persons to be heard and visits to industrial areas	11 April	1949
A/AC.26/SC.1/15	Hearing of Major-General Lee Eung Jun	13 April	1949
A/AC.26/SC.1/16	Hearing of Kim To Yeun, Minister of Finance	15 April	1949
A/AC.26/SC.1/17	Hearing of Kimm Kiusic, Chairman, National Independence Federation	23 April	1949

(a) SUB-COMMITTEE I (*continued*)

A/AC.26/SC.1/18	Hearing of Kim Pyang Hoi, Representative of Cholla Namdc, National Assembly	24 April	1949
A/AC.26/SC.1/19	Visits to industrial establishments (Seoul-Yongdung Po-Inchon area)	29 April	1949
A/AC.26/SC.1/20	Hearing of Sul Eui Sik, publisher of *Sai Han Minbo*	4 May	1949
A/AC.26/SC.1/21	Hearing of Kim Pyung Yen, Governor of Pyongan-Namdo Province (North Korea)	7 May	1949
A/AC.26/SC.1/22	Report: persons to be heard and contact with North Korea	16 May	1949
A/AC.26/SC.1/23	Letter from S. Y. Kim, Ministry of Foreign Affairs, to the Secretary of Sub-Committee I, concerning legal trade and exchange of mail between the south and the north	1 June	1949
A/AC.26/SC.1/24	Hearing of Kim Koo	6 June	1949
A/AC.26/SC.1/25	Hearing of Kwon Yun Ho, preacher: Shi Chun Kyo (Presbyterian group of Korea)	6 June	1949
A/AC.26/SC.1/26	Hearing of General Lee Chun Chun (Chi Tae Hyung), member of the National Assembly	8 June	1949
A/AC.26/SC.1/27	Report: broadcast to North Korea; Press release regarding hearings	9 June	1949
A/AC.26/SC.1/28	Summary of suggestions and opinions regarding unification of Korea and removal of economic and other barriers	14 June	1949
A/AC.26/SC.1/29	Report concerning trips to be made	17 June	1949
A/AC.26/SC.1/30	Final report to the Commission (period 9 February-24 June 1949)	25 June	1949
A/AC.26/SC.1/30/Rev.1	Final report to the Commission (period 9 February-30 June 1949)	6 July	1949
A/AC.26/SC.1/31	Report of Sub-Committee I	18 July	1949
A/AC.26/SC.1/31/Annex II/Rev.1	Revised draft of Annex II of the report of Sub-Committee I	21 July	1949

(b) SUB-COMMITTEE II

A/AC.26/SC.2/1	Report and recommendations	17 February	1949
A/AC.26/SC.2/1/Rev.1	Report and recommendations	22 February	1949
A/AC.26/SC.2/2	Hearing of Sin Ik Hi, President of the National Assembly	1 March	1949
A/AC.26/SC.2/3	Hearings of Yoo Chin O and L. G. Paik	7 March	1949
A/AC.26/SC.2/4	Hearing of Yun Chi Yung, former Minister of the Interior	11 March	1949
A/AC.26/SC.2/5	Chronology of important developments in Korea from 15 August 1948 to 31 January 1949	14 March	1949
A/AC.26/SC.2/5/Corr.1	Corrigendum to A/AC.26/SC.2/5	17 March	1949
A/AC.26/SC.2/6	Hearing of An Chai Hong, formerly Civil Administrator of the Interim Government	17 March	1949
A/AC.26/SC.2/7	Further list of persons to be heard and trips to the provinces	17 March	1949
A/AC.26/SC.2/8	Hearing of Bishop Ro, Vicar Apostolic of Seoul	25 March	1949
A/AC.26/SC.2/9	Hearing of Kim Bup Rin, President of Dong Kook University	2 April	1949
A/AC.26/SC.2/10	Hearing of Kim Song Soo, member of the Supreme Council of the Democratic Nationalist Party	5 April	1949
A/AC.26/SC.2/11	Hearing of Cho So Ang, Chairman of the Socialist Party	5 April	1949
A/AC.26/SC.2/12	Hearing of Colonel B. C. Limb, Minister of Foreign Affairs	8 April	1949
A/AC.26/SC.2/12/Corr.1	Corrigendum to A/AC.26/SC.2/12	14 April	1949
A/AC.26/SC.2/13	Hearing of Kim Hyo Suk, Minister of the Interior	19 April	1949
A/AC.26/SC.2/14	Summary and analysis of hearings	9 June	1949
A/AC.26/SC.2/15	Report on trips to the Provinces affected by recent disturbances	9 June	1949
A/AC.26/SC.2/16	Final report to the Commission	18 June	1949

A/AC.26/SC.3/1	Report of the *Ad Hoc* Committee regarding the access of Koreans to the Commission	22 February	1949
A/AC.26/SC.3/2	Report of the *Ad Hoc* Committee of the Whole on the question of observer teams	1 June	1949

(d) SUB-COMMITTEE III

A/AC.26/SC.4/1	Report and recommendations	16 June	1949
A/AC.26/SC.4/2	First progress report	2 July	1949
A/AC.26/SC.4/3	Summary record of 1st meeting	7 July	1949
A/AC.26/SC.4/4	Summary record of 2nd meeting	7 July	1949
A/AC.26/SC.4/5	Summary record of 3rd meeting	7 July	1949
A/AC.26/SC.4/6	Summary record of 4th meeting	8 July	1949
A/AC.26/SC.4/6/Corr.1	Corrigendum to the summary record of the 4th meeting	11 July	1949
A/AC.26/SC.4/7	Summary record of 5th meeting	7 July	1949
A/AC.26/SC.4/8	Summary record of 6th meeting	7 July	1949
A/AC.26/SC.4/9	Communications from Brigadier General W. L. Roberts concerning withdrawal of United States occupation forces	7 July	1949
A/AC.26/SC.4/10	Communication to the Chairman of Sub-Committee III from the Ambassador of the United States concerning withdrawal of US troops	11 July	1949
A/AC.26/SC.4/11	Communication dated 16 July 1949 to the Chairman of Sub-Committee III from Chief, United States Advisory Group to the Republic of Korea	20 July	1949
A/AC.26/SC.4/12	Communication under date of 25 July 1949 from the Ambassador of the United States to the Chairman of Sub-Committee III	26 July	1949
A/AC.26/SC.4/13	Second progress report	27 July	1949
A/AC.26/SC.4/14	Meeting with U.S. Ambassador Muccio	28 July	1949
A/AC.26/SC.4/15	Notes on observation of United States troop embarkation at Inchon, 21 June 1949	8 July	1949
A/AC.26/SC.4/16	Notes on observation of United States troop embarkation at Inchon, 29 June 1949	8 July	1949
A/AC.26/SC.4/17	Notes on inspection of former USAFIK installations at Camp Sobingo-Youngsan area, 30 June 1949	8 July	1949
A/AC.26/SC.4/18	Notes on inspection of Ascom-Inchon area, 1 July 1949	8 July	1949

8. PRESS RELEASES

Number

1[80]	Arrival of the advance party and objectives of the Commission	29 January	1949
1, Corr.1	Corrigendum to the above Press release	29 January	1949
2	First meeting of the Commission	2 February	1949
3	First public meeting of the Commission	12 February	1949
4	Regarding resolution on access of Koreans to the Commission, and first field trip	17 February	1949
5	Request to the Secretary-General to transmit to the USSR a message regarding contact with North Korea	22 February	1949
6	Misquotation of remarks of the Press Officer concerning "representative government"	28 February	1949
7	Resolution concerning social functions	1 March	1949
8	Arrival of the Delegate from El Salvador	26 March	1949
9	Message of congratulation addressed by the Chairman to President Rhee on his 75th birthday	28 March	1949
10	Trips to Cheju Do and Cholla Namdo	21 April	1949
11	Press questionnaire	23 April	1949

---

[80] This first Press release was prepared at Lake Success and the advance party brought it. A few corrections were subsequently made and a corrigendum released.

8. Press releases (*continued*)

ㄱ

ㄴ

ㄷ

ㄹ

ㅁ

한국문제 관련 유엔문서 자료집(下)

초판 인쇄 | 2017년 2월 20일
초판 발행 | 2017년 2월 27일

편   저 | 경희대학교 한국현대사연구원
발행인 | 한정희
발행처 | 경인문화사
총괄이사 | 김환기
편집부 | 김지선 나지은 박수진 문성연 유지혜
마케팅부 | 김선규 하재일 유인순
등록번호 | 제406-1973-000003호
주 소 | 경기도 파주시 회동길 445-1 경인빌딩 B동 4층
전 화 | 031) 955-9300 팩 스 | 031) 955-9310
전자우편 | kyungin@kyunginp.co.kr
홈페이지 | www.kyunginp.co.kr

값 45,000원
ISBN 978-89-499-4263-6 93910
      978-89-499-4261-2 (세트)